Practical Machine Learning Cookbook

Resolving and offering solutions to your machine learning problems with R

Atul Tripathi

Packt>

BIRMINGHAM - MUMBAI

Practical Machine Learning Cookbook

First published: April 2017

Production reference: 1070417

Published by Packt Publishing Ltd.
Livery Place
35 Livery Street
Birmingham
B3 2PB, UK.
ISBN 978-1-78528-051-1

www.packtpub.com

Credits

Author
Atul Tripathi

Reviewer
Ryota Kamoshida

Commissioning Editor
Akram Hussain

Acquisition Editor
Tushar Gupta

Content Development Editor
Aishwarya Pandere

Technical Editor
Prasad Ramesh

Copy Editor
Safis Editing

Project Coordinator
Nidhi Joshi

Proofreader
Safis Editing

Indexer
Tejal Daruwale Soni

Graphics
Tania Dutta

Production Coordinator
Shantanu Zagade

About the Author

Atul Tripathi has spent more than 11 years in the fields of machine learning and quantitative finance. He has a total of 14 years of experience in software development and research. He has worked on advanced machine learning techniques, such as neural networks and Markov models. While working on these techniques, he has solved problems related to image processing, telecommunications, human speech recognition, and natural language processing. He has also developed tools for text mining using neural networks. In the field of quantitative finance, he has developed models for Value at Risk, Extreme Value Theorem, Option Pricing, and Energy Derivatives using Monte Carlo simulation techniques.

About the Reviewer

Ryota Kamoshida is the developer of the Python library **MALSS (MAchine Learning Support System)**, (https://github.com/canard0328/malss) and now works as a senior researcher in the field of computer science at Hitachi, Ltd.

www.PacktPub.com

For support files and downloads related to your book, please visit www.PacktPub.com.

Did you know that Packt offers eBook versions of every book published, with PDF and ePub files available? You can upgrade to the eBook version at www.PacktPub.com and as a print book customer, you are entitled to a discount on the eBook copy. Get in touch with us at service@packtpub.com for more details.

At www.PacktPub.com, you can also read a collection of free technical articles, sign up for a range of free newsletters and receive exclusive discounts and offers on Packt books and eBooks.

Mapt

https://www.packtpub.com/mapt

Get the most in-demand software skills with Mapt. Mapt gives you full access to all Packt books and video courses, as well as industry-leading tools to help you plan your personal development and advance your career.

Why subscribe?

- Fully searchable across every book published by Packt
- Copy and paste, print, and bookmark content
- On demand and accessible via a web browser

Customer Feedback

Thanks for purchasing this Packt book. At Packt, quality is at the heart of our editorial process. To help us improve, please leave us an honest review on this book's Amazon page at https://www.amazon.com/dp/1785280511.

If you'd like to join our team of regular reviewers, you can e-mail us at customerreviews@packtpub.com. We award our regular reviewers with free eBooks and videos in exchange for their valuable feedback. Help us be relentless in improving our products!

Table of Contents

Preface

Data in today's world is the new **black gold** which is growing exponentially. This growth can be attributed to the growth of existing data, and new data in a structured and unstructured format from multiple sources such as social media, Internet, documents and the Internet of Things. The flow of data must be collected, processed, analyzed, and finally presented in real time to ensure that the consumers of the data are able to take informed decisions in today's fast-changing environment. Machine learning techniques are applied to the data using the context of the problem to be solved to ensure that fast arriving and complex data can be analyzed in a scientific manner using statistical techniques. Using machine learning algorithms that iteratively learn from data, hidden patterns can be discovered. The iterative aspect of machine learning is important because as models are exposed to new data, they are able to independently adapt and learn to produce reliable decisions from new data sets.

We will start by introducing the various topics of machine learning, that will be covered in the book. Based on real-world challenges, we explore each of the topics under various chapters, such as *Classification, Clustering, Model Selection and Regularization, Nonlinearity, Supervised Learning, Unsupervised Learning, Reinforcement Learning, Structured Prediction, Neural Networks, Deep Learning,* and finally the case studies. The algorithms have been developed using R as the programming language. This book is friendly for beginners in R, but familiarity with R programming would certainly be helpful for playing around with the code.

You will learn how to make informed decisions about the type of algorithms you need to use and how to implement these algorithms to get the best possible results. If you want to build versatile applications that can make sense of images, text, speech, or some other form of data, this book on machine learning will definitely come to your rescue!

What this book covers

Chapter 1, *Introduction to Machine Learning,* covers various concepts about machine learning. This chapter makes the reader aware of the various topics we shall be covering in the book.

Chapter 2, *Classification,* covers the following topics and algorithms: discriminant function analysis, multinomial logistic regression, Tobit regression, and Poisson regression.

Chapter 3, *Clustering,* covers the following topics and algorithms: hierarchical clustering, binary clustering, and k-means clustering.

Chapter 4, *Model Selection and Regularization,* covers the following topics and algorithms: shrinkage methods, dimension reduction methods, and principal component analysis.

Chapter 5, *Nonlinearity,* covers the following topics and algorithms: generalized additive models, smoothing splines, local regression.

Chapter 6, *Supervised Learning,* covers the following topics and algorithms: decision tree learning, Naive Bayes, random forest, support vector machine, and stochastic gradient descent.

Chapter 7, *Unsupervised Learning,* covers the following topics and algorithms: self-organizing map, and vector quantization.

Chapter 8, *Reinforcement Learning,* covers the following topics and algorithms: Markov chains, and Monte Carlo simulations.

Chapter 9, *Structured Prediction,* covers the following topic and algorithms: hidden Markov models.

Chapter 10, *Neural Networks,* covers the following topic and algorithms: neural networks.

Chapter 11, *Deep Learning,* covers the following topic and algorithms: recurrent neural networks.

Chapter 12, *Case Study - Exploring World Bank Data,* covers World Bank data analysis.

Chapter 13, *Case Study - Pricing Reinsurance Contracts,* covers pricing reinsurance contracts.

Chapter 14, *Case Study - Forecast of Electricity Consumption,* covers forecasting electricity consumption.

What you need for this book

This book is focused on building machine learning-based applications in R. We have used R to build various solutions. We focused on how to utilize various R libraries and functions in the best possible way to overcome real-world challenges. We have tried to keep all the code as friendly and readable as possible. We feel that this will enable our readers to easily understand the code and readily use it in different scenarios.

Who this book is for

This book is for students and professionals working in the fields of statistics, data analytics, machine learning, and computer science, or other professionals who want to build real-world machine learning-based applications. This book is friendly to R beginners, but being familiar with R would be useful for playing around with the code. The will also be useful for experienced R programmers who are looking to explore machine learning techniques in their existing technology stacks.

Sections

In this book, you will find headings that appear frequently (Getting ready and How to do it).

To give clear instructions on how to complete a recipe, we use these sections as follows:

Getting ready

This section tells you what to expect in the recipe, and describes how to set up any software or any preliminary settings required for the recipe.

How to do it...

This section contains the steps required to follow the recipe.

Conventions

In this book, you will find a number of text styles that distinguish between different kinds of information. Here are some examples of these styles and an explanation of their meaning.

Code words in text, database table names, folder names, filenames, file extensions, pathnames, dummy URLs, user input, and Twitter handles are shown as follows: "We will be saving the data to the `fitbit_details` frame:"

Any command-line input or output is written as follows:

```
install.packages("ggplot2")
```

New terms and **important words** are shown in bold. Words that you see on the screen, for example, in menus or dialog boxes, appear in the text like this: "**Monte Carlo v/s Market n Zero Rates**"

> Warnings or important notes appear in a box like this.

> Tips and tricks appear like this.

Reader feedback

Feedback from our readers is always welcome. Let us know what you think about this book-what you liked or disliked. Reader feedback is important for us as it helps us develop titles that you will really get the most out of.

To send us general feedback, simply e-mail feedback@packtpub.com, and mention the book's title in the subject of your message.

If there is a topic that you have expertise in and you are interested in either writing or contributing to a book, see our author guide at www.packtpub.com/authors .

Customer support

Now that you are the proud owner of a Packt book, we have a number of things to help you to get the most from your purchase.

Downloading the example code

You can download the example code files for this book from your account at http://www.packtpub.com. If you purchased this book elsewhere, you can visit http://www.packtpub.com/support and register to have the files e-mailed directly to you.

You can download the code files by following these steps:

1. Log in or register to our website using your e-mail address and password.
2. Hover the mouse pointer on the **SUPPORT** tab at the top.
3. Click on **Code Downloads & Errata**.
4. Enter the name of the book in the **Search** box.
5. Select the book for which you're looking to download the code files.
6. Choose from the drop-down menu where you purchased this book from.
7. Click on **Code Download**.

You can also download the code files by clicking on the **Code Files** button on the book's webpage at the Packt Publishing website. This page can be accessed by entering the book's name in the **Search** box. Please note that you need to be logged in to your Packt account.

Once the file is downloaded, please make sure that you unzip or extract the folder using the latest version of:

- WinRAR / 7-Zip for Windows
- Zipeg / iZip / UnRarX for Mac
- 7-Zip / PeaZip for Linux

The code bundle for the book is also hosted on GitHub at `https://github.com/PacktPublishing/Practical-Machine-Learning-Cookbook`. We also have other code bundles from our rich catalog of books and videos available at `https://github.com/PacktPublishing/`. Check them out!

Downloading the color images of this book

We also provide you with a PDF file that has color images of the screenshots/diagrams used in this book. The color images will help you better understand the changes in the output. You can download this file from `https://www.packtpub.com/sites/default/files/downloads/PracticalMachineLearningCookbook_ColorImages.pdf`.

Errata

Although we have taken every care to ensure the accuracy of our content, mistakes do happen. If you find a mistake in one of our books-maybe a mistake in the text or the code-we would be grateful if you could report this to us. By doing so, you can save other readers from frustration and help us improve subsequent versions of this book. If you find any errata, please report them by visiting http://www.packtpub.com/submit-errata, selecting your book, clicking on the **Errata Submission Form** link, and entering the details of your errata. Once your errata are verified, your submission will be accepted and the errata will be uploaded to our website or added to any list of existing errata under the Errata section of that title.

To view the previously submitted errata, go to https://www.packtpub.com/books/content/support and enter the name of the book in the search field. The required information will appear under the **Errata** section.

Piracy

Piracy of copyrighted material on the Internet is an ongoing problem across all media. At Packt, we take the protection of our copyright and licenses very seriously. If you come across any illegal copies of our works in any form on the Internet, please provide us with the location address or website name immediately so that we can pursue a remedy.

Please contact us at copyright@packtpub.com with a link to the suspected pirated material.

We appreciate your help in protecting our authors and our ability to bring you valuable content.

Questions

If you have a problem with any aspect of this book, you can contact us at questions@packtpub.com, and we will do our best to address the problem.

1
Introduction to Machine Learning

In this chapter, we will cover an introduction to machine learning and various topics covered under machine learning. In this chapter you will learn about the following topics:

- What is machine learning?
- An overview of classification
- An overview of clustering
- An overview of model selection and regularization
- An overview of non-linearity
- An overview of supervised learning
- An overview of unsupervised learning
- An overview of reinforcement learning
- An overview of structured prediction
- An overview of neural networks
- An overview of deep learning

What is machine learning?

Human beings are exposed to data from birth. The eyes, ears, nose, skin, and tongue are continuously gathering various forms of data which the brain translates to sight, sound, smell, touch, and taste. The brain then processes various forms of raw data it receives through sensory organs and translates it to speech, which is used to express opinion about the nature of raw data received.

In today's world, sensors attached to machines are applied to gather data. Data is collected from Internet through various websites and social networking sites. Electronic forms of old manuscripts that have been digitized also add to data sets. Data is also obtained from the Internet through various websites and social networking sites. Data is also gathered from other electronic forms such as old manuscripts that have been digitized. These rich forms of data gathered from multiple sources require processing so that insight can be gained and a more meaningful pattern may be understood.

Machine learning algorithms help to gather data from varied sources, transform rich data sets, and help us to take intelligent action based on the results provided. Machine learning algorithms are designed to be efficient and accurate and to provide general learning to do the following:

- Dealing with large scale problems
- Making accurate predictions
- Handling a variety of different learning problems
- Learning which can be derived and the conditions under which they can be learned

Some of the areas of applications of machine learning algorithms are as follows:

- Price prediction based on sales
- Prediction of molecular response for medicines
- Detecting motor insurance fraud
- Analyzing stock market returns
- Identifying risk ban loans
- Forecasting wind power plant predictions
- Tracking and monitoring the utilization and location of healthcare equipment
- Calculating efficient use of energy
- Understating trends in the growth of transportation in smart cities
- Ore reserve estimations for the mining industry

An overview of classification

Linear regression models present response variables that are quantitative in nature. However, certain responses are qualitative in nature. Responses such as attitudes (strongly disagree, disagree, neutral, agree, and strongly agree) are qualitative in nature. Predicting a qualitative response for an observation can be referred to as classifying that observation, since it involves assigning the observation to a category or class. Classifiers are an invaluable tool for many tasks today, such as medical or genomics predictions, spam detection, face recognition, and finance.

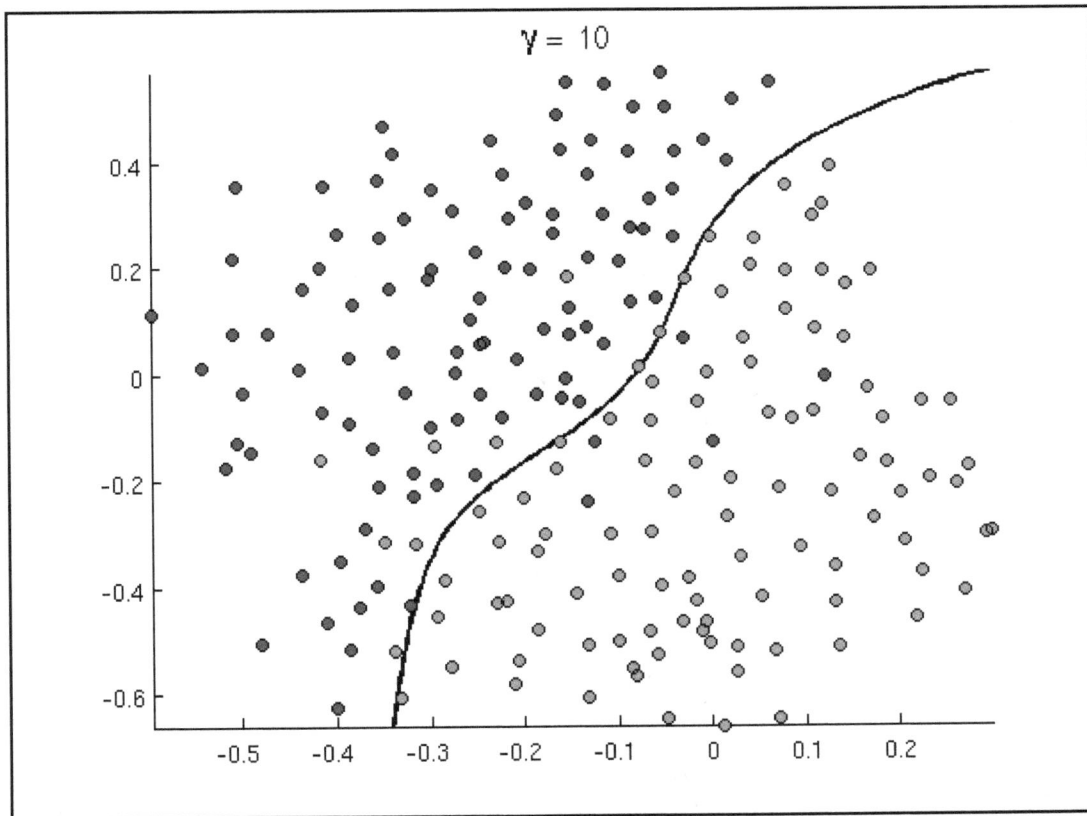

An overview of clustering

Clustering is a division of data into groups of similar objects. Each object (cluster) consists of objects that are similar between themselves and dissimilar to objects of other groups. The goal of clustering is to determine the intrinsic grouping in a set of unlabeled data. Clustering can be used in varied areas of application from data mining (DNA analysis, marketing studies, insurance studies, and so on.), text mining, information retrieval, statistical computational linguists, and corpus-based computational lexicography. Some of the requirements that must be fulfilled by clustering algorithms are as follows:

- Scalability
- Dealing with various types of attributes
- Discovering clusters of arbitrary shapes
- The ability to deal with noise and outliers
- Interpretability and usability

The following diagram shows a representation of clustering:

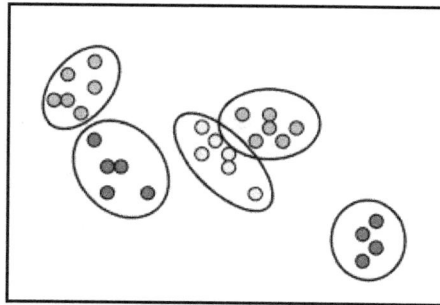

An overview of supervised learning

Supervised learning entails learning a mapping between a set of input variables (typically a vector) and an output variable (also called the supervisory signal) and applying this mapping to predict the outputs for unseen data. Supervised methods attempt to discover the relationship between input variables and target variables. The relationship discovered is represented in a structure referred to as a model. Usually models describe and explain phenomena, which are hidden in the dataset and can be used for predicting the value of the target attribute knowing the values of the input attributes.

Supervised learning is the machine learning task of inferring a function from supervised training data (set of training examples). The training data consists of a set of training examples. In supervised learning, each example is a pair consisting of an input object and a desired output value. A supervised learning algorithm analyzes the training data and produces an inferred function.

In order to solve the supervised learning problems, the following steps must be performed:

1. Determine the type of training examples.
2. Gather a training set.
3. Determine the input variables of the learned function.
4. Determine the structure of the learned function and corresponding learning algorithm.
5. Complete the design.
6. Evaluate the accuracy of the learned function.

The supervised methods can be implemented in a variety of domains such as marketing, finance, and manufacturing.

Some of the issues to consider in supervised learning are as follows:

- Bias-variance trade-off
- Function complexity and amount of training data
- Dimensionality of the input space
- Noise in the output values
- Heterogeneity of the data
- Redundancy in the data
- Presence of interactions and non-linearity

An overview of unsupervised learning

Unsupervised learning studies how systems can learn to represent particular input patterns in a way that reflects the statistical structure of the overall collection of input patterns. Unsupervised learning is important since it is likely to be much more common in the brain than supervised learning. For example, the activities of photoreceptors in the eyes are constantly changing with the visual world. They go on to provide all the information that is available to indicate what objects there are in the world, how they are presented, what the lighting conditions are, and so on. However, essentially none of the information about the contents of scenes is available during learning. This makes unsupervised methods essential, and allows them to be used as computational models for synaptic adaptation.

In unsupervised learning, the machine receives inputs but obtains neither supervised target outputs, nor rewards from its environment. It may seem somewhat mysterious to imagine what the machine could possibly learn given that it doesn't get any feedback from its environment. However, it is possible to develop a formal framework for unsupervised learning, based on the notion that the machine's goal is to build representations of the input that can be used for decision making, predicting future inputs, efficiently communicating the inputs to another machine, and so on. In a sense, unsupervised learning can be thought of as finding patterns in the data above and beyond what would be considered noise.

Some of the goals of unsupervised learning are as follows:

- Discovering useful structures in large data sets without requiring a target desired output
- Improving learning speed for inputs
- Building a model of the data vectors by assigning a score or probability to each possible data vector

An overview of reinforcement learning

Reinforcement learning is the problem of getting an agent to act in the world so as to maximize its rewards. It is about what to do and how to map situations to actions so as to maximize a numerical reward signal. The learner is not told which actions to take, as in most forms of machine learning, but instead must discover which actions yield the most reward by trying them. The two most important distinguishing features of reinforcement learning are trial and error and search and delayed reward. Some examples of reinforcement learning are as follows:

- A chess player making a move, the choice is informed both by planning anticipating possible replies and counter replies.
- An adaptive controller adjusts parameters of a petroleum refinery's operation in real time. The controller optimizes the yield/cost/quality trade-off on the basis of specified marginal costs without sticking strictly to the set points originally suggested by engineers.
- A gazelle calf struggles to its feet minutes after being born. Half an hour later it is running at 20 miles per hour.
- Teaching a dog a new trick--one cannot tell it what to do, but one can reward/punish it if it does the right/wrong thing. It has to figure out what it did that made it get the reward/punishment, which is known as the credit assignment problem.

Reinforcement learning is like trial and error learning. The agent should discover a good policy from its experiences of the environment without losing too much reward along the way. **Exploration** is about finding more information about the environment while **Exploitation** exploits known information to maximize reward. For example:

- **Restaurant selection**: Exploitation; go to your favorite restaurant. Exploration; try a new restaurant.
- **Oil drilling**: Exploitation; drill at the best-known location. Exploration; drill at a new location.

Major components of reinforcement learning are as follows:

- **Policy**: This is the agent's behavior function. It determines the mapping from perceived states of the environment to actions to be taken when in those states. It corresponds to what in psychology would be called a set of stimulus-response rules or associations.
- **Value Function**: This is a prediction of future reward. The value of a state is the total amount of reward an agent can expect to accumulate over the future, starting from that state. Whereas rewards determine the immediate, intrinsic desirability of environmental states, values indicate the long-term desirability of states after taking into account the states that are likely to follow, and the rewards available in those states.
- **Model**: The model predicts what the environment will do next. It predicts the next state and the immediate reward in the next state.

An overview of structured prediction

Structured prediction is an important area of application for machine learning problems in a variety of domains. Considering an input x and an output y in areas such as a labeling of time steps, a collection of attributes for an image, a parsing of a sentence, or a segmentation of an image into objects, problems are challenging because the y's are exponential in the number of output variables that comprise it. These are computationally challenging because prediction requires searching an enormous space, and also statistical considerations, since learning accurate models from limited data requires reasoning about commonalities between distinct structured outputs. Structured prediction is fundamentally a problem of representation, where the representation must capture both the discriminative interactions between x and y and also allow for efficient combinatorial optimization over y.

Structured prediction is about predicting structured outputs from input data in contrast to predicting just a single number, like in classification or regression. For example:

- **Natural language processing**--automatic translation (output: sentences) or sentence parsing (output: parse trees)
- **Bioinformatics**--secondary structure prediction (output: bipartite graphs) or enzyme function prediction (output: path in a tree)
- **Speech processing**--automatic transcription (output: sentences) or text to speech (output: audio signal)
- **Robotics**--planning (output: sequence of actions)

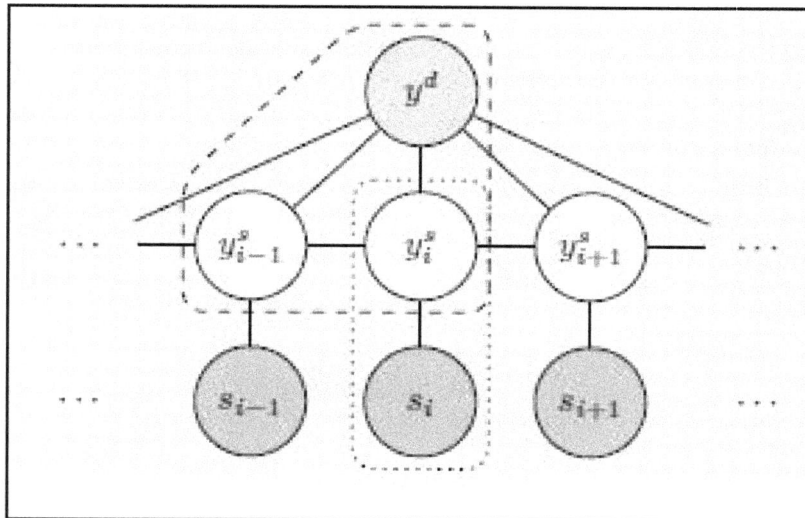

An overview of neural networks

Neural networks represent a brain metaphor for information processing. These models are biologically inspired rather than an exact replica of how the brain actually functions. Neural networks have been shown to be very promising systems in many forecasting applications and business classification applications due to their ability to learn from the data.

The artificial neural network learns by updating the network architecture and connection weights so that the network can efficiently perform a task. It can learn either from available training patterns or automatically learn from examples or input-output relations. The learning process is designed by one of the following:

- Knowing about available information
- Learning the paradigm--having a model from the environment
- Learning rules--figuring out the update process of weights
- Learning the algorithm--identifying a procedure to adjust weights by learning rules

There are four basic types of learning rules:

- Error correction rules
- Boltzmann
- Hebbian
- Competitive learning

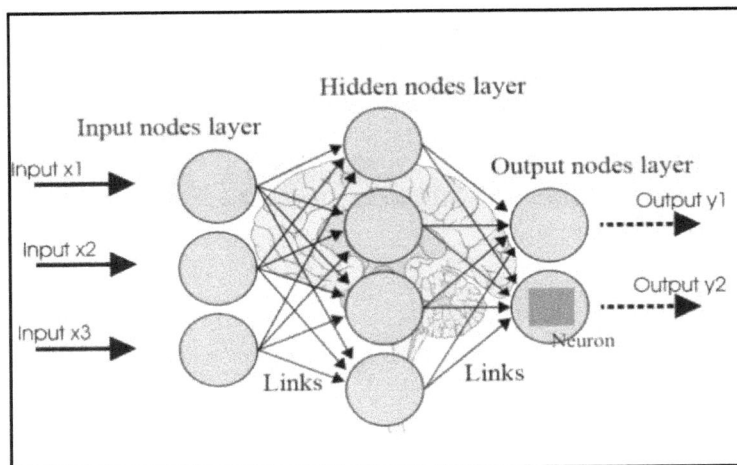

An overview of deep learning

Deep learning refers to a rather wide class of machine learning techniques and architectures, with the hallmark of using many layers of non-linear information processing that are hierarchical in nature. There are broadly three categories of deep learning architecture:

- Deep networks for unsupervised or generative learning
- Deep networks for supervised learning
- Hybrid deep networks

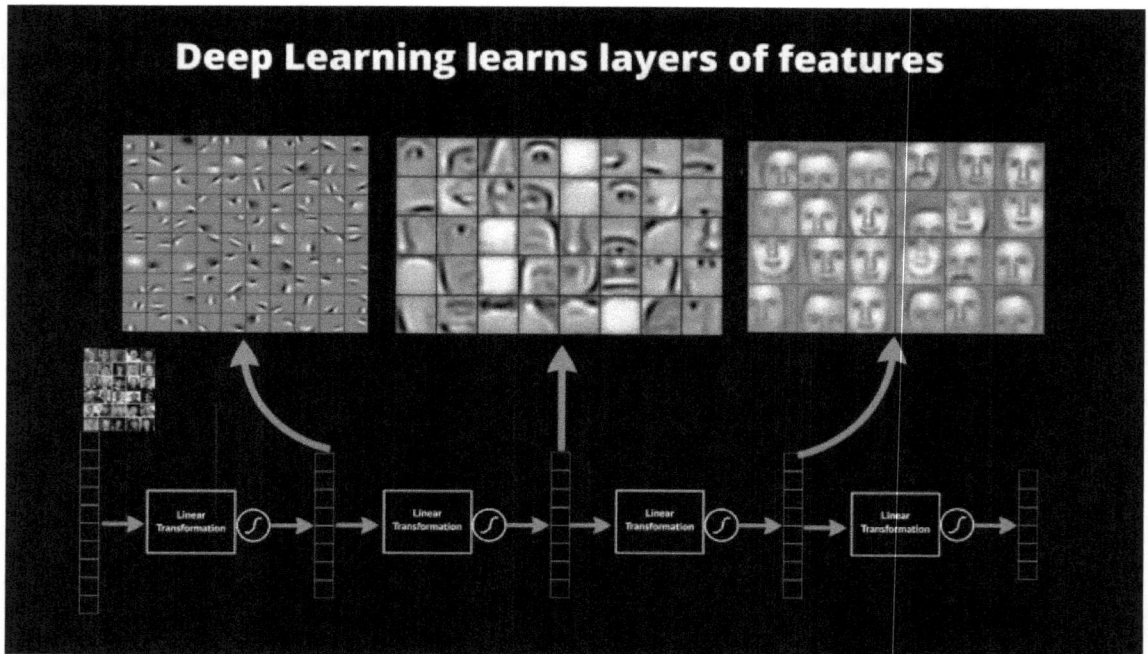

2
Classification

In this chapter, we will cover the following recipes:

- Discriminant function analysis - geological measurements on brines from wells
- Multinomial logistic regression - understanding program choices made by students
- Tobit regression - measuring students' academic aptitude
- Poisson regression - understanding species present in Galapagos Islands

Introduction

Discriminant analysis is used to distinguish distinct sets of observations and allocate new observations to previously defined groups. For example, if a study was to be carried out in order to investigate the variables that discriminate between fruits eaten by (1) primates, (2) birds, or (3) squirrels, the researcher could collect data on numerous fruit characteristics of those species eaten by each of the animal groups. Most fruits will naturally fall into one of the three categories. Discriminant analysis could then be used to determine which variables are the best predictors of whether a fruit will be eaten by birds, primates, or squirrels. Discriminant analysis is commonly used in biological species classification, in medical classification of tumors, in facial recognition technologies, and in the credit card and insurance industries for determining risk. The main goals of discriminant analysis are discrimination and classification. The assumptions regarding discriminant analysis are multivariate normality, equality of variance-covariance within group and low multicollinearity of the variables.

Multinomial logistic regression is used to predict categorical placement in or the probability of category membership on a dependent variable, based on multiple independent variables. It is used when the dependent variable has more than two nominal or unordered categories, in which dummy coding of independent variables is quite common. The independent variables can be either dichotomous (binary) or continuous (interval or ratio in scale). Multinomial logistic regression uses maximum likelihood estimation to evaluate the probability of categorical membership. It uses maximum likelihood estimation rather than the least squares estimation used in traditional multiple regression. The general form of the distribution is assumed. The starting values of the estimated parameters are used and the likelihood that the sample came from a population with those parameters is computed. The values of the estimated parameters are adjusted iteratively until the maximum likelihood value for the estimated parameters is obtained.

Tobit regression is used to describe the relationship between non-negative dependent variables and independent variables. It is also known as a censored regression model, designed to estimate linear relationships between variables when there is either left or right censoring in the dependent variable. Censoring takes place when cases with a value at or above some threshold, all take on the value of that threshold, so that the true value might be equal to the threshold, but it might also be higher. The Tobit model has been used in a large number of applications where the dependent variable is observed to be zero for some individuals in the sample (automobile expenditures, medical expenditures, hours worked, wages, and so on). This model is for metric dependent variables and then it is limited in the sense that we observe it only if it is above or below some cut off level. For example:

- The wages may be limited from below by the minimum wage
- The donation amount given to charity
- Top coding income
- Time used and leisure activity of individuals

Poisson regression deals with situations in which the dependent variable is a count. Poisson regression is similar to regular multiple regression except that the dependent (Y) variable is an observed count that follows the Poisson distribution. Thus, the possible values of Y are the nonnegative integers: 0, 1, 2, 3, and so on. It is assumed that large counts are rare. Hence, Poisson regression is similar to logistic regression, which also has a discrete response variable. However, the response is not limited to specific values as it is in logistic regression.

Discriminant function analysis - geological measurements on brines from wells

Let us assume that a study of ancient artifacts that have been collected from mines needs to be carried out. Rock samples have been collected from the mines. On the collected rock samples geochemical measurements have been carried out. A similar study has been carried out on the collected artifacts. In order to separate the samples into the mine from which they were excavated, DFA can be used as a function. The function can then be applied to the artifacts to predict which mine was the source of each artifact.

Getting ready

In order to perform discriminant function analysis we shall be using a dataset collected from mines.

Step 1 - collecting and describing data

The dataset on data analysis in geology titled BRINE shall be used. This can be obtained from http://www.kgs.ku.edu/Mathgeo/Books/Stat/ASCII/BRINE.TXT. The dataset is in a standard form, with rows corresponding to samples and columns corresponding to variables. Each sample is assigned to a stratigraphic unit, listed in the last column. There are 19 cases and eight variables in the dataset. The eight numeric measurements include the following:

- No
- HCO3
- SO4
- CL
- CA
- MG
- NA
- Group

How to do it...

Let's get into the details.

Step 2 - exploring data

The first step is to load the following package:

```
> library(MASS)
```

Version info: Code for this page was tested in R version 3.2.3 (2015-12-10)

Let's explore the data and understand the relationships among the variables. We'll begin by importing the txt data file named `brine.txt`. We will be saving the data to the `brine` data frame, as follows:

```
> brine <- read.table("d:/brine.txt", header=TRUE, sep=",",
row.names=1)
```

Next we shall print the `brine` data frame. The `head()` function returns the `brine` data frame. The `brine` data frame is passed as an input parameter. Use the following code:

```
> head(brine)
```

The results are as follows:

	HCO3	SO4	Cl	Ca	Mg	Na	GROUP
1	10.4	30.0	967.1	95.9	53.7	857.7	1
2	6.2	29.6	1174.9	111.7	43.9	1054.7	1
3	2.1	11.4	2387.1	348.3	119.3	1932.4	1
4	8.5	22.5	2186.1	339.6	73.6	1803.4	1
5	6.7	32.8	2015.5	287.6	75.1	1691.8	1
6	3.8	18.9	2175.8	340.4	63.8	1793.9	1

DFA assumes multivariate normality. The data must be checked to verify the normality before performing the analysis.

In order to verify the appropriateness of the transformation, plotting of the data is carried out. The `pairs()` function is used to plot the data. It produces a matrix of scatterplots. The cross-plots should only compare the measurement variables in columns 1-6, the last (7th column) is the name of the group. Consider the following:

```
> pairs(brine[ ,1:6])
```

The plot is as shown in the following screenshot:

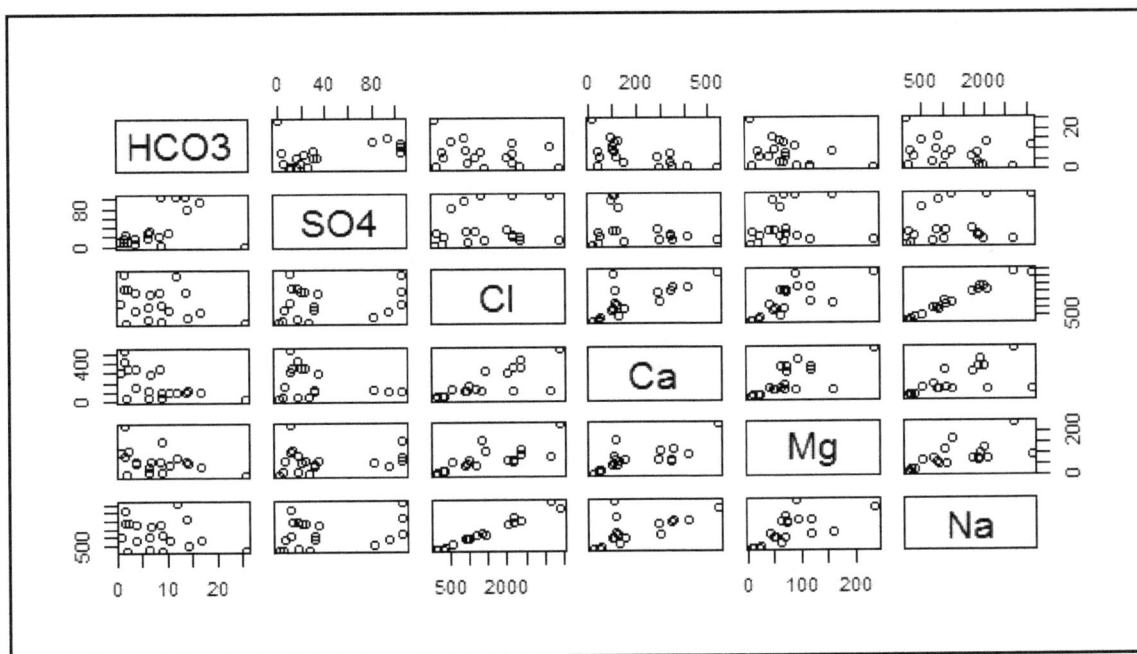

Step 3 - transforming data

It is visible that the data has a comet-shaped distribution pattern. This indicates that log transformation of the data is required, which is common for geochemical data. It is good practice to first make a copy of the entire dataset, and then apply the log transformation only to the geochemical measurements. Since the data includes zeros as well; `log+1` transformation should be carried out instead of `log` transformation on the dataset.

The `brine` data frame is copied to the `brine.log` data frame. The log transformation on the data frame is carried out. As stated earlier, log transformation is carried out. Look at the following code:

```
> brine.log <- brine
> brine.log[ ,1:6] <- log(brine[ ,1:6]+1)
> pairs(brine.log[ ,1:6])
```

After the data transformation, in order to re-evaluate the normality condition using the `pairs()` function data frame, `brine.log` is replotted. The distribution appears to be more normal. The skewness has been reduced compared to the earlier plot:

```
> pairs(brine.log[ ,1:6])
```

The plot is as shown in the following screenshot:

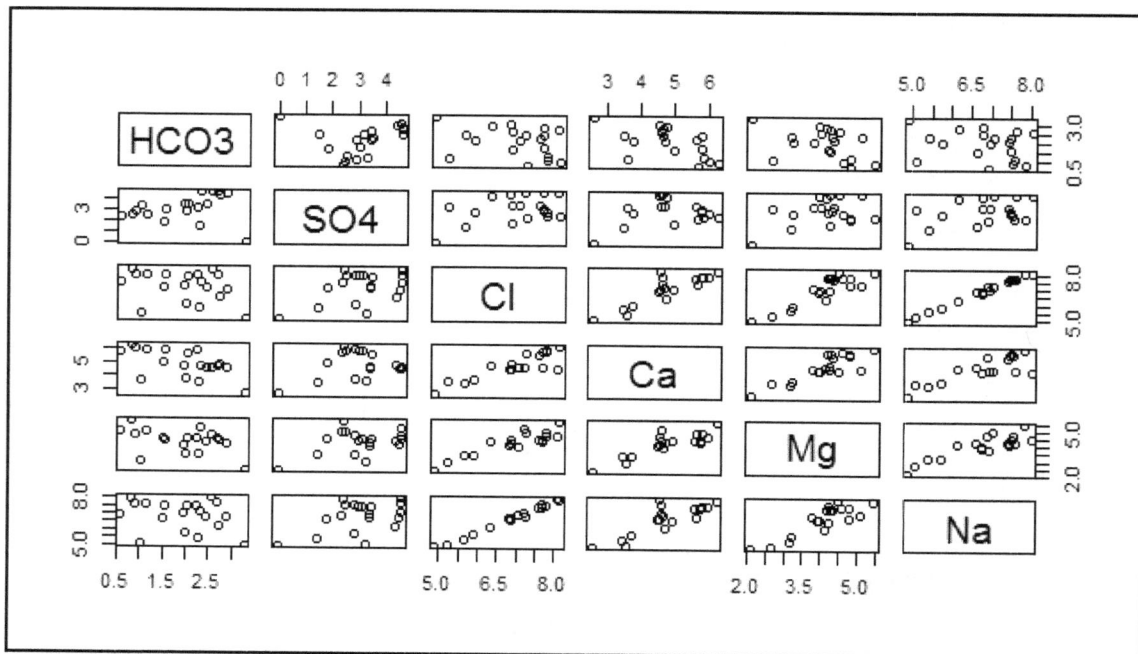

Step 4 - training the model

The next step is about training the model. This is carried out by discriminant function analysis. The `lda()` function is called to perform discriminant function analysis as follows:

```
> brine.log.lda <- lda(GROUP ~ HCO3 + SO4 + Cl + Ca + Mg + Na,
data=brine.log)
```

The format of this call is much like a linear regression or ANOVA, in that we specify a formula. Here, the GROUP variable should be treated as the dependent variable, with the geochemical measurements as the independent variables. In this case, no interactions between the variables are being modeled, so the variables are added with + instead of *. Because attach() was not called, the name of the data frame must be supplied to the data parameter. After running the DFA, the first step is to view the results, as follows:

```
> brine.log.lda
```

The results are as follows:

```
        Call:
lda(GROUP ~ HCO3 + SO4 + Cl + Ca + Mg + Na, data = brine.log)
Prior probabilities of groups:
           1                2                3
0.3684211        0.3157895        0.3157895
Group means:
          HCO3          SO4           Cl           Ca           Mg           Na
1     1.759502     3.129009     7.496891     5.500942     4.283490     7.320686
2     2.736481     3.815399     6.829565     4.302573     4.007725     6.765017
3     1.374438     2.378965     6.510211     4.641049     3.923851     6.289692
Coefficients of linear discriminants:
                    LD1              LD2
HCO3        -1.67799521       0.64415802
SO4          0.07983656       0.02903096
Cl          22.27520614      -0.31427770
Ca          -1.26859368       2.54458682
Mg          -1.88732009      -2.89413332
Na         -20.86566883       1.29368129
Proportion of trace:
        LD1          LD2
     0.7435       0.2565
```

- The first part of the output displays the formula that was fitted.
- The second section is the prior probabilities of the groups, which reflects the proportion of each group within the dataset. In other words, if you had no measurements and the number of measured samples represented the actual relative abundances of the groups, the prior probabilities would describe the probability that any unknown sample would belong to each of the groups.
- The third section shows the group means, which is a table of the average value of each of the variables for each of your groups. Scanning this table can help you to see if the groups are distinctive in terms of one or more of the variables.

- The fourth section reports the coefficients of the discriminant function (a, b, and c). Because there are three groups, there are 3-1 linear discriminants (if you had only two groups, you would need only 1 [2-1] linear discriminants). For each linear discriminant (LD1 and LD2), there is one coefficient corresponding, in order, to each of the variables.
- Finally, the fifth section shows the proportion of the trace, which gives the variance explained by each discriminant function. Here, first the discriminant explains 75% of the variance, with the remainder explained by the second discriminant.

Step 5 - classifying the data

The predict() function, also part of the MASS package, uses the lda() results to assign the samples to the groups. In other words, since lda() derived a linear function that should classify the groups, predict() allows you to apply this function to the same data to see how successful the classification function is. Following the statistical convention that x-hat is the prediction of x, (hat is added to the object name to make it clear that these are the predictions). Consider the following:

```
> brine.log.hat <- predict(brine.log.lda)
```

Let us print brine.log.hat as follows:

```
> brine.log.hat
```

The results are as follows:

```
      $class
       [1] 2 1 1 1 1 1 1 2 2 2 2 2 2 3 3 3 3 3 3
      Levels: 1 2 3


      $posterior
                    1                2                3
      1     2.312733e-01     7.627845e-01     5.942270e-03
      2     9.488842e-01     3.257237e-02     1.854347e-02
      3     8.453057e-01     9.482540e-04     1.537461e-01
      4     9.990242e-01     8.794725e-04     9.632578e-05
      5     9.965920e-01     2.849903e-03     5.581176e-04
      6     9.984987e-01     1.845534e-05     1.482872e-03
      7     8.676660e-01     7.666611e-06     1.323263e-01
      8     4.938019e-03     9.949035e-01     1.584755e-04
      9     4.356152e-03     9.956351e-01     8.770078e-06
      10    2.545287e-05     9.999439e-01     3.066264e-05
      11    2.081510e-02     9.791728e-01     1.210748e-05
```

12	1.097540e-03	9.989023e-01	1.455693e-07
13	1.440307e-02	9.854613e-01	1.356671e-04
14	4.359641e-01	2.367602e-03	5.616683e-01
15	6.169265e-02	1.540353e-04	9.381533e-01
16	7.500357e-04	4.706701e-09	9.992500e-01
17	1.430433e-03	1.095281e-06	9.985685e-01
18	2.549733e-04	3.225658e-07	9.997447e-01
19	6.433759e-02	8.576694e-03	9.270857e-01

```
$x
            LD1            LD2
1      -1.1576284     -0.1998499
2      -0.1846803      0.6655823
3       1.0179998      0.6827867
4      -0.3939366      2.6798084
5      -0.3167164      2.0188002
6       1.0061340      2.6434491
7       2.0725443      1.5714400
8      -2.0387449     -0.9731745
9      -2.6054261     -0.2774844
10     -2.5191350     -2.8304663
11     -2.4915044      0.3194247
12     -3.4448401      0.1869864
13     -2.0343204     -0.4674925
14      1.0441237     -0.0991014
15      1.6987023     -0.6036252
16      3.9138884     -0.7211078
17      2.7083649     -1.3896956
18      2.9310268     -1.9243611
19      0.7941483     -1.2819190
```

The output starts with the assigned classifications of each of our samples. Next, it lists the posterior probabilities of each sample to each group, with the probabilities in each row (that is, for each sample) summing to 1.0. These posterior probabilities measure the strength of each classification. If one of these probabilities for a sample is much greater than all the others, that sample is assigned to one group with a high degree of certainty. If two or more of the probabilities are nearly equal, the assignment is much less certain.

If there are many groups, the following command is a quick way to find the maximum probability for each sample:

```
> apply(brine.log.hat$posterior, MARGIN=1, FUN=max)
```

```
          1         2         3 4         5         6
7         8
0.7627845 0.9488842 0.8453057 0.9990242 0.9965920 0.9984987 0.8676660
0.9949035
          9        10        11        12        13        14
```

```
15          16
0.9956351 0.9999439 0.9791728 0.9989023 0.9854613 0.5616683 0.9381533
0.9992500
        17          18          19
0.9985685 0.9997447 0.9270857
```

Since most of the probabilities in the dataset are large (>0.9), this indicates that most of the samples in the set have been assigned to one group.

If most of these probabilities are large, the overall classification is successful. The last part of the `predict()` output lists the scores of each sample for each discriminant function axis. These scores can be plotted to show graphically how the groups are distributed in the discriminant function, just as scores from a principal components analysis could be plotted, as follows:

```
> plot(brine.log.lda)
```

The three groups occupy distinctly different and non-overlapping regions. There is just one case of group 1 being close to group 2, so one can clearly state that the discrimination has been successful.

The plot is as shown in the following figure:

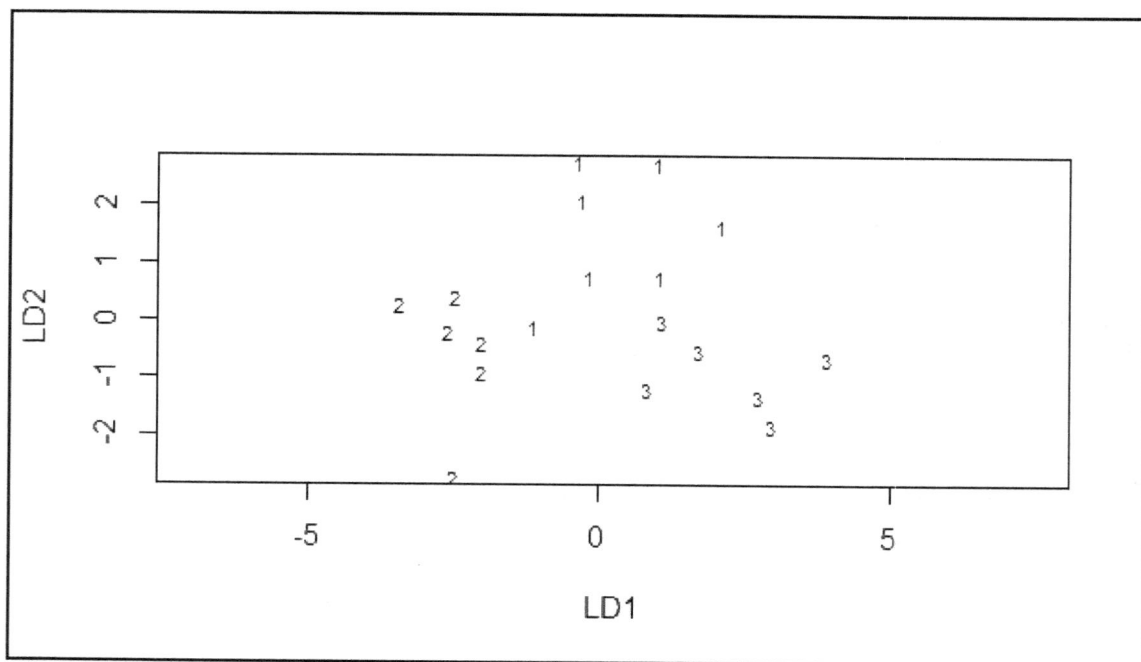

A second type of plot shows the data plot along a particular discriminant function axis as follows:

```
> plot(brine.log.lda, dimen=1, type="both")
```

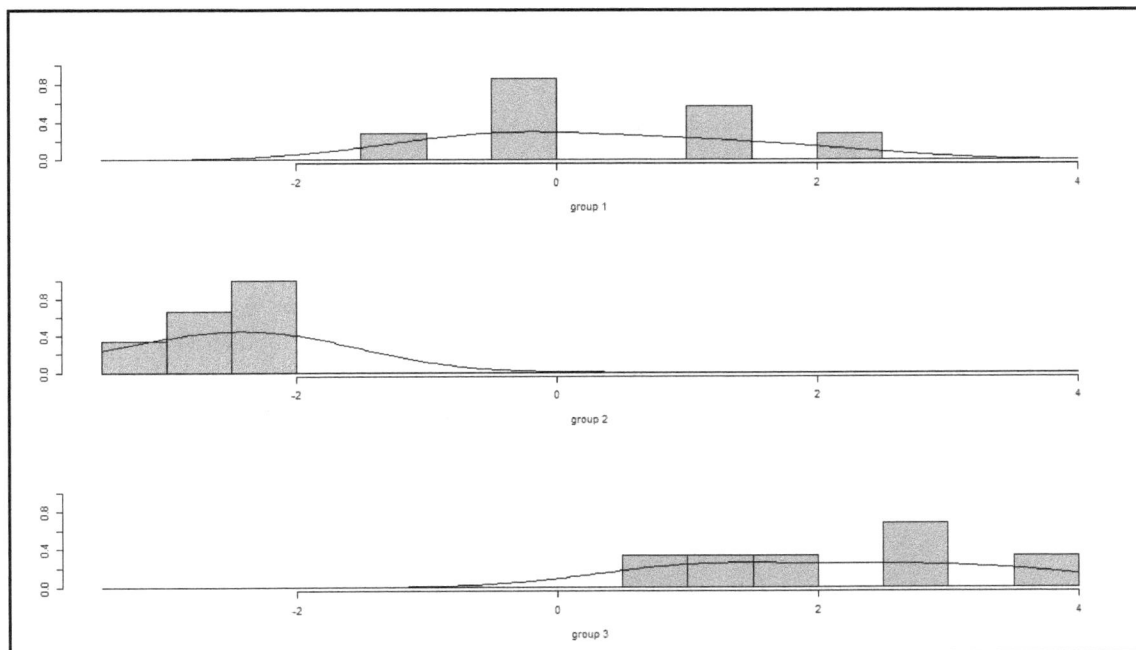

Again, note the good separation of the groups along discriminant function 1, and particularly so for group 2.

Step 6 - evaluating the model

The effectiveness of DFA in classifying the groups must be evaluated, and this is done by comparing the assignments made by predict() to the actual group assignments. The table() function is most useful for this. By convention, it is called with the actual assignments as the first argument and the fitted assignments as the second argument, as follows:

```
> tab <- table(brine.log$GROUP, brine.log.hat$class)
```

Printing the value of tab.

```
> tab
```

The results are as follows:

```
     1   2   3
1    6   1   0
2    0   6   0
3    0   0   6
```

The rows in the output correspond to the groups specified in the original data and the columns correspond to the classification made by the DFA. In a perfect classification, large values would lie along the diagonal, with zeroes off the diagonal, which would indicate that all samples that belong to group 1 were discriminated by the DFA as belonging to group 1, and so on. The form of this table can give you considerable insight into which groups are reliably discriminated. It can also show which groups are likely to be confused and which types of misclassification are more common than others.

The following command will calculate the overall predictive accuracy, that is, the proportion of cases that lie along the diagonal:

```
> sum(tab[row(tab) == col(tab)]) / sum(tab)
```

The result is as follows:

```
[1] 0.9473684
```

Here the predictive accuracy is almost 95%, quite a success. This approach measures what is called the resubstitution error, how well the samples are classified when all the samples are used to develop the discriminant function.

A second approach for evaluating a DFA is leave-one-out cross-validation (also called jackknifed validation), which excludes one observation. This approach of evaluating DFA uses the data that has been left out, that is, excluding one observation. We are now left with n - 1 observation. This cross-validation technique is done automatically for each sample in the dataset. To do this, add CV=TRUE (think Cross-validation) to the lda() call as follows:

```
> brine.log.lda <- lda(GROUP ~ HCO3 + SO4 + Cl + Ca + Mg + Na,
    data=brine.log, CV=TRUE)
```

The success of the discrimination can be measured similarly, as follows:

```
> tab <- table(brine.log$GROUP, brine.log.lda$class)
```

Print the value of tab as follows:

```
> tab
```

The result is as follows:

```
      1   2   3
1   6   1   0
2   1   4   1
3   1   0   5
```

```
> sum(tab[row(tab) == col(tab)]) / sum(tab)
```

The result is as follows:

```
[1] 0.7894737
```

In this dataset, the jackknifed validation is considerably less accurate (only 79% accurate), reflecting that the resubstitution error always overestimates the performance of a DFA. Such a discrepancy is particularly common with small datasets such as this, and discriminant function analysis is often much more successful with large datasets.

Multinomial logistic regression - understanding program choices made by students

Let's assume that high school students are to be enrolled on a program. The students are given the opportunity to choose programs of their choice. The choices of the students are based on three options. These choices are general program, vocational program, and academic program. The choice of each student is based on each student's writing score and social economic status.

Getting ready

In order to complete this recipe we shall be using a student's dataset. The first step is collecting the data.

Step 1 - collecting data

The student's dataset titled `hsbdemo` is being utilized. The dataset is available at: `http://voia.yolasite.com/resources/hsbdemo.csv` in an MS Excel format.

There are 201 data rows and 13 variables in the dataset. The eight numeric measurements are as follows:

- `id`
- `read`
- `write`
- `math`
- `science`
- `socst`
- `awards`
- `cid`

The non-numeric measurements are as follows:

- `gender`
- `ses`
- `schtyp`
- `prog`
- `honors`

How to do it...

Let's get into the details.

Step 2 - exploring data

The first step is loading the packages. The `library ()` returns an error if the package does not exist. Use the following commands:

```
> library(foreign)
> library (nnet)
> library (ggplot2)
> library (reshape2)
```

Version info: Code for this page was tested in R version 3.2.3 (2015-12-10).

Exploring the data throws some light on the relationships of the data. The CSV file titled `hsbdemo.csv` needs to be imported in the R environment. The imported data is saved in the data frame titled `ml` as follows:

```
> ml <- read.table("d:/hsbdemo.csv", header=TRUE, sep=",",
row.names="id")
```

Exploring the descriptive statistics of the variables that are of interest is to be carried out using the `with()` function as follows:

```
> with(ml, table(ses, prog))
```

The results are as follows:

```
          prog
ses         academic        general     vocation
   high           42              9            7
   low            19             16           12
   middle         44             20           31
```

Let us obtain the mean and the standard deviation as follows:

```
> with(ml, do.call(rbind, tapply(write, prog, function(x) c(M =
mean(x), SD = sd(x)))))
```

The results are as follows:

```
                      M              SD
academic        56.25714        7.943343
general         51.33333        9.397775
vocation        46.76000        9.318754
```

The mean is the highest for academic and the standard deviation is the highest for general.

Step 3 - training the model

In order to estimate multinomial logistic regression, the `multinom()` function is used. The `multinom()` function does not require the reshaping of the data.

It is important to choose a reference group for the outcome. We can choose the level of our outcome that we wish to use as our baseline. This is specified in the `relevel ()` function. Then, we run our model using the `multinom()` function. Since no p-value calculations are carried out for the regression coefficients, p-value tests are carried out using Wald tests (z-tests). The formula mentioned in the `multinom()` function is of the form response ~ predictors. The data frame `ml` is the data frame to interpret the variables occurring in the formula, as follows:

```
> ml$prog2 <- relevel(ml$prog, ref = "academic")
> test <- multinom(prog2 ~ ses + write, data = ml)
```

The results are as follows:

```
    # weights:   15 (8 variable)
 initial  value        219.722458
 iter     10 value     179.983731
 final    value        179.981726
 converged

  > summary(test)
```

The results are as follows:

```
    Call:
 multinom(formula = prog2 ~ ses + write, data = ml)
 Coefficients:
            (Intercept)      seslow    sesmiddle        write
 general    1.689478     1.1628411   0.6295638   -0.05793086
 vocation   4.235574     0.9827182   1.2740985   -0.11360389

    Std. Errors:
            (Intercept)      seslow    sesmiddle        write
 general    1.226939     0.5142211   0.4650289   0.02141101
 vocation   1.204690     0.5955688   0.5111119   0.02222000
 Residual Deviance: 359.9635
 AIC: 375.9635
```

Next, the test summary of coefficients is divided by the test summary of standard errors, as follows:

```
> z <- summary(test)$coefficients/summary(test)$standard.errors
```

Display the value of z as follows:

```
> z
```

The results are as follows:

```
           (Intercept)      seslow    sesmiddle       write
general       1.376987    2.261364     1.353816   -2.705658
vocation      3.515904    1.650050     2.492798   -5.112687
```

Step 4 - testing the results of the model

A two-tailed z test is carried out as follows:

```
> p <- (1 - pnorm(abs(z), 0, 1))*2
```

Display the value of p as follows:

```
> p
```

The results are as follows:

```
           (Intercept)         seslow     sesmiddle        write
general    0.1685163893    0.02373673     0.1757949   6.816914e-03
vocation   0.0004382601    0.09893276     0.0126741   3.176088e-07
```

Step 5 - model improvement performance

Relative risk is defined as the ratio between choosing one outcome category and choosing the baseline category. The relative risk is the exponential of the right-hand side of the linear equation. The exponential regression coefficients are relative risk ratios for a unit change in the predictor variable.

Extract the coefficients from the model and perform an exponential on it as follows:

```
> exp(coef(test))
```

The results are as follows:

```
                (Intercept)    seslow      sesmiddle       write
  general           5.416653   3.199009     1.876792    0.9437152
  vocation         69.101326   2.671709     3.575477    0.8926115
```

The relative risk ratio for a one-unit increase in the variable write is .9437 for being in a general program versus an academic program. The relative risk ratio switching from `ses` = 1 to 3 is .3126 for being in a general program versus an academic program. Use the probabilities that have been predicted to get an insight into the model. The `fitted()` function is used to calculate predicted probabilities for each of our outcome levels as follows:

```
> head(pp <- fitted(test))
```

The results are as follows:

```
         academic      general     vocation
  45     .1482721    0.3382509    0.5134769
  108    0.1201988   0.1806335    0.6991678
  15     0.4186768   0.2368137    0.3445095
  67     0.1726839   0.3508433    0.4764728
  153    0.1001206   0.1689428    0.7309367
  51     0.3533583   0.2378047    0.4088370
```

Examine the changes in probability associated with one of the two variables, `ses` and `write`. Create small datasets varying one variable while holding the other one constant. First, hold the write variable at its mean and then examine the predicted probability for each level of the `ses` variable as follows:

```
> dses <- data.frame(ses = c("low", "middle", "high"),write =
mean(ml$write))
> predict(test, newdata = dses, "probs")
```

The results are as follows:

```
      academic       general      vocation
  1   0.4396813    0.3581915    0.2021272
  2   0.4777451    0.2283359    0.2939190
  3   0.7009046    0.1784928    0.1206026
```

Looking at the average predicted probabilities for different values of the continuous predictor variable, using predicted probabilities as follows:

```
> dwrite <- data.frame(ses = rep(c("low", "middle", "high"), each =
41), write = rep(c(30:70), 3))
```

Store the predicted probabilities for each value of `ses` and write as follows:

```
> pp.write <- cbind(dwrite, predict(test, newdata = dwrite, type =
"probs", se = TRUE))
```

Calculate the mean probabilities within each level of `ses` as follows:

```
> by(pp.write[, 3:5], pp.write$ses, colMeans)
```

The results are as follows:

```
      pp.write$ses: high
    academic      general      vocation
   0.6164348    0.1808049    0.2027603
---------------------------------------------------------------
pp.write$ses: low
    academic      general      vocation
   0.3972955    0.3278180    0.2748864
---------------------------------------------------------------
pp.write$ses: middle
    academic      general      vocation
   0.4256172    0.2010877    0.3732951
```

Sometimes, a couple of plots can convey a good deal of information. Using the predictions we generated for the `pp.write` object previously, we can plot the predicted probabilities against the writing score by the level of `ses` for different levels of the outcome variable. The `melt()` function takes data in wide format and stacks a set of columns into a single column of data. The `lpp` data frame is used to specify the data frame as follows:

```
> lpp <- melt(pp.write, id.vars = c("ses", "write"), value.name =
"probability")
```

Print the values for `head` as follows:

```
> head(lpp)
```

The results are as follows:

```
        ses   write   variable    probability
   1    low     30    academic    0.09843258
   2    low     31    academic     0.10716517
   3    low     32    academic     0.11650018
   4    low     33    academic     0.12645441
   5    low     34    academic     0.13704163
   6    low     35    academic     0.14827211
```

Next we plot predicted probabilities across write values for each level of `ses` facetted by program type as follows:

```
> ggplot(lpp, aes(x = write, y = probability, colour = ses)) +
+     geom_line() +
+     facet_grid(variable ~ ., scales="free")
```

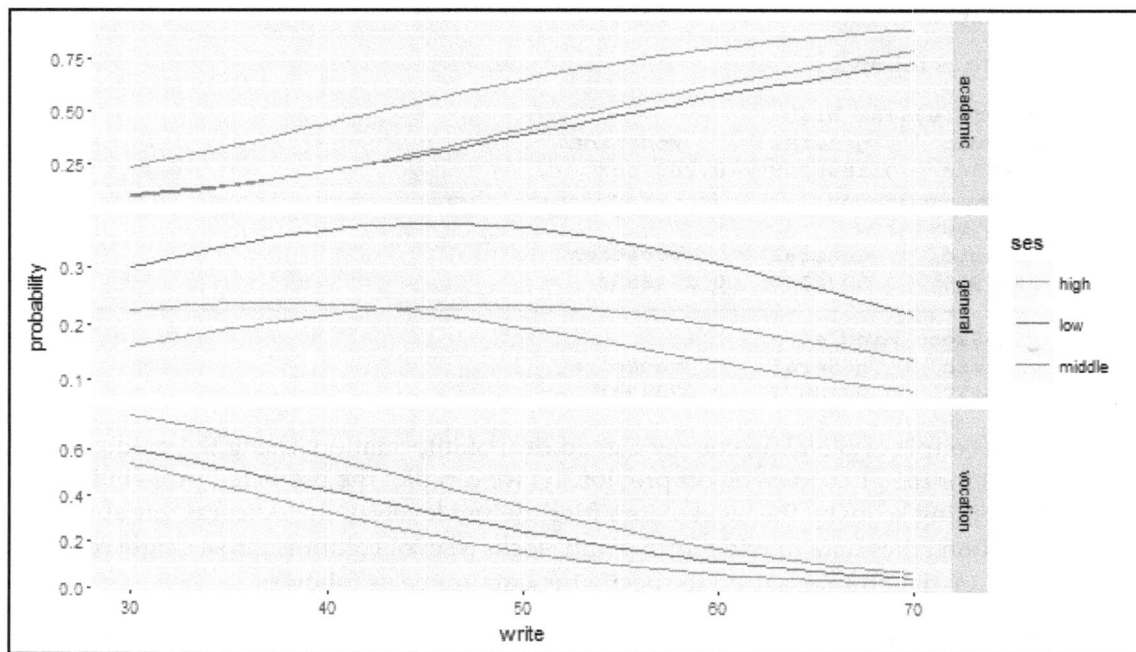

Tobit regression - measuring the students' academic aptitude

Let us measure the academic aptitude of a student on a scale of 200-800. This measurement is based on the model using reading and math scores. The nature of the program in which the student has been enrolled is also to be taken into consideration. There are three types of programs: academic, general, and vocational. The problem is that some students may answer all the questions on the academic aptitude test correctly and score 800 even though it is likely that these students are not truly equal in aptitude. This may be true for all the students who may answer all the questions incorrectly and score 200.

Getting ready

In order to complete this recipe we shall be using a student's dataset. The first step is collecting the data.

Step 1 - collecting data

To develop the Tobit regression model we shall use the student dataset titled tobit, which is available at `http://www.ats.ucla.edu/stat/data/tobit.csv` in an MS Excel format. There are 201 data rows and five variables in the dataset. The four numeric measurements are as follows:

- `id`
- `read`
- `math`
- `apt`

The non-numeric measurement is as follows:

- `prog`

How to do it...

Let's get into the details.

Step 2 - exploring data

The first step is to load the following packages. The `require()` function is designed for use inside other functions; it returns `FALSE` and gives a warning (rather than an error as `library ()` does by default) if the package does not exist. Use the following commands:

```
> require(ggplot2)
> require(GGally)
> require(VGAM)
```

Version info: Code for this page was tested in R version 3.2.3 (2015-12-10)

Explore the data and understand the relationships among the variables. Begin by importing the CSV data file named `gala.txt`. This will save the data to the `dat` data frame as follows:

```
> dat <- read.table("d:/tobit.csv", header=TRUE, sep=",",
row.names="id")
```

In this dataset, the lowest value of `apt` is 352. This indicates that no student has received the lowest score of 200. Even though censoring from below was possible, it is not required in this dataset. Use the following command:

```
> summary(dat)
```

The results are as follows:

```
      Id             read           math        prog              apt
Min.   :  1.0   Min.   :28.0   Min.   :33.0   academic  : 45   Min.   :352
1st Qu.: 50.8   1st Qu.:44.0   1st Qu.:45.0   general   :105   1st Qu.:576
Median :100.5   Median :50.0   Median :52.0   vocational: 50   Median :633
Mean   :100.5   Mean   :52.2   Mean   :52.6                    Mean   :640
3rd Qu.:150.2   3rd Qu.:60.0   3rd Qu.:59.0                    3rd Qu.:705
Max.   :200.0   Max.   :76.0   Max.   :75.0                    Max.   :800
```

Step 3 - plotting data

Write is a function that gives the density of a normal distribution for a given mean and standard deviation, which has been scaled on the count metric. In order to generate the histogram formulate count as *density * sample size * bin* width use the following code:

```
> f <- function(x, var, bw = 15) {
dnorm(x, mean = mean(var), sd(var)) * length(var) * bw
}
```

Now we shall set up the base plot as follows:

```
> p <- ggplot(dat, aes(x = apt, fill=prog))
```

Now we shall prepare a histogram, colored by proportion in different programs with a normal distribution overlaid as follows:

```
> p + stat_bin(binwidth=15) +
stat_function(fun = f, size = 1,
args = list(var = dat$apt))
```

The histogram plotted is shown in the following figure:

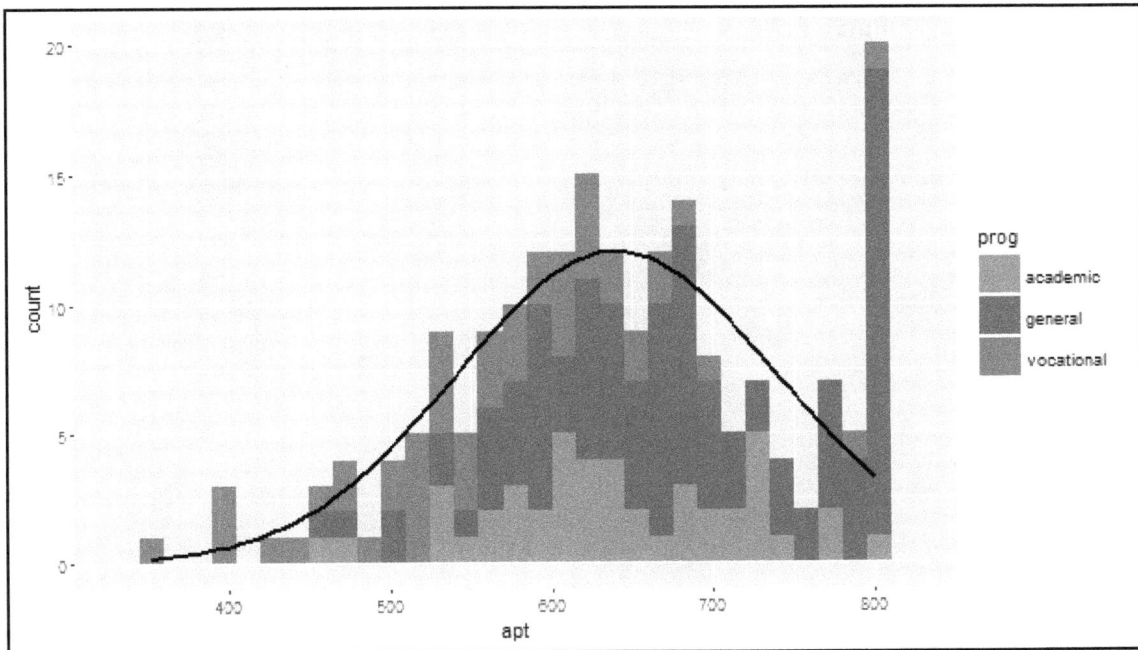

Looking at the preceding histogram, we can see the censoring in the values of apt, that is, there are far more cases with scores between 750 to 800 than one would expect compared to the rest of the distribution.

In the following alternative histogram, the excess of cases where apt=800 have been highlighted. In the following histogram, the breaks option produces a histogram where each unique value of apt has its own bar (by setting breaks equal to a vector containing values from the minimum of apt to the maximum of apt). Because apt is continuous, most values of apt are unique in the dataset, although close to the center of the distribution there are a few values of apt that have two or three cases.

The spike on the far right of the histogram is the bar for cases where apt=800, the height of this bar, relative to all the others, clearly shows the excess number of cases with this value. Use the following command:

```
> p + stat_bin(binwidth = 1) + stat_function(fun = f, size = 1, args =
list(var = dat$apt,
      bw = 1))
```

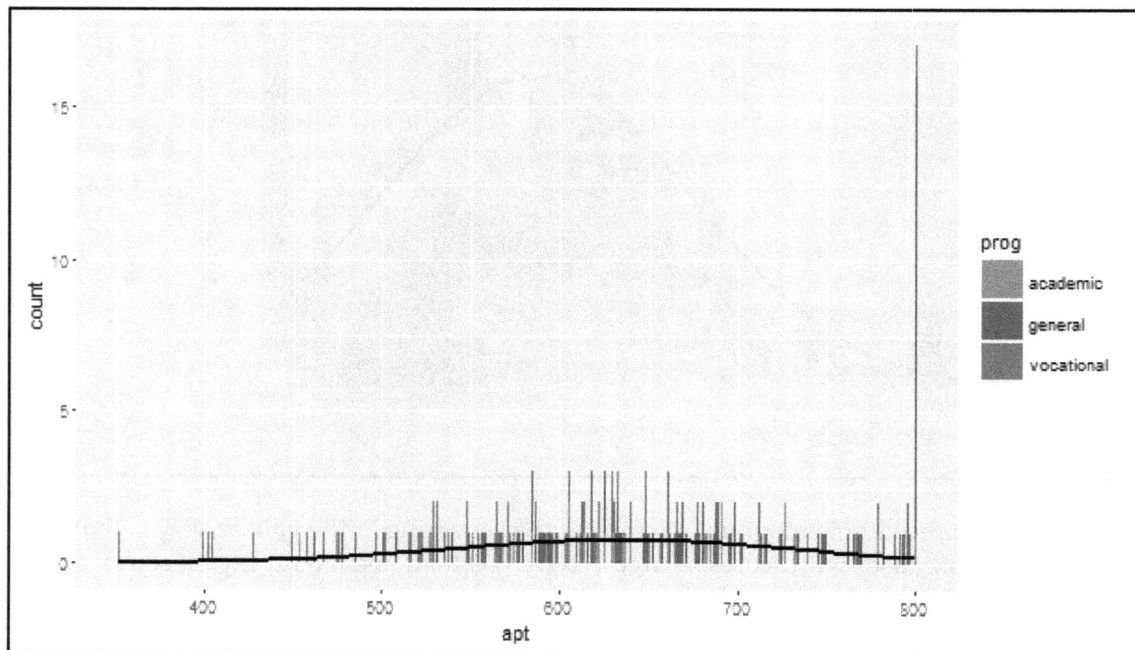

Step 4 - exploring relationships

The following command enables use to explore the bivariate relationships in the dataset:

```
> cor(dat[, c("read", "math", "apt")])
```

The results are as follows:

```
                    read          math            apt
    read     1.0000000     0.6622801      0.6451215
    math     0.6622801     1.0000000      0.7332702
    apt      0.6451215     0.7332702      1.0000000
```

Now plot the matrix as follows:

```
> ggpairs(dat[, c("read", "math", "apt")])
```

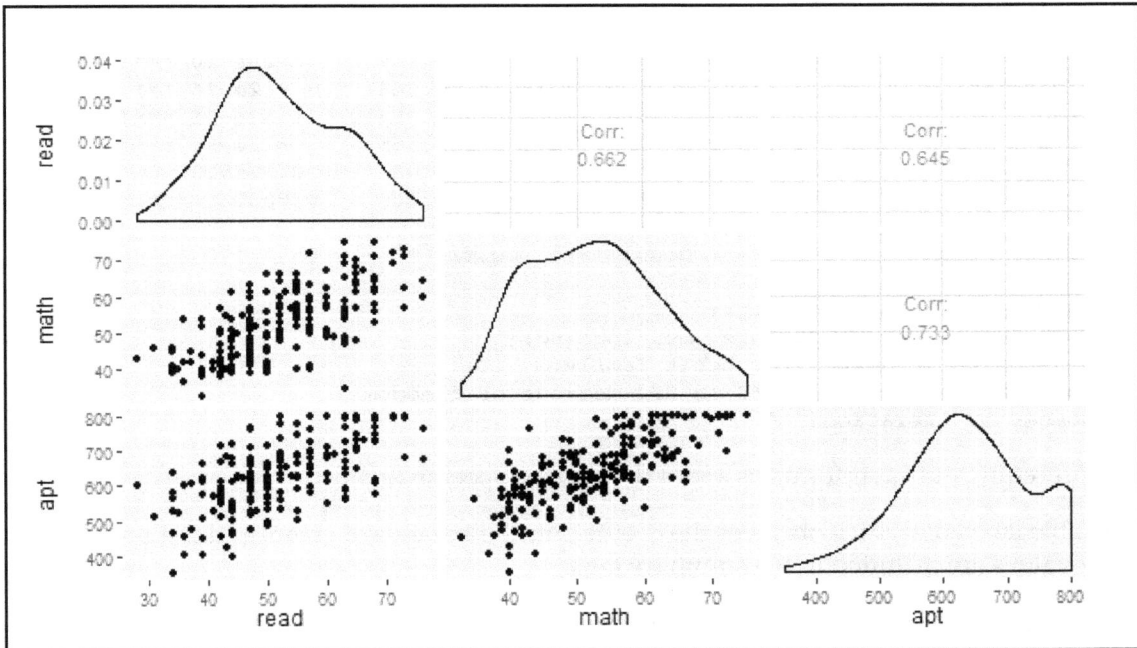

In the first row of the scatterplot matrix, the scatterplots display a relationship between read and apt. The relationship between math and apt is also established.

Step 5 - training the model

Run the Tobit model, using the `vglm` function of the VGAM package using this command:

```
> summary(m <- vglm(apt ~ read + math + prog, tobit(Upper = 800), data
= dat))
```

The results are as follows:

```
Call:
vglm(formula = apt ~ read + math + prog, family = tobit(Upper = 800),
    data = dat)

Pearson residuals:
                 Min        1Q       Median        3Q       Max
mu           -2.5684    -0.7311     -0.03976     0.7531     2.802
loge(sd)     -0.9689    -0.6359     -0.33365     0.2364     4.845

Coefficients:
                 Estimate Std.       Error      z value      Pr(>|z|)
(Intercept):1    209.55956      32.54590        6.439      1.20e-10 ***
(Intercept):2      4.18476       0.05235       79.944       < 2e-16 ***
read               2.69796       0.61928        4.357      1.32e-05 ***
math               5.91460       0.70539        8.385       < 2e-16 ***
proggeneral      -12.71458      12.40857       -1.025      0.305523
progvocational   -46.14327      13.70667       -3.366      0.000761 ***
---
Signif. codes:     0 '***'   0.001 '**'   0.01 '*'   0.05 '.' 0.1 ' ' 1

Number of linear predictors:   2
Names of linear predictors: mu, loge(sd)
Dispersion Parameter for tobit family:    1
Log-likelihood: -1041.063 on 394 degrees of freedom
Number of iterations: 5
```

The preceding output informs us about the options specified.

The table labeled coefficients gives the coefficients their standard errors and the z-statistic. No p-values are included in the summary table.

The interpretation of the Tobit regression coefficients is similar to that of OLS regression coefficients. The linear coefficients effect is on the uncensored latent variable:

- For a one-unit increase in read, there is a 2.6981 point increase in the predicted value of apt.
- A one-unit increase in math is associated with a 5.9146 unit increase in the predicted value of apt.
- The terms for prog have a slightly different interpretation. The predicted value of apt is -46.1419 points lower for students in a vocational program than for students in an academic program.
- The coefficient labeled (Intercept):1 is the intercept or constant for the model.

- The coefficient labeled (Intercept):2 is an ancillary statistic. Exponential of this value, is analogous to the square root of the residual variance in OLS regression. The value of 65.6773 can be compared to the standard deviation of academic aptitude, which was 99.21, a substantial reduction.

The final log likelihood, -1041.0629, is shown toward the bottom of the output; it can be used in comparisons of nested models.

Step 6 - testing the model

Calculate the p - values for each of the coefficients in the model. Calculate the p - value for each of the coefficients using z - values and then display them in a tabular manner.
The coefficients for read, math, and prog = 3 (vocational) are statistically significant as follows:

```
> ctable <- coef(summary(m))
> pvals <- 2 * pt(abs(ctable[, "z value"]), df.residual(m), lower.tail
= FALSE)
> cbind(ctable, pvals)
```

The results are as follows:

	Estimate	Std. Error	z value	Pr(>|z|)	pvals
(Intercept):1	209.559557	32.54589921	6.438893	1.203481e-10	3.505839e-10
(Intercept):2	4.184759	0.05234618	79.943922	0.000000e+00	1.299833e-245
read	2.697959	0.61927743	4.356625	1.320835e-05	1.686815e-05
math	5.914596	0.70538721	8.384892	5.077232e-17	9.122434e-16
proggeneral	-12.714581	12.40856959	-1.024661	3.055230e-01	3.061517e-01
progvocational	-46.143271	13.70667208	-3.366482	7.613343e-04	8.361912e-04

We can test the significance of the program type overall by fitting a model without a program in it and using a likelihood ratio test as follows:

```
> m2 <- vglm(apt ~ read + math, tobit(Upper = 800), data = dat)
> (p <- pchisq(2 * (logLik(m) - logLik(m2)), df = 2, lower.tail =
FALSE))
```

The results are as follows:

```
[1] 0.003155176
```

The statistical significance of the prog variable is indicated by the p - value equal to 0.0032. We calculate the upper and lower 95% confidence intervals for the coefficients as follows:

```
> b <- coef(m)
> se <- sqrt(diag(vcov(m)))
> cbind(LL = b - qnorm(0.975) * se, UL = b + qnorm(0.975) * se)
```

The results are as follows:

	LL	UL
(Intercept):1	145.770767	273.348348
(Intercept):2	4.082163	4.287356
read	1.484198	3.911721
math	4.532062	7.297129
proggeneral	-37.034931	11.605768
progvocational	-73.007854	-19.278687

By plotting residuals to one, we can assess the absolute as well as relative (Pearson) values and assumptions such as normality and homogeneity of variance. This shall help in examining the model and the data fit.

We may also wish to examine how well our model fits the data. One way to start is with plots of the residuals to assess their absolute as well as relative (Pearson) values and assumptions such as normality and homogeneity of variance. Use the following commands:

```
> dat$yhat <- fitted(m)[,1]
> dat$rr <- resid(m, type = "response")
> dat$rp <- resid(m, type = "pearson")[,1]

> par(mfcol = c(2, 3))

> with(dat, {
  plot(yhat, rr, main = "Fitted vs Residuals")
  qqnorm(rr)
  plot(yhat, rp, main = "Fitted vs Pearson Residuals")
  qqnorm(rp)
  plot(apt, rp, main = "Actual vs Pearson Residuals")
  plot(apt, yhat, main = "Actual vs Fitted")
})
```

The plot is as shown in the following screenshot:

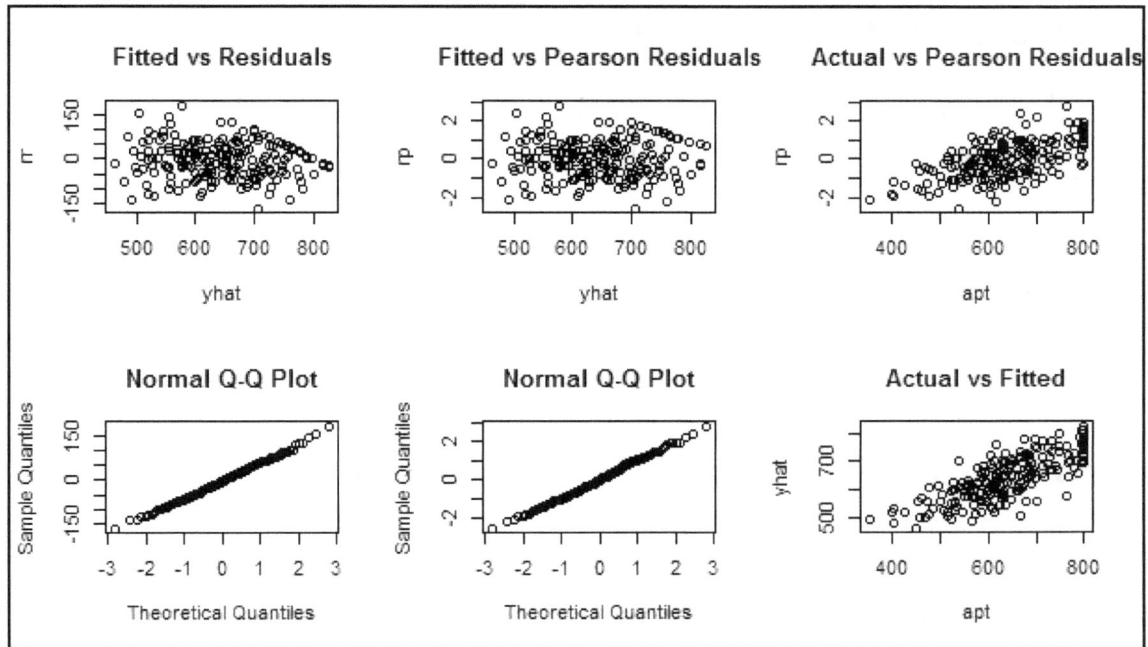

Establish the correlation as follows:

```
> (r <- with(dat, cor(yhat, apt)))
```

The results are as follows:

```
[1] 0.7825
```

Variance accounted for is calculated as follows:

```
> r^2
```

The results are as follows:

```
[1] 0.6123
```

The correlation between the predicted and observed values of apt is 0.7825. If we square this value, we get the multiple squared correlation, this indicates that the predicted values share 61.23% of their variance with apt.

Poisson regression - understanding species present in Galapagos Islands

The Galapagos Islands are situated in the Pacific Ocean about 1000 km from the Ecuadorian coast. The archipelago consists of 13 islands, five of which are inhabited. The islands are rich in flora and fauna. Scientists are still perplexed by the fact that such a diverse set of species can flourish in such a small and remote group of islands.

Getting ready

In order to complete this recipe we shall be using species dataset. The first step is collecting the data.

Step 1 - collecting and describing the data

We will utilize the number of species dataset titled `gala` that is available at `https://github.com/burakbayramli/kod/blob/master/books/Practical_Regression_Ano ve_Using_R_Faraway/gala.txt`.

The dataset includes 30 cases and seven variables in the dataset. The seven numeric measurements include the following:

- Species
- Endemics
- Area
- Elevation
- Nearest
- Scruz
- Adjcacent

How to do it...

Let's get into the details.

Step 2 - exploring the data

Exploring the data will throw some light on the relationships. Begin by importing the txt data file named gala.txt. We will be saving the data to the gala data frame as follows:

```
> gala <- read.table("d:/gala.txt")
```

The regpois() gives the Poisson regression on the variables that are expected to be important from an ecological point of view as follows:

```
> regpois <- glm( Species ~ Area + Elevation + Nearest, family=poisson,
data=gala)
```

Next provide the summary of the data as follows:

```
> summary(regpois)
```

The summary function will provide deviance residuals, coefficients, signif codes, null deviance, residual deviance, AIC, and number of Fisher scoring iterations.The results are as follows:

```
Deviance residuals:
      Min        1Q     Median         3Q        Max
 -17.1900    -6.1715    -2.7125     0.7063    21.4237

Coefficients:
                Estimate    Std. Error    z value    Pr(>|z|)
(Intercept)    3.548e+00    3.933e-02     90.211     < 2e-16  ***
Area          -5.529e-05    1.890e-05     -2.925     0.00344  **
Elevation      1.588e-03    5.040e-05     31.502     < 2e-16  ***
Nearest        5.921e-03    1.466e-03      4.039     5.38e-05 ***
---

Signif. codes:
     0 '***' 0.001 '**' 0.01 '*' 0.05 '.' 0.1 ' ' 1
```

(Dispersion parameter for Poisson family taken to be 1)

```
Null deviance:
3510.7  on 29   degrees of freedom

Residual deviance:
    1797.8  on 26   degrees of freedom

AIC:
    1966.7
```

Number of Fisher Scoring iterations:

```
    5
> plot(regpois$fit,gala$Species)
```

The plot is shown in the following screenshot:

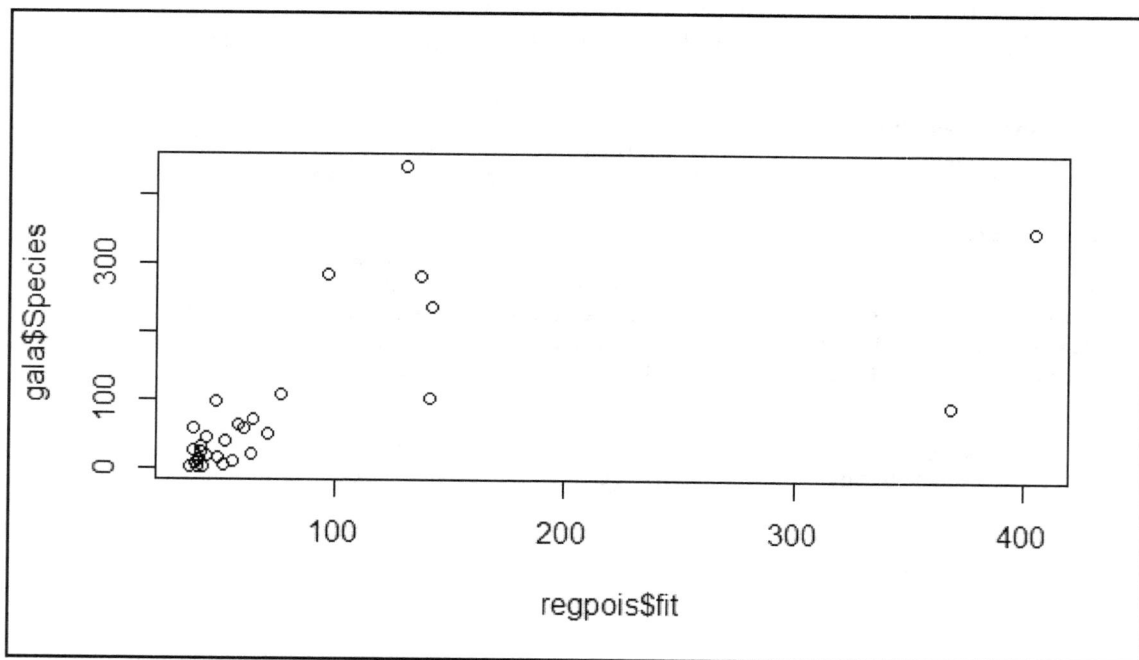

Step 3 - plotting data and testing empirical data

`ppois()` is the distribution function of a Poisson where the parameter is `lambda=regpois$fit` and it is computed in `gala$Species` as follows:

```
> p <- ppois(gala$Species, regpois$fit)
```

The values should be close to uniform in nature.
Check the uniformity by plotting the values as follows:

```
> hist(p, breaks=10)
```

The plot result is shown in the screenshot:

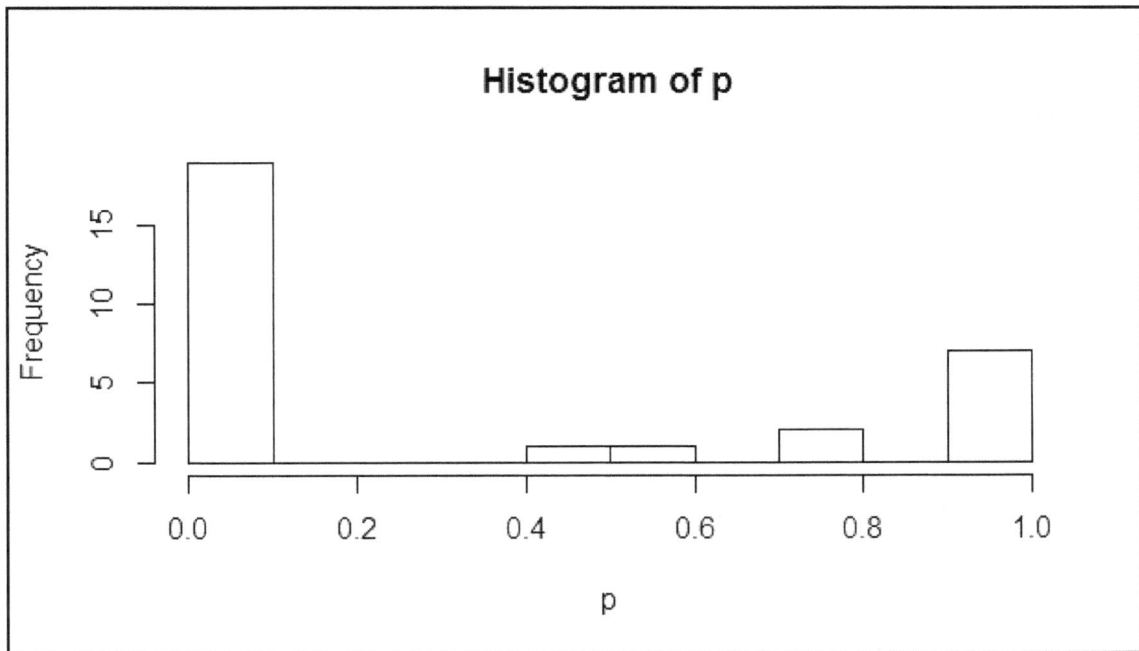

The plot clearly shows that they are not in uniform.

Now carry out the Kolmogorov-Smirnov test on whether empirical data fits a given distribution.

The Kolmogorov-Smirnov test is a test for goodness of fit and it usually involves examining a random sample from some unknown distribution in order to test the null hypothesis that the unknown distribution function is in fact a known, specified function. We usually use the Kolmogorov-Smirnov test to check the normality assumption in the analysis of variance.

The Kolmogorov-Smirnov test is constructed as a statistical hypothesis test. We determine a null hypothesis, H_0, that the two samples we are testing come from the same distribution. Then we search for evidence that this hypothesis should be rejected and express this in terms of a probability. If the likelihood of the samples being from different distributions exceeds a confidence level we demand that the original hypothesis is rejected in favor of the hypothesis, H_1, that the two samples are from different distributions.

To do this we devise a single number calculated from the samples, that is, a statistic. The trick is to find a statistic that has a range of values that do not depend on things we do not know, such as the actual underlying distributions in this case.

The test statistic in the Kolmogorov-Smirnov test is very easy; it is just the maximum vertical distance between the empirical cumulative distribution functions of the two samples. The empirical cumulative distribution of a sample is the proportion of the sample values that are less than or equal to a given value.

One sample Kolmogorov-Smirnov test is as follows:

```
> ks.test(p, "punif")
```

The results are as follows:

```
        One-sample Kolmogorov-Smirnov test
  data:  p
  D = 0.57731, p-value = 4.134e-09
  alternative hypothesis: two-sided
```

Therefore, we can safely conclude that the model is not adequate.

Step 4 - rectifying discretization of the Poisson model

Now make a correction since Poisson is discrete. The change is as follows:

```
    p = 1/2*(F(Y)+F(Y-1))
; where Y are the data,
; and F are the distribution functions coming from Poisson
```

A correction of the procedure is carried out, taking into account discrete distribution as follows:

```
> p <- 0.5*(ppois(gala$Species,regpois$fit) +
ppois(gala$Species-1,regpois$fit))
```

Let us check the uniformity by plotting the values as follows:

```
> hist(p,breaks=10)
```

The plot result is shown in the following figure:

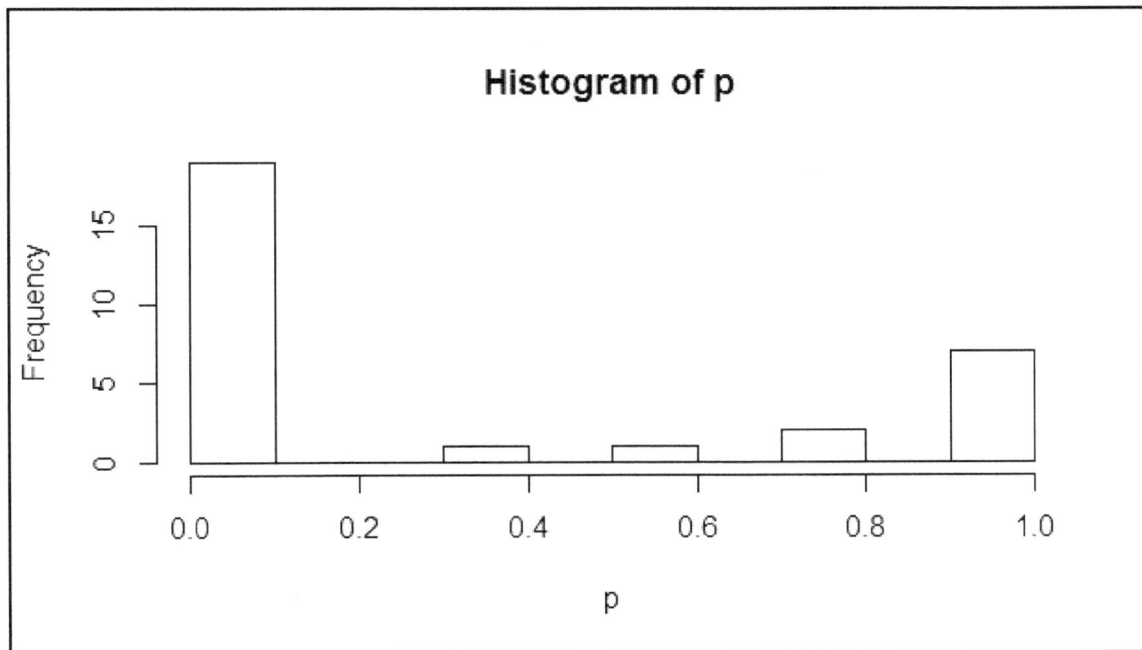

The correction does not make much of a difference. The plot clearly shows that they are not in uniform.

Now let us carry out the Kolmogorov-Smirnov test again to verify whether empirical data fits a given distribution as follows:

```
> ks.test(p, "punif")
```

The results are as follows:

```
     One-sample Kolmogorov-Smirnov test
data:  p
D = 0.58571, p-value = 2.3e-09
alternative hypothesis: two-sided
```

Step 5 - training and evaluating the model using the link function

We shall see how generalized linear models fit using the `glm( )` function as follows:

```
> regpois2 <- glm( Species ~ Area + Elevation + Nearest,
family=poisson(link=sqrt), data=gala)
```

Let us print the results of `regpois2` as follows:

```
> summary(regpois2)
```

The results are as follows:

```
Call:
glm(formula = Species ~ Area + Elevation + Nearest, family = poisson(link =
sqrt),
     data = gala)
Deviance Residuals:
    Min          1Q        Median          3Q            Max
-19.108      -5.129      -1.335        1.846         16.918

Coefficients:
                 Estimate    Std. Error    z value      Pr(>|z|)
(Intercept)     4.1764222    0.1446592     28.871      < 2e-16 ***
Area           -0.0004844    0.0001655     -2.926        0.00343 **
Elevation       0.0110143    0.0003372     32.664      < 2e-16 ***
Nearest         0.0083908    0.0065858      1.274        0.20264
---
Signif. codes:    0 '***' 0.001 '**' 0.01 '*' 0.05 '.' 0.1 ' ' 1
(Dispersion parameter for poisson family taken to be 1)
Null deviance:    3510.7 on 29 degrees of freedom
Residual deviance:    1377.5 on 26 degrees of freedom
AIC: 1546.3
Number of Fisher Scoring iterations: 5
```

Step 6 - revaluating using the Poisson model

A correction of the procedure is carried out, taking into account discrete distribution as follows:

```
> p2 <- 0.5*(ppois(gala$Species,regpois2$fit) +
ppois(gala$Species-1,regpois2$fit))
```

Check the uniformity by plotting the values as follows:

```
> hist(p,breaks=10)
```

The plot result is shown in the following figure:

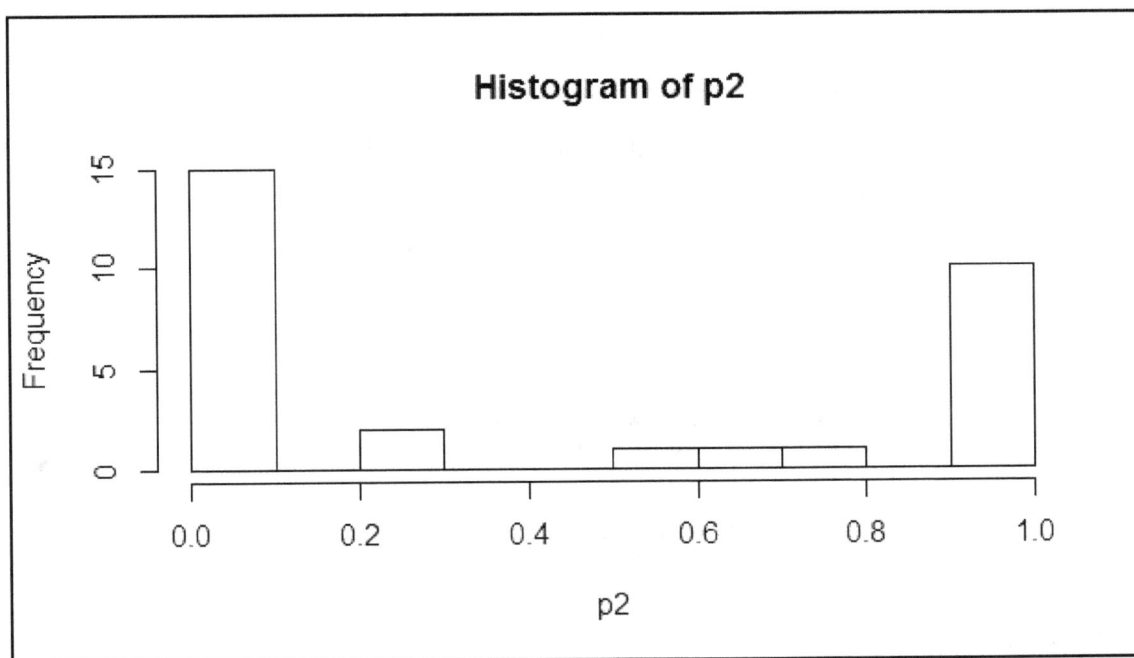

Carry out the Kolmogorov-Smirnov test again to verify whether empirical data fits a given distribution as follows:

```
> ks.test(p2,"punif")
```

A one sample Kolmogorov-Smirnov test is carried out as follows:

```
      data:  p2
D = 0.47262, p-value = 3.023e-06
alternative hypothesis: two-sided
```

The result still does not pass the test.

Step 7 - revaluating using the linear model

Applying usual the linear model: `lm()` function is used to fit linear models. It can be used to carry out regression, single stratum analysis of variance, and analysis of covariance (although `aov` may provide a more convenient interface for these).

The `reg` data frame is used to store the results returned from the `lm()` function as follows:

```
> reg <- lm(Species ~ Area+Elevation+Nearest, data=gala)
```

Let us now view the results of the `reg` data frame using the following command:

```
> summary(reg)
```

The results are as follows:

```
      Call:
lm(formula = Species ~ Area + Elevation + Nearest, data = gala)

Residuals:
      Min          1Q        Median          3Q           Max
-191.856      -33.111      -18.626        5.673       262.209

Coefficients:
                Estimate    Std. Error    t value     Pr(>|t|)
(Intercept)     16.46471     23.38884      0.704      0.48772
Area             0.01908      0.02676      0.713      0.48216
Elevation        0.17134      0.05452      3.143      0.00415  **
Nearest          0.07123      1.06481      0.067      0.94718
---
Signif. codes:    0 '***' 0.001 '**' 0.01 '*' 0.05 '.' 0.1 ' ' 1

Residual standard error:   80.84 on 26 degrees of freedom
Multiple R-squared:       0.5541,   Adjusted R-squared:   0.5027
F-statistic:          10.77 on 3 and 26 DF,   p-value: 8.817e-05
```

Now let us plot the reg data frame as follows:

```
> plot(reg)
```

The **Residuals vs Fitted** plot is shown in the folllowing figure:

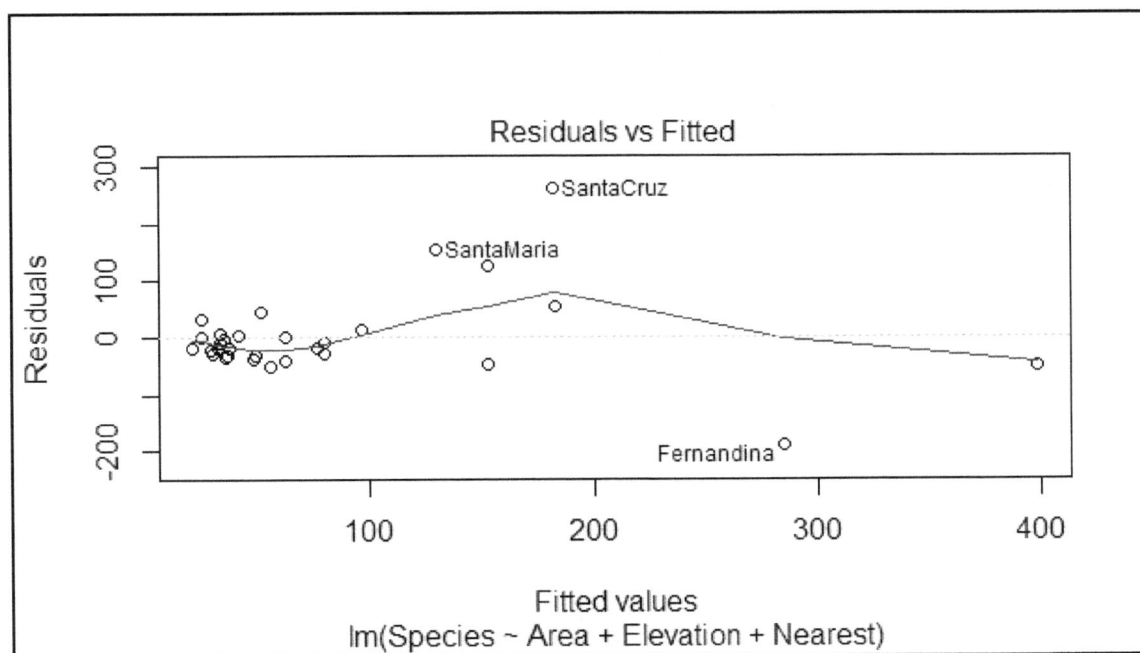

The Normal Q-Q linear model plot is shown in the following screenshot:

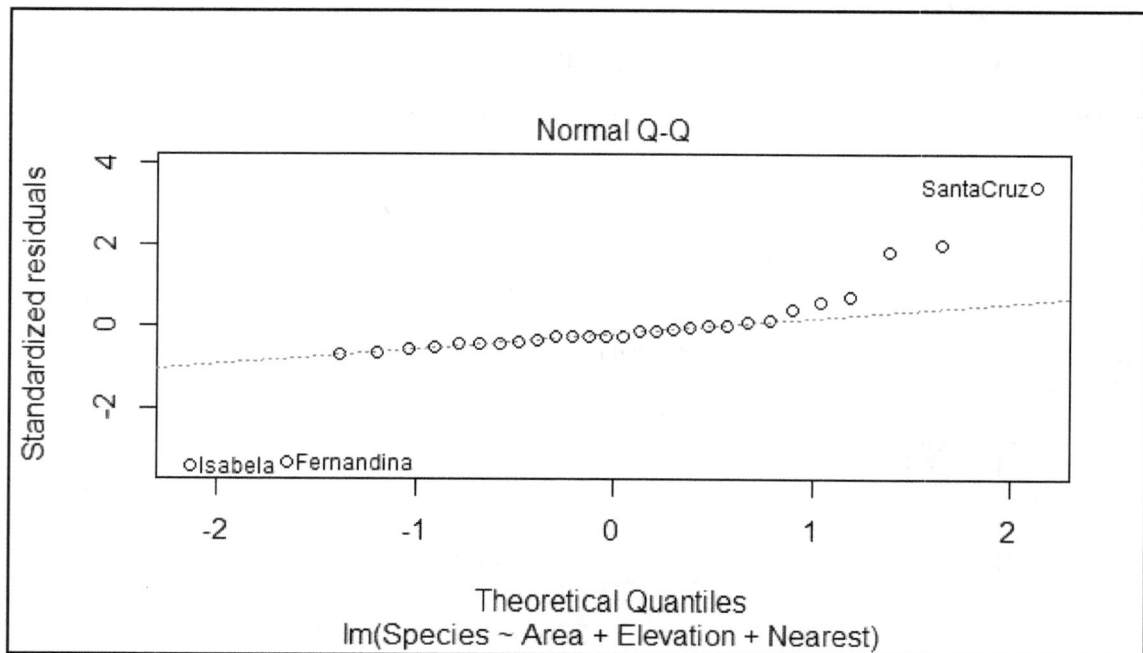

The **Scale-Location** linear model plot is shown in the following figure:

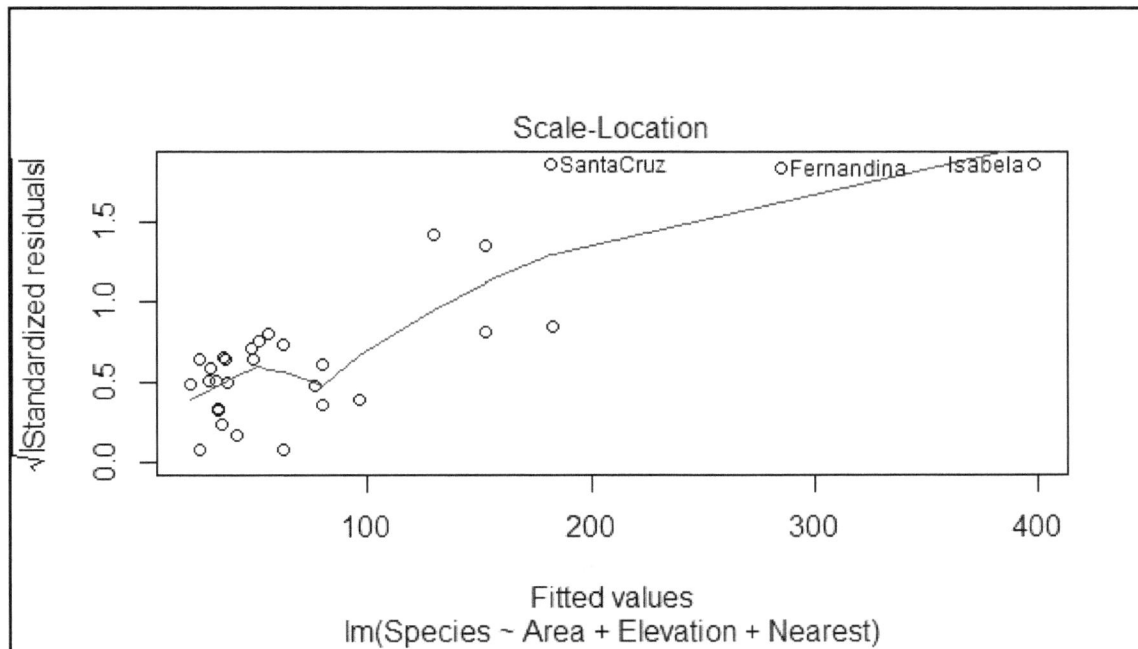

Now let us apply a transformation by using the following square root function. The reg2 data frame is used to store the results returned from the lm function:

```
> reg2 <- lm(sqrt(Species) ~ Area+Elevation+Nearest, data=gala)
```

Let us now view the results of the reg data frame as follows:

```
> summary(reg2)
```

The results are as follows:

```
Call:
lm(formula = sqrt(Species) ~ Area + Elevation + Nearest, data = gala)
Residuals:
     Min        1Q     Median        3Q         Max
 -8.8057   -2.1775    -0.2086    1.3943      8.8730

Coefficients:
                Estimate    Std. Error    t value    Pr(>|t|)
(Intercept)     3.744e+00    1.072e+00      3.492    0.001729 **
Area           -2.253e-05    1.227e-03     -0.018    0.985485
```

```
Elevation       9.795e-03    2.499e-03    3.920 0.  000576 ***
Nearest         2.002e-02    4.880e-02    0.410     0.685062
---
Signif. codes:  0 '***' 0.001 '**' 0.01 '*' 0.05 '.' 0.1 ' ' 1

Residual standard error:   3.705 on 26 degrees of freedom
Multiple R-squared:     0.5799,  Adjusted R-squared:  0.5315
F-statistic:      11.96 on 3 and 26 DF,  p-value: 4.144e-05
```

Now let us plot the `reg2` data frame as follows:

```
> plot(reg2)
```

The **Residual vs Fitted** plot is shown in the following figure:

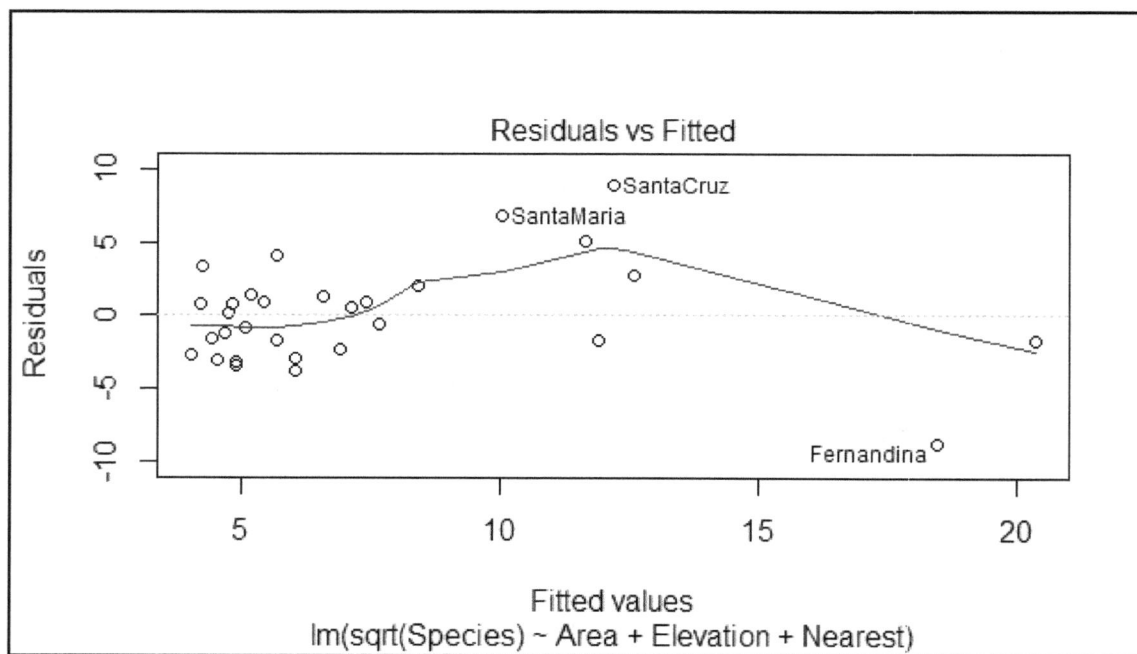

The **Normal Q-Q** linear model plot is shown in the following figure:

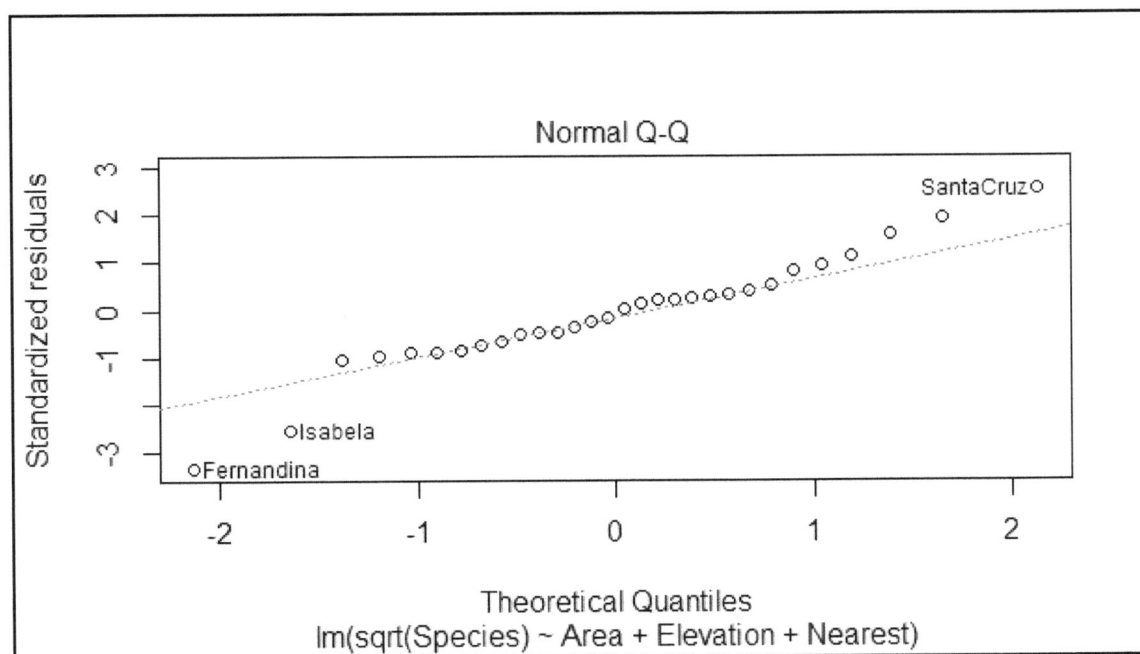

The Poisson regression **Scale-Location** linear model plot is shown in the following screenshot:

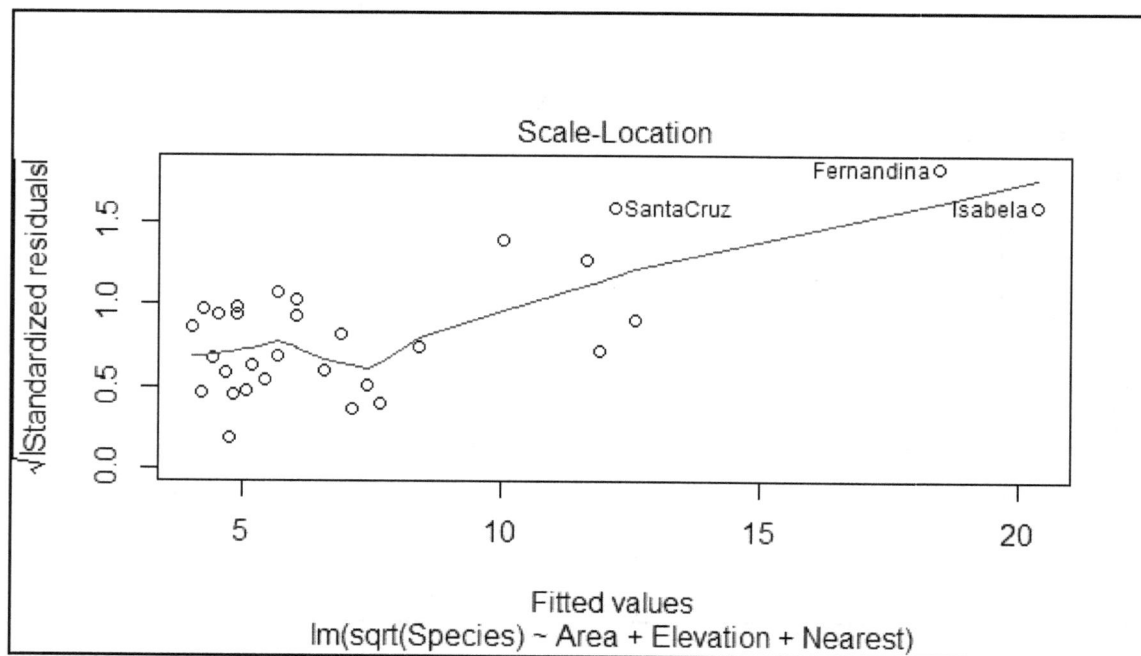

The **Scale-Location** linear model plot is shown in the following figure:

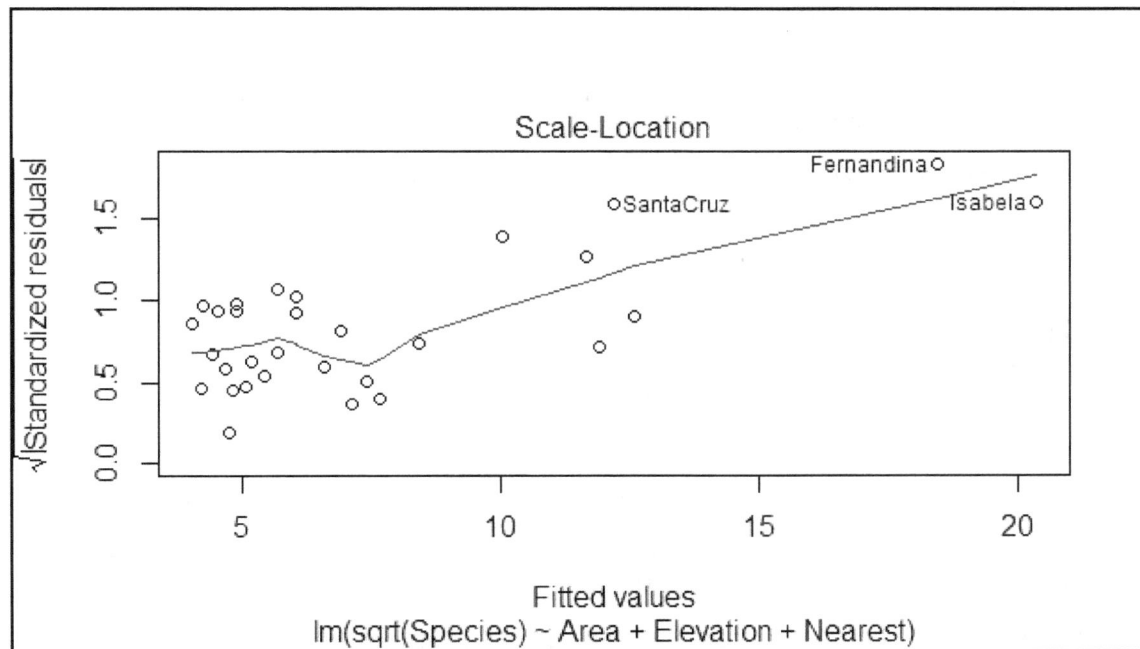

Let us carry out the Shapiro test. Given a sample X1, . . . , Xn of n real-valued observations, the Shapiro-Wilk test (Shapiro and Wilk, 1965) is a test of the composite hypothesis that the data is **i.i.d.** (**independent and identically distributed**) and normal, that is, $N(\mu, \sigma 2)$ for some unknown real μ and some $\sigma > 0$. Use the following command:

```
> shapiro.test(reg2$res)
```

The results are as follows:

```
        Shapiro-Wilk normality test
data:   reg2$res
W = 0.9633, p-value = 0.375
```

Now let us apply a transformation by using the log function as follows.

The `reg3` data frame is used to store the results returned from the `lm()` function as follows:

```
> reg3 <- lm(log(Species) ~ Area+Elevation+Nearest, data=gala)
```

Let us now view the results of the `reg3` data frame as follows:

```
> summary(reg3)
```

The results are as follows:

```
Call:
lm(formula = log(Species) ~ Area + Elevation + Nearest, data = gala)
Residuals:
      Min       1Q    Median       3Q      Max
  -2.0739  -0.5161    0.3307   0.7472   1.6271

Coefficients:
                Estimate    Std. Error    t value      Pr(>|t|)
(Intercept)    2.3724325     0.3448586      6.879      2.65e-07 ***
Area          -0.0002687     0.0003946     -0.681       0.50197
Elevation      0.0029096     0.0008039      3.620       0.00125 **
Nearest        0.0133869     0.0157001      0.853       0.40163
---
Signif. codes:  0 '***' 0.001 '**' 0.01 '*' 0.05 '.' 0.1 ' ' 1

Residual standard error:   1.192 on 26 degrees of freedom
Multiple R-squared:        0.4789,  Adjusted R-squared:  0.4187
F-statistic:          7.964 on 3 and 26 DF,  p-value: 0.0006281
```

Now let us plot the `reg3` data frame as follows:

```
> plot(reg3)
```

The **Residuals vs Fitted** plot is shown in the following figure:

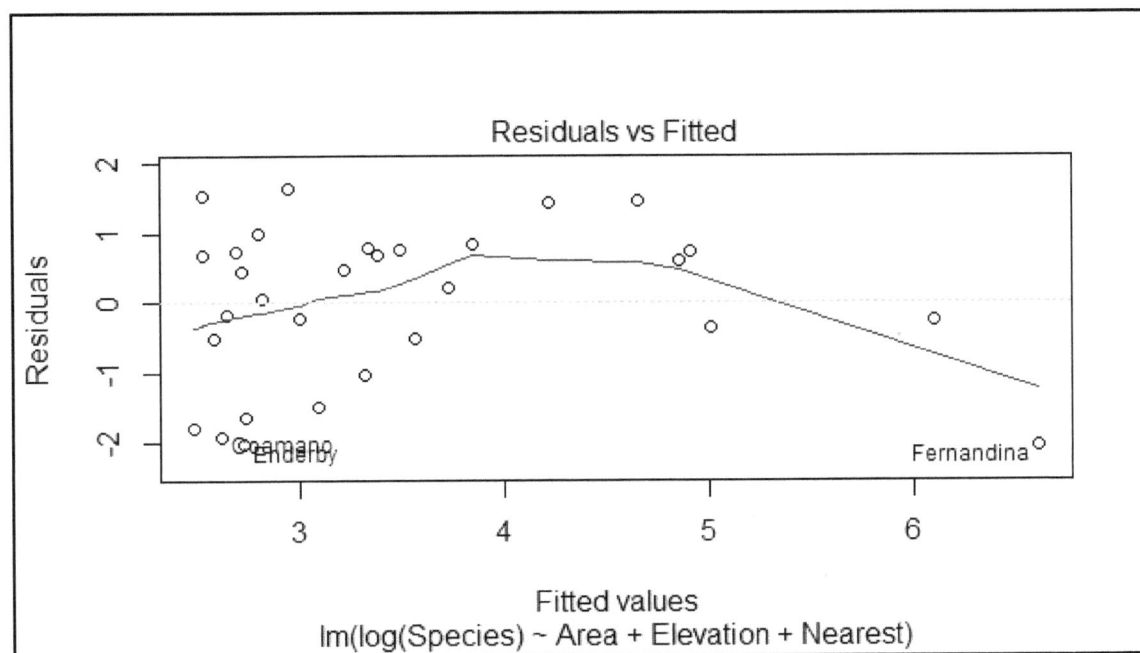

The Normal Q-Q linear model plot is shown in the following figure:

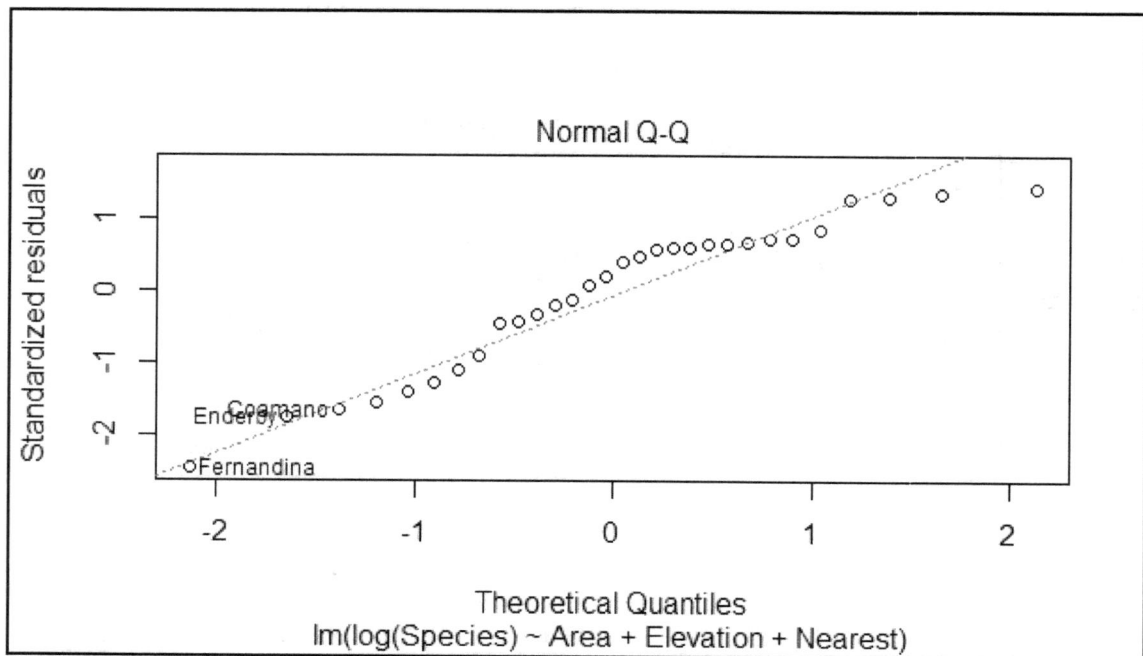

The **Scale-Location** linear model plot is shown in the following figure:

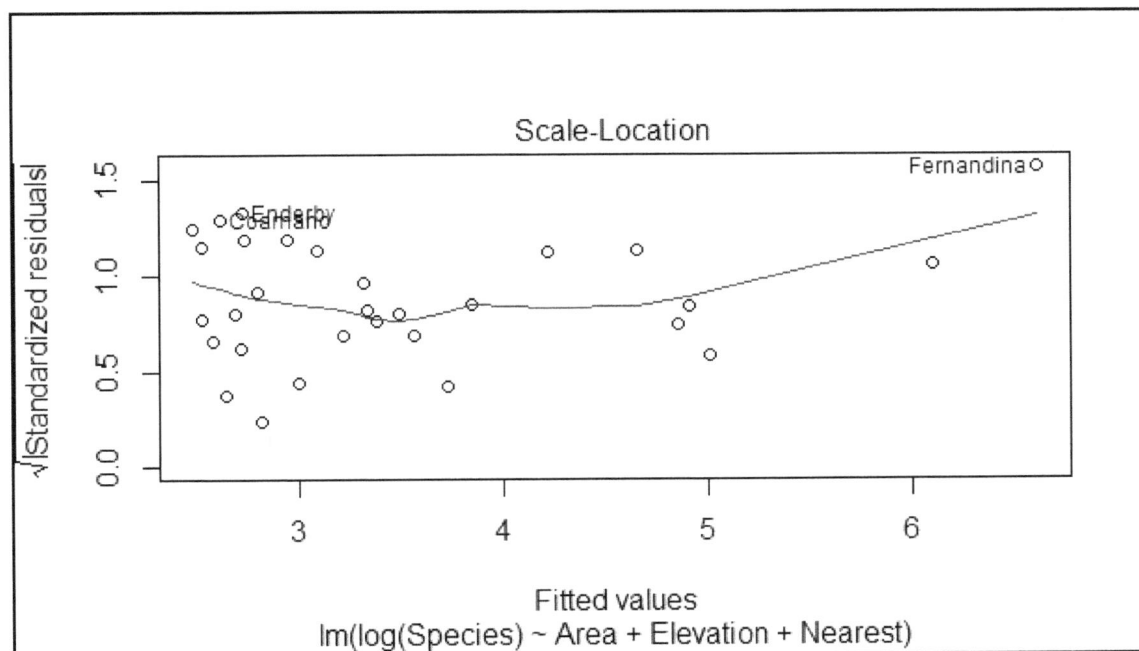

Let us carry out a Shapiro test as follows:

```
> shapiro.test(reg3$res)
```

The result is:

```
        Shapiro-Wilk normality test
data:   reg3$res
W = 0.91925, p-value = 0.02565
```

3
Clustering

In this chapter, we will cover the following recipes:

- Hierarchical clustering - World Bank
- Hierarchical clustering - Amazon rainforest burned between 1999-2010
- Hierarchical clustering - gene clustering
- Binary clustering - math test
- K-means clustering - European countries protein consumption
- K-means clustering - foodstuff

Introduction

Hierarchical clustering: One of the most important methods in unsupervised learning is Hierarchical clustering. In Hierarchical clustering for a given set of data points, the output is produced in the form of a binary tree (dendrogram). In the binary tree, the leaves represent the data points while internal nodes represent nested clusters of various sizes. Each object is assigned a separate cluster. Evaluation of all the clusters takes place based on a pairwise distance matrix. The distance matrix will be constructed using distance values. The pair of clusters with the shortest distance must be considered. The identified pair should then be removed from the matrix and merged together. The merged clusters' distance must be evaluated with the other clusters and the distance matrix should be updated. The process is to be repeated until the distance matrix is reduced to a single element.

An ordering of the objects is produced by hierarchical clustering. This helps with informative data display. The smaller clusters produced help in the discovery of information. The main disadvantage of hierarchical clustering is that, if the objects have been incorrectly grouped at an early stage then, there is no provision for a relocation of objects. Use of different distance metrics for measuring distances between clusters may result in the generation of different results.

K-means clustering: The K-means clustering algorithm is a method for estimating the mean (vectors) of a set of K-groups. The K-Means clustering method is unsupervised, non-deterministic, and iterative in nature. The method produces a specific number of disjointed, flat (non-hierarchical) clusters. K denotes the number of clusters. These clusters are based on the data at hand. Each of the clusters has at least one data point. The clusters are non-overlapping and non-hierarchical in nature. The dataset is partitioned into K number of clusters. The data points are randomly assigned to each of the clusters. This results in an almost equal distribution of data points among the clusters at the early stage. If a data point is closest to its own cluster, it is not changed. If a data point is not close to its own cluster, it is moved to the cluster to which it is closest. The steps are repeated for all the data points till no data points are moving from one cluster to another. At this point the clusters are stabilized and the clustering process ends. The choice of initial an partition can greatly affect the final clusters that result, in terms of inter-cluster and intra-cluster distances and cohesion.

The main advantage of K-means clustering is that it is relatively computationally, less expensive in terms of time compared to hierarchical clustering. The main challenge is that there is a difficulty in determining the number of clusters.

Hierarchical clustering - World Bank sample dataset

One of the main goals for establishing the World Bank was to fight and eliminate poverty. Continuous evolution and fine-tuning its policies in the ever-evolving world has been helping the institution to achieve the goal of poverty elimination. The barometer of success in the elimination of poverty is measured in terms of improvement of each of the parameters in health, education, sanitation, infrastructure, and other services needed to improve the lives of the poor. The development gains that will ensure the goals must be pursued in an environmentally, socially, and economically sustainable manner.

Getting ready

In order to perform Hierarchical clustering, we shall be using a dataset collected from the World Bank dataset.

Step 1 - collecting and describing data

The dataset titled `WBClust2013` shall be used. This is available in the CSV format titled `WBClust2013.csv`. The dataset is in standard format. There are 80 rows of data and 14 variables. The numeric variables are:

- `new.forest`
- `Rural`
- `log.CO2`
- `log.GNI`
- `log.Energy.2011`
- `LifeExp`
- `Fertility`
- `InfMort`
- `log.Exports`
- `log.Imports`
- `CellPhone`
- `RuralWater`
- `Pop`

The non-numeric variable is:

- `Country`

How to do it...

Let's get into the details.

Step 2 - exploring data

Version info: Code for this page was tested in R version 3.2.3 (2015-12-10)

Let's explore the data and understand the relationships between variables. We'll begin by importing the CSV file named WBClust2013.csv. We will be saving the data to the wbclust data frame:

```
> wbclust=read.csv("d:/WBClust2013.csv",header=T)
```

Next, we shall print the wbclust data frame. The head() function returns the wbclust data frame. The wbclust data frame is passed as an input parameter:

```
> head(wbclust)
```

The results are as follows:

```
        Country new.forest   Rural      log.CO2   log.GNI log.Energy.2011  LifeExp Fertility InfMort log.Exports
1         China  -5.929375  46.832 1.83973304   8.651724      7.615477 75.19951    1.6630    10.9    3.350966
2         India  -2.735634  68.006 0.56883558   7.346010      6.419537 66.21085    2.5050    41.4    3.172485
3 United States  -1.688899  18.723 2.87153773  10.865707      8.858293 78.74146    1.8805     5.9    2.604613
4     Indonesia   4.636429  47.748 0.64354020   8.137396      6.753775 70.60724    2.3700    24.5    3.271911
5        Brazil   3.222813  14.829 0.81104934   9.362203      7.223405 73.61788    1.8110    12.3    2.475628
6      Pakistan   6.053449  62.140 0.03161348   7.130899      6.177147 66.43588    3.2640    69.0    2.636213
  log.Imports CellPhone RuralWater         Pop
1    3.259900  88.70833       84.9 1357380000
2    3.408213  70.78318       90.7 1252139596
3    2.844193  95.52955       98.0  316128839
4    3.216865 121.54341       76.4  249865631
5    2.535485 135.30505       85.3  200361925
6    2.942568  70.13038       89.0  182142594
```

Step 3 - transforming data

Centering variables and creating z-scores are two common data analysis activities to standardize data. The numeric variables mentioned above need to create z-scores. The scale() function is a generic function whose default method centers and/or scales the columns of a numeric matrix. The data frame, wbclust is passed to the scale function. Only numeric fields are considered. The result is then stored in another data frame, wbnorm.

```
> wbnorm <- scale(wbclust[,2:13])
> wbnorm
```

The results are as follows:

```
        new.forest       Rural     log.CO2      log.GNI log.Energy.2011       LifeExp    Fertility
 [1,]   -1.5868009   0.33809236   0.73384701   0.032982395     0.4788446547   0.442646915  -0.822234191
 [2,]   -0.8025212   1.35749860  -0.24330597  -0.869172134    -0.7378944563  -0.593232631  -0.159983330
 [3,]   -0.5454767  -1.01519422   1.52716910   1.562685765     1.7432739991   0.850831828  -0.651165827
 [4,]    1.0078203   0.38219249  -0.18586795  -0.322381497    -0.3978432411  -0.086579641  -0.266163694
 [5,]    0.6606817  -1.20266791  -0.05707545   0.523872116     0.0799536232   0.260374726  -0.705829052
 [6,]    1.3557946   1.07508446  -0.65635910  -1.017798652    -0.9844993561  -0.567300156   0.436986270
 [7,]    1.6450615   0.67866475  -1.08103307  -0.550027966    -0.5744934561  -2.218369066   2.590481349
 [8,]    0.3497634   1.32095712  -1.25862465  -1.300715181    -1.8548802689  -0.122580415  -0.393580130
 [9,]   -0.1747622  -0.65767506   1.25049678   0.586262385     1.4190262396  -0.103436031  -0.879650240
[10,]   -0.2368652  -1.55508378   1.03273482   1.498270384     1.0649522402   1.352672723  -1.021224058
[11,]    0.5746262  -0.89069320   0.35853091   0.399324140     0.2110563885   0.665706675  -0.387287961
[12,]   -1.1822396   0.74900349  -0.70159339  -0.424525130    -1.1103654624  -0.323232448   0.289120282
[13,]    1.1735015   2.00282406  -2.02269355  -1.788005101    -1.2227708545  -0.967184767   1.520812500
[14,]   -1.8746588   1.34233316  -0.21681716  -0.869172134    -0.6086747631   0.489570472  -0.739649464
[15,]   -2.0615030   0.82641943   0.08947721  -0.417534229    -0.2637797596  -0.052006755   0.077546076
[16,]   -0.5644195  -0.70769693   1.02684921   1.460760873     1.1200997628   1.098744717  -1.044819694
[17,]   -1.2162839  -0.58637343   0.42838526   0.472760143     0.1976392919   0.403801606  -0.509985270
[18,]    0.2801866   0.58964604   0.48373630  -0.026258292     0.3509491664   0.326074452  -1.019651015
[19,]   -0.9229715  -0.90821771   0.65157461   1.408179559     1.1353905714   1.291565851  -0.549311330
[20,]   -0.9411997  -1.05443178   0.91454541   1.346769294     0.8673628225   1.168733729  -0.635828664
[21,]   -1.2980378  -0.40901003   0.81045102   1.280754422     0.8133720930   1.334290068  -1.029089270
[22,]   -0.1307375  -0.17319952   1.02062379   0.216483671     0.7846175740  -1.758631201  -0.233129803
[23,]    0.2599093  -1.06199043   1.20295976   1.042015543     1.4423618992   1.153555388  -1.110100955
[24,]    1.0048703   1.44406195  -1.73971591  -1.560358631    -1.0590872047  -1.211443610   2.028118682
[25,]    0.3322161  -0.75550416  -0.25947626   0.173495699    -0.6463659711   0.278720842  -0.308635839
[26,]   -1.5639512  -0.91178038   0.68271981   1.162638223     0.7642100131   1.269922662  -1.092010967
[27,]   -0.6911546  -0.43731885   0.78693642  -0.279306870     0.7940268971  -0.047754009  -0.926054991
[28,]    0.5232651   1.70481118  -1.37793791  -1.268194911    -0.9876392491  -1.184161949   1.376879119
[29,]    0.7039651  -0.44868089   0.26734982  -0.064126848    -0.1365866710  -0.054896262   0.087770852
[30,]    2.3249406   1.28691914  -1.36457894  -0.910502419    -1.2946081464  -1.094182501   1.402047797
[31,]   -0.1307375  -1.02458235   1.39001657   1.539876352     1.7858879570   1.138545697  -0.863919815
[32,]   -0.5276118  -0.43674112   0.34646874   0.080812552    -0.0009236421  -0.243922811   1.083506706
[33,]   -0.4797723   0.04768627  -0.27296128  -0.433957743    -0.8698178137  -0.082444949  -0.001892567
```

All data frames have a `rownames` attribute. In order to retrieve or set the row or column names of a matrix-like object, the `rownames()` function is used. The data frame `wbclust` with the first column is passed to the `rownames()` function.

```
> rownames(wbnorm)=wbclust[,1]
> rownames(wbnorm)
```

The call to the function `rownames(wbnorm)` results in displaying of the values from the first column. The results are as follows:

```
 [1] "China"               "India"         "United States"        "Indonesia"          "Brazil"
 [6] "Pakistan"            "Nigeria"       "Bangladesh"           "Russian Federation" "Japan"
[11] "Mexico"              "Philippines"   "Ethiopia"             "Vietnam"            "Egypt, Arab Rep."
[16] "Germany"             "Turkey"        "Thailand"             "France"             "United Kingdom"
[21] "Italy"               "South Africa"  "Korea, Rep."          "Tanzania"           "Colombia"
[26] "Spain"               "Ukraine"       "Kenya"                "Algeria"            "Sudan"
[31] "Canada"              "Iraq"          "Morocco"              "Peru"               "Uzbekistan"
[36] "Malaysia"            "Saudi Arabia"  "Nepal"                "Ghana"              "Mozambique"
[41] "Australia"           "Cameroon"      "Angola"               "Sri Lanka"          "Cote d'Ivoire"
[46] "Chile"               "Kazakhstan"    "Netherlands"          "Ecuador"            "Guatemala"
[51] "Cambodia"            "Zambia"        "Zimbabwe"             "Senegal"            "Belgium"
[56] "Greece"              "Tunisia"       "Bolivia"              "Czech Republic"     "Portugal"
[61] "Dominican Republic"  "Benin"         "Haiti"                "Hungary"            "Sweden"
[66] "Belarus"             "Azerbaijan"    "United Arab Emirates" "Austria"            "Tajikistan"
[71] "Honduras"            "Switzerland"   "Israel"               "Bulgaria"           "Serbia"
[76] "Togo"                "Paraguay"      "Jordan"               "El Salvador"        "Nicaragua"
```

Step 4 - training and evaluating the model performance

The next step is about training the model. The first step is to calculate the distance matrix. The `dist()` function is used. Using the specified distance measure, distances between the rows of a data matrix are computed. The distance measure used can be Euclidean, maximum, Manhattan, Canberra, binary, or Minkowski. The distance measure used is Euclidean. The Euclidean distance calculates the distance between two vectors as $sqrt(sum((x\_i - y\_i)^2))$. The result is then stored in a new data frame, `dist1`.

```
> dist1 <- dist(wbnorm, method="euclidean")
```

The next step is to perform clustering using Ward's method. The `hclust()` function is used. In order to perform cluster analysis on a set of dissimilarities of *n* objects, the `hclust()` function is used. At the first stage, each of the objects is assigned to its own cluster. After this, at each stage the algorithm iterates and joins two of the most similar clusters. This process continues till there is just a single cluster left. The `hclust()` function requires that we provide the data in the form of a distance matrix. The `dist1` data frame is passed. By default, the complete linkage method is used. There are multiple agglomeration methods which can be used, some of them could be `ward.D`, `ward.D2`, `single`, `complete`, and `average`.

```
> clust1 <- hclust(dist1,method="ward.D")
> clust1
```

The call to the function `clust1` results in displaying the agglomeration methods used, the manner in which the distance is calculated, and the number of objects. The results are as follows:

```
Call:
hclust(d = dist1, method = "ward.D")

Cluster method   : ward.D
Distance         : euclidean
Number of objects: 80
```

Step 5 - plotting the model

The `plot()` function is a generic function for plotting R objects. Here, the `plot()` function is used to draw the dendrogram:

```
> plot(clust1,labels= wbclust$Country, cex=0.7,
xlab="",ylab="Distance",main="Clustering for 80 Most Populous Countries")
```

The result is as follows:

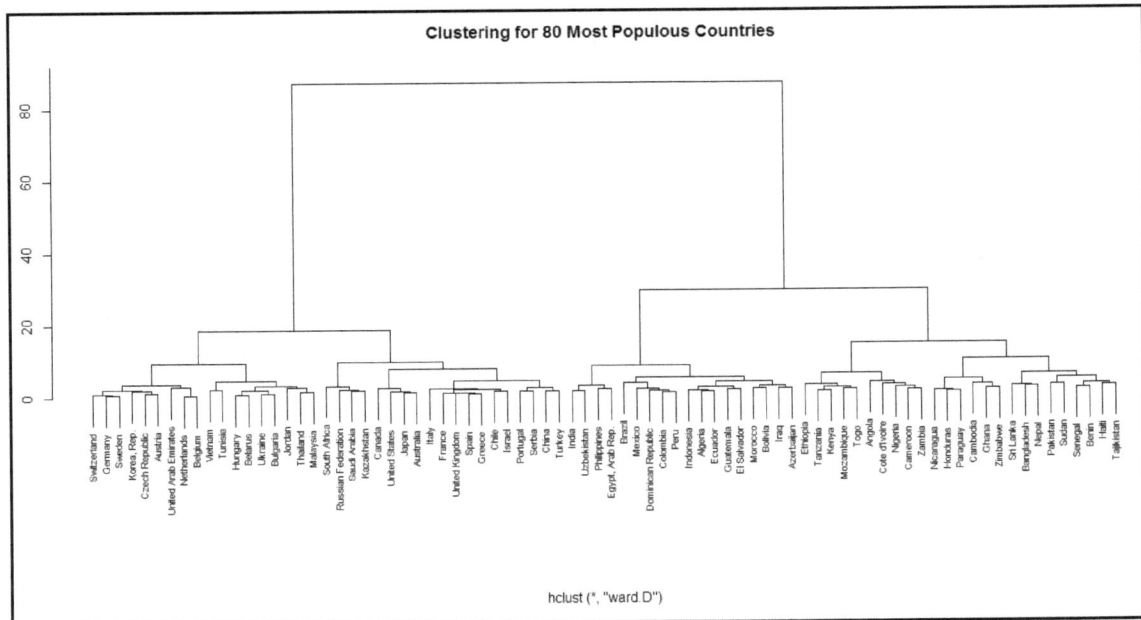

The `rect.hclust()` function highlights the clusters and draws the rectangles around the branches of the dendrogram. The dendrogram is first cut at a certain level followed by drawing a rectangle around the selected branches.

The object `clust1` is passed as an object to the function along with the number of clusters to be formed:

```
> rect.hclust(clust1, k=5)
```

The result is as follows:

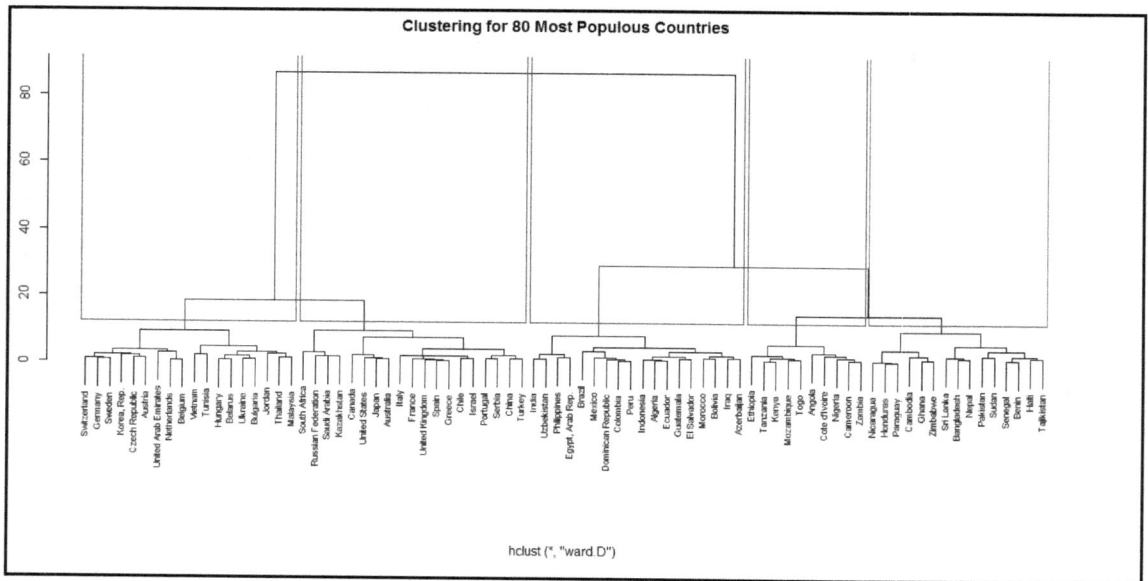

Clustering for 80 Most Populous Countries

The `cuts()` function shall cut the tree into multiple groups on the basis of the desired number of groups or the cut height. Here, `clust1` is passed as an object to the function along with the number of the desired group:

```
> cuts=cutree(clust1, k=5)
> cuts
```

The result is as follows:

China	India	United States	Indonesia	Brazil
1	2	1	2	2
Pakistan	Nigeria	Bangladesh	Russian Federation	Japan
3	4	3	1	1
Mexico	Philippines	Ethiopia	Vietnam	Egypt, Arab Rep.
2	2	4	5	2
Germany	Turkey	Thailand	France	United Kingdom
5	1	5	1	1
Italy	South Africa	Korea, Rep.	Tanzania	Colombia
1	1	5	4	2
Spain	Ukraine	Kenya	Algeria	Sudan
1	5	4	2	3
Canada	Iraq	Morocco	Peru	Uzbekistan
1	2	2	2	2
Malaysia	Saudi Arabia	Nepal	Ghana	Mozambique
5	1	3	3	4
Australia	Cameroon	Angola	Sri Lanka	Cote d'Ivoire
1	4	4	3	4
Chile	Kazakhstan	Netherlands	Ecuador	Guatemala
1	1	5	2	2
Cambodia	Zambia	Zimbabwe	Senegal	Belgium
3	4	3	3	5
Greece	Tunisia	Bolivia	Czech Republic	Portugal
1	5	2	5	1
ominican Republic	Benin	Haiti	Hungary	Sweden
2	3	3	5	5
Belarus	Azerbaijan	United Arab Emirates	Austria	Tajikistan
5	2	5	5	3
Honduras	Switzerland	Israel	Bulgaria	Serbia
3	5	1	5	1
Togo	Paraguay	Jordan	El Salvador	Nicaragua
4	3	5	2	3

Getting the list of countries in each group:

```
for (i in 1:5){
print(paste("Countries in Cluster ",i))
print(wbclust$Country[cuts==i])
print (" ")
}
```

The result is as follows:

```
[1] "Countries in Cluster  1"
 [1] China            United States    Russian Federation Japan          Turkey
 [6] France           United Kingdom   Italy              South Africa   Spain
[11] Canada           Saudi Arabia     Australia          Chile          Kazakhstan
[16] Greece           Portugal         Israel             Serbia
80 Levels: Algeria Angola Australia Austria Azerbaijan Bangladesh Belarus Belgium Benin Bolivia ... Zimbabwe
[1] " "
[1] "Countries in Cluster  2"
 [1] India            Indonesia        Brazil             Mexico         Philippines
 [6] Egypt, Arab Rep. Colombia         Algeria            Iraq           Morocco
[11] Peru             Uzbekistan       Ecuador            Guatemala      Bolivia
[16] Dominican Republic Azerbaijan     El Salvador
80 Levels: Algeria Angola Australia Austria Azerbaijan Bangladesh Belarus Belgium Benin Bolivia ... Zimbabwe
[1] " "
[1] "Countries in Cluster  3"
 [1] Pakistan   Bangladesh Sudan      Nepal      Ghana    Sri Lanka Cambodia  Zimbabwe   Senegal
[10] Benin      Haiti      Tajikistan Honduras   Paraguay Nicaragua
80 Levels: Algeria Angola Australia Austria Azerbaijan Bangladesh Belarus Belgium Benin Bolivia ... Zimbabwe
[1] " "
[1] "Countries in Cluster  4"
 [1] Nigeria       Ethiopia     Tanzania     Kenya       Mozambique    Cameroon    Angola
 [8] Cote d'Ivoire Zambia       Togo
80 Levels: Algeria Angola Australia Austria Azerbaijan Bangladesh Belarus Belgium Benin Bolivia ... Zimbabwe
[1] " "
[1] "Countries in Cluster  5"
 [1] Vietnam          Germany          Thailand           Korea, Rep.    Ukraine
 [6] Malaysia         Netherlands      Belgium            Tunisia        Czech Republic
[11] Hungary          Sweden           Belarus            United Arab Emirates Austria
[16] Switzerland      Bulgaria         Jordan
80 Levels: Algeria Angola Australia Austria Azerbaijan Bangladesh Belarus Belgium Benin Bolivia ... Zimbabwe
[1] " "
```

Hierarchical clustering - Amazon rainforest burned between 1999-2010

Between 1999-2010, 33,000 square miles (85,500 square kilometers), or 2.8 percent of the Amazon rainforest burned down. This was found by NASA-led research. The main purpose of the research was to measure the extent of fire smolders under the forest canopy. The research found that burning forests destroys a much larger area compared to when forest lands are cleared for agriculture and cattle pasture. Yet, no correlation could be established between the fires and deforestation.

The answer to the query of no correlation between fires and deforestation lay in humidity data from the **Atmospheric Infrared Sounder** (**AIRS**) instrument aboard NASA's Aqua satellite. The fire frequency coincides with low night-time humidity, which allowed the low-intensity surface fires to continue burning.

Getting ready

In order to perform hierarchical clustering, we shall be using a dataset collected on the Amazon rainforest, which burned from 1999-2010.

Step 1 - collecting and describing data

The `NASAUnderstory` dataset shall be used. This is available in CSV format as `NASAUnderstory.csv`. The dataset is in standard format. There are 64 rows of data and 32 variables. The numeric variables are:

- `PlotID`
- `SPHA`
- `BLIT`
- `ASMA`
- `MOSS`
- `LEGR`
- `CHCA`
- `GRAS`
- `SEDG`
- `SMTR`
- `PTAQ`
- `COCA`
- `VAAN`
- `GAHI`
- `ARNU`
- `LYOB`
- `PIMA`
- `RUBU`
- `VAOX`
- `ACSP`
- `COCO`
- `ACRU`
- `TRBO`
- `MACA`

- CLOB
- STRO
- FUNG
- DILO
- ERIO
- GATR

The non-numeric variables are:

- Overstory Species
- Labels

How to do it...

Let's get into the details.

Step 2 - exploring data

Version info: Code for this page was tested in R version 3.2.3 (2015-12-10)

Let's explore the data and understand the relationships among the variables. We'll begin by importing the file named NASAUnderstory.csv. We will be saving the data to the NASA data frame:

```
> NASA = read.csv("d:/NASAU    nderstory.csv",header=T)
```

Next, we shall obtain the long version of each of the species column labels:

```
> NASA.lab=NASA$Labels
```

Next, we shall print the `NASA.lab` data frame. This contains the complete name of each of the species as obtained.

The results are as follows:

```
 [1] Sphagnum Moss          Brown Litter             Big-leaved Aster        Mosses (Non-Sphagnum)      Labrador Tea
 [6] Leatherleaf            Grasses (Unidentified)   Sedges (Unidentified)   Bog False Solomon Seal     Bracken Fern
[11] Bunchberry             Lowbush Blueberry        Creeping Snowberry      Wild Sarsaparilla          Ground Pine
[16] Spruce (Black)         Brier                    Small Cranberry         Maple (Mountain)           Hazelnut (Beaked)
[21] Maple (Red)            Starflower               Canadian Mayflower      Blue-bead Lily             Twisted Stalk
[26] Fungi                  Bush Honeysuckle         Cotton Grass            Bedstraw (Narrow Leaves)
[31]
[36]
[41]
[46]
[51]
[56]
[61]
30 Levels:  Bedstraw (Narrow Leaves) Big-leaved Aster Blue-bead Lily Bog False Solomon Seal Bracken Fern Brier Brown Litter   ... Wild Sarsaparilla
```

Next, we shall pass the entire data content to the `NASA` data frame:

> `NASA=NASA[,-32]`

Printing the `NASA` data frame shall results in displaying the entire data content.

> `NASA`

The results are as follows:

	PlotID	Overstory.Species	SPHA	BLIT	ASMA	MOSS	LEGR	CHCA	GRAS	SEDG	SMTR	PTAQ	COCA	VAAN	GAHI	ARNU	LYOB	PIMA	RUBU	VAOX	ACSP	COCO	ACRU	TRBO	MACA
1	2	Aspen	68	14	0	3	33	5	5	0	14	0	0	4	28	0	0	1	0	6	0	0	0	0	0
2	3	Spruce	0	6	18	2	0	0	5	0	0	2	0	0	0	7	0	0	6	0	2	1	2	2	2
3	12	Aspen	60	1	0	0	5	9	12	1	14	0	0	0	2	0	0	3	0	4	0	0	0	0	0
4	14	Aspen	16	14	0	72	14	1	2	0	13	0	0	5	7	0	0	2	0	1	0	0	0	0	0
5	15	Aspen	68	7	0	30	27	8	4	0	12	0	0	5	13	0	0	3	0	3	0	0	0	0	0
6	16	Spruce	0	14	14	3	0	0	2	0	0	1	0	0	0	2	1	0	1	0	17	6	10	1	0
7	18	Aspen	62	7	0	3	6	12	4	0	0	0	0	0	0	0	0	13	0	5	0	0	0	0	0
8	19	Aspen	62	5	0	0	6	28	1	0	0	0	0	0	0	0	0	15	0	5	0	0	0	0	0
9	20	Spruce	0	5	8	14	0	0	4	6	0	14	10	3	0	0	6	0	0	0	1	8	1	1	0
10	21	Spruce	0	16	26	5	0	0	1	0	0	18	6	10	0	10	11	0	3	0	1	5	5	4	4
11	36	Spruce	0	25	38	3	0	5	3	0	6	7	0	0	0	0	1	0	0	3	6	4	4
12	38	Aspen	82	10	0	10	24	12	8	0	6	0	0	4	2	0	0	2	0	1	0	0	0	0	0
13	39	Aspen	60	3	0	34	24	0	5	0	9	0	1	5	4	0	1	6	0	4	0	0	0	0	0
14	41	Aspen	72	17	0	4	6	0	3	0	5	0	0	5	6	0	1	1	0	0	0	0	0	0	0
15	42	Aspen	34	14	0	36	15	1	0	5	6	0	4	9	8	0	1	4	0	2	0	0	0	1	0
16	43	Aspen	32	13	0	34	28	3	0	0	6	0	0	5	5	0	0	2	0	1	0	0	0	0	0
17	45	Aspen	55	25	0	8	7	4	0	10	4	0	0	5	3	0	0	0	0	2	0	0	0	0	0
18	47	Aspen	64	8	0	5	9	8	1	32	20	0	0	5	4	0	0	2	0	5	0	0	0	0	0
19	48	Aspen	64	12	0	13	6	0	10	2	10	0	0	0	1	0	7	1	0	0	0	0	0	0	0
20	49	Aspen	48	5	0	6	1	0	5	14	5	0	1	2	2	0	0	0	0	1	0	0	0	0	0
21	50	Aspen	38	18	0	38	11	0	2	6	4	0	2	0	3	0	0	0	0	1	0	0	1	0	0
22	51	Aspen	74	3	0	2	34	17	1	0	2	0	0	0	0	0	0	6	0	3	0	0	0	0	0
23	52	Aspen	86	3	0	5	36	9	17	1	0	0	0	4	0	0	1	0	2	0	0	0	0	0
24	54	Aspen	62	16	0	0	22	10	5	0	7	1	0	4	3	0	0	1	0	2	0	0	0	0	0
25	55	Aspen	38	30	0	18	4	2	0	2	6	0	0	5	6	0	0	4	0	2	0	0	0	0	0
26	56	Aspen	68	13	0	6	34	5	0	5	2	0	0	2	3	0	0	6	0	4	0	0	0	0	0
27	57	Aspen	72	5	0	4	17	20	0	14	0	0	0	4	0	0	0	3	0	4	0	0	0	0	0
28	62	Aspen	66	1	0	12	7	20	17	6	0	0	0	0	0	0	0	4	0	4	0	0	0	0	0
29	63	Aspen	56	8	0	1	12	12	6	0	0	0	0	0	0	0	0	8	0	3	0	0	0	0	0
30	64	Aspen	56	0	0	6	6	24	0	34	0	0	0	0	0	0	0	7	0	4	0	0	0	0	0
31	68	Aspen	62	8	0	9	4	5	1	10	1	0	0	0	5	0	0	1	0	5	0	0	0	0	0
32	69	Spruce	1	15	11	5	0	0	2	0	0	2	17	7	1	1	3	0	0	0	0	2	1	1	3
33	71	Spruce	1	20	16	5	0	0	2	2	0	4	5	3	0	4	2	0	3	0	0	1	2	0	2
34	72	Spruce	0	32	14	4	0	0	1	0	0	0	4	0	0	5	5	0	4	0	3	2	2	5	4

Step 3 - transforming data

Next, data standardization shall be carried out. The `scale()` function shall center and scale the columns of all the numeric variables as mentioned earlier:

```
> NASAscale <- scale(NASA[,3:31])
```

This shall scale all the numeric values between columns 3 to 31 of the `NASA` data frame.

Printing the `NASAscale` data frame results in displaying all the scaled and centered values of the `NASAscale`.

```
> NASAscale
```

The results are as follows:

```
            SPHA         BLIT         ASMA         MOSS         LEGR         CHCA         GRAS         SEDG         SMTR
 [1,]  1.2641384  -0.24208432  -0.77255673  -0.50604541   2.54875930   0.19309198   0.36896403  -0.49052647   2.6140567
 [2,] -0.9204396  -0.95979313   0.65894545  -0.58972221  -0.65297519  -0.55782127   0.36896403  -0.49052647  -0.5529735
 [3,]  1.0071292  -1.40836113  -0.77255673  -0.75707581  -0.16786391   0.79382257   2.37776818  -0.35498626   2.6140567
 [4,] -0.4064213  -0.24208432  -0.77255673   5.26765381   0.70533641  -0.40763862  -0.49195204  -0.49052647   2.3878403
 [5,]  1.2641384  -0.87007953  -0.77255673   1.75322820   1.96662576   0.64363992   0.08199201  -0.49052647   2.1616238
 [6,] -0.9204396  -0.24208432   0.34083385  -0.50604541  -0.65297519  -0.55782127  -0.49195204  -0.49052647  -0.5529735
 [7,]  1.0713815  -0.87007953  -0.77255673  -0.50604541  -0.07084165   1.24437052   0.08199201  -0.49052647  -0.5529735
 [8,]  1.0713815  -1.04950673  -0.77255673  -0.75707581  -0.07084165   3.64729290  -0.77892406  -0.49052647  -0.5529735
 [9,] -0.9204396  -1.04950673  -0.13633354   0.41439939  -0.65297519  -0.55782127   0.08199201   0.32271478  -0.5529735
[10,] -0.9204396  -0.06265712   1.29516864  -0.33869181  -0.65297519  -0.55782127  -0.77892406  -0.49052647  -0.5529735
[11,] -0.9204396   0.74476529   2.24950342  -0.50604541  -0.65297519  -0.55782127   0.36896403  -0.08390584  -0.5529735
[12,]  1.7139045  -0.60093872  -0.77255673   0.07969219   1.67555898   1.24437052   1.22988009  -0.49052647   0.8043251
[13,]  1.0071292  -1.22893393  -0.77255673   2.08793540   1.67555898  -0.55782127   0.36896403  -0.49052647   1.4829745
[14,]  1.3926430   0.02705648  -0.77255673  -0.42236861  -0.07084165  -0.55782127  -0.20498002  -0.49052647   0.5781087
[15,]  0.1718494  -0.24208432  -0.77255673   2.25528900   0.80235867  -0.40763862  -1.06589608   0.18717457   0.8043251
[16,]  0.1075971  -0.33179792  -0.77255673   2.08793540   2.06364801  -0.10727332  -1.06589608  -0.49052647   0.8043251
[17,]  0.8464985   0.74476529  -0.77255673  -0.08766141   0.02618061   0.04290093  -1.06589608   0.86487561   0.3518923
[18,]  1.1356338  -0.78036593  -0.77255673  -0.33869181   0.22022512   0.64363992  -0.77892406   3.84676019   3.9713554
[19,]  1.1356338  -0.42151152  -0.77255673   0.33072259  -0.07084165  -0.55782127   1.80382414  -0.21944605   1.7091909
[20,]  0.6216155  -1.04950673  -0.77255673  -0.25501501  -0.55595294  -0.55782127   0.36896403   1.40703644   0.5781087
[21,]  0.3003540   0.11677008  -0.77255673   2.42264260   0.41426964  -0.55782127  -0.49195204   0.32271478   0.3518923
[22,]  1.4568953  -1.22893393  -0.77255673  -0.58972221   2.64578156   1.99528376  -0.77892406  -0.49052647  -0.1005406
[23,]  1.8424091  -1.22893393  -0.77255673  -0.33869181   2.83982607   0.79382257   3.81262829  -0.35498626  -0.5529735
[24,]  1.0713815  -0.06265712  -0.77255673  -0.75707581   1.48151447   0.94400522   0.36896403  -0.49052647   1.0305416
[25,]  0.3003540   1.19333330  -0.77255673   0.74910659  -0.26488616  -0.25745597  -1.06589608  -0.21944605   0.8043251
[26,]  1.2641384  -0.33179792  -0.77255673  -0.25501501   2.64578156   0.19309198  -1.06589608   0.18717457  -0.1005406
[27,]  1.3926430  -1.04950673  -0.77255673  -0.42236861   0.99640318   2.44583171  -1.06589608   1.40703644  -0.5529735
[28,]  1.1998861  -1.40836113  -0.77255673   0.24704579   0.02618061   2.44583171   3.81262829   0.32271478  -0.5529735
[29,]  0.8786246  -0.78036593  -0.77255673  -0.67339901   0.51129190   1.24437052   0.65593605  -0.49052647  -0.5529735
[30,]  0.8786246  -1.49807473  -0.77255673  -0.25501501  -0.07084165   3.04656230  -1.06589608   4.11784060  -0.5529735
[31,]  1.0713815  -0.78036593  -0.77255673  -0.00398461  -0.26488616   0.19309198  -0.77892406   0.86487561  -0.3267571
[32,] -0.8883135  -0.15237072   0.10225016  -0.33869181  -0.65297519  -0.55782127  -0.49195204  -0.49052647  -0.5529735
[33,] -0.8883135   0.29619729   0.49988965  -0.33869181  -0.65297519  -0.55782127  -0.49195204  -0.21944605  -0.5529735
```

In order to encode a vector as a factor, the function factor is used. If the argument ordered is TRUE, the factor levels are assumed to be ordered. Here, we are passing the `OverstorySpecies` column as a value to the factor function:

```
> rownames(NASAscale)=as.factor(NASA$Overstory.Species)
```

The `as.factor()` returns a data frame with the row names.

Printing the data frame `rownames(NASAscale)` results in displaying all the values of the `OverstorySpecies` column:

```
> rownames(NASAscale)
```

The results are as follows:

```
 [1] "Aspen"  "Spruce" "Aspen"  "Aspen"  "Aspen"  "Spruce" "Aspen"  "Aspen"  "Spruce" "Spruce" "Spruce"
[12] "Aspen"  "Aspen"  "Aspen"  "Aspen"  "Aspen"  "Aspen"  "Aspen"  "Aspen"  "Aspen"  "Aspen"  "Aspen"
[23] "Aspen"  "Aspen"  "Aspen"  "Aspen"  "Aspen"  "Aspen"  "Aspen"  "Aspen"  "Aspen"  "Spruce" "Spruce"
[34] "Spruce" "Spruce" "Spruce" "Spruce" "Spruce" "Spruce" "Spruce" "Spruce" "Spruce" "Spruce" "Spruce"
[45] "Spruce" "Spruce" "Spruce" "Spruce" "Spruce" "Spruce" "Spruce" "Spruce" "Spruce" "Spruce" "Spruce"
[56] "Spruce" "Spruce" "Spruce" "Aspen"  "Spruce" "Aspen"  "Aspen"  "Aspen"
```

Step 4 - training and evaluating model performance

The next step is about training the model. The first step is to calculate the distance matrix. The `dist()` function is used. The function computes and returns the distance matrix, using the specified distance measure to compute the distances between the rows of a data matrix. The distance measure used can be Euclidean, maximum, Manhattan, Canberra, binary, or Minkowski. The distance measure used is Euclidean. The Euclidean distance calculates the distance between two vectors as $sqrt(sum((x\_i - y\_i)^2))$. The result is then stored in a new data frame `dist1`.

```
> dist1 <- dist(NASAscale, method="euclidean")
```

The next step is to perform clustering using Ward's method. The `hclust()` function is used. In order to perform cluster analysis on a set of dissimilarities of *n* objects, the `hclust()` function is used. At the first stage, each of the objects is assigned to its own cluster. The algorithm then proceeds iteratively at each stage joining the two most similar clusters. This process continues till there is just a single cluster left. The `hclust()` function requires us to provide the data in the form of a distance matrix. The `dist1` data frame is passed. By default, the complete linkage method is used. There can be multiple agglomeration methods which can be used, some of them could be `ward.D`, `ward.D2`, `single`, `complete`, and `average`.

```
> clust1 <- hclust(dist1,method="ward.D")
> clust1
```

The call to the function, `clust1` results in display of the agglomeration method used, the manner in which the distance is calculated, and the number of objects. The results are as follows:

```
call:
hclust(d = dist1, method = "ward.D")

Cluster method   : ward.D
Distance         : euclidean
Number of objects: 63
```

Step 5 - plotting the model

The `plot()` function is a generic function for the plotting R objects. Here, the `plot()` function is used to draw the dendrogram:

```
> plot(clust1, labels= NASA[,2], cex=0.5,
xlab="",ylab="Distance",main="Clustering for NASA Understory Data")
```

The result is as follows:

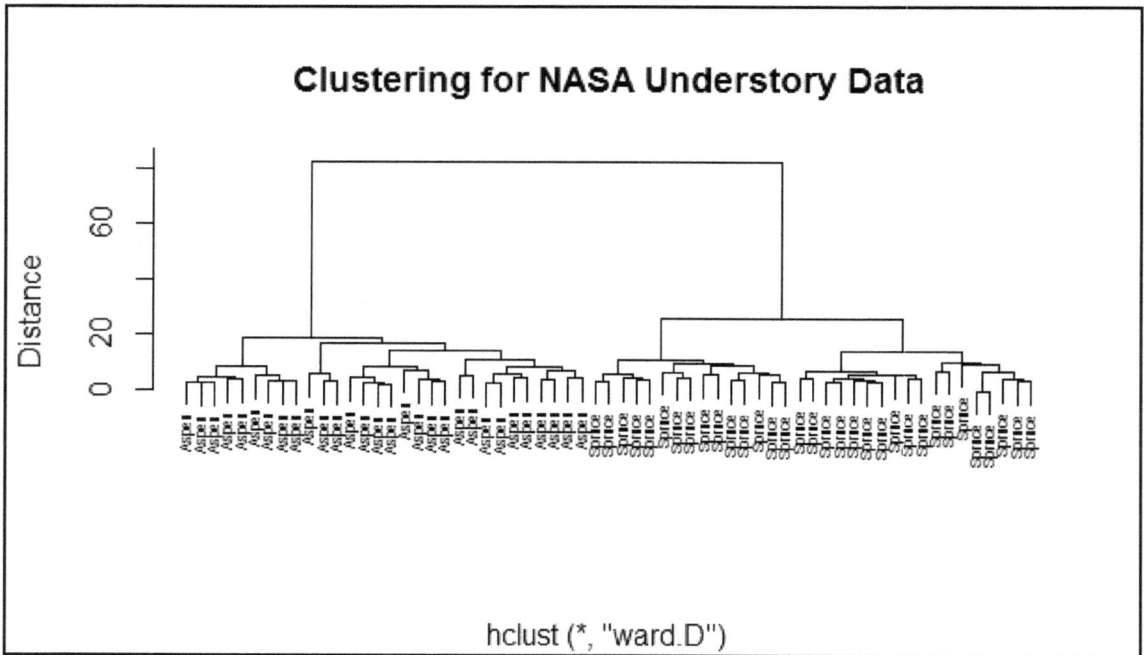

The `rect.hclust()` function highlights clusters and draws rectangles around the branches of the dendrogram. The dendrogram is first cut at a certain level followed by drawing a rectangle around selected branches.

The object, `clust1` is passed as an object to the function along with the number of clusters to be formed:

```
> rect.hclust(clust1,k=2)
```

The result is as follows:

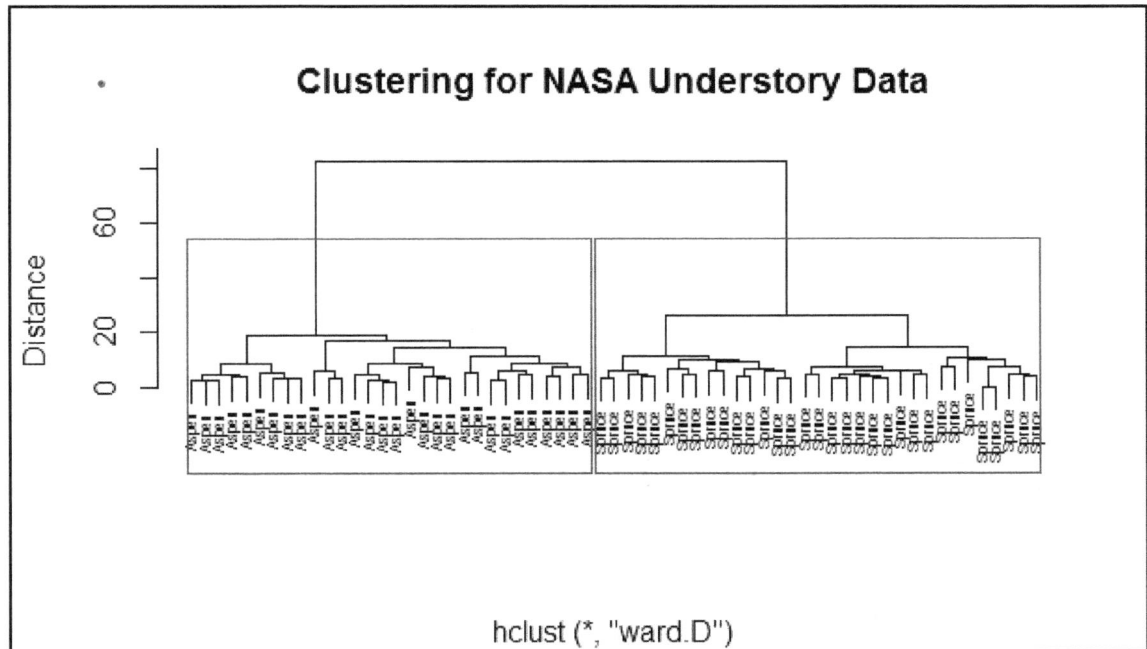

The `cuts()` function shall cut the tree into multiple groups on the basis of the desired number of groups or the cut height. Here, `clust1` is passed as an object to the function along with the number of desired groups:

```
> cuts=cutree(clust1,k=2)
> cuts
```

The result is as follows:

```
Aspen Spruce  Aspen  Aspen  Aspen Spruce  Aspen  Aspen Spruce Spruce Spruce  Aspen  Asp
en  Aspen
      1       2      1      1      1      2      1      1      2      2      2      1
1     1
Aspen Aspen  Aspen  Aspen  Aspen  Aspen  Aspen  Aspen  Aspen  Aspen  Aspen  Aspen  Asp
en  Aspen
      1      1      1      1      1      1      1      1      1      1      1      1
1     1
Aspen Aspen  Aspen Spruce Spruce Spruce Spruce Spruce Spruce Spruce Spruce Spruce Spru
ce Spruce
      1      1      1      2      2      2      2      2      2      2      2      2
2     2
Spruce Spruce Spruce Spruce Spruce Spruce Spruce Spruce Spruce Spruce Spruce Spruce Spru
ce Spruce
      2       2      2      2      2      2      2      2      2      2      2     `2
2     2
Spruce Spruce  Aspen Spruce  Aspen  Aspen  Aspen
      2       2      1      2      1      1      1
```

Step 6 - improving model performance

The following package needs to be loaded as a first step:

```
> library(vegan)
```

The vegan library is primarily used by community and vegetation ecologists. It contains ordination methods, diversity analysis, and other functions. Some of the popular tools are **diversity analysis, species abundance models, analysis of species richness, dissimilarity analyses, and so on.**

The next step is about improving the model by training using the distance method, jaccard. The first step is to calculate the distance matrix. The vegdist() function is used. The function calculates pairwise distance. The result is then stored in a new data frame, dist1. The jaccard coefficient measures similarity between finite sample sets. This is calculated by dividing the size of the intersection by the size of the union of the sample sets:

```
> dist1 <- vegdist(NASA[,3:31], method="jaccard", upper=T)
```

The next step is to perform clustering using Ward's method. The hclust() function is used:

```
> clust1 <- hclust(dist1,method="ward.D")
> clust1
```

The call to the function, `clust1` results in display of the agglomeration methods used, the manner in which the distance is calculated, and the number of objects. The results are as follows:

```
call:
hclust(d = dist1, method = "ward.D")

Cluster method   : ward.D
Distance         : jaccard
Number of objects: 63
```

The `plot()` function is a generic function for the plotting R objects:

```
> plot(clust1,labels= NASA[,2], cex=0.5,
xlab="",ylab="Distance",main="Clustering for NASA Understory Data")
```

The `clust1` data frame is passed as an object to the function. `cex` gives the numerical value of the amount by which plotting text and symbols can be magnified relative to the default.

The result is as follows:

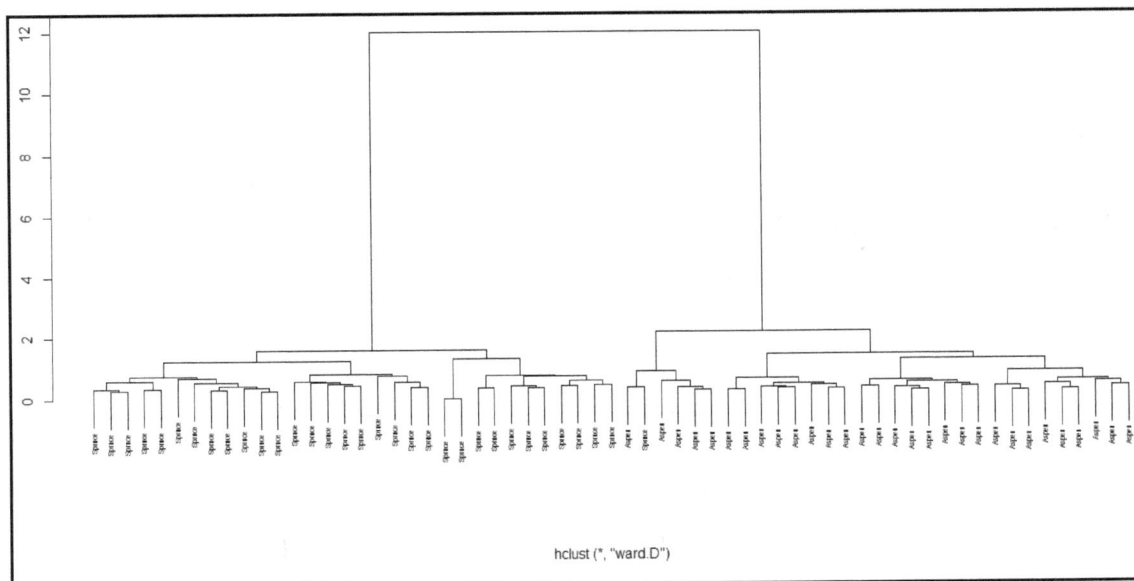

The object `clust1` is passed as an object to the function along with the number of clusters to be formed:

```
> rect.hclust(clust1,k=2)
```

The result is as follows:

The `cuts()` function shall cut the tree into multiple groups on the basis of the desired number of groups or the cut height:

```
> cuts=cutree(clust1,k=2)
> cuts
```

The result is as follows:

```
[1] 1 2 1 1 1 2 1 1 2 2 2 1 1 1 1 1 1 1 1 1 1 1 1 1 1 1 1 1 1 1 2 2 2 2 2 2 2 2 2 2 2 2 2 2 2 2
[47] 2 2 2 2 2 2 2 2 2 2 2 1 1 1 1 1
```

Using principal components lets us plot of two cluster solutions.

The `clusplot()` function shall draw a two-dimensional clustering plot. Here, the NASA data frame is passed as an object.

The result is as follows:

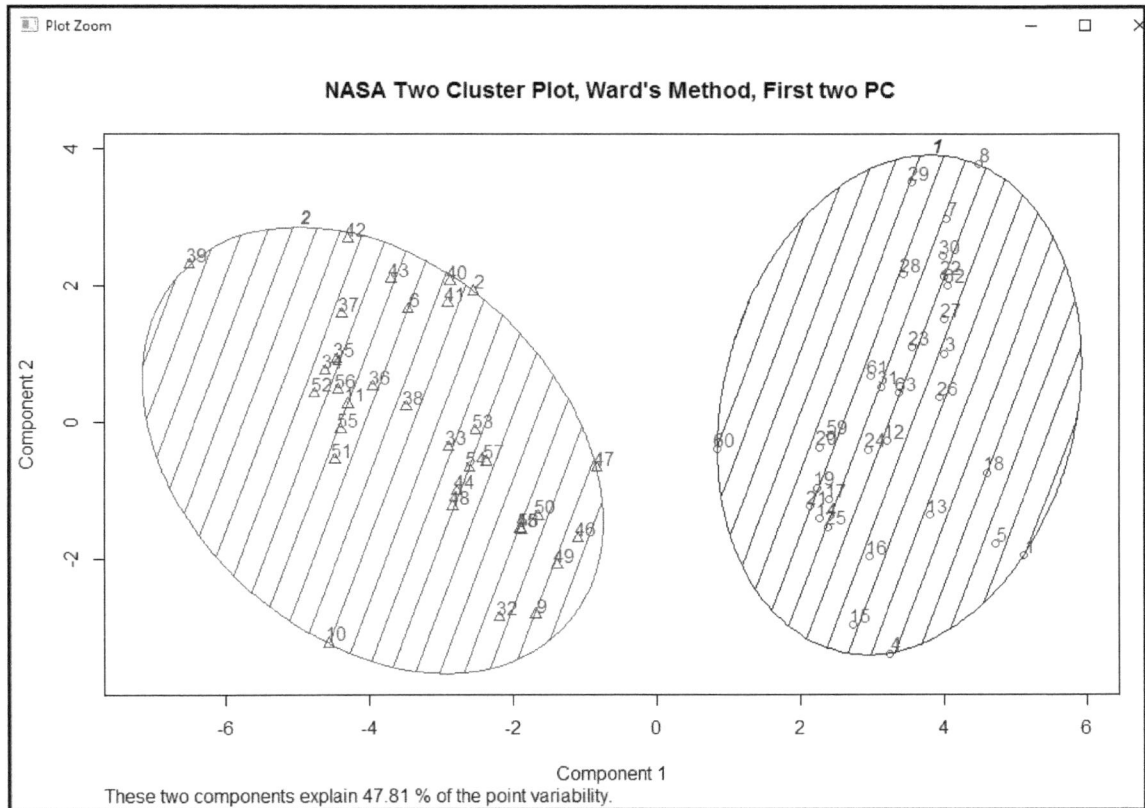

Using discriminant functions lets us plot two cluster solutions.

The `plotcluster()` function plots using projection methods in order to distinguish the given classes. Various projection methods include classical discriminant coordinates, methods to project differences in mean and covariance structure, asymmetric methods (separation of a homogeneous class from a heterogeneous one), local neighborhood-based methods and methods based on robust covariance matrices.

The `clusplot()` function shall draw a two-dimensional clustering plot. Here, the NASA data frame is passed as an object:

```
> clusplot(NASA, cuts, color=TRUE, shade=TRUE, labels=2, lines=0,
main="NASA Two Cluster  Plot, Ward's Method, First two PC")
```

The result is as follows:

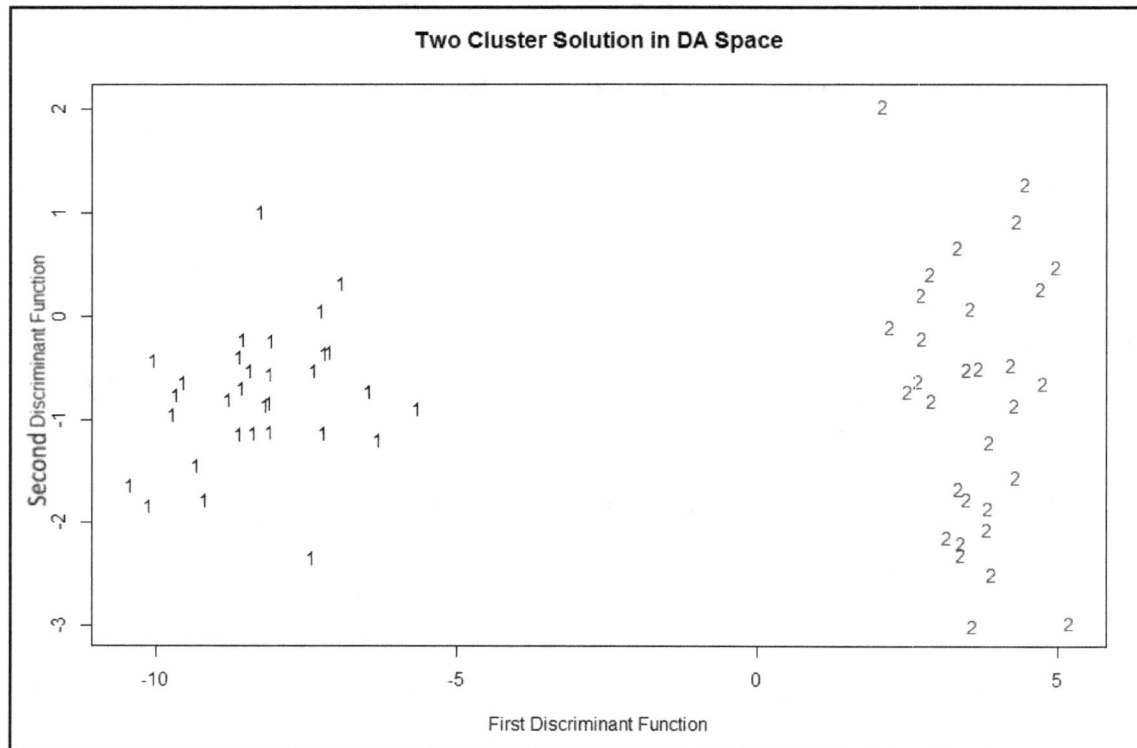
Two Cluster Solution in DA Space

Next, transposing the NASAscale data frame takes place using the t() function:

```
> library(fpc)
> NASAtrans=t(NASAscale)
```

The next step is about improving the model by training using the Minkowski distance method. The first step is to calculate the distance matrix. The `dist()` function is used.

The Minkowski distance is often used when variables are measured on ratio scales with an absolute zero value.

```
> dist1 <- dist(NASAtrans, method="minkowski", p=3)
```

The next step is to perform clustering using Ward's method. The `hclust()` function is used.

```
> clust1 <- hclust(dist1,method="ward.D")
> clust1
```

The call to the `clust1` function results in display of the agglomeration method used, the manner in which the distance is calculated, and the number of objects. The results are as follows:

```
Call:
hclust(d = dist1, method = "ward.D")

Cluster method    : ward.D
Distance          : minkowski
Number of objects: 29
```

The `plot()` function is a generic function for the plotting R objects. Here, the `plot()` function is used to draw the dendrogram:

```
> plot(clust1,labels= NASA.lab[1:29], cex=1,
xlab="",ylab="Distance",main="Clustering for NASA Understory Data")
```

The result is as follows:

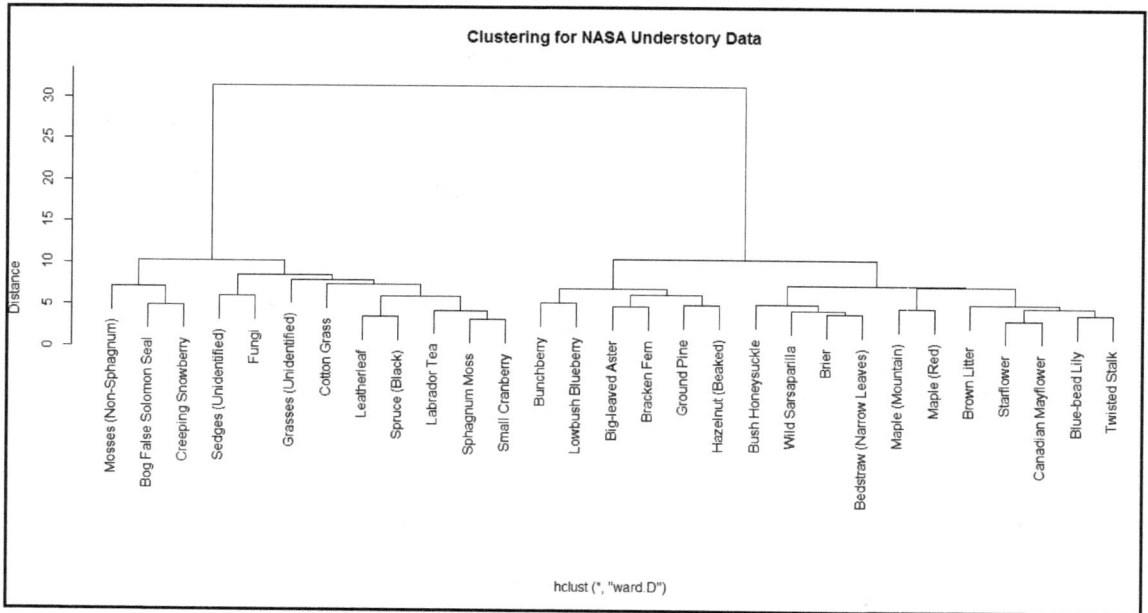

Clustering for NASA Understory Data

hclust (*, "ward.D")

The `rect.hclust()` function shall draw rectangles around the branches of the dendrogram highlighting the corresponding clusters. First, the dendrogram is cut at a certain level, and then a rectangle is drawn around selected branches.

The `clust1` object is passed as an object to the function along with the number of clusters to be formed:

```
> rect.hclust(clust1,k=3)
```

The result is as follows:

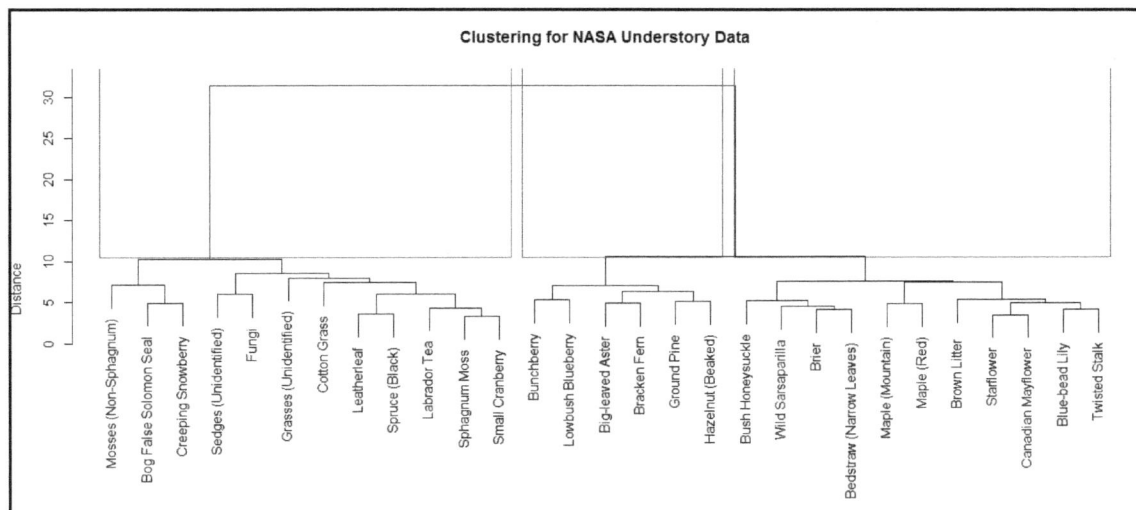

The cuts() function shall cut the tree into multiple groups on the basis of the desired number of groups or the cut height. Here, clust1 is passed as an object to the function along with the number of the desired group:

```
> cuts=cutree(clust1,k=3)
> cuts
```

The result is as follows:

SPHA	BLIT	ASMA	MOSS	LEGR	CHCA	GRAS	SEDG	SMTR	PTAQ	COCA	VAAN	GAHI	ARNU	LYOB	PIMA	RUBU	VAOX	ACSP	COCO	ACRU	TRBO	MACA	CLBO
1	2	3	1	1	1	1	1	1	3	3	3	1	2	3	1	2	1	2	3	2	2	2	2

STRO	FUNG	DILO	ERIO	GATR
2	1	2	1	2

Hierarchical clustering - gene clustering

The ability to gather genome-wide expression data is a computationally complex task. The human brain with its limitations cannot solve the problem. However, data can be fine-grained to an easily comprehensible level by subdividing the genes into a smaller number of categories and then analyzing them.

The goal of clustering is to subdivide a set of genes in such a way that similar items fall into the same cluster, whereas dissimilar items fall into different clusters. The important questions to be considered are decisions on similarity and usage for the items that have been clustered. Here we shall explore clustering genes and samples using the photoreceptor time series for the two genotypes.

Getting ready

In order to perform Hierarchical clustering, we shall be using a dataset collected on mice.

Step 1 - collecting and describing data

The datasets titled GSE4051_data and GSE4051_design shall be used. These are available in the CSV format titled GSE4051_data.csv and GSE4051_design.csv. The dataset is in standard format.

In GSE4051_data there are 29,949 rows of data and 39 variables. The numeric variables are:

- Sample_21
- Sample_22
- Sample_23
- Sample_16
- Sample_17
- Sample_6
- Sample_24
- Sample_25
- Sample_26
- Sample_27
- Sample_14
- Sample_3
- Sample_5
- Sample_8
- Sample_28
- Sample_29
- Sample_30
- Sample_31

- `Sample_1`
- `Sample_10`
- `Sample_4`
- `Sample_7`
- `Sample_32`
- `Sample_33`
- `Sample_34`
- `Sample_35`
- `Sample_13`
- `Sample_15`
- `Sample_18`
- `Sample_19`
- `Sample_36`
- `Sample_37`
- `Sample_38`
- `Sample_39`
- `Sample_11`
- `Sample_12`
- `Sample_2`
- `Sample_9`

In the `GSE4051_design` dataset there are 39 rows of data and 4 variables. The numeric variable is:

- `sidNum`

The non-numeric variables are:

- `sidChar`
- `devStage`
- `gType`

How to do it...

Let's get into the details.

Step 2 - exploring data

Version info: Code for this page was tested in R version 3.2.3 (2015-12-10)

The RColorBrewer package is an R package from http://colorbrewer2.org and provides color schemes for maps and other graphics.

The pvclust package is used for assessing uncertainty in hierarchical cluster analysis. In hierarchical clustering, each of the clusters calculates p-values via multi-scale bootstrap resampling. The p-value of a cluster is measured between 0 and 1. There are two types of p-value available: **approximatelyunbiased** (**AU**) and **bootstrap probability** (**BP**) value. The AU p-value is calculated using the multi-scale bootstrap resampling method, while the ordinary bootstrap resampling method is used to calculate the BP p-value. The AU p-value has superiority bias compared to the BP p-value.

LaTeX-formatted tables are produced by the xtable package. Using xtable, package-specific R objects can be turned into xtables. These xtables can then be output in either LaTeX or HTML formats.

The plyr package is used as a tool for carrying out **split-apply-combine** (**SAC**) procedures. It breaks a big problem down into manageable pieces, operates on each piece, and then puts all the pieces back together.

The following packages must be loaded:

```
> library(RColorBrewer)
> library(cluster)
> library(pvclust)
> library(xtable)
> library(plyr)
```

Let's explore the data and understand the relationships among the variables. We'll begin by importing the CSV file named GSE4051_data.csv. We will be saving the data to the GSE4051_data data frame:

```
> GSE4051_data =read.csv("d:/ GSE4051_data.csv",header=T)
```

Next, we shall print information about the GSE4051_data data frame. The str() function returns the provided information about the structure of the GSE4051_data data frame. It compactly displays the internal structure of the GSE4051_data data frame. max.level indicates the maximal level of nesting applied to display nested structures:

```
> str(GSE4051_data, max.level = 0)
```

The result is as follows:

```
'data.frame':   29949 obs. of   39 variables:
```

Next, we shall import the CSV file named GSE4051_design.csv. We will be saving the data to the GSE4051_design data frame:

```
> GSE4051_design =read.csv("d:/ GSE4051_design.csv",header=T)
```

The preceding line prints the internal structure of the GSE4051_design data frame.

The result is as follows:

```
'data.frame':   39 obs. of   4 variables:
 $ sidChar : Factor w/ 39 levels "Sample_1","Sample_10",..: 13 14 15 16 8 9 36 17 18 19 ...
 $ sidNum  : int  20 21 22 23 16 17 6 24 25 26 ...
 $ devStage: Factor w/ 5 levels "4_weeks","E16",..: 2 2 2 2 2 2 2 4 4 4 ...
 $ gType   : Factor w/ 2 levels "NrlKO","wt": 2 2 2 2 1 1 1 2 2 2 ...
```

Step 3 - transforming data

In order to ease visualization at a later stage, the rows are rescaled. Since the absolute differences in the expression between genes at the currently required, rescaling of the rows is carried out.

Centering variables and creating z-scores are two common data analysis activities. The scale function centers and/or scales the columns of a numeric matrix.

Transposing the matrix. The GSE4051_data data frame is passed for transposition of the data frame:

```
> trans_GSE4051_data <- t(scale(t(GSE4051_data)))
```

Next, we shall print information about the GSE4051_data data frame. With give.attr = FALSE, attributes as sub structures are not displayed.

```
> str(trans_GSE4051_data, max.level = 0, give.attr = FALSE)
```

The result is as follows:

```
num [1:29949, 1:39] 0.0838 0.1758 0.7797 -0.3196 0.8358 ...
```

The head() function returns the first part of a vector, matrix, table, data frame, or function. The GSE4051_data and trans_GSE4051_data data frames are passed as objects. The rowMeans() function calculates the means of rows. The data.frame() function creates data frames that are tightly coupled collections of variables and share many of the properties of matrices:

```
> round(data.frame(avgBefore = rowMeans(head(GSE4051_data)),
                   avgAfter = rowMeans(head(trans_GSE4051_data)),
                   varBefore = apply(head(GSE4051_data), 1, var),
                   varAfter = apply(head(trans_GSE4051_data),
   1, var)), 2)
```

The result is as follows:

	avgBefore	avgAfter	varBefore	varAfter
1	7.22	0	0.02	1
2	9.37	0	0.35	1
3	9.70	0	0.15	1
4	8.42	0	0.03	1
5	8.47	0	0.02	1
6	9.67	0	0.03	1

Step 4 - training the model

The next step is training the model. The first step is to calculate the distance matrix. The `dist()` function is used. The function computes and returns the distance matrix, using the specified distance measure to compute the distances between the rows of a data matrix. The distance measure used can be Euclidean, maximum, Manhattan, Canberra, binary, or Minkowski. The distance measure used is Euclidean. The Euclidean distance calculates the distance between two vectors as *sqrt(sum((x_i - y_i)^2))*. The transposed `trans_GSE4051_data` data frame is used to calculate the distance. The result is then stored in the `pair_dist_GSE4051_data` data frame.

```
> pair_dist_GSE4051_data <- dist(t(trans_GSE4051_data), method =
'euclidean')
```

Next, the `interaction()` function is used, which computes and returns an unordered factor with the interaction of the `gType`, `devStage` variables. The result of unordered factors is passed to the `with()` function along with the data frame, `GSE4051_design`. This creates a new factor representing the interaction of `gType`, `devStage` variables:

```
> GSE4051_design$group <- with(GSE4051_design, interaction(gType,
devStage))
```

The `summary()` function is used to produce result summaries of the data frame, `GSE4051_design$group`:

```
> summary(GSE4051_design$group)
```

The result is as follows:

NrlKO.4_weeks	wt.4_weeks	NrlKO.E16	wt.E16	NrlKO.P10	wt.P10	NrlKO.P2	wt.P2	NrlKO.P6
4	4	3	4	4	4	4	4	4
wt.P6								
4								

Next, the computing of hierarchical clustering using various linkage types is carried out.

The `hclust()` function is used. In order to perform cluster analysis on a set of dissimilarities of *n* objects, the `hclust()` function is used. At the first stage, each of the objects is assigned to its own cluster. The algorithm then proceeds iteratively at each stage joining the two most similar clusters. This process continues till there is just a single cluster left. The `hclust()` function requires we provide the data in the form of a distance matrix. The `pair_dist_GSE4051_data` data frame is passed.

The agglomeration method, single, is used as the first case:

```
> pr.hc.single <- hclust(pair_dist_GSE4051_data, method = 'single')
```

The call to pr.hc.single results in display of the agglomeration method used, the manner in which the distance is calculated and the number of objects:

```
> pr.hc.single
```

The result is as follows:

```
call:
hclust(d = pair_dist_GSE4051_data, method = "single")

Cluster method   : single
Distance         : euclidean
Number of objects: 39
```

The agglomeration method, complete is used as the second case:

```
> pr.hc.complete <- hclust(pair_dist_GSE4051_data, method = 'complete')
```

The call to pr.hc.complete results in display of the agglomeration method used, the manner in which the distance is calculated and the number of objects:

```
> pr.hc.complete
```

The result is as follows:

```
call:
hclust(d = pair_dist_GSE4051_data, method = "complete")

Cluster method   : complete
Distance         : euclidean
Number of objects: 39
```

The agglomeration method average is used as the third case:

```
> pr.hc.average <- hclust(pair_dist_GSE4051_data, method = 'average')
```

The call to `pr.hc.average` results in display of the agglomeration method used, the manner in which the distance is calculated, and the number of objects:

```
> pr.hc.average
```

The result is as follows:

```
Call:
hclust(d = pair_dist_GSE4051_data, method = "average")

Cluster method   : average
Distance         : euclidean
Number of objects: 39
```

The agglomeration method ward is used as the fourth case:

```
> pr.hc.ward <- hclust(pair_dist_GSE4051_data, method = 'ward.D2')
```

The call to `pr.hc.ward` results in display of the agglomeration method used, the manner in which the distance is calculated, and the number of objects:

```
> pr.hc.ward
```

The result is as follows:

```
Call:
hclust(d = pair_dist_GSE4051_data, method = "ward.D2")

Cluster method   : ward.D2
Distance         : euclidean
Number of objects: 39
```

```
> op <- par(mar = c(0,4,4,2), mfrow = c(2,2))
```

The `plot()` function is a generic function for plotting R objects.

The first call to the `plot()` function passes the `pr.hc.single` data frame as an object:

```
> plot(pr.hc.single, labels = FALSE, main = "Single Linkage
  Representation", xlab = "")
```

The result is as follows:

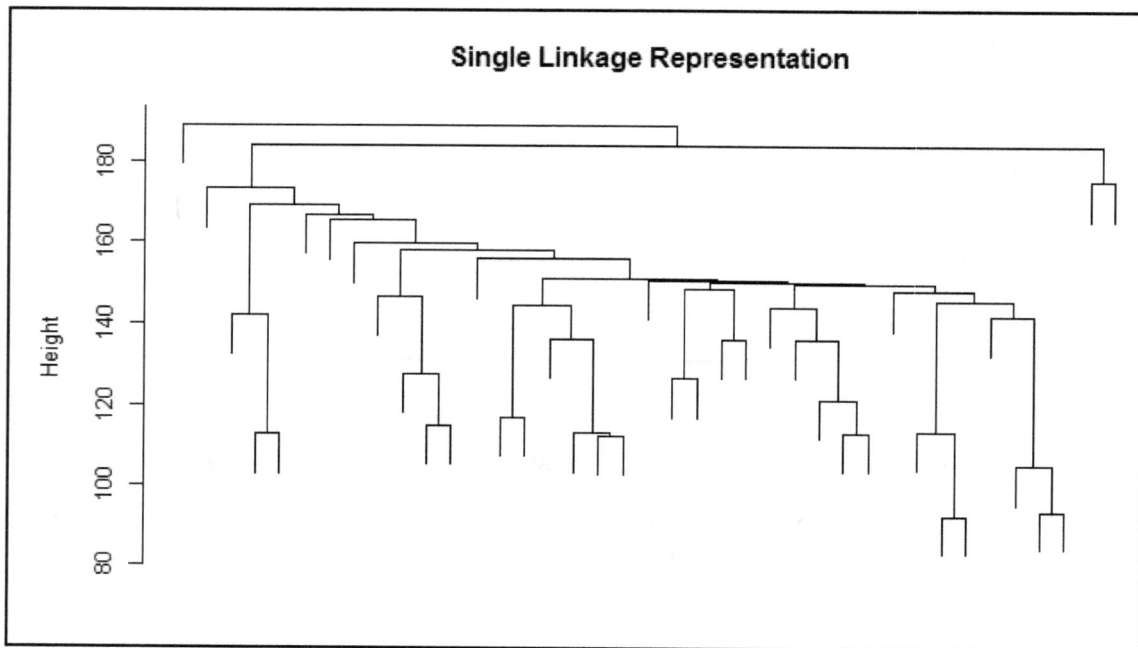

Single Linkage Representation

The second call to the `plot()` function passes the `pr.hc.complete` data frame as an object:

```
> plot(pr.hc.complete, labels = FALSE, main = "Complete Linkage
Representation", xlab = "")
```

The result is as follows:

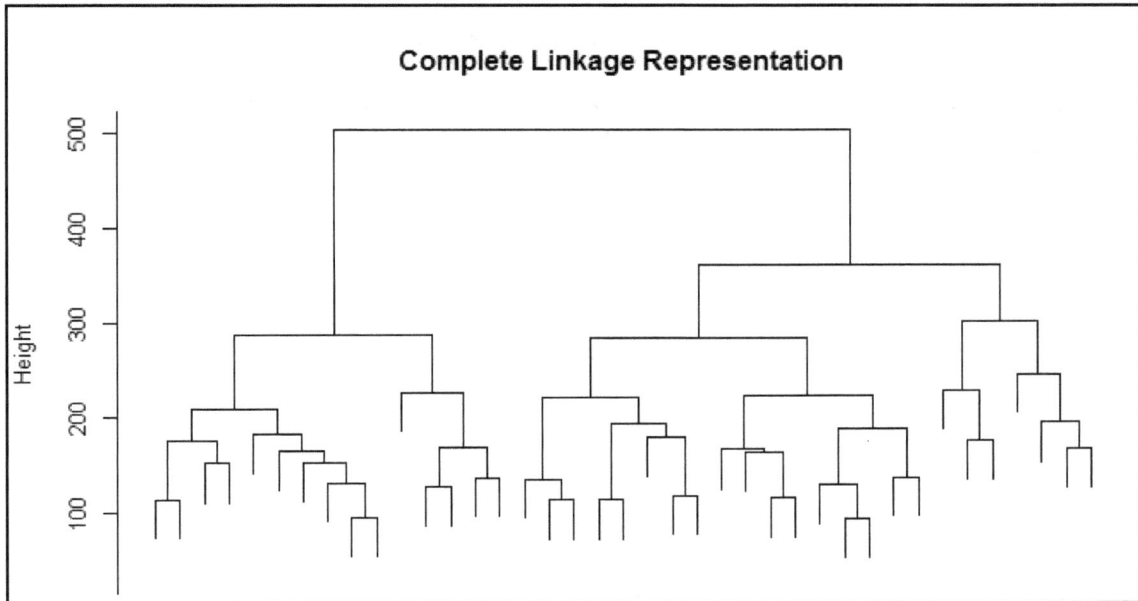

The third call to the `plot()` function passes the `pr.hc.average` data frame as an object:

```
> plot(pr.hc.average, labels = FALSE, main = "Average Linkage
Representation", xlab = "")
```

The result is as follows:

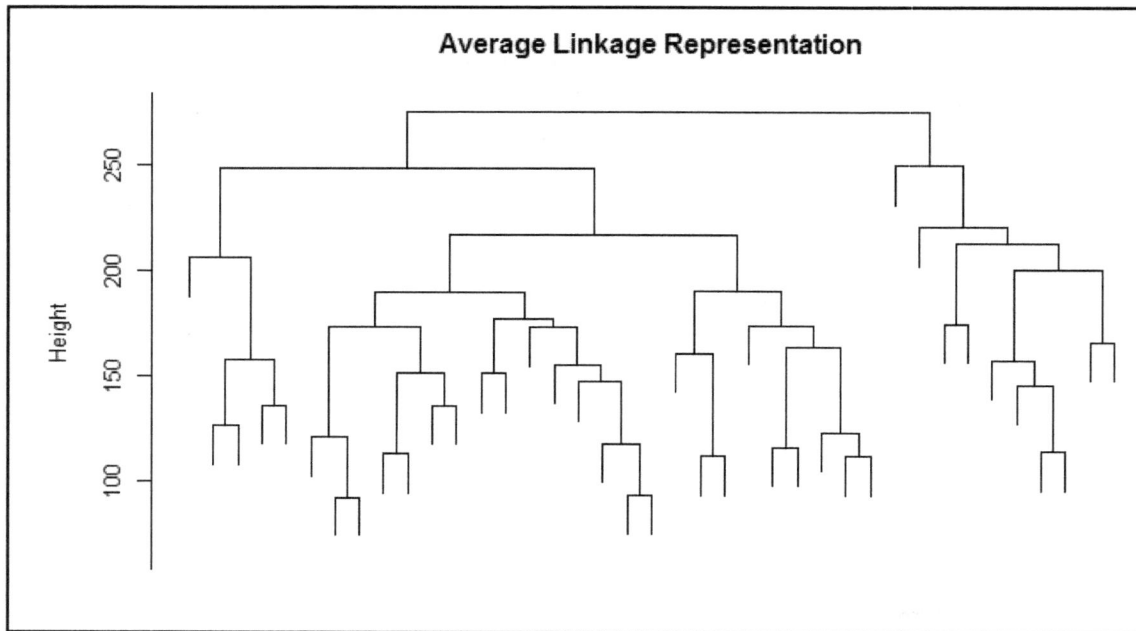

Average Linkage Representation

The fourth call to the plot () function passes the pr.hc.ward data frame as an object:

```
> plot(pr.hc.ward, labels = FALSE, main = "Ward Linkage
Representation", xlab = "")
```

The result is as follows:

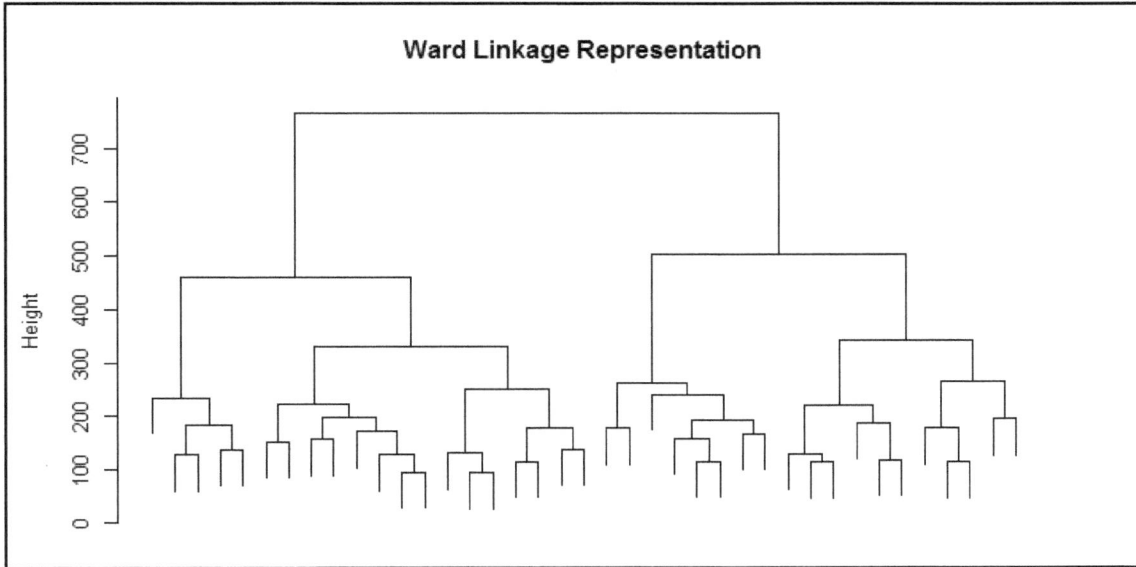

Ward Linkage Representation

```
> par(op)
> op <- par(mar = c(1,4,4,1))
```

Step 5 - plotting the model

The plot() function is a generic function for the plotting R objects. Here, the plot() function is used to draw the dendrogram.

The rect.hclust() function shall draw rectangles around the branches of the dendrogram highlighting the corresponding clusters. First the dendrogram is cut at a certain level, and then a rectangle is drawn around selected branches.

RColorBrewer uses the work from http://colorbrewer2.org/ to choose sensible color schemes for figures in R.

The colors are split into three groups:

- Sequential: Low data--light colors; high data--dark colors
- Diverging: Mid-range data--light colors; low and high range data--contrasting dark colors
- Qualitative: Colors have been designed to highlight the maximum visual difference between classes

One of the important functions of RColorBrewer is brewer.pal(). This function allows one to choose from the display.brewer.all() function by passing the number of colors and the name of the palette.

As a first case, pr.hc.single is passed as an object to the plot() function:

```
> plot(pr.hc.single, labels = GSE4051_design$group, cex = 0.6, main =
"Single Hierarchical Cluster - 10 clusters")
> rect.hclust(clust1,k=5)
```

The result is as follows:

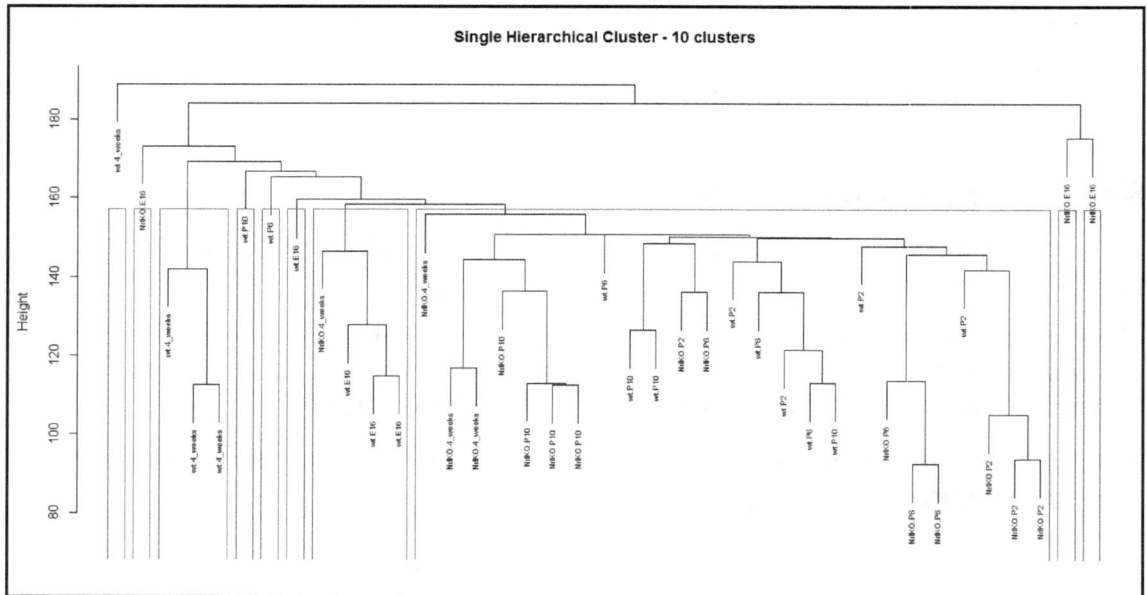

Next, we create the heat maps using the `single` agglomeration method. By default, the `heatmap()` function uses the agglomeration method `euclidean`:

```
> par(op)
> jGraysFun <- colorRampPalette(brewer.pal(n = 9, "Blues"))
> gTypeCols <- brewer.pal(9, "Spectral")[c(4,7)]
> heatmap(as.matrix(trans_GSE4051_data), Rowv = NA, col =
jGraysFun(256), hclustfun = function(x) hclust(x, method = 'single'),
    scale = "none", labCol = GSE4051_design$group, labRow = NA, margins =
c(8,1),
 ColSideColor = gTypeCols[unclass(GSE4051_design$gType)])
    > legend("topright", legend = levels(GSE4051_design$gType), col =
gTypeCols, lty = 1, lwd = 5, cex = 0.5)
```

The result is as follows:

As a second case, `pr.hc.complete` is passed as an object to the `plot()` function:

```
> plot(pr.hc.complete, labels = GSE4051_design$group, cex = 0.6, main =
"Complete Hierarchical Cluster - 10 clusters")
> rect.hclust(pr.hc.complete, k = 10)
```

The result is as follows:

Next we create heat maps using the `complete` agglomeration method.

```
> par(op)
> jGraysFun <- colorRampPalette(brewer.pal(n = 9, "Greens"))
> gTypeCols <- brewer.pal(11, "PRGn")[c(4,7)]
> heatmap(as.matrix(trans_GSE4051_data), Rowv = NA, col =
jGraysFun(256), hclustfun = function(x) hclust(x, method = 'complete'),
 scale = "none", labCol = GSE4051_design$group, labRow = NA, margins =
c(8,1),
  ColSideColor = gTypeCols[unclass(GSE4051_design$gType)])
> legend("topright", legend = levels(GSE4051_design$gType), col =
gTypeCols, lty = 1, lwd = 5, cex = 0.5)
```

The result is as follows:

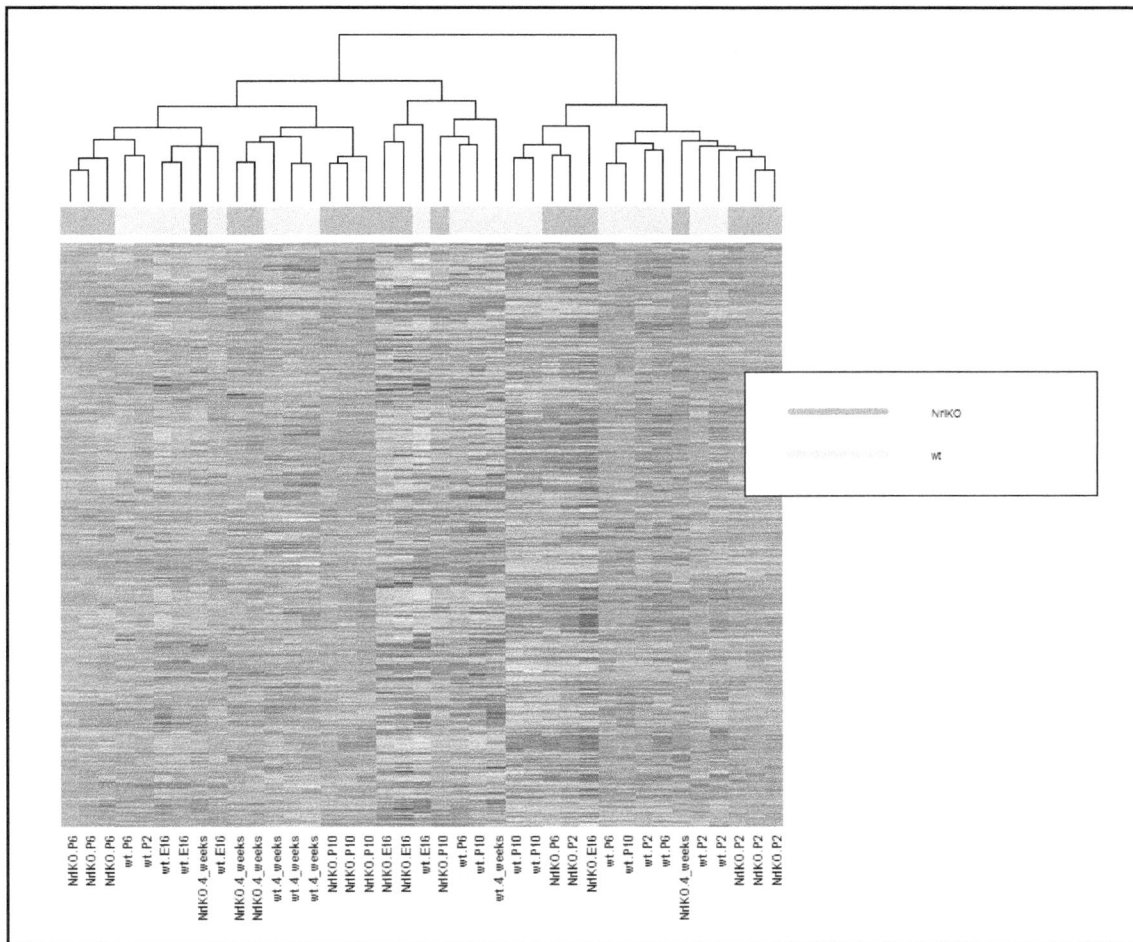

As a third case, pr.hc.average is passed as an object to the plot() function:

```
> plot(pr.hc.average, labels = GSE4051_design$group, cex = 0.6, main =
"Average Hierarchical Cluster - 10 clusters")
> rect.hclust(pr.hc.average, k = 10)
```

The result is as follows:

Average Hierarchical Cluster - 10 clusters

Next, we create heat maps using the `average` agglomeration method:

```
> jGraysFun <- colorRampPalette(brewer.pal(n = 9, "Oranges"))
> gTypeCols <- brewer.pal(9, "Oranges")[c(4,7)]
> heatmap(as.matrix(trans_GSE4051_data), Rowv = NA, col =
jGraysFun(256), hclustfun = function(x) hclust(x, method = 'average'),
    scale = "none", labCol = GSE4051_design$group, labRow = NA, margins =
c(8,1),
  ColSideColor = gTypeCols[unclass(GSE4051_design$gType)])
> legend("topright", legend = levels(GSE4051_design$gType), col =
gTypeCols, lty = 1, lwd = 5, cex = 0.5)
```

The result is as follows:

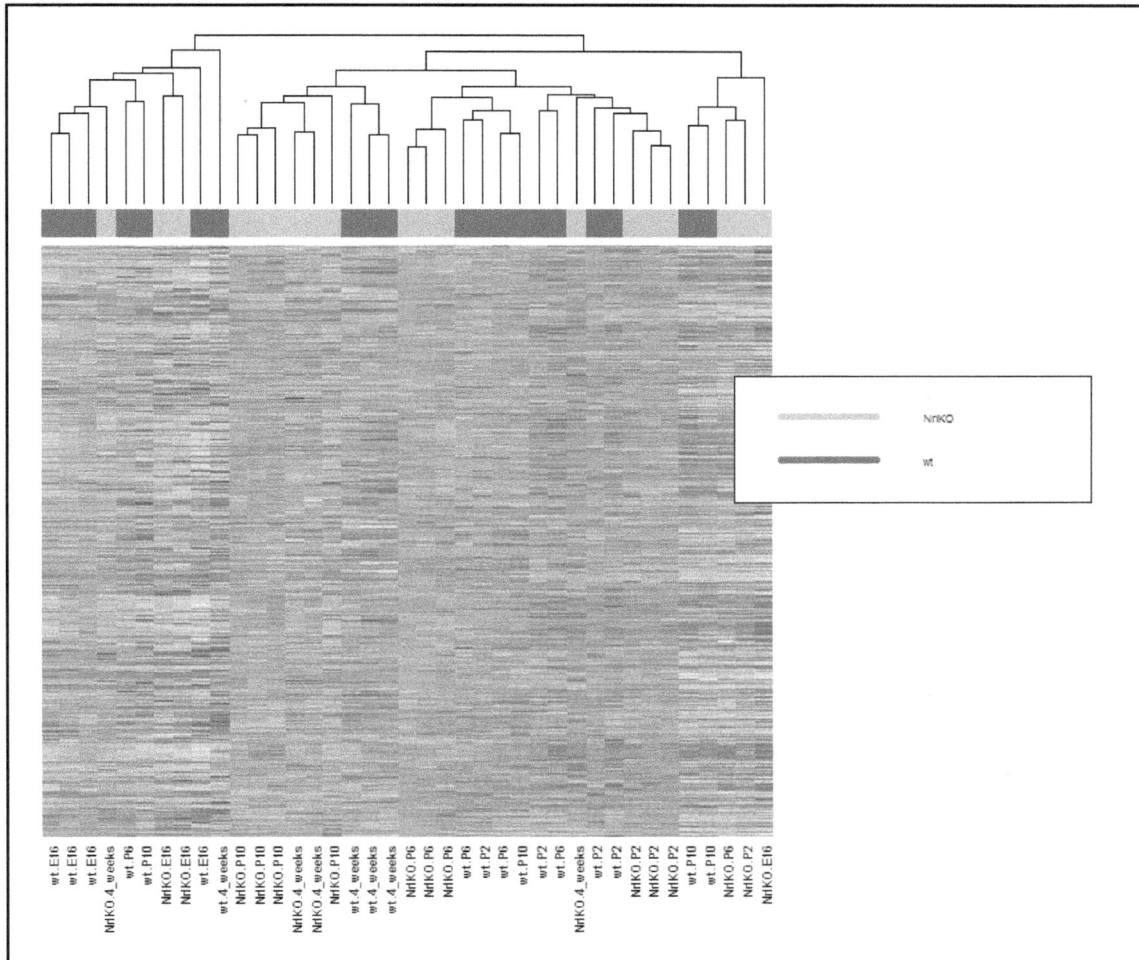

As a fourth case, `pr.hc.ward` is passed as an object to the `plot()` function:

```
> plot(pr.hc.ward, labels = GSE4051_design$group, cex = 0.6, main =
"Ward Hierarchical Cluster - 10 clusters")
> rect.hclust(pr.hc.ward, k = 10)
```

The result is as follows:

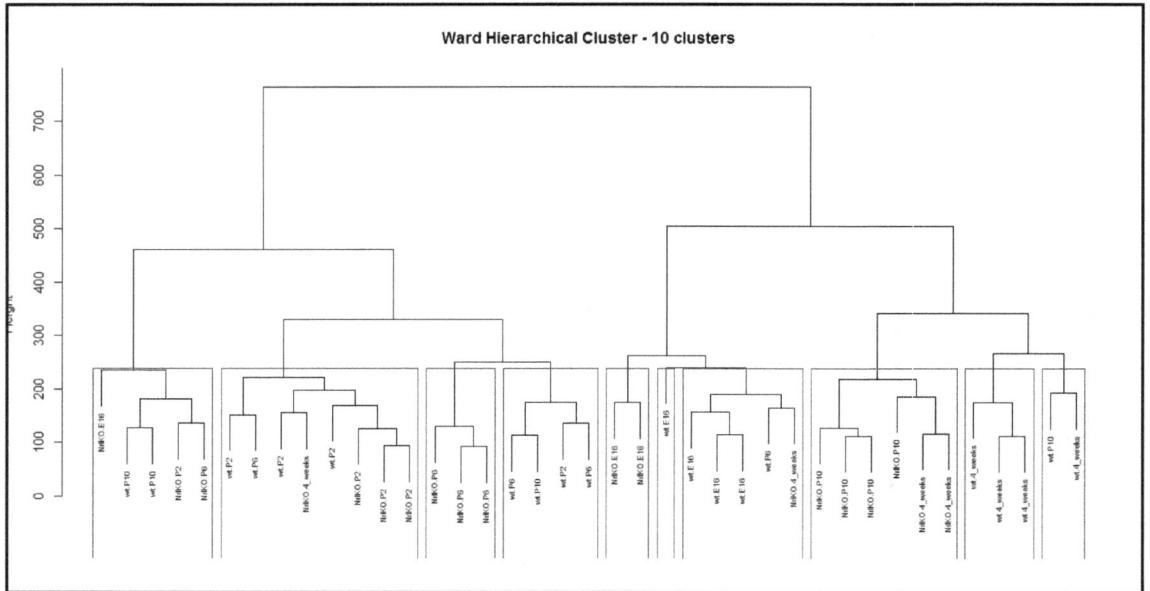

Ward Hierarchical Cluster - 10 clusters

Next, we create heat maps using the `ward` agglomeration method:

```
> jGraysFun <- colorRampPalette(brewer.pal(n = 9, "Reds"))
> gTypeCols <- brewer.pal(9, "Reds")[c(4,7)]
> heatmap(as.matrix(trans_GSE4051_data), Rowv = NA, col =
jGraysFun(256), hclustfun = function(x) hclust(x, method = 'ward.D2'),
    scale = "none", labCol = GSE4051_design$group, labRow = NA, margins =
c(8,1),
    ColSideColor = gTypeCols[unclass(GSE4051_design$gType)])
> legend("topright", legend = levels(GSE4051_design$gType), col =
gTypeCols, lty = 1, lwd = 5, cex = 0.5)
```

The result is as follows:

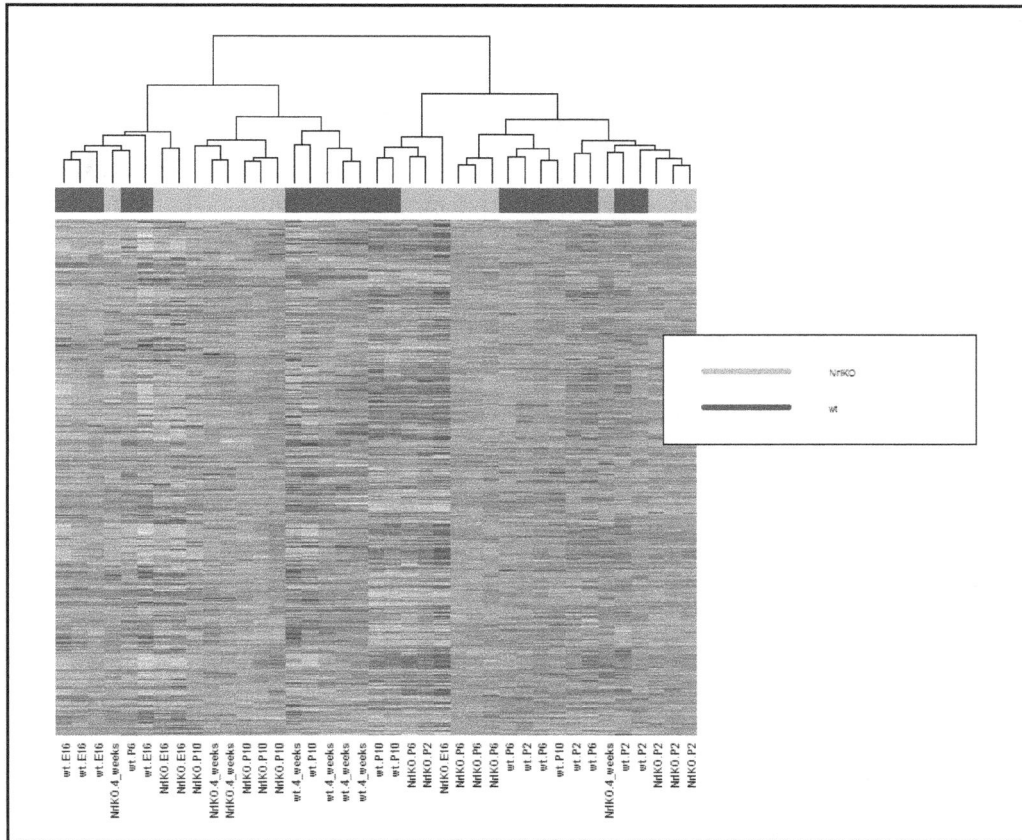

Binary clustering - math test

In the education system tests and examinations are major features. The advantage of examination system is that it can be one of the ways to differentiate between good and poor performers. The examination system puts the onus on students to upgrade for next standard for which they should appear and pass exams. It creates responsibility on students to study on regular basis. The exam systems prepare the students to meet the challenges of future. It helps them to analyze reason and communicate their ideas effectively in a fixed time period. On the other hand few draw backs are noticed such as slow learners cannot perform well in test and this creates inferior complexity among students.

Getting ready

In order to perform binary clustering, we shall be using a dataset collected on math tests.

Step 1 - collecting and describing data

The dataset titled `math test` shall be used. This is available in the TXT format titled `math test.txt`. The dataset is in standard format. There are 60 rows of data. There are 60 columns. The columns are scores on items for 55 male students.

How to do it...

Let's get into the details.

Step 2 - exploring data

Version info: Code for this page was tested in R version 3.2.3 (2015-12-10)

Let's explore the data and understand relationships among the variables. We'll begin by importing the TXT file named `ACT math test.txt`. We will be saving the data to the `Mathtest` data frame:

```
> Mathtest = read.table("d:/math test.txt",header=T)
```

Step 3 - training and evaluating model performance

Next, we shall perform clustering of the items. Groups of items based on the students' scores shall be clustered together.

First, we shall count the total mismatches based on the squared Euclidean distance.

The `dist()` function is called. The `Mathtest` data frame is passed as input to the `dist()` function. Counting the total mismatches based on the squared Euclidean distance, the result shall be stored in the, `dist.items` data frame:

```
> dist.items <- dist(Mathtest[,-1], method='euclidean')^2
```

Next, we shall print the `dist.items` data frame.

```
> dist.items
```

The result is as follows:

```
     1  2  3  4  5  6  7  8  9 10 11 12 13 14 15 16 17 18 19 20 21 22 23 24 25 26 27 28 29 30 31 32 33 34 35 36 37 38 39 40
2   16
3   17 17
4   26 22 19
5   17  9 12 19
6   13 13 14 23 16
7    7 16 16 17 18 21 15
8   18 22 15 22 19 19 20
9   19 15 14 23 14 10 17 21
10  24 24 25 20 25 23 20 20 23
11  23 25 16 19 22 14 21 17 20 23
12  20 18 21 26 19 15 16 16 19 18 21
13  25 19 14 17 16 20 21 21 20 21 18 25
14  17 17 16 21 18 16 15 19 18 27 20 23 22
15  22 22 19 14 19 21 22 20 23 18 19 20 19 21
16  25 15 22 21 20 22 15 25 20 23 26 23 22 20 23
17  30 26 17 26 23 25 32 22 21 30 23 30 21 25 26 29
18  28 26 21 22 23 25 24 20 27 26 15 28 21 21 18 29 18
19  31 27 22 23 22 24 25 21 22 21 28 27 26 26 29 28 25 25
20  20 22 17 26 17 25 26 16 23 28 27 22 19 23 26 31 18 24 25
21  28 26 21 20 21 31 26 18 25 22 23 24 23 16 29 22 16 25 20
22  18 18 19 22 21 17 20 18 21 22 21 22 17 19 18 23 22 14 27 18 18
23  23 17 14 19 20 16 19 19 18 21 20 23 22 20 25 22 19 23 20 25 19 17
24  20 16 17 18 17 17 16 22 17 26 23 24 19 15 26 19 24 26 23 24 22 20 15
25  29 25 22 23 22 24 27 21 22 15 20 21 24 28 15 26 25 19 22 23 17 19 22 29
26  20 20 24 21 23 20 20 21 22 25 24 19 19 20 25 28 26 21 24 20 24 21 20 21
27  31 27 18 17 22 26 25 19 18 21 20 27 14 24 21 22 19 19 22 23 21 25 22 29 20 19
28  25 25 14 19 22 22 19 17 18 21 20 25 18 20 17 28 15 22 19 15 19 18 23 20 19 16
29  28 34 25 24 31 25 28 20 25 28 19 28 23 27 24 27 18 22 21 26 28 26 27 30 27 26 17 19
30  24 24 21 24 25 19 20 16 21 24 21 18 21 21 24 27 20 22 21 22 20 20 15 18 27 20 21 15 14
31  22 22 23 28 23 21 24 20 23 22 23 28 19 23 22 25 20 20 25 26 20 18 21 20 25 16 25 21 24 18
32  26 30 25 24 27 27 32 18 25 18 19 26 21 23 22 31 20 24 25 22 20 24 25 24 25 24 25 24 23 23 20 20 22
33  21 23 16 25 24 20 19 21 16 21 22 23 22 22 21 18 25 23 24 25 19 17 22 19 24 18 23 21 23 15 23 21 21
34  19 23 16 25 20 20 23 15 24 25 18 21 20 22 25 24 27 21 22 19 21 17 20 21 26 23 24 22 23 21 23 22 19 21
35  21 25 18 17 20 22 21 17 20 19 20 21 20 16 17 24 23 21 24 25 21 23 20 17 24 21 18 20 21 21 21 21 22 24
36  30 26 25 24 23 27 26 18 29 24 23 22 17 33 22 25 20 22 27 22 26 22 27 28 25 28 17 23 18 22 28 24 25 25 21
37  26 30 19 20 23 23 24 16 19 20 19 24 21 23 24 31 22 18 19 22 18 20 19 24 19 24 17 17 20 20 28 18 21 23 19 20
38  24 24 23 22 23 19 22 18 21 26 21 20 23 21 20 31 20 16 25 22 20 18 25 30 25 22 19 17 18 14 22 24 25 21 23 20 14
```

Next, the distance measure ignores `0-0` matches altogether. The binary method shall be used in the `dist()` function. In the binary method, the non-zero elements are on and zero-elements are off since the vectors are considered binary bits.

```
> dist.items.2 <- dist(Mathtest[,-1], method='binary')
```

Next, we shall print the data frame, `dist.items.2`, to observe the result.

The result is as follows:

```
        1         2         3         4         5         6         7
2  0.3018868
3  0.3333333 0.3333333
4  0.4814815 0.4230769 0.3958333
5  0.3207547 0.1836735 0.2500000 0.3800000
6  0.2549020 0.2549020 0.2857143 0.4423077 0.3076923
7  0.3200000 0.3200000 0.3541667 0.3829787 0.4038462 0.3061224
8  0.3829787 0.4489796 0.3488372 0.4888889 0.4042553 0.4042553 0.4444444
9  0.3725490 0.3061224 0.3043478 0.4693878 0.2916667 0.2173913 0.3617021
10 0.4800000 0.4800000 0.5208333 0.4545455 0.5000000 0.4693878 0.4444444
11 0.4600000 0.4901961 0.3636364 0.4318182 0.4489796 0.3111111 0.4565217
12 0.4081633 0.3750000 0.4468085 0.5416667 0.3958333 0.3260870 0.3636364
13 0.4807692 0.3877551 0.3181818 0.3863636 0.3404255 0.4081633 0.4468085
14 0.3400000 0.3400000 0.3404255 0.4375000 0.3600000 0.3265306 0.3260870
15 0.4400000 0.4400000 0.4130435 0.3333333 0.3958333 0.4285714 0.4680851
16 0.4716981 0.3125000 0.4489796 0.4468085 0.4000000 0.4313725 0.3333333
17 0.5882353 0.5306122 0.4047619 0.5777778 0.4893617 0.5208333 0.6530612
18 0.5714286 0.5416667 0.4883721 0.5238095 0.5000000 0.5319149 0.5454545
19 0.6078431 0.5510204 0.5000000 0.5348837 0.4782609 0.5106383 0.5555556
20 0.4166667 0.4489796 0.3863636 0.5531915 0.3695652 0.5000000 0.5416667
21 0.5714286 0.5416667 0.4883721 0.4878049 0.4666667 0.6200000 0.5777778
22 0.3829787 0.3829787 0.4222222 0.4888889 0.4375000 0.3695652 0.4444444
23 0.4509804 0.3541667 0.3181818 0.4222222 0.4081633 0.3404255 0.4130435
24 0.3846154 0.3200000 0.3541667 0.3829787 0.3400000 0.3400000 0.3404255
25 0.5686275 0.5102041 0.4888889 0.5227273 0.4680851 0.5000000 0.5744681
26 0.4255319 0.4255319 0.4666667 0.5333333 0.4468085 0.4791667 0.4545455
27 0.6078431 0.5510204 0.4285714 0.4250000 0.4782609 0.5416667 0.5555556
28 0.5208333 0.5208333 0.3500000 0.4634146 0.4782609 0.4782609 0.4523810
29 0.5833333 0.6666667 0.5681818 0.5714286 0.6326531 0.5434783 0.6222222
30 0.5000000 0.5000000 0.4772727 0.5454545 0.5208333 0.4222222 0.4651163
31 0.4583333 0.4583333 0.5000000 0.5957447 0.4791667 0.4468085 0.5217391
32 0.5416667 0.6000000 0.5555556 0.5581395 0.5625000 0.5625000 0.6666667
33 0.4375000 0.4693878 0.4444444 0.5434783 0.4897959 0.4255319 0.4318182
34 0.3958333 0.4600000 0.3636364 0.5319149 0.4166667 0.4166667 0.4893617
35 0.4285714 0.4901961 0.4000000 0.3953488 0.4166667 0.4489796 0.4565217
36 0.6000000 0.5416667 0.5555556 0.5581395 0.5000000 0.5625000 0.5777778
```

Next, the distance measure ignores 1–1 matches altogether. The binary method shall be used in the dist() function. In the binary method, the non-zero elements are on and zero-elements are off since the vectors are considered binary bits.

```
> dist.items.3 <- dist(1 - Mathtest[,-1], method='binary')
```

Next, we shall print the data frame, dist.items.3, to observe the result.

The result is as follows:

```
        1         2         3         4         5         6         7         8         9        10
2  0.8888889
3  0.8095238 0.8095238
4  0.9629630 0.8800000 0.7307692
5  0.8947368 0.6000000 0.6315789 0.7916667
6  0.7647059 0.7647059 0.7000000 0.8846154 0.8421053
7  0.7619048 0.7619048 0.7083333 0.6923077 0.8750000 0.7142857
8  0.6923077 0.7857143 0.5555556 0.6875000 0.7037037 0.7037037 0.6666667
9  0.8260870 0.7142857 0.6086957 0.7931034 0.6666667 0.5263158 0.6800000 0.6774194
10 0.8275862 0.8275862 0.7812500 0.6451613 0.8333333 0.7931034 0.6666667 0.5882353 0.7187500
11 0.8214286 0.8620690 0.5925926 0.6333333 0.7857143 0.5833333 0.7000000 0.5312500 0.6666667 0.6571429
12 0.7692308 0.7200000 0.7241379 0.7878788 0.7307692 0.6250000 0.5925926 0.5161290 0.6551724 0.5625000
13 0.8928571 0.7600000 0.5600000 0.6071429 0.6666667 0.7692308 0.7241379 0.6363636 0.6896552 0.6363636
14 0.7727273 0.7727273 0.6666667 0.7500000 0.7826087 0.7272727 0.6250000 0.6333333 0.6923077 0.7941176
15 0.8148148 0.8148148 0.6785714 0.5185185 0.7307692 0.7777778 0.7333333 0.6060606 0.7419355 0.5625000
16 0.9259259 0.6818182 0.7857143 0.7241379 0.8000000 0.8461538 0.6000000 0.7352941 0.7142857 0.6969697
17 0.8823529 0.8125000 0.5666667 0.7222222 0.7419355 0.7812500 0.8421053 0.5945946 0.6363636 0.7317073
18 0.8235294 0.7878788 0.6363636 0.6285714 0.7187500 0.7575758 0.6857143 0.5405405 0.7297297 0.6500000
19 0.8857143 0.8181818 0.6666667 0.6571429 0.7096774 0.7500000 0.7142857 0.5675676 0.6470588 0.5675676
20 0.7407407 0.7857143 0.6071429 0.7647059 0.6538462 0.8333333 0.7878788 0.5000000 0.7187500 0.7368421
21 0.8235294 0.7878788 0.6363636 0.5882353 0.6774194 0.8611111 0.7222222 0.5000000 0.6944444 0.5789474
22 0.6923077 0.6923077 0.6551724 0.6875000 0.7500000 0.6538462 0.6666667 0.5454545 0.6774194 0.6285714
23 0.8518519 0.7083333 0.5600000 0.6551724 0.7692308 0.6666667 0.6785714 0.5937500 0.6428571 0.6363636
24 0.8695652 0.7619048 0.7083333 0.6923077 0.7727273 0.7727273 0.6666667 0.7096774 0.6800000 0.7878788
25 0.8787879 0.8064516 0.6875000 0.6764706 0.7333333 0.7741935 0.7714286 0.5833333 0.6666667 0.4545455
26 0.7142857 0.7142857 0.6774194 0.7058824 0.7241379 0.7666667 0.6451613 0.5714286 0.6562500 0.6111111
27 0.8857143 0.8181818 0.5806452 0.5312500 0.7096774 0.7878788 0.7142857 0.5277778 0.5625000 0.5675676
28 0.7812500 0.7812500 0.4827586 0.5757576 0.7096774 0.7096774 0.5937500 0.4857143 0.5625000 0.5675676
29 0.8000000 0.8947368 0.6944444 0.6486486 0.8378378 0.7352941 0.7368421 0.5263158 0.6756757 0.6666667
30 0.7741935 0.7741935 0.6562500 0.6857143 0.7812500 0.6551724 0.6250000 0.4705882 0.6363636 0.6315789
31 0.7586207 0.7586207 0.7187500 0.7777778 0.7666667 0.7241379 0.7272727 0.5714286 0.6969697 0.6111111
32 0.7878788 0.8571429 0.7142857 0.6666667 0.7941176 0.7941176 0.8205128 0.6944444 0.5000000
33 0.7500000 0.7931034 0.6666667 0.7352941 0.8000000 0.7142857 0.8333333 0.6000000 0.5517241 0.6000000
34 0.7307692 0.8214286 0.5925926 0.7575758 0.7407407 0.7407407 0.7419355 0.4838710 0.7500000 0.6944444
35 0.7777778 0.8620690 0.6428571 0.5862069 0.7407407 0.7857143 0.7000000 0.5312500 0.6666667 0.5757576
36 0.8571429 0.7878788 0.7142857 0.6666667 0.7187500 0.7941176 0.7222222 0.5000000 0.7631579 0.6153846
```

The next step is to perform clustering using the `complete` method. The `hclust()` function is used. In order to perform cluster analysis on a set of dissimilarities for *n* objects, the `hclust()` function is used. At the first stage, each of the objects is assigned to its own cluster. The algorithm then proceeds iteratively at each stage joining the two most similar clusters. This process continues till there is just a single cluster left. The `hclust()` function requires us to provide the data in the form of a distance matrix. The `dist1` data frame is passed. By default, the complete linkage method is used. There can be multiple agglomeration methods which can be used, some of them could be `ward.D`, `ward.D2`, `single`, `complete`, or `average`.

The method used is complete. When the complete method is used, the cluster that is formed has the maximum distance between any object in the cluster and the other object:

```
> items.complete.link <- hclust(dist.items, method='complete')
> items.complete.link
```

The call to the `items.complete.link` function results in display of the agglomeration method used, the manner in which the distance is calculated, and the number of objects. The results are as follows:

```
Call:
hclust(d = dist.items, method = "complete")

Cluster method   : complete
Distance         : euclidean
Number of objects: 59
```

Step 4 - plotting the model

The `plot()` function is a generic function for the plotting R objects. Here, the `plot()` function is used to plot the complete linkage dendrogram.

Complete linkage is used for hierarchical clustering, and ensures the distance between two clusters is the maximum distance. At each step of the algorithm when using complete linkage, two of the nearest clusters are merged together. The process is iterated until the entire dataset is merged into a single cluster:

```
> plot(items.complete.link, labels=Mathtest[,1], ylab="Distance")
```

The result is as follows:

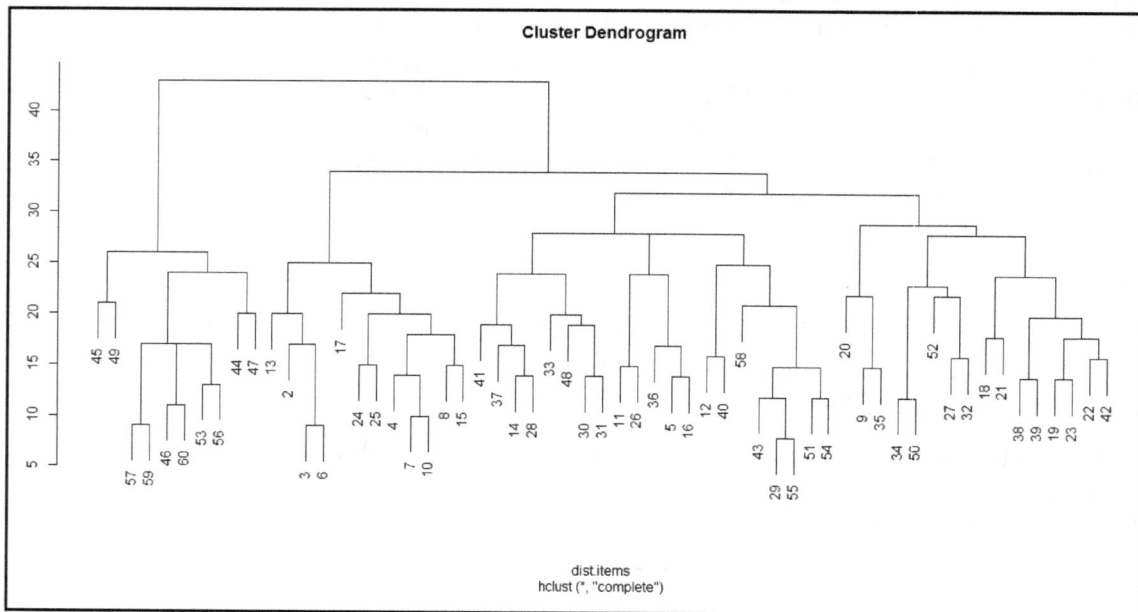

Next, we shall be performing single linkage on the dendrogram. In single linkage hierarchical clustering, each step is merged into two clusters based on the smallest distance to other objects, or the smallest minimum pairwise distance between the clusters:

```
> items.sing.link <- hclust(dist.items, method='single')
> items.sing.link
```

The call to the items.sing.link function results in display of the agglomeration method used, the manner in which the distance is calculated, and the number of objects. The results are as follows:

```
Call:
hclust(d = dist.items, method = "single")

Cluster method   : single
Distance         : euclidean
Number of objects: 59
```

Here, the `plot()` function is used to plot the complete linkage dendrogram. `items.sing.link` is passed as a data frame:

```
> plot(items.sing.link, labels=Mathtest[,1], ylab="Distance")
```

The result is as follows:

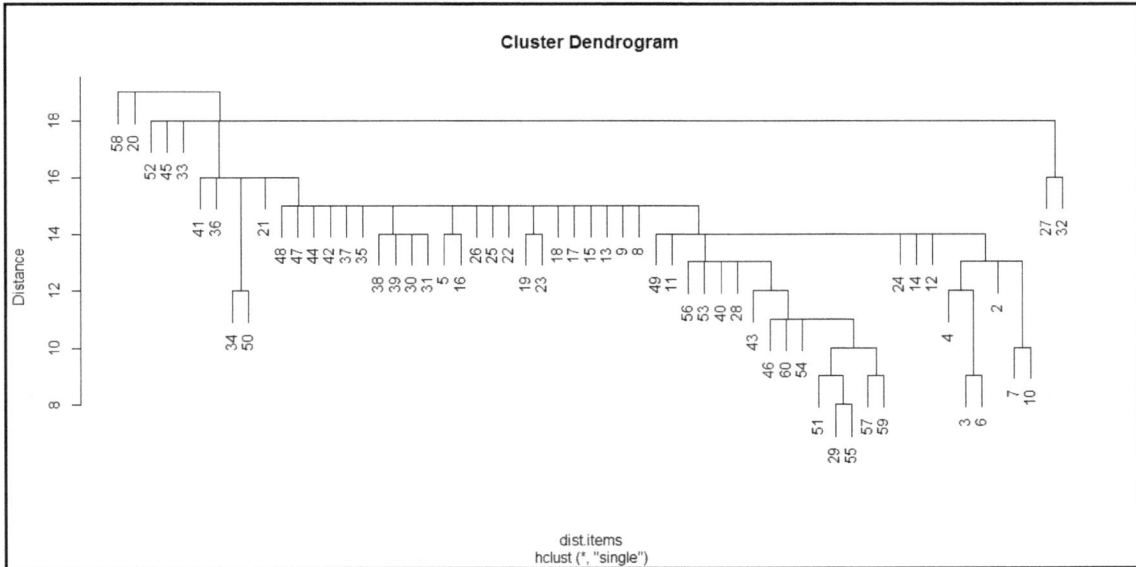

Step 5 - K-medoids clustering

Loading the `cluster()` library:

```
> library(cluster)
```

In order to calculate the average silhouette width, we write a function.

Silhouette refers to a method for interpreting and validating consistency within clusters of data. In order to provide the position of the object in the cluster, the technique uses graphical representation. The silhouette range of is between -1 and 1, with 1 indicating the highest match and -1 indicating the poorest match of the object to its own cluster. In a cluster, if most of the objects have a high value, for instance closer to 1, the clustering configuration is appropriate.

```
> my.k.choices <- 2:8
```

rep() is a generic function that is used to replicate the values of my.k.choices. The result is stored in the data frame avg.sil.width:

```
> avg.sil.width <- rep(0, times=length(my.k.choices))
```

PAM stands for **Partitioning Around Medoids**. PAM requires that one be aware of the number of clusters desired (like k-means clustering), but it does more computation than k-means in order to ensure that the medoids it finds are truly representative of the observations within a given cluster.

```
> for (ii in (1:length(my.k.choices)) ){
+ avg.sil.width[ii] <- pam(dist.items,
k=my.k.choices[ii])$silinfo$avg.width
+ }
```

Printing the value of choices with silhouette values calculated.

```
> print( cbind(my.k.choices, avg.sil.width) )
```

The result is as follows:

```
     my.k.choices avg.sil.width
[1,]            2    0.15613282
[2,]            3    0.09740046
[3,]            4    0.08061349
[4,]            5    0.07817696
[5,]            6    0.07483902
[6,]            7    0.07018717
[7,]            8    0.04567235
```

Performing clustering on the basis of 2 clusters:

```
> items.kmed.2 <- pam(dist.items, k=2, diss=T)
> items.kmed.2
```

The result is as follows:

```
Medoids:
      ID
[1,]  3  3
[2,] 53 53
Clustering vector:
 [1] 1 1 1 1 1 1 1 1 1 2 1 1 1 1 1 1 1 2 2 1 2 1 1 1 2 2 2 2 2 2 2 2 1 1 2 2 1 2 2 2 2 2 2 2 2 2 2 2 2
 2 2 2 2 2 2
[58] 2 2
objective function:
   build    swap
17.54237 16.98305

Available components:
[1] "medoids"    "id.med"    "clustering" "objective" "isolation" "clusinfo" "silinfo"   "diss"

[9] "call"
```

The `lapply()` function returns a list of the same length as X, each element of which is the result of applying FUN to the corresponding element of X:

```
> items.2.clust <- lapply(1:2, function(nc)
Mathtest[,1][items.kmed.2$clustering==nc])
> items.2.clust
```

The result is as follows:

```
[[1]]
 [1]  2  3  4  5  6  7  8  9 10 12 13 14 15 16 17 18 21 23 24 25 35 36 39

[[2]]
 [1] 11 19 20 22 26 27 28 29 30 31 32 33 34 37 38 40 41 42 43 44 45 46 47 48 49 50 51 52 53 54 55 56 57
58 59 60
```

Performing clustering on the basis of 3 clusters.

```
> items.kmed.3 <- pam(dist.items, k=3, diss=T)
> items.kmed.3
```

The result is as follows:

```
Medoids:
      ID
[1,]  6  6
[2,] 28 28
[3,] 56 56
Clustering vector:
 [1] 1 1 1 2 1 1 1 2 1 2 1 1 2 1 2 1 2 2 2 2 2 1 1 1 2 2 2 2 2 2 1 2 2 1 2 3 2 2 3 3 3 2 3 3 3 3 2 3 2 3 2 3
 3 3 3 2 3 3 2
[58] 3 3
Objective function:
   build     swap
15.81356 15.81356

Available components:
[1] "medoids"    "id.med"     "clustering" "objective"  "isolation"  "clusinfo"   "silinfo"    "diss"

[9] "call"
```

```
> items.3.clust <- lapply(1:3, function(nc)
Mathtest[,1][items.kmed.3$clustering==nc])
> items.3.clust
```

The result is as follows:

```
[[1]]
 [1]   2   3   4   6   7   8  10  12  13  15  17  23  24  25  32  35

[[2]]
 [1]   5   9  11  14  16  18  19  20  21  22  26  27  28  29  30  31  33  34  36  38  39  43  48  50  55  58

[[3]]
 [1]  37  40  41  42  44  45  46  47  49  51  52  53  54  56  57  59  60
```

K-means clustering - European countries protein consumption

A food consumption pattern is of great interest in the field of medicine and nutrition. Food consumption is correlated to the overall health of an individual, the nutritional value of the food, the economics involved in purchasing a food item, and the environment in which it is consumed. This analysis is concerned with the relationship between meat and other food items in 25 European countries. It is interesting to observe the correlation between meat and other food items. The data includes measures of red meat, white meat, eggs, milk, fish, cereals, starchy foods, nuts (including pulses and oil-seeds), fruits, and vegetables.

Getting ready

In order to perform K-means clustering, we shall be using a dataset collected on protein consumption for 25 European countries.

Step 1 - collecting and describing data

The dataset titled `protein` which is in the CSV format shall be used. The dataset is in standard format. There are 25 rows of data and are 10 variables.

The numeric variables are:

- `RedMeat`
- `WhiteMeat`
- `Eggs`
- `Milk`

- Fish
- Cereals
- Starch
- Nuts
- Fr&Veg

The non-numeric variable is:

- Country

How to do it...

Let's get into the details.

Step 2 - exploring data

Version info: Code for this page was tested in R version 3.2.3 (2015-12-10)

Let's explore the data and understand relationships among the variables. We'll begin by importing the CSV file named `protein.csv`. We will be saving the data to the `protein` data frame:

```
> protein = read.csv("d:/Europenaprotein.csv",header=T)
```

The `head()` returns the first or last parts of a vector, matrix, table, data frame, or function. The `protein` data frame is passed to the `head()` function.

```
> head(protein)
```

The result is as follows:

	Country	RedMeat	WhiteMeat	Eggs	Milk	Fish	Cereals	Starch	Nuts	Fr.Veg
1	Albania	10.1	1.4	0.5	8.9	0.2	42.3	0.6	5.5	1.7
2	Austria	8.9	14.0	4.3	19.9	2.1	28.0	3.6	1.3	4.3
3	Belgium	13.5	9.3	4.1	17.5	4.5	26.6	5.7	2.1	4.0
4	Bulgaria	7.8	6.0	1.6	8.3	1.2	56.7	1.1	3.7	4.2
5	Czechoslovakia	9.7	11.4	2.8	12.5	2.0	34.3	5.0	1.1	4.0
6	Denmark	10.6	10.8	3.7	25.0	9.9	21.9	4.8	0.7	2.4

Step 3 - clustering

Start clustering on the basis of three clusters.

In order to find a random number of clusters at the initial stage, call the `set.seed()` function. The `set.seed()` function results in the generation of random numbers:

```
> set.seed(123456789)
```

The `kmeans()` function shall carry out the K-means clustering on the data matrix. The `protein` data matrix is passed as an object that can be coerced to a numeric matrix of data. `centers=3` signifies the number of initial (distinct) cluster centers. Since, the number of clusters is denoted by a number, `nstart=10` defines the number of random sets to be chosen:

```
> groupMeat <- kmeans(protein[,c("WhiteMeat","RedMeat")], centers=3,
nstart=10)
> groupMeat
```

The result is as follows:

```
K-means clustering with 3 clusters of sizes 8, 12, 5

Cluster means:
  WhiteMeat    RedMeat
1 12.062500   8.837500
2  4.658333   8.258333
3  9.000000  15.180000

Clustering vector:
 [1] 2 1 3 2 1 1 1 2 3 2 1 3 2 1 2 1 2 2 2 2 3 3 2 1 2

Within cluster sum of squares by cluster:
[1] 39.45750 69.85833 35.66800
 (between_SS / total_SS =  75.7 %)

Available components:

[1] "cluster"     "centers"    "totss"      "withinss"    "tot.withinss" "betweens
s"
[7] "size"        "iter"       "ifault"
```

Next, the listing of cluster assignments takes place. The `order()` function returns a permutation that rearranges its first argument, produced in ascending or descending order. The data frame `groupMeat` is passed as a data frame object:

```
> o=order(groupMeat$cluster)
```

The call to the `data.frame()` function results in displaying the countries and the clusters in which they are placed:

```
> data.frame(protein$Country[o],groupMeat$cluster[o])
```

The result is as follows:

```
       protein.Country.o.  groupMeat.cluster.o.
1                Austria                      1
2         Czechoslovakia                      1
3                Denmark                      1
4              E Germany                      1
5                Hungary                      1
6            Netherlands                      1
7                 Poland                      1
8              W Germany                      1
9                Albania                      2
10              Bulgaria                      2
11               Finland                      2
12                Greece                      2
13                 Italy                      2
14                Norway                      2
15              Portugal                      2
16               Romania                      2
17                 Spain                      2
18                Sweden                      2
19                  USSR                      2
20            Yugoslavia                      2
21               Belgium                      3
22                France                      3
23               Ireland                      3
24           Switzerland                      3
25                    UK                      3
```

The `plot()` function is a generic function for the plotting R objects. The argument type signifies the type of plot to be drawn. The `xlim` argument means arguments should be given the extremes of the range, not a range. `xlab` and `ylab` provide the title for the *x*-axis and *y*-axis respectively:

```
> plot(protein$Red, protein$White, type="n", xlim=c(3,19), xlab="Red
Meat", ylab="White Meat")
> text(x=protein$Red, y=protein$White,
labels=protein$Country,col=groupMeat$cluster+1)
```

The result is as follows:

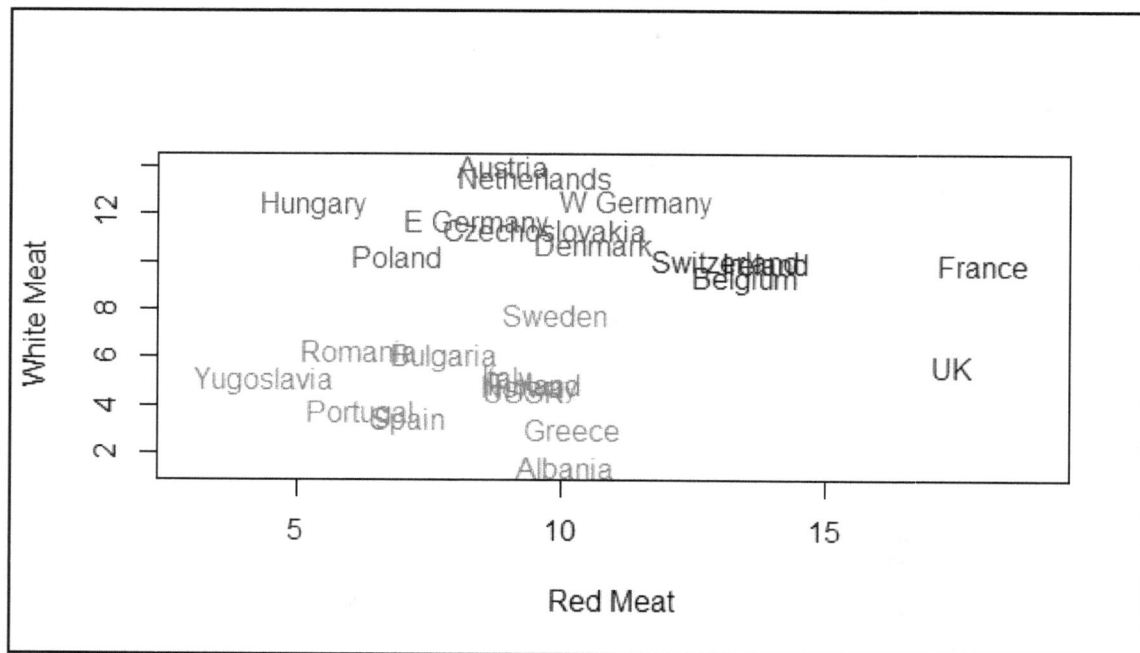

Step 4 - improving the model

Next, clustering on all the nine protein groups takes place and seven clusters are created. There is a close significance between the colored scatter-plot for white meat against red meat. Countries in close geographic proximity tend to be clustered into the same group.

The `set.seed()` function results in the generation of random numbers:

```
> set.seed(123456789)
```

`centers=7` signifies the number of initial (distinct) cluster centers:

```
> groupProtein <- kmeans(protein[,-1], centers=7, nstart=10)
> o=order(groupProtein$cluster)
> data.frame(protein$Country[o],groupProtein$cluster[o])
```

Seven different clusters are formed. Each of the 25 countries is placed in one of the clusters.

The result is as follows:

```
    protein.Country.o.  groupProtein.cluster.o.
1             Austria                        1
2           E Germany                        1
3         Netherlands                        1
4           W Germany                        1
5            Portugal                        2
6               Spain                        2
7             Albania                        3
8              Greece                        3
9               Italy                        3
10               USSR                        3
11      Czechoslovakia                        4
12             Hungary                        4
13              Poland                        4
14            Bulgaria                        5
15             Romania                        5
16          Yugoslavia                        5
17             Denmark                        6
18             Finland                        6
19              Norway                        6
20              Sweden                        6
21             Belgium                        7
22              France                        7
23             Ireland                        7
24         Switzerland                        7
25                  UK                        7
```

```
> library(cluster)
```

The `clustplot()` function creates a bivariate plot that can be visualized as a partition (clustering) of the data. All observations are represented by points in the plot, using principal components. Around each cluster, an ellipse is drawn. The data frame, protein is passed as an object:

```
> clusplot(protein[,-1], groupProtein$cluster, main='2D representation
of the Cluster solution', color=TRUE, shade=TRUE, labels=2, lines=0)
```

The result is as follows:

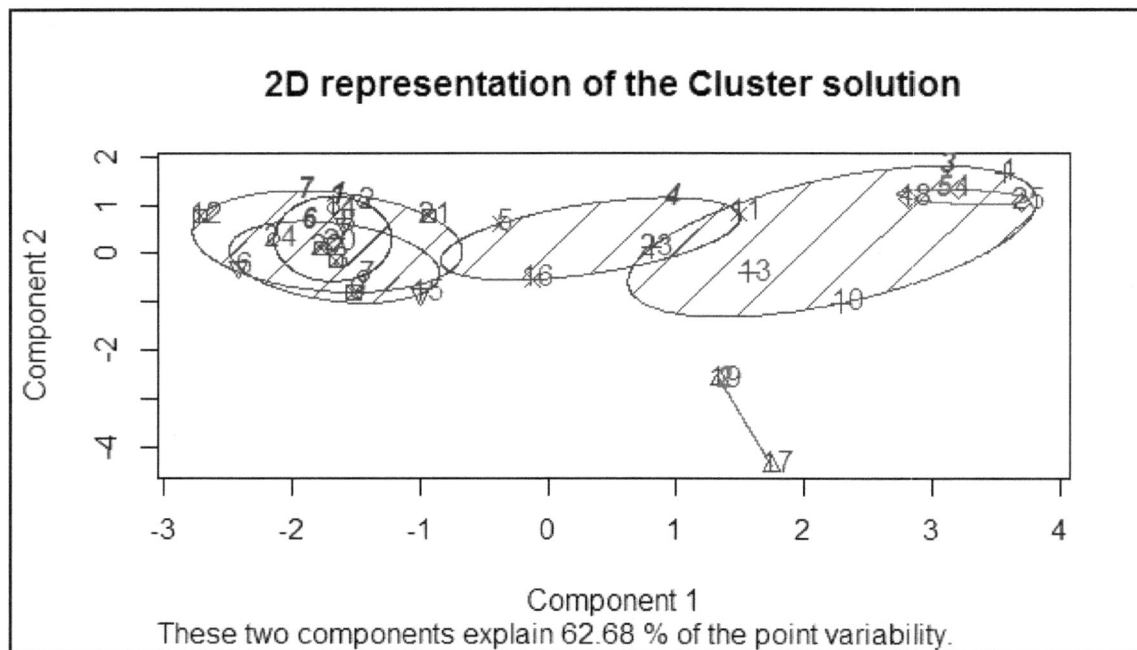

2D representation of the Cluster solution

Component 1

These two components explain 62.68 % of the point variability.

Another approach is to view it in hierarchical form. The agnes() function is used. By putting diss=FALSE, the dissimilarity matrix is used for calculating from raw data. metric="euclidean" indicates the use of the Euclidean distance measure:

```
> foodagg=agnes(protein,diss=FALSE,metric="euclidean")
> foodagg
```

The result is as follows:

```
call:    agnes(x = protein, diss = FALSE, metric = "euclidian")
Agglomerative coefficient:  0.6448106
Order of objects:
 [1]  1   4 18 25 23  2  3  5  7 10 13 16 11 17 19  6 12 14  9 15 20 21 22 24  8
Height (summary):
   Min. 1st Qu.  Median    Mean 3rd Qu.    Max.
  7.115   9.631  11.710  13.380  16.250  29.130

Available components:
[1] "order"   "height"  "ac"        "merge"  "diss"    "call"    "method" "data"
```

```
> plot(foodagg, main='Dendrogram')
```

The result is as follows:

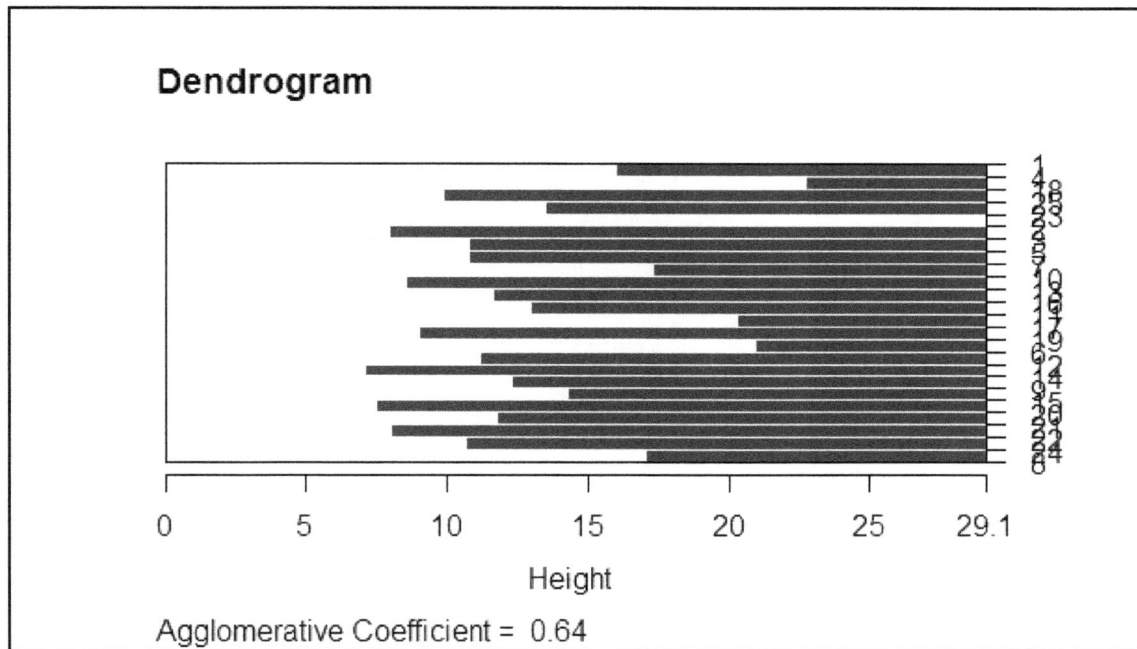

Dendrogram

Height

Agglomerative Coefficient = 0.64

The `cutree()` function cuts a tree into several groups by specifying either the desired number(s) of groups or the cut height(s):

```
> groups <- cutree(foodagg, k=4)
```

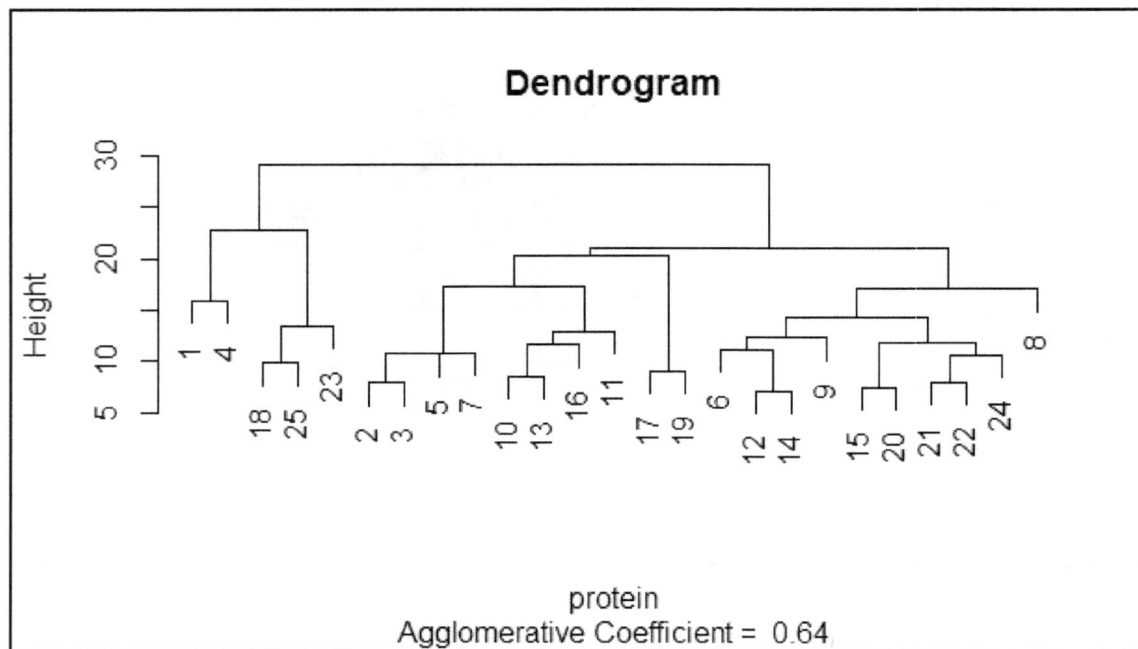

Dendrogram

protein
Agglomerative Coefficient = 0.64

```
> rect.hclust(foodagg, k=4, border="red")
```

The result is as follows:

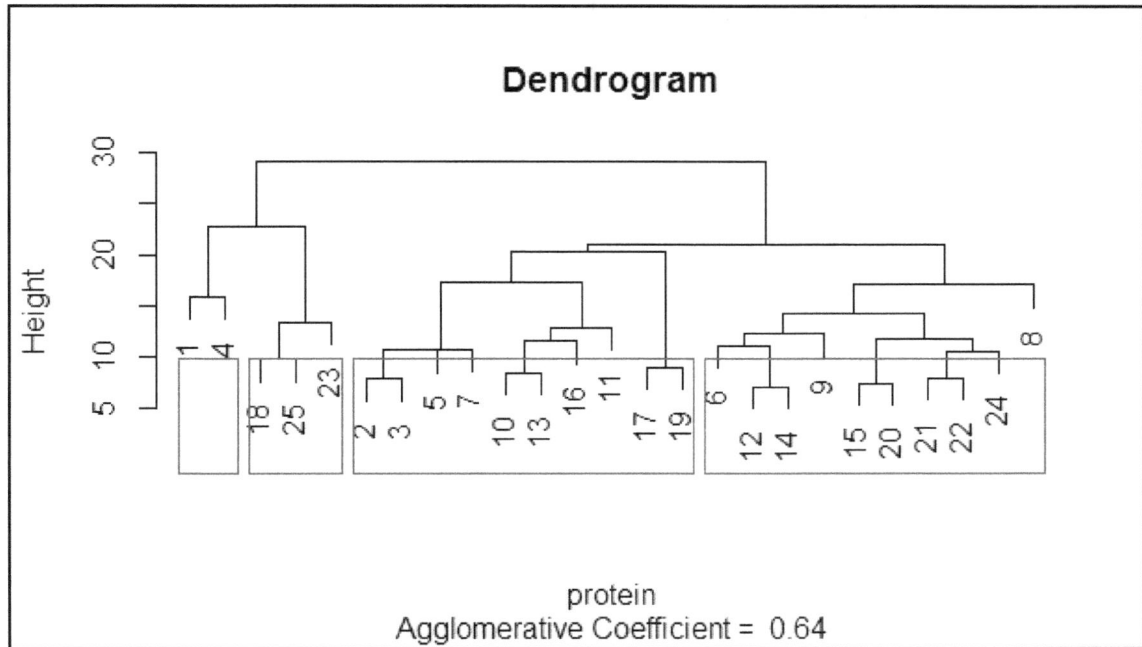

Dendrogram

protein
Agglomerative Coefficient = 0.64

K-means clustering - foodstuff

Nutrients in the food we consume can be classified by the role they play in building body mass. These nutrients can be divided into either macronutrients or essential micronutrients. Some examples of macronutrients are carbohydrates, protein, and fat while some examples of essential micronutrients are vitamins, minerals, and water.

Getting ready

Let's get started with the recipe.

Step 1 - collecting and describing data

In order to perform K-means clustering we shall be using a dataset collected on various food items and their respective `Energy`, `Protein`, `Fat`, `Calcium`, and `Iron` content. The numeric variables are:

- `Energy`
- `Protein`
- `Fat`
- `Calcium`
- `Iron`

The non-numeric variable is:

- `Food`

How to do it...

Let's get into the details.

Step 2 - exploring data

> Version info: Code for this page was tested in R version 3.2.3 (2015-12-10).

Loading the `cluster()` library.

```
> library(cluster)
```

Let's explore the data and understand relationships among the variables. We'll begin by importing the text file named `foodstuffs.txt`. We will be saving the data to the `food.energycontent` data frame:

```
> food.energycontent <- read.table("d:/foodstuffs.txt", header=T)
```

The head() returns the first or last parts of a vector, matrix, table, data frame, or function. The food.energycontent data frame is passed to the head() function:

```
> head(food.energycontent)
```

The result is as follows:

```
  Food Energy Protein Fat Calcium Iron
1   BB    340      20  28       9  2.6
2   HR    245      21  17       9  2.7
3   BR    420      15  39       7  2.0
4   BS    375      19  32       9  2.5
5   BC    180      22  10      17  3.7
6   CB    115      20   3       8  1.4
```

The str() function returns the provided information on the structure of the food.energycontent data frame. It compactly displays the internal structure:

```
> str(food.energycontent)
```

The result is as follows:

```
'data.frame':   27 obs. of  6 variables:
 $ Food    : Factor w/ 27 levels "AC","AR","BB",..: 3 14 6 7 4 9 10 5 16 17 ...
 $ Energy  : int   340 245 420 375 180 115 170 160 265 300 ...
 $ Protein : int   20 21 15 19 22 20 25 26 20 18 ...
 $ Fat     : int   28 17 39 32 10 3 7 5 20 25 ...
 $ Calcium : int   9 9 7 9 17 8 12 14 9 9 ...
 $ Iron    : num   2.6 2.7 2 2.5 3.7 1.4 1.5 5.9 2.6 2.3 ...
```

Step 3 - transforming data

The apply() function carries out entry-by-entry changes to data frames and matrices. It returns a vector, array, or list of values obtained by applying a function to margins of an array or matrix. 2 indicates column subscripts the function will be applied over. sd is for standard deviation function, which is to be applied on the data frame:

```
> standard.deviation <- apply(food.energycontent[,-1], 2, sd)
> standard.deviation
```

The result is as follows:

```
    Energy    Protein       Fat   Calcium      Iron
101.207806   4.251696 11.257033 78.034254  1.460857
```

The sweep() function returns an array obtained from an input array by sweeping out a summary statistic. food.energycontent[,-1] is passed as an array. 2 indicates column subscripts which the function will be applied over. standard.deviation is the summary statistic which is to be swept out:

```
> foodergycnt.stddev <-
sweep(food.energycontent[,-1],2,standard.deviation,FUN="/")
    > foodergycnt.stddev
```

The result is as follows:

	Energy	Protein	Fat	Calcium	Iron
1	3.3594247	4.704005	2.48733386	0.11533397	1.7797775
2	2.4207619	4.939205	1.51016699	0.11533397	1.8482304
3	4.1498775	3.528003	3.46450074	0.08970420	1.3690596
4	3.7052478	4.468804	2.84266727	0.11533397	1.7113245
5	1.7785189	5.174405	0.88833352	0.21785305	2.5327602
6	1.1362760	4.704005	0.26650006	0.10251908	0.9583417
7	1.6797123	5.880006	0.62183347	0.15377862	1.0267947
8	1.5809057	6.115206	0.44416676	0.17940839	4.0387258
9	2.6183751	4.704005	1.77666704	0.11533397	1.7797775
10	2.9641982	4.233604	2.22083381	0.11533397	1.5744185
11	3.3594247	4.704005	2.48733386	0.11533397	1.7113245
12	3.3594247	4.468804	2.57616721	0.11533397	1.7113245
13	3.5076346	4.468804	2.66500057	0.11533397	1.6428715
14	2.0255355	4.233604	1.24366693	0.08970420	1.7113245
15	1.8279223	5.409605	0.79950017	0.11533397	1.8482304
16	1.3338892	5.174405	0.35533341	0.32037213	0.4107179
17	0.6916463	2.587203	0.08883335	1.05082059	4.1071788
18	0.4446297	1.646402	0.08883335	0.94830150	3.6964609
19	0.8892595	3.292803	0.17766670	0.48696564	0.5476238
20	1.3338892	3.763204	0.44416676	0.19222328	0.3422649
21	1.9761322	4.468804	1.15483358	0.06407443	0.6845298
22	1.5315024	3.763204	0.79950017	2.01193697	1.2321536
23	1.9267289	3.763204	0.97716687	0.17940839	0.8898887
24	1.1856793	3.998404	0.44416676	2.03756674	0.4791709
25	1.7785189	5.174405	0.79950017	4.70306286	1.7113245
26	1.6797123	5.880006	0.62183347	0.08970420	0.8214358
27	1.0868727	5.409605	0.08883335	1.25585875	1.7797775

Step 4 - clustering

The kmeans() function shall carry out K-means clustering on the data matrix. The data matrix foodergycnt.stddev is passed as an object that can be coerced to the numeric matrix of data. centers=5 signifies the number of initial (distinct) cluster centers. iter.max=100 means the maximum number of iterations allowed. Since the number of clusters is denoted by a number, nstart=25 defines the number of random sets to be chosen:

```
> food.5cluster <- kmeans(foodergycnt.stddev, centers=5, iter.max=100,
nstart=25)
> food.5cluster
```

The result is as follows:

```
K-means clustering with 5 clusters of sizes 2, 8, 8, 8, 1

Cluster means:
    Energy  Protein        Fat   Calcium       Iron
1 0.568138 2.116802 0.08883335 0.9995610 3.9018198
2 1.414170 4.116004 0.57741679 0.6743833 0.6930864
3 1.759993 5.380205 0.77729183 0.2771219 1.9509099
4 3.377951 4.410004 2.56506304 0.1121302 1.6599848
5 1.778519 5.174405 0.79950017 4.7030629 1.7113245

Clustering vector:
 [1] 4 3 4 4 3 2 3 3 4 4 4 4 3 3 2 1 1 2 2 2 2 2 5 3 3

Within cluster sum of squares by cluster:
[1]  0.5626614 10.2035285 13.0477424  4.3254549  0.0000000
 (between_SS / total_SS =  78.4 %)

Available components:

[1] "cluster"     "centers"     "totss"       "withinss"     "tot.withinss" "betweens
s"
[7] "size"        "iter"        "ifault"
```

```
> food.4cluster <- kmeans(foodergycnt.stddev, centers=4, iter.max=100,
nstart=25)
> food.4cluster
```

The result is as follows:

```
K-means clustering with 4 clusters of sizes 3, 8, 2, 14

Cluster means:
    Energy  Protein      Fat   Calcium     Iron
1 1.498567 4.312004 0.68105570 2.9175222 1.140883
2 3.377951 4.410004 2.56506304 0.1121302 1.659985
3 0.568138 2.116802 0.08883335 0.9995610 3.901820
4 1.619723 4.872005 0.68528586 0.2544670 1.388618

Clustering vector:
 [1] 2 4 2 2 4 4 4 2 2 2 2 2 4 4 4 3 3 4 4 4 1 4 1 1 4 4

Within cluster sum of squares by cluster:
[1]  6.9589520  4.3254549  0.5626614 28.9804747
 (between_SS / total_SS =  68.6 %)

Available components:

[1] "cluster"     "centers"     "totss"      "withinss"    "tot.withinss" "betweens
s"
[7] "size"        "iter"        "ifault"
```

Printing the clustering vector for the 4-cluster solution:

```
> food.4cluster$cluster
```

The result is as follows:

```
[1] 2 4 2 2 4 4 4 2 2 2 2 2 4 4 4 3 3 4 4 4 1 4 1 1 4 4
```

Next, we shall be printing the clusters for the 4-cluster solution in terms of food labels.

The `lapply()` function returns a list of the same length as X:

```
> food.4cluster.clust <- lapply(1:4, function(nc)
protein[food.4cluster$cluster==nc])
> food.4cluster.clust
```

The result is as follows:

```
[[1]]
[1] MC SC DC
Levels: AC AR BB BC BH BR BS BT CB CC DC FB HF HR HS LL LS MB MC PF PR PS RC SC TC UC VC

[[2]]
[1] BB BR BS LL LS HS PR PS
Levels: AC AR BB BC BH BR BS BT CB CC DC FB HF HR HS LL LS MB MC PF PR PS RC SC TC UC VC

[[3]]
[1] AR AC
Levels: AC AR BB BC BH BR BS BT CB CC DC FB HF HR HS LL LS MB MC PF PR PS RC SC TC UC VC

[[4]]
 [1] HR BC CB CC BH BT VC FB TC HF MB PF UC RC
Levels: AC AR BB BC BH BR BS BT CB CC DC FB HF HR HS LL LS MB MC PF PR PS RC SC TC UC VC
```

Step 5 - visualizing the clusters

Using the pairs() function, a matrix of scatterplots is produced.
food.energycontent[,-1] provides the coordinates of points given as numeric columns
of a matrix or data frame.

```
> pairs(food.energycontent[,-1], panel=function(x,y)
text(x,y,food.4cluster$cluster))
```

The result is as follows:

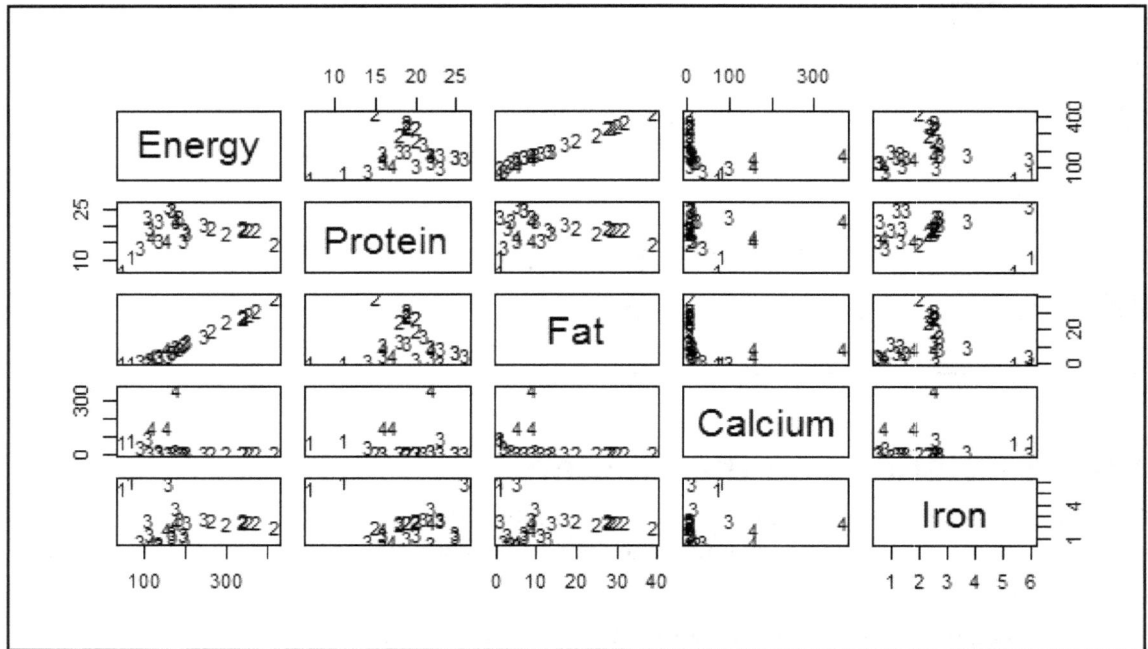

The `princomp()` function performs a principal components analysis on the given numeric data matrix. The function produces an unrotated principal component analysis. `cor=T` signifies a logical value indicating that the calculation should use the correlation matrix:

```
> food.pc <- princomp(food.energycontent[,-1],cor=T)
> my.color.vector <- rep("green", times=nrow(food.energycontent))
> my.color.vector[food.4cluster$cluster==2] <- "blue"
> my.color.vector[food.4cluster$cluster==3] <- "red"
> my.color.vector[food.4cluster$cluster==4] <- "orange"
```

The `par()` function combines multiple plots into one overall graph. `s` generates a square plotting region:

```
> par(pty="s")
```

Plotting the cluster:

```
      > plot(food.pc$scores[,1], food.pc$scores[,2],
  ylim=range(food.pc$scores[,1]),
      + xlab="PC 1", ylab="PC 2", type ='n', lwd=2)
      > text(food.pc$scores[,1], food.pc$scores[,2], labels=Food, cex=0.7,
  lwd=2,
      + col=my.color.vector)
```

The result is as follows:

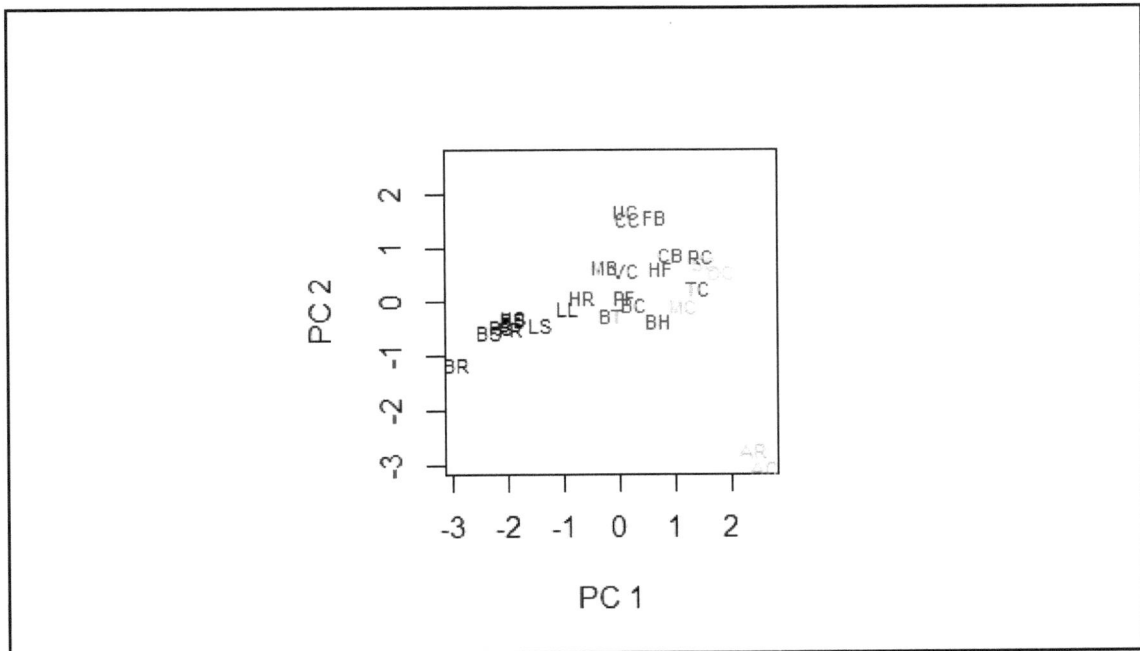

4
Model Selection and Regularization

In this chapter, we will cover the following recipes:

- Shrinkage methods - calories burned per day
- Dimension reduction methods - Delta's Aircraft Fleet
- Principal component analysis - understanding world cuisine

Introduction

Subset selection: The use of labeled examples to induce a model that classifies objects into a finite set of known classes is one of the main challenges of supervised classification in machine learning. Vectors of numeric or nominal features are used to describe the various examples. In the feature subset selection problem, a learning algorithm is faced with the problem of selecting some subset of features upon which to focus its attention, while ignoring the rest.

When fitting a linear regression model, a subset of variables that best describe the data are of interest. There are a number of different ways the best subset, applying a number of different strategies, can be adopted when searching for a variables set. If there are m variables and the best regression model consists of p variables, $p \leq m$, then a more general approach to pick the best subset might be to try all possible combinations of p variables and select the model that fits the data the best.

However, there are $m!\,p!(m-p)!$ possible combinations, which increases with the increase in the value of m, for example, $m = 20$ and $p = 4$ gives 4,845 possible combinations. In addition, through the usage of fewer features, we may reduce the cost of acquiring the data and improve the comprehensibility of the classification model.

Shrinkage methods: Shrinkage regression refers to shrinkage methods of estimation or prediction in regression situations; useful when there is multi co-linearity among the regressors. In cases where the dataset is small compared to the number of co-variables studied, shrinkage techniques may improve predictions. The common shrinkage methods are as follows:

- Linear shrinkage factor--shrinks all coefficients with the same factor
- Ridge regression--penalized maximum likelihood, penalty factor is added to the likelihood function such that coefficients are shrunk individually according to the variance of each co-variable
- Lasso--shrinks some coefficients to zero by setting a constraint on the sum of the absolute values of the coefficients of standardized co-variables

Shrinkage methods retain a subset of the predictors, while discarding the rest. The subset selection produces a model that is interpretable and produces possibly lower prediction-errors than the full model, while not reducing the prediction error of the full model. Shrinkage methods more continuous and don't suffer as much from high variability. When there are many correlated variables in a linear regression model, their coefficients are poorly determined and exhibit high variance.

Dimension reduction methods: One of the significant challenges across a wide variety of information-processing fields, including pattern recognition, data compression, machine learning, and database navigation, is manifold learning. The measured data vectors are high-dimensional and, in many cases, the data lies near a lower-dimensional manifold. The main challenges of high-dimensional data are that it is multiple; it indirectly measures the underlying source, which typically cannot be directly measured. Dimensionality reduction may also be seen as the process of deriving a set of degrees of freedom, which can be used to reproduce most of the variability of a dataset.

Shrinkage methods - calories burned per day

In order to compare the metabolic rate of humans, the concept of **basal metabolic rate (BMR)** is critical, in a clinical context, as a means of determining thyroid status in humans. The BMR of mammals varies with body mass, with the same allometric exponent as field metabolic rate, and with many physiological and biochemical rates. Fitbit, as a device, uses BMR and activities performed during the day to estimate calories burned throughout the day.

Getting ready

In order to perform shrinkage methods, we shall be using a dataset collected from Fitbit and a calories-burned dataset.

Step 1 - collecting and describing data

The dataset titled `fitbit_export_20160806.csv` which is in CSV format shall be used. The dataset is in standard format. There are 30 rows of data and 10 variables. The numeric variables are as follows:

- `Calories Burned`
- `Steps`
- `Distance`
- `Floors`
- `Minutes Sedentary`
- `Minutes Lightly Active`
- `Minutes Fairly Active`
- `ExAng`
- `Minutes Very Active`
- `Activity Calories`

The non-numeric variables are as follows:

- `Date`

How to do it...

Let's get into the details.

Step 2 - exploring data

As the first step, the following packages need to be loaded:

```
> install.packages("glmnet")
> install.packages("dplyr")
> install.packages("tidyr")
> install.packages("ggplot2")
> install.packages("caret")
> install.packages("boot")
> install.packages("RColorBrewer")
> install.packages("Metrics")
> library(dplyr)
> library(tidyr)
> library(ggplot2)
> library(caret)
> library(glmnet)
> library(boot)
> library(RColorBrewer)
> library(Metrics)
```

> Version info: Code for this page was tested in R version 3.3.0 (2016-05-03)

Let's explore the data and understand the relationships among the variables. We'll begin by importing the csv data file named `fitbit_export_20160806.csv`. We will be saving the data to the `fitbit_details` frame:

```
> fitbit_details <-
read.csv("https://raw.githubusercontent.com/ellisp/ellisp.github.io/source/
data/fitbit_export_20160806.csv",
+ skip = 1, stringsAsFactors = FALSE) %>%
+ mutate(
+ Calories.Burned = as.numeric(gsub(",", "", Calories.Burned)),
+ Steps = as.numeric(gsub(",", "", Steps)),
+ Activity.Calories = as.numeric(gsub(",", "", Activity.Calories)),
+ Date = as.Date(Date, format = "%d/%m/%Y")
+ )
```

Storing the `fitbit_details` data frame to the `fitbit` data frame:

```
> fitbit <- fitbit_details
```

Printing data frame `fitbit`. The `head()` function returns the first part of the `fitbit` data frame. The `fitbit` data frame is passed as an input parameter:

```
> head(fitbit)
```

The result is as follows:

```
    Date Calories.Burned Steps Distance Floors Minutes.Sedentary Minutes.Lightly.Active Minutes.Fairly.Active Minutes.Very.Active
1 2016-07-07            2682 12541     9.02     13               667                    171                     18                  60
2 2016-07-08            2423  8029     5.70     35               760                    208                     13                   6
3 2016-07-09            2875 10801     7.67      3               496                    148                     18                  46
4 2016-07-10            2638 11997     8.52     22               771                    248                      3                  27
5 2016-07-11            2423  9039     6.42     12               714                    232                     10                  16
6 2016-07-12            3102 17721    12.58      8               519                    226                     30                 107
  Activity.Calories
1              1248
2               928
3              1040
4              1285
5              1044
6              1805
```

Setting `Activity.Calories` and `Date` values as NULL:

```
> fitbit$Activity.Calories <- NULL
```

```
> fitbit$Date <- NULL
```

Scaling coefficients to calories per thousand steps. The result is then set to the `fitbit$Steps` data frame:

```
> fitbit$Steps <- fitbit$Steps / 1000
```

Printing the `fitbit$Steps` data frame:

```
> fitbit$Steps
```

The result is as follows:

```
 [1] 12.541  8.029 10.801 11.997  9.039 17.721 10.544 10.047  4.733 12.056 11.791 10.721 13.007 13.401 15.281 11.337  7.738
[18] 11.767 13.324  5.957 10.206 11.557 11.013 10.168 11.686 13.991 13.444 12.398 11.986 12.858
```

Exploring all the candidate variables. Function for calculating correlation coefficients:

```
> panel_correlations <- function(x, y, digits = 2, prefix = "",
cex.cor, ...){
    # combining multiple plots into one overall graph
+ usr <- par("usr")
```

```
+ on.exit(par(usr))
+ par(usr = c(0, 1, 0, 1))

# computing the absolute value
+ r <- abs(cor(x, y))

# Formatting object
+ txt <- format(c(r, 0.123456789), digits = digits)[1]
+ txt <- paste0(prefix, txt)

+ if(missing(cex.cor)) cex.cor <- 0.8/strwidth(txt)

+ text(0.5, 0.5, txt, cex = cex.cor * r)
+ }
```

Producing a matrix of scatterplots. The `pairs()` function produces the scatter plots in matrix form. `fitbit` is the dataset for scatter plots. Distance can be calculated almost exactly directly from `Steps`:

```
> pairs(fitbit[ , -1], lower.panel = panel_correlations, main =
"Pairwise Relationship - Fitbit's Measured Activities")
```

The result is as follows:

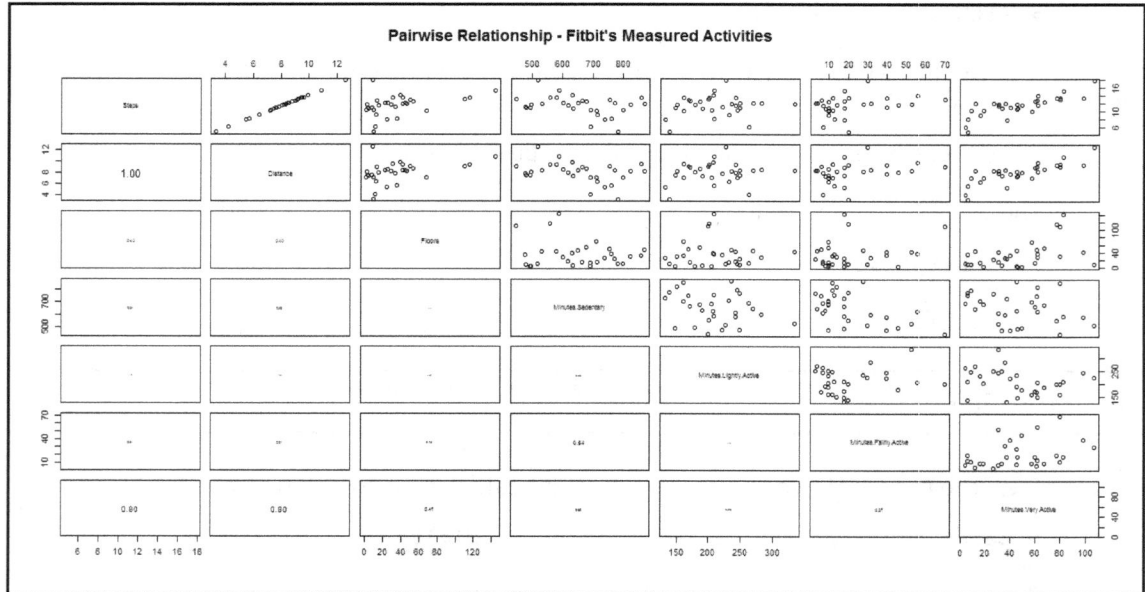

Printing `fitbit data frame`:

```
> ggplot(fitbit, aes(x = Distance / Steps)) + geom_rug() +
geom_density() +ggtitle("Stride Length Reverse- Engineered from Fitbit
Data", subtitle = "Not all strides identical, due to rounding or other
jitter")
```

The result is as follows:

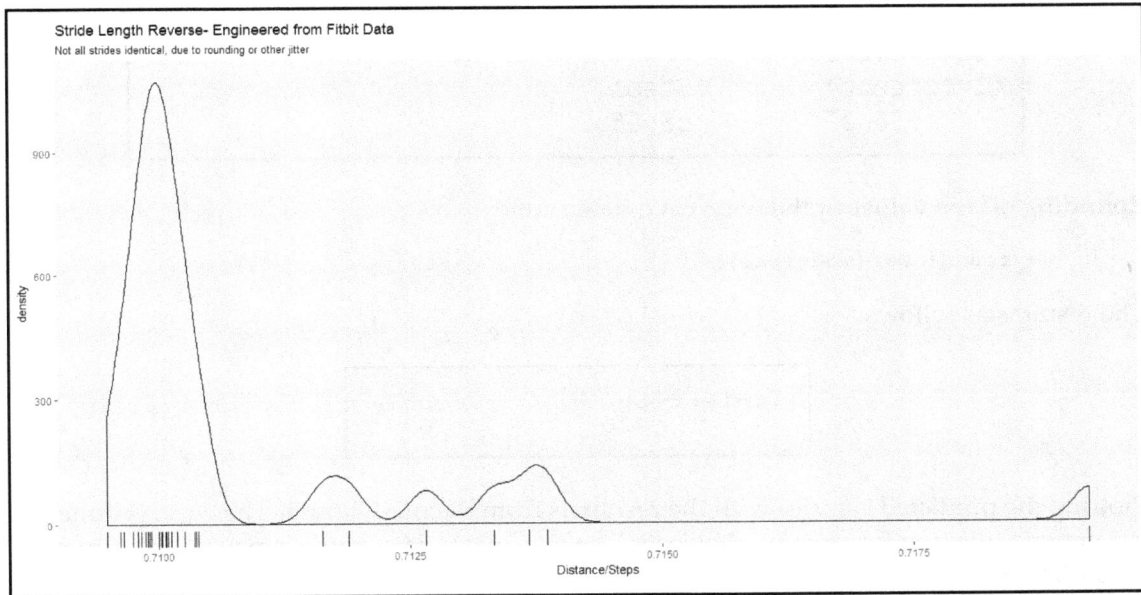

Step 3 - building the model

Building ordinary least squares estimation with Steps as the sole explanatory variable and `Calories.Burned` as the response variable. `lm()` as a function is used to fit linear models. `Calories.Burned ~ Steps` is the formula, while `fitbit` is the data frame. The result is then stored in the moderate data frame:

```
> moderate <- lm(Calories.Burned ~ Steps, data = fitbit)
```

Printing the `moderate` data frame:

```
> moderate
```

The result is as follows:

```
Call:
lm(formula = Calories.Burned ~ Steps, data = fitbit)

Coefficients:
(Intercept)        Steps
   1926.27        68.55
```

Rounding off the values of the `moderate` data frame:

```
> round(coef(moderate))
```

The result is as follows:

```
(Intercept)        Steps
       1926           69
```

Plotting the predicted calories with the residuals from the model used. The `plot()` function is a generic function for plotting R objects. The `moderate` data frame is passed as a function value. The `bty` parameter determines the type of box drawn about plots:

```
> plot(moderate, which = 1, bty = "l", main = "Predicted Calories
compared with Residuals")
```

The result is as follows:

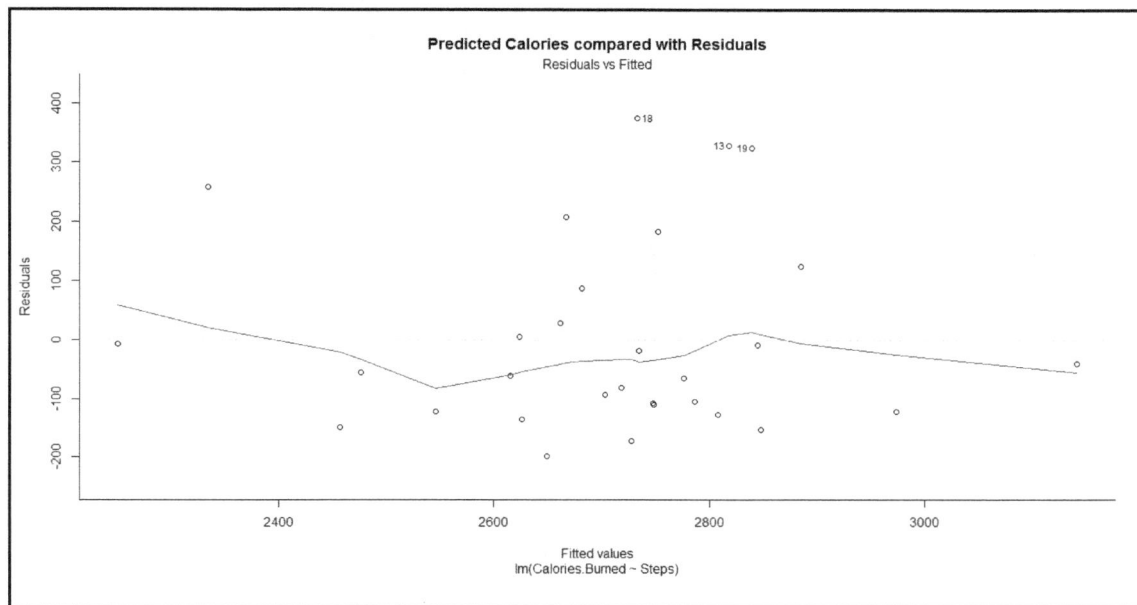

Checking the partial autocorrelation function of residuals. `pacf()` is used for partial autocorrelations. `resid()` as a function computes the difference between the observed data of the dependent variable. `moderate` is passed as a data frame to the `resid()` function, to compute the difference between the observed data of the dependent variable:

```
> pacf(resid(moderate), main = "Partial Autocorrelation of residuals
from single variable regression")
```

The `grid()` function adds the grids to the plotted data:

```
> grid()
```

The result is as follows:

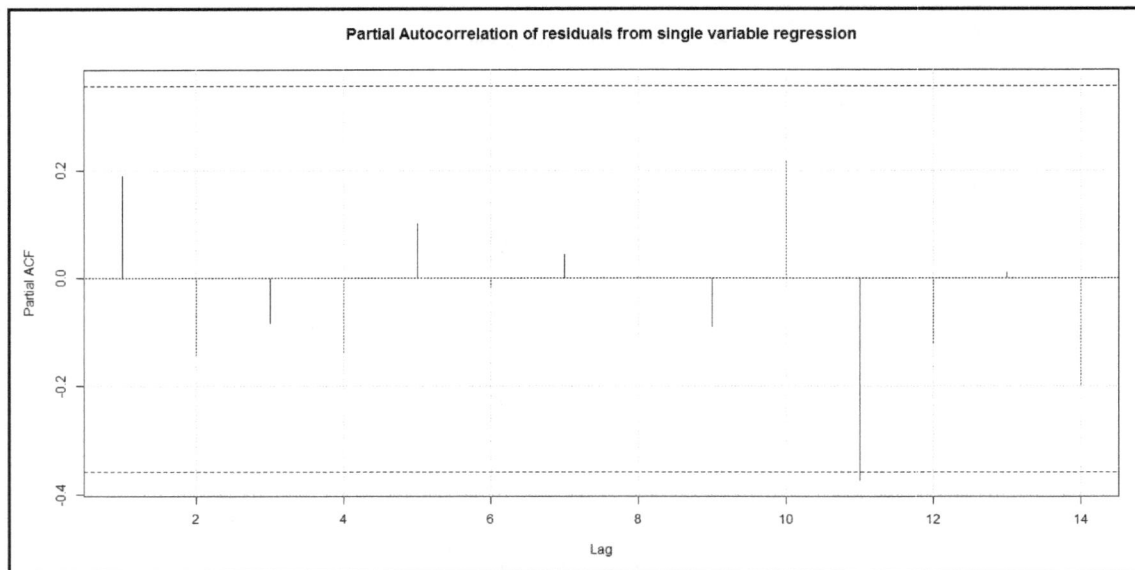

Partial Autocorrelation of residuals from single variable regression

Step 4 - improving the model

Predicting daily calories based on all seven explanatory variables. Fitting the model to multiple samples at different values of alpha, using the fit model to predict the out of bag points from the original sample that weren't in the re-sample. It is about creating the balance between the extremes of ridge regression and lasso estimation by choosing an appropriate value of alpha.

Creating the matrix X by standardizing. The `as.matrix()` function turns `fitbit[ , -1]` that is, apart from date column into matrix:

```
> X <- as.matrix(fitbit[ , -1])
```

Printing the X data frame. The `head()` function returns the first part of the X data frame. The X data frame is passed as an input parameter:

```
> head(X)
```

The result is as follows:

	Steps	Distance	Floors	Minutes.Sedentary	Minutes.Lightly.Active	Minutes.Fairly.Active	Minutes.Very.Active
[1,]	12.541	9.02	13	667	171	18	60
[2,]	8.029	5.70	35	760	208	13	6
[3,]	10.801	7.67	3	496	148	18	46
[4,]	11.997	8.52	22	771	248	3	27
[5,]	9.039	6.42	12	714	232	10	16
[6,]	17.721	12.58	8	519	226	30	107

Creating the vector Y by standardizing:

```
> Y <- fitbit$Calories.Burned
```

Printing the Y data frame:

```
> Y
```

The result is as follows:

```
[1] 2682 2423 2875 2638 2423 3102 2450 2555 2245 2936 2717 2690 3147 2837 2851 2611 2307 3109 3164 2593 2490 263
8 2769 2629
[25] 2555 3010 2694 2713 2640 2680
```

```
> set.seed(123)
```

Generating regular sequences:

```
> alphas <- seq(from = 0, to  = 1, length.out = 10)
> res <- matrix(0, nrow = length(alphas), ncol = 6)
```

Creating five repeats of each CV run:

```
> for(i in 1:length(alphas)){
+ for(j in 2:6){
# k-fold cross-validation for glmnet
+ cvmod <- cv.glmnet(X, Y, alpha = alphas[i])
+ res[i, c(1, j)] <- c(alphas[i], sqrt(min(cvmod$cvm)))
+ }
+ }
```

Creating the dataset to be used. The data.frame() function is used to create data frames based on a tightly coupled set of variables. These variables share the properties of matrices:

```
> res <- data.frame(res)
```

Printing the `res` data frame:

```
> res
```

The result is as follows:

```
         X1       X2       X3       X4       X5       X6
1  0.0000000 109.5889 107.0899 104.8613 111.7505 113.1563
2  0.1111111 108.6981 109.3370 110.0573 106.2842 109.0958
3  0.2222222 106.9779 108.4218 113.9708 102.3784 110.2811
4  0.3333333 111.2883 109.3242 106.8881 111.5851 110.8253
5  0.4444444 109.0175 110.8455 107.9398 117.3966 109.8615
6  0.5555556 107.8713 109.9792 106.3763 107.8555 110.9318
7  0.6666667 106.9289 113.0265 106.6506 103.0891 100.5173
8  0.7777778 108.6405 107.2741 110.9709 109.0754 107.5905
9  0.8888889 110.3589 116.6443 105.5138 108.3451 106.8064
10 1.0000000 105.8732 111.4563 107.1465 115.6756 108.3659
```

Creating a vector of `average_rmse`:

```
> res$average_rmse <- apply(res[ , 2:6], 1, mean)
```

Printing the `res$average_rmse`vector:

```
> res$average_rmse
```

The result is as follows:

```
[1] 109.2894 108.6945 108.4060 109.9822 111.0122 108.6028 106.0425 108.7103 109.5337 109.7035
```

Arranging the `res$average_rmse` in ascending order. The result is then stored in the `res` data frame:

```
> res <- res[order(res$average_rmse), ]
```

Printing the `res` data frame:

```
> res
```

The result is as follows:

```
          X1       X2       X3       X4       X5       X6 average_rmse
7  0.6666667 106.9289 113.0265 106.6506 103.0891 100.5173     106.0425
3  0.2222222 106.9779 108.4218 113.9708 102.3784 110.2811     108.4060
6  0.5555556 107.8713 109.9792 106.3763 107.8555 110.9318     108.6028
2  0.1111111 108.6981 109.3370 110.0573 106.2842 109.0958     108.6945
8  0.7777778 108.6405 107.2741 110.9709 109.0754 107.5905     108.7103
1  0.0000000 109.5889 107.0899 104.8613 111.7505 113.1563     109.2894
9  0.8888889 110.3589 116.6443 105.5138 108.3451 106.8064     109.5337
10 1.0000000 105.8732 111.4563 107.1465 115.6756 108.3659     109.7035
4  0.3333333 111.2883 109.3242 106.8881 111.5851 110.8253     109.9822
5  0.4444444 109.0175 110.8455 107.9398 117.3966 109.8615     111.0122
```

```
> names(res)[1] <- "alpha"
> res %>%
+ select(-average_rmse) %>%
+ gather(trial, rmse, -alpha) %>%
+ ggplot(aes(x = alpha, y = rmse)) +
+ geom_point() +
+ geom_smooth(se = FALSE) +
+ labs(y = "Root Mean Square Error") +
+ ggtitle("Cross Validation best RMSE for differing values of alpha")
```

The result is as follows:

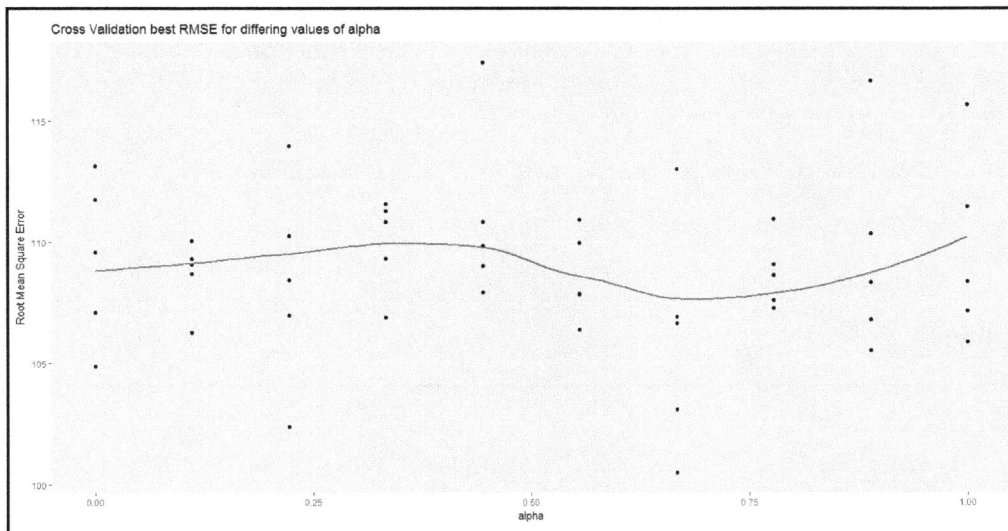

```
> bestalpha <- res[1, 1]
```

Printing the `bestalpha` data frame:

> **bestalpha**

```
[1] 0.6666667
```

Comparing ordinary least squares equivalents with the estimated values of the eight coefficients (seven explanatory variables plus an intercept) by using elastic net.

Determining lambda at best value of alpha. Computing k-fold cross-validation for `glmnet` by calling the `cv.glmnet()` function:

> **crossvalidated <- cv.glmnet(X, Y, alpha = bestalpha)**

Creating the model. `glmnet()` fits a generalized linear model via penalized maximum likelihood. The regularization path is computed for the lasso or `elasticnet` penalty at a grid of values for the regularization parameter lambda. `X` is the input matrix, while `Y` is the response variable. `alpha` is the `elasticnet` mixing parameter, with $0 \leq \alpha \leq 1$:

> **moderate1 <- glmnet(X, Y, alpha = bestalpha)**

Building an ordinary least squares estimation, with `fitbit` as the sole explanatory variable and `Calories.Burned` as the response variable. `lm()` as a function is used to fit linear models. `Calories.Burned ~ Steps` is the formula, while `fitbit` is the data frame. The result is then stored in the `OLSmodel` data frame:

> **OLSmodel <- lm(Calories.Burned ~ ., data = fitbit)**

Printing the `OLSmodel` data frame:

> **OLSmodel**

The result is as follows:

```
Call:
lm(formula = Calories.Burned ~ ., data = fitbit)

Coefficients:
           (Intercept)                  Steps               Distance        Floors    Minutes.Sedentary
              1941.1889               -66.8266               116.0772        0.0274              -0.2458
  Minutes.Lightly.Active   Minutes.Fairly.Active   Minutes.Very.Active
                  2.2466                  4.4016                 3.8955
```

Comparing ordinary least squares equivalents with the estimated values of the eight coefficients (seven explanatory variables plus an intercept). The result is then stored in the `coeffs` data frame:

```
> coeffs <- data.frame(original = coef(OLSmodel),
    + shrunk = as.vector(coef(moderate1, s =
crossvalidated$lambda.min)),
    + very.shrunk = as.vector(coef(moderate1, s =
crossvalidated$lambda.1se)))
```

Printing the `coeffs` data frame:

```
> coeffs
```

The result is as follows:

	original	shrunk	very.shrunk
(Intercept)	1941.18889510	1953.9193828	2176.9301681
Steps	-66.82663867	7.7214570	15.9566697
Distance	116.07718793	14.3140006	22.1799747
Floors	0.02740202	0.0000000	0.0000000
Minutes.Sedentary	-0.24578123	-0.2388018	-0.1801439
Minutes.Lightly.Active	2.24661181	2.1139746	0.7914329
Minutes.Fairly.Active	4.40164035	4.4040703	3.7619668
Minutes.Very.Active	3.89545935	3.6009476	0.8484609

Rounding off the values of the `moderate` data frame to three significant digits:

```
> round(coeffs, 3)
```

The result is as follows:

	original	shrunk	very.shrunk
(Intercept)	1941.189	1971.199	2157.172
Steps	-66.827	9.176	15.703
Distance	116.077	15.045	21.835
Floors	0.027	0.000	0.000
Minutes.Sedentary	-0.246	-0.236	-0.187
Minutes.Lightly.Active	2.247	1.985	0.888
Minutes.Fairly.Active	4.402	4.384	3.842
Minutes.Very.Active	3.895	3.295	1.019

Creating the model. `glmnet()` fits a generalized linear model via a penalized maximum likelihood:

```
> moderate2 <- glmnet(X, Y, lambda = 0)
```

Printing the `moderate2` data frame:

```
> moderate2
```

The result is as follows:

```
Call:  glmnet(x = X, y = Y, lambda = 0)

        Df    %Dev Lambda
[1,]   7 0.8806      0
```

Rounding off the values to three significant digits:

```
> round(data.frame("elastic, lambda = 0" = as.vector(coef(moderate2)),
  "lm" = coef(OLSmodel), check.names = FALSE), 3)
```

The result is as follows:

```
                        elastic, lambda = 0         lm
(Intercept)                     1937.924   1941.189
Steps                             15.455    -66.827
Distance                           0.653    116.077
Floors                             0.011      0.027
Minutes.Sedentary                 -0.241     -0.246
Minutes.Lightly.Active             2.236      2.247
Minutes.Fairly.Active              4.415      4.402
Minutes.Very.Active                3.894      3.895
```

Creating the model. `glmnet()` fits a generalized linear model via a penalized maximum likelihood after eliminating the distance column:

```
> moderate3 <- glmnet(X[ , -2], Y, lambda = 0)
```

Printing the `moderate3` data frame:

```
> moderate3
```

The result is as follows:

```
call:   glmnet(x = X[, -2], y = Y, lambda = 0)

        Df   %Dev Lambda
[1,]   6 0.8806      0
```

Building ordinary least squares estimation `Y ~ X[ , -2]` is the formula. The result is then stored in the `moderate4` data frame:

```
> moderate4 <- lm(Y ~ X[ , -2])
```

Printing the `moderate4` data frame:

```
> moderate4
```

The result is as follows:

```
call:
lm(formula = Y ~ X[, -2])

coefficients:
                (Intercept)            X[, -2]steps             X[, -2]Floors    X[, -2]Minutes.Sedentary
                  1.938e+03               1.580e+01                 9.739e-03                  -2.406e-01
X[, -2]Minutes.Lightly.Active   X[, -2]Minutes.Fairly.Active    X[, -2]Minutes.very.Active
                  2.239e+00               4.413e+00                 3.906e+00
```

Rounding off the values to three significant digits:

```
> round(data.frame("elastic, lambda = 0" = as.vector(coef(moderate3)),
"lm" = coef(moderate4), check.names = FALSE), 3)
```

The result is as follows:

```
                             elastic, lambda = 0        lm
(Intercept)                           1938.103  1938.129
X[, -2]steps                            15.885    15.798
X[, -2]Floors                            0.011     0.010
X[, -2]Minutes.Sedentary                -0.241    -0.241
X[, -2]Minutes.Lightly.Active            2.236     2.239
X[, -2]Minutes.Fairly.Active             4.415     4.413
X[, -2]Minutes.very.Active               3.897     3.906
```

Step 5 - comparing the model

Comparing the predictive strength of different models by using bootstrapping, where the modeling approach is applied to bootstrap re-samples of the data. The estimate model is then used to predict the full, original dataset.

Function to feed to boot that does elastic modeling:

```
> modellingfucn1 <- function(data, i){
+ X <- as.matrix(data[i , -1])
+ Y <- data[i , 1]
# k-fold cross-validation for glmnet
+ crossvalidated <- cv.glmnet(X, Y, alpha = 1, nfolds = 30)
# Fitting a generalized linear model via penalized maximum likelihood
+ moderate1 <- glmnet(X, Y, alpha = 1)
# Computing the root mean squared error
+ rmse(predict(moderate1, newx = as.matrix(data[ , -1]), s =
crossvalidated$lambda.min), data[ , 1])
+ }
```

Generating an R bootstrap replica of a statistic applied to data. `fitbit` is the dataset, `statistic = modellingfucn1` is the function, which, when applied to `fitbit`, returns a vector containing the statistics of interest. `R = 99` indicates the number of bootstrap replicates:

```
> elastic_boot <- boot(fitbit, statistic = modellingfucn1, R = 99)
```

Printing the `elastic_boot` data frame:

```
> elastic_boot
```

The result is as follows:

```
ORDINARY NONPARAMETRIC BOOTSTRAP


Call:
boot(data = fitbit, statistic = modellingfucn1, R = 99)


Bootstrap Statistics :
     original    bias    std. error
t1*  81.87882  13.92733   9.038867
```

Function to feed to boot that does OLS modeling:

```
> modellingOLS <- function(data, i){
+ mod0 <- lm(Calories.Burned ~ Steps, data = data[i, ])
+ rmse(predict(moderate, newdata = data), data[ , 1])
+ }
```

Generating an R bootstrap replica of a statistic applied to data. `fitbit` is the dataset, `statistic = modellingOLS` is the function, which, when applied to `fitbit`, returns a vector containing the statistics of interest. `R = 99` indicates the number of bootstrap replicates:

```
> lmOLS_boot <- boot(fitbit, statistic = modellingOLS, R = 99)
```

Printing the `lmOLS_boot` data frame:

```
> lmOLS_boot
```

The result is as follows:

```
ORDINARY NONPARAMETRIC BOOTSTRAP


Call:
boot(data = fitbit, statistic = modellingfucn2, R = 99)


Bootstrap Statistics :
        original    bias    std. error
t1* 81.55149  18.15953     16.66511
```

Generating an R bootstrap replica of a statistic applied to data. `fitbit` is the dataset, `statistic = modellingfucn2` is the function, which, when applied to `fitbit`, returns a vector containing the statistics of interest. `R = 99` indicates the number of bootstrap replicates:

```
> lm_boot <- boot(fitbit, statistic = modellingfucn2, R = 99)
```

Printing the `lm_boot` data frame:

```
> lm_boot
```

The result is as follows:

```
ORDINARY NONPARAMETRIC BOOTSTRAP


Call:
boot(data = fitbit, statistic = modellingOLS, R = 99)


Bootstrap Statistics :
    original  bias     std. error
t1* 159.7195      0            0
```

```
> round(c("elastic modelling" = mean(elastic_boot$t),
+ "OLS modelling" = mean(lm_boot$t),
+ "OLS modelling, only one explanatory variable" =
mean(lmOLS_boot$t)), 1)
```

The result is as follows:

```
                          elastic modelling                    OLS modelling
                                     95.8                              99.7
OLS modelling, only one explanatory variable
                                    159.7
```

Refitting the model with scaled variables.

Creating the model. `glmnet()` fits a generalized linear model via a penalized maximum likelihood.

```
> ordering <- c(7,5,6,2,1,3,4)
> par(mar = c(5.1, 4.1, 6.5, 1), bg = "grey90")
> model_scaled <- glmnet(scale(X), Y, alpha = bestalpha)
> the_palette <- brewer.pal(7, "Set1")
> plot(model_scaled, xvar = "dev", label = TRUE, col = the_pallete, lwd
= 2, main = "Increasing contribution of different explanatory variablesnas
penalty for including them is relaxed")

> legend("topleft", legend = colnames(X)[ordering], text.col =
the_palette[ordering], lwd = 2, bty = "n", col = the_palette[ordering])
```

The result is as follows:

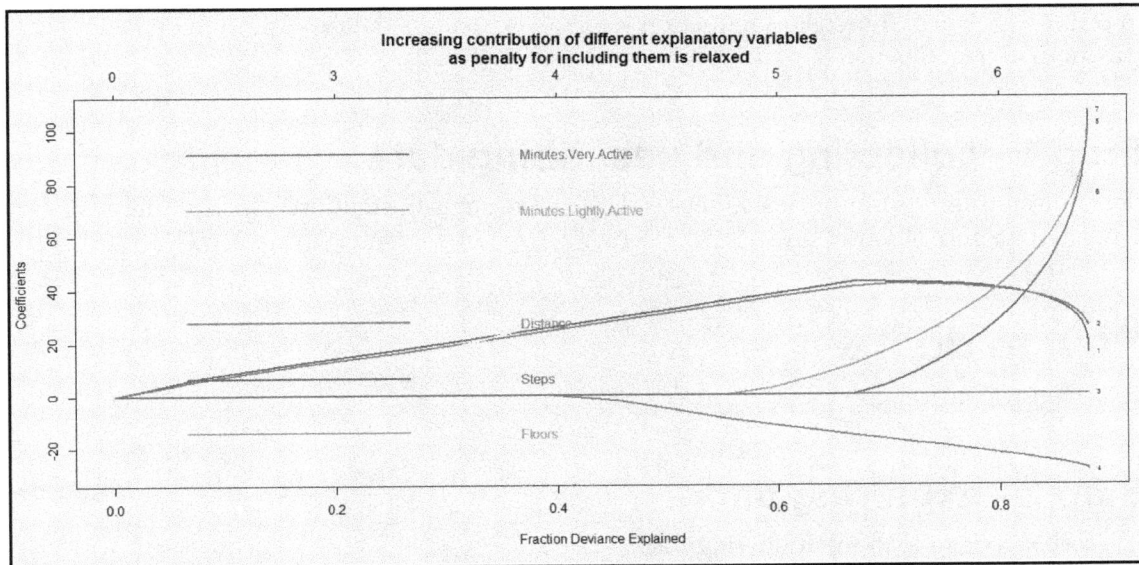

Increasing contribution of different explanatory variables
as penalty for including them is relaxed

Dimension reduction methods - Delta's Aircraft Fleet

Fleet planning is a part of the strategic planning process for any airline company. Fleet is the total number of aircraft that an airline operates, as well as the specific aircraft types that comprise the total fleet. Airline selection criteria for aircraft acquisition are based on technical/performance characteristics, economic and financial impact, environmental regulations and constraints, marketing considerations, and political realities. Fleet composition is a critical long-term strategic decision for an airline company. Each aircraft type has different technical performance characteristics, for example, the capacity to carry the payload over a maximum flight distance or range. It affects financial position, operating costs, and especially the ability to serve specific routes.

Getting ready

In order to perform dimension reduction we shall be using a dataset collected on Delta Airlines Aircraft Fleet.

Step 1 - collecting and describing data

The dataset titled `delta.csv` shall be used. The dataset is in standard format. There are 44 rows of data and 34 variables.

How to do it...

Let's get into the details.

Step 2 - exploring data

The first step is to load the following packages:

```
> install.packages("rgl")
> install.packages("RColorBrewer")
> install.packages("scales")
> library(rgl)
> library(RColorBrewer)
> library(scales)
```

Version info: Code for this page was tested in R version 3.3.2 (2016-10-31)

Let's explore the data and understand the relationships among the variables. We'll begin by importing the csv data file named `delta.csv`. We will be saving the data to the delta frame:

```
> delta <- read.csv(file="d:/delta.csv", header=T, sep=",",
row.names=1)
```

Exploring the internal structure of the `delta` data frame. The `str()` function displays the internal structure of the data frame. The details passed as an R object to the `str()` function:

```
> str(delta)
```

The result is as follows:

```
'data.frame':    44 obs. of   33 variables:
 $ Seat.Width..Club.          : num  0 19.4 0 0 0 0 0 0 0 0 ...
 $ Seat.Pitch..Club.          : int  0 44 0 0 0 0 0 0 0 0 ...
 $ Seat..Club.                : int  0 12 0 0 0 0 0 0 0 0 ...
 $ Seat.Width..First.Class.   : num  21 19.4 21 21 0 0 0 0 19.6 21 ...
 $ Seat.Pitch..First.Class.   : num  36 40 36 36 0 0 0 0 37 37 ...
 $ Seats..First.Class.        : int  12 28 12 12 0 0 0 0 12 12 ...
 $ Seat.Width..Business.      : num  0 21 0 0 21 21 21 20 0 0 ...
 $ Seat.Pitch..Business.      : num  0 59 0 0 60 80 80 60 0 0 ...
 $ Seats..Business.           : int  0 14 0 0 32 34 34 34 0 0 ...
 $ Seat.Width..Eco.Comfort.   : num  17.2 0 17.2 17.2 18 18 18 18 18.1 17.2 ...
 $ Seat.Pitch..Eco.Comfort.   : num  34 0 34 34 35 35 35 35 34 34 ...
 $ Seats..Eco.Comfort.        : int  18 0 18 18 30 32 32 32 15 18 ...
 $ Seat.Width..Economy.       : num  17.2 0 17.2 17.2 18 18 18 18 18.1 17.2 ...
 $ Seat.Pitch..Economy.       : num  30.5 0 31.5 31.5 30.5 30.5 30.5 30.5 31 30.5 ...
 $ Seats..Economy.            : int  96 0 120 120 181 168 227 232 83 94 ...
 $ Accommodation              : int  126 54 150 150 243 243 293 298 110 124 ...
 $ Cruising.Speed..mph.       : int  517 517 517 517 531 531 531 531 504 517 ...
 $ Range..miles.              : int  2399 3119 2420 2420 6536 6536 5343 5343 1510 2925 ...
 $ Engines                    : int  2 2 2 2 2 2 2 2 2 2 ...
 $ Wingspan..ft.              : num  112 112 112 112 198 ...
 $ Tail.Height..ft.           : num  38.6 38.6 38.6 38.6 59.8 ...
 $ Length..ft.                : num  111 111 123 123 189 ...
 $ Wifi                       : int  1 1 1 1 0 0 0 0 1 1 ...
 $ Video                      : int  0 1 0 0 1 1 1 1 0 1 ...
 $ Power                      : int  0 0 0 0 1 1 1 1 1 1 ...
 $ Satellite                  : int  0 0 0 0 0 0 0 0 0 1 ...
 $ Flat.bed                   : int  0 0 0 0 1 0 1 0 0 0 ...
 $ Sleeper                    : int  0 0 0 0 0 1 0 1 0 0 ...
 $ Club                       : int  0 1 0 0 0 0 0 0 0 0 ...
 $ First.Class                : int  1 1 1 1 0 0 0 0 1 1 ...
 $ Business                   : int  0 1 0 0 1 1 1 1 0 0 ...
 $ Eco.Comfort                : int  1 0 1 1 1 1 1 1 1 1 ...
 $ Economy                    : int  1 0 1 1 1 1 1 1 1 1 ...
```

Exploring the intermediary quantitative variables related to the aircraft's physical characteristics: Accommodation, Cruising Speed, Range, Engines, Wing Span, Tail Height, and Length. Scatter plot matrix. The plot() function is a generic function for plotting Robjects. The delta[,16:22] data frame is passed as a function value:

```
> plot(delta[,16:22], main = "Aircraft Physical Characteristics", col =
"red")
```

The result is as follows:

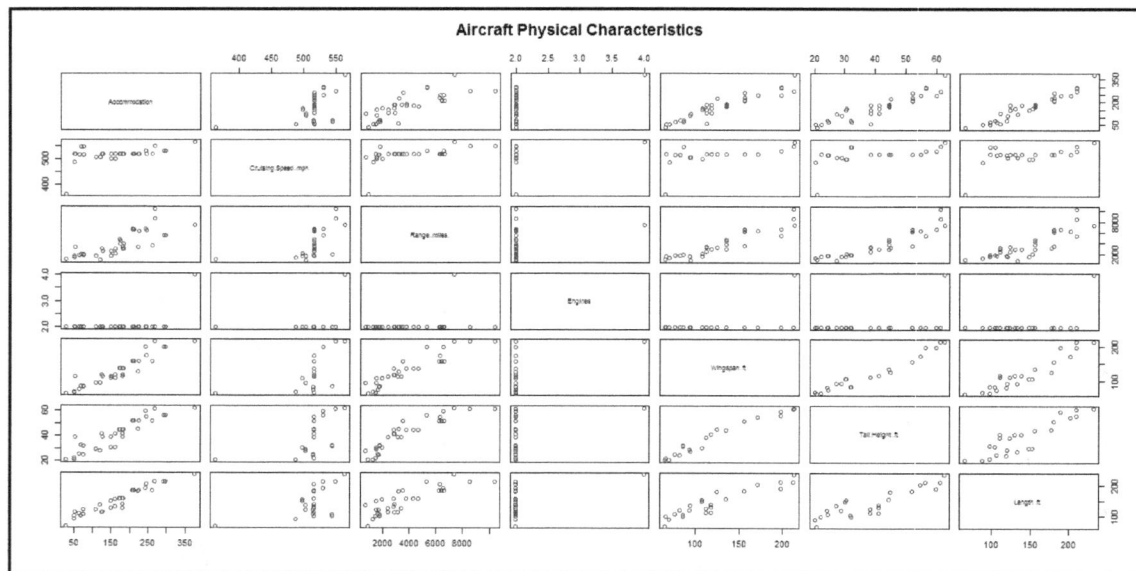

Aircraft Physical Characteristics

There is a positive correlation between all these variables as all of them are related to the aircraft's overall size.

Step 3 - applying principal components analysis

Visualizing a high-dimensional dataset, such as the number of engines. Applying principle components analysis to data. The `princomp()` function performs principal components analysis on the `delta` datamatrix. The result is `principal_comp_analysis`, which is an object of class `princomp`:

```
> principal_comp_analysis <- princomp(delta)
```

Printing the `principal_comp_analysis` data frame:

```
> principal_comp_analysis
```

The result is as follows:

```
Call:
princomp(x = delta)

Standard deviations:
     Comp.1      Comp.2      Comp.3      Comp.4      Comp.5      Comp.6      Comp.7      Comp.8      Comp.9     Comp.10
Comp.11
2.259237e+03 6.907940e+01 2.871764e+01 2.259929e+01 1.482962e+01 1.049014e+01 9.152229e+00 7.937495e+00 4.523039e+00 3.623724e+00 2.606
872e+00
    Comp.12     Comp.13     Comp.14     Comp.15     Comp.16     Comp.17     Comp.18     Comp.19     Comp.20     Comp.21
Comp.22
1.929074e+00 1.760506e+00 1.563002e+00 1.245856e+00 4.772154e-01 3.806455e-01 3.493458e-01 2.724929e-01 2.153123e-01 1.991243e-01 1.669
167e-01
    Comp.23     Comp.24     Comp.25     Comp.26     Comp.27     Comp.28     Comp.29     Comp.30     Comp.31     Comp.32
Comp.33
1.340994e-01 1.209009e-01 6.524198e-02 4.241346e-02 2.373915e-02 2.016179e-03 2.452124e-05 0.000000e+00 0.000000e+00 0.000000e+00 0.000
000e+00

 33  variables and  44 observations.
```

Plotting `principal_comp_analysis` data:

```
> plot(principal_comp_analysis, main ="Principal Components Analysis of
Raw Data", col ="blue")
```

The result is as follows:

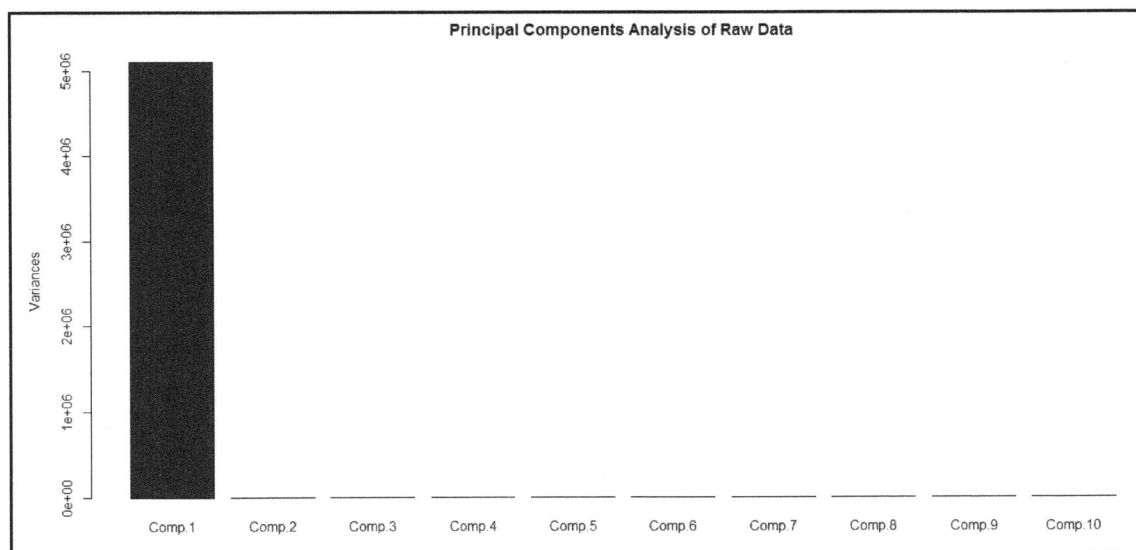

It is demonstrable that the first principal component has a standard deviation, which accounts for over 99.8% of the variance in the data.

Printing loadings of principal components analysis. The `loadings()` function uses the `principal_comp_analysis` principal components-analysis data object as input:

```
> loadings(principal_comp_analysis)
```

The result is as follows:

Loadings:	Comp.1	Comp.2	Comp.3	Comp.4	Comp.5	Comp.6	Comp.7	Comp.8	Comp.9	Comp.10	Comp.11	Comp.12	Comp.13	Comp.14	Comp.15	Comp.16
Seat.width..Club.				-0.144	-0.110						-0.165					0.105
Seat.Pitch..Club.				-0.327	-0.248		0.189				-0.374		0.121	0.174	0.119	0.239
Seat..Club.											-0.102					
Seat.width..First.Class.		0.250		-0.160		-0.156	0.136		-0.246			0.341	-0.128	0.429	0.371	-0.210
Seat.Pitch..First.Class.		0.515	-0.110	-0.386	0.112	-0.130	0.183	0.161	-0.307	0.211	-0.389				-0.424	
Seats..First.Class.		0.258	-0.124	-0.307	-0.109	0.160	0.149		0.313			0.172	-0.242	-0.659	0.361	
Seat.width..Business.			-0.154	0.142	-0.108				0.244	-0.480			0.255	-0.232	-0.393	-0.229
Seat.Pitch..Business.			-0.514	0.446	-0.298	0.154	-0.172	0.379	0.285		0.401					
Seats..Business.			-0.225	0.187					-0.287	-0.608	-0.294	-0.133	-0.503	-0.294		
Seat.width..Eco.Comfort.						0.285	-0.224				-0.113	0.111				0.546
Seat.Pitch..Eco.Comfort.		0.159				0.544	-0.442				-0.268	0.260	0.120			-0.124
Seats..Eco.Comfort.						0.200	-0.160		-0.208	0.318		-0.733		0.156	0.437	-0.107
Seat.width..Economy.					0.125	0.110					0.186		-0.110			0.427
Seat.Pitch..Economy.					0.227	0.190		-0.130			0.262		-0.104	-0.132		-0.165
Seats..Economy.	0.597			-0.136	0.345	-0.165		0.168	0.597		-0.205	-0.127				
Accommodation	0.697			-0.104				0.233	-0.592		0.183	0.153	0.152			
Cruising.Speed..mph.		0.463	0.809	0.289	-0.144	0.115										
Range..miles.	0.999															

Looking at the first column of loadings, it is clear that the first principle component is just the range, in miles. The scale of each variable in the dataset is different.

Plotting variance on regular scaling. `barplot()` plots both vertical and horizontal bars. `sapply()` is a wrapper function that returns a list of the same length as `delta`. `horiz=T` signifies a logical value that the bars are to be drawn horizontally, with the first at the bottom:

```
> mar <- par()$mar
> par(mar=mar+c(0,5,0,0))

> barplot(sapply(delta, var), horiz=T, las=1, cex.names=0.8, main =
"Regular Scaling of Variance", col = "Red", xlab = "Variance")
```

The result is as follows:

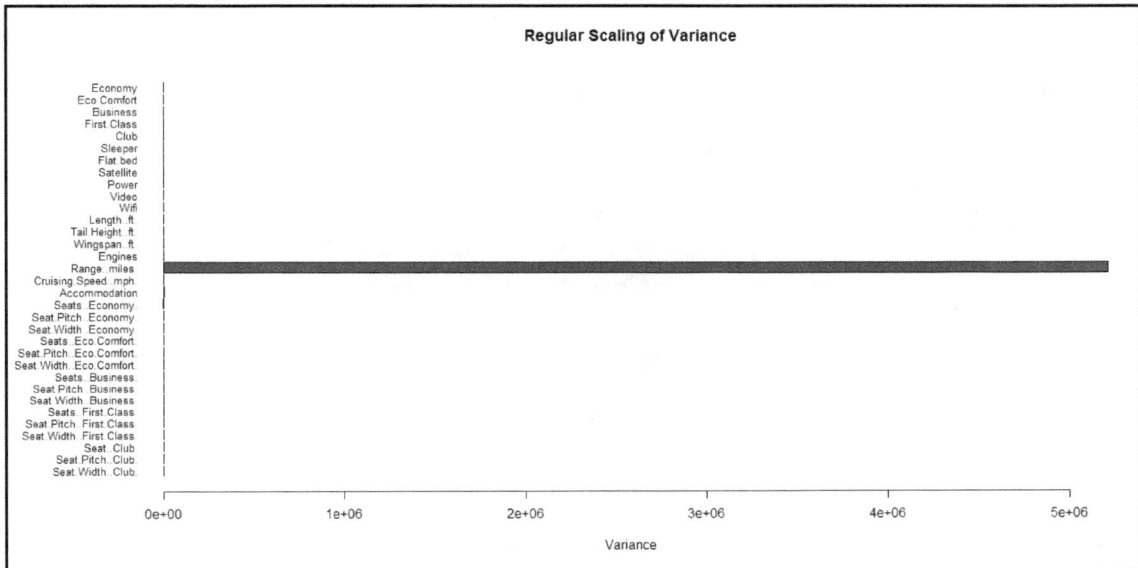

Plotting variance on a logarithmic scale. `barplot()` plots both vertical and horizontal bars:

```
> barplot(sapply(delta, var), horiz=T, las=1, cex.names=0.8, log='x',
main = "Logarithmic  Scaling of Variance", col = "Blue", xlab = "Variance")
```

The result is as follows:

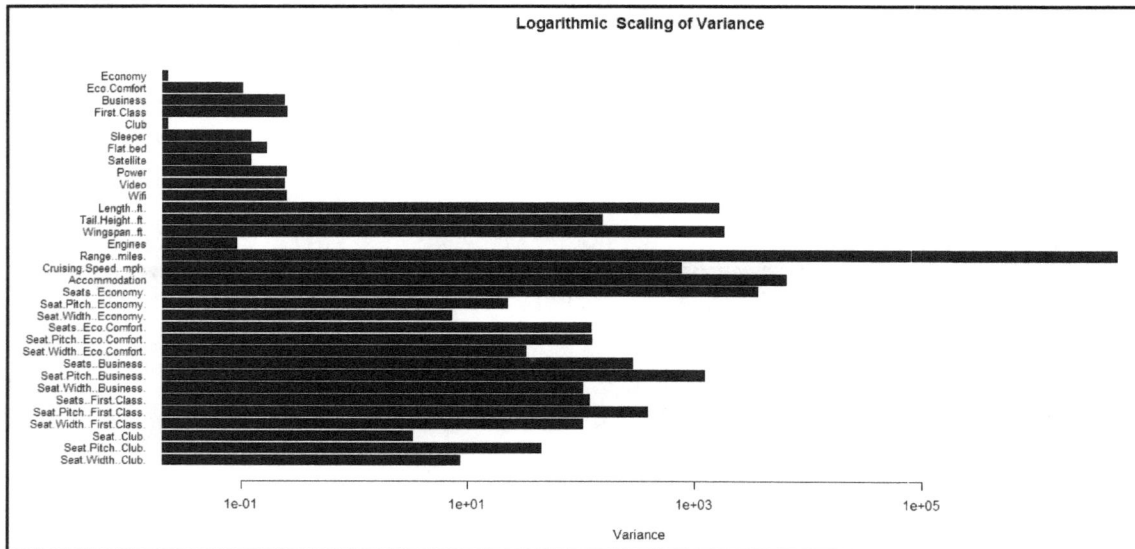

```
> par(mar=mar)
```

Step 4 - scaling the data

The scaling of `delta` data is useful under certain circumstances, since the variables span different ranges. `scale()` as a function centers and/or scales the columns of the `delta` matrix. The result is then stored in the `delta2` data frame:

```
> delta2 <- data.frame(scale(delta))
```

Verifying whether the variance is uniform:

```
> plot(sapply(delta2, var), main = "Variances Across Different
Variables", ylab = "Variances")
```

The result is as follows:

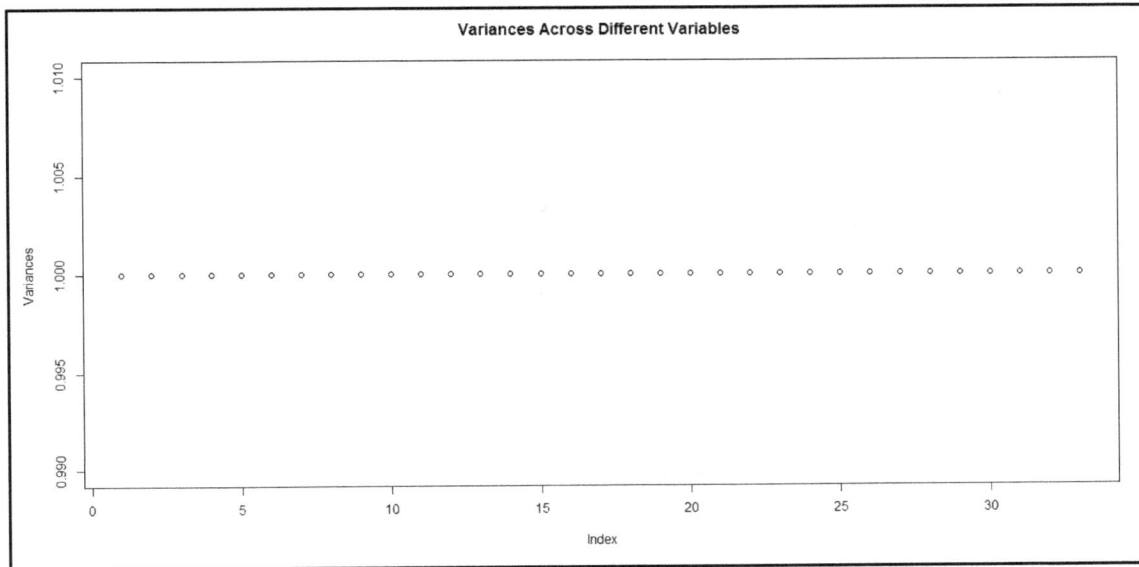

The variance is now constant across variables.

Applying principal components to the scaled data `delta2`. The `princomp()` function performs principal components analysis on the `delta2` datamatrix. The result is `principal_comp_analysis`, which is an object of class `princomp`:

```
> principal_comp_analysis <- princomp(delta2)
```

Plotting the `principal_comp_analysis` object:

```
> plot(principal_comp_analysis, main ="Principal Components Analysis of
Scaled Data", col ="red")
```

The result is as follows:

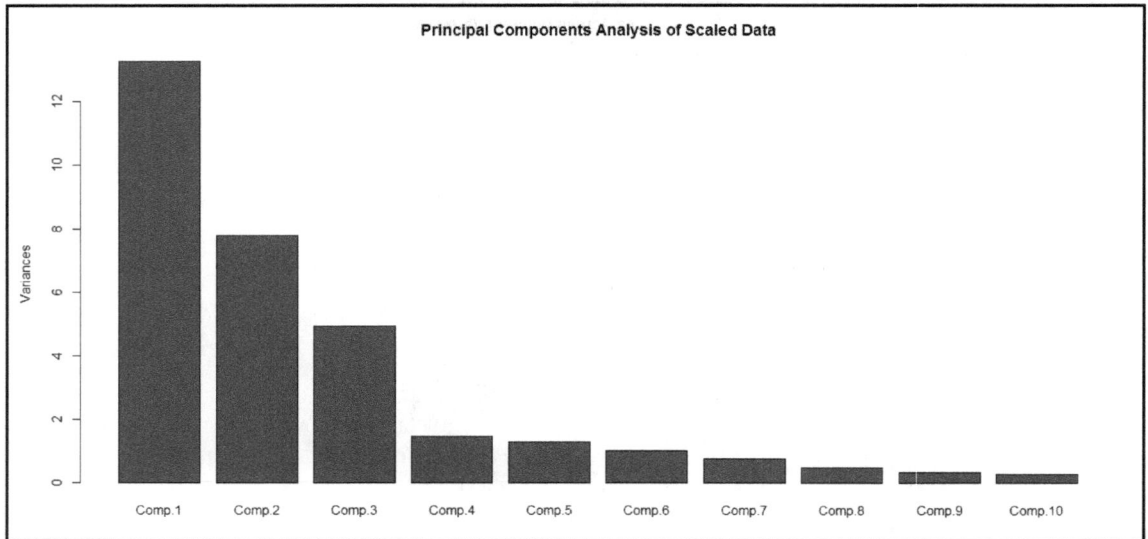

Principal Components Analysis of Scaled Data

```
> plot(principal_comp_analysis, type='l', main ="Principal Components
Analysis of Scaled Data")
```

The result is as follows:

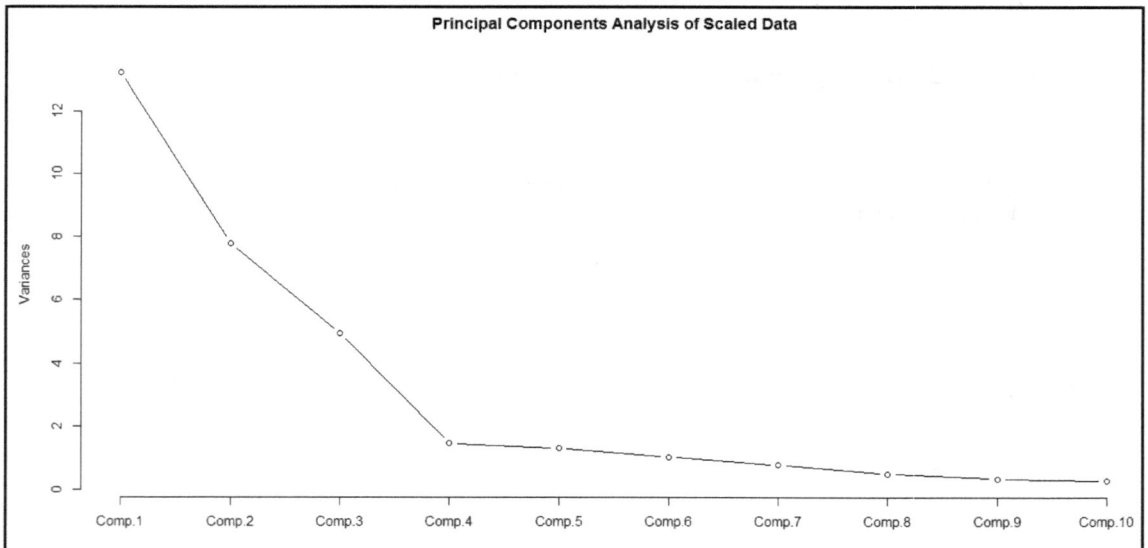

Principal Components Analysis of Scaled Data

The `summary()` function is used to produce summaries of the results of various model-fitting functions:

```
> summary(principal_comp_analysis)
```

The result is as follows:

```
Importance of components:
                          Comp.1     Comp.2     Comp.3     Comp.4     Comp.5     Comp.6     Comp.7     Comp.8     Comp.9     Comp.10     Comp.11
standard deviation       3.6401340  2.7883991  2.2225223  1.21058843 1.14073049 1.01495084 0.87821658 0.70479857 0.5848836 0.529084330 0.407860804
Proportion of Variance   0.4108706  0.2410905  0.1531661  0.04544262 0.04034933 0.03194187 0.02391517 0.01540282 0.0106074 0.008680007 0.005158153
Cumulative Proportion    0.4108706  0.6519611  0.8051271  0.85056976 0.89091910 0.92286097 0.94677614 0.96217896 0.9727864 0.981466375 0.986624528
                          Comp.12    Comp.13    Comp.14    Comp.15    Comp.16    Comp.17    Comp.18    Comp.19    Comp.20     Comp.21
standard deviation       0.362177038 0.298829473 0.238584294 0.1981036 0.1757588137 0.1444047596 0.1385927988 0.1173372505 0.1045097508 0.0853608392
Proportion of Variance   0.004067355 0.002768963 0.001765038 0.0012169 0.0009578654 0.0006465964 0.0005955958 0.0004269157 0.0003386756 0.0002259371
Cumulative Proportion    0.990691883 0.993460846 0.995225884 0.9964428 0.9974006493 0.9980472457 0.9986428415 0.9990697572 0.9994084328 0.9996343699
                          Comp.22    Comp.23    Comp.24    Comp.25    Comp.26    Comp.27    Comp.28    Comp.29    Comp.30
standard deviation       0.0791201165 5.177928e-02 4.469526e-02 0.0221107242 1.530274e-02 1.080092e-02 3.619390e-03 4.267325e-08 4.071751e-08
Proportion of Variance   0.0001941083 8.313469e-05 6.194314e-05 0.0000151592 7.261202e-06 3.617359e-06 4.062012e-07 5.646532e-17 5.140824e-17
Cumulative Proportion    0.9998284782 9.999116e-01 9.999736e-01 0.9999887152 9.999960e-01 9.999996e-01 1.000000e+00 1.000000e+00 1.000000e+00
                          Comp.31    Comp.32 Comp.33
standard deviation       9.643864e-09 7.10068e-09       0
Proportion of Variance   2.883848e-18 1.56340e-18       0
Cumulative Proportion    1.000000e+00 1.00000e+00       1
```

Applying principal components to the scaled data `delta2`. The `prcomp()` function performs principal components analysis on the `delta2` datamatrix. The result is `principal_comp_analysis`, which is an object of class `prcomp`:

```
> principal_comp_vectors <- prcomp(delta2)
```

Creating a data frame of `principal_comp_vectors`:

```
> comp <- data.frame(principal_comp_vectors$x[,1:4])
```

Applying k means with `k = 4`. The `kmeans()` function performs k-means clustering on comp. `nstart=25` signifies the number of random sets to be chosen. `iter.max=1000` is the maximum number of iterations allowed:

```
> k_means <- kmeans(comp, 4, nstart=25, iter.max=1000)
```

Creating a vector of nine contiguous colors:

```
> palette(alpha(brewer.pal(9,'Set1'), 0.5))
```

Plotting comp:

```
> plot(comp, col=k_means$clust, pch=16)
```

The result is as follows:

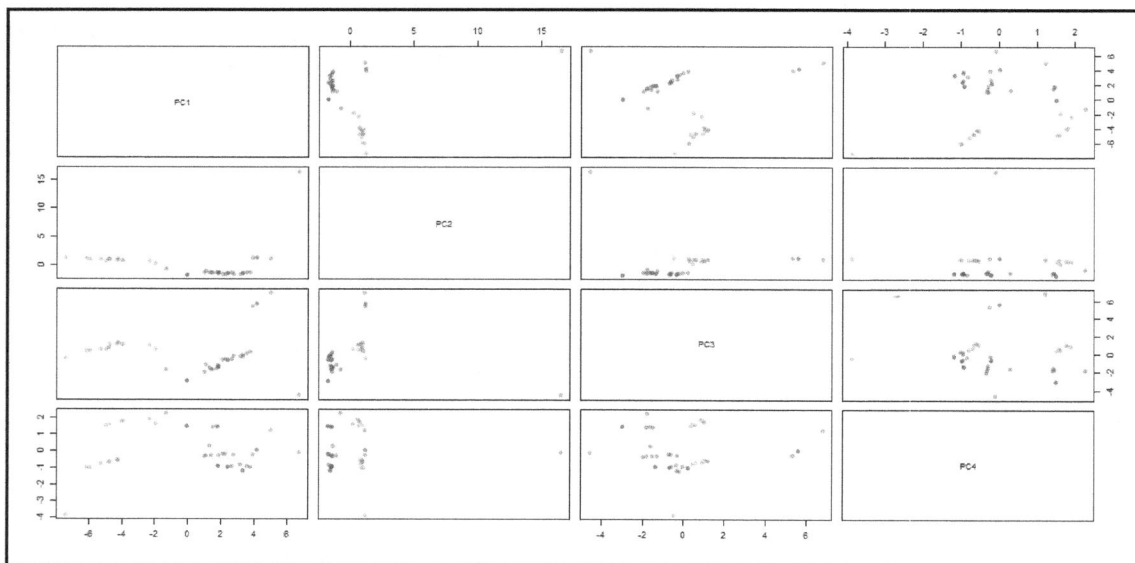

Step 5 - visualizing in 3D plot

Plotting in 3D comp$PC1, comp$PC2, comp$PC3:

```
> plot3d(comp$PC1, comp$PC2, comp$PC3, col=k_means$clust)
```

The result is as follows:

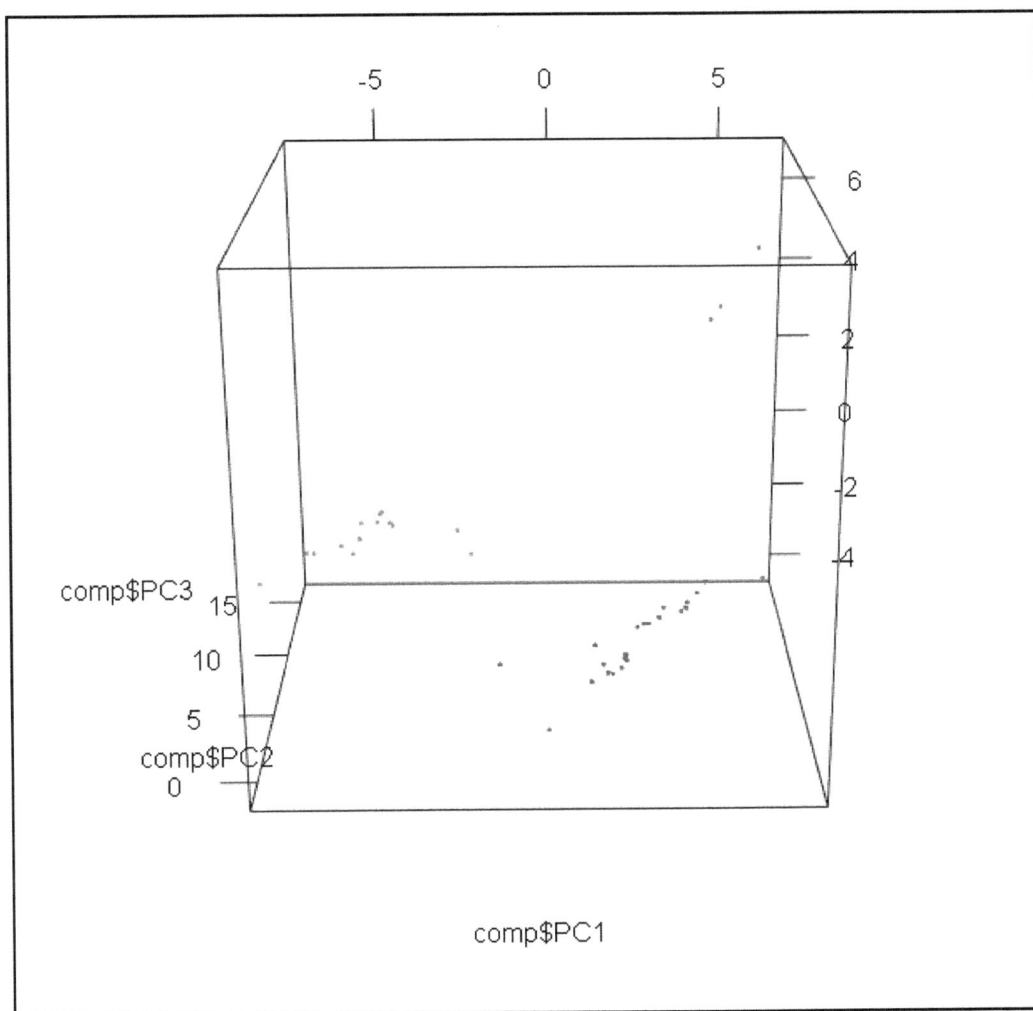

Plotting in 3D comp$PC1, comp$PC3, comp$PC4:

```
> plot3d(comp$PC1, comp$PC3, comp$PC4, col=k_means$clust)
```

The result is as follows:

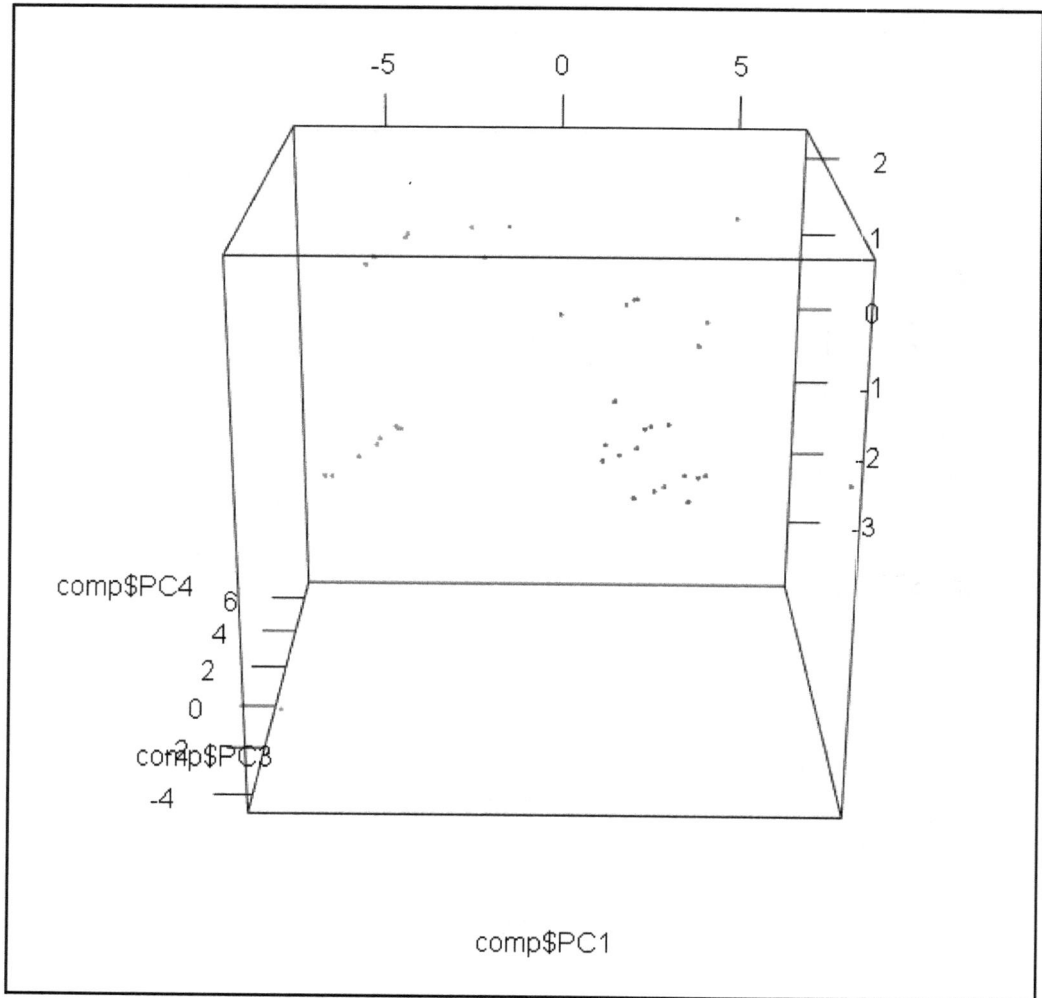

Examining the clusters in order of increasing size:

```
> sort(table(k_means$clust))
```

The result is as follows:

```
2   4   3   1
1   4  15  24
```

```
> clust <- names(sort(table(k_means$clust)))
```

Names as displayed in the first cluster:

```
> row.names(delta[k_means$clust==clust[1],])
```

The result is as follows:

```
[1] "Airbus A319 VIP"
```

Names as displayed in the second cluster:

```
> row.names(delta[k_means$clust==clust[2],])
```

The result is as follows:

```
[1] "CRJ 100/200 Pinnacle/Skywest" "CRJ 100/200 ExpressJet"      "E120"                   "ERJ-145"
```

Names as displayed in the third cluster:

```
> row.names(delta[k_means$clust==clust[3],])
```

The result is as follows:

```
[1] "Airbus A330-200"        "Airbus A330-200 (3L2)"  "Airbus A330-200 (3L3)"  "Airbus A330-300"     "Boeing 747-400 (74S)"
[6] "Boeing 757-200 (75E)"   "Boeing 757-200 (75X)"   "Boeing 767-300 (76G)"   "Boeing 767-300 (76L)" "Boeing 767-300 (76T)"
[11] "Boeing 767-300 (76Z V.1)" "Boeing 767-300 (76Z V.2)" "Boeing 767-400 (76D)" "Boeing 777-200ER"   "Boeing 777-200LR"
```

Names as displayed in the fourth cluster:

```
> row.names(delta[k_means$clust==clust[4],])
```

The result is as follows:

```
 [1] "Airbus A319"           "Airbus A320"           "Airbus A320 32-R"      "Boeing 717"            "Boeing 737-700 (73W)"
 [6] "Boeing 737-800 (738)"  "Boeing 737-800 (73H)"  "Boeing 737-900ER (739)" "Boeing 757-200 (75A)"  "Boeing 757-200 (75M)"
[11] "Boeing 757-200 (75N)"  "Boeing 757-200 (757)"  "Boeing 757-200 (75V)"  "Boeing 757-300"        "Boeing 767-300 (76P)"
[16] "Boeing 767-300 (76Q)"  "Boeing 767-300 (76U)"  "CRJ 700"               "CRJ 900"               "E170"
[21] "E175"                  "MD-88"                 "MD-90"                 "MD-DC9-50"
```

Principal component analysis - understanding world cuisine

Food is a powerful symbol of who we are. There are many types of food identification, such as ethnic, religious, and class identifications. Ethnic food preferences become identity markers in the presence of gustatory foreigners, such as when one goes abroad, or when those foreigners visit the home shores.

Getting ready

In order to perform principal component analysis, we shall be using a dataset collected on the Epicurious recipe dataset.

Step 1 - collecting and describing data

The dataset titled `epic_recipes.txt` shall be used. The dataset is in standard format.

How to do it...

Let's get into the details.

Step 2 - exploring data

The first step is to load the following packages:

```
> install.packages("glmnet")
> library(ggplot2)
> library(glmnet)
```

Version info: Code for this page was tested in R version 3.3.2 (2016-10-31)

Let's explore the data and understand the relationships among the variables. We'll begin by importing the TXT data file named `epic_recipes.txt`. We will be saving the data to the `datafile` frame:

```
> datafile <- file.path("d:","epic_recipes.txt")
```

Reading a file in table format and creating a data frame from it. `datafile` is the file name, which is passed as an input:

```
> recipes_data <- read.table(datafile, fill=TRUE,
col.names=1:max(count.fields(datafile)), na.strings=c("", "NA"),
stringsAsFactors = FALSE)
```

Step 3 - preparing data

Splitting the data into subsets. `aggregate()` splits `recipes_data[,-1]` and computes summary statistics. `recipes_data[,-1]` list of grouping elements, each as long as the variables in the data frame. The result is then stored in the `agg` data frame:

```
> agg <- aggregate(recipes_data[,-1], by=list(recipes_data[,1]), paste,
collapse=",")
```

Creating a vector, array, or list of values:

```
> agg$combined <- apply(agg[,2:ncol(agg)], 1, paste, collapse=",")
```

Replacing all occurrence of patterns. `gsub()` as a function replaces each `,NA` with `""` after searching `agg$combined`:

```
> agg$combined <- gsub(",NA","",agg$combined)
```

Extracting the names of all cuisines:

```
> cuisines <- as.data.frame(table(recipes_data[,1]))
```

Printing the cuisines data frame:

```
> cuisines
```

The result is as follows:

```
                         Var1 Freq
1                     African  115
2                    American 4988
3                       Asian 1176
4                Cajun_Creole  146
5         Central_SouthAmerican  241
6                     Chinese  226
7      EasternEuropean_Russian  146
8             English_Scottish  204
9                      French  996
10                     German   52
11                      Greek  225
12                     Indian  274
13                      Irish   86
14                    Italian 1715
15                   Japanese  136
16                     Jewish  320
17              Mediterranean  289
18                    Mexican  622
19              MiddleEastern  248
20                    Moroccan  137
21               Scandinavian   92
22           Southern_SoulFood  346
23                Southwestern  108
24          Spanish_Portuguese  291
25                        Thai  164
26                  Vietnamese   65
```

Extracting the frequency of ingredients:

```
> ingredients_freq <- lapply(lapply(strsplit(a$combined,","), table),
as.data.frame)
> names(ingredients_freq) <- agg[,1]
```

Normalizing the frequency of ingredients:

```
> proportion <- lapply(seq_along(ingredients_freq), function(i) {
+ colnames(ingredients_freq[[i]])[2] <- names(ingredients_freq)[i]
+ ingredients_freq[[i]][,2] <- ingredients_freq[[i]][,2]/cuisines[i,2]
+ ingredients_freq[[i]]}
+ )
```

List of 26 elements, one for each cuisine:

```
> names(proportion) <- a[,1]
> final <- Reduce(function(...) merge(..., all=TRUE, by="Var1"),
proportion)
> row.names(final) <- final[,1]
> final <- final[,-1]
> final[is.na(final)] <- 0
> prop_matrix <- t(final)
> s <- sort(apply(prop_matrix, 2, sd), decreasing=TRUE)
```

The scale() function centers and/or scales the columns of the prop_matrix matrix. The result is then stored in the final_impdata frame:

```
> final_imp <- scale(subset(prop_matrix, select=names(which(s > 0.1))))
```

Creating heatmap. final_imp is the data frame passed as an input.
trace="none" signifies the character string, indicating whether a solid "trace" line should be drawn across rows or down columns, "both" or "none". The key=TRUE value represents that a color-key should be shown:

```
> heatmap.2(final_imp, trace="none", margins = c(6,11),
col=topo.colors(7), key=TRUE, key.title=NA, keysize=1.2,
density.info="none")
```

The result is as follows:

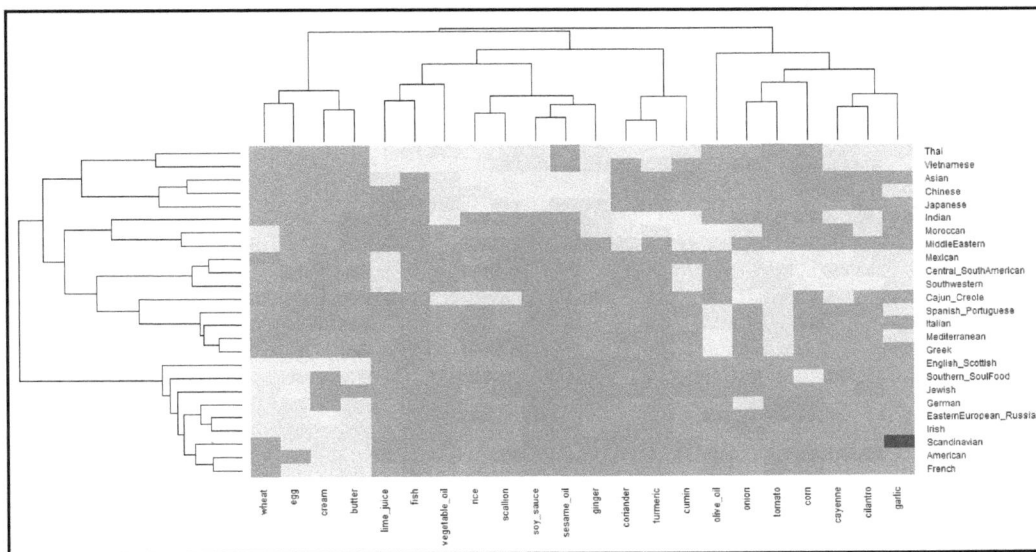

Step 4 - applying principal components analysis

Applying principle components analysis to data. `princomp()` performs principal components analysis on the `final_imp` datamatrix. The result is `pca_computation`, which is an object of class `princomp`:

```
> pca_computation <- princomp(final_imp)
```

Printing the `pca_computation` data frame:

```
> pca_computation
```

The result is as follows:

```
Call:
princomp(x = final_imp)

Standard deviations:
   Comp.1     Comp.2     Comp.3     Comp.4     Comp.5     Comp.6     Comp.7     Comp.8     Comp.9    Comp.10    Comp.11    Comp.12
Comp.13
2.95664772 2.22248409 1.54442468 1.44724581 1.10369661 0.75612298 0.57781510 0.47944174 0.42994264 0.39243338 0.30441262 0.24488043 0.1
9478279
  Comp.14    Comp.15    Comp.16    Comp.17    Comp.18    Comp.19    Comp.20    Comp.21    Comp.22
0.16134688 0.13102208 0.10750934 0.10266234 0.08372124 0.04197352 0.03426400 0.02328061 0.01466105

 22  variables and  25 observations.
```

Producing a biplot. `pca_computation` is an object of class `princomp`. `pc.biplot=TRUE` means it is a principal component biplot:

```
> biplot(pca_computation, pc.biplot=TRUE, col=c("black","red"),
cex=c(0.9,0.8), xlim=c(-2.5,2.5), xlab="PC1, 39.7%", ylab="PC2, 24.5%")
```

The result is as follows:

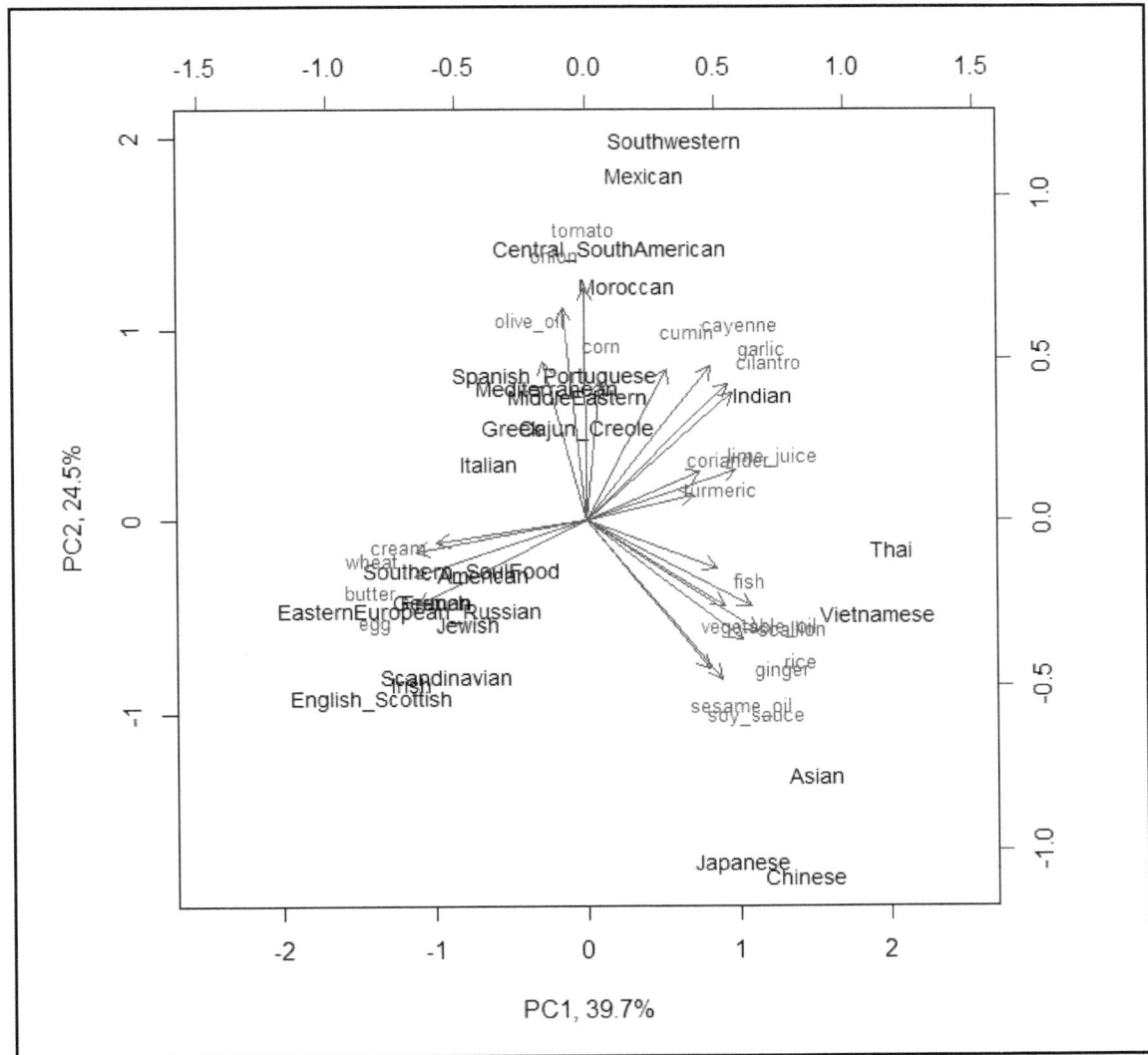

5
Nonlinearity

In this chapter, we will cover the following recipes:

- Generalized additive models - measuring the household income of New Zealand
- Smoothing splines - understanding cars and speed
- Local regression - understanding drought warnings and impact

Generalized additive models - measuring the household income of New Zealand

An income survey provides a snapshot of income levels for people and households. It gives median and average weekly income from most sources. There are income comparisons across different population groups. Income is only received intermittently, whereas consumption is smoothed over time. As a consequence, it is reasonable to expect that consumption is more directly related to current living standards than current income, at least for short reference periods.

Getting ready

In order to perform shrinkage methods, we will be using a dataset collected on the New Zealand Census 2013.

Step 1 - collecting and describing data

The `nzcensus` package contains demographic values of New Zealand that are more than 60 in number. These values have been accumulated at the level of mesh block, area unit, territorial authority, and regional council.

How to do it...

Let's get into the details.

Step 2 - exploring data

The first step is to load the following packages:

```
> devtools::install_github("ellisp/nzelect/pkg2")
> library(leaflet)
> library(nzcensus)
> library(Metrics)
> library(ggplot2)
> library(scales)
> library(boot)
> library(dplyr)
> library(Hmisc)
> library(mgcv)
> library(caret)
> library(grid)
> library(stringr)
> library(ggrepel)
> library(glmnet)
> library(maps)
```

Removing Chatham Islands from the dataset. `AreaUnits2013` is an esriGeometryPolygon Geometry Type object. It defines area units from the 2013 Census pattern:

```
> tmp <- AreaUnits2013[AreaUnits2013$WGS84Longitude> 0 &
!is.na(AreaUnits2013$MedianIncome2013), ]
```

Creating a color palette function:

```
> palette <- colorQuantile("RdBu", NULL, n = 10)
```

Creating labels for popups. The `paste0()` function concatenates vectors after converting to character:

```
> labels <- paste0(tmp$AU_NAM, " $", format(tmp$MedianIncome2013,
big.mark = ","))
```

Drawing the map:

```
> leaflet() %>%
+  addProviderTiles("CartoDB.Positron") %>%
+  addCircles(lng = tmp$WGS84Longitude, lat = tmp$WGS84Latitude,
+             color = pal(-tmp$MedianIncome2013),
+             popup = labs,
+             radius = 500) %>%
+  addLegend(
+      pal = pal,
+      values = -tmp$MedianIncome2013,
+      title = "Quantile of median<br>household income",
+      position = "topleft",
+      bins = 5)
```

The result is as follows:

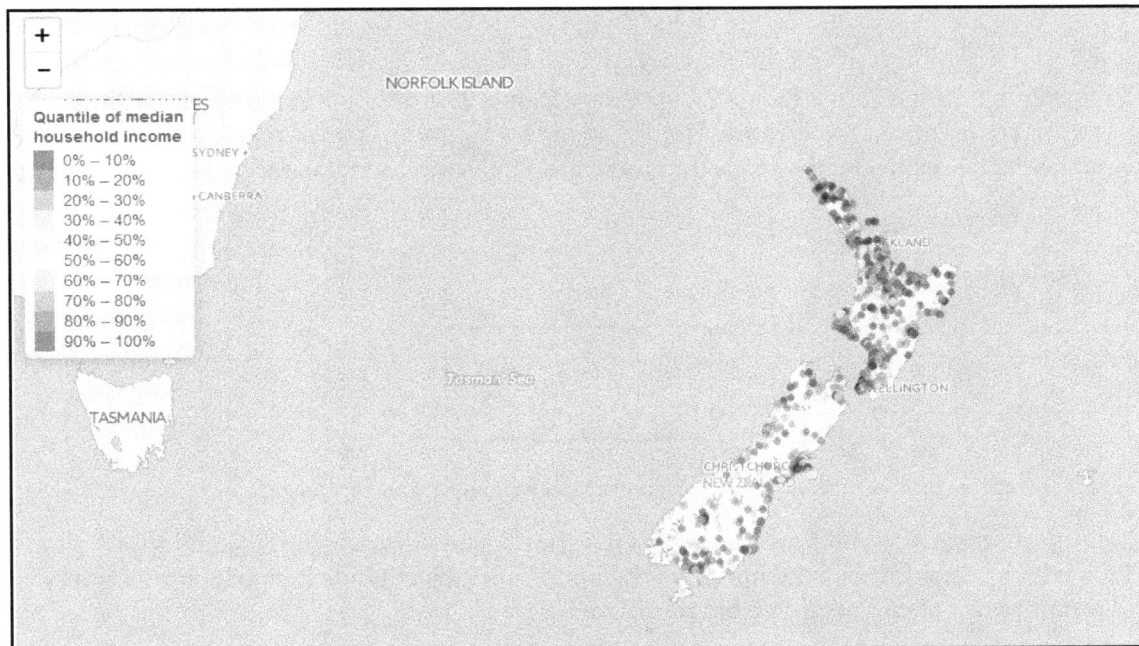

Step 3 - setting up the data for the model

Getting the data into a convenient shape. Eliminate the area's code and name, and the redundant coordinate system:

```
> au <- AreaUnits2013 %>%
+   select(-AU2014, -AU_NAM, -NZTM2000Easting, -NZTM2000Northing) %>%
+   select(-PropWorked40_49hours2013, -Prop35to39_2013, -PropFemale2013)

> row.names(au) <- AreaUnits2013$AU_NAM
```

Replacing all occurrences of a repetitive pattern. The gsub() function searches for patterns "_2013", "2013", and "Prop", and then replaces them with names(au):

```
> names(au) <- gsub("_2013", "", names(au))
> names(au) <- gsub("2013", "", names(au))
> names(au) <- gsub("Prop", "", names(au))
```

Fetching a logical vector indicating that a set of cases is complete:

```
> au <- au[complete.cases(au), ]
```

Providing a generic name:

```
> data_use <- au
```

Exploring the dimension of the data_use data frame. The dim() function returns the dimension of the data_use frame. The data_usedata frame is passed as an input parameter. The result clearly states that there are 1785 rows of data and 69 columns:

```
> dim(data_use)
```

The result is as follows:

```
[1] 1785   69
```

```
> data_use <- data_use[the_data$WGS84Longitude > 100, ]
```

Creating syntactically valid names out of character vectors and setting them. The names() function sets the names of the data_use object while it creates syntactically valid names out of character vectors returned:

```
> names(data_use) <- make.names(names(data_use))
```

Displaying the names created from the `data_use` data frame:

> `names(data_use)`

The result is as follows:

```
[1] "MeanBedrooms"       "PrivateDwellings"      "SeparateHouse"       "NumberInHH"              "MultiPersonHH"
[6] "InternetHH"         "NotOwnedHH"            "MedianRentHH"        "LandlordPublic"          "NoMotorVehicle"
[11] "AreChildren"       "SameResidence5YearsAgo" "Overseas5YearsAgo"  "NZBorn"                  "European"
[16] "Maori"             "Pacific"               "Asian"               "Male"                    "X20to24"
[21] "X25to29"           "X30to34"               "X40to44"             "X45to49"                 "X50to54"
[26] "X55to59"           "X60to64"               "X65AndOlder"         "NoReligion"              "Smoker"
[31] "Separated"         "Partnered"             "OwnResidence"        "NoChildren"              "NoQualification"
[36] "Bachelor"          "Doctorate"             "FTStudent"           "PTStudent"               "MedianIncome"
[41] "SelfEmployed"      "UnemploymentBenefit"   "StudentAllowance"    "FullTimeEmployed"        "PartTimeEmployed"
[46] "Unemployed"        "Employee"              "Employer"            "SelfEmployedNoEmployees" "Managers"
[51] "Professionals"     "Trades"                "Labourers"           "AgForFish"               "PubAdmin"
[56] "FinServices"       "ProfServices"          "worked1_9hours"      "worked10_19hours"        "worked20_29hours"
[61] "worked30_39hours"  "worked50_59hours"      "workedover60hours"   "workedHome"              "PublicTransport"
[66] "WalkJogBike"       "NoUnpaidActivities"    "WGS84Longitude"      "WGS84Latitude"
```

Step 4 - building the model

Estimating the strength of the non-parametric model. `spearman2()` computes the square of Spearman's rho rank correlation, and a generalization of it in which x can relate non-monotonically to y. This is done by computing the Spearman multiple rho-squared between $(rank(x), rank(x)^2)$, and y:

> `reg_data <- spearman2(MedianIncome ~ ., data = data_use)`

Ordering data in descending order:

> `reg_data[order(-reg_data[ ,6])[1:15], ]`

The result is as follows:

	rho2	F	df1	df2	P	Adjusted rho2	n
FullTimeEmployed	0.7129141	4427.6847	1	1783	0	0.7127531	1785
InternetHH	0.5834990	2497.9024	1	1783	0	0.5832654	1785
NoQualification	0.4470782	1441.6876	1	1783	0	0.4467681	1785
UnemploymentBenefit	0.4308350	1349.6595	1	1783	0	0.4305158	1785
Smoker	0.4094793	1236.3689	1	1783	0	0.4091481	1785
Partnered	0.3866362	1123.9207	1	1783	0	0.3862922	1785
Managers	0.3854095	1118.1189	1	1783	0	0.3850648	1785
Bachelor	0.3723224	1057.6304	1	1783	0	0.3719704	1785
SelfEmployed	0.3664151	1031.1455	1	1783	0	0.3660598	1785
NoMotorVehicle	0.3584018	995.9976	1	1783	0	0.3580419	1785
Unemployed	0.3570226	990.0367	1	1783	0	0.3566620	1785
Labourers	0.3378065	909.5664	1	1783	0	0.3374351	1785
worked50_59hours	0.3311392	882.7264	1	1783	0	0.3307640	1785
workedover60hours	0.3311392	882.7264	1	1783	0	0.3307640	1785
Separated	0.3122424	809.4831	1	1783	0	0.3118567	1785

Allocating flexible splines to the first 15 variables. The `terms()` function extracts `terms` objects from multiple R data objects:

```
> reg_formula <- terms(MedianIncome ~
s(FullTimeEmployed, k = 6) +
s(InternetHH, k = 6) +
s(NoQualification, k = 5) +
s(UnemploymentBenefit, k = 5) +
s(Smoker, k = 5) +
s(Partnered, k = 5) +
s(Managers, k = 4) +
s(Bachelor, k = 4) +
s(SelfEmployed, k = 4) +
s(NoMotorVehicle, k = 4) +
s(Unemployed, k = 3) +
s(Labourers, k = 3) +
s(Worked50_59hours, k = 3) +
s(Separated, k = 3) +
s(Maori, k = 3) +
s(WGS84Longitude, WGS84Latitude) +
.,
data = data_use)
```

Fitting the generalized additive model. `reg_formula` is the formula, while `data_use` is the dataset.

```
> gam_model <- gam(reg_formula, data = data_use)
```

Plotting `gam_model`.

```
> par(bty = "l", mar = c(5,4, 2, 1))
> par(mar = rep(2, 4))
> plot(gam_model, residuals = TRUE, pages = 1, shade = TRUE, seWithMean
= TRUE, ylab = "")
```

The result is as follows:

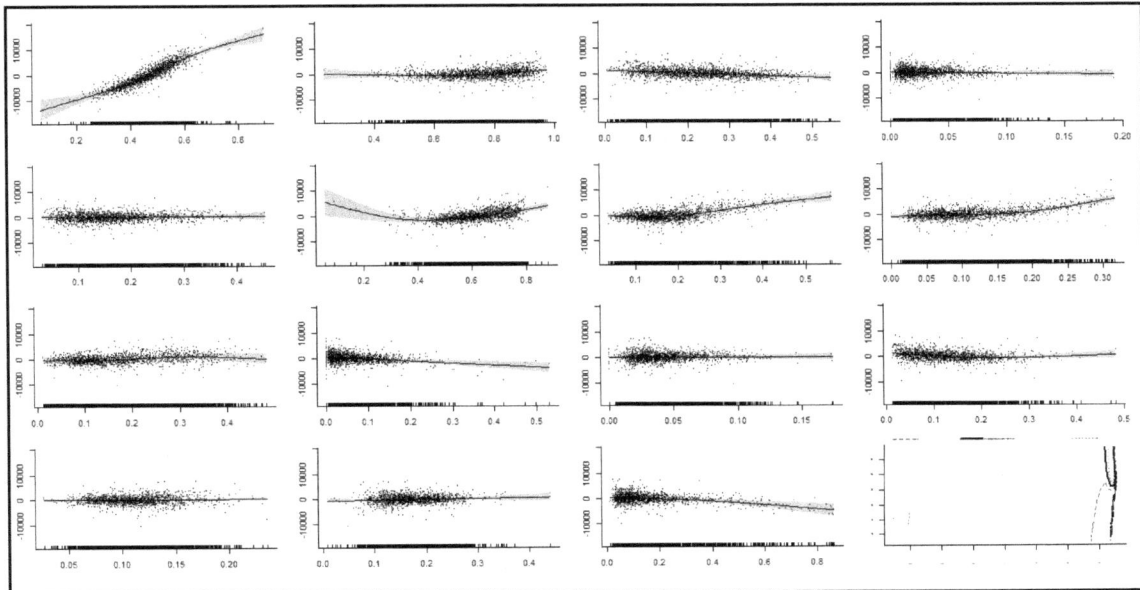

```
> rmses_gam_boot <- boot(data = data_use, statistic = fit_gam, R = 99)
```

Printing the rmses_gam_boot data frame:

```
> rmses_gam_boot
```

The result is as follows:

```
ORDINARY NONPARAMETRIC BOOTSTRAP


Call:
boot(data = data_use, statistic = fit_gam, R = 99)


Bootstrap Statistics :
     original    bias    std. error
t1*  1639.39  244.9502    387.2537
```

Calculating the mean of `rmses_gam_boot$t`:

```
> gam_rmse <- mean(rmses_gam_boot$t)
```

Printing the `gam_rmse` data frame:

```
> gam_rmse
```

The result is as follows:

```
[1] 1884.34
```

Smoothing splines - understanding cars and speed

In order to determine the parameters required in statistics for fitting a model, multiple methods can be used. In each of the cases, fitting involves the estimating of a small number of parameters from the data. Apart from estimating parameters, two important stages are the identification of a suitable model and the verification of the model. These smoothing methods can be used in a variety of ways: to aid understanding and produce smoothed plots, to identify a suitable parametric model from the shape of the smoothed data, or to focus on the effects of interest in order to eliminate complex effects which are of no use.

How to do it...

Let's get into the details.

Step 1 - exploring the data

The first step is to load the following packages:

```
> install.packages("graphics")
> install.packages("splines")
> library(graphics)
> library(splines)
```

Creating a matrix. The `cbind()` function takes the sequence of numbers and creates a matrix. The result is then passed to the `matrix()` function, which creates the matrix with two rows. The result is then stored in the matrix:

```
> matrx = matrix(cbind(1,.99,  .99,1),nrow=2)
```

Step 2 - creating the model

Cholesky factorization creates positive-definite matrix *A*, which can be factored as $A=LL^T$, where *L* is lower triangular with positive diagonal elements. The `chol()` function computes Cholesky factorization of a real, symmetrical, positive-definite square matrix. The result is then stored in `cholsky`:

```
> cholsky = t(chol(matrx))
> nvars = dim(cholsky)[1]
```

```
[1] 2
```

Number of observations for density distribution:

```
> numobs = 1000
> set.seed(1)
```

Calculating a matrix using normal distribution. `rnorm()` calculates normal distribution, with `numobs` as the number of observations to be used. The result is then used by the `matrix()` function to the compute matrix, with `nrow=nvars` as two rows and `ncol=numobs` as 1,000 columns. The result is stored in `random_normal`:

```
> random_normal = matrix(rnorm(nvars*numobs,10,1), nrow=nvars,
ncol=numobs)
```

Performing matrix multiplication. `cholsky` is multiplied with matrix `random_normal`:

```
> X = cholsky %*% random_normal
```

Transposing matrix X:

```
> newX = t(X)
```

Creating a data frame of the matrix. The `as.data.frame()` function creates the data frame raw, tightly coupled collections of variables which share many of the properties of matrix newX:

```
> raw = as.data.frame(newX)
```

Printing the raw data frame. The `head()` function returns the first part of the raw data frame. The raw data frame is passed as an input parameter:

```
> head(raw)
```

The result is as follows:

```
         V1         V2
1   9.113850  10.162218
2  11.619701  12.987429
3   9.944150  11.353624
4  10.053516  11.178816
5   7.876934   9.179485
6   9.687213  10.851732
```

Creating a transposed data frame of `random_normal`. The `t()` function creates a transposed matrix of the `random_normal` matrix, which is then converted to tightly coupled collections of variables. These share many of the properties of the matrix:

```
> raw_original = as.data.frame(t(random_normal))
```

Combining the names response and `predictor1`. The `c()` function combines the arguments response and `predictor1` to form a vector:

```
> names(raw) = c("response","predictor1")
```

Exponential rise of `raw$predictor1` to power 3:

```
> raw$predictor1_3 = raw$predictor1^3
```

Printing the `raw$predictor1_3` data frame. The `head()` function returns the first part of the `raw$predictor1_3` data frame. The `raw$predictor1_3`data frame is passed as an input parameter:

```
> head(raw$predictor1_3)
```

The result is as follows:

```
[1] 1049.4591 2190.6329 1463.5364 1396.9711  773.4905 1277.9010
```

Exponential rise of `raw$predictor1` to power 2:

```
> raw$predictor1_2 = raw$predictor1^2
```

Printing the `raw$predictor1_2` data frame. The `head()` function returns the first part of the `raw$predictor1_2` data frame. The `raw$predictor1_2` data frame is passed as an input parameter:

```
> head(raw$predictor1_2)
```

The result is as follows:

```
[1] 103.27068 168.67332 128.90478 124.96592  84.26295 117.76010
```

Building an ordinary least squares estimation with `raw$response ~ raw$predictor1_3` as the formula. The `lm()` function is used to fit linear models. `raw$response ~ raw$predictor1_3` is the formula. The result is then stored in the fit data frame:

```
> fit = lm(raw$response ~ raw$predictor1_3)
```

Printing the fit data frame:

```
> fit
```

The result is as follows:

```
Call:
lm(formula = raw$response ~ raw$predictor1_3)

Coefficients:
      (Intercept)    raw$predictor1_3
         6.304595            0.002496
```

Plotting the ordinary least squares estimation formula. The plot() function is a Generic function for plotting R objects. The raw$response ~ raw$predictor1_3 formula is passed as a function value:

```
> plot(raw$response ~ raw$predictor1_3, pch=16, cex=.4,
xlab="Predictor", ylab="Response", col ="red", main="Simulated Data with
Slight Curve")
```

The result is as follows:

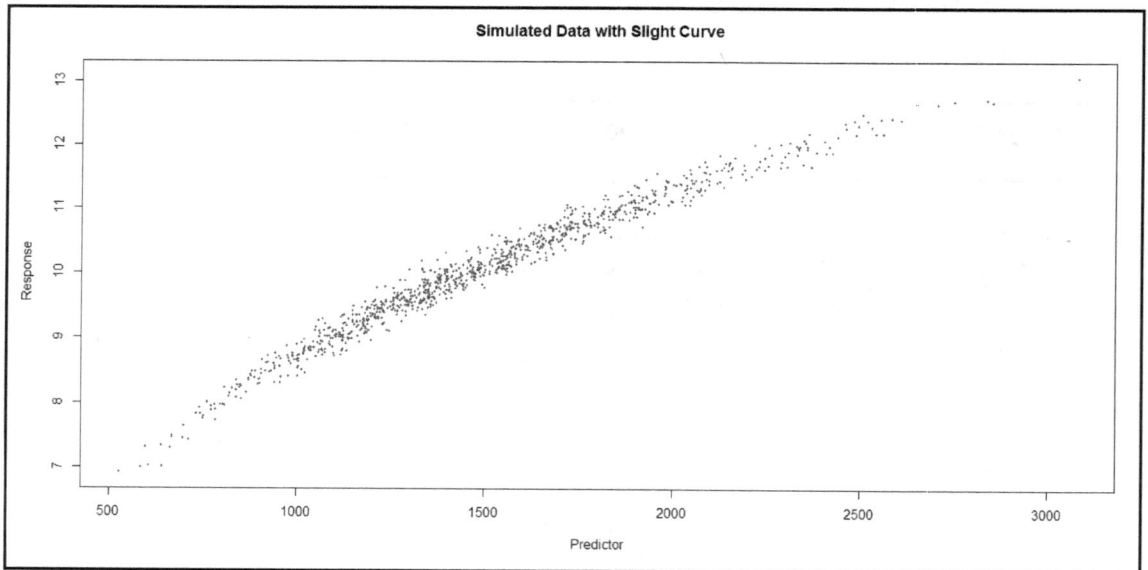

Adding a straight function through the current plot:

```
> abline(fit)
```

The result is as follows:

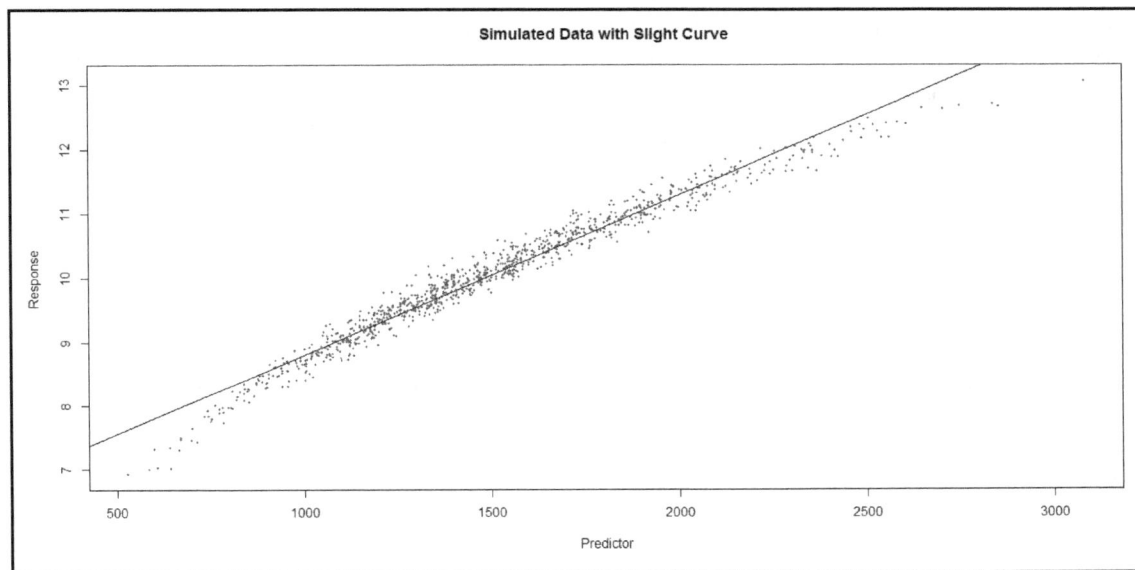

Fitting the value of cars and speeds on the *x* axis:

```
> x_axis <- with(cars, speed)
```

Fitting the value of cars and speeds on the y axis:

```
> y_axis <- with(cars, dist)
```

Setting the number of points for smooth curve evaluation:

```
> eval_length = 50
```

Step 3 - fitting the smooth curve model

Fitting a smooth curve between two variables is a non-parametric method, because the linearity assumptions of conventional regression methods have been relaxed. It is called **local regression**, because the fitting at, say, point *x*, is weighted toward the data nearest to *x*.

The `loess.smooth()` function plots and adds a smooth curve computed to a scatter plot. `x_axis`, `y_axis` are the arguments provided to the x and y coordinates of the plot. `evaluation = eval.length` for example `eval_length = 50`, represents the points for smooth curve evaluation. `span=.75` is the smoothness parameter. `degree=1` is the degree of the local polynomial:

```
> fit_loess <- loess.smooth(x_axis, y_axis, evaluation = eval_length,
family="gaussian", span=.75, degree=1)
```

Printing the `fit_loess` data frame:

```
> fit_loess
```

The result is as follows:

```
$x
 [1]  4.000000  4.428571  4.857143  5.285714  5.714286  6.142857  6.571429  7.000000  7.428571  7.857143  8.285714  8.714286  9.142857
 9.571429
[15] 10.000000 10.428571 10.857143 11.285714 11.714286 12.142857 12.571429 13.000000 13.428571 13.857143 14.285714 14.714286 15.142857
15.571429
[29] 16.000000 16.428571 16.857143 17.285714 17.714286 18.142857 18.571429 19.000000 19.428571 19.857143 20.285714 20.714286 21.142857
21.571429
[43] 22.000000 22.428571 22.857143 23.285714 23.714286 24.142857 24.571429 25.000000

$y
 [1]  3.272340  4.649135  6.007926  7.355284  8.697776 10.041974 11.394447 12.761764 14.150494 15.567208 16.984996 18.326847 19.644429
20.998786
[15] 22.450966 23.928844 25.355833 26.786293 28.274581 29.857278 31.391655 32.967213 34.604079 36.239846 37.998521 39.935642 41.616790
43.001795
[29] 44.220676 45.361214 46.511191 47.778778 49.244460 50.845164 52.509776 54.167182 56.025692 58.263629 60.764900 63.413415 66.093080
68.687803
[43] 71.081492 73.386173 75.774481 78.221236 80.701256 83.189361 85.660370 88.089103
```

Fitting a polynomial surface on the basis of one or more numerical predictors, using local fitting. The `loess()` function fits the polynomial surface. `y_axis ~ x_axis` represents the formula. `span=.75` is the smoothness parameter. `degree=1` is the degree of the local polynomial:

```
> fit_loess_2 <- loess(y_axis ~ x_axis, family="gaussian", span=.75,
degree=1)
```

Printing the `fit_loess_2` data frame:

```
> fit_loess_2
```

The result is as follows:

```
Call:
loess(formula = y_axis ~ x_axis, span = 0.75, degree = 1, family = "gaussian")

Number of Observations: 50
Equivalent Number of Parameters: 3.13
Residual Standard Error: 15.25
```

Generating regular sequences of minimum and maximum values of the *y* axis.
The Seq() function takes in length.out=eval_length for example eval_length = 50,
which indicates the desired length of the sequence to be generated from the minimum and
maximum values of the *x* axis:

```
> new_x_axis = seq(min(x_axis),max(x_axis), length.out=eval_length)
```

Printing the new_x_axis data frame:

```
> new_x_axis
```

The result is as follows:

```
 [1]  4.000000  4.428571  4.857143  5.285714  5.714286  6.142857  6.571429  7.000000  7.428571  7.857143  8.285714  8.714286  9.142857
 9.571429
[15] 10.000000 10.428571 10.857143 11.285714 11.714286 12.142857 12.571429 13.000000 13.428571 13.857143 14.285714 14.714286 15.142857
15.571429
[29] 16.000000 16.428571 16.857143 17.285714 17.714286 18.142857 18.571429 19.000000 19.428571 19.857143 20.285714 20.714286 21.142857
21.571429
[43] 22.000000 22.428571 22.857143 23.285714 23.714286 24.142857 24.571429 25.000000
```

Setting a confidence level of 95% on the fit.loess model:

```
> conf_int = cbind(
+ predict(fit_loess_2, data.frame(x=new_x_axis)),
+ predict(fit_loess_2, data.frame(x=new_x_axis))+
+ predict(fit_loess_2, data.frame(x=new_x_axis),
se=TRUE)$se.fit*qnorm(1-.05/2),
+ predict(fit_loess_2, data.frame(x=new_x_axis))-
+ predict(fit_loess_2, data.frame(x=new_x_axis),
se=TRUE)$se.fit*qnorm(1-.05/2)
+ )
```

Building an ordinary least squares estimation with y_axis ~ x_axis as the formula.
The lm() function is used to fit linear models. y_axis ~ x_axis is the formula. The result
is then stored in the fit_lm data frame:

```
> fit_lm = lm(y_axis ~ x_axis)
```

Printing the `fit_lm` data frame:

> `fit_lm`

The result is as follows:

```
Call:
lm(formula = y_axis ~ x_axis)

Coefficients:
(Intercept)          x_axis
    -17.579           3.932
```

Building a polynomial function. `y_axis ~ poly(x_axis,3)` is a polynomial function with three degrees of freedom. The `lm()` function is used to fit linear models. `y_axis ~ poly(x_axis,3)` is the formula. The result is then stored in the `fit_poly` data frame:

> `fit_poly = lm(y_axis ~ poly(x_axis,3) )`

Printing the `fit_poly` data frame:

> `fit_poly`

The result is as follows:

```
Call:
lm(formula = y_axis ~ poly(x_axis, 3))

Coefficients:
    (Intercept)   poly(x_axis, 3)1   poly(x_axis, 3)2   poly(x_axis, 3)3
          42.98             145.55              23.00              13.80
```

Building a natural spline function. `y_axis ~ ns(x_axis, 3)` is the natural spline function with degree 3 of freedom. The `lm()` function is used to fit linear models. `y_axis ~ ns(x_axis, 3)` is the formula. The result is then stored in the `fit_nat_spline` data frame:

> `fit_nat_spline = lm(y_axis ~ ns(x_axis, 3) )`

Printing the `fit_nat_spline` data frame:

> **fit_nat_spline**

The result is as follows:

```
Call:
lm(formula = y_axis ~ ns(x_axis, 3))

Coefficients:
    (Intercept)   ns(x_axis, 3)1   ns(x_axis, 3)2   ns(x_axis, 3)3
          2.594           35.959           96.444           72.986
```

Smoothing of the spline:

> **fit_smth_spline <- smooth.spline(y_axis ~ x_axis, nknots=15)**

Printing the `fit_smth_spline` data frame:

> **fit_smth_spline**

The result is as follows:

```
Call:
smooth.spline(x = y_axis ~ x_axis, nknots = 15)

Smoothing Parameter  spar= 0.7274958  lambda= 0.1118473 (15 iterations)
Equivalent Degrees of Freedom (Df): 2.632293
Penalized Criterion: 4189.645
GCV: 244.1153
```

Step 4 - plotting the results

Plotting the model:

```
> plot(x_axis, y_axis, xlim=c(min(x_axis),max(x_axis)),
ylim=c(min(y_axis),max(y_axis)), pch=16, cex=.5, ylab = "Stopping Distance
(feet)", xlab= "Speed (MPH)", main="Comparison of Models", sub="Splines")
```

The result is as follows:

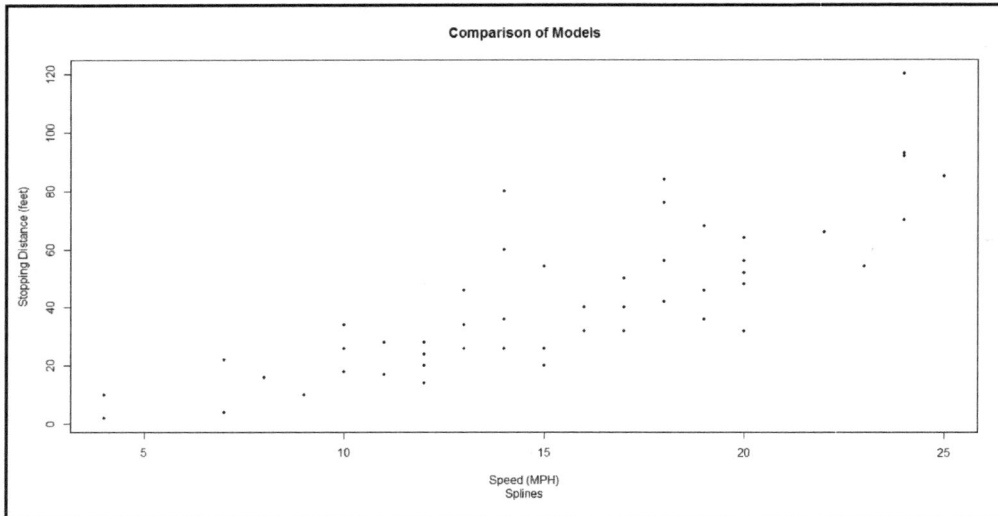

Adding additional models to the graph. Plotting LOESS with Confidence Intervals:

```
> matplot(new_x_axis, conf_int, lty = c(1,2,2), col=c(1,2,2), type =
"l", add=T)
```

The result is as follows:

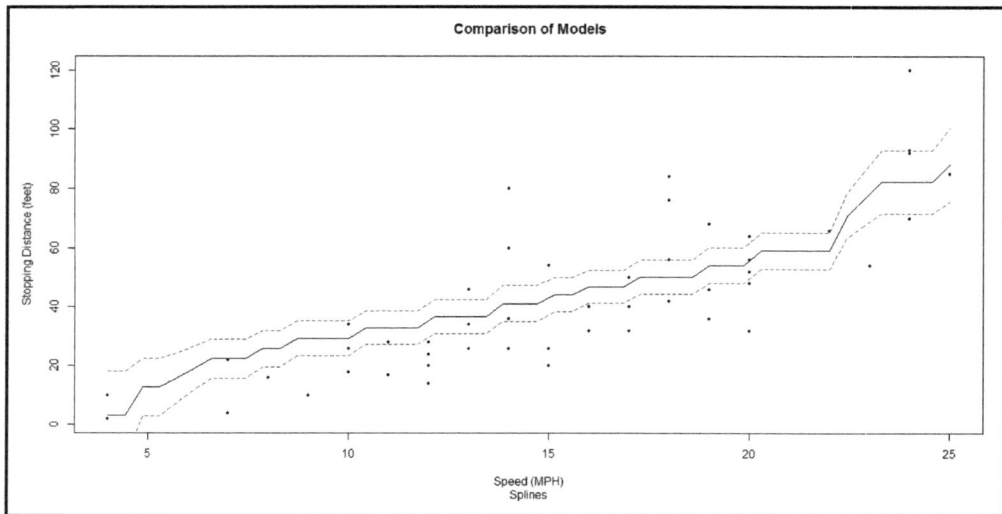

Plotting an ordinary least squares estimation. The `predict()` function predicts values based on linear models. `fit_lm` is an object of class `lm`:

```
> lines(new_x_axis, predict(fit_lm, data.frame(x=new_x_axis)),
col="red", lty=3)
```

The result is as follows:

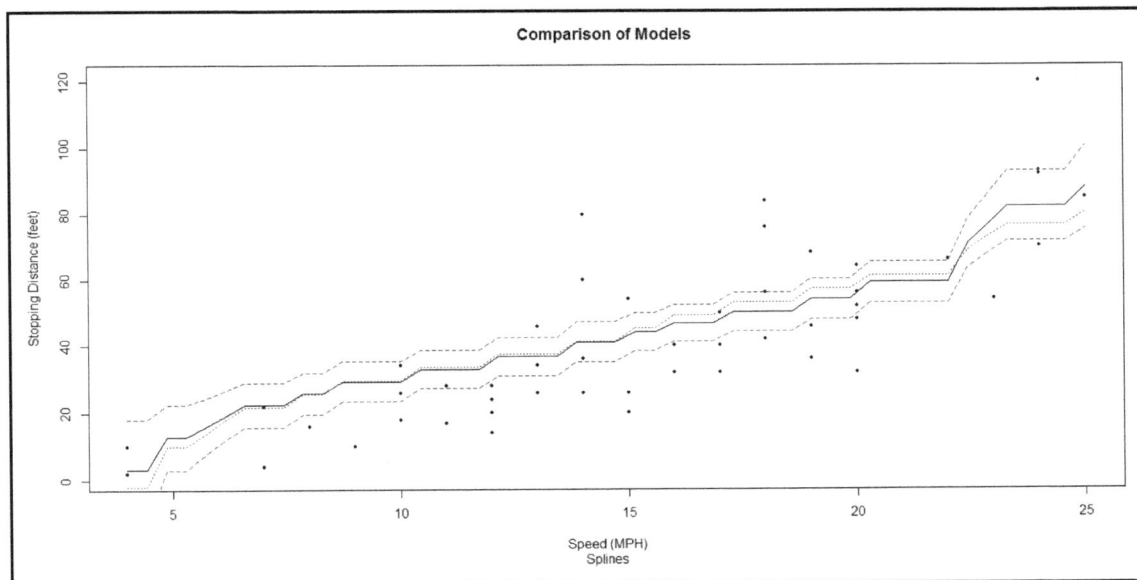

Plotting a polynomial function estimation:

```
> lines(new_x_axis, predict(fit_poly, data.frame(x=new_x_axis)),
col="blue", lty=4)
```

The result is as follows:

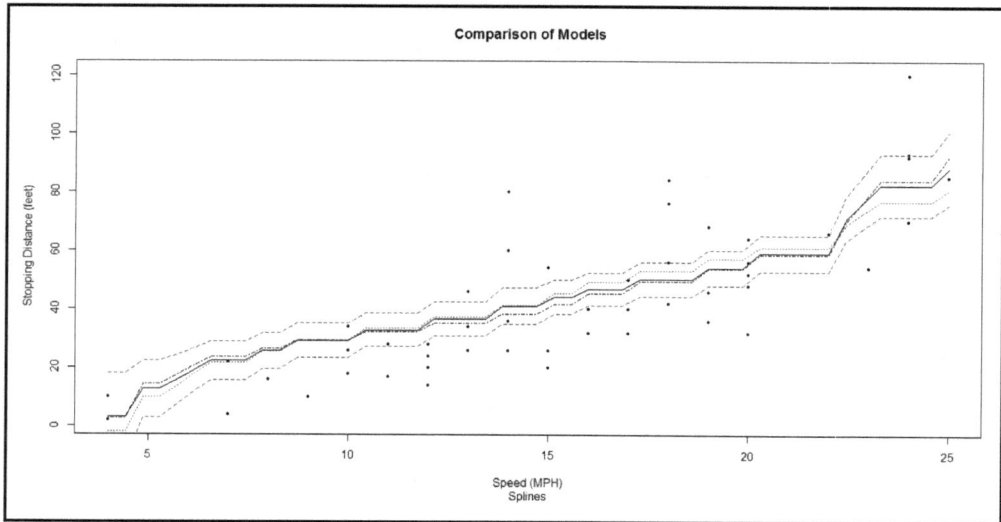

Plotting a natural spline function:

```
> lines(new_x_axis, predict(fit_nat_spline, data.frame(x=new_x_axis)),
col="green", lty=5)
```

The result is as follows:

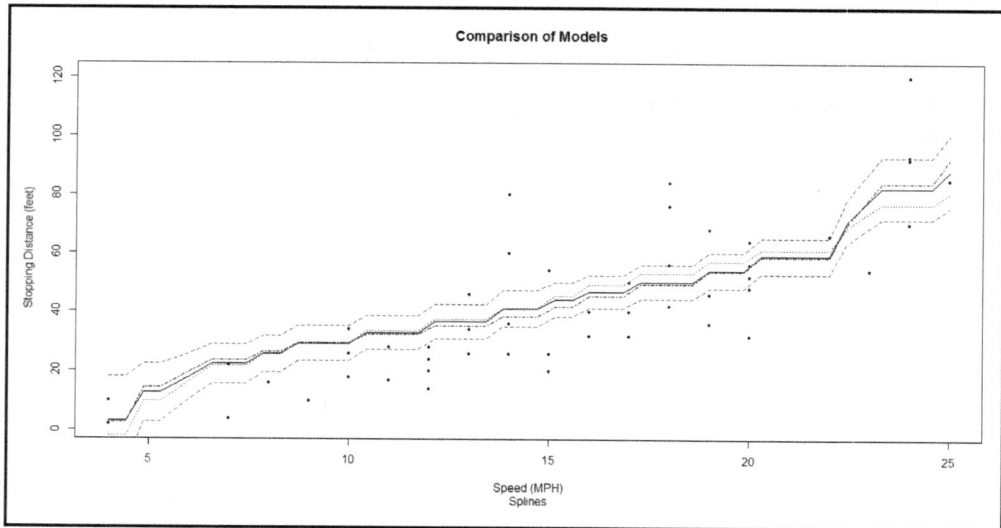

Plotting a smoothed spline:

```
> lines(fit_smth_spline, col="dark grey", lty=6)
```

The result is as follows:

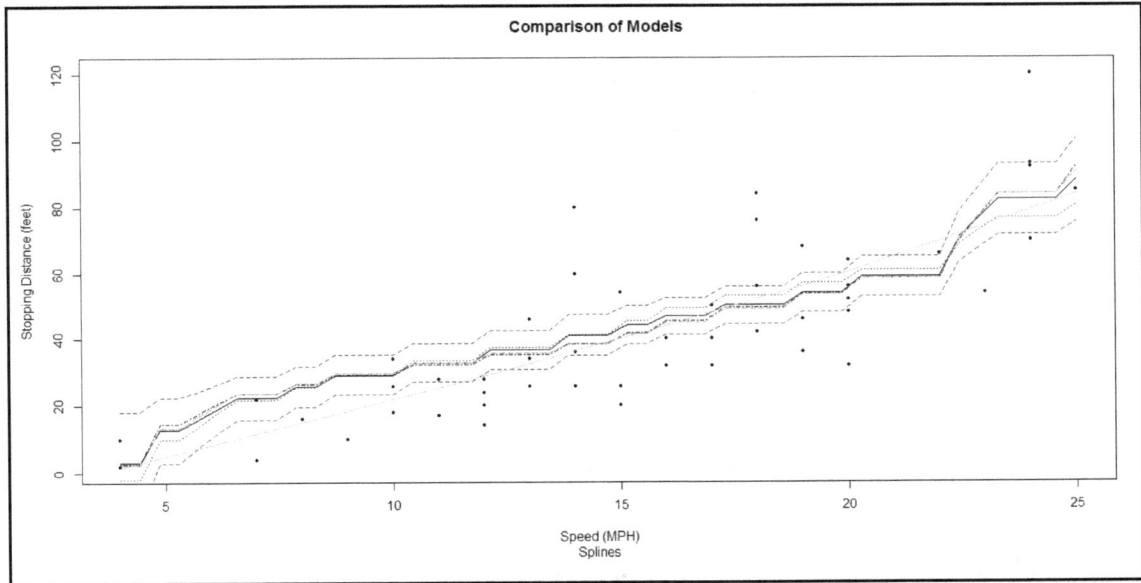

Plotting a kernel curve. The `ksmooth()` function:

```
> lines(ksmooth(x_axis, y_axis, "normal", bandwidth = 5), col =
'purple', lty=7)
```

The result is as follows:

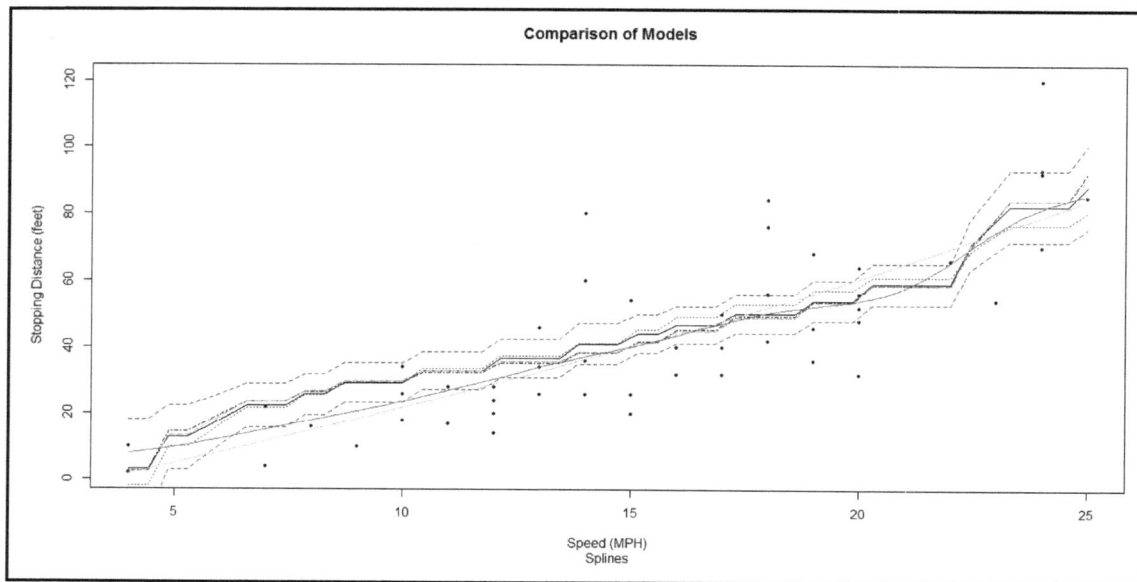

Comparison of Models

Local regression - understanding drought warnings and impact

Drought is a natural hazard which is measured and characterized by lower-than-expected or lower-than-normal rainfall. This condition, when prolonged over a longer-than-normal time period is insufficient to meet the demands of human activities and hazardous to the environment. Drought is a temporary phenomenon. Three main distinguishing features of droughts are intensity, duration, and spatial coverage. A drought early warning system can help to identify the climatic changes, understand water supply trends, and prepare for upcoming emergencies. The drought warning can help decision-makers take appropriate measures to face the upcoming challenge. They can then measure the severity of the impact and understand the underlying causes of vulnerability to reduce risk for a particular location and for a specific group of people or economic sector.

Getting ready

Let's get started with the recipe.

Step 1 - collecting and describing data

The dataRetrieval package is a collection of functions to help retrieve **US Geological Survey (USGS)** and **US Environmental Protection Agency (EPA)**.

How to do it...

Let's get into the details.

Step 2 - collecting and exploring data

The first step is to load the following packages:

```
> library(dataRetrieval)
> library(dplyr)
```

Retrieving the site number. The site number is usually an eight-digit number, which is represented as a string or vector:

```
> siteNumber <- c("01538000")
```

Retrieving parameter codes:

```
> parameterCd <- "00060"
```

Using site number and parameter codes importing data from NWIS web service. The result is then stored in the Q_daily data frame:

```
> Q_daily <- readNWISdv(siteNumber, parameterCd)
```

Printing the Q_daily data frame. The tail() function returns the last part of the Q_daily data frame. The Q_daily data frame is passed as an input parameter:

```
> tail(Q_daily)
```

The result is as follows:

```
        agency_cd site_no      Date X_00060_00003 X_00060_00003_cd
35553   USGS 01538000 2017-01-31            71                 P
35554   USGS 01538000 2017-02-01            66                 P
35555   USGS 01538000 2017-02-02            61                 P
35556   USGS 01538000 2017-02-03       -999999             P Ice
35557   USGS 01538000 2017-02-04       -999999             P Ice
35558   USGS 01538000 2017-02-05       -999999             P Ice
```

Exploring the internal structure of the `Q_daily` data frame. The `str()` function displays the internal structure of the data frame. The `Q_daily` is passed as an R object to the `str()` function:

```
> str(Q_daily)
```

The result is as follows:

```
'data.frame':   35558 obs. of  5 variables:
 $ agency_cd       : chr  "USGS" "USGS" "USGS" "USGS" ...
 $ site_no         : chr  "01538000" "01538000" "01538000" "01538000" ...
 $ Date            : Date, format: "1919-10-01" "1919-10-02" "1919-10-03" "1919-10-04" ...
 $ X_00060_00003   : num  25 25 25 25 25 30 30 30 30 30 ...
 $ X_00060_00003_cd: chr  "A" "A" "A" "A" ...
 - attr(*, "url")= chr "https://waterservices.usgs.gov/nwis/dv/?site=01538000&format=waterml,1.1&ParameterCd=00060&StatCd=00003&startDT=1
851-01-01"
 - attr(*, "siteInfo")='data.frame':    1 obs. of  13 variables:
  ..$ station_nm        : chr "Wapwallopen Creek near wapwallopen, PA"
  ..$ site_no           : chr "01538000"
  ..$ agency_cd         : chr "USGS"
  ..$ timeZoneOffset    : chr "-05:00"
  ..$ timeZoneAbbreviation: chr "EST"
  ..$ dec_lat_va        : num 41.1
  ..$ dec_lon_va        : num -76.1
  ..$ srs               : chr "EPSG:4326"
  ..$ siteTypeCd        : chr "ST"
  ..$ hucCd             : chr "02050107"
  ..$ stateCd           : chr "42"
  ..$ countyCd          : chr "42079"
  ..$ network           : chr "NWIS"
 - attr(*, "variableInfo")='data.frame':    1 obs. of  7 variables:
  ..$ variableCode       : chr "00060"
  ..$ variableName       : chr "Streamflow, ft&#179;/s"
  ..$ variableDescription: chr "Discharge, cubic feet per second"
  ..$ valueType          : chr "Derived Value"
  ..$ unit               : chr "ft3/s"
  ..$ options            : chr "Mean"
  ..$ noDataValue        : logi NA
 - attr(*, "disclaimer")= chr "Provisional data are subject to revision. Go to http://waterdata.usgs.gov/nwis/help/?provisional for more
information."
 - attr(*, "statisticInfo")='data.frame':    1 obs. of  2 variables:
  ..$ statisticCd  : chr "00003"
  ..$ statisticName: chr "Mean"
 - attr(*, "queryTime")= POSIXct, format: "2017-02-06 23:42:00"
```

Renaming columns--the `renameNWISColumns()` function renames columns retrieved from NWIS. `Q_daily` is the daily or unit-values dataset retrieved from NWIS Web:

```
> Q_daily <- renameNWISColumns(Q_daily)
```

Printing the renamed `Q_daily` data frame. The `tail()` function returns the last part of the `Q_daily` data frame. The `Q_daily` data frame is passed as an input parameter:

```
> tail(Q_daily)
```

The result is as follows:

```
       agency_cd   site_no        Date Flow Flow_cd   rollMean day.of.year
35552       USGS 01538000 2017-01-30   79       P -199942.8          30
35553       USGS 01538000 2017-01-31   71       P -199941.2          31
35554       USGS 01538000 2017-02-01   66       P -199939.9          32
35555       USGS 01538000 2017-02-02   61       P -199938.9          33
35556       USGS 01538000 2017-02-03   54       P -199939.4          34
35557       USGS 01538000 2017-02-04   65       P -199938.7          35
```

Importing data from the USGS file site. The `readNWISsite()` function uses `siteNumber` 8 digit number which represents the USGS site number. The result is then stored in the `stationInfo` data frame:

```
> stationInfo <- readNWISsite(siteNumber)
```

Step 3 - calculating the moving average

Checking for missing days:

```
> if(as.numeric(diff(range(Q_daily$Date))) != (nrow(Q_daily)+1)){
+   fullDates <- seq(from=min(Q_daily$Date),
+             to = max(Q_daily$Date), by="1 day")
+   fullDates <- data.frame(Date = fullDates,
+   agency_cd = Q_daily$agency_cd[1],
+             site_no = Q_daily$site_no[1],
+             stringsAsFactors = FALSE)
+   Q_daily <- full_join(Q_daily, fullDates,
+             by=c("Date","agency_cd","site_no")) %>%
+   arrange(Date)
+ }
```

Calculating the moving average for 30 days. The `filter()` function applies linear filtering to a time series. `sides=1`, the filter coefficients are applied for past values only:

```
> moving_avg <- function(x,n=30){stats::filter(x,rep(1/n,n), sides=1)}
```

```
> Q_daily <- Q_daily %>% mutate(rollMean =
as.numeric(moving_avg(Flow)), day.of.year = as.numeric(strftime(Date,
format = "%j")))
```

Printing the `Q_daily` data frame. The `tail()` function returns the last part of the `Q_daily` data frame. The `Q_daily` data frame is passed as an input parameter:

```
> tail(Q_daily)
```

The result is as follows:

	agency_cd	site_no	Date	Flow	Flow_cd	rollMean	day.of.year
35552	USGS	01538000	2017-01-30	79	P	-199942.8	30
35553	USGS	01538000	2017-01-31	71	P	-199941.2	31
35554	USGS	01538000	2017-02-01	66	P	-199939.9	32
35555	USGS	01538000	2017-02-02	61	P	-199938.9	33
35556	USGS	01538000	2017-02-03	54	P	-199939.4	34
35557	USGS	01538000	2017-02-04	65	P	-199938.7	35

Step 4 - calculating percentiles

Calculating historical percentiles. The various quantiles are calculated using respective probabilities. Then, the data frame is collapsed into a single row, using the summarize() function. Finally, using the function group_by(), the results, which are in table form, are converted and grouped into a table:

```
> Q_summary <- Q_daily %>%
+     group_by(day.of.year) %>%
+     summarize(p75 = quantile(rollMean, probs = .75, na.rm = TRUE),
+               p25 = quantile(rollMean, probs = .25, na.rm = TRUE),
+               p10 = quantile(rollMean, probs = 0.1, na.rm = TRUE),
+               p05 = quantile(rollMean, probs = 0.05, na.rm = TRUE),
+               p00 = quantile(rollMean, probs = 0, na.rm = TRUE))
```

Obtaining the current year from the system:

```
> current_year <- as.numeric(strftime(Sys.Date(), format = "%Y"))

> summary.0 <- Q_summary %>% mutate(Date = as.Date(day.of.year - 1,
origin = paste0(current_year-2,"-01-01")), day.of.year = day.of.year - 365)

> summary.1 <- Q_summary %>% mutate(Date = as.Date(day.of.year - 1,
origin = paste0(current_year-1,"-01-01")))

> summary.2 <- Q_summary %>% mutate(Date = as.Date(day.of.year - 1,
origin = paste0(current_year,"-01-01")), day.of.year = day.of.year + 365)
```

Combining each of the data frames:

```
> Q_summary <- bind_rows(summary.0, summary.1, summary.2)
```

Printing the Q_summary data frame:

```
> Q_summary
```

The result is as follows:

```
# A tibble: 1,098 × 7
   day.of.year      p75       p25       p10       p05        p00        Date
         <dbl>    <dbl>     <dbl>     <dbl>     <dbl>      <dbl>      <date>
1         -364 101.69167 40.11667 21.07333 14.30450 -233307.0 2015-01-01
2         -363 105.92500 41.60833 22.66567 16.89083 -233307.2 2015-01-02
3         -362 106.45000 41.31667 23.32900 17.16283 -233307.0 2015-01-03
4         -361 104.86667 40.76667 23.79767 17.22783 -233305.7 2015-01-04
5         -360 103.88333 41.01667 23.59900 17.33067 -233305.1 2015-01-05
6         -359 101.73333 41.61417 23.66900 17.77900 -233305.5 2015-01-06
7         -358  99.96667 42.16417 23.86900 19.86667 -233305.8 2015-01-07
8         -357 101.54167 42.05750 23.82867 20.04667 -266640.2 2015-01-08
9         -356  94.99167 41.66667 24.42333 20.98333 -299974.5 2015-01-09
10        -355  92.70000 41.41667 24.69333 20.83167 -333308.6 2015-01-10
# ... with 1,088 more rows
```

```
> smooth.span <- 0.3
```

Predicting values based on a linear model and fitting a polynomial surface.
The loess() function fits the polynomial surface. p75~day.of.year represents the
formula, while span = smooth.span for example smooth.span= 0.3, controls the
degree of smoothing:

```
> Q_summary$sm.75 <- predict(loess(p75~day.of.year, data = Q_summary,
span = smooth.span))
```

Printing the Q_summary$sm.75 data frame:

```
> head(Q_summary$sm.75)
```

The result is as follows:

```
[1] 80.59694 81.44816 82.29218 83.12881 83.95787 84.77917
```

```
> Q_summary$sm.25 <- predict(loess(p25~day.of.year, data = Q_summary,
span = smooth.span))
```

Printing the Q_summary$sm.25 data frame:

```
> head(summaryQ$sm.25)
```

The result is as follows:

```
[1] 36.16151 36.16151 36.58664 37.00671 37.42077 37.82784
```

```
> Q_summary$sm.10 <- predict(loess(p10~day.of.year, data = Q_summary,
span = smooth.span))
```

Printing the Q_summary$sm.10 data frame:

```
> head(summaryQ$sm.10)
```

The result is as follows:

```
[1] 22.41312 22.41312 22.72999 23.04434 23.35553 23.66293
```

```
> Q_summary$sm.05 <- predict(loess(p05~day.of.year, data = Q_summary,
span = smooth.span))
```

Printing the Q_summary$sm.05 data frame:

```
> head(summaryQ$sm.05)
```

The result is as follows:

```
[1] 16.23024 16.23024 16.48055 16.73002 16.97826 17.22487
```

```
> Q_summary$sm.00 <- predict(loess(p00~day.of.year, data = Q_summary,
span = smooth.span))
```

Printing the Q_summary$sm.05 data frame:

```
> head(summaryQ$sm.00)
```

The result is as follows:

```
[1] -109716.7 -109716.7 -110200.7 -110650.7 -111063.8 -111437.1
```

```
> Q_summary <- select(Q_summary, Date, day.of.year, sm.75, sm.25,
sm.10, sm.05, sm.00) %>% filter(Date >=
as.Date(paste0(current_year-1,"-01-01")))
```

Printing the Q_summary data frame:

```
> Q_summary
```

The result is as follows:

```
# A tibble: 733 × 7
         Date day.of.year     sm.75     sm.25     sm.10     sm.05      sm.00
       <date>        <dbl>     <dbl>     <dbl>     <dbl>     <dbl>      <dbl>
1  2016-01-01           1  90.99353  36.16151  22.41312  16.23024  -109716.7
2  2016-01-01           1  90.99353  36.16151  22.41312  16.23024  -109716.7
3  2016-01-02           2  91.56954  36.58664  22.72999  16.48055  -110200.7
4  2016-01-03           3  92.13778  37.00671  23.04434  16.73002  -110650.7
5  2016-01-04           4  92.69719  37.42077  23.35553  16.97826  -111063.8
6  2016-01-05           5  93.24672  37.82784  23.66293  17.22487  -111437.1
7  2016-01-06           6  93.78531  38.22699  23.96590  17.46943  -111767.7
8  2016-01-07           7  94.31193  38.61726  24.26381  17.71154  -112052.9
9  2016-01-08           8  94.82552  38.99769  24.55602  17.95079  -112289.7
10 2016-01-09           9  95.32503  39.36733  24.84190  18.18678  -112475.3
# ... with 723 more rows
```

```
> latest.years <- Q_daily %>% filter(Date >=
as.Date(paste0(current_year-1,"-01-01"))) %>% mutate(day.of.year =
1:nrow(.))
```

Step 5 - plotting results

Plotting the data:

```
> title.text <- paste0(stationInfo$station_nm,"n", "Provisional Data -
Subject to changen", "Record Start = ", min(Q_daily$Date), " Number of
years = ", as.integer (as.numeric(difftime(time1 = max(Q_daily$Date), time2
= min(Q_daily$Date), units = "weeks"))/52.25), "nDate of plot =
",Sys.Date(), "  Drainage Area = ",stationInfo$drain_area_va, "mi^2")
```

```
> mid.month.days <- c(15, 45, 74, 105, 135, 166, 196, 227, 258, 288,
319, 349)

> month.letters <- c("J","F","M","A","M","J","J","A","S","O","N","D")

> start.month.days <- c(1, 32, 61, 92, 121, 152, 182, 214, 245, 274,
305, 335)

> label.text <- c("Normal","DroughtWatch","DroughtWarning","Drought
Emergency")

> year1_summary <- data.frame(Q_summary[2:366,])

> head(year1_summary)
```

The result is as follows:

	Date	day.of.year	sm.75	sm.25	sm.10	sm.05	sm.00
1	2016-01-01	1	90.99353	36.16151	22.41312	16.23024	-109716.7
2	2016-01-02	2	91.56954	36.58664	22.72999	16.48055	-110200.7
3	2016-01-03	3	92.13778	37.00671	23.04434	16.73002	-110650.7
4	2016-01-04	4	92.69719	37.42077	23.35553	16.97826	-111063.8
5	2016-01-05	5	93.24672	37.82784	23.66293	17.22487	-111437.1
6	2016-01-06	6	93.78531	38.22699	23.96590	17.46943	-111767.7

```
> year2_summary <- data.frame(Q_summary[367:733,])

> head(year2_summary)
```

The result is as follows:

	Date	day.of.year	sm.75	sm.25	sm.10	sm.05	sm.00
1	2016-12-31	366	90.55267	35.63442	22.02318	15.95450	-109125.5
2	2017-01-01	366	90.55267	35.63442	22.02318	15.95450	-109125.5
3	2017-01-02	367	91.13212	36.10354	22.39240	16.25584	-109351.1
4	2017-01-03	368	91.71522	36.58013	22.76842	16.56302	-109564.3
5	2017-01-04	369	92.30089	37.06284	23.15014	16.87519	-109764.4
6	2017-01-05	370	92.88805	37.55033	23.53646	17.19149	-109951.0

```
> simple.plot <- ggplot(data = Q_summary, aes(x = day.of.year)) +
+ geom_ribbon(aes(ymin = sm.25, ymax = sm.75, fill = "Normal")) +
+ geom_ribbon(aes(ymin = sm.10, ymax = sm.25, fill =
"Drought Watch")) +
+ geom_ribbon(aes(ymin = sm.05, ymax = sm.10, fill = "Drought
Warning")) +
+ geom_ribbon(aes(ymin = sm.00, ymax = sm.05, fill = "Drought
```

```
Emergency")) +
    + scale_y_log10(limits = c(1,1000)) +
    + geom_line(data = latest.years, aes(x=day.of.year, y=rollMean, color =
"30-Day Mean"),size=2) +
    + geom_vline(xintercept = 365)

> simple.plot
```

The result is as follows:

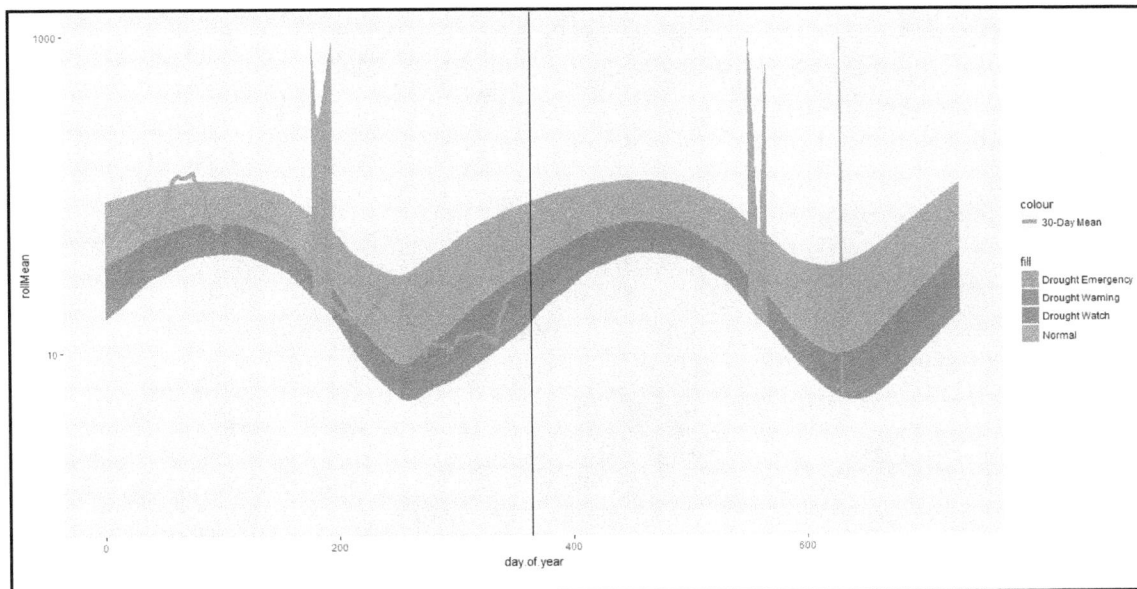

6
Supervised Learning

In this chapter, we will cover the following recipes:

- Decision tree learning - Advance Health Directive for patients with chest pain
- Decision tree learning - income-based distribution of real estate values
- Decision tree learning - predicting the direction of stock movement
- Naive Bayes - predicting the direction of stock movement
- Random forest - currency trading strategy
- Support vector machine - currency trading strategy
- Stochastic gradient descent - adult income

Introduction

Decision tree learning: Decision trees are very popular tools for classification and prediction problems. A decision tree is a classifier which recursively partitions the instance space or the variable set. Decision trees are represented as a tree structure where each node can be classified as either a leaf node or a decision node. A leaf node holds the value of the target attribute, while a decision node specifies the rule to be implemented on a single attribute-value. Each decision node splits the instance space into two or more sub-spaces according to a certain discrete function of the input attributes-values. Each test considers a single attribute, such that the instance space is partitioned according to the attribute's value. In the case of numeric attributes, the condition refers to a range. After implementing the rule on the decision node, a sub-tree is an outcome. Each of the leaf nodes holds a probability vector indicating the probability of the target attribute having a certain value. Instances are classified by navigating them from the root of the tree down to a leaf, according to the outcome of the tests along the path.

The key requirements to mine data with decision trees are as follows:

- **Attribute-value description**: The object can be expressed as a fixed set of properties or attributes
- **Predefined classes**: The categories to which examples are to be assigned must be supervised data
- **Sufficient data**: Use of multiple training cases

Naive Bayes: The naive Bayes is a supervised learning method. It is a linear classifier. It is based on the Bayes' theorem, which states that the presence of a particular feature of a class is unrelated to the presence of any other feature. It is a robust and efficient algorithm. Bayesian classifiers can predict class membership probabilities such as the probability that a given tuple belongs to a particular class. Bayesian belief networks is joint conditional probability distribution. It allows class-conditional independencies to be defined between subsets of variables. It provides a graphical model of a causal relationship on which learning can be performed.

Random forest: Random forests are collections of decision trees that provide predictions into the structure of data. They are a tool that pulls the power of multiple decision trees in judicious randomization, and ensemble learning to produce predictive models.
They provide variable rankings, missing values, segmentations, and reporting for each record to ensure deep data understanding. After each tree is built, all the data is run down the tree. For each of the pairs of cases, vicinities are computed. If two cases occupy the same terminal node, their vicinities are increased by one. At the end of the run, normalization is carried out by dividing by the number of trees. Proximities are used in replacing missing data, locating outliers, and producing to reveal low-dimensional understandings of the data. The training data, which is out-of-bag data, is used to estimate classification error and to calculate the importance of variables.

Random forests run very efficiently on large databases, producing accurate results. They handle multiple variables without deletion, giving estimates of the importance of the variables to solve the classification problems. They generate an internal unbiased estimate of the generalization error as the forest building progresses. A random forest is an effective method for estimating missing data, and maintains accuracy when a large proportion of the data is missing.

Support vector machines: Machine learning algorithms use right set of features to solve learning problems. SVMs make use of a (nonlinear) mapping function φ which transforms data in the input space to data in the feature space in such a way as to render a problem linearly separable. The SVM then discovers the optimal separating hyperplane which is then mapped back into input space via φ-1. Among the possible hyperplanes, we select the one where the distance of the hyperplane from the closest data points (the margin) is as large as possible.

Decision tree learning - Advance Health Directive for patients with chest pain

An Advance Health Directive document states the directions regarding the future health care for an individual on various medical conditions. It guides an individual to make the right decision in case of emergency or as required. The document helps an individual to understand the nature and consequences of their health care decisions, understand the nature and effect of the directive, freely and voluntarily make these decisions, and communicate the decisions in some way.

Getting ready

In order to perform decision tree classification, we will be using a dataset collected from the heart patients dataset.

Step 1 - collecting and describing the data

The dataset titled `Heart.csv` which is available in CSV format, will be used. The dataset is in standard format. There are 303 rows of data. There are 15 variables. The numeric variables are as follows:

- Age
- Sex
- RestBP
- Chol
- Fbs
- RestECG
- MaxHR

- ExAng
- Oldpeak
- Slope
- Ca

The non-numeric variables are as follows:

- ChestPain
- Thal
- AHD

How to do it...

Let's get into the details.

Step 2 - exploring the data

The following packages need to be loaded as the first step to be carried out:

```
> install.packages("tree")
> install.packages("caret")
> install.packages("e1071")
> library(tree)
> library(caret)
```

Version info: Code for this page was tested in R version 3.3.0 (2016-05-03).

Let's explore the data and understand the relationships between the variables. We'll begin by importing the CSV data file named Heart.csv. We will be saving the data to the AHD_data data frame:

```
> AHD_data <- read.csv("d:/Heart.csv", header = TRUE)
```

Exploring the internal structure of the `AHD_data` data frame. The `str()` function displays the internal structure of the data frame. The `AHD_data` is passed as an R object to the `str()` function:

```
> str(AHD_data)
```

The result is as follows:

```
'data.frame':    303 obs. of  15 variables:
 $ X        : int  1 2 3 4 5 6 7 8 9 10 ...
 $ Age      : int  63 67 67 37 41 56 62 57 63 53 ...
 $ Sex      : int  1 1 1 1 0 1 0 0 1 1 ...
 $ ChestPain: Factor w/ 4 levels "asymptomatic",..: 4 1 1 2 3 3 1 1 1 1 ...
 $ RestBP   : int  145 160 120 130 130 120 140 120 130 140 ...
 $ Chol     : int  233 286 229 250 204 236 268 354 254 203 ...
 $ Fbs      : int  1 0 0 0 0 0 0 0 0 1 ...
 $ RestECG  : int  2 2 2 0 2 0 2 0 2 2 ...
 $ MaxHR    : int  150 108 129 187 172 178 160 163 147 155 ...
 $ ExAng    : int  0 1 1 0 0 0 0 1 0 1 ...
 $ Oldpeak  : num  2.3 1.5 2.6 3.5 1.4 0.8 3.6 0.6 1.4 3.1 ...
 $ Slope    : int  3 2 2 3 1 1 3 1 2 3 ...
 $ Ca       : int  0 3 2 0 0 0 2 0 1 0 ...
 $ Thal     : Factor w/ 3 levels "fixed","normal",..: 1 2 3 2 2 2 2 2 3 3 ...
 $ AHD      : Factor w/ 2 levels "No","Yes": 1 2 2 1 1 1 2 1 2 2 ...
```

Printing the `AHD_data` data frame. The `head()` function returns the first part of the `AHD_data` data frame. The `AHD_data` data frame is passed as an input parameter:

```
> head(AHD_data)
```

The result is as follows:

```
  X Age Sex    ChestPain RestBP Chol Fbs RestECG MaxHR ExAng Oldpeak Slope Ca      Thal AHD
1 1  63   1      typical    145  233   1       2   150     0     2.3     3  0     fixed  No
2 2  67   1 asymptomatic    160  286   0       2   108     1     1.5     2  3    normal Yes
3 3  67   1 asymptomatic    120  229   0       2   129     1     2.6     2  2 reversable Yes
4 4  37   1   nonanginal    130  250   0       0   187     0     3.5     3  0    normal  No
5 5  41   0   nontypical    130  204   0       2   172     0     1.4     1  0    normal  No
6 6  56   1   nontypical    120  236   0       0   178     0     0.8     1  0    normal  No
.
```

Exploring the dimensions of the AHD_data data frame. The dim() function returns the dimensions of the AHD_data frame. The AHD_data data frame is passed as an input parameter. The result clearly states that there are 303 rows of data and 15 columns:

```
> dim(AHD_data)
```

The result is as follows:

```
[1] 303  15
```

Step 3 - preparing the data

The data needs to be prepared for carrying out the model building and testing. Data is split into two parts--one for building the model and the other for testing the model which will be prepared.

The createDataPartition() function is used for creating splits of the data. AHD_data is passed as an argument to the function. Random sampling takes place. The percentage of data that goes to training is denoted by p. Here, the value of p is 0.5, which means that 50% of the data is used for the training. List = 'FALSE' avoids returning the data as a list. The result is then stored in the data frame split:

```
> split <- createDataPartition(y=AHD_data$AHD, p = 0.5, list=FALSE)
```

The call to the data frame split displays training set data for training purposes:

```
> split
```

The result is as follows:

```
        Resample1
 [1,]          1
 [2,]          3
 [3,]          4
 [4,]          5
 [5,]          7
 [6,]          8
 [7,]         13
 [8,]         18
 [9,]         19
[10,]         21
[11,]         23
[12,]         24
[13,]         26
[14,]         27
[15,]         28
[16,]         29
[17,]         30
[18,]         31
[19,]         32
[20,]         33
[21,]         34
[22,]         37
[23,]         38
[24,]         40
[25,]         41
[26,]         43
[27,]         44
[28,]         45
[29,]         48
```

The training data will be created. The split data frame is used to create the training data. The train data frame is used to store the values of the training data:

```
> train <- AHD_data[split,]
```

Printing the training data frame:

```
> train
```

The result is as follows:

	X	Age	Sex	ChestPain	RestBP	Chol	Fbs	RestECG	MaxHR	ExAng	Oldpeak	Slope	Ca	Thal	AHD
1	1	63	1	typical	145	233	1	2	150	0	2.3	3	0	fixed	No
3	3	67	1	asymptomatic	120	229	0	2	129	1	2.6	2	2	reversable	Yes
4	4	37	1	nonanginal	130	250	0	0	187	0	3.5	3	0	normal	No
5	5	41	0	nontypical	130	204	0	2	172	0	1.4	1	0	normal	No
7	7	62	0	asymptomatic	140	268	0	2	160	0	3.6	3	2	normal	Yes
8	8	57	0	asymptomatic	120	354	0	0	163	1	0.6	1	0	normal	No
13	13	56	1	nonanginal	130	256	1	2	142	1	0.6	2	1	fixed	Yes
18	18	54	1	asymptomatic	140	239	0	0	160	0	1.2	1	0	normal	No
19	19	48	0	nonanginal	130	275	0	0	139	0	0.2	1	0	normal	No
21	21	64	1	typical	110	211	0	2	144	1	1.8	2	0	normal	No
23	23	58	1	nontypical	120	284	0	2	160	0	1.8	2	0	normal	Yes
24	24	58	1	nonanginal	132	224	0	2	173	0	3.2	1	2	reversable	Yes
26	26	50	0	nonanginal	120	219	0	0	158	0	1.6	2	0	normal	No
27	27	58	0	nonanginal	120	340	0	0	172	0	0.0	1	0	normal	No
28	28	66	0	typical	150	226	0	0	114	0	2.6	3	0	normal	No
29	29	43	1	asymptomatic	150	247	0	0	171	0	1.5	1	0	normal	No
30	30	40	1	asymptomatic	110	167	0	2	114	1	2.0	2	0	reversable	Yes
31	31	69	0	typical	140	239	0	0	151	0	1.8	1	2	normal	No
32	32	60	1	asymptomatic	117	230	1	0	160	1	1.4	1	2	reversable	Yes
33	33	64	1	nonanginal	140	335	0	0	158	0	0.0	1	0	normal	Yes
34	34	59	1	asymptomatic	135	234	0	0	161	0	0.5	2	0	reversable	No
37	37	43	1	asymptomatic	120	177	0	2	120	1	2.5	2	0	reversable	Yes
38	38	57	1	asymptomatic	150	276	0	2	112	1	0.6	2	1	fixed	Yes
40	40	61	1	nonanginal	150	243	1	0	137	1	1.0	2	0	normal	No
41	41	65	0	asymptomatic	150	225	0	2	114	0	1.0	2	3	reversable	Yes
43	43	71	0	nontypical	160	302	0	0	162	0	0.4	1	2	normal	No
44	44	59	1	nonanginal	150	212	1	0	157	0	1.6	1	0	normal	No
45	45	61	0	asymptomatic	130	330	0	2	169	0	0.0	1	0	normal	Yes

The testing data will be created. The `split` data frame is used to create the testing data. The – sign before the `split` data frame denotes all those rows of data which have not been considered for training purposes. The test data frame is used to store the values of the testing data:

```
> test <- AHD_data[-split,]
```

Printing the testing data frame:

```
> test
```

The result is as follows:

	X	Age	Sex	ChestPain	RestBP	Chol	Fbs	RestECG	MaxHR	ExAng	Oldpeak	Slope	Ca	Thal	AHD
2	2	67	1	asymptomatic	160	286	0	2	108	1	1.5	2	3	normal	Yes
6	6	56	1	nontypical	120	236	0	0	178	0	0.8	1	0	normal	No
9	9	63	1	asymptomatic	130	254	0	2	147	0	1.4	2	1	reversable	Yes
10	10	53	1	asymptomatic	140	203	1	2	155	1	3.1	3	0	reversable	Yes
11	11	57	1	asymptomatic	140	192	0	0	148	0	0.4	2	0	fixed	No
12	12	56	0	nontypical	140	294	0	2	153	0	1.3	2	0	normal	No
14	14	44	1	nontypical	120	263	0	0	173	0	0.0	1	0	reversable	No
15	15	52	1	nonanginal	172	199	1	0	162	0	0.5	1	0	reversable	No
16	16	57	1	nonanginal	150	168	0	0	174	0	1.6	1	0	normal	No
17	17	48	1	nontypical	110	229	0	0	168	0	1.0	3	0	reversable	Yes
20	20	49	1	nontypical	130	266	0	0	171	0	0.6	1	0	normal	No
22	22	58	0	typical	150	283	1	2	162	0	1.0	1	0	normal	No
25	25	60	1	asymptomatic	130	206	0	2	132	1	2.4	2	2	reversable	Yes
35	35	44	1	nonanginal	130	233	0	0	179	1	0.4	1	0	normal	No
36	36	42	1	asymptomatic	140	226	0	0	178	0	0.0	1	0	normal	No
39	39	55	1	asymptomatic	132	353	0	0	132	1	1.2	2	1	reversable	Yes
42	42	40	1	typical	140	199	0	0	178	1	1.4	1	0	reversable	No
46	46	58	1	nonanginal	112	230	0	2	165	0	2.5	2	1	reversable	Yes
47	47	51	1	nonanginal	110	175	0	0	123	0	0.6	1	0	normal	No
50	50	53	1	nonanginal	130	197	1	2	152	0	1.2	3	0	normal	No
55	55	60	1	asymptomatic	130	253	0	0	144	1	1.4	1	1	reversable	Yes
56	56	54	1	asymptomatic	124	266	0	2	109	1	2.2	2	1	reversable	Yes
60	60	51	1	typical	125	213	0	2	125	1	1.4	1	1	normal	No
61	61	51	0	asymptomatic	130	305	0	0	142	1	1.2	2	0	reversable	Yes
65	65	54	1	asymptomatic	120	188	0	0	113	0	1.4	2	1	reversable	Yes
66	66	60	1	asymptomatic	145	282	0	2	142	1	2.8	2	2	reversable	Yes
71	71	65	0	nonanginal	155	269	0	0	148	0	0.8	1	0	normal	No

Step 4 - training the model

The model will now be prepared and trained on the training dataset. Decision trees are used when datasets are divided into groups, as compared to investigating a numerical response and its relationship to a set of descriptor variables. The implementation of classification trees in R is carried out using the `tree()` function.

The `tree()` function is used to implement classification trees. A tree is grown by binary recursive partitioning. The AHD field on the training dataset is used to form classification trees. The resulting data frame is stored in the `trees` data frame:

```
> trees <- tree(AHD ~., train)
```

A graphical version of the trees data frame will be displayed. The `plot()` function is a generic function for the plotting of R objects. The trees data frame is passed as a function value:

```
> plot(trees)
```

The result is as follows:

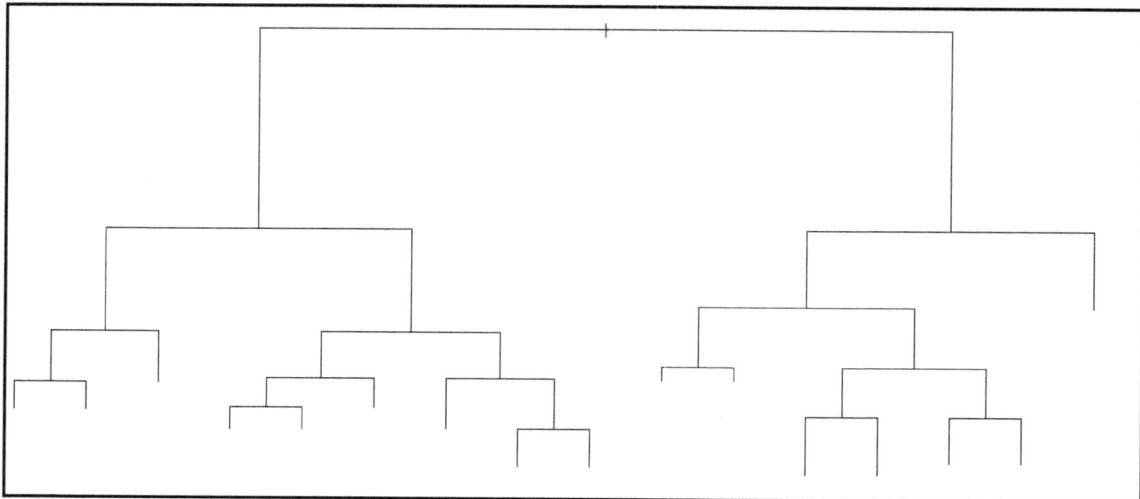

Find the deviance or number of misclassifications by running a cross-validation experiment. The cv.tree() function will be used. The trees data frame object is passed. FUN=prune.misclass obtains a nested sequence of subtrees of the supplied data frame trees by recursively snipping off the least important splits. The result is stored in the cv.trees data frame:

```
> cv.trees <- cv.tree(trees, FUN=prune.misclass)
```

Printing the results of data frame cv.trees:

```
> cv.trees
```

The $dev field gives the deviance for each K.

The result is as follows:

```
$size
[1] 16 12 10  9  8  5  2  1

$dev
[1] 36 36 35 39 46 50 52 71

$k
[1]        -Inf  0.000000  0.500000  1.000000  2.000000  2.666667  3.666667 30.000000

$method
[1] "misclass"

attr(,"class")
[1] "prune"            "tree.sequence"
```

Using the `plot()` function data frame, `cv.trees` is displayed. The `$dev` value is on the *y* axis (right side). The `$k` value is on the top. The `$size` value is on the *x* axis.

As can be clearly seen, when `$size = 1`, `$k = 30.000000`, `$dev = 1`. We plot the data frame using:

```
> plot(cv.trees)
```

The result is as follows:

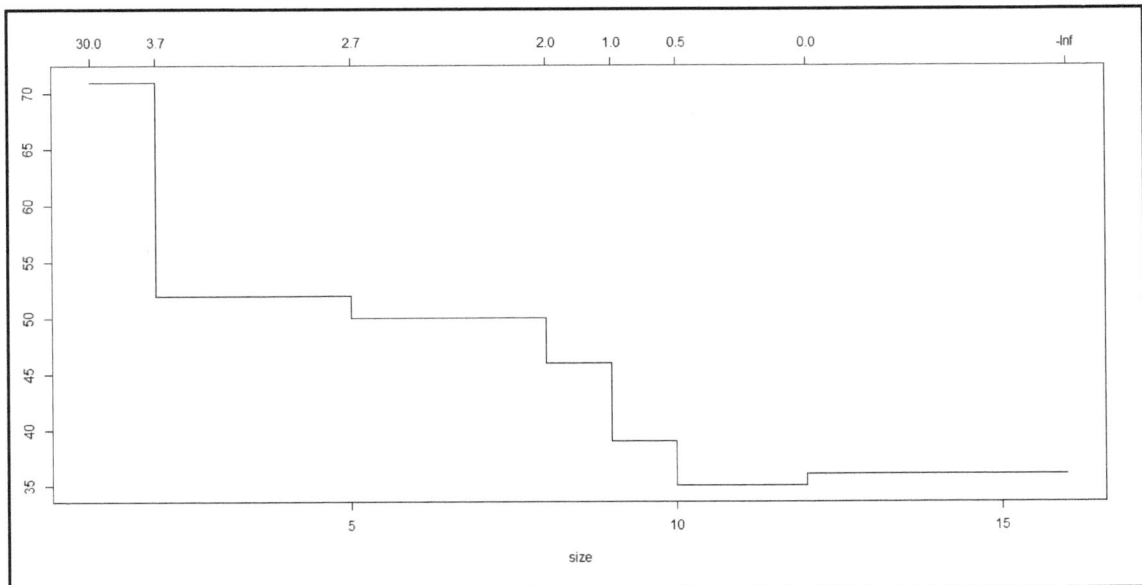

Step 5- improving the model

Let us improve the model by splitting the tree with the lowest deviance. The `prune.misclass()` function is called to split the tree. `prune.misclass` obtains a nested sequence of subtrees of the supplied data frame trees by recursively snipping off the least important splits. The result is stored in the `prune.trees` data frame. `best=4` indicates the size (for example, the number of terminal nodes) of a specific subtree in the cost-complexity sequence that is to be returned:

```
> prune.trees <- prune.misclass(trees, best=4)
```

Using the `plot()` function data frame, `prune.trees` is displayed:

```
> plot(prune.trees)
```

The result is as follows:

Adding the text to the preceding pruned tree:

```
> text(prune.trees, pretty=0)
```

The result is as follows:

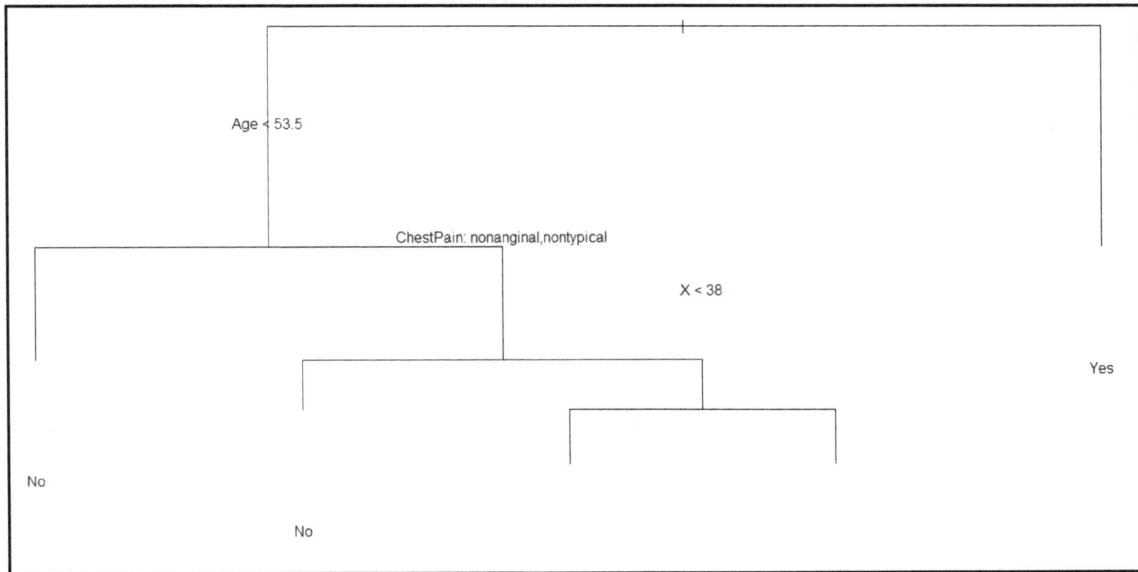

In order to predict the value based on a linear model object, we will use the predict() function. prune.trees is passed as an object. The test data object is passed as an object in which to look for variables with which to predict. The result will be stored in the tree.pred data frame:

```
> tree.pred <- predict(prune.trees, test, type='class')
```

Displaying the variable test.pred values:

```
> tree.pred
```

The result is as follows:

```
 [1] No  No  Yes Yes Yes No  Yes Yes No  Yes No  No  Yes No  No  Yes Yes Yes No  No  Yes Yes No  Yes Yes Yes
No  Yes Yes Yes
[31] No  Yes No  Yes No  No  No  Yes Yes Yes No  No  Yes No  No  No  Yes No  Yes Yes Yes Yes Yes Yes No  No
Yes Yes Yes Yes
[61] No  Yes No  Yes Yes Yes Yes Yes No  No  Yes No  Yes Yes Yes Yes Yes Yes No  No  Yes Yes Yes Yes Yes Yes
Yes Yes No  Yes
[91] Yes Yes No  Yes No  No  Yes Yes Yes Yes No  No  No  Yes Yes No  No  No  No  Yes No  Yes No  No  Yes No
No  No  Yes Yes
[121] No  Yes Yes Yes Yes No  Yes Yes No  Yes No  Yes Yes No  No  Yes Yes Yes No  Yes Yes No  Yes No  Yes Yes
No  Yes Yes Yes
[151] No
Levels: No Yes
```

Summarizing the results of the model. The `confusionMatrix()` calculates the cross-tabulation of the observed and predicted classes. `tree.pred` is passed as a factor of predicted classes:

```
> confusionMatrix(tree.pred, test$AHD)
```

The result is as follows:

```
Confusion Matrix and Statistics

          Reference
Prediction No Yes
       No  54   6
       Yes 28  63

               Accuracy : 0.7748
                 95% CI : (0.6998, 0.8387)
    No Information Rate : 0.543
    P-Value [Acc > NIR] : 2.86e-09

                  Kappa : 0.5575
 Mcnemar's Test P-Value : 0.0003164

            Sensitivity : 0.6585
            Specificity : 0.9130
         Pos Pred Value : 0.9000
         Neg Pred Value : 0.6923
             Prevalence : 0.5430
         Detection Rate : 0.3576
   Detection Prevalence : 0.3974
      Balanced Accuracy : 0.7858

       'Positive' Class : No
```

Decision tree learning - income-based distribution of real estate values

Income has been an essential component of the attractive long-term total returns provided by real estate as an asset class. The annual income returns generated from investing in real estate have been more than 2.5 times higher than stocks and lagged bonds by only 50 basis points. Real estate often provides a steady source of income based on the rent paid by tenants.

Getting ready

In order to perform decision tree classification, we will be using a dataset collected from the real estate dataset.

Step 1 - collecting and describing the data

The dataset titled `RealEstate.txt` will be used. This dataset is available in TXT format, titled `RealEstate.txt`. The dataset is in standard format. There are 20,640 rows of data. The 9 numerical variables are as follows:

- `MedianHouseValue`
- `MedianIncome`
- `MedianHouseAge`
- `TotalRooms`
- `TotalBedrooms`
- `Population`
- `Households`
- `Latitude`
- `Longitude`

How to do it...

Let's get into the details.

Step 2 - exploring the data

The following package needs to be loaded as the first step to be carried out:

```
> install.packages("tree")
```

Version info: Code for this page was tested in R version 3.3.0 (2016-05-03).

Let's explore the data and understand the relationships between the variables. We'll begin by importing the TXT data file named `RealEstate.txt`. We will be saving the data to the `realEstate` data frame:

```
> realEstate <- read.table("d:/RealEstate.txt", header=TRUE)
```

Exploring the dimensions of the `realEstate` data frame. The `dim()` function returns the dimensions of the `realEstate` frame. The `realEstate` data frame is passed as an input parameter. The result clearly states that there are 20,640 rows of data and 9 columns:

```
> dim(realEstate)
```

The result is as follows:

```
[1] 20640        9
```

Exploring the internal structure of the `realEstate` data frame. The `str()` function displays the internal structure of the data frame. The `realEstate` is passed as an R object to the `str()` function:

```
> str(realEstate)
```

The result is as follows:

```
'data.frame':    20640 obs. of  9 variables:
 $ MedianHouseValue: num  452600 358500 352100 341300 342200 ...
 $ MedianIncome    : num  8.33 8.3 7.26 5.64 3.85 ...
 $ MedianHouseAge  : num  41 21 52 52 52 52 52 52 42 52 ...
 $ TotalRooms      : num  880 7099 1467 1274 1627 ...
 $ TotalBedrooms   : num  129 1106 190 235 280 ...
 $ Population       : num  322 2401 496 558 565 ...
 $ Households      : num  126 1138 177 219 259 ...
 $ Latitude        : num  37.9 37.9 37.9 37.9 37.9 ...
 $ Longitude       : num  -122 -122 -122 -122 -122 ...
```

Printing the `realEstate` data frame. The `head()` function returns the first part of the `realEstate` data frame. The `realEstate` data frame is passed as an input parameter:

```
> head(realEstate)
```

The result is as follows:

```
   MedianHouseValue MedianIncome MedianHouseAge TotalRooms TotalBedrooms Population Households Latitude Longitude
1            452600       8.3252             41        880           129        322        126    37.88   -122.23
2            358500       8.3014             21       7099          1106       2401       1138    37.86   -122.22
3            352100       7.2574             52       1467           190        496        177    37.85   -122.24
4            341300       5.6431             52       1274           235        558        219    37.85   -122.25
5            342200       3.8462             52       1627           280        565        259    37.85   -122.25
6            269700       4.0368             52        919           213        413        193    37.85   -122.25
```

Printing the summary of the `realEstate` data frame. The `summary()` function is a multipurpose function. `summary()` is a generic function that provides a summary of the data related to the individual object or data frame. The `realEstate` data frame is passed as an R object to the `summary()` function:

```
> summary(realEstate)
```

The result is as follows:

```
MedianHouseValue  MedianIncome     MedianHouseAge   TotalRooms     TotalBedrooms   Population
Min.   : 14999   Min.   : 0.4999   Min.   : 1.00   Min.   :    2   Min.   :   1.0  Min.   :    3
1st Qu.:119600   1st Qu.: 2.5634   1st Qu.:18.00   1st Qu.: 1448   1st Qu.: 295.0  1st Qu.:  787
Median :179700   Median : 3.5348   Median :29.00   Median : 2127   Median : 435.0  Median : 1166
Mean   :206856   Mean   : 3.8707   Mean   :28.64   Mean   : 2636   Mean   : 537.9  Mean   : 1425
3rd Qu.:264725   3rd Qu.: 4.7432   3rd Qu.:37.00   3rd Qu.: 3148   3rd Qu.: 647.0  3rd Qu.: 1725
Max.   :500001   Max.   :15.0001   Max.   :52.00   Max.   :39320   Max.   :6445.0  Max.   :35682
   Households       Latitude        Longitude
Min.   :   1.0   Min.   :32.54   Min.   :-124.3
1st Qu.: 280.0   1st Qu.:33.93   1st Qu.:-121.8
Median : 409.0   Median :34.26   Median :-118.5
Mean   : 499.5   Mean   :35.63   Mean   :-119.6
3rd Qu.: 605.0   3rd Qu.:37.71   3rd Qu.:-118.0
Max.   :6082.0   Max.   :41.95   Max.   :-114.3
```

Step 3 - training the model

The model will now be prepared on the dataset. Decision trees are a tool for classification and prediction. They represent rules which can be understood by humans and used in knowledge systems such as a database. They classify instances by starting at the root of the tree and moving through it until they reach a leaf node. The node specifies a test on a single attribute, the leaf indicates the value of the target attribute, and the edge splits off one attribute.

The `tree()` function is used to implement classification trees. A tree is grown by binary recursive partitioning. These models are computationally intensive techniques, since they recursively partition response variables into subsets based on their relationship to one or more predictor variables.

The formula expression is based on the sum of the variables `Latitude` and `Longitude`. The result of the sum is stored in the log value of `MedianHouseValue`. `data=realEstate` represents the data frame in which to preferentially interpret formula, weights, and subset.

The resulting data frame is stored in data frame `treeModel`:

```
> treeModel <- tree(log(MedianHouseValue) ~ Longitude + Latitude,
data=realEstate)
```

A summary of the `treeModel` will be displayed. The summary displays the formula used, along with the number of terminal nodes or leaves in the trees. The statistical distribution of the residuals is also displayed.

The `summary()` function is used to display the statistical summary of `treeModel`. It is a generic that is used to produce the summaries of the results for various fitting functions. The data frame on which the summary is desired is `treeModel`, which is passed as an input parameter.

Deviance here means the mean squared error:

```
> summary(treeModel)
```

The result is as follows:

```
Regression tree:
tree(formula = log(MedianHouseValue) ~ Longitude + Latitude,
    data = realEstate)
Number of terminal nodes:  12
Residual mean deviance:  0.1662 = 3429 / 20630
Distribution of residuals:
    Min.   1st Qu.    Median     Mean   3rd Qu.      Max.
-2.75900 -0.26080 -0.01359  0.00000  0.26310  1.84100
```

A graphical version of the `treeModel` data frame will be displayed. The `plot()` function is a generic function for plotting R objects. The `treeModel` data frame is passed as a function value:

```
> plot(treeModel)
```

The result is as follows:

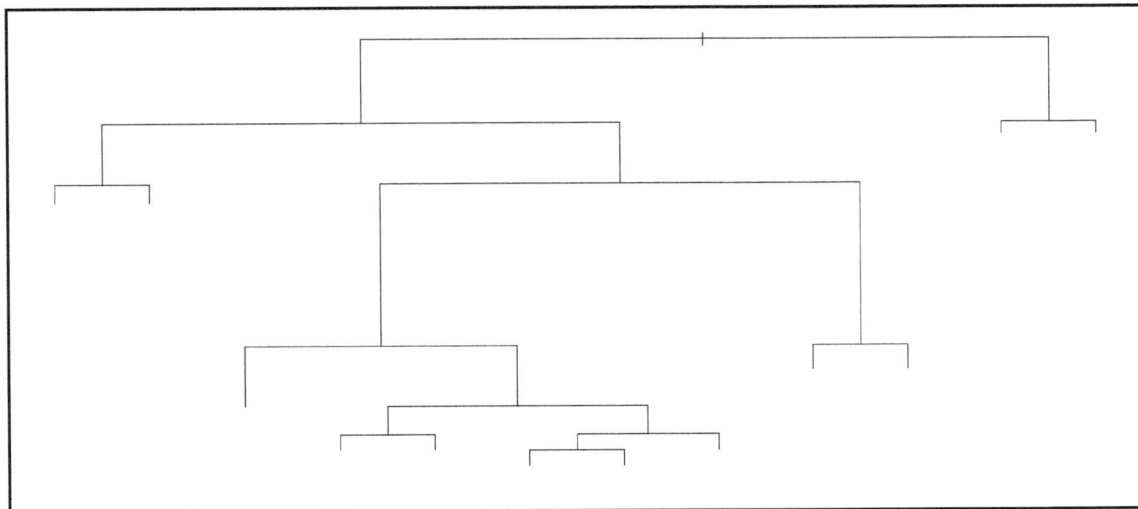

After the graphical version of the `treeModel` data frame is displayed, text needs to be inserted to display the value at each node and the leaves. The `text()` function is used to insert strings given in the labels vector at the given coordinates:

```
> text(treeModel, cex=.75)
```

The result is as follows:

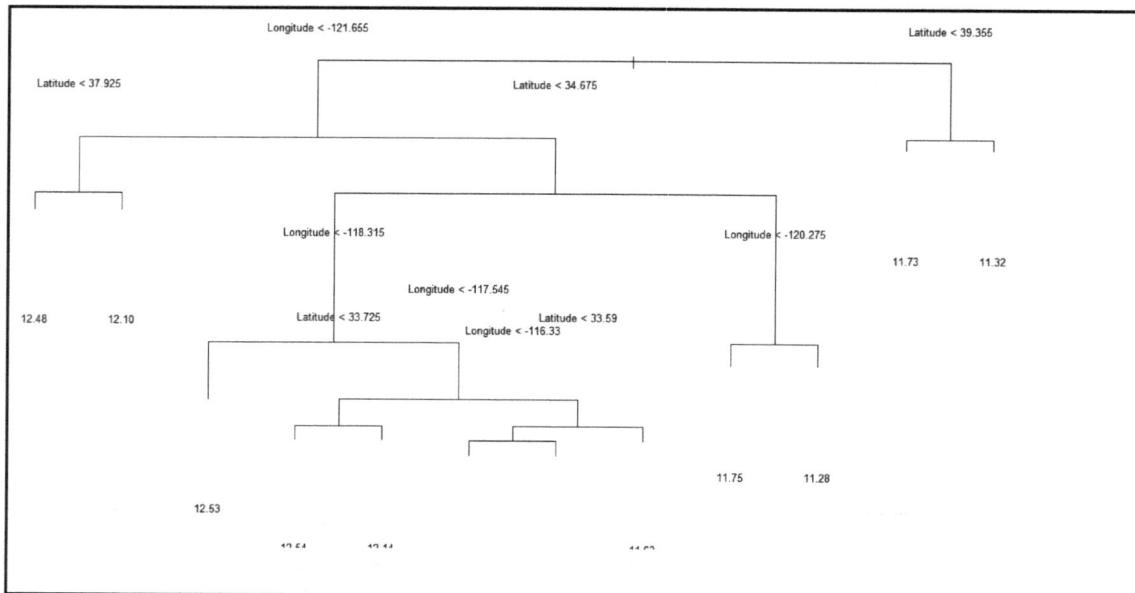

Step 4 - comparing the predictions

Comparing the predictions with the dataset which reflect the global price trend. We wish to summarize the frequency distribution of MedianHouseValue for ease of reporting or comparison. The most direct method is to use quantiles. Quantiles are points in a distribution that relate to the rank order of values in that distribution. The quantiles will divide the MedianHouseValue distribution such that there is a given proportion of an observation below the quantile.

The quantile() function produces sample quantiles corresponding to the given probabilities. realEstate$MedianHouseValue is the numeric vector whose sample quantiles are wanted. The quantile() function returns priceDecilesas a vector of length:

```
> priceDeciles <- quantile(realEstate$MedianHouseValue, 0:10/10)
```

Displaying the value of the `priceDeciles` data frame:

```
> priceDeciles
```

The result is as follows:

```
  0%    10%    20%    30%    40%    50%    60%    70%    80%    90%    100%
14999  82300 107200 134000 157300 179700 209400 241930 290000 376600 500001
```

Next, a summary of the `priceDeciles` will be displayed. The `summary()` function is used to display the statistical summary of the `priceDeciles`. The data frame for which the summary is desired is `priceDeciles`, which is passed as an input parameter:

```
> summary(priceDeciles)
```

The result is as follows:

```
   Min. 1st Qu.  Median    Mean 3rd Qu.    Max.
  15000  120600  179700  208500  266000  500000
```

Dividing the `priceDeciles` vector into different ranges. The `cut()` function divides the range of intervals according to which interval they fall into. The numeric vector `MedianHouseValue` of the `realEstate` data frame is to be converted to a factor by cutting:

```
> cutPrices <- cut(realEstate$MedianHouseValue, priceDeciles,
  include.lowest=TRUE)
```

Printing the `cutPrices` data frame. The `head()` function returns the first part of the `cutPrices` data frame. The `cutPrices` data frame is passed as an input parameter:

```
> head(cutPrices)
```

The result is as follows:

```
[1] (3.77e+05,5e+05]    (2.9e+05,3.77e+05] (2.9e+05,3.77e+05] (2.9e+05,3.77e+05] (2.9e+05,3.77e+05]
[6] (2.42e+05,2.9e+05]
10 Levels: [1.5e+04,8.23e+04] (8.23e+04,1.07e+05] (1.07e+05,1.34e+05] ... (3.77e+05,5e+05]
```

A summary of `cutPrices` will be displayed. The `summary()` function is used to display the statistical summary of the `treeModel`. The data frame on which the summary is desired is `cutPrices`, which is passed as an input parameter:

```
> summary(cutPrices)
```

The result is as follows:

```
[1.5e+04,8.23e+04] (8.23e+04,1.07e+05] (1.07e+05,1.34e+05] (1.34e+05,1.57e+05]
              2066                2063                2064                2065
(1.57e+05,1.8e+05]  (1.8e+05,2.09e+05] (2.09e+05,2.42e+05]  (2.42e+05,2.9e+05]
              2065                2067                2058                2067
(2.9e+05,3.77e+05]   (3.77e+05,5e+05]
              2062                2063
```

Plotting the value of the `cutPrices`. The `plot()` function is a generic function for the plotting of R objects. The `cutPrices` data frame is passed as a function value. The longitude variable of the `realEstate` dataset represents the *x* coordinates of points in the plot. The latitude variable of the `realEstate` dataset represents the *y* coordinates of points in the plot. `col=grey(10:2/11)` represents the plot color. `pch=20` represents the size of the symbol to be used as the default in plotting points. `xlab="Longitude"` represents the title for the x axis, while `ylab="Latitude"` represents the title for the *y* axis:

```
> plot(realEstate$Longitude, realEstate$Latitude,
  col=grey(10:2/11)[cutPrices], pch=20, xlab="Longitude",ylab="Latitude")
```

The result is as follows:

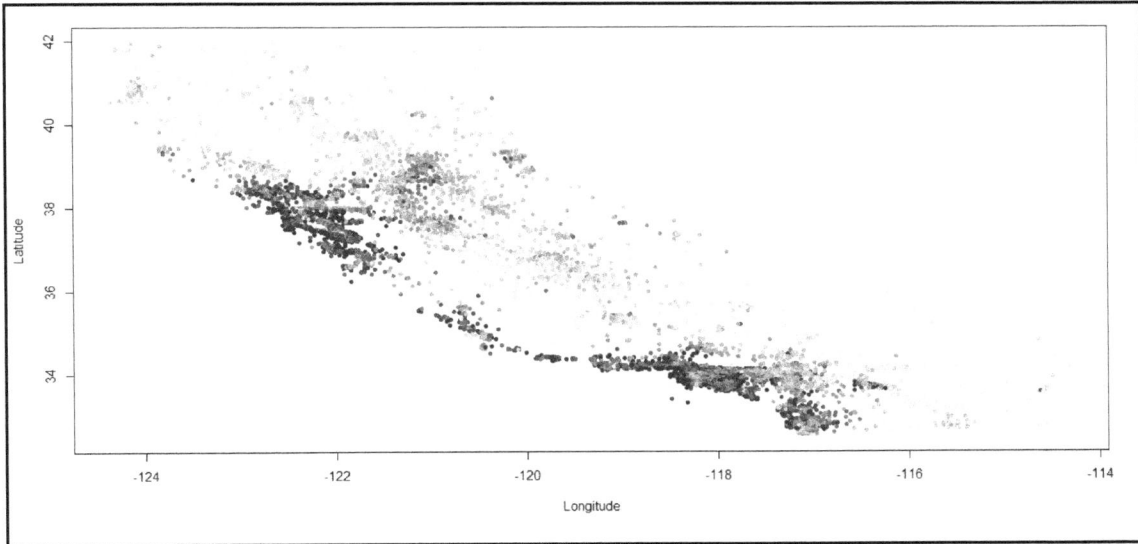

A summary of `Longitude` will be displayed. The `summary()` function is used to display the statistical summary:

```
> summary(realEstate$Longitude)
```

The result is as follows:

```
   Min. 1st Qu.  Median    Mean 3rd Qu.    Max.
 -124.4  -121.8  -118.5  -119.6  -118.0  -114.3
```

Printing the `Longitude` data frame. The `head()` function returns the first part of the `Longitude` data frame:

```
> head(realEstate$Longitude)
```

The result is as follows:

```
[1] -122.23 -122.22 -122.24 -122.25 -122.25 -122.25
```

A summary of `Latitude` will be displayed. The `summary()` function is used to display the statistical summary:

```
> summary(realEstate$Latitude)
```

The result is as follows:

```
  Min. 1st Qu.  Median    Mean 3rd Qu.    Max.
 32.54   33.93   34.26   35.63   37.71   41.95
```

Printing the `Latitude` data frame. The `head()` function returns the first part of the `Latitude` data frame:

```
> head(realEstate$Latitude)
```

The result is as follows:

```
[1] 37.88 37.86 37.85 37.85 37.85 37.85
```

The `partition.tree()` function is used to partition a tree where two or more variables are involved. `treeModel` is passed as a tree object. `ordvars=c("Longitude","Latitude")` indicates the ordering in which the variables are to be used to plot. Longitude represents the *x* axis, while `Latitude` represents the y axis. `add=TRUE` means adding to the existing plot:

```
> partition.tree(treeModel, ordvars=c("Longitude","Latitude"),
add=TRUE)
```

The result is as follows:

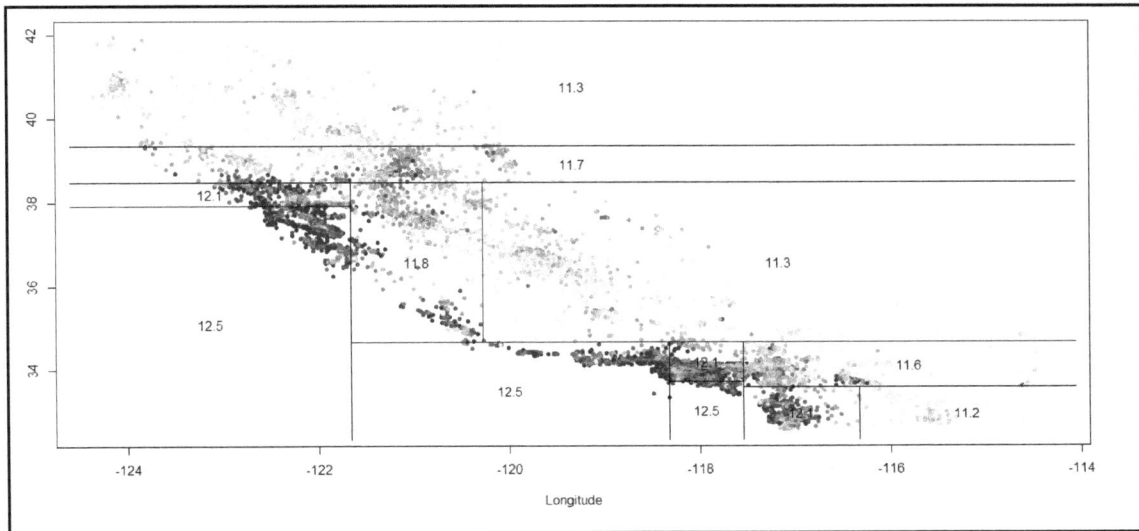

Step 5 - improving the model

The number of leaves in a tree controls the flexibility of the tree. The number of leaves indicates how many cells they partition the tree into. Each node has to contain a certain number of points, and adding a node has to reduce the error by at least a certain amount. The default value for `min.dev` is 0.01.

Next, we will reduce the value of `min.dev` to 0.001.

The `tree()` function is used to implement classification trees. The formula expression is based on the sum of the variables `Latitude` and `Longitude`. The result of the sum is stored in the log value of `MedianHouseValue`. `data=realEstate` represents the data frame in which to preferentially interpret formula, weights, and subset. The value for `min.dev` denotes the deviance that must be at least 0.001 times of the root node for the node to be split.

The resulting data frame is stored in the `treeModel2` data frame:

```
> treeModel2 <- tree(log(MedianHouseValue) ~ Longitude + Latitude,
data=realEstate, mindev=0.001)
```

A summary of the `treeModel2` will be displayed. The summary displays the formula used, along with the number of terminal nodes or the leaves in the trees. The statistical distribution of the residuals is also displayed.

The `summary()` function is used to display the statistical summary of the `treeModel2`. The data frame on which the summary is desired is `treeModel2`, which is passed as an input parameter.

Deviance here means the mean squared error:

```
> summary(treeModel2)
```

The result is as follows:

```
Regression tree:
tree(formula = log(MedianHouseValue) ~ Longitude + Latitude,
    data = realEstate, mindev = 0.001)
Number of terminal nodes:  68
Residual mean deviance:  0.1052 = 2164 / 20570
Distribution of residuals:
    Min.  1st Qu.   Median      Mean  3rd Qu.     Max.
-2.94700 -0.19790 -0.01872  0.00000  0.19970  1.60600
```

When compared with the summary of `treeModel`, the value of leaves in `treeModel2` increases from 12 to 68. The value of deviance changes from 0.1666 to 0.1052 for `treeModel` and `treeModel2`, respectively.

A graphical version of the `treeModel2` data frame will be displayed. The `plot()` function is a generic function for plotting R objects. The `treeModel2` data frame is passed as a function value:

```
> plot(treeModel2)
```

The result is as follows:

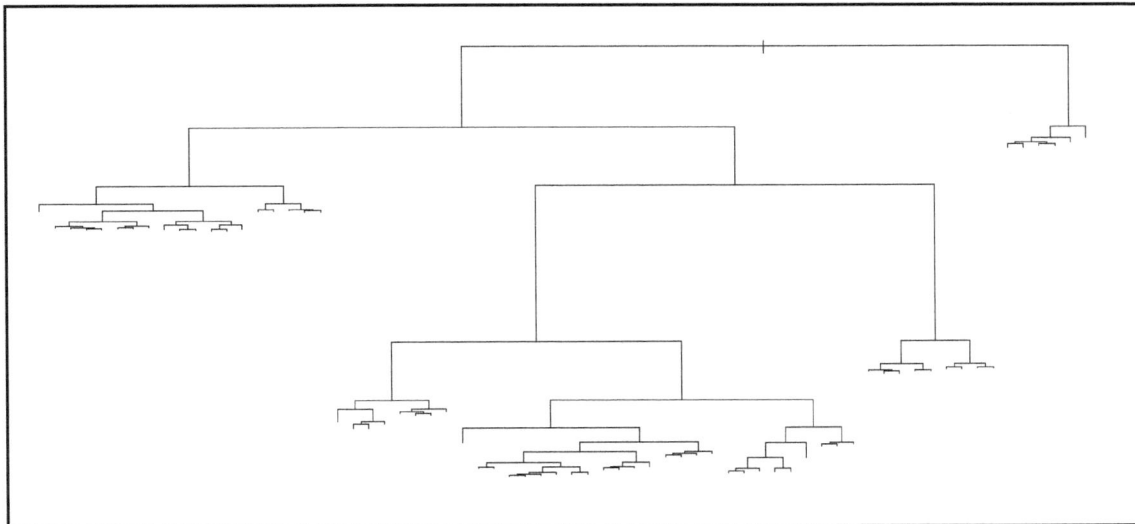

After the graphical version of the `treeModel2` data frame is displayed, text needs to be inserted to display the value at each node and the leaves. The `text()` function is used to insert strings given in the vector labels at the given coordinates:

```
> text(treeModel2, cex=.65)
```

The result is as follows:

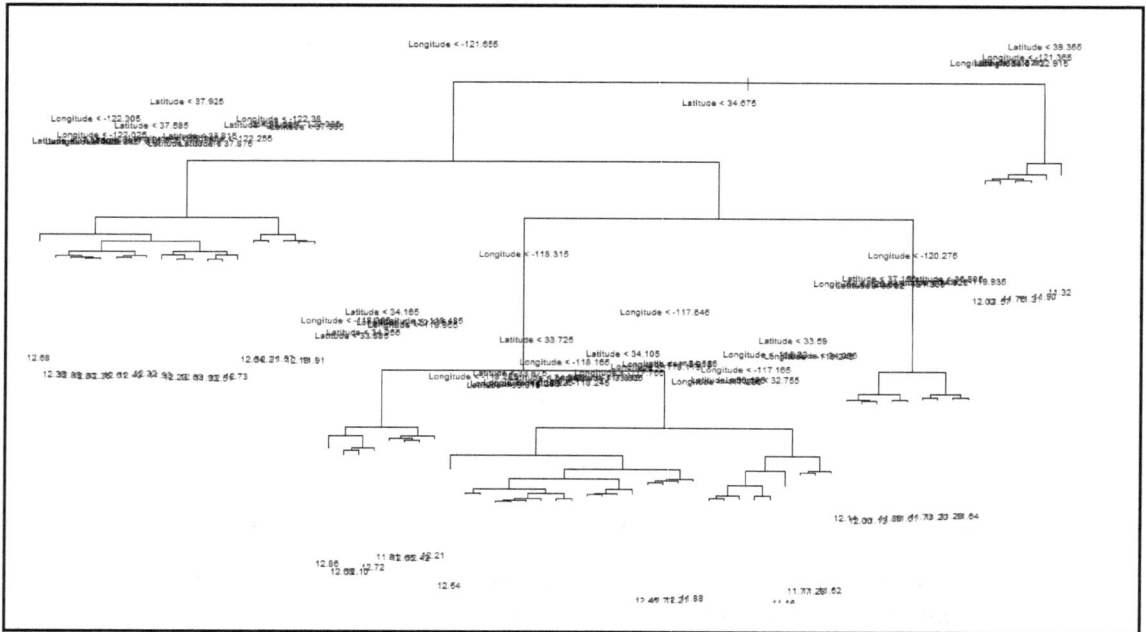

Including all the variables in the formula extension.

The `tree()` function is used to implement classification trees. The formula expression is based on all the variables.

The resulting data frame is stored in the `treeModel3` data frame:

```
> treeModel3 <- tree(log(MedianHouseValue) ~ ., data=realEstate)
```

A summary of `treeModel3` will be displayed. The summary displays the formula used along with the number of terminal nodes or the leaves in the trees. The statistical distribution of the residuals is also displayed.

The `summary()` function is used to display the statistical summary of `treeModel3`. The data frame on which the summary is desired is `treeModel3`, which is passed as an input parameter.

Deviance here means the mean squared error:

```
> summary(treeModel3)
```

The result is as follows:

```
Regression tree:
tree(formula = log(MedianHouseValue) ~ ., data = realEstate)
Variables actually used in tree construction:
[1] "MedianIncome"  "Latitude"     "Longitude"     "MedianHouseAge"
Number of terminal nodes:  15
Residual mean deviance:  0.1321 = 2724 / 20620
Distribution of residuals:
    Min.   1st Qu.   Median     Mean  3rd Qu.      Max.
-2.86000 -0.22650 -0.01475  0.00000  0.20740   2.03900
```

The formula clearly states that all the variables of the realEstate dataset.

A graphical version of treeModel3 data frame will be displayed. The plot() function is a generic function for plotting R objects. The treeModel3 data frame is passed as a function value:

```
> plot(treeModel3)
```

The result is as follows:

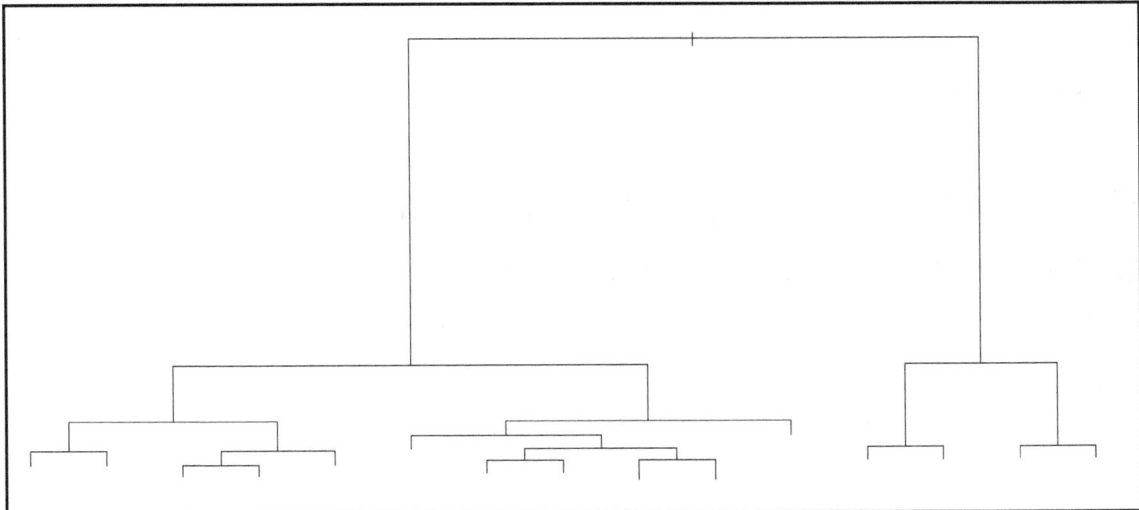

After a graphical version of the `treeModel3` data frame is displayed, text needs to be inserted to display the value at each node and the leaves. The `text()` function is used to insert strings given in the vector labels at the given coordinates:

```
> text(treeModel3, cex=.75)
```

The result is as follows:

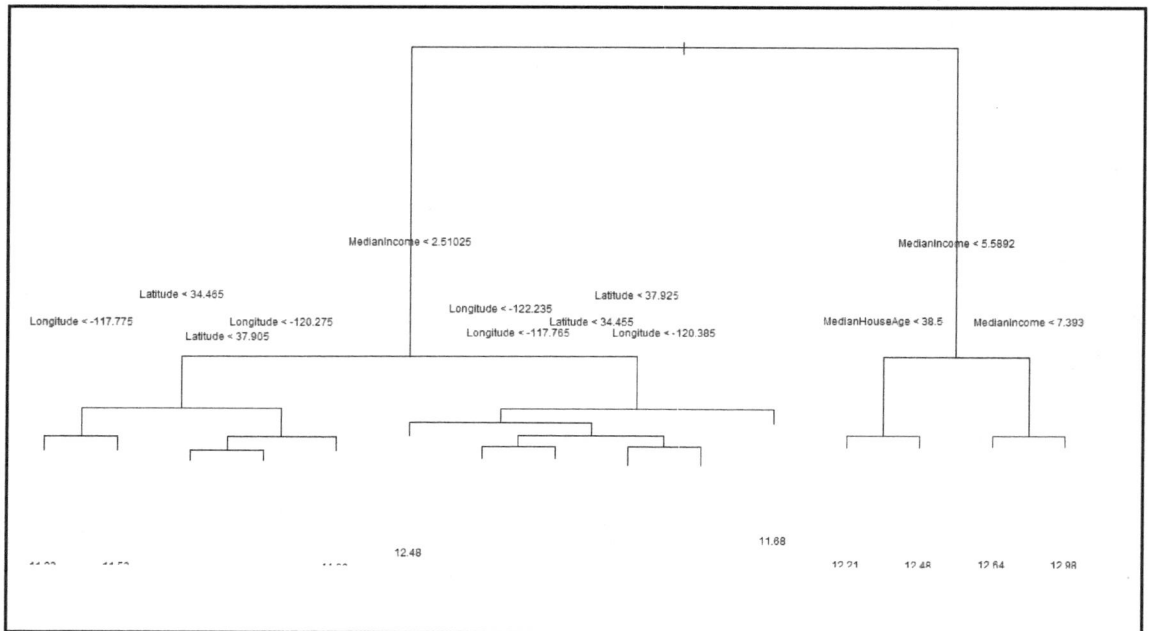

Decision tree learning - predicting the direction of stock movement

Stock trading is one of the most challenging problems statisticians are trying to solve. There are multiple technical indicators, such as trend direction, momentum or lack of momentum in the market, volatility for profit potential, and volume measures to monitor the popularity in the market, to name a few. These indicators can be used to create strategy to high-probability trading opportunities. Days/weeks/months can be spent discovering the relationships between technical indicators. An efficient and less time-consuming tool, such as a decision tree, can be used. The main advantage of a decision tree is that it is a powerful and easily interpretable algorithm, which gives a good head start.

Getting ready

In order to perform decision tree classification, we will be using a dataset collected from the stock markets dataset.

Step 1 - collecting and describing the data

The dataset to be used is the Bank of America's daily closing stock value between 1st January, 2012 and 1st January, 2014. This dataset is freely available on `https://yahoo.com/`, from where we will be downloading the data.

How to do it...

Let's get into the details.

Step 2 - exploring the data

The following package needs to be loaded as the first step to be carried out:

```
> install.packages("quantmod")
> install.packages("rpart")
> install.packages("rpart.plot")
```

Version info: Code for this page was tested in R version 3.3.0 (2016-05-03).

Each of the preceding libraries needs to be installed:

```
> library("quantmod")
> library("rpart")
> library("rpart.plot")
```

Let's download the data. We will begin by marking the start and end date for the time period in which the data is desired.

The `as.Date()` function is used to convert the character representation and objects of the `Date` class, which represents the calendar dates.

The start date for the dataset is stored in `startDate`, which represents the character vector representation of the calendar date. The format for representation is *YYYY-MM-DD*:

```
> startDate = as.Date("2012-01-01")
```

The end date for the dataset is stored in `endDate`, which represents the character vector representation of the calendar date. The format for representation is *YYYY-MM-DD*:

```
> endDate = as.Date("2014-01-01")
```

Load the data using the `getSymbols()` function. The function loads data from multiple sources, either local or remote. Data is fetched and saved in the `env` specified. The default value is `.GlobalEnv` for `env`. `BAC` is the character vector that specifies the name of the symbol to be loaded. `src = yahoo` specifies the sourcing method:

```
> getSymbols("BAC", env = .GlobalEnv,  src = "yahoo", from = startDate,
to = endDate)
```

Step 3 - calculating the indicators

Relative Strength Index is calculated. It is a ratio of recent upward price movements to the absolute price movement. The `RSI()` function is used to calculate the Relative Strength Index. The `BAC` symbol is used as a price series. `n = 3` represents the number of periods for moving averages. The result is then stored in the `relativeStrengthIndex3` data frame:

```
> relativeStrengthIndex3 <- RSI(Op(BAC), n= 3)
```

Displaying the `relativeStrengthIndex3` value:

```
> relativeStrengthIndex3
```

The result is as follows:

```
                      EMA
2012-01-03           NA
2012-01-04           NA
2012-01-05           NA
2012-01-06  92.592593
2012-01-09  93.495935
2012-01-10  96.078431
2012-01-11  97.435897
2012-01-12  98.868258
2012-01-13  47.664109
2012-01-17  57.014319
2012-01-18  45.653652
2012-01-19  79.354816
2012-01-20  59.192256
2012-01-23  67.711649
2012-01-24  65.434854
2012-01-25  71.828809
2012-01-26  84.090916
2012-01-27  51.691301
2012-01-30  43.341684
2012-01-31  49.463943
2012-02-01  61.835597
2012-02-02  79.102066
2012-02-03  88.807546
2012-02-06  91.969539
2012-02-07  94.722215
2012-02-08  94.886539
2012-02-09  98.059105
2012-02-10  57.977139
2012-02-13  72.331575
2012-02-14  56.532020
2012-02-15  40.898355
2012-02-16  21.651993
2012-02-17  55.896895
2012-02-21  54.807992
```

Calculating the moving averages. The **exponential moving average** is used for technical analysis and as a technical indicator. In a **simple moving average**, each value in the series carries equal weight. The values outside of the time series are not included in the average. However, the exponential moving average is a cumulative calculation, including all data. There is a diminishing value of the past data, while the more recent data values have greater contribution.

`EMA()` uses the `BAC` symbol and is used as a price series. n = 5 represents the time period to average over. The result is then stored in the `exponentialMovingAverage5` data frame:

```
> exponentialMovingAverage5 <- EMA(Op(BAC),n=5)
```

Displaying the `exponentialMovingAverage5` value:

```
> exponentialMovingAverage5
```

The result is as follows:

```
2012-01-13  -0.0130370370
2012-01-17   0.0846419753
2012-01-18  -0.0302386831
2012-01-19   0.4531742112
2012-01-20   0.1287828075
2012-01-23   0.2058552050
2012-01-24   0.1239034700
2012-01-25   0.1426023133
2012-01-26   0.2617348756
2012-01-27   0.0144899170
2012-01-30  -0.0436733886
2012-01-31  -0.0024489258
2012-02-01   0.0517007162
2012-02-02   0.1544671441
2012-02-03   0.2563114294
2012-02-06   0.2575409529
2012-02-07   0.2783606353
2012-02-08   0.1922404235
2012-02-09   0.3614936157
2012-02-10   0.0676624105
2012-02-13   0.1917749403
2012-02-14   0.0478499602
2012-02-15  -0.0614333599
2012-02-16  -0.2409555732
2012-02-17   0.0593629512
2012-02-21   0.0329086341
2012-02-22   0.0419390894
2012-02-23  -0.0320406071
2012-02-24   0.0319729286
2012-02-27  -0.1520180476
2012-02-28   0.0719879683
```

Exploring the dimensions of the exponentialMovingAverage5 data frame. The dim() function returns the dimensions of the exponentialMovingAverage5 frame. The exponentialMovingAverage5 data frame is passed as an input parameter. The result clearly states that there are 502 rows of data and 1 column:

```
> dim(exponentialMovingAverage5)
```

The result is as follows:

```
[1] 502    1
```

Exploring the internal structure of the exponentialMovingAverage5 data frame. The str() function displays the internal structure of the data frame. The exponentialMovingAverage5 is passed as an R object to the str() function:

```
> str(exponentialMovingAverage5)
```

The result is as follows:

```
An 'xts' object on 2012-01-03/2013-12-31 containing:
  Data: num [1:502, 1] NA NA NA NA 5.94 ...
 - attr(*, "dimnames")=List of 2
  ..$ : NULL
  ..$ : chr "EMA"
  Indexed by objects of class: [Date] TZ: UTC
  xts Attributes:
List of 2
 $ src    : chr "yahoo"
 $ updated: POSIXct[1:1], format: "2016-07-22 15:13:25"
```

Calculating the difference between the price and our calculated exponentialMovingAverage5, for example, the five-year exponential moving average values. The result is stored in the exponentialMovingAverageDiff data frame:

```
> exponentialMovingAverageDiff <- Op(BAC)-exponentialMovingAverage5
```

Comparing the fast-moving average of a BAC series with a slow-moving average of a BAC series. BAC is passed as the price matrix. fast = 12 represents the periods for fast-moving average, slow = 26 represents the periods for slow-moving average, signal = 9 represents the signal for moving average:

```
> MACD <- MACD(Op(BAC),fast = 12, slow = 26, signal = 9)
```

Displaying the MACD value:

```
> MACD
```

The result is as follows:

	macd	signal
2012-01-03	NA	NA
2012-01-04	NA	NA
2012-01-05	NA	NA
2012-01-06	NA	NA
2012-01-09	NA	NA
2012-01-10	NA	NA
2012-01-11	NA	NA
2012-01-12	NA	NA
2012-01-13	NA	NA
2012-01-17	NA	NA
2012-01-18	NA	NA
2012-01-19	NA	NA
2012-01-20	NA	NA
2012-01-23	NA	NA
2012-01-24	NA	NA
2012-01-25	NA	NA
2012-01-26	NA	NA
2012-01-27	NA	NA
2012-01-30	NA	NA
2012-01-31	NA	NA
2012-02-01	NA	NA
2012-02-02	NA	NA
2012-02-03	NA	NA
2012-02-06	NA	NA
2012-02-07	NA	NA
2012-02-08	7.805070032	NA
2012-02-09	8.085846209	NA
2012-02-10	7.922208050	NA
2012-02-13	7.922024506	NA
2012-02-14	7.696811589	NA
2012-02-15	7.283884784	NA
2012-02-16	6.569682439	NA
2012-02-17	6.272487938	NA
2012-02-21	5.955405657	7.279269023
2012-02-22	5.667469977	6.956909214

Printing the MACD data frame. The head() function returns the first part of the MACD data frame. The MACD data frame is passed as an input parameter:

```
> head(MACD)
```

The result is as follows:

```
           macd signal
2012-01-03  NA    NA
2012-01-04  NA    NA
2012-01-05  NA    NA
2012-01-06  NA    NA
2012-01-09  NA    NA
2012-01-10  NA    NA
```

Grabbing the signal line to use as an indicator. The result is stored in the MACDsignal data frame:

```
> MACDsignal <- MACD[,2]
```

Displaying the MACDsignal value:

```
> MACDsignal
```

The result is as follows:

```
2012-01-17         NA
2012-01-18         NA
2012-01-19         NA
2012-01-20         NA
2012-01-23         NA
2012-01-24         NA
2012-01-25         NA
2012-01-26         NA
2012-01-27         NA
2012-01-30         NA
2012-01-31         NA
2012-02-01         NA
2012-02-02         NA
2012-02-03         NA
2012-02-06         NA
2012-02-07         NA
2012-02-08         NA
2012-02-09         NA
2012-02-10         NA
2012-02-13         NA
2012-02-14         NA
2012-02-15         NA
2012-02-16         NA
2012-02-17         NA
2012-02-21  7.279269023
2012-02-22  6.956909214
2012-02-23  6.622470704
2012-02-24  6.298893029
2012-02-27  5.932154164
2012-02-28  5.596629643
2012-02-29  5.307348654
```

Determining the close to the midpoint of the high/low range. In order to determine the location of each day's close relative to the high/low range, a stochastic oscillator is used. The SMI() function is used for the momentum indicator.

BAC is the matrix which contains high-low-close prices. n = 13 indicates the number of periods. slow=25 indicates the number of periods for double smoothing. fast=2 indicates the number of periods for initial smoothing. signal=9 indicates the number of periods for the signal line. The results are stored in the stochasticOscillator data frame:

```
> stochasticOscillator <- SMI(Op(BAC),n=13,slow=25,fast=2,signal=9)
```

Displaying the stochasticOscillator value:

```
> stochasticOscillator
```

The result is as follows:

2012-01-12	NA	NA
2012-01-13	NA	NA
2012-01-17	NA	NA
2012-01-18	NA	NA
2012-01-19	NA	NA
2012-01-20	NA	NA
2012-01-23	NA	NA
2012-01-24	NA	NA
2012-01-25	NA	NA
2012-01-26	NA	NA
2012-01-27	NA	NA
2012-01-30	NA	NA
2012-01-31	NA	NA
2012-02-01	NA	NA
2012-02-02	NA	NA
2012-02-03	NA	NA
2012-02-06	NA	NA
2012-02-07	NA	NA
2012-02-08	80.3129074	NA
2012-02-09	82.8992932	NA
2012-02-10	81.1582428	NA
2012-02-13	81.7157047	NA
2012-02-14	81.1498062	NA
2012-02-15	78.4958391	NA
2012-02-16	71.6591168	NA
2012-02-17	68.1994284	NA
2012-02-21	65.4572862	76.78306943
2012-02-22	62.9139401	74.00924356
2012-02-23	59.2364325	71.05468134
2012-02-24	56.2995258	68.10365022
2012-02-27	50.2837296	64.53966610

Grabbing the oscillator to use as an indicator. The result is stored in the stochasticOscillatorSignal data frame:

```
> stochasticOscillatorSignal <- stochasticOscillator[,1]
```

Displaying the stochasticOscillatorSignal value:

```
> stochasticOscillatorSignal
```

The result is as follows:

```
2012-02-03           NA              NA
2012-02-06           NA              NA
2012-02-07           NA              NA
2012-02-08   80.3129074              NA
2012-02-09   82.8992932              NA
2012-02-10   81.1582428              NA
2012-02-13   81.7157047              NA
2012-02-14   81.1498062              NA
2012-02-15   78.4958391              NA
2012-02-16   71.6591168              NA
2012-02-17   68.1994284              NA
2012-02-21   65.4572862     76.78306943
2012-02-22   62.9139401     74.00924356
2012-02-23   59.2364325     71.05468134
2012-02-24   56.2995258     68.10365022
2012-02-27   50.2837296     64.53966610
2012-02-28   46.8890757     61.00954803
2012-02-29   46.3290434     58.07344711
2012-03-01   45.7386847     55.60649462
2012-03-02   46.5724049     53.79967668
2012-03-05   47.5768473     52.55511079
2012-03-06   43.9686727     50.83782317
2012-03-07   39.0152520     48.47330894
2012-03-08   37.8043691     46.33952098
2012-03-09   38.6988311     44.81138300
2012-03-12   38.4206230     43.53323099
2012-03-13   38.8030183     42.58718845
2012-03-14   43.5628586     42.78232248
2012-03-15   50.4453915     44.31493628
2012-03-16   58.2642458     47.10479819
2012-03-19   65.7203944     50.82791743
```

Step 4 - preparing variables to build datasets

Calculating the difference between the closing and opening prices. `Cl` stands for closing prices and `Op` for opening prices. The results are stored in the `PriceChange` data frame:

```
> PriceChange <- Cl(BAC) - Op(BAC)
```

Displaying the `PriceChange` value:

```
> PriceChange
```

The result is as follows:

```
2012-01-26          NA
2012-01-27          NA
2012-01-30          NA
2012-01-31          NA
2012-02-01          NA
2012-02-02          NA
2012-02-03          NA
2012-02-06          NA
2012-02-07          NA
2012-02-08   80.3129074
2012-02-09   82.8992932
2012-02-10   81.1582428
2012-02-13   81.7157047
2012-02-14   81.1498062
2012-02-15   78.4958391
2012-02-16   71.6591168
2012-02-17   68.1994284
2012-02-21   65.4572862
2012-02-22   62.9139401
2012-02-23   59.2364325
2012-02-24   56.2995258
2012-02-27   50.2837296
2012-02-28   46.8890757
2012-02-29   46.3290434
2012-03-01   45.7386847
2012-03-02   46.5724049
2012-03-05   47.5768473
2012-03-06   43.9686727
2012-03-07   39.0152520
2012-03-08   37.8043691
2012-03-09   38.6988311
```

Creating a binary classification variable. The `ifelse()` function uses a test expression to return the value, which is itself a vector, and is of the same length as the test expression. The vector returned has an element from x if the corresponding value of the `test` expression is TRUE, or from y if the corresponding value of `test` expression is FALSE.

Here, `PriceChange>0` is the test function, which is to be tested in a logical mode. UP and DOWN perform the logical test. The result is then stored in the `binaryClassification` data frame:

```
> binaryClassification <- ifelse(PriceChange>0,"UP","DOWN")
```

Displaying the `binaryClassification` value:

```
> binaryClassification
```

The result is as follows:

```
           BAC.Close
2012-01-03 "UP"
2012-01-04 "UP"
2012-01-05 "UP"
2012-01-06 "DOWN"
2012-01-09 "UP"
2012-01-10 "UP"
2012-01-11 "UP"
2012-01-12 "DOWN"
2012-01-13 "UP"
2012-01-17 "DOWN"
2012-01-18 "UP"
2012-01-19 "DOWN"
2012-01-20 "UP"
2012-01-23 "UP"
2012-01-24 "UP"
2012-01-25 "UP"
2012-01-26 "DOWN"
2012-01-27 "UP"
2012-01-30 "DOWN"
2012-01-31 "DOWN"
2012-02-01 "UP"
2012-02-02 "UP"
2012-02-03 "UP"
2012-02-06 "UP"
2012-02-07 "DOWN"
2012-02-08 "UP"
2012-02-09 "DOWN"
2012-02-10 "UP"
2012-02-13 "DOWN"
```

Exploring the internal structure of the `binaryClassification` data frame. The `str()` function displays the internal structure of the data frame. `binaryClassification` is passed as an R object to the `str()` function:

```
> str(binaryClassification)
```

The result is as follows:

```
An 'xts' object on 2012-01-03/2013-12-31 containing:
  Data: chr [1:502, 1] "UP" "UP" "UP" "DOWN" "UP" "UP" "UP" "DOWN" "UP" "DOWN" "UP" ...
 - attr(*, "dimnames")=List of 2
  ..$ : NULL
  ..$ : chr "BAC.Close"
  Indexed by objects of class: [Date] TZ:
  xts Attributes:
 NULL
```

Creating the dataset to be used. The `data.frame()` function is used to create data frames based on a tightly coupled set of variables. These variables share the properties of matrices. The variables passed as parameters to `data.frame()` are `relativeStrengthIndex3`, `exponentialMovingAverageDiff`, `MACDsignal`, `stochasticOscillator`, and `binaryClassification`.

The result is then stored in the `DataSet` data frame:

```
> DataSet <- data.frame(relativeStrengthIndex3,
exponentialMovingAverageDiff, MACDsignal, stochasticOscillator,
binaryClassification)
```

Displaying the `DataSet` value:

```
> DataSet
```

The result is as follows:

	EMA	BAC.Open	signal	SMI	BAC.Close
2012-01-03	NA	NA	NA	NA	UP
2012-01-04	NA	NA	NA	NA	UP
2012-01-05	NA	NA	NA	NA	UP
2012-01-06	92.592593	NA	NA	NA	DOWN
2012-01-09	93.495935	0.3240000000	NA	NA	UP
2012-01-10	96.078431	0.3360000000	NA	NA	UP
2012-01-11	97.435897	0.3306666667	NA	NA	UP
2012-01-12	98.868258	0.4804444444	NA	NA	DOWN
2012-01-13	47.664109	-0.0130370370	NA	NA	UP
2012-01-17	57.014319	0.0846419753	NA	NA	DOWN
2012-01-18	45.653652	-0.0302386831	NA	NA	UP
2012-01-19	79.354816	0.4531742112	NA	NA	DOWN
2012-01-20	59.192256	0.1287828075	NA	NA	UP
2012-01-23	67.711649	0.2058552050	NA	NA	UP
2012-01-24	65.434854	0.1239034700	NA	NA	UP
2012-01-25	71.828809	0.1426023133	NA	NA	UP
2012-01-26	84.090916	0.2617348756	NA	NA	DOWN
2012-01-27	51.691301	0.0144899170	NA	NA	UP
2012-01-30	43.341684	-0.0436733886	NA	NA	DOWN
2012-01-31	49.463943	-0.0024489258	NA	NA	DOWN
2012-02-01	61.835597	0.0517007162	NA	NA	UP
2012-02-02	79.102066	0.1544671441	NA	NA	UP
2012-02-03	88.807546	0.2563114294	NA	NA	UP
2012-02-06	91.969539	0.2575409529	NA	NA	UP
2012-02-07	94.722215	0.2783606353	NA	NA	DOWN
2012-02-08	94.886539	0.1922404235	NA	80.3129074	UP
2012-02-09	98.059105	0.3614936157	NA	82.8992932	DOWN
2012-02-10	57.977139	0.0676624105	NA	81.1582428	UP
2012-02-13	72.331575	0.1917749403	NA	81.7157047	DOWN

Printing the `DataSet` data frame. The `head()` function returns the first part of the `DataSet` data frame. The `DataSet` data frame is passed as an input parameter:

```
> head(DataSet)
```

The result is as follows:

	EMA	BAC.Open	signal	SMI	BAC.Close
2012-01-03	NA	NA	NA	NA	UP
2012-01-04	NA	NA	NA	NA	UP
2012-01-05	NA	NA	NA	NA	UP
2012-01-06	92.59259	NA	NA	NA	DOWN
2012-01-09	93.49593	0.324	NA	NA	UP
2012-01-10	96.07843	0.336	NA	NA	UP

Exploring the internal structure of the `DataSet` data frame. The `str()` function displays the internal structure of the data frame. The `DataSet` is passed as an R object to the `str()` function:

```
> str(DataSet)
```

The result is as follows:

```
'data.frame':    502 obs. of  5 variables:
 $ EMA       : num  NA NA NA 92.6 93.5 ...
 $ BAC.Open  : num  NA NA NA NA 0.324 ...
 $ signal    : num  NA NA NA NA NA NA NA NA NA NA ...
 $ SMI       : num  NA NA NA NA NA NA NA NA NA NA ...
 $ BAC.Close : Factor w/ 2 levels "DOWN","UP": 2 2 2 1 2 2 2 1 2 1 ...
```

Naming the columns. The `c()` function is used to combine the arguments into vectors.

The variables passed as parameters to `c()` are `relativeStrengthIndex3`, `exponentialMovingAverageDiff`, `MACDsignal`, `stochasticOscillator`, and `binaryClassification`:

```
> colnames(DataSet) <- c("relativeStrengthIndex3",
"exponentialMovingAverageDiff", "MACDsignal", "stochasticOscillator",
"binaryClassification")
```

Displaying the `colnames(DataSet)` value:

```
> colnames(DataSet)
```

The result is as follows:

```
[1] "relativeStrengthIndex3"       "exponentialMovingAverageDiff" "MACDsignal"
[4] "stochasticOscillator"         "binaryClassification"
```

Eliminating the data where the indicators are to be calculated:

```
> DataSet <- DataSet[-c(1:33),]
```

Displaying the `DataSet` value:

```
> DataSet
```

The result is as follows:

	relativeStrengthIndex3	exponentialMovingAverageDiff	MACDsignal	stochasticOscillator	binaryClassification
2012-02-21	54.807992	0.0329086341	7.279269023	65.4572862	UP
2012-02-22	58.450340	0.0419390894	6.956909214	62.9139401	DOWN
2012-02-23	42.893436	-0.0320406071	6.622470704	59.2364325	UP
2012-02-24	57.851032	0.0319729286	6.298893029	56.2995258	DOWN
2012-02-27	25.408018	-0.1520180476	5.932154164	50.2837296	UP
2012-02-28	59.487389	0.0719879683	5.596629643	46.8890757	UP
2012-02-29	68.593445	0.1213253122	5.307348654	46.3290434	DOWN
2012-03-01	56.476240	0.0342168748	5.035722759	45.7386847	UP
2012-03-02	59.539437	0.0361445832	4.781732933	46.5724049	UP
2012-03-05	53.854072	0.0107630555	4.537052201	47.5768473	DOWN
2012-03-06	16.724239	-0.1994912964	4.238735482	43.9686727	DOWN
2012-03-07	24.300395	-0.1129941976	3.918826916	39.0152520	UP
2012-03-08	65.318323	0.0980038683	3.645464627	37.8043691	DOWN
2012-03-09	70.006417	0.0986692455	3.417166445	38.6988311	DOWN
2012-03-12	48.411252	-0.0075538363	3.199182324	38.4206230	DOWN
2012-03-13	58.807692	0.0349641091	3.003753810	38.8030183	UP
2012-03-14	89.630630	0.4166427394	2.942658473	43.5628586	UP
2012-03-15	93.554439	0.4910951596	3.022805761	50.4453915	UP
2012-03-16	96.343401	0.6140634397	3.259451282	58.2642458	UP
2012-03-19	97.653738	0.6560422932	3.638235347	65.7203944	DOWN
2012-03-20	80.181102	0.3373615288	4.044359154	69.8327010	UP

Printing the `DataSet` data frame. The `head()` function returns the first part of the `DataSet` data frame. The `DataSet` data frame is passed as an input parameter:

```
> head(DataSet)
```

The result is as follows:

```
           relativeStrengthIndex3 exponentialMovingAverageDiff MACDsignal stochasticoscillator
2012-02-21                54.80799                   0.03290863   7.279269             65.45729
2012-02-22                58.45034                   0.04193909   6.956909             62.91394
2012-02-23                42.89344                  -0.03204061   6.622471             59.23643
2012-02-24                57.85103                   0.03197293   6.298893             56.29953
2012-02-27                25.40802                  -0.15201805   5.932154             50.28373
2012-02-28                59.48739                   0.07198797   5.596630             46.88908
           binaryClassification
2012-02-21                   UP
2012-02-22                 DOWN
2012-02-23                   UP
2012-02-24                 DOWN
2012-02-27                   UP
2012-02-28                   UP
```

Exploring the internal structure of the `DataSet` data frame. The `str()` function displays the internal structure of the data frame. The `DataSet` is passed as an R object to the `str()` function:

```
> str(DataSet)
```

The result is as follows:

```
'data.frame':   469 obs. of  5 variables:
 $ relativeStrengthIndex3    : num  54.8 58.5 42.9 57.9 25.4 ...
 $ exponentialMovingAverageDiff: num  0.0329 0.0419 -0.032 0.032 -0.152 ...
 $ MACDsignal                : num  7.28 6.96 6.62 6.3 5.93 ...
 $ stochasticOscillator      : num  65.5 62.9 59.2 56.3 50.3 ...
 $ binaryClassification      : Factor w/ 2 levels "DOWN","UP": 2 1 2 1 2 2 1 2 2 1 ...
```

Exploring the dimensions of the `DataSet` data frame. The `dim()` function returns the dimensions of the `DataSet` frame. The `DataSet` data frame is passed as an input parameter. The result clearly states that there are 469 rows of data and 5 columns:

```
> dim(DataSet)
```

The result is as follows:

```
[1] 469    5
```

Building a training dataset. Two-thirds of the elements in the `DataSet` data frame will be used as a training dataset, while one-third of the elements in the `DataSet` data frame will be used as a testing dataset.

The training dataset will be stored in `TrainingDataSet`:

```
> TrainingDataSet <- DataSet[1:312,]
```

Displaying the `TrainingDataSet` value:

```
> TrainingDataSet
```

The result is as follows:

	relativeStrengthIndex3	exponentialMovingAverageDiff	MACDsignal	stochasticOscillator	binaryClassification
2012-02-21	54.807992	0.0329086341	7.279269023	65.4572862	UP
2012-02-22	58.450340	0.0419390894	6.956909214	62.9139401	DOWN
2012-02-23	42.893436	-0.0320406071	6.622470704	59.2364325	UP
2012-02-24	57.851032	0.0319729286	6.298893029	56.2995258	DOWN
2012-02-27	25.408018	-0.1520180476	5.932154164	50.2837296	UP
2012-02-28	59.487389	0.0719879683	5.596629643	46.8890757	UP
2012-02-29	68.593445	0.1213253122	5.307348654	46.3290434	DOWN
2012-03-01	56.476240	0.0342168748	5.035722759	45.7386847	UP
2012-03-02	59.539437	0.0361445832	4.781732933	46.5724049	UP
2012-03-05	53.854072	0.0107630555	4.537052201	47.5768473	DOWN
2012-03-06	16.724239	-0.1994912964	4.238735482	43.9686727	DOWN
2012-03-07	24.300395	-0.1129941976	3.918826916	39.0152520	UP
2012-03-08	65.318323	0.0980038683	3.645464627	37.8043691	DOWN
2012-03-09	70.006417	0.0986692455	3.417166445	38.6988311	DOWN
2012-03-12	48.411252	-0.0075538363	3.199182324	38.4206230	DOWN
2012-03-13	58.807692	0.0349641091	3.003753810	38.8030183	UP
2012-03-14	89.630630	0.4166427394	2.942658473	43.5628586	UP
2012-03-15	93.554439	0.4910951596	3.022805761	50.4453915	UP
2012-03-16	96.343401	0.6140634397	3.259451282	58.2642458	UP
2012-03-19	97.653738	0.6560422932	3.638235347	65.7203944	DOWN
2012-03-20	80.181102	0.3373615288	4.044359154	69.8327010	UP
2012-03-21	87.538815	0.4449076858	4.492232419	74.3646318	DOWN

Exploring the internal structure of the `TrainingDataSet` data frame. The `str()` function displays the internal structure of the data frame. The `TrainingDataSet` is passed as an R object to the `str()` function:

```
> str(TrainingDataSet)
```

The result is as follows:

```
'data.frame':   312 obs. of  5 variables:
 $ relativeStrengthIndex3      : num   54.8 58.5 42.9 57.9 25.4 ...
 $ exponentialMovingAverageDiff: num   0.0329 0.0419 -0.032 0.032 -0.152 ...
 $ MACDsignal                  : num   7.28 6.96 6.62 6.3 5.93 ...
 $ stochasticOscillator        : num   65.5 62.9 59.2 56.3 50.3 ...
 $ binaryClassification        : Factor w/ 2 levels "DOWN","UP": 2 1 2 1 2 2 1 2 2 1 ...
```

The training dataset will be stored in `TestDataSet`:

```
> TestDataSet <- DataSet[313:469,]
```

Displaying the `TestDataSet` value:

```
> TestDataSet
```

The result is as follows:

	relativeStrengthIndex3	exponentialMovingAverageDiff	MACDsignal	stochasticOscillator	binaryClassification
2013-05-20	65.325949	0.0730539531	1.98313400	69.6679580	UP
2013-05-21	78.156846	0.1420359687	2.13036094	72.0639927	DOWN
2013-05-22	67.458592	0.0680239792	2.25183036	73.9600584	DOWN
2013-05-23	17.410830	-0.3279840139	2.27747286	69.4201295	UP
2013-05-24	44.080812	-0.0586560093	2.26575090	65.3480900	UP
2013-05-28	66.024066	0.1742293272	2.26484286	64.7048951	DOWN
2013-05-29	49.601280	-0.0038471152	2.24360230	63.2583992	UP
2013-05-30	63.841750	0.1241019232	2.22847156	63.6817730	UP
2013-05-31	81.114361	0.3560679488	2.26183097	65.8115477	DOWN
2013-06-03	58.588063	0.0907119659	2.29181066	65.8819964	DOWN
2013-06-04	43.695489	-0.0595253561	2.29123360	63.3093314	DOWN
2013-06-05	29.805575	-0.1863502374	2.24007639	57.6419193	DOWN
2013-06-06	20.482875	-0.2642334916	2.12973132	49.0406161	UP
2013-06-07	48.979815	-0.0094889944	2.01314398	42.7848515	UP
2013-06-10	62.039679	0.1003406704	1.91329325	39.3458410	DOWN
2013-06-11	32.449075	-0.1864395531	1.77933613	32.8078058	UP
2013-06-12	45.731641	-0.0376263687	1.64254716	26.5032382	DOWN
2013-06-13	29.609063	-0.1850842458	1.47858272	18.2167820	UP
2013-06-14	53.284086	0.0299438361	1.33046817	12.2603547	DOWN
2013-06-17	47.086977	-0.0200374426	1.18979644	6.6571619	UP
2013-06-18	53.803044	0.0199750383	1.06447974	1.9930456	UP
2013-06-19	63.525236	0.0599833589	0.96136615	-0.1580052	DOWN

Exploring the internal structure of the `TestDataSet` data frame. The `str()` function displays the internal structure of the data frame. The `TestDataSet` is passed as an R object to the `str()` function:

```
> str(TestDataSet)
```

The result is as follows:

```
'data.frame':    157 obs. of  5 variables:
 $ relativeStrengthIndex3      : num  65.3 78.2 67.5 17.4 44.1 ...
 $ exponentialMovingAverageDiff: num  0.0731 0.142 0.068 -0.328 -0.0587 ...
 $ MACDsignal                  : num  1.98 2.13 2.25 2.28 2.27 ...
 $ stochasticOscillator        : num  69.7 72.1 74 69.4 65.3 ...
 $ binaryClassification        : Factor w/ 2 levels "DOWN","UP": 2 1 1 2 2 1 2 2 1 1 ...
```

Step 5 - building the model

Building the tree model by specifying the indicators. The `rpart()` function will be used. It will fit the model. `binaryClassification` is the outcome, using the sum of `relativeStrengthIndex3`, `exponentialMovingAverageDiff`, `MACDsignal`, and `stochasticOscillator` as the predictors. `data=TrainingDataSet` represents the data frame. `cp=.001` represents the complexity parameter. The main role of the parameter is to save computing time by pruning off splits. The result is then stored in the `DecisionTree` data frame:

```
> DecisionTree <-
rpart(binaryClassification~relativeStrengthIndex3+exponentialMovingAverageD
iff+MACDsignal+stochasticOscillator,data=TrainingDataSet,  cp=.001)
```

Plotting the tree model. The `prp()` function will be used to plot the `DecisionTree` data frame. `type=2` shifts alternate nodes vertically:

```
> prp(DecisionTree,type=2)
```

The result is as follows:

Displaying the `cp` table for the `DecisionTree` data frame. The `printcp()` function is used. `DecisionTree` is passed as an input:

```
> printcp(DecisionTree)
```

The result is as follows:

```
Regression tree:
rpart(formula = binaryClassification ~ relativeStrengthIndex3 +
    exponentialMovingAverageDiff + MACDsignal + stochasticOscillator,
    data = TrainingDataSet, cp = 0.001)

variables actually used in tree construction:
[1] exponentialMovingAverageDiff MACDsignal                stochasticOscillator

Root node error: 379763/312 = 1217.2

n= 312

          CP nsplit rel error    xerror       xstd
1  0.6161391      0  1.000000  1.006621  0.0805080
2  0.1385847      1  0.383861  0.425413  0.0258015
3  0.1279509      2  0.245276  0.239488  0.0171030
4  0.0234300      3  0.117325  0.148520  0.0100709
5  0.0184278      4  0.093895  0.112485  0.0088131
6  0.0139817      5  0.075468  0.093846  0.0074399
7  0.0114713      6  0.061486  0.090516  0.0073090
8  0.0109389      7  0.050015  0.083841  0.0068419
9  0.0024909      8  0.039076  0.055447  0.0044426
10 0.0020731      9  0.036585  0.049021  0.0037592
11 0.0018220     10  0.034512  0.047577  0.0036377
12 0.0017162     11  0.032690  0.046951  0.0036975
13 0.0015551     12  0.030973  0.045004  0.0034110
14 0.0015058     13  0.029418  0.044700  0.0034306
15 0.0010804     14  0.027913  0.042956  0.0032516
16 0.0010000     15  0.026832  0.041428  0.0032116
```

Plotting the geometric mean for trees. `plotcp()` function is used. It provides the visual representation of the cross-validation results of the `DecisionTree` data frame:

```
> plotcp(DecisionTree,upper="splits")
```

The result is as follows:

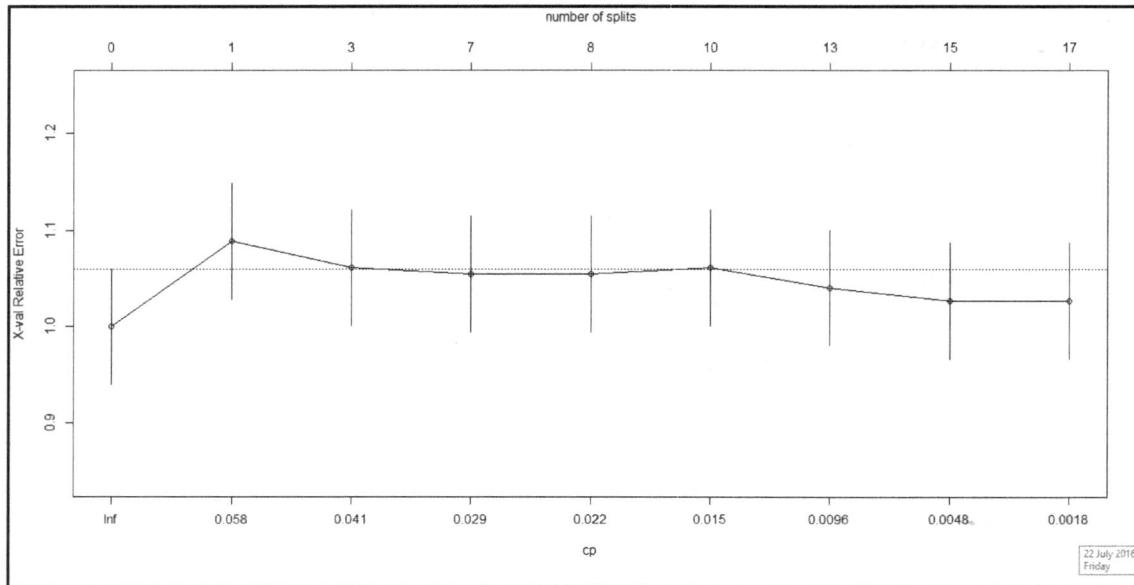

Step 6 - improving the model

Improving the model after pruning the tree. `prune()` is the function used. `DecisionTree` is the data frame that is passed as an input. `cp=0.041428` has been taken, since this is the lowest cross-validation error value (x error):

```
> PrunedDecisionTree <- prune(DecisionTree,cp=0.041428)
```

Plotting the `tree` model. The `prp()` function will be used to plot the `DecisionTree` data frame. `type=4` shifts alternate nodes vertically:

```
> prp(PrunedDecisionTree, type=4)
```

The result is as follows:

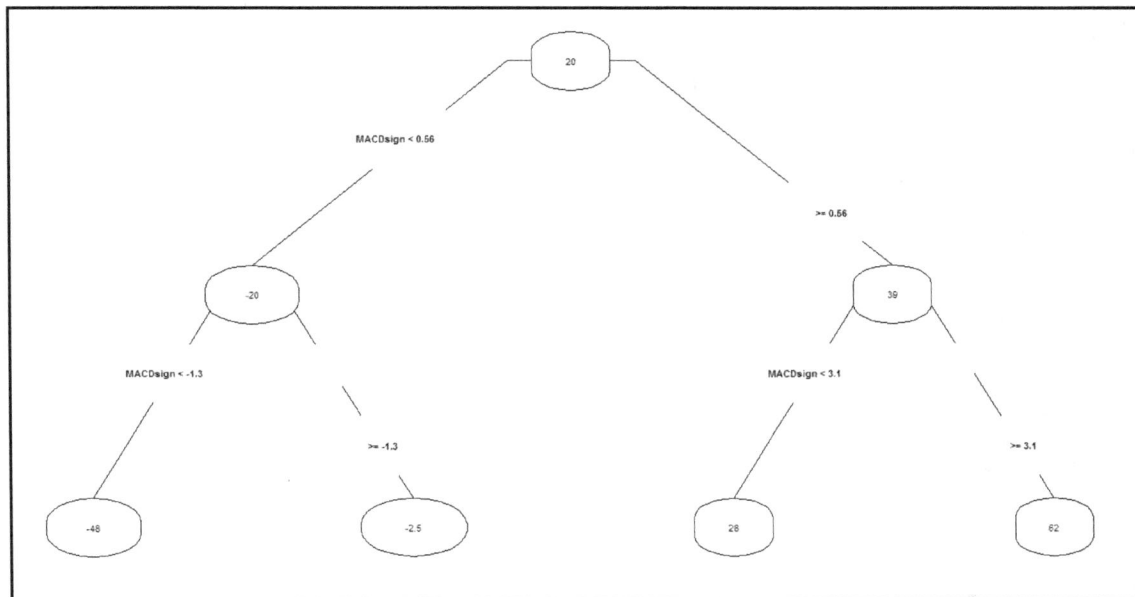

Testing the model:

```
> table(predict(PrunedDecisionTree,TestDataSet), TestDataSet[,5],
dnn=list('predicted','actual'))
```

The result is as follows:

```
                 actual
predicted DOWN  UP
     DOWN   64  53
     UP     23  17
```

Naive Bayes - predicting the direction of stock movement

Stock trading is one of the most challenging problems statisticians are trying to solve. There are multiple technical indicators, such as trend direction, momentum or lack of momentum in the market, volatility for profit potential, and volume measures to monitor the popularity in the market, to name a few. These indicators can be used to create strategy to high-probability trading opportunities. Days/weeks/months can be spent discovering the relationships between technical indicators. An efficient and less time-consuming tool, such as a decision tree, can be used. The main advantage of a decision tree is that it is a powerful and easily interpretable algorithm, which gives a good head start.

Getting ready

In order to perform naive Bayes, we will be using a dataset collected from the stock markets dataset.

Step 1 - collecting and describing the data

The dataset to be used is the Apple Inc. daily closing stock value between January 1, 2012 and January 1, 2014. This dataset is freely available on `https://www.yahoo.com/`, from where we will be downloading the data.

How to do it...

Let's get into the details.

Step 2 - exploring the data

The following packages need to be loaded as the first step to be carried out:

```
> install.packages("quantmod")
> install.packages("lubridate")
> install.packages("e1071")
```

Version info: Code for this page was tested in R version 3.3.0 (2016-05-03)

Each of the following libraries needs to be installed:

```
> library("quantmod")
> library("lubridate")
> library("e1071")
```

Let's download the data. We will begin by marking the start and end date for the time period in which the data is desired.

The as.Date() function is used to convert the character representation and objects of the *Date* class, which represents the calendar dates.

The start date for the dataset is stored in startDate, which represents the character vector representation of the calendar date. The format for representation is *YYYY-MM-DD*:

```
> startDate = as.Date("2012-01-01")
```

The end date for the dataset is stored in endDate, which represents the character vector representation of the calendar date. The format for representation is YYYY-MM-DD:

```
> endDate = as.Date("2014-01-01")
```

Loading the data using the getSymbols() function. The function loads data from multiple sources, either local or remote. Data is fetched and saved in the env specified. The default value is .GlobalEnv for env. AAPL is the character vector, which specifies the name of the symbol to be loaded. src = yahoo specifies the sourcing method:

```
> getSymbols("AAPL", env = .GlobalEnv, src = "yahoo", from = startDate,
  to = endDate)
```

```
    As of 0.4-0, 'getSymbols' uses env=parent.frame() and
auto.assign=TRUE by default.

This behavior will be phased out in 0.5-0 when the call will
default to use auto.assign=FALSE. getOption("getSymbols.env") and
getOptions("getSymbols.auto.assign") are now checked for alternate defaults

This message is shown once per session and may be disabled by setting
options("getSymbols.warning4.0"=FALSE). See ?getSymbols for more details.
[1] "AAPL"
```

Exploring the days of the week when data is available. The `wday()` function is used. The function returns the day of the week in decimal format. `AAPL` represents the data frame. `label = TRUE` displays the day of the week as a character string, for example, Sunday. The result is then stored in the `weekDays` data frame:

```
> weekDays <- wday(AAPL, label=TRUE)
```

Printing the `weekDays` data frame. The `head()` function returns the first part of the `weekDays` data frame. The `weekDays` data frame is passed as an input parameter:

```
> head(weekDays)
```

The result is as follows:

```
[1] Tues   wed    Thurs Fri    Mon    Tues
Levels: Sun < Mon < Tues < Wed < Thurs < Fri < Sat
```

Step 3 - preparing variables to build datasets

Calculating the difference between closing and opening prices. `Cl` stands for closing prices and `Op` for opening prices. The results are stored in the `changeInPrices` data frame:

```
> changeInPrices <- Cl(AAPL) - Op(AAPL)
```

Printing the `changeInPrices` data frame. The `head()` function returns the first part of the `changeInPrices` data frame. The `changeInPrices` data frame is passed as an input parameter:

```
> head(changeInPrices)
```

The result is as follows:

```
            AAPL.Close
2012-01-03   1.830002
2012-01-04   3.439999
2012-01-05   3.079990
2012-01-06   2.629994
2012-01-09  -3.769992
2012-01-10  -2.669994
```

Exploring the summary of change in prices. The `summary()` function is used. The function provides a range of descriptive statistics to produce result summaries of the `changeInPrices` data frame:

```
> summary(changeInPrices)
```

The result is as follows:

```
     Index                 AAPL.Close
Min.   :2012-01-03    Min.   :-30.1200
1st Qu.:2012-07-02    1st Qu.: -5.0075
Median :2013-01-02    Median : -0.1500
Mean   :2013-01-01    Mean   : -0.5479
3rd Qu.:2013-07-02    3rd Qu.:  3.7325
Max.   :2013-12-31    Max.   : 30.7600
```

Exploring the dimensions of the `changeInPrices` data frame. The `dim()` function returns the dimensions of the `changeInPrices` frame. The `changeInPrices` data frame is passed as an input parameter. The result clearly states that there are 502 rows of data and 1 column:

```
> dim(changeInPrices)
```

The result is as follows:

```
[1] 502    1
```

Creating a binary classification variable. The `ifelse()` function uses a test expression to return the value, which is itself a vector, and is of the same length as the test expression. The vector returned has an element from x if the corresponding value of the test expression is TRUE, or from y if the corresponding value of the test expression is FALSE.

Here, `changeInPrices>0` is the test function which is to test a logical mode. UP and DOWN perform the logical test. The result is then stored in the `binaryClassification` data frame:

```
> binaryClassification <- ifelse(changeInPrices>0,"UP","DOWN")
```

Displaying the `binaryClassification` value:

```
> binaryClassification
```

The result is as follows:

```
            AAPL.Close
2012-01-03  "UP"
2012-01-04  "UP"
2012-01-05  "UP"
2012-01-06  "UP"
2012-01-09  "DOWN"
2012-01-10  "DOWN"
2012-01-11  "DOWN"
2012-01-12  "DOWN"
2012-01-13  "UP"
2012-01-17  "UP"
2012-01-18  "UP"
2012-01-19  "DOWN"
2012-01-20  "DOWN"
2012-01-23  "UP"
2012-01-24  "DOWN"
2012-01-25  "DOWN"
2012-01-26  "DOWN"
2012-01-27  "UP"
2012-01-30  "UP"
2012-01-31  "UP"
2012-02-01  "DOWN"
2012-02-02  "DOWN"
2012-02-03  "UP"
2012-02-06  "UP"
2012-02-07  "UP"
2012-02-08  "UP"
2012-02-09  "UP"
2012-02-10  "UP"
2012-02-13  "UP"
```

Exploring the summary of change in prices. The `summary()` function is used. The function provides a range of descriptive statistics to produce result summaries of the `binaryClassification` data frame:

> **summary(binaryClassification)**

The result is as follows:

```
      Index              AAPL.Close
Min.    :2012-01-03     DOWN:257
1st Qu.:2012-07-02      UP  :245
Median :2013-01-02
Mean    :2013-01-01
3rd Qu.:2013-07-02
Max.    :2013-12-31
```

Creating the dataset to be used. The `data.frame()` function is used to create data frames based on a tightly coupled set of variables. These variables share the properties of matrices.

The variables passed as parameters to `data.frame()` are `weekDays` and `binaryClassification`. The result is then stored in the `DataSet` data frame:

> **AAPLDataSet <- data.frame(weekDays,binaryClassification)**

Displaying the `AAPLDataSet` value:

> **AAPLDataSet**

The result is as follows:

	weekDays	AAPL.Close
2012-01-03	Tues	UP
2012-01-04	Wed	UP
2012-01-05	Thurs	UP
2012-01-06	Fri	UP
2012-01-09	Mon	DOWN
2012-01-10	Tues	DOWN
2012-01-11	Wed	DOWN
2012-01-12	Thurs	DOWN
2012-01-13	Fri	UP
2012-01-17	Tues	UP
2012-01-18	Wed	UP
2012-01-19	Thurs	DOWN
2012-01-20	Fri	DOWN
2012-01-23	Mon	UP
2012-01-24	Tues	DOWN
2012-01-25	Wed	DOWN
2012-01-26	Thurs	DOWN
2012-01-27	Fri	UP
2012-01-30	Mon	UP
2012-01-31	Tues	UP
2012-02-01	Wed	DOWN
2012-02-02	Thurs	DOWN
2012-02-03	Fri	UP
2012-02-06	Mon	UP
2012-02-07	Tues	UP
2012-02-08	Wed	UP
2012-02-09	Thurs	UP
2012-02-10	Fri	UP

Printing the `AAPLDataSet` data frame. The `head()` function returns the first part of the `AAPLDataSet` data frame. The `AAPLDataSet` data frame is passed as an input parameter:

```
> head(AAPLDataSet)
```

The result is as follows:

	weekDays	AAPL.Close
2012-01-03	Tues	UP
2012-01-04	Wed	UP
2012-01-05	Thurs	UP
2012-01-06	Fri	UP
2012-01-09	Mon	DOWN
2012-01-10	Tues	DOWN

Exploring the dimensions of the `AAPLDataSet` data frame. The `dim()` function returns the dimensions of the `AAPLDataSet` data frame. The `AAPLDataSet` data frame is passed as an input parameter. The result clearly states that there are 502 rows of data and 2 columns:

> **dim(AAPLDataSet)**

The result is as follows:

```
[1] 502    2
```

Step 4 - building the model

Building the naives Bayes classifier by specifying the indicators. The `naiveBayes()` function will be used. It uses the Bayes rule to compute posterior probabilities for a given set of class variables given independent predictor variables. The function assumes a Gaussian distribution of metric predictors. `NaiveBayesclassifier` is the outcome of the function, where the independent variable is `AAPLDataSet[,1]` and the dependent variable is `AAPLDataSet[,2]`:

> **NaiveBayesclassifier <- naiveBayes(AAPLDataSet[,1], AAPLDataSet[,2])**

Displaying the `NaiveBayesclassifier` result:

> **NaiveBayesclassifier**

The result is as follows:

```
Naive Bayes Classifier for Discrete Predictors

Call:
naiveBayes.default(x = AAPLDataSet[, 1], y = AAPLDataSet[, 2])

A-priori probabilities:
AAPLDataSet[, 2]
     DOWN        UP
0.5119522 0.4880478

Conditional probabilities:
                  x
AAPLDataSet[, 2]       Sun       Mon      Tues       Wed     Thurs       Fri       Sat
           DOWN 0.0000000 0.1284047 0.1906615 0.2295720 0.2373541 0.2140078 0.0000000
           UP   0.0000000 0.2530612 0.2163265 0.1755102 0.1632653 0.1918367 0.0000000
```

The result is over the entire dataset, and shows the probability of a price increase or decrease. It is bearish in nature.

Step 5 - creating data for a new, improved model

Developing a sophisticated strategy, looking ahead more than a day. Calculating moving average to the model for a period of 5 years. EMA() uses the AAPL symbol as a price series. n = 5 represents the time period to average over. The result is then stored in the exponentialMovingAverage5 data frame:

```
> exponentialMovingAverage5 <- EMA(Op(AAPL),n = 5)
```

Displaying the exponentialMovingAverage5 value:

```
> exponentialMovingAverage5
```

The result is as follows:

```
                      EMA
2012-01-03            NA
2012-01-04            NA
2012-01-05            NA
2012-01-06            NA
2012-01-09  415.9240
2012-01-10  419.2527
2012-01-11  420.3951
2012-01-12  421.0234
2012-01-13  420.5823
2012-01-17  421.7882
2012-01-18  423.5121
2012-01-19  425.7247
2012-01-20  426.3132
2012-01-23  425.0988
2012-01-24  425.0992
2012-01-25  434.8795
2012-01-26  439.3730
2012-01-27  441.0286
2012-01-30  442.5891
2012-01-31  446.9227
2012-02-01  450.7518
2012-02-02  452.4679
2012-02-03  454.0786
2012-02-06  455.5124
2012-02-07  458.7583
2012-02-08  462.6722
2012-02-09  468.7015
2012-02-10  476.1210
2012-02-13  483.9240
2012-02-14  490.8360
2012-02-15  498.6440
2012-02-16  496.2627
2012-02-17  498.5451
2012-02-21  501.3234
```

Exploring the summary of change in prices. The `summary()` function is used. The function provides a range of descriptive statistics to produce result summaries of the `exponentialMovingAverage5` data frame:

```
> summary(exponentialMovingAverage5)
```

The result is as follows:

```
     Index                    EMA
 Min.   :2012-01-03   Min.    :400.1
 1st Qu.:2012-07-02   1st Qu.:454.5
 Median :2013-01-02   Median :522.1
 Mean   :2013-01-01   Mean    :525.0
 3rd Qu.:2013-07-02   3rd Qu.:581.8
 Max.   :2013-12-31   Max.    :697.8
                      NA's    :4
```

Calculating moving average to the model for a period of 10 years.

`EMA()` uses the AAPL symbol as a price series. `n = 10` represents the time period to average over. The result is then stored in the `exponentialMovingAverage10` data frame:

```
> exponentialMovingAverage10 <- EMA(Op(AAPL),n = 10)
```

Displaying the `exponentialMovingAverage10` value:

```
> exponentialMovingAverage10
```

The result is as follows:

```
                       EMA
2012-01-03              NA
2012-01-04              NA
2012-01-05              NA
2012-01-06              NA
2012-01-09              NA
2012-01-10              NA
2012-01-11              NA
2012-01-12              NA
2012-01-13              NA
2012-01-17        419.4390
2012-01-18        420.8065
2012-01-19        422.5053
2012-01-20        423.4116
2012-01-23        423.2768
2012-01-24        423.6083
2012-01-25        429.2140
2012-01-26        432.6951
2012-01-27        434.8124
2012-01-30        436.7938
2012-01-31        440.2112
2012-02-01        443.5201
2012-02-02        445.7710
2012-02-03        447.8672
2012-02-06        449.7786
2012-02-07        452.5916
2012-02-08        455.8477
2012-02-09        460.3772
2012-02-10        465.9377
2012-02-13        472.0454
2012-02-14        477.9753
2012-02-15        484.5725
2012-02-16        485.8321
2012-02-17        488.9735
2012-02-21        492.2292
2012-02-22        496.0203
```

Exploring the summary of change in prices. The `summary()` function is used. The function provides a range of descriptive statistics to produce result summaries of the `exponentialMovingAverage10` data frame:

```
> summary(exponentialMovingAverage10)
```

The result is as follows:

```
          Index                      EMA
   Min.    :2012-01-03    Min.    :408.2
   1st Qu.:2012-07-02    1st Qu.:452.5
   Median :2013-01-02    Median :521.4
   Mean    :2013-01-01    Mean    :525.3
   3rd Qu.:2013-07-02    3rd Qu.:579.2
   Max.    :2013-12-31    Max.    :690.9
                         NA's    :9
```

Exploring the dimensions of the exponentialMovingAverage10 data frame. The dim() function returns the dimensions of the exponentialMovingAverage10 frame. The exponentialMovingAverage10 data frame is passed as an input parameter. The result clearly states that there are 502 rows of data and 1 column:

```
> dim(exponentialMovingAverage10)
```

The result is as follows:

```
[1] 502    1
```

Calculating the difference between exponentialMovingAverage5 and exponentialMovingAverage10:

```
> exponentialMovingAverageDiff <- exponentialMovingAverage5 -
exponentialMovingAverage10
```

Displaying the exponentialMovingAverageDiff value:

```
> exponentialMovingAverageDiff
```

The result is as follows:

	EMA
2012-01-03	NA
2012-01-04	NA
2012-01-05	NA
2012-01-06	NA
2012-01-09	NA
2012-01-10	NA
2012-01-11	NA
2012-01-12	NA
2012-01-13	NA
2012-01-17	2.349176968
2012-01-18	2.705663418
2012-01-19	3.219465214
2012-01-20	2.901570272
2012-01-23	1.822016650
2012-01-24	1.490928211
2012-01-25	5.665426292
2012-01-26	6.677857137
2012-01-27	6.216280801
2012-01-30	5.795342146
2012-01-31	6.711473809
2012-02-01	7.231704486
2012-02-02	6.696875947
2012-02-03	6.211406080
2012-02-06	5.733787451
2012-02-07	6.166676687
2012-02-08	6.824514652
2012-02-09	8.324272958
2012-02-10	10.183279127
2012-02-13	11.878594211
2012-02-14	12.860669002
2012-02-15	14.071458191
2012-02-16	10.430590131
2012-02-17	9.571593757
2012-02-21	9.094168840

Exploring the summary of change in prices. The `summary()` function is used. The function provides a range of descriptive statistics to produce result summaries of the `exponentialMovingAverageDiff` data frame:

```
> summary(exponentialMovingAverageDiff)
```

The result is as follows:

```
        Index                  EMA
   Min.    :2012-01-03    Min.    :-17.3855
   1st Qu.:2012-07-02    1st Qu.: -4.3898
   Median :2013-01-02    Median :  1.2982
   Mean    :2013-01-01    Mean    :  0.7234
   3rd Qu.:2013-07-02    3rd Qu.:  5.5539
   Max.    :2013-12-31    Max.    : 15.0582
                          NA's    :9
```

Rounding off the `exponentialMovingAverageDiff` data frame to two significant digits:

```
> exponentialMovingAverageDiffRound <-
round(exponentialMovingAverageDiff, 2)
```

Exploring the summary of change in prices. The `summary()` function is used. The function provides a range of descriptive statistics to produce result summaries of the `exponentialMovingAverageDiffRound` data frame:

```
> summary(exponentialMovingAverageDiffRound)
```

The result is as follows:

```
        Index                  EMA
   Min.    :2012-01-03    Min.    :-17.3900
   1st Qu.:2012-07-02    1st Qu.: -4.3900
   Median :2013-01-02    Median :  1.3000
   Mean    :2013-01-01    Mean    :  0.7233
   3rd Qu.:2013-07-02    3rd Qu.:  5.5500
   Max.    :2013-12-31    Max.    : 15.0600
      .                   NA's    :9
```

Step 6 - improving the model

Creating the dataset to be used. The `data.frame()` function is used to create data frames based on a tightly coupled set of variables. These variables share the properties of matrices. The variables passed as parameters to `data.frame()` are `weekDays`, `exponentialMovingAverageDiffRound`, and `binaryClassification`. The result is then stored in the `AAPLDataSetNew` data frame:

```
> AAPLDataSetNew <-
data.frame(weekDays,exponentialMovingAverageDiffRound,
binaryClassification)
```

Displaying the `AAPLDataSetNew` value:

```
> AAPLDataSetNew
```

The result is as follows:

	weekDays	EMA	AAPL.Close
2012-01-03	Tues	NA	UP
2012-01-04	Wed	NA	UP
2012-01-05	Thurs	NA	UP
2012-01-06	Fri	NA	UP
2012-01-09	Mon	NA	DOWN
2012-01-10	Tues	NA	DOWN
2012-01-11	Wed	NA	DOWN
2012-01-12	Thurs	NA	DOWN
2012-01-13	Fri	NA	UP
2012-01-17	Tues	2.35	UP
2012-01-18	Wed	2.71	UP
2012-01-19	Thurs	3.22	DOWN
2012-01-20	Fri	2.90	DOWN
2012-01-23	Mon	1.82	UP
2012-01-24	Tues	1.49	DOWN
2012-01-25	Wed	5.67	DOWN
2012-01-26	Thurs	6.68	DOWN
2012-01-27	Fri	6.22	UP
2012-01-30	Mon	5.80	UP
2012-01-31	Tues	6.71	UP
2012-02-01	Wed	7.23	DOWN
2012-02-02	Thurs	6.70	DOWN
2012-02-03	Fri	6.21	UP
2012-02-06	Mon	5.73	UP
2012-02-07	Tues	6.17	UP
2012-02-08	Wed	6.82	UP
2012-02-09	Thurs	8.32	UP
2012-02-10	Fri	10.18	UP
2012-02-13	Mon	11.88	UP
2012-02-14	Tues	12.86	UP
2012-02-15	Wed	14.07	DOWN
2012-02-16	Thurs	10.43	UP
2012-02-17	Fri	9.57	DOWN
2012-02-21	Tues	9.09	UP

Exploring the summary of change in prices. The `summary()` function is used. The function provides a range of descriptive statistics to produce result summaries of the `AAPLDataSetNew` data frame:

```
> summary(AAPLDataSetNew)
```

The result is as follows:

```
   weekDays          EMA           AAPL.Close
Sun   :   0    Min.    :-17.3900   DOWN:257
Mon   :  95    1st Qu.: -4.3900    UP  :245
Tues  : 102    Median :  1.3000
Wed   : 102    Mean   :  0.7233
Thurs : 101    3rd Qu.:  5.5500
Fri   : 102    Max.   : 15.0600
Sat   :   0    NA's    :9
```

```
> AAPLDataSetNew <- AAPLDataSetNew[-c(1:10),]
```

The result is as follows:

```
            weekDays    EMA  AAPL.Close
2012-01-18       Wed   2.71          UP
2012-01-19     Thurs   3.22        DOWN
2012-01-20       Fri   2.90        DOWN
2012-01-23       Mon   1.82          UP
2012-01-24      Tues   1.49        DOWN
2012-01-25       Wed   5.67        DOWN
2012-01-26     Thurs   6.68        DOWN
2012-01-27       Fri   6.22          UP
2012-01-30       Mon   5.80          UP
2012-01-31      Tues   6.71          UP
2012-02-01       Wed   7.23        DOWN
2012-02-02     Thurs   6.70        DOWN
2012-02-03       Fri   6.21          UP
2012-02-06       Mon   5.73          UP
2012-02-07      Tues   6.17          UP
2012-02-08       Wed   6.82          UP
2012-02-09     Thurs   8.32          UP
2012-02-10       Fri  10.18          UP
2012-02-13       Mon  11.88          UP
2012-02-14      Tues  12.86          UP
2012-02-15       Wed  14.07        DOWN
2012-02-16     Thurs  10.43          UP
2012-02-17       Fri   9.57        DOWN
2012-02-21      Tues   9.09          UP
2012-02-22       Wed   9.22        DOWN
2012-02-23     Thurs   9.04          UP
2012-02-24       Fri   9.08          UP
2012-02-27       Mon   8.81          UP
2012-02-28      Tues   9.13          UP
2012-02-29       Wed  10.81          UP
2012-03-01     Thurs  12.08        DOWN
2012-03-02       Fri  11.44          UP
2012-03-05       Mon  10.58        DOWN
2012-03-06      Tues   6.17          UP
```

Exploring the summary of change in prices. The `summary()` function is used. The function provides a range of descriptive statistics to produce result summaries of the `AAPLDataSetNew` data frame:

```
> summary(AAPLDataSetNew)
```

The result is as follows:

```
    weekDays           EMA              AAPL.close
 Sun   :  0     Min.    :-17.390     DOWN:253
 Mon   : 94     1st Qu.: -4.395      UP  :239
 Tues  : 99     Median :  1.285
 Wed   :100     Mean    :  0.720
 Thurs : 99     3rd Qu.:  5.553
 Fri   :100     Max.    : 15.060
 Sat   :  0
```

Exploring the dimensions of the `AAPLDataSetNew` data frame. The `dim()` function returns the dimensions of the `AAPLDataSetNew` frame. The `AAPLDataSetNew` data frame is passed as an input parameter. The result clearly states that there are 492 rows of data and 3 columns:

```
> dim(AAPLDataSetNew)
```

The result is as follows:

```
[1] 492   3
```

Building a training dataset. Two-thirds of the elements in the `AAPLDataSetNew` data frame will be used as the training dataset, while one-third of the elements in the `AAPLDataSetNew` data frame will be used as the testing dataset.

The training dataset will be stored in the `trainingDataSet` data frame:

```
> trainingDataSet <- AAPLDataSetNew[1:328,]
```

Exploring the dimensions of the `trainingDataSet` data frame. The `dim()` function returns the dimensions of the `trainingDataSet` data frame. The `trainingDataSet` data frame is passed as an input parameter. The result clearly states that there are 328 rows of data and 3 columns:

> **dim(trainingDataSet)**

The result is as follows:

```
[1] 328    3
```

Exploring the summary of change in prices. The `trainingDataSet()` function is used. The function provides a range of descriptive statistics to produce result summaries of the `trainingDataSet` data frame:

> **summary(trainingDataSet)**

The result is as follows:

```
   weekDays          EMA              AAPL.Close
 Sun   : 0    Min.   :-17.3900     DOWN:171
 Mon   :62    1st Qu.: -5.5075     UP  :157
 Tues  :65    Median :  0.7800
 Wed   :68    Mean   :  0.1318
 Thurs :67    3rd Qu.:  5.8125
 Fri   :66    Max.   : 15.0600
 Sat   : 0
```

The training dataset will be stored in the `TestDataSet` data frame:

> **TestDataSet <- AAPLDataSetNew[329:492,]**

Exploring the dimensions of the `TestDataSet` data frame. The `dim()` function returns the dimensions of the `TestDataSet` frame. The `TestDataSet` data frame is passed as an input parameter. The result clearly states that there are 164 rows of data and 3 columns:

> **dim(TestDataSet)**

The result is as follows:

```
[1] 164    3
```

```
> summary(TestDataSet)
```

The result is as follows:

```
weekDays            EMA              AAPL.Close
Sun   : 0    Min.    :-10.470    DOWN:82
Mon   :32    1st Qu.: -0.535    UP  :82
Tues  :34    Median :  1.630
Wed   :32    Mean   :  1.896
Thurs :32    3rd Qu.:  4.418
Fri   :34    Max.   : 11.940
Sat   : 0
```

Building the naives Bayes classifier by specifying the indicators. The naiveBayes() function will be used. It uses the Bayes rule to compute posterior probabilities for a given set of class variables given independent predictor variables. The function assumes a Gaussian distribution of metric predictors.

exponentialMovingAverageDiffRoundModel is the outcome of the function, where the independent variable is trainingDataSet[,1:2] and the dependent variable is trainingDataSet[,3]:

```
> exponentialMovingAverageDiffRoundModel <-
naiveBayes(trainingDataSet[,1:2],trainingDataSet[,3])
```

Displaying the `exponentialMovingAverageDiffRoundModel` result:

```
> exponentialMovingAverageDiffRoundModel
```

The result is as follows:

```
Naive Bayes Classifier for Discrete Predictors

Call:
naiveBayes.default(x = trainingDataSet[, 1:2], y = trainingDataSet[,
    3])

A-priori probabilities:
trainingDataSet[, 3]
     DOWN        UP
0.5213415 0.4786585

Conditional probabilities:
                   weekDays
trainingDataSet[, 3]     Sun       Mon      Tues      Wed      Thurs       Fri       Sat
              DOWN 0.0000000 0.1169591 0.1871345 0.2514620 0.2514620 0.1929825 0.0000000
              UP   0.0000000 0.2675159 0.2101911 0.1592357 0.1528662 0.2101911 0.0000000

                   EMA
trainingDataSet[, 3]     [,1]      [,2]
              DOWN -0.2464912 6.938301
              UP    0.5437580 7.209192
```

Testing the result:

```
> table(predict(exponentialMovingAverageDiffRoundModel,TestDataSet),
TestDataSet[,3],dnn=list('Predicted','Actual'))
```

The result is as follows:

```
          Actual
Predicted DOWN UP
     DOWN   46 49
     UP     36 33
```

Random forest - currency trading strategy

The goal of forecasting future price trends for forex markets can be scientifically achieved after carrying out technical analysis. Forex traders develop strategies based on multiple technical analyses such as market trend, volume, range, support and resistance levels, chart patterns and indicators, as well as conducting a multiple time frame analysis using different time-frame charts. Based on statistics of past market action, such as past prices and past volume, a technical analysis strategy is created for evaluating the assets. The main goal for analysis is not to measure an asset's underlying value but to calculate future performance of markets indicated by the historical performance.

Getting ready

In order to perform random forest, we will be using a dataset collected from the US Dollar and GB Pound dataset.

Step 1 - collecting and describing the data

The dataset titled `PoundDollar.csv` will be used. The dataset is in standard format. There are 5,257 rows of data and 6 variables. The numeric variables are as follows:

- Date
- Open
- High
- Low
- Close
- Volume

How to do it...

Let's get into the details.

Step 2 - exploring the data

The following packages need to be loaded as the first step to be carried out:

```
> install.packages("quantmod")
> install.packages("randomForest")
> install.packages("Hmisc")
```

Version info: Code for this page was tested in R version 3.3.0 (2016-05-03).

Each of the following libraries needs to be installed:

```
> library("quantmod")
> library("randomForest")
> library("Hmisc")
```

Let's explore the data and understand the relationships between the variables. We'll begin by importing the CSV data file named PoundDollar.csv. We will be saving the data to the PoundDollar data frame:

```
> PoundDollar <- read.csv("d:/PoundDollar.csv")
```

Printing the PoundDollar data frame. The head() function returns the first part of the PoundDollar data frame. The PoundDollar data frame is passed as an input parameter:

```
> head(PoundDollar)
```

The result is as follows:

```
    X       Date   Open    High     Low   Close Volume
1 1   1/2/12 6:00 1.55051 1.55411 1.54845 1.55170   4803
2 2  1/2/12 10:00 1.55170 1.55230 1.54746 1.54797   2263
3 3  1/2/12 14:00 1.54797 1.55147 1.54668 1.55036   2375
4 4  1/2/12 18:00 1.55036 1.55155 1.54810 1.55095   1767
5 5  1/2/12 22:00 1.55095 1.55342 1.54967 1.55272   4271
6 6   1/3/12 2:00 1.55272 1.55547 1.55200 1.55457   4383
```

Printing the summary of the `PoundDollar` data frame. The `summary()` function is a multipurpose function. `summary()` is a generic function, which provides a summary of the data related to the individual object or data frame. The `PoundDollar` data frame is passed as an R object to the `summary()` function:

```
> summary(PoundDollar)
```

The result is as follows:

```
      X                 Date           Open            High            Low            Close          Volume
Min.   :   1   1/10/12 10:00:   1   Min.   :1.459   Min.   :1.463   Min.   :1.456   Min.   :1.459   Min.   :     2
1st Qu.:1315   1/10/12 14:00:   1   1st Qu.:1.550   1st Qu.:1.552   1st Qu.:1.548   1st Qu.:1.550   1st Qu.:  7106
Median :2629   1/10/12 18:00:   1   Median :1.588   Median :1.590   Median :1.586   Median :1.588   Median : 14113
Mean   :2629   1/10/12 2:00 :   1   Mean   :1.590   Mean   :1.592   Mean   :1.588   Mean   :1.590   Mean   : 17938
3rd Qu.:3943   1/10/12 22:00:   1   3rd Qu.:1.626   3rd Qu.:1.627   3rd Qu.:1.624   3rd Qu.:1.626   3rd Qu.: 23321
Max.   :5257   1/10/12 6:00 :   1   Max.   :1.717   Max.   :1.719   Max.   :1.716   Max.   :1.717   Max.   :155384
               (Other)      :5251
```

Exploring the dimensions of the `PoundDollar` data frame. The `dim()` function returns the dimensions of the `PoundDollar` frame. The `PoundDollar` data frame is passed as an input parameter. The result clearly states that there are 5,257 rows of data and 7 columns:

```
> dim(PoundDollar)
```

The result is as follows:

```
[1] 5257      7
```

Step 3 - preparing variables to build datasets

Representing calendar dates and times. The `as.POSIXlt()` function manipulates the objects to represent date and time. `PoundDollar` is passed as an argument. `format="%m/%d/%y %H:%M"` represents the date-time format. The results are stored in the `DateAndTime` data frame:

```
> DateAndTime <- as.POSIXlt(PoundDollar[,2],format="%m/%d/%y %H:%M")
```

Capturing the `High`, `Low`, and `Close` values:

```
> HighLowClose <- PoundDollar[,4:6]
```

The `PoundDollar` data frame captures the `High`, `Low`, and `Close` values located in the fourth, fifth, and sixth columns. Printing the `HighLowClose` data frame. The `head()` function returns the first part of the `HighLowClose` data frame. The `HighLowClose` data frame is passed as an input parameter:

```
> head(HighLowClose)
```

The result is as follows:

```
      High     Low   Close
1 1.55411 1.54845 1.55170
2 1.55230 1.54746 1.54797
3 1.55147 1.54668 1.55036
4 1.55155 1.54810 1.55095
5 1.55342 1.54967 1.55272
6 1.55547 1.55200 1.55457
```

Printing the summary of the `HighLowClose` data frame. The `summary()` function is a multipurpose function. `summary()` is a generic function, which provides a summary of the data related to the individual object or data frame. The `HighLowClose` data frame is passed as an R object to the `summary()` function:

```
> summary(HighLowClose)
```

The result is as follows:

```
      High              Low               Close
 Min.    :1.463    Min.    :1.456    Min.    :1.459
 1st Qu.:1.552     1st Qu.:1.548     1st Qu.:1.550
 Median :1.590     Median :1.586     Median :1.588
 Mean    :1.592    Mean    :1.588    Mean    :1.590
 3rd Qu.:1.627     3rd Qu.:1.624     3rd Qu.:1.626
 Max.    :1.719    Max.    :1.716    Max.    :1.717
```

Exploring the internal structure of the `HighLowClose` data frame. The `str()` function displays the internal structure of the data frame. The `HighLowClose` is passed as an R object to the `str()` function:

```
> str(HighLowClose)
```

The result is as follows:

```
'data.frame':     5257 obs. of  3 variables:
 $ High : num  1.55 1.55 1.55 1.55 1.55 ...
 $ Low  : num  1.55 1.55 1.55 1.55 1.55 ...
 $ Close: num  1.55 1.55 1.55 1.55 1.55 ...
```

Creating the dataset to be used. The `data.frame()` function is used to create data frames based on a tightly coupled set of variables. These variables share the properties of matrices. The variable passed as parameter to `data.frame()` is `HighLowClose`. The result is then stored in the `HighLowClosets` data frame. `row.names=DateAndTime` represents a single integer string specifying a column to be used as row names. The result is stored in the `HighLowClose` data frame:

```
> HighLowClosets <- data.frame(HighLowClose, row.names=DateAndTime)
```

Describing the dataset. The `describe()` function provides the item analysis. `HighLowClosets` is passed as an input argument:

```
> describe(HighLowClosets)
```

The result is as follows:

```
HighLowClosets

 3  Variables      5257  observations
-----------------------------------------------------------------------------------
High
         n missing  unique    Info    Mean     .05     .10     .25     .50     .75     .90     .95
      5257       0    4581       1   1.592   1.504   1.518   1.552   1.590   1.627   1.676   1.689

lowest : 1.463 1.463 1.464 1.465 1.465, highest: 1.717 1.717 1.718 1.718 1.719
-----------------------------------------------------------------------------------
Low
         n missing  unique    Info    Mean     .05     .10     .25     .50     .75     .90     .95
      5257       0    4590       1   1.588   1.501   1.513   1.548   1.586   1.624   1.673   1.686

lowest : 1.456 1.458 1.459 1.460 1.460, highest: 1.715 1.715 1.715 1.716 1.716
-----------------------------------------------------------------------------------
close
         n missing  unique    Info    Mean     .05     .10     .25     .50     .75     .90     .95
      5257       0    4610       1    1.59   1.502   1.516   1.550   1.588   1.626   1.674   1.687

lowest : 1.459 1.460 1.461 1.462 1.462, highest: 1.716 1.716 1.717 1.717 1.717
-----------------------------------------------------------------------------------
```

Creating time series objects. The `as.xts()` function is used. It converts the data objects of arbitrary classes to class `xts` without losing any attributes of the original format. `HighLowClosets` is passed as an input object:

```
> HighLowClosexts <- as.xts(HighLowClosets)
```

Calculating the Bollinger Bands. Bollinger Bands are range-bound indicators that calculate standard deviation from the moving average. Bollinger Bands operate under the logic that a currency pair's price is most likely to gravitate toward its average, and hence when it strays too far, such as two standard deviations away, it is due to retrace back to its moving average. The `BBands()` function is used to calculate Bollinger Bands. `HighLowClosexts` is passed as an object that is changed to a matrix, which contains high-low-close prices. `n=20` indicates the number of periods for moving average. SMA names the function to be called. `sd=2` indicates two standard deviations:

```
> BollingerBands <- BBands(HighLowClosexts,n=20,SMA,sd=2)
```

Describing the dataset. The `describe()` function provides item analysis. `BollingerBands` is passed as an input argument:

```
> describe(BollingerBands)
```

The result is as follows:

```
BollingerBands

 4 variables     5257 observations
------------------------------------------------------------------------------------------------
dn
       n missing  unique     Info    Mean     .05     .10     .25     .50     .75     .90     .95
    5238      19    5238        1   1.582   1.489   1.506   1.541   1.581   1.618   1.669   1.681

lowest : 1.451 1.451 1.452 1.452 1.453, highest: 1.713 1.713 1.713 1.713 1.713
------------------------------------------------------------------------------------------------
mavg
       n missing  unique     Info    Mean     .05     .10     .25     .50     .75     .90     .95
    5238      19    5235        1   1.591   1.504   1.515   1.551   1.588   1.624   1.675   1.687

lowest : 1.467 1.467 1.467 1.467 1.467, highest: 1.715 1.715 1.715 1.715 1.715
------------------------------------------------------------------------------------------------
up
       n missing  unique     Info    Mean     .05     .10     .25     .50     .75     .90     .95
    5238      19    5238        1   1.599   1.516   1.525   1.559   1.597   1.633   1.681   1.692

lowest : 1.476 1.477 1.477 1.477 1.478, highest: 1.720 1.721 1.721 1.721 1.721
------------------------------------------------------------------------------------------------
pctB
        n missing  unique     Info     Mean      .05      .10      .25      .50      .75      .90      .95
    5238      19    5238        1   0.5018 -0.03586  0.04628  0.21201  0.50380  0.78954  0.94882  1.03015

lowest : -0.3462 -0.3427 -0.3341 -0.3166 -0.2988, highest:  1.3657  1.3718  1.3738  1.3972  1.4310
------------------------------------------------------------------------------------------------
```

Building the upper band:

```
> Upper <- BollingerBands$up - HighLowClosexts$Close
```

Printing the summary of the `Upper` data frame. The `summary()` function is a multipurpose function. `summary()` is a generic function, which provides a summary of the data related to the individual object or data frame. The `Upper` data frame is passed as an R object to the `summary()` function:

```
> summary(Upper)
```

The result is as follows:

```
      Index                            up
Min.    :2012-01-02 06:00:00   Min.     :-0.012491
1st Qu. :2012-11-02 05:00:00   1st Qu. : 0.002766
Median  :2013-09-03 01:00:00   Median  : 0.006554
Mean    :2013-09-01 03:57:22   Mean     : 0.008594
3rd Qu. :2014-06-30 17:00:00   3rd Qu. : 0.012562
Max.    :2015-04-26 21:00:00   Max.     : 0.051020
                               NA's     :19
```

Building the lower band:

```
> Lower <- BollingerBands$dn - HighLowClosexts$Close
```

Printing the summary of the `Lower` data frame. The `summary()` function is a multipurpose function. `summary()` is a generic function, which provides a summary of the data related to the individual object or data frame. The Lower data frame is passed as an R object to the `summary()` function:

```
> summary(Upper)
```

The result is as follows:

```
      Index                            dn
 Min.    :2012-01-02 06:00:00    Min.    :-0.042220
 1st Qu.:2012-11-02 05:00:00    1st Qu.:-0.012141
 Median :2013-09-03 01:00:00    Median :-0.006606
 Mean   :2013-09-01 03:57:22    Mean    :-0.008372
 3rd Qu.:2014-06-30 17:00:00    3rd Qu.:-0.002868
 Max.   :2015-04-26 21:00:00    Max.    : 0.008861
                                NA's    :19
```

Building the middle band:

```
> Middle <- BollingerBands$mavg - HighLowClosexts$Close
```

Printing the summary of the `Middle` data frame. The `summary()` function is a multipurpose function. `summary()` is a generic function which provides a summary of the data related to the individual object or data frame. The `Middle` data frame is passed as an R object to the `summary()` function:

```
> summary(Middle)
```

The result is as follows:

```
      Index                          mavg
 Min.    :2012-01-02 06:00:00    Min.    :-0.026222
 1st Qu.:2012-11-02 05:00:00    1st Qu.:-0.004377
 Median :2013-09-03 01:00:00    Median :-0.000038
 Mean   :2013-09-01 03:57:22    Mean    : 0.000111
 3rd Qu.:2014-06-30 17:00:00    3rd Qu.: 0.004425
 Max.   :2015-04-26 21:00:00    Max.    : 0.025714
                                NA's    :19
```

Calculating the percentage change. The `Delt()` function is used to calculate the percentage change from one period to another of a given series. `k=1` indicates the change over the periods. The result is stored in the `PercentageChngpctB` data frame:

```
> PercentageChngpctB <- Delt(BollingerBands$pctB, k=1)
```

Describing the dataset. The `describe()` function provides item analysis. `PercentageChngpctB` is passed as an input argument:

```
> describe(PercentageChngpctB)
```

The result is as follows:

```
PercentageChngpctB

 1  Variables      5257  Observations
-----------------------------------------------------------------------------------------
Delt.1.arithmetic
      n   missing   unique    Info      Mean       .05       .10       .25       .50       .75       .90       .95
   5237        20     5237       1    -2.016  -1.07295  -0.54484  -0.14324  -0.01858   0.16710   0.57484   1.13343

lowest : -8426.29 -2130.42   -83.18   -75.28   -74.12, highest:    36.73    37.56    57.70    58.12    74.48
-----------------------------------------------------------------------------------------
```

Calculating the percentage change of the `Upper` data frame. `k=1` indicates the change over the periods:

```
> PercentageChngUp <- Delt(Upper, k=1)
```

Describing the dataset. The `describe()` function provides item analysis. `PercentageChngUp` is passed as an input argument:

```
> describe(PercentageChngUp)
```

The result is as follows:

```
PercentageChngUp

 1  Variables      5257  Observations
-----------------------------------------------------------------------------------------
Delt.1.arithmetic
      n   missing   unique    Info      Mean       .05       .10       .25       .50       .75       .90       .95
   5237        20     5237       1   0.03257  -1.37131  -0.69452  -0.23013  -0.02814   0.19289   0.74148   1.50053

lowest : -1363.07  -861.89   -98.12   -48.49   -38.79, highest:    46.20    52.45    66.20   107.11  2230.24
-----------------------------------------------------------------------------------------
```

Calculating the percentage change of the `Lower` data frame. `k=1` indicates the change over the periods:

> ```
> > PercentageChngLow <- Delt(Lower, k=1)
> ```

Describing the dataset. The `describe()` function provides item analysis. `PercentageChngLow`is passed as an input argument:

> ```
> > describe(PercentageChngLow)
> ```

The result is as follows:

```
PercentageChngLow

 1  variables    5257  observations
-------------------------------------------------------------------------------------------------------
Delt.1.arithmetic
      n  missing   unique    Info    Mean     .05      .10      .25      .50      .75      .90      .95
   5237       20     5237       1  0.3371 -1.47272 -0.74089 -0.23429 -0.02817  0.17183  0.70740  1.43229

lowest : -278.00 -268.28 -217.24  -82.49  -71.47, highest: 105.26 251.08 507.36 868.97 1003.04
-------------------------------------------------------------------------------------------------------
```

Calculating the percentage change of the `Middle` data frame. `k=1` indicates the change over the periods:

> ```
> > PercentageChngMid <- Delt(Middle, k=1)
> ```

Describing the dataset. The `describe()` function provides item analysis. `PercentageChngMid` is passed as an input argument:

> ```
> > describe(PercentageChngMid)
> ```

The result is as follows:

```
PercentageChngMid

 1  Variables    5257  observations
-------------------------------------------------------------------------------------------------------
Delt.1.arithmetic
      n  missing   unique    Info    Mean     .05      .10      .25      .50      .75      .90      .95
   5237       20     5237       1 -0.3783 -2.20895 -1.06928 -0.35203 -0.08207  0.19687  0.92735  2.15286

lowest : -959.5 -847.8 -737.4 -366.2 -227.7, highest: 152.7 241.3 312.5 377.0 591.9
-------------------------------------------------------------------------------------------------------
```

Calculating the percentage change of the `HighLowClosexts$Close` variable. `k=1` indicates the change over the periods:

> ```
> > Returns <- Delt(HighLowClosexts$Close, k=1)
> ```

Step 4 - building the model

Creating a binary classification variable. The `ifelse()` function uses a test expression to return the value, which is itself a vector, and is of the same length as the test expression. The vector returned has an element from x if the corresponding value of the test expression is TRUE, or from y if the corresponding value of the test expression is FALSE.

Here, `Returns>0` is the test function, which is to be tested in a logical mode. UP and DOWN perform the logical test. The result is then stored in the `binaryClassification` data frame:

```
> binaryClassification <- ifelse(Returns>0,"Up","Down")
```

Exploring the summary of change in prices. The `summary()` function is used. The function provides a range of descriptive statistics to produce result summaries of the `binaryClassification` data frame:

```
> summary(binaryClassification)
```

The result is as follows:

```
        Index                    Delt.1.arithmetic
Min.    :2012-01-02 06:00:00     Down:2618
1st Qu. :2012-11-02 05:00:00     Up  :2638
Median  :2013-09-03 01:00:00     NA's:   1
Mean    :2013-09-01 03:57:22
3rd Qu. :2014-06-30 17:00:00
Max.    :2015-04-26 21:00:00
```

Shifting class back one:

```
> ClassShifted <- binaryClassification[-1]
```

Combining all the features. The `data.frame()` function is used to create data frames based on a tightly coupled set of variables. These variables share the properties of matrices.

The variables passed as parameters to `data.frame()` are Upper, Lower, Middle, `BollingerBands$pctB`, `PercentageChngpctB`, `PercentageChngUp`, `PercentageChngLow`, and `PercentageChngMid`. The result is then stored in the `FeaturesCombined` data frame:

```
> FeaturesCombined <- data.frame(Upper, Lower, Middle,
  BollingerBands$pctB, PercentageChngpctB, PercentageChngUp,
  PercentageChngLow, PercentageChngMid)
```

Exploring the summary of change in prices. The `summary()` function is used. The function provides a range of descriptive statistics to produce result summaries of the `FeaturesCombined` data frame:

```
> summary(FeaturesCombined)
```

The result is as follows:

```
      up                   dn                    mavg                  pctB              Delt.1.arithmetic    Delt.1.arithmetic.1   Delt.1.arithmetic.2
 Min.   :-0.012491    Min.   :-0.042220    Min.   :-0.026222    Min.   :-0.3462    Min.   :-8426.293    Min.   :-1363.0732    Min.   :-278.0016
 1st Qu.: 0.002766    1st Qu.:-0.012141    1st Qu.:-0.004377    1st Qu.: 0.2120    1st Qu.:   -0.143    1st Qu.:   -0.2301    1st Qu.:  -0.2343
 Median : 0.006554    Median :-0.006606    Median :-0.000038    Median : 0.5038    Median :   -0.019    Median :   -0.0281    Median :  -0.0282
 Mean   : 0.008594    Mean   :-0.008372    Mean   : 0.000111    Mean   : 0.5018    Mean   :   -2.016    Mean   :    0.0326    Mean   :   0.3371
 3rd Qu.: 0.012562    3rd Qu.:-0.002868    3rd Qu.: 0.004425    3rd Qu.: 0.7895    3rd Qu.:    0.167    3rd Qu.:    0.1929    3rd Qu.:   0.1718
 Max.   : 0.051020    Max.   : 0.008861    Max.   : 0.025714    Max.   : 1.4310    Max.   :   74.480    Max.   : 2230.2382    Max.   :1003.0420
 NA's   :19           NA's   :19           NA's   :19           NA's   :19         NA's   :20           NA's   :20            NA's   :20
 Delt.1.arithmetic.3
 Min.   :-959.4667
 1st Qu.:  -0.3520
 Median :  -0.0821
 Mean   :  -0.3783
 3rd Qu.:   0.1969
 Max.   : 591.9231
 NA's   :20
```

Matching the class:

```
> FeaturesShifted <- FeaturesCombined[-5257,]
```

Combining the `FeaturesShifted` and `ClassShifted` data frames. The variables passed as parameters to `data.frame()` are `FeaturesShifted` and `ClassShifted`. The result is then stored in the `FeaturesClassData` data frame:

```
> FeaturesClassData <- data.frame(FeaturesShifted, ClassShifted)
```

Exploring the summary of change in prices. The `summary()` function is used. The function provides a range of descriptive statistics to produce result summaries of the `FeaturesClassData` data frame:

```
> summary(FeaturesClassData)
```

The result is as follows:

```
      up                   dn                    mavg                  pctB              Delt.1.arithmetic    Delt.1.arithmetic.1   Delt.1.arithmetic.2
 Min.   :-0.012491    Min.   :-0.042220    Min.   :-0.026222    Min.   :-0.3462    Min.   :-8426.293    Min.   :-1363.0732    Min.   :-278.0016
 1st Qu.: 0.002766    1st Qu.:-0.012137    1st Qu.:-0.004376    1st Qu.: 0.2119    1st Qu.:   -0.143    1st Qu.:   -0.2301    1st Qu.:  -0.2343
 Median : 0.006555    Median :-0.006606    Median :-0.000037    Median : 0.5036    Median :   -0.019    Median :   -0.0282    Median :  -0.0282
 Mean   : 0.008595    Mean   :-0.008369    Mean   : 0.000113    Mean   : 0.5017    Mean   :   -2.017    Mean   :    0.0324    Mean   :   0.3372
 3rd Qu.: 0.012564    3rd Qu.:-0.002868    3rd Qu.: 0.004426    3rd Qu.: 0.7895    3rd Qu.:    0.167    3rd Qu.:    0.1922    3rd Qu.:   0.1718
 Max.   : 0.051020    Max.   : 0.008861    Max.   : 0.025714    Max.   : 1.4310    Max.   :   74.480    Max.   : 2230.2382    Max.   :1003.0420
 NA's   :19           NA's   :19           NA's   :19           NA's   :19         NA's   :20           NA's   :20            NA's   :20
 Delt.1.arithmetic.3  Delt.1.arithmetic.4
 Min.   :-959.4667    Down:2618
 1st Qu.:  -0.3520    Up  :2638
 Median :  -0.0821
 Mean   :  -0.3784
 3rd Qu.:   0.1969
 Max.   : 591.9231
 NA's   :20
```

Calculated indicators being removed:

```
> FinalModelData <- FeaturesClassData[-c(1:20),]
```

Naming the columns. The `c()` function is used to combine the arguments into vectors:

```
> colnames(FinalModelData) <-
c("pctB","LowDiff","UpDiff","MidDiff","PercentageChngpctB","PercentageChngU
p","PercentageChngLow","PercentageChngMid","binaryClassification")
```

Exploring the internal structure of the `FinalModelData` data frame. The `str()` function displays the internal structure of the data frame. The `FinalModelData` is passed as an R object to the `str()` function:

```
> str(FinalModelData)
```

The result is as follows:

```
'data.frame':    5236 obs. of  9 variables:
 $ pctB                 : num  0.0198 0.0198 0.0191 0.0212 0.0197 ...
 $ LowDiff              : num  -0.00265 -0.00264 -0.00333 -0.0016 -0.00366 ...
 $ UpDiff               : num  0.00855 0.00859 0.00787 0.00981 0.00801 ...
 $ MidDiff              : num  0.096 0.111 0.136 0.103 0.163 ...
 $ PercentageChngpctB   : num  -0.564 0.159 0.221 -0.243 0.581 ...
 $ PercentageChngUp     : num  0.02176 0.00271 -0.0378 0.11363 -0.07314 ...
 $ PercentageChngLow    : num  0.1391 -0.00506 0.26256 -0.51833 1.2865 ...
 $ PercentageChngMid    : num  0.00572 0.00392 -0.08388 0.24726 -0.18416 ...
 $ binaryClassification: Factor w/ 2 levels "Down","Up": 1 2 1 2 1 1 2 1 2 2 ...
```

Setting initial random variables:

```
> set.seed(1)
```

Evaluating the features (columns 1 to 9) using the class (column 9) to find the optimal number of features per tree. `FinalModelData[,-9]` indicates the data frame of predictor variables, and `FinalModelData[,9]` indicates the data frame of response variables. `ntreeTry=100` indicates the number of trees used at the tuning step. `stepFactor=1.5` indicates each iteration; `mtry` is inflated (or deflated) by this value, and `improve=0.01` means the (relative) improvement in out-of-bag error must be by this much for the search to continue. `trace=TRUE` indicates whether to print the progress of the search. `dobest=FALSE` means whether to run a forest using the optimal `mtry` found:

```
> FeatureNumber <- tuneRF(FinalModelData[,-9], FinalModelData[,9],
ntreeTry=100, stepFactor=1.5, improve=0.01, trace=TRUE, plot=TRUE,
dobest=FALSE)
```

Using all the features to predict the class, with two features per tree. The randomForest() function is used. data=FinalModelData indicates the data frame containing the variables in the model. mtry=2 indicates the number of variables randomly sampled as candidates at each split. ntree=2000 indicates the number of trees to grow. keep.forest=TRUE indicates that the forest will be retained in the output object. importance=TRUE indicates the importance of predictors to be assessed:

```
> RandomForest <- randomForest(binaryClassification~.,
data=FinalModelData, mtry=2,  ntree=2000, keep.forest=TRUE,
importance=TRUE)
```

The result is as follows:

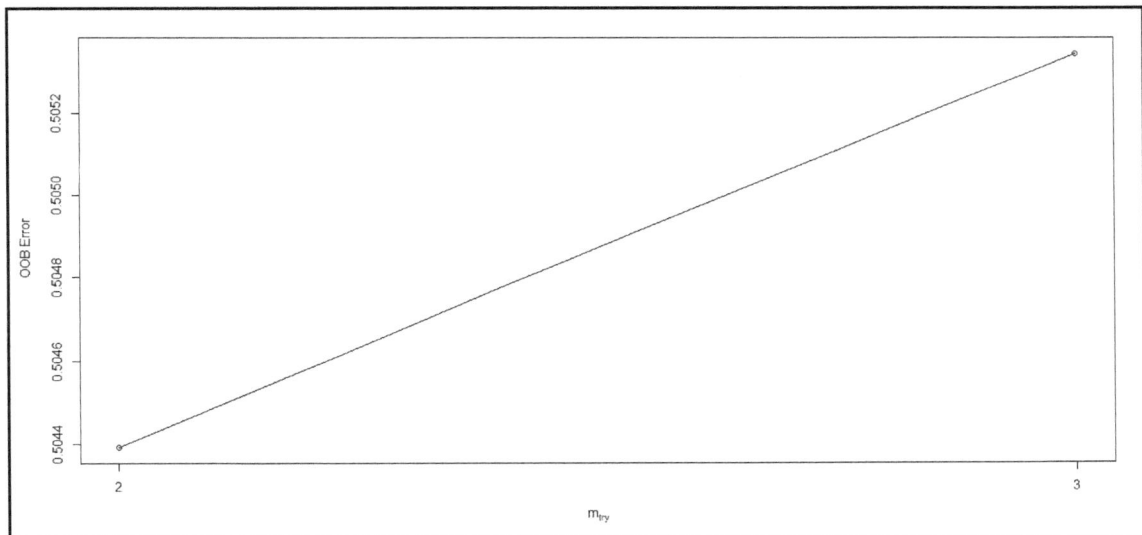

Plotting the random forest:

```
> varImpPlot(RandomForest, main = 'Random Forest: Measurement of
  Importance of Each Feature',pch=16,col='blue' )
```

The result is as follows:

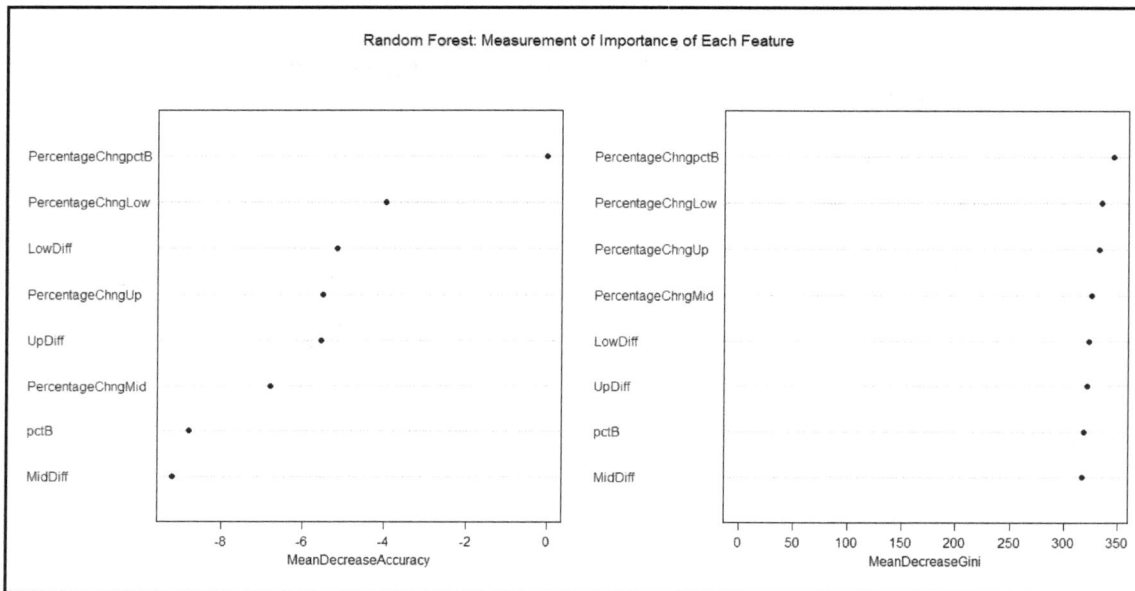

Support vector machine - currency trading strategy

The forex market is an international trading market where the currencies of every country are sold and bought freely. The price of one currency determined only by market participants is driven by supply and demand. The trading is conducted through individual contracts. The standard contract size (also called a lot) is usually 100,000 units. This means that for every standard contract acquired, the control is of 100,000 units of the base currency. For this contract size, each pip (the smallest price increment) is worth $10. Depending on the trading strategy of a trader, a position can be maintained for a very short time or for longer periods, even years. There are several tools that allow the trader to be able to understand and make decisions on the market, grouped basically under fundamental or technical analysis. Fundamental analysis takes into account the constant exchange of political and economic information. Technical analysis is based essentially on prices, time, and volume--the lowest and highest prices that a currency has reached, time of period, number of transactions performed, and so on. Technical analysis also assumes the repetitiveness of the market, which it most probably will perform again in the future as it has already performed in the past. It analyzes past quotes and predicts the prices to come based on statistical and mathematical calculations.

Getting ready

In order to perform Support Vector Machine, we will be using a dataset collected from the US Dollar and GB Pound dataset.

Step 1 - collecting and describing the data

The dataset titled `PoundDollar.csv` will be used. The dataset is in standard format. There are 5,257 rows of data and 6 variables. The numeric variables are as follows:

- `Date`
- `Open`
- `High`
- `Low`
- `Close`
- `Volume`

How to do it...

Let's get into the details.

Step 2 - exploring the data

The following packages need to be loaded as the first step to be carried out:

```
> install.packages("quantmod")
> install.packages("e1071")
> install.packages("Hmisc")
> install.packages("ggplot2")
```

Version info: Code for this page was tested in R version 3.3.0 (2016-05-03).

Each of the following libraries needs to be installed:

```
> library("quantmod")
> library("e1071")
> library("Hmisc")
> install.packages("ggplot2")
```

Let's explore the data and understand the relationships between the variables. We'll begin by importing the CSV data file named `PoundDollar.csv`. We will be saving the data to the `PoundDollar` data frame:

```
> PoundDollar <- read.csv("d:/PoundDollar.csv")
```

Printing the `PoundDollar` data frame. The `head()` function returns the first part of the `PoundDollar` data frame. The `PoundDollar` data frame is passed as an input parameter:

```
> head(PoundDollar)
```

The result is as follows:

```
  X         Date  Open    High    Low     Close   Volume
1 1  1/2/12  6:00 1.55051 1.55411 1.54845 1.55170 4803
2 2 1/2/12 10:00 1.55170 1.55230 1.54746 1.54797 2263
3 3 1/2/12 14:00 1.54797 1.55147 1.54668 1.55036 2375
4 4 1/2/12 18:00 1.55036 1.55155 1.54810 1.55095 1767
5 5 1/2/12 22:00 1.55095 1.55342 1.54967 1.55272 4271
6 6  1/3/12  2:00 1.55272 1.55547 1.55200 1.55457 4383
```

Exploring the internal structure of the `PoundDollar` data frame. The `str()` function displays the internal structure of the data frame. The `PoundDollar` is passed as an R object to the `str()` function:

```
> str(PoundDollar)
```

The result is as follows:

```
'data.frame':   5257 obs. of  7 variables:
 $ X      : int  1 2 3 4 5 6 7 8 9 10 ...
 $ Date   : Factor w/ 5257 levels "1/10/12 10:00",..: 171 167 168 169 170 369 371 366 367 368 ...
 $ Open   : num  1.55 1.55 1.55 1.55 1.55 ...
 $ High   : num  1.55 1.55 1.55 1.55 1.55 ...
 $ Low    : num  1.55 1.55 1.55 1.55 1.55 ...
 $ Close  : num  1.55 1.55 1.55 1.55 1.55 ...
 $ Volume : int  4803 2263 2375 1767 4271 4383 15191 22655 23244 10215 ...
```

Step 3 - calculating the indicators

The Relative Strength Index is calculated. It is a ratio of recent upward price movements to absolute price movement. The `RSI()` function is used to calculate the Relative Strength Index. The `PoundDollar` data frame is used as a price series. `n = 3` represents the number of the period for moving averages. The result is then stored in the `relativeStrengthIndex3` data frame:

```
> relativeStrengthIndex3 <- RSI(Op(PoundDollar), n= 3)
```

Exploring the summary of change in prices. The `summary()` function is used. The function provides a range of descriptive statistics to produce result summaries of the `relativeStrengthIndex3` data frame:

```
> summary(relativeStrengthIndex3)
```

The result is as follows:

```
    Min. 1st Qu.  Median    Mean 3rd Qu.    Max.   NA's
  0.2408 29.2700 51.6300 50.5800 72.0000 99.7900      3
```

Calculating **moving averages (MA)** of the `PoundDollar` series. `SMA` calculates the arithmetic mean of the series over the past set of observations. `n=50` indicates the number of periods to average over:

```
> SeriesMeanAvg50 <- SMA(Op(PoundDollar), n=50)
```

Printing the summary of the `SeriesMeanAvg50` data frame. The `summary()` function is a multipurpose function. `summary()` is a generic function, which provides a summary of the data related to the individual object or data frame. The `SeriesMeanAvg50` data frame is passed as an R object to the `summary()` function:

```
> summary(SeriesMeanAvg50)
```

The result is as follows:

```
   Min. 1st Qu.  Median    Mean 3rd Qu.    Max.    NA's
  1.477   1.551   1.590   1.591   1.626   1.714      49
```

Describing the dataset. The `describe()` function provides the item analysis. `SeriesMeanAvg50` is passed as an input argument:

```
> describe(SeriesMeanAvg50)
```

The result is as follows:

```
SeriesMeanAvg50
      n missing  unique    Info    Mean     .05     .10     .25     .50     .75     .90     .95
   5208      49    5204       1   1.591   1.505   1.516   1.551   1.590   1.626   1.676   1.688

lowest : 1.477 1.477 1.477 1.477 1.477, highest: 1.714 1.714 1.714 1.714 1.714
```

Measuring the trend. Finding the difference between opening price and the 50-period simple moving average:

```
> Trend <- Op(PoundDollar) - SeriesMeanAvg50
```

Printing the summary of the `SeriesMeanAvg50` data frame. The `Trend` data frame is passed as an R object to the `summary()` function:

```
> summary(Trend)
```

The result is as follows:

```
    Min.  1st Qu.   Median     Mean 3rd Qu.      Max.     NA's
-0.03636 -0.00725  0.00031 -0.00021 0.00745  0.03877       49
```

Calculating the price difference between closing and opening prices. The result is stored in the data frame `PriceDiff`:

```
> PriceDiff <- Cl(PoundDollar) - Op(PoundDollar)
```

Printing the summary of the `PriceDiff` data frame. The `Trend` data frame is passed as an R object to the `summary()` function:

```
> summary(PriceDiff)
```

The result is as follows:

```
      Min.    1st Qu.     Median       Mean    3rd Qu.       Max.
-1.844e-02 -1.220e-03  2.000e-05 -6.253e-06  1.200e-03  2.699e-02
```

Step 4 - preparing variables to build datasets

Creating a binary classification variable. The `ifelse()` function uses a test expression to return the value, which is itself a vector and is of the same length as the test expression. The vector returned has an element from x if the corresponding value of the test expression is TRUE, or from y if the corresponding value of the test expression is FALSE.

Here, `PriceChange>0` is the test function, which is to be tested in a logical mode. UP and DOWN perform the logical test. The result is then stored in the `binaryClassification` data frame:

```
> binaryClassification <- ifelse(PriceDiff>0,"UP","DOWN")
```

Printing the summary of the `binaryClassification` data frame. The `Trend` data frame is passed as an R object to the `summary()` function:

```
> summary(binaryClassification)
```

The result is as follows:

```
        Length      Class       Mode
        5257    character   character
```

Combining the relative StrengthIndex3, Trend, and binaryClassification data frames. The variables passed as parameters to data.frame() are relativeStrengthIndex3, Trend, and binaryClassification. The result is then stored in the DataSet data frame:

```
> DataSet <- data.frame(relativeStrengthIndex3, Trend,
binaryClassification)
```

Printing the summary of the DataSet data frame. The Trend data frame is passed as an R object to the summary() function:

```
> summary(DataSet)
```

The result is as follows:

```
relativeStrengthIndex3        Trend              binaryClassification
Min.    : 0.6199      Min.     :-0.03636      DOWN:2618
1st Qu.:28.8542       1st Qu.:-0.00725        UP  :2639
Median :50.6667       Median : 0.00031
Mean    :50.3598      Mean     :-0.00021
3rd Qu.:72.0845       3rd Qu.: 0.00745
Max.    :99.5032      Max.     : 0.03877
NA's    :3            NA's     :49
```

Exploring the internal structure of the DataSet data frame. The str() function displays the internal structure of the data frame. The DataSet is passed as an R object to the str() function:

```
> str(DataSet)
```

The result is as follows:

```
'data.frame':   5257 obs. of  3 variables:
 $ relativeStrengthIndex3: num   NA NA NA 49 54.5 ...
 $ Trend                 : num   NA NA NA NA NA NA NA NA NA NA ...
 $ binaryClassification  : Factor w/ 2 levels "DOWN","UP": 2 1 2 2 2 2 2 2 2 1 ...
```

Calculating the indicators, creating a dataset, and removing the points:

```
> DataSet <- DataSet[-c(1:49),]
```

Exploring the dimensions of the `DataSet` data frame. The `dim()` function returns the dimensions of the `DataSet` frame. The `DataSet` data frame is passed as an input parameter. The result clearly states that there are 5,208 rows of data and 3 columns:

```
> dim(DataSet)
```

The result is as follows:

```
[1] 5208    3
```

Separating the training dataset:

```
> TrainingDataSet <- DataSet[1:4528,]
```

Exploring the dimensions of the `TrainingDataSet` data frame. The `dim()` function returns the dimensions of the `TrainingDataSet` frame. The `TrainingDataSet` data frame is passed as an input parameter. The result clearly states that there are 4,528 rows of data and 3 columns:

```
> dim(TrainingDataSet)
```

The result is as follows:

```
[1] 4528    3
```

Printing the summary of the `TrainingDataSet` data frame. The `TrainingDataSet` data frame is passed as an R object to the `summary()` function:

```
> summary(TrainingDataSet)
```

The result is as follows:

```
relativeStrengthIndex3        Trend                binaryClassification
Min.    : 0.6199       Min.    :-0.0363598    DOWN:2247
1st Qu.:29.1705       1st Qu.:-0.0071439    UP  :2281
Median :50.8829       Median : 0.0006596
Mean   :50.7597       Mean    : 0.0001243
3rd Qu.:72.5465       3rd Qu.: 0.0077117
Max.    :99.5032       Max.    : 0.0387742
```

Separating the testing dataset:

```
> TestDataSet <- DataSet[4529:6038,]
```

Exploring the dimensions of the `TestDataSet` data frame. The `dim()` function returns the dimensions of the `TestDataSet` frame. The `TestDataSet` data frame is passed as an input parameter. The result clearly states that there are 1,510 rows of data and 3 columns:

```
> dim(TestDataSet)
```

```
[1] 1510      3
```

Printing the summary of the `TestDataSet` data frame. The `TestDataSet` data frame is passed as an R object to the `summary()` function:

```
> summary(TestDataSet)
```

The result is as follows:

```
relativeStrengthIndex3        Trend                binaryClassification
Min.    : 0.966        Min.    :-0.0363      DOWN:347
1st Qu.:26.358        1st Qu.:-0.0082      UP  :333
Median :49.089        Median :-0.0014      NA's:830
Mean   :48.071        Mean    :-0.0025
3rd Qu.:69.500        3rd Qu.: 0.0059
Max.    :96.014        Max.    : 0.0240
NA's    :830          NA's    :830
```

Step 5 - building the model

Building support vector machines using the `svm()` function.
`binaryClassification~relativeStrengthIndex3+Trend` is used as the formula.
`data=TrainingDataSet` is used as a data frame which contains the variables of the model.
`kernel="radial"` means that the radial basis kernel function is used in training and
predicting. `cost=1` indicates the cost of constraints violation. `gamma=1/2` indicates the
parameter needed for all kernel functions except linear:

```
> SVM <- svm(binaryClassification~relativeStrengthIndex3+Trend,
  data=TrainingDataSet, kernel="radial", cost=1, gamma=1/2)
```

Printing the summary of the SVM data frame. The SVM data frame is passed as an R object to
the `summary()` function:

```
> summary(SVM)
```

The result is as follows:

```
Call:
svm(formula = binaryClassification ~ relativeStrengthIndex3 + Trend, data = TrainingDataSet, kernel = "radial",
    cost = 1, gamma = 1/2)


Parameters:
  SVM-Type:  C-classification
 SVM-Kernel:  radial
      cost:  1
     gamma:  0.5

Number of Support Vectors:  4401

 ( 2202 2199 )


Number of Classes:  2

Levels:
 DOWN UP
```

In order to predict the value based on the model object, we will use the `predict()`
function. SVM is passed as an object. The `TrainingDataSet` data object is passed as an
object in which to look for variables with which to predict:

```
> TrainingPredictions <- predict(SVM, TrainingDataSet, type="class")
```

Printing the summary of the `TrainingPredictions` data frame. The SVM data frame is passed as an R object to the `summary()` function:

```
> summary(TrainingPredictions)
```

The result is as follows:

```
DOWN    UP
2205  2323
```

Describing the dataset. The `describe()` function provides item analysis. `TrainingPredictions` is passed as an input argument:

```
> describe(TrainingPredictions)
```

The result is as follows:

```
TrainingPredictions
      n  missing   unique
   4528        0        2

DOWN (2205, 49%), UP (2323, 51%)
```

Combining the `TrainingDataSet` and `TrainingPredictions` data frames. The variables passed as parameters to `data.frame()` are `TrainingDataSet` and `TrainingPredictions`. The result is then stored in the `TrainingDatadata` frame:

```
> TrainingData <- data.frame (TrainingDataSet, TrainingPredictions)
```

Printing the summary of the `TrainingData` data frame. The `TrainingData` data frame is passed as an R object to the `summary()` function:

```
> summary(TrainingData)
```

The result is as follows:

```
relativeStrengthIndex3      Trend                 binaryClassification TrainingPredictions
Min.    : 0.6199      Min.     :-0.0363598      DOWN:2247            DOWN:2205
1st Qu.:29.1705      1st Qu.:-0.0071439      UP  :2281            UP  :2323
Median :50.8829      Median : 0.0006596
Mean    :50.7597      Mean     : 0.0001243
3rd Qu.:72.5465      3rd Qu.: 0.0077117
Max.    :99.5032      Max.     : 0.0387742
```

Printing the `TrainingData`:

```
> ggplot(TrainingData,aes(x=Trend,y=relativeStrengthIndex3))
+stat_density2d(geom="contour",aes(color=TrainingPredictions))
+labs(,x="Open - SMA50",y="RSI3",color="Training Predictions")
```

The result is as follows:

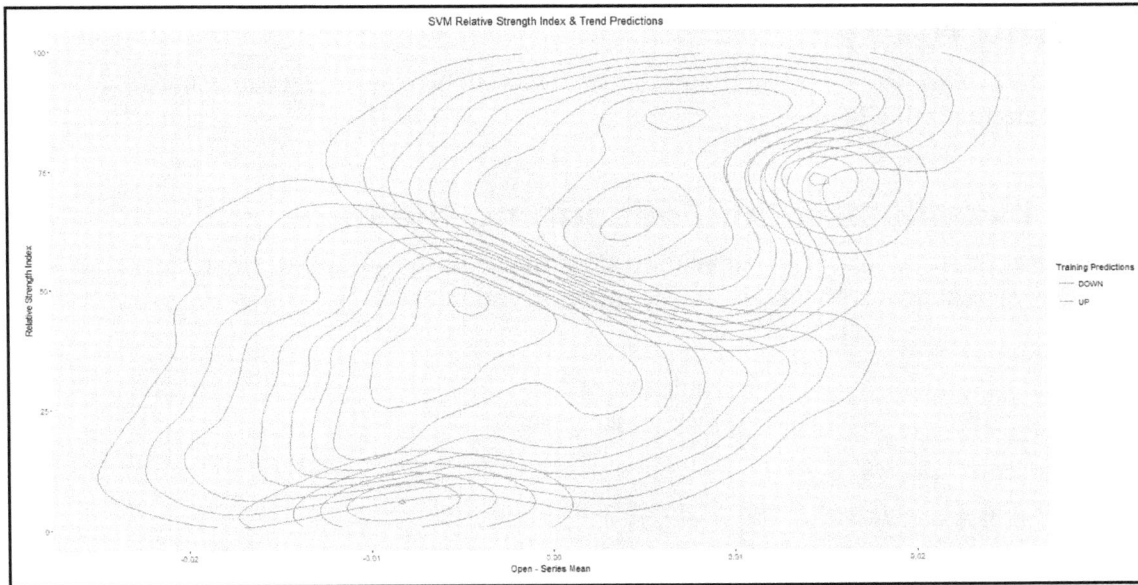

Stochastic gradient descent - adult income

Stochastic gradient descent also known as **incremental** gradient descent, is a stochastic approximation of the gradient descent optimization method for minimizing an objective function that is written as a sum of differentiable functions. It tries to find minima or maxima by iteration. In stochastic gradient descent, the true gradient of $Q(w)$ is approximated by a gradient at a single example:

$$w := w - \alpha \nabla Q_i(w)$$

As the algorithm sweeps through the training set, it performs the above update for each training example. Several passes can be made over the training set until the algorithm converges. If this is done, the data can be shuffled for each pass to prevent cycles. Typical implementations may use an adaptive learning rate so that the algorithm converges.

Getting ready

In order to perform stochastic gradient descent, we will be using a dataset collected from census data to predict income.

Step 1 - collecting and describing the data

The dataset titled `adult.txt` will be used. The dataset is in standard format. There are 32,561 rows of data and 15 variables. The numeric variables are as follows:

- `age`
- `fnlwgt`
- `education-num`
- `capital-gain`
- `capital-loss`
- `hours-per-week`

The non-numeric variables are as follows:

- `workclass`
- `education`
- `marital-status`
- `occupation`
- `relationship`
- `race`
- `sex`
- `native-country`
- `incomerange`

How to do it...

Let's get into the details.

Step 2 - exploring the data

Each of the following libraries is required to be installed:

```
> library("klar")
> library("caret")
> library ("stringr")
```

Version info: Code for this page was tested in R version 3.3.0 (2016-05-03).

Let's explore the data and understand the relationships between the variables. We'll begin by importing the TXT data file named `adult.txt`. We will be saving the data to the labels data frame:

```
> labels <- read.csv("d:/adult.txt")
```

Exploring the internal structure of the `allData` data frame. The `str()` function displays the internal structure of the data frame. `allData` is passed as an R object to the `str()` function:

```
> str(allData)
```

The result is as follows:

```
'data.frame':   32561 obs. of  15 variables:
 $ V1 : Factor w/ 73 levels "17,","18,","19,",..: 23 34 22 37 12 21 33 36 15 26 ...
 $ V2 : Factor w/ 9 levels "?,","Federal-gov,",..: 8 7 5 5 5 5 5 7 5 5 ...
 $ V3 : Factor w/ 21648 levels "100009,","100029,",..: 20430 20692 10269 11554 16171 14136 4680 9797 18599 4604 ...
 $ V4 : Factor w/ 16 levels "10th,","11th,",..: 10 10 12 2 10 13 7 12 13 10 ...
 $ V5 : Factor w/ 16 levels "1,","10,","11,",..: 5 5 16 14 5 6 12 16 6 5 ...
 $ V6 : Factor w/ 7 levels "Divorced,","Married-AF-spouse,",..: 5 3 1 3 3 3 4 3 5 3 ...
 $ V7 : Factor w/ 15 levels "?,","Adm-clerical,",..: 2 5 7 7 11 5 9 5 11 5 ...
 $ V8 : Factor w/ 6 levels "Husband,","Not-in-family,",..: 2 1 2 1 6 6 2 1 2 1 ...
 $ V9 : Factor w/ 5 levels "Amer-Indian-Eskimo,",..: 5 5 5 3 3 5 3 5 5 5 ...
 $ V10: Factor w/ 2 levels "Female,","Male,": 2 2 2 2 1 1 1 2 1 2 ...
 $ V11: Factor w/ 119 levels "0,","10520,",..: 34 1 1 1 1 1 1 1 13 95 ...
 $ V12: Factor w/ 92 levels "0,","1092,","1138,",..: 1 1 1 1 1 1 1 1 1 1 ...
 $ V13: Factor w/ 94 levels "1,","10,","11,",..: 35 5 35 35 35 35 8 40 46 35 ...
 $ V14: Factor w/ 42 levels "?,","Cambodia,",..: 40 40 40 40 6 40 24 40 40 40 ...
 $ V15: Factor w/ 2 levels "<=50K",">50K": 1 1 1 1 1 1 1 2 2 2 ...
```

Step 3 - preparing the data

Grabbing the labels from the main file. The `as.factor()` function is used to encode the `allData[,15]` vector as a factor. This is to ensure format compatibility. The result is then stored in the `labels` data frame:

```
> labels <- as.factor(allData[,15])
```

Grabbing all the features of the data after removing the labels. The result is stored in the `allFeatures` data frame:

```
> allFeatures <- allData[,-c(15)]
```

Printing the `allFeatures` data frame. The `head()` function returns the first part of the `allFeatures` data frame. The `allFeatures` data frame is passed as an input parameter:

```
> head(allFeatures)
```

The result is as follows:

```
     V1              V2      V3         V4  V5                  V6                V7            V8      V9     V10
1 39,        State-gov,  77516, Bachelors, 13,      Never-married,      Adm-clerical, Not-in-family, white,   Male,
2 50, Self-emp-not-inc,  83311, Bachelors, 13, Married-civ-spouse,   Exec-managerial,       Husband, white,   Male,
3 38,          Private, 215646,   HS-grad,  9,           Divorced, Handlers-cleaners, Not-in-family, white,   Male,
4 53,          Private, 234721,      11th,  7, Married-civ-spouse, Handlers-cleaners,       Husband, Black,   Male,
5 28,          Private, 338409, Bachelors, 13, Married-civ-spouse,    Prof-specialty,         wife, Black, Female,
6 37,          Private, 284582,   Masters, 14, Married-civ-spouse,   Exec-managerial,         wife, white, Female,
     V11 V12 V13            V14
1 2174,   0,  40, United-States,
2    0,   0,  13, United-States,
3    0,   0,  40, United-States,
4    0,   0,  40, United-States,
5    0,   0,  40,          Cuba,
6    0,   0,  40, United-States,
```

Normalizing the features. The mean and scale are converted to z scores so that the variance = 1. `scale()` function's default method centers and/or scales the columns of a numeric matrix. `continuousFeatures` is the numeric matrix. The result is then stored in the `continuousFeatures` data frame:

```
> continuousFeatures <- scale(continuousFeatures)
```

Printing the `continuousFeatures` data frame. The `head()` function returns the first part of the `continuousFeatures` data frame. The `continuousFeatures` data frame is passed as an input parameter:

```
> head(continuousFeatures)
```

The result is as follows:

```
               V1          V3          V5         V11        V12         V13
[1,]    0.03067009  -1.0635944   1.1347213   0.1484506  -0.2166562  -0.0354289
[2,]    0.83709613  -1.0086915   1.1347213  -0.1459182  -0.2166562  -2.2221190
[3,]   -0.04264137   0.2450747  -0.4200532  -0.1459182  -0.2166562  -0.0354289
[4,]    1.05703050   0.4257948  -1.1974404  -0.1459182  -0.2166562  -0.0354289
[5,]   -0.77575595   1.4081541   1.1347213  -0.1459182  -0.2166562  -0.0354289
[6,]   -0.11595283   0.8981871   1.5234150  -0.1459182  -0.2166562  -0.0354289
```

Converting labels into a 1 or -1. The rep() function is used to replicate values. The result is then stored in the labels.n data frame:

```
> labels.n = rep(0,length(labels))
> labels.n[labels==" <=50K"] = -1
> labels.n[labels==" >50K"] = 1
> labels = labels.n
> rm(labels.n)
```

Separating training datasets. The createDataPartition() function creates a set of training data partitions. y=labels indicates the vector for outcomes. p=.8 means 80% of the data is used for training datasets:

```
> trainingData <- createDataPartition(y=labels, p=.8, list=FALSE)
```

Exploring the dimensions of the trainingData data frame. The dim() function returns the dimensions of the trainingData frame. The trainingData data frame is passed as an input parameter. The result clearly states that there are 26,049 rows of data and a single column:

```
> dim(trainingData)
```

The result is as follows:

```
[1] 26049        1
```

Creating training features and training labels of the trainingData data frame:

```
> trainingFeatures <- continuousFeatures[trainingData,]
> trainingLabels <- labels[trainingData]
```

Figuring out the remaining 20% of data for testing and validation:

```
> remainingLabels <- labels[-trainingData]
> remainingFeatures <- continuousFeatures[-trainingData,]
```

Creating the testing features and testing labels of the `trainingData` data frame. Of the 20% data, 50% of that data is used for testing purposes, while the remaining 50% is used for validation purposes.

The `createDataPartition()` function creates a set of training data partitions. `y=remainingLabels` indicates the vector for outcomes. `p=.5` means 50% of the data is used for training datasets. The result is then stored in the `testingData` data frame:

```
> testingData <- createDataPartition(y=remainingLabels, p=.5,
list=FALSE)
> testingLabels <- remainingLabels[testingData]
> testingFeatures <- remainingFeatures[testingData,]
```

Creating validation features and testing labels of the `testingData` data frame:

```
> validationLabels <- remainingLabels[-testingData]
> validationFeatures <- remainingFeatures[-testingData,]
```

Defining the accuracy measure required:

```
> getAccuracy <- function(a,b,features,labels){
+       estFxn = features %*% a + b;
+       predictedLabels = rep(0,length(labels));
+       predictedLabels[estFxn < 0] = -1 ;
+       predictedLabels[estFxn >= 0] = 1 ;
+       return(sum(predictedLabels == labels) / length(labels))
+ }
```

Step 4 - building the model

Setting up the initial parameters:

```
> numEpochs = 100
> numStepsPerEpoch = 500
> nStepsPerPlot = 30
> evalidationSetSize = 50
> c1 = 0.01
> c2 = 50
```

Combining a set of arguments. The result is stored in the `lambda_vals` data frame:

```
> lambda_vals = c(0.001, 0.01, 0.1, 1)
> bestAccuracy = 0
```

Exploring the internal structure of the `lambda_vals` data frame. The `str()` function displays the internal structure of the data frame. The `lambda_vals` is passed as an R object to the `str()` function:

```
> str(lambda_vals)
```

The result is as follows:

```
num [1:4] 0.001 0.01 0.1 1
```

Creating a matrix for each epoch from a given set of values. The `matrix()` function is used. `nrow = (numStepsPerEpoch/nStepsPerPlot)*numEpochs+1` denotes the number of rows of the matrix, and `ncol = length(lambda_vals)` denotes the number of columns of the matrix:

```
> accMat <- matrix(NA, nrow =
(numStepsPerEpoch/nStepsPerPlot)*numEpochs+1, ncol = length(lambda_vals))
```

Creating a matrix for accuracy on a validation set from a given set of values. The `matrix()` function is used. `nrow = (numStepsPerEpoch/nStepsPerPlot)*numEpochs+1` denotes the number of rows of the matrix, and `ncol = length(lambda_vals)` denotes the number of columns of the matrix:

```
> accMatv <- matrix(NA, nrow =
(numStepsPerEpoch/nStepsPerPlot)*numEpochs+1, ncol = length(lambda_vals))
```

Setting up the classifier model:

```
for(i in 1:4){
  lambda = lambda_vals[i]
  accMatRow = 1
  accMatCol = i
  a = rep(0,ncol(continuousFeatures))
  b = 0
  stepIndex = 0
   for (e in 1:numEpochs){
```

The `#createDataPartition()` function creates a set of training data partitions. `y=trainingLabels` indicates the vector for outcomes. `p = (1 - evalidationSetSize/length(trainingLabels))` % of data is used for training datasets. The result is then stored in the `etrainingData` data frame:

```
etrainingData <- createDataPartition(y=trainingLabels, p=(1 -
evalidationSetSize/length(trainingLabels)), list=FALSE)
 etrainingFeatures <- trainingFeatures[etrainingData,]
 etrainingLabels <- trainingLabels[etrainingData]
 evalidationFeatures <- trainingFeatures[-etrainingData,]
 evalidationLabels <- trainingLabels[-etrainingData]
 steplength = 1 / (e*c1 + c2)

    for (step in 1:numStepsPerEpoch){
      stepIndex = stepIndex+1
      index = sample.int(nrow(etrainingFeatures),1)
      xk = etrainingFeatures[index,]
      yk = etrainingLabels[index]
       costfxn = yk * (a %*% xk + b)
       if(costfxn >= 1){

        a_dir = lambda * a
        a = a - steplength * a_dir

      } else {

        a_dir = (lambda * a) - (yk * xk)
        a = a - steplength * a_dir
        b_dir = -yk
        b = b - (steplength * b_dir)

      }
```

Logging in the accuracy. `getAccuracy()` is called:

```
    if (stepIndex %% nStepsPerPlot == 1){{#30}{
    accMat[accMatRow,accMatCol] =
 getAccuracy(a,b,evalidationFeatures,evalidationLabels)
    accMatv[accMatRow,accMatCol] =
 getAccuracy(a,b,validationFeatures,validationLabels)
    accMatRow = accMatRow + 1
    }

    }

    }
    tempAccuracy = getAccuracy(a,b,validationFeatures,validationLabels)
```

```
       print(str_c("tempAcc = ", tempAccuracy," and bestAcc = ", bestAccuracy)
)

       if(tempAccuracy > bestAccuracy){
       bestAccuracy = tempAccuracy
       best_a = a
       best_b = b
       best_lambdaIndex = i
       }

       }
```

Calculating the accuracy of the model. `getAccuracy()`, as defined previously, is used:

```
> getAccuracy(best_a,best_b, testingFeatures, testingLabels)
```

Step 5 - plotting the model

Plotting the accuracy of the model during training. The `c()` function is used to combine the arguments into vectors:

```
> colors = c("red","blue","green","black")
```

Setting the vectors to be used in the graph:

```
> xaxislabel = "Step"
> yaxislabels = c("Accuracy on Randomized Epoch Validation
Set","Accuracy on Validation Set")
>
> ylims=c(0,1)
> stepValues = seq(1,15000,length=500)
```

Creating a generic vector. `list()` is called, which concatenates the `accMat` and `accMatv` data frames:

```
> mats =  list(accMat,accMatv)
```

Plotting the graph:

```
> for(j in 1:length(mats)){

  mat = mats[[j]]

  for(i in 1:4){

    if(i == 1){
```

The # `plot()` function is a generic function for plotting R objects. The `stepValues` data frame is passed as a function value:

```
        plot(stepValues, mat[1:500,i], type = "l",xlim=c(0, 15000),
ylim=ylims,
            col=colors[i],xlab=xaxislabel,ylab=yaxislabels[j],main=title)
        } else{
            lines(stepValues, mat[1:500,i], type = "l",xlim=c(0, 15000),
ylim=ylims,
            col=colors[i],xlab=xaxislabel,ylab=yaxislabels[j],main=title)
        }
        Sys.sleep(1)
      }

legend(x=10000,y=.5,legend=c("lambda=.001","lambda=.01","lambda=.1","lambda
=1"),fill=colors)
      }
```

The resulting graph will look like the following:

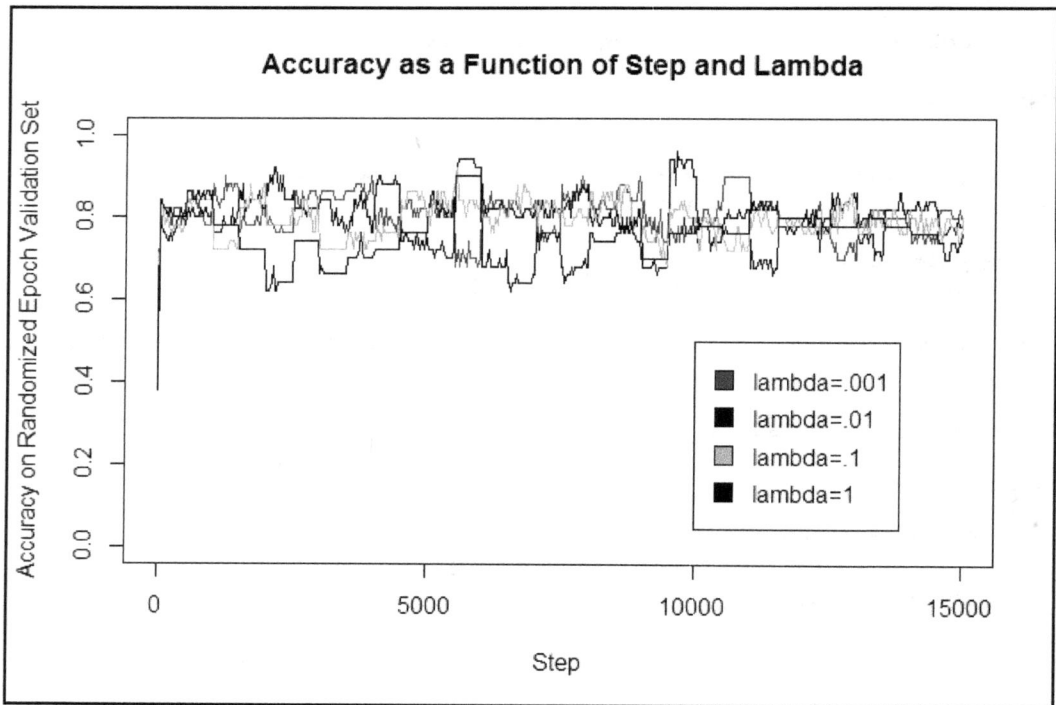

7

Unsupervised Learning

In this chapter, we will cover the following recipes:

- **Self-organizing map** - visualizing heatmaps
- **Vector quantization**--Image clustering

Introduction

Self-organizing map (SOM): The self-organizing map belongs to a class of unsupervised learning that is based on competitive learning, in which output neurons compete amongst themselves to be activated, with the result that only one is activated at any one time. This activated neuron is called the winning neuron. Such competition can be induced/implemented by having lateral inhibition connections (negative feedback paths) between the neurons, resulting in the neurons organizing themselves. SOM can be imagined as a sheet-like neural network, with nodes arranged as regular, usually two-dimensional grids. The principal goal of a SOM is to transform an incoming arbitrary dimensional signal into a one- or two-dimensional discrete map, and to perform this transformation adaptively in a topologically ordered fashion. The neurons are selectively tuned to various input patterns (stimuli) or classes of input patterns during the course of the competitive learning. The locations of the neurons so tuned (the winning neurons) become ordered, and a meaningful coordinate system for input features is created on the lattice. The SOM thus forms the required topographic map of the input patterns.

Vector quantization: Quantization is the process of mapping an infinite set of scalar or vector quantities by a finite set of scalar or vector quantities. Quantization has applications in the areas of signal processing, speech processing, and image processing. Vector quantization performs quantization over blocks of data, instead of a single scalar value. The quantization output is an index value that indicates another data block (vector) from a finite set of vectors, called the codebook. The selected vector is usually an approximation of the input data block. Reproduction vectors are known as encoders and decoders. The encoder takes an input vector, which determines the best representing reproduction vector, and transmits the index of that vector. The decoder takes that index and forms the reproduction vector.

Self-organizing map - visualizing of heatmaps

Over the past decade, there has been exponential growth in information. Gaining new knowledge from such databases is difficult, costly, and time-consuming if done manually. It may even be impossible when the data exceeds certain limits of size and complexity. As a result, the automated analysis and visualization of massive multidimensional datasets have been the focus of much scientific research over the last few years. The principal objective of this analysis and visualization is to find regularities and relationships in the data, thereby gaining access to hidden and potentially useful knowledge. A self-organizing map (SOM) is an unsupervised neural network algorithm that projects high-dimensional data onto a two-dimensional map. The projection preserves the topology of the data so that similar data items will be mapped to nearby locations on the map.

How to do it...

Let's get into the details.

Step 1 - exploring data

The following packages first need to be loaded:

```
> install.packages("kohonen")
> library(kohonen)
```

> Version info: Code for this page was tested in R version 3.3.2 (2016-10-31)

Create a sample dataset:

```
> training_frame <- data[, c(2,4,5,8)]
```

Changing the data frame with training data to a matrix: `scale()` as a function centers and scales the columns of a `training_frame` matrix. The `as.matrix()` function creates a matrix from the result of `scale(training_frame)`.

```
> training_matrix <- as.matrix(scale(training_frame))
```

Printing the `training_matrix`:

```
> training_matrix
```

The result is as follows:

```
           zn        chas         nox           dis
1    0.28454827 -0.2723291 -0.14407485  0.1400749840
2   -0.48724019 -0.2723291 -0.73953036  0.5566090496
3   -0.48724019 -0.2723291 -0.73953036  0.5566090496
4   -0.48724019 -0.2723291 -0.83445805  1.0766711351
5   -0.48724019 -0.2723291 -0.83445805  1.0766711351
6   -0.48724019 -0.2723291 -0.83445805  1.0766711351
7    0.04872402 -0.2723291 -0.26489191  0.8384142195
8    0.04872402 -0.2723291 -0.26489191  1.0236248974
9    0.04872402 -0.2723291 -0.26489191  1.0861216287
10   0.04872402 -0.2723291 -0.26489191  1.3283202075
11   0.04872402 -0.2723291 -0.26489191  1.2117799501
12   0.04872402 -0.2723291 -0.26489191  1.1547920492
13   0.04872402 -0.2723291 -0.26489191  0.7863652700
14  -0.48724019 -0.2723291 -0.14407485  0.4333252240
15  -0.48724019 -0.2723291 -0.14407485  0.3166899868
16  -0.48724019 -0.2723291 -0.14407485  0.3341187865
17  -0.48724019 -0.2723291 -0.14407485  0.3341187865
18  -0.48724019 -0.2723291 -0.14407485  0.2198105553
19  -0.48724019 -0.2723291 -0.14407485  0.0006920764
20  -0.48724019 -0.2723291 -0.14407485  0.0006920764
21  -0.48724019 -0.2723291 -0.14407485  0.0013569352
22  -0.48724019 -0.2723291 -0.14407485  0.1031753182
23  -0.48724019 -0.2723291 -0.14407485  0.0863638874
24  -0.48724019 -0.2723291 -0.14407485  0.1425444597
25  -0.48724019 -0.2723291 -0.14407485  0.2871037683
26  -0.48724019 -0.2723291 -0.14407485  0.3132232229
27  -0.48724019 -0.2723291 -0.14407485  0.4212152950
28  -0.48724019 -0.2723291 -0.14407485  0.3126533438
29  -0.48724019 -0.2723291 -0.14407485  0.3132707128
30  -0.48724019 -0.2723291 -0.14407485  0.2108349609
31  -0.48724019 -0.2723291 -0.14407485  0.2079855659
32  -0.48724019 -0.2723291 -0.14407485  0.1804414138
```

```
attr(,"scaled:center")
        zn        chas         nox         dis
11.36363636  0.06916996  0.55469506  3.79504269
attr(,"scaled:scale")
        zn        chas         nox         dis
23.3224530   0.2539940   0.1158777   2.1057101
```

Step 2 - training the model

Creating the SOM Grid: `somgrid()` plots the functions of the self-organizing map's grids. `xdim = 20` and `ydim=20` are the dimensions of the grid, while `topo="hexagonal"` represents the topology of the grid:

```
> som_grid <- somgrid(xdim = 20, ydim=20, topo="hexagonal")
```

Training the Self Organizing Maps: `som()` is a function of self-organizing maps that is used to map high-dimensional spectra or patterns to 2D. The Euclidean distance measure is used. `training_matrix` is the data matrix, `rlen=1000` is the number of times the complete dataset will be presented to the network for training, and alpha is the learning rate. `keep.data = TRUE` means that the data needs to be saved in the return object and `n.hood="circular"` indicates the shape of the neighborhood:

```
> som_model <- som(training_matrix,
+                  grid=som_grid,
+                  rlen=1000,
+                  alpha=c(0.05,0.01),
+                  keep.data = TRUE,
+                  n.hood="circular")
```

Step 3 - plotting the model

Plotting the `som_model` object:

```
> plot(som_model, main ="Training Progress", type="changes", col =
"red")
```

The result is as follows:

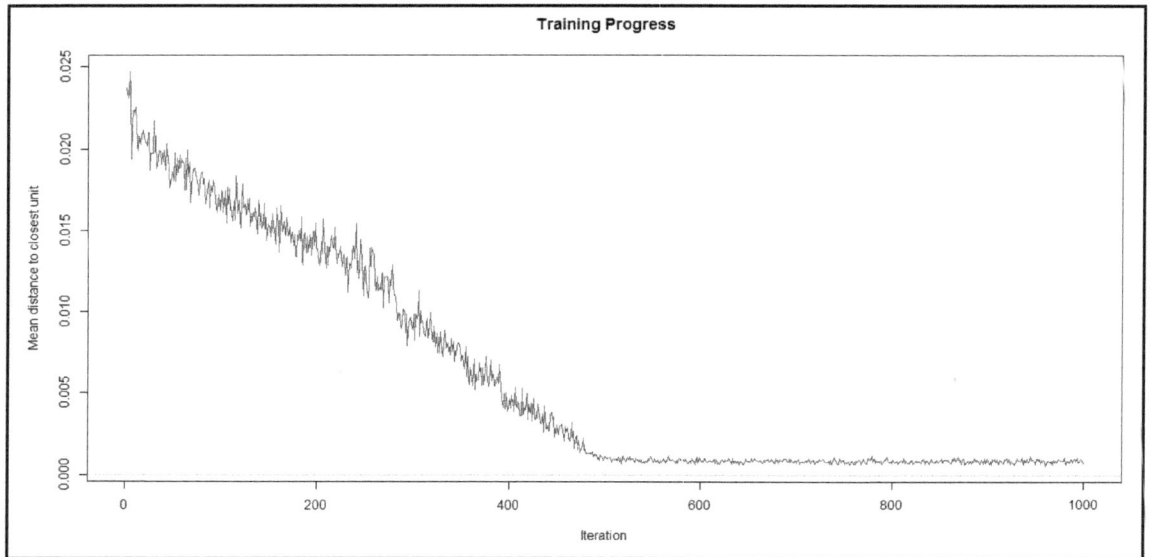

Plotting the model based on node count:

```
> plot(som_model, main ="Node Count", type="count")
```

The result is as follows:

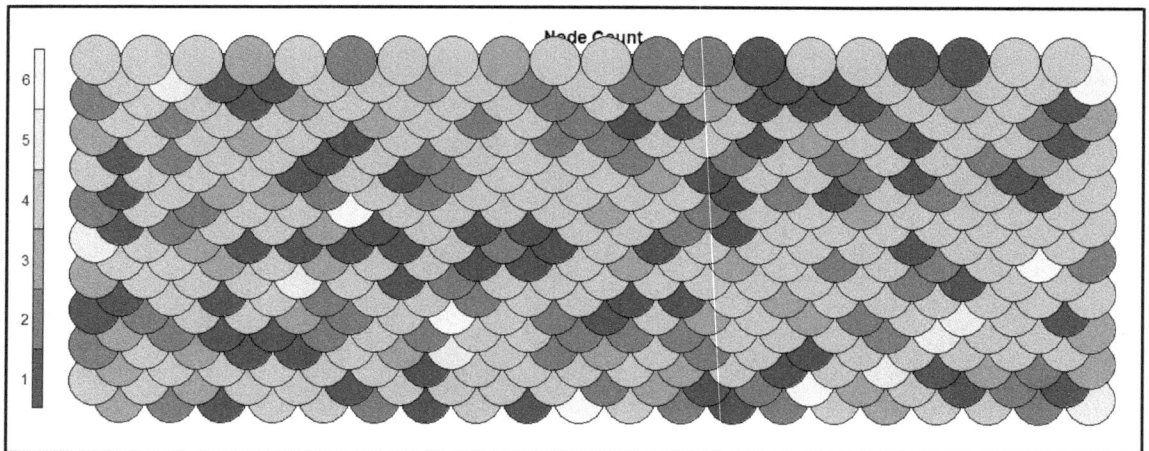

Plotting the model based on the neighborhood distance.

```
> plot(som_model, main ="Neighbour Distances", type="dist.neighbours")
```

The result is as follows:

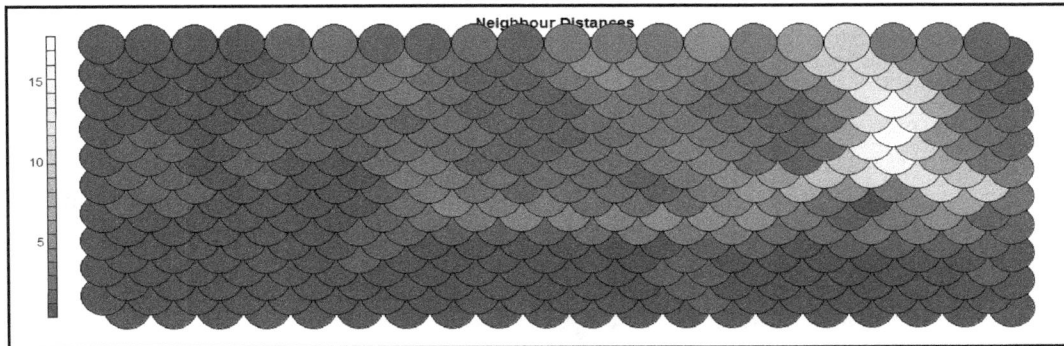

The following code plots the model based on the `type = "codes"`.

```
> plot(som_model, type="codes")
```

The result is as follows:

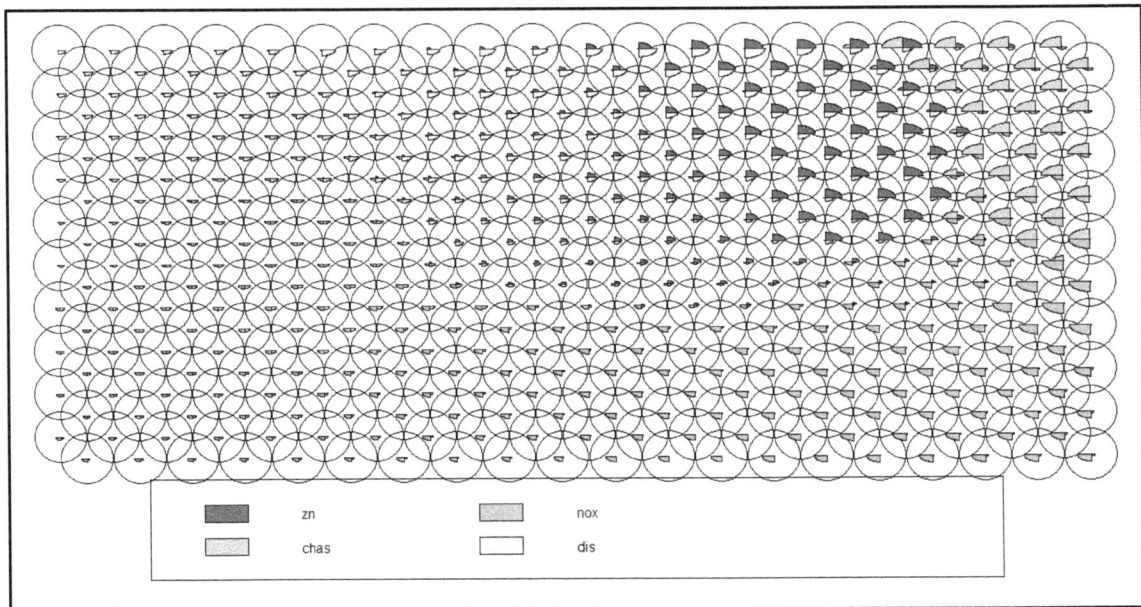

The following code plots the model based on property plot.

```
> plot(som_model, type = "property", property = som_model$codes[,4],
main=names(som_model$data)[4])
```

The result is as follows:

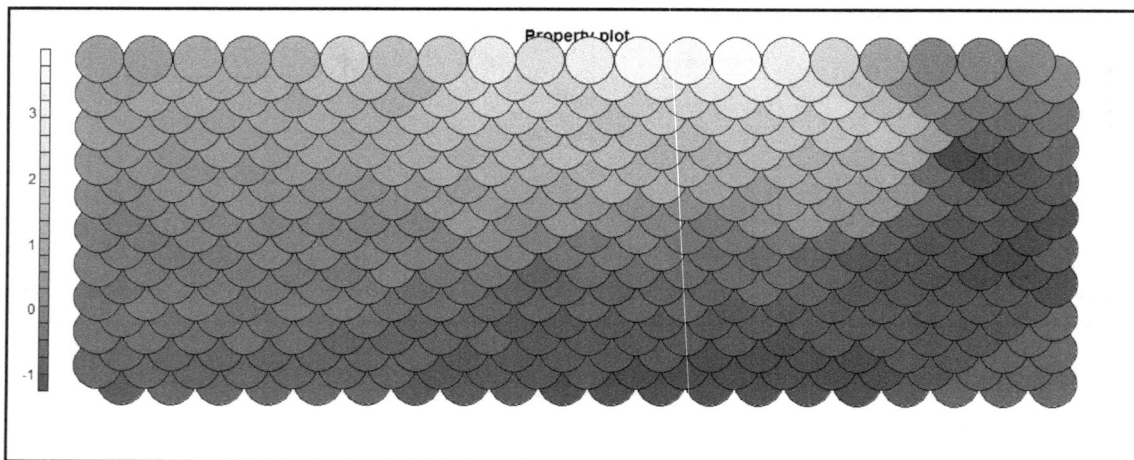

Vector quantization - image clustering

The development of technology in the field of digital media generates huge amounts of non-textual information in the form of images. If programs could comprehend the significance of these images and understand what they mean, this could result in a vast number of different applications. One such application could be the use of robots to extract malign tissue from hospital patients using body scan images to interpret the location of the tissue. Images are considered one of the most important media for conveying information. The potential for the retrieval of information is vast, so much so that users may be overwhelmed by the sheer amount of information retrieved. The unstructured format of images challenges classification and clustering techniques. Machine learning algorithms are used to extract information to understand images. One of the first steps towards understanding images is to segment them and identify the different objects within them. To do this, features like histogram plots and frequency domain transform can be used.

Getting ready

Let's get started.

Step 1 - collecting and describing data

The JPEG file is used.

How to do it...

Let's get into the details.

Step 2 - exploring data

The following packages first need to be loaded:

```
> install.packages("jpeg")
> install.packages("ggplot2")
> library(jpeg)
> library(ggplot2)
```

Version info: Code for this page was tested in R version 3.3.2

The readJPEG() function is used to read an image in the JPEG file format, and converts it into a raster array:.

```
> img <- readJPEG("d:/Image.jpg")
```

Step 3 - data cleaning

Exploring the dimensions of the img: the dim() function returns the dimensions of the img frame. The img data frame is passed as an input parameter:

```
> img_Dim <- dim(img)
```

Now let's print the img_Dim:

```
> img_Dim
```

The result is as follows:

```
[1] 526 800    3
```

Now, we are assigning RGB (red, green, and blue--RGB channels roughly follow the color receptors in the human eye) channels to the data frame. The result is then stored in the `img_RGB_channels` data frame:

```
> img_RGB_channels  <- data.frame(
+       x = rep(1:img_Dim[2], each = img_Dim[1]),
+       y = rep(img_Dim[1]:1, img_Dim[2]),
+       R = as.vector(img[,,1]),
+       G = as.vector(img[,,2]),
+       B = as.vector(img[,,3])
+ )
```

Step 4 - visualizing cleaned data

Let's plot the original image:

```
> plotTheme <- function() {
  theme(
  panel.background = element_rect(
size = 3,
 colour = "black",
   fill = "white"),
    axis.ticks = element_line(
  size = 2),
    panel.grid.major = element_line(
colour = "gray80",
  linetype = "dotted"),
    panel.grid.minor = element_line(
    colour = "gray90",
    linetype = "dashed"),
   axis.title.x = element_text(
  size = rel(1.2),
    face = "bold"),
   axis.title.y = element_text(
size = rel(1.2),
  face = "bold"),
    plot.title = element_text(
size = 20,
  face = "bold",
```

```
            vjust = 1.5)
      )
}

> ggplot(data = img_RGB_channels, aes(x = x, y = y)) +
+      geom_point(colour = rgb(img_RGB_channels[c("R", "G", "B")])) +
+      labs(title = "Original Image: Colorful Bird") +
+      xlab("x") +
+      ylab("y") +
+      plotTheme()
```

The result is as follows:

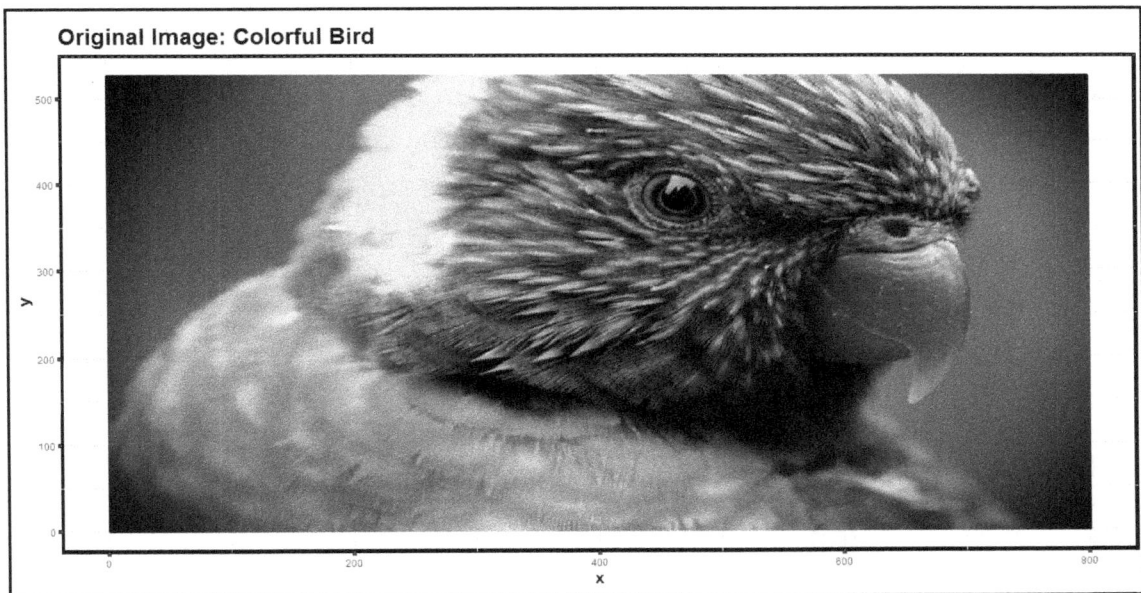

Step 5 - building the model and visualizing it

Assigning the clustering colors:

```
> kClusters <- 3
```

Performing k-means clustering: `kmeans()` as a function performs clustering on the data matrix `img_RGB_channels`. `centers = kClusters` signifies the number of initial clusters:

```
> kMeans_clst <- kmeans(img_RGB_channels[, c("R", "G", "B")], centers =
kClusters)
```

Creating colours corresponding to the given intensities of red, green and blue primaries.

```
> kColours <- rgb(kMeans_clst$centers[kMeans_clst$cluster,])
```

Plotting the image with three clusters:

```
> ggplot(data = img_RGB_channels, aes(x = x, y = y)) +
+     geom_point(colour = kColours) +
+     labs(title = paste("k-Means Clustering of", kClusters, "Colours"))
+
+     xlab("x") +
+     ylab("y") +
+     plotTheme()
```

The result is as follows:

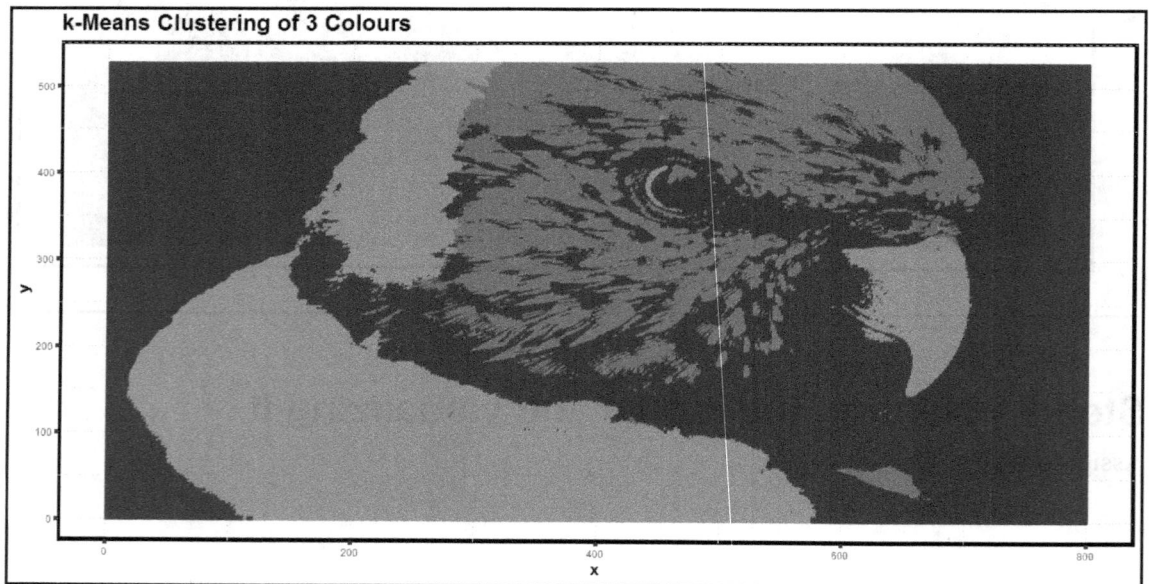

k-Means Clustering of 3 Colours

Assigning the clustering colors:

```
> kClusters <- 5
```

Performing k-means clustering:

```
> kMeans_clst <- kmeans(img_RGB_channels[, c("R", "G", "B")], centers =
kClusters)
```

Creating colours corresponding to the given intensities of red, green and blue primaries.

```
> kColours <- rgb(kMeans_clst$centers[kMeans_clst$cluster,])
```

Plotting the image with five clusters:

```
> ggplot(data = img_RGB_channels, aes(x = x, y = y)) +
+     geom_point(colour = kColours) +
+     labs(title = paste("k-Means Clustering of", kClusters, "Colours"))
+
+     xlab("x") +
+     ylab("y") +
+     plotTheme()
```

The result is as follows:

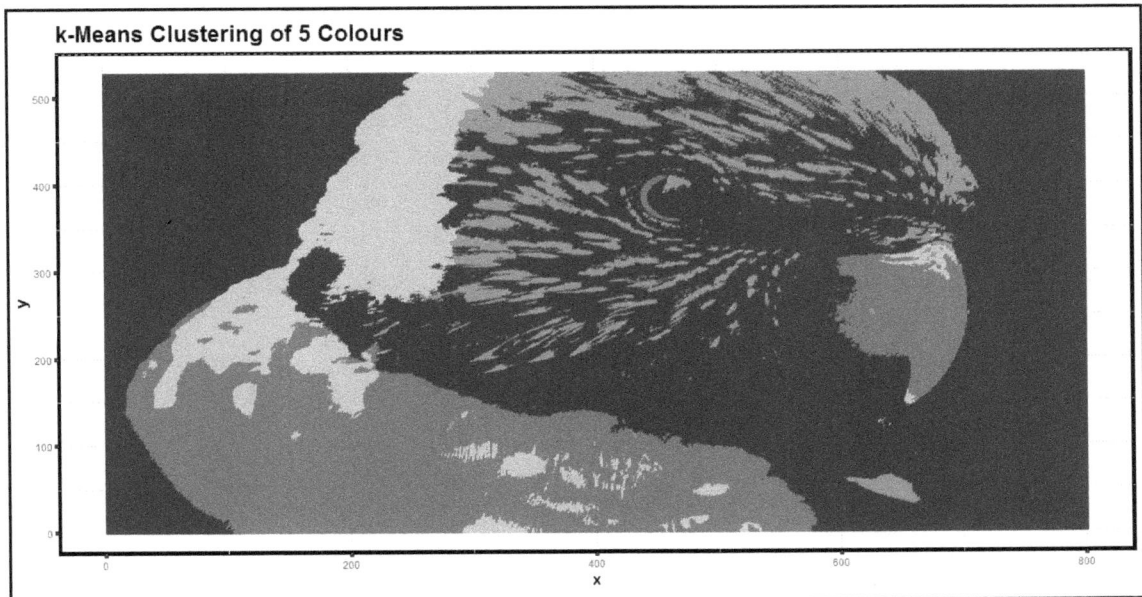

8
Reinforcement Learning

In this chapter, we will cover the following recipes:

- Markov chains - the stocks regime switching model
- Markov chains - the multi-channel attribution model
- Markov chains - the car rental agency service
- Continuous Markov chains - vehicle service at the gas station
- Monte Carlo simulations - calibrated hull and white short-rates

Introduction

The Markov chain: A sequence of trials of an experiment is a Markov chain if the outcome of each experiment is one of the set of discrete states, and the outcome of the experiment is dependent only on the present state and not of any of the past states. The probability of changing from one state to another state is represented as p_{ij}. It is called a transition probability. The transition probability matrix is an n × n matrix such that each element of the matrix is non-negative and each row of the matrix sums to one.

Continuous time Markov chains: Continuous-time Markov chains can be labeled as transition systems augmented with rates that have discrete states. The states have continuous time-steps and the delays are exponentially distributed. Continuous-time Markov chains are suited to model reliability models, control systems, biological pathways, chemical reactions, and so on.

Monte Carlo simulations: Monte Carlo simulation is a stochastic simulation of system behavior. The simulation uses sampling experiments to be performed on the model and then conducts numerical experiments using the computer to obtain a statistical understanding of the system behavior. Monte Carlo simulations are used to construct theories for observed behavior of complicated systems, predict future behavior of a system, and study effects on final results based upon input and parameter changes within a system. The stochastic simulation is a way of experimenting with a system to find ways to improve or better understand the system behavior. It uses random numbers that are uniformly distributed over the interval [0, 1]. These uniformly distributed random numbers are used for the generation of stochastic variables from various probability distributions. Sampling experiments are then generated, which are associated with the modeling of system behavior.

Markov chains - the stocks regime switching model

In the last few decades, a lot of studies have been conducted on the analysis and forecasting of volatility. Volatility is the degree of variation of a trading price series over time as measured by the standard deviation of returns. Models of stock returns assume that the returns follow a geometric Brownian motion. This implies that over any discrete time interval, the return on stocks is log normally distributed and that returns in non-overlapping intervals are independent. Studies have found that this model fails to capture extreme price movements and stochastic variability in the volatility parameter. Stochastic volatility takes discrete values, switching between these values randomly. This is the basis of the **regime-switching lognormal process (RSLN)**.

Getting ready

In order to perform the Markov chains regime switching model we shall be using data collected from the Stock's dataset.

Step 1 - collecting and describing the data

The dataset called `StocksRegimeSwitching.csv` shall be used. This dataset is available in csv format and called `StocksRegimeSwitching.csv`. The dataset is in the standard format. There are 66 rows of data. There are seven variables. The numeric variables are as follows:

- `LRY`
- `LRV`
- `INT`
- `LRC`
- `LVS`
- `LGS`

The non-numeric variable is as follows:

- `DATE`

How to do it...

Let's get into the details.

Step 2 - exploring the data

The first step is to load the following packages:

```
>install.packages("MSwM")
>library(MSwM)
```

Version info: Code for this page was tested in R version 3.2.2 (2015-08-14).

Let's explore the data and understand the relationships between the variables. We'll begin by importing the CSV data file called `StocksRegimeSwitching.csv`. We will be saving the data to the `MarkovSwitchData` data frame:

```
> MarkovSwitchData <- read.csv("d:/StocksRegimeSwitching.csv", header =
TRUE)
```

Attaching the dataset. The `attach()` function attaches the dataset to the search path. The dataset is searched when evaluating the variables. `MarkovSwitchData` is passed as a parameter:

```
> attach(MarkovSwitchData)
```

Printing the `MarkovSwitchData` data frame. The `head()` function returns the first part of the `MarkovSwitchData` data frame. The `MarkovSwitchData` data frame is passed as an input parameter:

```
> head(MarkovSwitchData)
```

The results are as follows:

```
    DATE    LRY    LRV    INT    LRC   LVS   LGS
1 1997Q3 11.49   6.74 10.73 13.35 4.95 4.90
2 1997Q4 11.51 12.97 11.09 13.33 4.63 4.43
3 1998Q1 11.44 13.41 12.45 13.30 4.36 3.99
4 1998Q2 11.42   4.26 13.51 13.31 4.55 4.20
5 1998Q3 11.39 33.71 12.55 13.28 4.05 3.83
6 1998Q4 11.39   3.54 10.00 13.31 3.90 3.36
```

Exploring the dimension of the `MarkovSwitchData` data frame. The `dim()` function returns the dimension of the `MarkovSwitchData` frame. The `MarkovSwitchData` data frame is passed as an input parameter. The result clearly states that there are 66 rows of data and seven single columns:

```
> dim(MarkovSwitchData)
```

The result is as follows:

```
[1] 66   7
```

Printing the summary of the `MarkovSwitchData` data frame. The `summary()` function is a multipurpose function. The `summary()` function is a generic function that provides a summary of the data related to the individual object or data frame. The `MarkovSwitchData` data frame is passed as an R object to the `summary()` function:

```
> summary(MarkovSwitchData)
```

The result is as follows:

```
     DATE          LRY             LRV              INT             LRC             LVS
1997Q3 : 1    Min.   :11.39   Min.   : 0.1100   Min.   : 4.520   Min.   :13.22   Min.   :3.900
1997Q4 : 1    1st Qu.:11.57   1st Qu.: 0.3125   1st Qu.: 5.015   1st Qu.:13.31   1st Qu.:4.705
1998Q1 : 1    Median :11.83   Median : 0.6100   Median : 6.215   Median :13.36   Median :4.875
1998Q2 : 1    Mean   :11.80   Mean   : 1.9211   Mean   : 6.619   Mean   :13.43   Mean   :4.896
1998Q3 : 1    3rd Qu.:12.00   3rd Qu.: 1.5275   3rd Qu.: 7.025   3rd Qu.:13.54   3rd Qu.:5.170
1998Q4 : 1    Max.   :12.21   Max.   :33.7100   Max.   :13.510   Max.   :13.85   Max.   :5.400
(Other):60
     LGS
Min.   :3.360
1st Qu.:3.853
Median :3.935
Mean   :3.978
3rd Qu.:4.140
Max.   :4.900
```

Step 3 - preparing the regression model

A regression model will be prepared on the dataset. Regression analysis is used when two or more variables are thought to be systematically connected by a linear relationship. Regression models are used to predict one variable from another variable. They provide a prediction about the past, present, and future events, based on information.

Defining the dependent variable. The `cbind()` function is used to define the dependent variable. The function takes in the `LVS` data frame. The resulting data frame is stored in the `yLogValueStocks` data frame:

```
> yLogValueStocks <- cbind(LVS)
```

Printing the `yLogValueStocks` frame. The `head()` function returns the first part of the `yLogValueStocks` frame. The `yLogValueStocks` frame is passed as an input parameter:

```
> head(yLogValueStocks)
```

The result is as follows:

```
            LVS
[1,]   4.95
[2,]   4.63
[3,]   4.36
[4,]   4.55
[5,]   4.05
[6,]   3.90
```

The cbind () function takes in the LGS data frame. The resulting data frame is stored in the yLogGrowthStocks data frame.

Printing the yLogGrowthStocks frame. The head() function returns the first part of the yLogGrowthStocks data frame. The yLogGrowthStocks frame is passed as an input parameter:

```
> head(yLogGrowthStocks)
```

The result is as follows:

```
            LGS
[1,]   4.90
[2,]   4.43
[3,]   3.99
[4,]   4.20
[5,]   3.83
[6,]   3.36
```

Defining the independent variable The cbind() function is used to define the dependent variable. The function takes in the LRY, LRC, INT, LRV data frames. The resulting data frame is stored in the x data frame:

```
> x <- cbind(LRY, LRC, INT, LRV)
```

Creating an **ordinary least square (OLS)** regression equation. The lm() function is used to fit linear models. The model to be fitted is represented symbolically by yLogValueStocks~x. The result is then stored in the olsLogValueStocks data frame:

```
> olsLogValueStocks <- lm(yLogValueStocks~x)
```

Printing the summary of the `olsLogValueStocks` data frame. The `summary()` function is used to provide a summary of the data related to the individual object or data frame. The `olsLogValueStocks` data frame is passed as an R object to the `summary()` function:

```
> summary(olsLogValueStocks)
```

The result is as follows:

```
Call:
lm(formula = yLogValueStocks ~ x)

Residuals:
     Min       1Q   Median       3Q      Max
-0.57390 -0.07711 -0.00725  0.07179  0.39578

Coefficients:
             Estimate Std. Error t value Pr(>|t|)
(Intercept) -9.151035   1.950114  -4.693 1.57e-05 ***
XLRY         1.043820   0.200840   5.197 2.48e-06 ***
XLRC         0.123601   0.210845   0.586   0.5599
XINT         0.013357   0.020907   0.639   0.5253
XLRV        -0.012112   0.005686  -2.130   0.0372 *
---
Signif. codes:  0 '***' 0.001 '**' 0.01 '*' 0.05 '.' 0.1 ' ' 1

Residual standard error: 0.1431 on 61 degrees of freedom
Multiple R-squared:  0.8042,    Adjusted R-squared:  0.7914
F-statistic: 62.64 on 4 and 61 DF,  p-value: < 2.2e-16
```

Creating an ordinary least square regression equation. The model to be fitted is represented symbolically by `yLogGrowthStocks~x`. The result is then stored in the `olsLogGrowthStocks` data frame:

```
> olsLogGrowthStocks <- lm(yLogGrowthStocks~x)
```

Printing the summary of the `olsLogGrowthStocks` data frame. The `olsLogGrowthStocks` data frame is passed as an R object to the `summary()` function:

```
> summary(olsLogGrowthStocks)
```

The result is as follows:

```
Call:
lm(formula = yLogGrowthStocks ~ x)

Residuals:
     Min       1Q   Median       3Q      Max
-0.62267 -0.11945  0.01245  0.07490  0.78002

Coefficients:
             Estimate Std. Error t value Pr(>|t|)
(Intercept) -7.711885   2.663863  -2.895  0.00525 **
XLRY         0.827857   0.274348   3.018  0.00371 **
XLRC         0.089680   0.288015   0.311  0.75658
XINT         0.110447   0.028559   3.867  0.00027 ***
XLRV        -0.009277   0.007767  -1.194  0.23691
---
Signif. codes:  0 '***' 0.001 '**' 0.01 '*' 0.05 '.' 0.1 ' ' 1

Residual standard error: 0.1954 on 61 degrees of freedom
Multiple R-squared:  0.2924,    Adjusted R-squared:  0.246
F-statistic: 6.303 on 4 and 61 DF,  p-value: 0.0002596
```

Step 4 - preparing the Markov-switching model

The Markov switching model involves multiple equations that can characterize the time series behaviors in different regimes. The model is able to capture complex dynamic patterns by switching between structures. The current value of the state variable depends on the immediate past value, which is controlled by the Markovian property.

Creating a Markov switching model for the value of stocks. The msmFit() function implements a Markov switching models using the EM algorithm, as follows. olsLogValueStocks is of the object class of the lm type. k = 2 represents the estimated number of regimes. The result is stored in the MarkovSwtchLogValueStocks data frame:

```
> MarkovSwtchLogValueStocks <- msmFit(olsLogValueStocks, k = 2, sw =
rep(TRUE, 6))
```

Printing the summary of the `MarkovSwtchLogValueStocks` data frame as follows. The `MarkovSwtchLogValueStocks` data frame is passed as an R object to the `summary()` function:

```
> summary(MarkovSwtchLogValueStocks)
```

The result is as follows:

```
Markov Switching Model

Call: msmFit(object = olsLogValueStocks, k = 2, sw = rep(TRUE, 6))

        AIC       BIC    logLik
  -102.0478 -38.25474 61.02392

Coefficients:

Regime 1
---------
                Estimate Std. Error  t value  Pr(>|t|)
(Intercept)(S) -10.7330     0.5460 -19.6575 < 2.2e-16 ***
xLRY(S)           1.6984     0.0303  56.0528 < 2.2e-16 ***
xLRC(S)          -0.3478     0.0414  -8.4010 < 2.2e-16 ***
xINT(S)           0.0411     0.0020  20.5500 < 2.2e-16 ***
xLRV(S)          -0.0139     0.0015  -9.2667 < 2.2e-16 ***
---
Signif. codes:  0 '***' 0.001 '**' 0.01 '*' 0.05 '.' 0.1 ' ' 1

Residual standard error: 0.03610862
Multiple R-squared: 0.9893

Standardized Residuals:
          Min            Q1           Med            Q3           Max
-8.340128e-02 -1.065220e-02 -3.682609e-16  1.117322e-02  7.650599e-02

Regime 2
---------
                Estimate Std. Error t value  Pr(>|t|)
(Intercept)(S)  13.6836     2.1896  6.2494 4.120e-10 ***
xLRY(S)           0.7522     0.1799  4.1812 2.900e-05 ***
xLRC(S)          -1.2801     0.1608 -7.9608 1.776e-15 ***
xINT(S)          -0.1005     0.0388 -2.5902 0.009592  **
xLRV(S)           0.0487     0.0201  2.4229 0.015397   *
---
Signif. codes:  0 '***' 0.001 '**' 0.01 '*' 0.05 '.' 0.1 ' ' 1
```

```
Residual standard error: 0.1515668
Multiple R-squared: 0.5145

Standardized Residuals:
        Min          Q1         Med          Q3         Max
-0.48074613  -0.02481690  0.00113687  0.02751167  0.46264470

Transition probabilities:
           Regime 1   Regime 2
Regime 1  0.8255604  0.1692358
Regime 2  0.1744396  0.8307642
```

Creating a Markov switching model for growth stocks. The `msmFit()` function implements the Markov switching model using the EM algorithm. `olsLogGrowthStocks` is of the object class of the `lm` type. `k = 2` represents the estimated number of regimes. The result is stored in the `MarkoSwtchLogGrowthStocks` data frame:

```
> MarkoSwtchLogGrowthStocks<- msmFit(olsLogGrowthStocks, k = 2, sw =
rep(TRUE, 6))
```

Printing the summary of the `MarkoSwtchLogGrowthStocksdata` frame. The `MarkoSwtchLogGrowthStocks` data frame is passed as an R object to the `summary()` function:

```
> summary(MarkoSwtchLogGrowthStocks)
```

The result is as follows:

```
Markov Switching Model

Call: msmFit(object = olsLogGrowthStocks, k = 2, sw = rep(TRUE, 6))

        AIC        BIC    logLik
  -65.43317  -1.640072  42.71658

Coefficients:

Regime 1
---------
               Estimate  Std. Error  t value   Pr(>|t|)
(Intercept)(S)  14.9726     4.1217    3.6326   0.0002806 ***
XLRY(S)          1.4894     0.3053    4.8785   1.069e-06 ***
XLRC(S)         -2.1932     0.2741   -8.0015   1.332e-15 ***
XINT(S)          0.1022     0.0651    1.5699   0.1164384
XLRV(S)          0.0466     0.0309    1.5081   0.1315289
---
Signif. codes:  0 '***' 0.001 '**' 0.01 '*' 0.05 '.' 0.1 ' ' 1

Residual standard error: 0.2376528
Multiple R-squared: 0.4281

Standardized Residuals:
        Min            Q1           Med            Q3           Max
-0.573535743  -0.021589934  0.004829526  0.018767748  0.681347620

Regime 2
---------
               Estimate  Std. Error   t value   Pr(>|t|)
(Intercept)(S)  -8.5099     0.8361   -10.1781   < 2.2e-16 ***
XLRY(S)          0.5287     0.0940     5.6245   1.860e-08 ***
XLRC(S)          0.4282     0.0871     4.9162   8.824e-07 ***
XINT(S)          0.0718     0.0100     7.1800   6.972e-13 ***
XLRV(S)         -0.0081     0.0029    -2.7931   0.005221  **
---
Signif. codes:  0 '***' 0.001 '**' 0.01 '*' 0.05 '.' 0.1 ' ' 1
```

```
  Residual standard error: 0.0676098
  Multiple R-squared: 0.803

  Standardized Residuals:
           Min            Q1            Med            Q3            Max
  -1.356430e-01  -2.402493e-02  6.076829e-06  3.124204e-02  1.493800e-01

  Transition probabilities:
             Regime 1   Regime 2
  Regime 1  0.8809933  0.08517424
  Regime 2  0.1190067  0.91482576
```

Step 5 - plotting the regime probabilities

Next we shall be plotting the regime probabilities that have been calculated.

Plotting the regime probabilities for the value of stocks. The par() function is used to query the graphical parameters as follows:

```
> par(mar=c(3,3,3,3))
```

The plotProb() function creates each plot for each regime. The plot contains smoothed and filtered probabilities. MarkovSwtchLogValueStocks is passed as an object of type MSM.lm. The which = 1 value represents the subset of the plots that is required. Use the following command:

```
> plotProb(MarkovSwtchLogValueStocks, which=1)
```

The result is as follows:

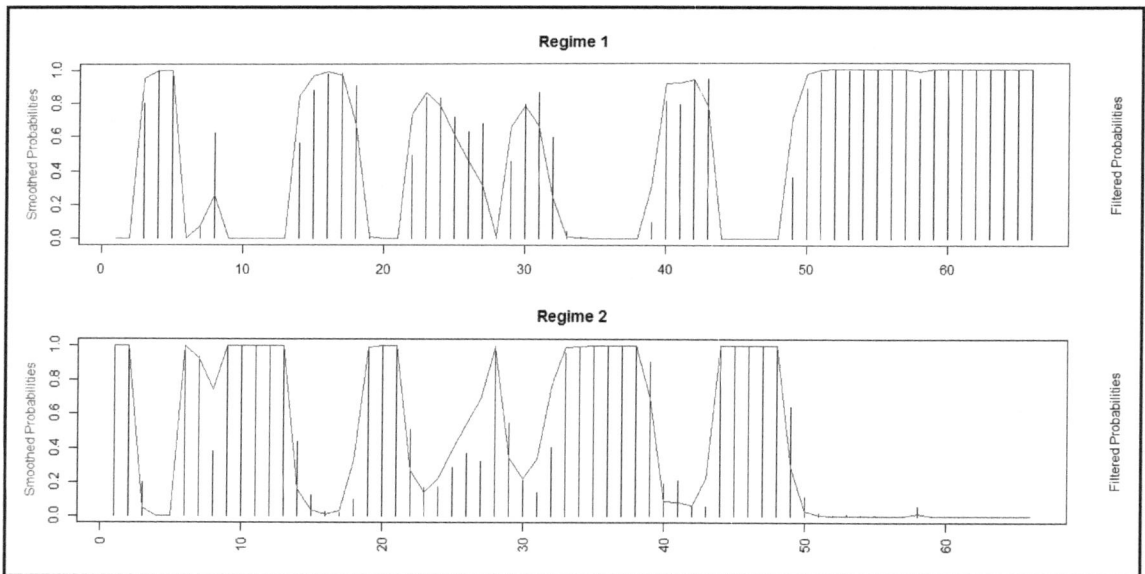

The plotProb() function creates each plot for each regime. The plot contains smoothed and filtered probabilities. MarkovSwtchLogValueStocks is passed as an object of the MSM.lm type. The which = 2 value represents the plot of the regime with the response variable against the smoothed probabilities. Use the following command:

```
> plotProb(MarkovSwtchLogValueStocks, which=2)
```

The result is as follows:

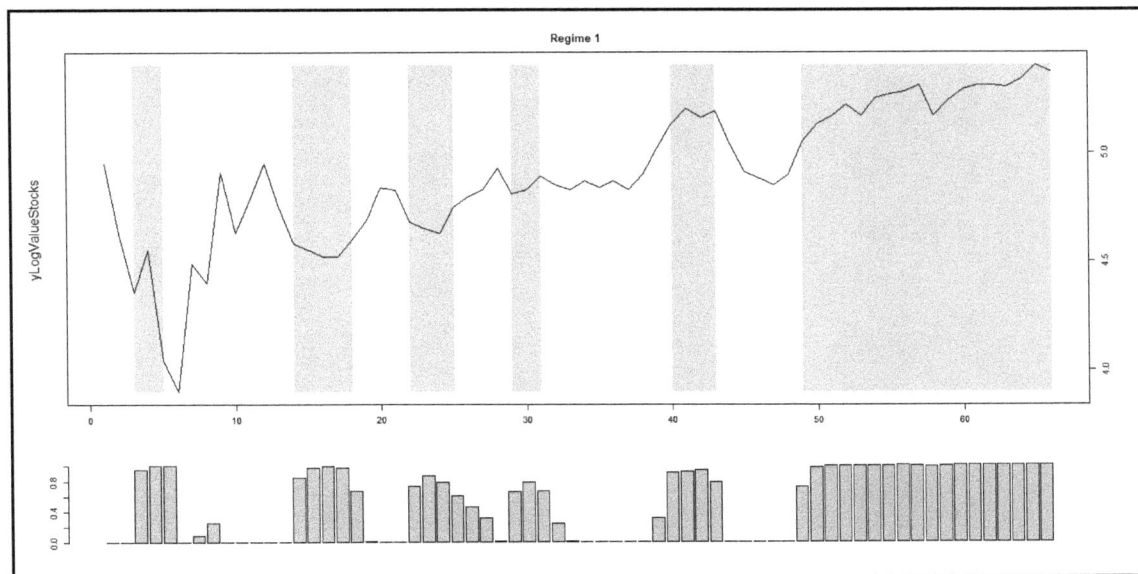

The `plotProb()` function creates each plot for each regime.
`MarkoSwtchLogGrowthStocks` is passed as an object of the `MSM.lm` type. The `which = 1` value represents the subset of the plots that is required:

```
> plotProb(MarkoSwtchLogGrowthStocks, which=1)
```

The result is as follows:

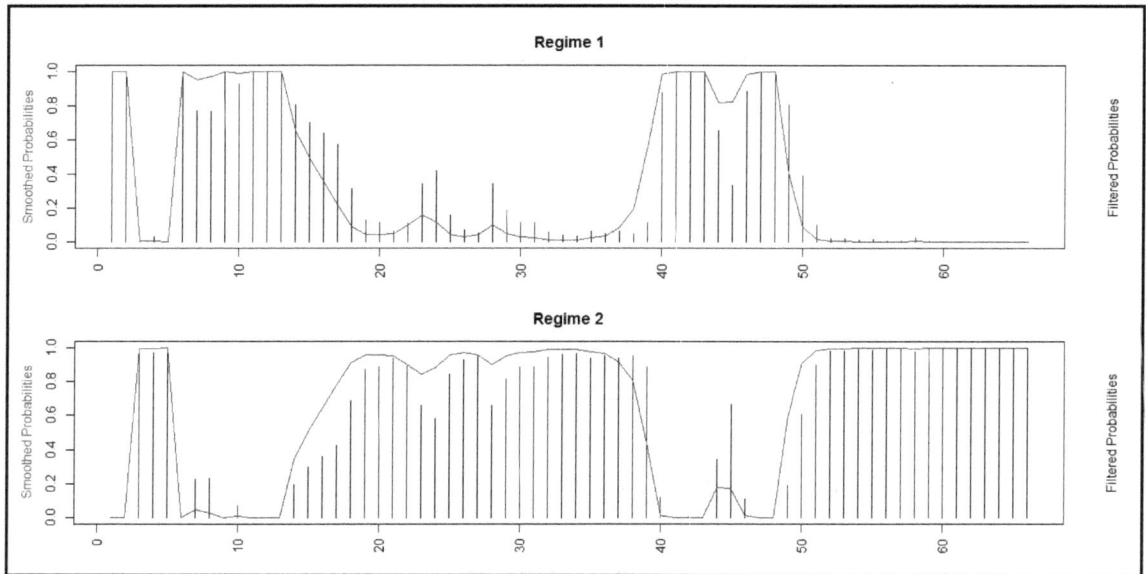

The `plotProb()` function creates each plot for each regime. `MarkoSwtchLogGrowthStocks` is passed as an object of the `MSM.lm` type. The `which = 2` value represents the plot of the regime with the response variable against the smoothed probabilities. Use the following command:

```
> plotProb(MarkoSwtchLogGrowthStocks, which=2)
```

The result is as follows:

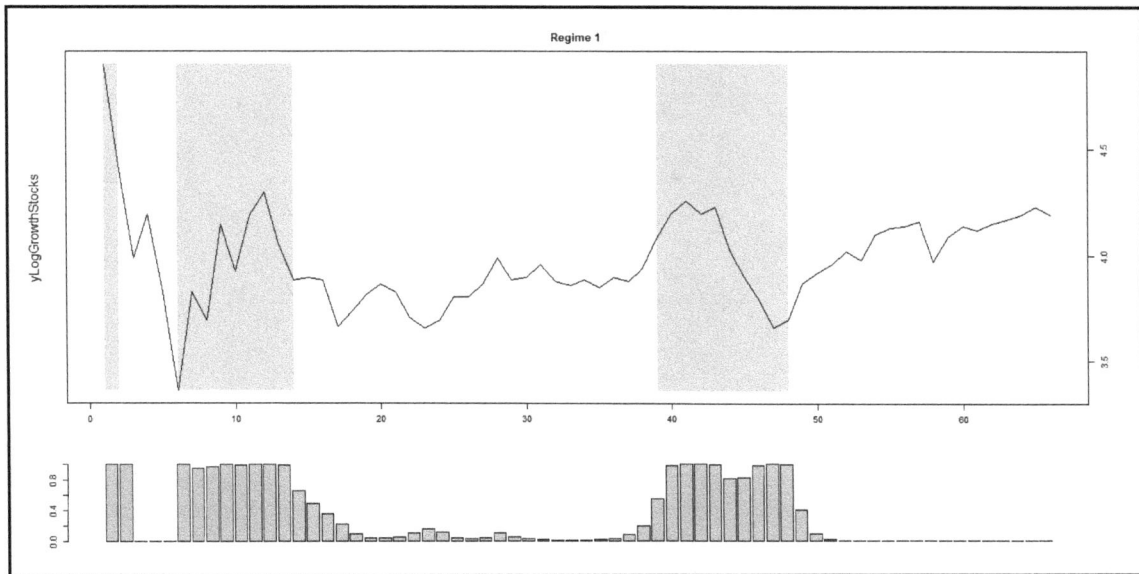

Step 6 - testing the Markov switching model

Next we shall run a set of diagnostic tests on the Markov switching model.

Ploting the regime probabilities for the value of stocks. The `par()` function is used to query graphical parameters:

```
> par(mar=c(3,3,3,3))
```

Creating the plots for the residual analysis. The `plotDiag()` function plots the residuals against the fitted values. `MarkovSwtchLogValueStocks` is passed as an object of the `MSM.lm` type. The `which = 1` value represents the subset of the plots is that required. The `which=1` value represents the plot of residuals against fitted values:

```
> plotDiag(MarkovSwtchLogValueStocks, regime=1, which=1)
```

The result is as follows:

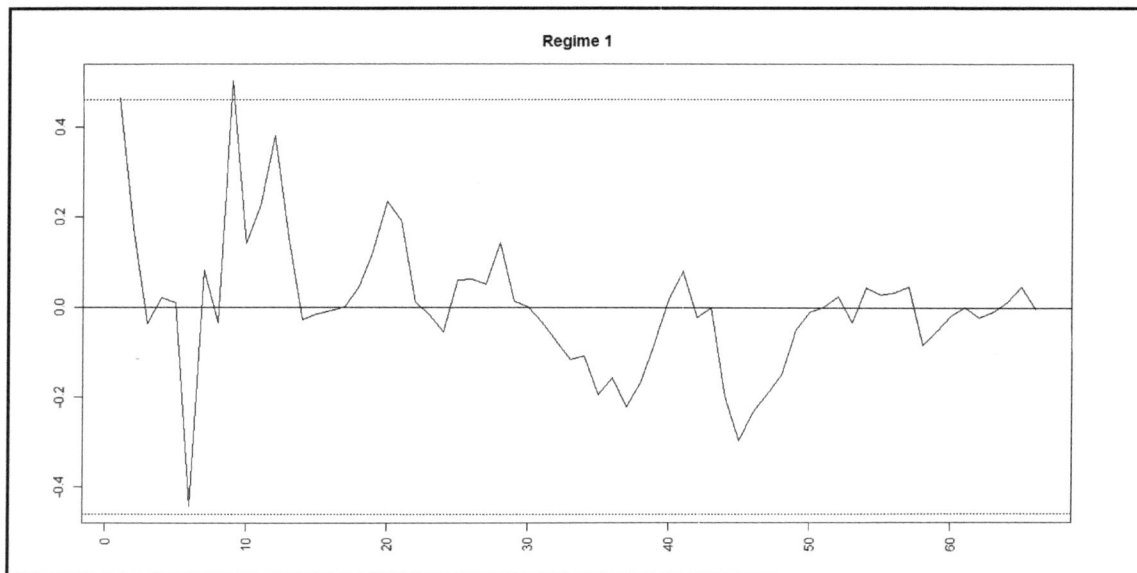

The `plotDiag()` function plots the residuals against the fitted values.
`MarkovSwtchLogValueStocks` is passed as an object of the `MSM.lm` type. `which = 2`
represents the subset of the plots that is required. `which=2` represents the Normal Q-Q plot:

```
> plotDiag(MarkovSwtchLogValueStocks, regime=1, which=2)
```

The result is as follows:

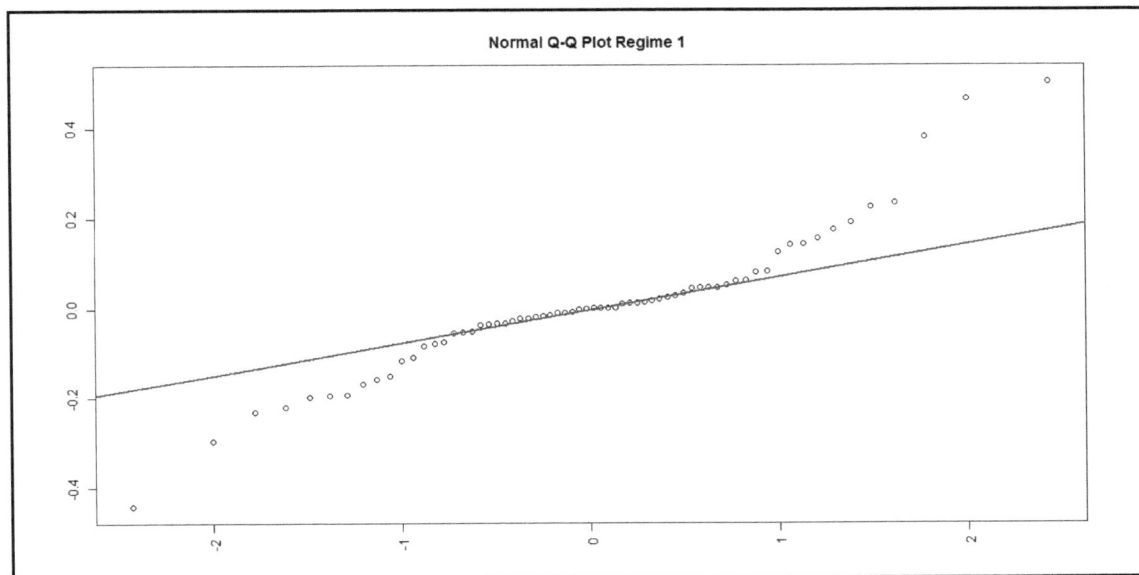

Normal Q-Q Plot Regime 1

The `plotDiag()` function plots the residuals against the fitted values.
`MarkoSwtchLogGrowthStocks` is passed as an object of the `MSM.lm` type. `which = 3`
represents the subset of the plots that is required. `which=3` represents the ACF/PACF of
residuals and the ACF/PACF of square residuals:

```
> plotDiag(MarkoSwtchLogGrowthStocks, regime=1, which=3)
```

The result is as follows:

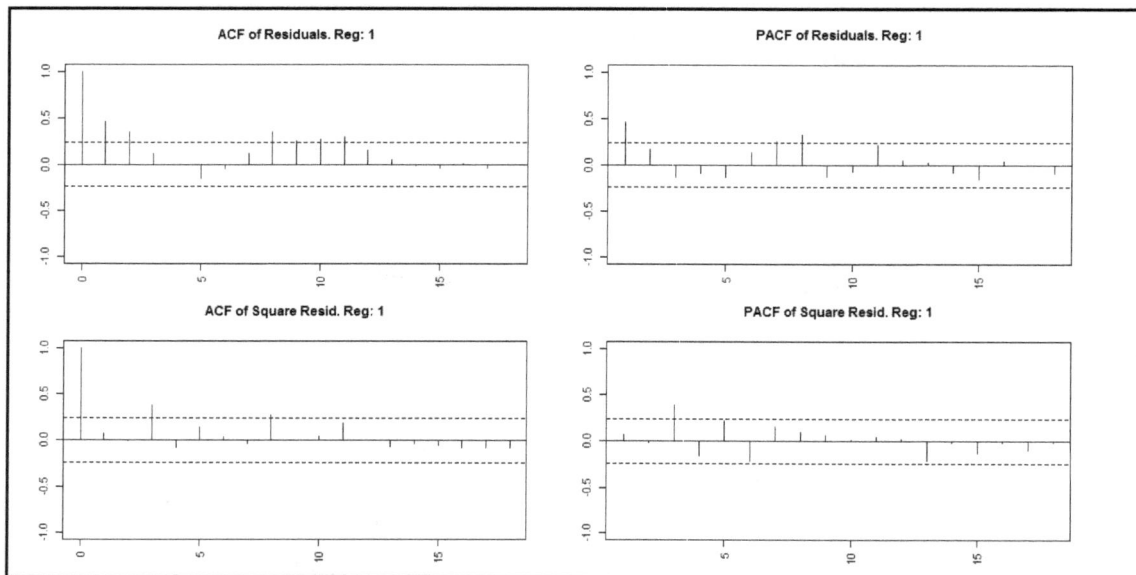

The `plotDiag()` function plots the residuals against the fitted values. `MarkoSwtchLogGrowthStocks` is passed as an object of the `MSM.lm` type. `which = 1` represents the subset of the plots that is required. `which = 1` represents the plot of residuals against fitted values:

```
> plotDiag(MarkoSwtchLogGrowthStocks, regime=1, which=1)
```

The result is as follows:

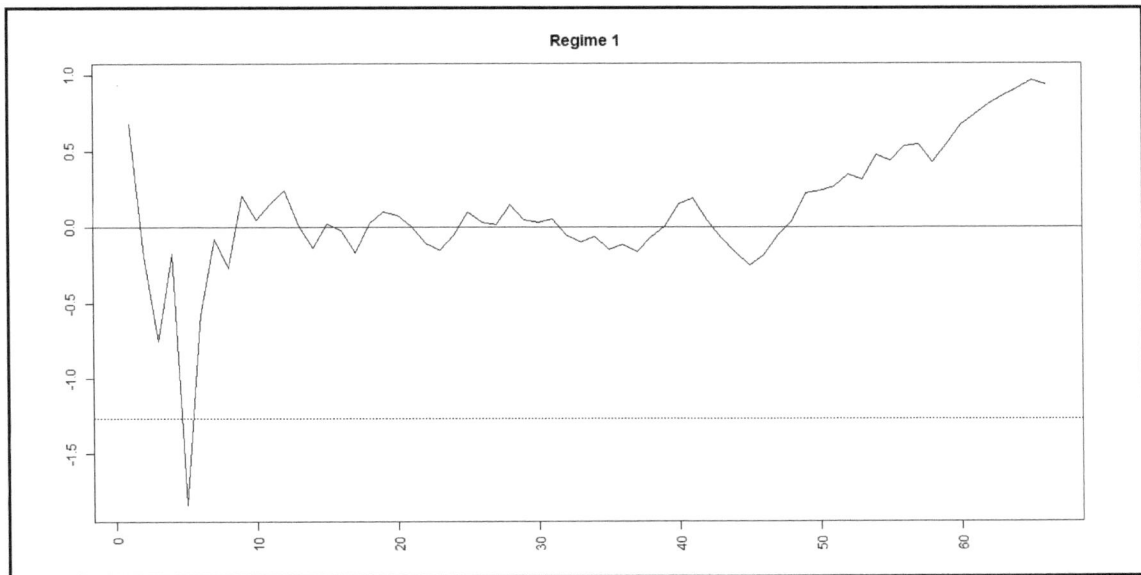

The `plotDiag()` function plots the residuals against the fitted values.
`MarkoSwtchLogGrowthStocks` is passed as an object of the `MSM.lm` type. `which = 2` represents the subset of the plots that is required. `which=2` represents the Normal Q-Q plot:

```
> plotDiag(MarkoSwtchLogGrowthStocks, regime=1, which=2)
```

The result is as follows:

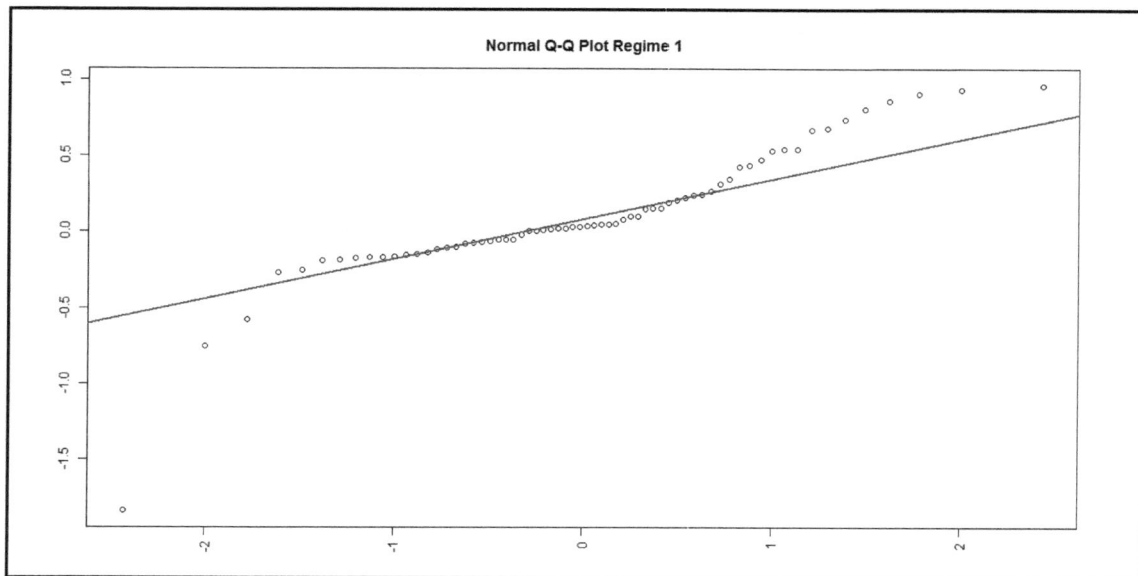

The `plotDiag()` function plots the residuals against the fitted values.
`MarkoSwtchLogGrowthStocks` is passed as an object of the `MSM.lm` type. `which = 3` represents the subset of the plots that is required. `which=3` represents the ACF/PACF of residuals and the ACF/PACF of square residuals:

```
> plotDiag(MarkoSwtchLogGrowthStocks, regime=1, which=3)
```

The result is as follows:

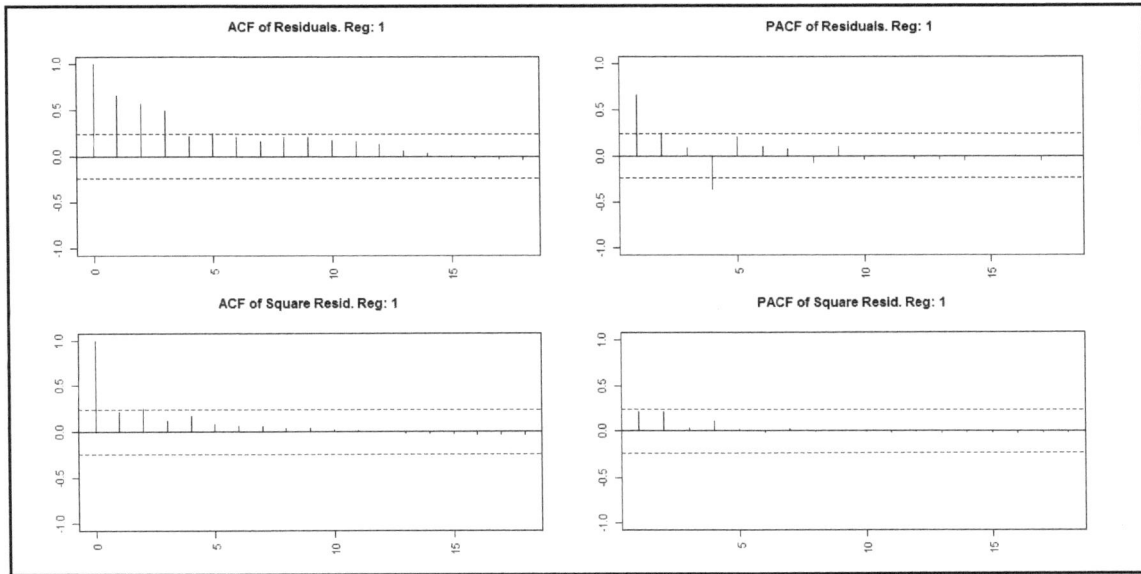

Markov chains - the multi-channel attribution model

A customer's journey undergoes a path of different channels before a purchase on an e-commerce website. Multi-channel attribution assigns a value to each step in the journey. The question is how one can identify the value in the actions people take on your website that lead to a conversion. Commonly, businesses use "last click" attribution, which means assigning all the conversion value to the last step in the journey or "first click" attribution. The first step in developing multi-channel attribution analytics is to understand the customer's journey - from awareness through purchase to after-purchase support. The ultimate goal is to develop loyal customers who spend a significant money on purchases, recommend the brand to others, and it potentially becomes a brand.

Getting ready

In order to perform a Markov chains multi-channel attribution model we shall be simulating customer journeys containing three unique channels.

How to do it...

Let's get into the details.

Step 1 - preparing the dataset

First load the following packages:

```
> install.packages("dplyr")
> install.packages("reshape2")
> install.packages("ggplot2")
> install.packages("ChannelAttribution")
> install.packages("markovchain")
> library(dplyr)
> library(reshape2)
> library(ggplot2)
> library(ChannelAttribution)
> library(markovchain)
```

Version info: Code for this page was tested in R version 3.2.2 (2015-08-14).

Creating the data sample: The `c()` function combines arguments to form a vector. All the arguments passed to the function are combined to form a common type that is the type of the returned value. The `data.frame()` function creates a tightly coupled data frame that is the collection of variables that share many of the properties of matrices and of lists. We will be saving the data to the `datafrm1` data frame as follows:

```
> datafrm1 <- data.frame(path = c('c1 > c2 > c3', 'c1', 'c2 > c3'),
conv = c(1, 0, 0), conv_null = c(0, 1, 1))
```

Print the `datafrm1` data frame as follows:

```
> datafrm1
```

The result is as follows:

```
                path conv conv_null
1 c1 > c2 > c3     1         0
2             c1     0         1
3        c2 > c3     0         1
```

Step 2 - preparing the model

Preparing the Markov model. The `markov_model()` function estimates the k-order Markov model from customer journey data. `datafrm1` is the data frame that contains the customer journeys as defined. The `var_path` variable has the names of the columns that contain the journey path. The `var_conv` variable represents the name of the columns containing total conversions. The `var_null` variable represents the columns containing total paths that do not lead to conversions. `out_more = TRUE` returns the transition probabilities between channels and removal effects.

The result of the estimated k-order Markov model is stored in the `model1` data frame as follows:

```
> model1 <- markov_model(datafrm1, var_path = 'path', var_conv =
'conv', var_null = 'conv_null', out_more = TRUE)
```

Printing the `model1` data frame:

```
> model1
```

The result is as follows:

```
$result
  channel_name total_conversions
1           c1         0.2001447
2           c2         0.3999276
3           c3         0.3999276

$transition_matrix
  channel_from   channel_to transition_probability
1      (start)           c1              0.6666667
2      (start)           c2              0.3333333
3           c1           c2              0.5000000
4           c1        (null)             0.5000000
5           c2           c3              1.0000000
6           c3 (conversion)              0.5000000
7           c3        (null)             0.5000000

$removal_effects
  channel_name removal_effects
1           c1       0.5004524
2           c2       1.0000000
3           c3       1.0000000
```

Extract the result attribution from the `model1data` frame as follows. The result is then stored in the `datafrmresult1` data frame:

```
> datafr{BS}l1$result
```

Extracting the `transition_matrix` attribution from the `model1data` frame as follows. The result is then stored in the `datafrmtransmatrix1` data frame:

```
> datafrmtransmatrix1 <- model1$transition_matrix
```

Reshaping the data frame. The result of the reshaped data frame is stored in `datafrmtransmatrix`:

```
> datafrmtransmatrix <- dcast(datafrmtransmatrix1, channel_from ~
channel_to, value.var = 'transition_probability')
```

Printing the `datafrmtransmatrix` data frame:

```
> datafrmtransmatrix
```

The result is as follows:

	channel_from	(conversion)	(null)	c1	c2	c3
1	(start)	NA	NA	0.6666667	0.3333333	NA
2	c1	NA	0.5	NA	0.5000000	NA
3	c2	NA	NA	NA	NA	1
4	c3	0.5	0.5	NA	NA	NA

Step 3 - plotting the Markov graph

Extracting the `transition_matrix` attribution from the `model1` data frame. The result is then stored in the `datafrmtransmatrix` data frame:

```
> datafrmtransmatrix <- model1$transition_matrix
```

Print the `datafrmtransmatrix` data frame as follows:

```
> datafrmtransmatrix
```

The result is as follows:

	channel_from	channel_to	transition_probability
1	(start)	c1	0.6666667
2	(start)	c2	0.3333333
3	c1	c2	0.5000000
4	c1	(null)	0.5000000
5	c2	c3	1.0000000
6	c3	(conversion)	0.5000000
7	c3	(null)	0.5000000

Creating the `datafrmdummy` data sample. The `c()` function combines arguments to form a vector. All the arguments passed to the function are combined to form a common type that is the type of the returned value. The `data.frame()` function creates a tightly coupled data frame that is the collection of variables that share many of the properties of matrices and of lists. We will be saving the data to the `datafrmdummy` data frame as follows:

```
> datafrmdummy <- data.frame(channel_from = c('(start)',
'(conversion)', '(null)'), channel_to = c('(start)', '(conversion)',
'(null)'), transition_probability = c(0, 1, 1))
```

Printing the `datafrmtransmatrix` data frame:

```
> datafrmtransmatrix
```

The result is as follows:

	channel_from	channel_to	transition_probability
1	(start)	(start)	0
2	(conversion)	(conversion)	1
3	(null)	(null)	1

Combining the columns as follows. `rbind()` takes a sequence of data frames and combines them. `datafrmtransmatrix` and `df_dummy` are passed as input parameters. The result is then the `datafrmtransmatrix` data frame:

```
> datafrmtransmatrix <- rbind(datafrmtransmatrix, datafrmdummy)
```

Printing the `datafrmtransmatrix` data frame:

```
> datafrmtransmatrix
```

The result is as follows:

```
      channel_from    channel_to transition_probability
1        (start)            c1            0.6666667
2        (start)            c2            0.3333333
3           c1              c2            0.5000000
4           c1           (null)            0.5000000
5           c2              c3            1.0000000
6           c3    (conversion)            0.5000000
7           c3          (null)            0.5000000
8        (start)        (start)            0.0000000
9    (conversion)  (conversion)            1.0000000
10       (null)          (null)            1.0000000
```

Order the channels as follows. `factor()` as a function is used to encode a vector as a factor. `datafrmtransmatrix$channel_from` is passed as a vector of data. `levels = c('(start)', '(conversion)', '(null)', 'c1', 'c2', 'c3')` represents an optional vector of the values:

```
> datafrmtransmatrix$channel_from <-
factor(datafrmtransmatrix$channel_from, levels = c('(start)',
'(conversion)', '(null)', 'c1', 'c2', 'c3'))
```

Printing the `datafrmtransmatrix$channel_from` data frame as follows:

```
> datafrmtransmatrix$channel_from
```

The result is as follows:

```
 [1] (start)      (start)      c1           c1           c2         c3         c3         (start)      (conversion)
[10] (null)
Levels: (start) (conversion) (null) c1 c2 c3
```

Ordering the channels as follows. `datafrmtransmatrix$channel_to` is passed as a vector of data:

```
> datafrmtransmatrix$channel_to <-
factor(datafrmtransmatrix$channel_to, levels = c('(start)', '(conversion)',
'(null)', 'c1', 'c2', 'c3'))
```

Print `datafrmtransmatrix$channel_to` the data frame:

```
> datafrmtransmatrix$channel_to
```

The result is as follows:

```
[1] c1          c2          c2          (null)      c3          (conversion) (null)      (start)
[9] (conversion) (null)
Levels: (start) (conversion) (null) c1 c2 c3
```

Reshaping the data frame. The result of the reshaped data frame is stored in `datafrmtransmatrix`:

```
> datafrmtransmatrix <- dcast(datafrmtransmatrix, channel_from ~
channel_to, value.var = 'transition_probability')
```

Printing the `datafrmtransmatrix` data frame:

```
> datafrmtransmatrix
```

The result is as follows:

```
  channel_from (start) (conversion) (null)       c1        c2 c3
1      (start)       0           NA     NA 0.6666667 0.3333333 NA
2 (conversion)      NA          1.0     NA        NA        NA NA
3       (null)      NA           NA    1.0        NA        NA NA
4           c1      NA           NA    0.5        NA 0.5000000 NA
5           c2      NA           NA     NA        NA        NA  1
6           c3      NA           NA    0.5       0.5        NA NA
```

Creating the Markov chain object. `matrix()` as a function creates a matrix from a given set of values:

```
> transitionmatrix <- matrix(data = as.matrix(datafrmtransmatrix[,
-1]), nrow = nrow(datafrmtransmatrix[, -1]), ncol =
ncol(datafrmtransmatrix[, -1]), dimnames = list
(c(as.character(datafrmtransmatrix[, 1])), c(colnames(datafrmtransmatrix[,
-1])))))
```

Printing the `transitionmatrix` data frame:

```
> transitionmatrix
```

The result is as follows:

```
                (start) (conversion) (null)        c1        c2 c3
(start)            0           NA      NA 0.6666667 0.3333333 NA
(conversion)      NA          1.0      NA        NA        NA NA
(null)            NA           NA     1.0        NA        NA NA
c1                NA           NA     0.5        NA 0.5000000 NA
c2                NA           NA      NA        NA        NA  1
c3                NA          0.5     0.5        NA        NA NA
```

```
> transitionmatrix[is.na(transitionmatrix)] <- 0
```

Creating a Markov chain object. The `transitionMatrix` will be a transition matrix, that is, all entries will be probabilities and either all rows or all columns will sum up to one:

```
> transitionmatrix1 <- new("markovchain", transitionMatrix =
transitionmatrix)
```

Printing the `transitionmatrix1` data frame:

```
> transitionmatrix1
```

The result is as follows:

```
Unnamed Markov chain
 A  6 - dimensional discrete Markov Chain defined by the following states:
 (start), (conversion), (null), c1, c2, c3
 The transition matrix  (by rows)  is defined as follows:
             (start) (conversion) (null)        c1        c2 c3
(start)         0          0.0     0.0 0.6666667 0.3333333  0
(conversion)    0          1.0     0.0 0.0000000 0.0000000  0
(null)          0          0.0     1.0 0.0000000 0.0000000  0
c1              0          0.0     0.5 0.0000000 0.5000000  0
c2              0          0.0     0.0 0.0000000 0.0000000  1
c3              0          0.5     0.5 0.0000000 0.0000000  0
```

Plotting the graph:

```
> plot(transitionmatrix1, edge.arrow.size = 0.5, main = "Markov Graph
Transition Matrix - transitionmatrix1")
```

The result is as follows:

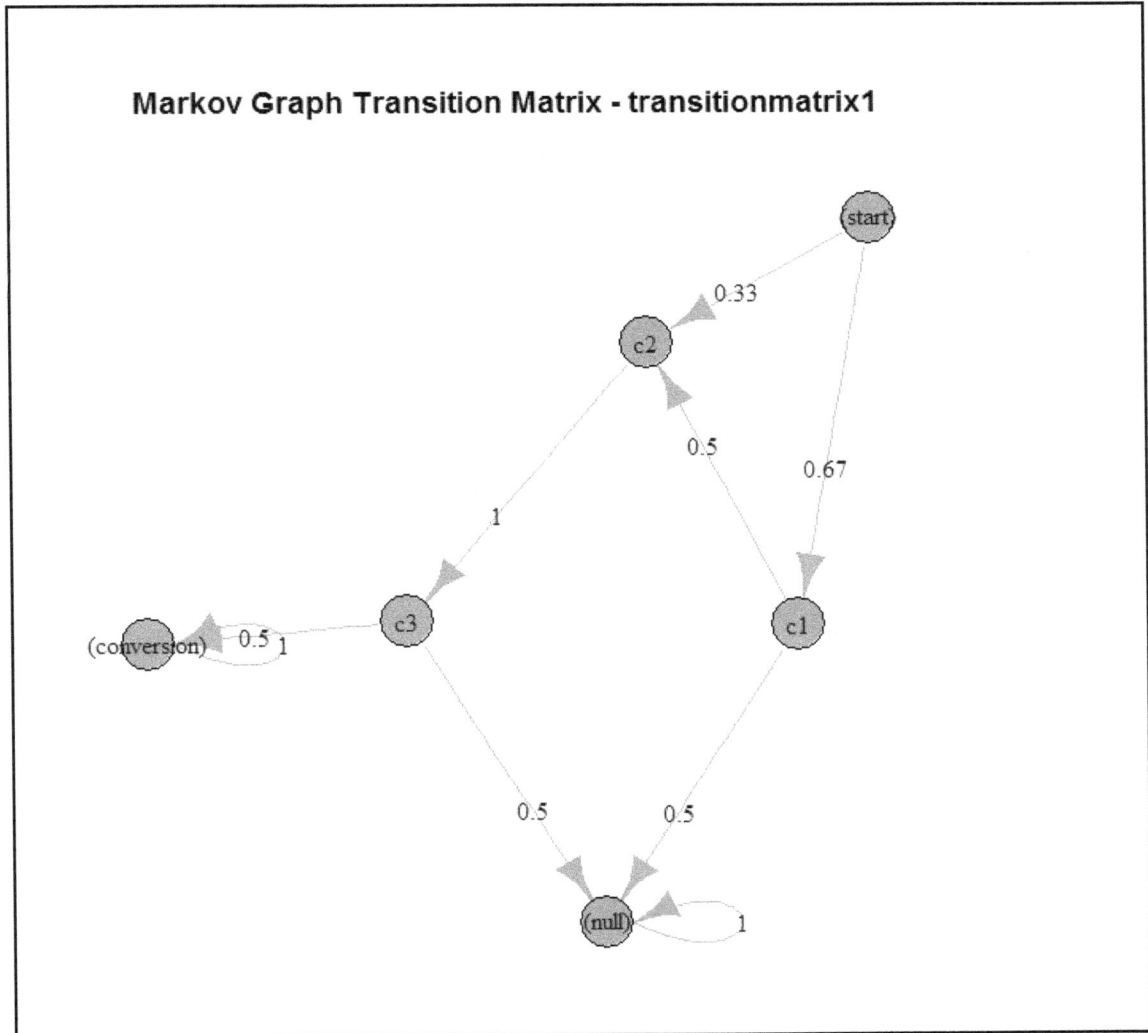

Step 4 - simulating the dataset of customer journeys

The `data.frame()` function creates a tightly coupled data frame that is the collection of variables that share many of the properties of matrices and of lists. We will be saving the data to the `datafrm2` data frame as follows:

```
> set.seed(354)
> datafrm2 <- data.frame(client_id = sample(c(1:1000), 5000, replace =
TRUE), date = sample(c(1:32), 5000, replace = TRUE), channel =
sample(c(0:9), 5000, replace = TRUE, prob = c(0.1, 0.15, 0.05, 0.07, 0.11,
0.07, 0.13, 0.1, 0.06, 0.16)))
```

Printing the `datafrm2` frame. The `head()` function returns the first part of the `datafrm2` frame. The `datafrm2` frame is passed as an input parameter:

```
> head(datafrm2)
```

The result is as follows:

```
  client_id       date channel
1       411 2016-01-05       5
2       761 2016-01-31       6
3       509 2016-01-09       6
4       541 2016-02-02       8
5       156 2016-01-04       9
6       934 2016-01-26       8
```

Converting the character objects to date objects. `datafrm2$date` represents the object to be converted. `origin = "2016-01-01"` represents the `Date` object:

```
> datafrm2$date <- as.Date(datafrm2$date, origin = "2016-01-01")
```

Concatenating the vectors after converting to characters. Add the `channel_` object to the channel. `datafrm2$channel` represents the data frame:

```
> datafrm2$channel <- paste0('channel_', datafrm2$channel)
```

Printing the `datafrm2` frame. The `head()` function returns the first part of the `datafrm2` frame. The `datafrm2` frame is passed as an input parameter:

```
> head(datafrm2)
```

The result is as follows:

```
      client_id        date   channel
1           411  2016-01-05  channel_5
2           761  2016-01-31  channel_6
3           509  2016-01-09  channel_6
4           541  2016-02-02  channel_8
5           156  2016-01-04  channel_9
6           934  2016-01-26  channel_8
```

Aggregating the channels to the paths for each customer:

```
> datafrm2 <- datafrm2 %>% group_by(client_id) %>% summarise(path =
paste(channel, collapse = ' > '), conv = 1, conv_null = 0) %>% ungroup()
```

Printing the `datafrm2` data frame:

```
> datafrm2
```

The result is as follows:

```
# A tibble: 990 x 4
   client_id
       <int>
1          1
2          2
3          3
4          4
5          5
6          6
7          7
8          8
9          9
10        10
# ... with 980 more rows, and 3 more variables: path <chr>, conv <dbl>, conv_null <dbl>
```

Preparing the Markov models. The `markov_model()` function estimates the k-order Markov model from customer journey data. `datafrm2` is the data frame that contains the customer journeys as defined. `var_path` has the names of the columns that contain the journey path. `var_conv` represents the name of the columns containing total conversions. `var_null` represents the columns containing total paths that do not lead to conversions. `out_more = TRUE` returns the transition probabilities between channels and removal effects.

The result of the estimated k-order Markov model is stored in the `model2` data frame as follows:

```
> model2 <- markov_model(datafrm2, var_path = 'path', var_conv =
'conv', var_null = 'conv_null', out_more = TRUE)

> datafrmheuristic <- datafrm2 %>% mutate(channel_name_ft = sub('>.*',
'', path), channel_name_ft = sub(' ', '', channel_name_ft), channel_name_lt
= sub('.*>', '', path), channel_name_lt = sub(' ', '', channel_name_lt))
```

Printing the `datafrmheuristic` data frame:

```
> datafrmheuristic
```

The result is as follows:

```
# A tibble: 990 x 6
   client_id                                                                                              path  conv conv_null
     <int>                                                                                               <chr> <dbl>    <dbl>
1       1                                                                                           channel_3     1        0
2       2             channel_4 > channel_9 > channel_9 > channel_6 > channel_2 > channel_1 > channel_0     1        0
3       3   channel_7 > channel_9 > channel_9 > channel_8 > channel_8 > channel_5 > channel_0 > channel_0     1        0
4       4                                         channel_1 > channel_9 > channel_0 > channel_6     1        0
5       5             channel_4 > channel_6 > channel_4 > channel_9 > channel_2 > channel_7     1        0
6       6                             channel_1 > channel_1 > channel_4 > channel_7 > channel_6     1        0
7       7             channel_6 > channel_5 > channel_6 > channel_6 > channel_7 > channel_7 > channel_6     1        0
8       8   channel_4 > channel_5 > channel_5 > channel_3 > channel_5 > channel_6 > channel_8 > channel_4 > channel_1     1        0
9       9                                                         channel_4 > channel_8     1        0
10     10                             channel_0 > channel_4 > channel_1 > channel_1     1        0
# ... with 980 more rows, and 2 more variables: channel_name_ft <chr>, channel_name_lt <chr>
```

```
> datafrmfirsttouch <- datafrmheuristic %>% group_by(channel_name_ft)
%>% summarise(first_touch_conversions = sum(conv)) %>% ungroup()
```

Printing the `datafrmfirsttouch` data frame:

```
> datafrmfirsttouch
```

The result is as follows:

```
# A tibble: 10 × 2
   channel_name_ft first_touch_conversions
             <chr>                   <dbl>
1        channel_0                      82
2        channel_1                     159
3        channel_2                      60
4        channel_3                      71
5        channel_4                     102
6        channel_5                      75
7        channel_6                     142
8        channel_7                      83
9        channel_8                      50
10       channel_9                     166
```

```
> datafrmlasttouch <- datafrmheuristic %>% group_by(channel_name_lt)
%>% summarise(last_touch_conversions = sum(conv)) %>% ungroup()
```

Printing the datafrmfirsttouch data frame:

```
> datafrmfirsttouch
```

The result is as follows:

```
# A tibble: 10 × 2
   channel_name_lt last_touch_conversions
             <chr>                   <dbl>
1        channel_0                      92
2        channel_1                     166
3        channel_2                      50
4        channel_3                      71
5        channel_4                     114
6        channel_5                      64
7        channel_6                     139
8        channel_7                      88
9        channel_8                      46
10       channel_9                     160
```

Merging the two data frames by common columns. The result is stored in the heuristicmodel2 data frame:

```
> heuristicmodel2 <- merge(datafrmfirsttouch, datafrmlasttouch, by.x =
'channel_name_ft', by.y = 'channel_name_lt')
```

Printing the `heuristicmodel2` data frame:

```
> heuristicmodel2
```

The result is as follows:

	channel_name_ft	first_touch_conversions	last_touch_conversions
1	channel_0	82	92
2	channel_1	159	166
3	channel_2	60	50
4	channel_3	71	71
5	channel_4	102	114
6	channel_5	75	64
7	channel_6	142	139
8	channel_7	83	88
9	channel_8	50	46
10	channel_9	166	160

Merging all the models:

```
> allmodels <- merge(heuristicmodel2, model2$result, by.x =
'channel_name_ft', by.y = 'channel_name')
```

Printing the `allmodels` data frame:

```
> allmodels
```

The result is as follows:

	channel_name_ft	first_touch_conversions	last_touch_conversions	total_conversions
1	channel_0	82	92	97.59677
2	channel_1	159	166	139.07908
3	channel_2	60	50	57.98764
4	channel_3	71	71	73.53247
5	channel_4	102	114	110.94456
6	channel_5	75	64	82.25067
7	channel_6	142	139	126.11034
8	channel_7	83	88	98.86641
9	channel_8	50	46	65.69749
10	channel_9	166	160	137.93456

Step 5 - preparing a transition matrix heat map for real data

Plotting the heatmap.

```
> colnames(allmodels)[c(1, 4)] <- c('channel_name',
'attrib_model_conversions')
> dataframplottransition <- model2$transition_matrix
> cols <- c("#e7f0fa", "#c9e2f6", "#95cbee", "#0099dc", "#4ab04a",
"#ffd73e", "#eec73a", "#e29421", "#e29421", "#f05336", "#ce472e")
```

Return the maximum value of all the arguments present in the dataframplottransition$transition_probability data frame:

```
> t <- max(dataframplottransition$transition_probability)
```

Printing the value of t:

```
> t
```

The result is as follows:

```
[1] 0.2391931
```

```
> ggplot(dataframplottransition, aes(y = channel_from, x = channel_to,
fill = transition_probability)) + theme_minimal() + geom_tile(colour =
"white", width = .9, height = .9) + scale_fill_gradientn(colours = cols,
limits = c(0, t), breaks = seq(0, t, by = t/4), labels = c("0",
round(t/4*1, 2), round(t/4*2, 2), round(t/4*3, 2), round(t/4*4, 2)), guide
= guide_colourbar(ticks = T, nbin = 50, barheight = .5, label = T, barwidth
= 10)) + geom_text(aes(label = round(transition_probability, 2)), fontface
= "bold", size = 4) + theme(legend.position = 'bottom', legend.direction =
"horizontal", panel.grid.major = element_blank(), panel.grid.minor =
element_blank(), plot.title = element_text(size = 20, face = "bold", vjust
= 2, color = 'black', lineheight = 0.8), axis.title.x = element_text(size =
24, face = "bold"), axis.title.y = element_text(size = 24, face = "bold"),
axis.text.y = element_text(size = 8, face = "bold", color = 'black'),
axis.text.x = element_text(size = 8, angle = 90, hjust = 0.5, vjust = 0.5,
face = "plain")) + ggtitle("Heatmap - Transition Matrix ")
```

The result is as follows:

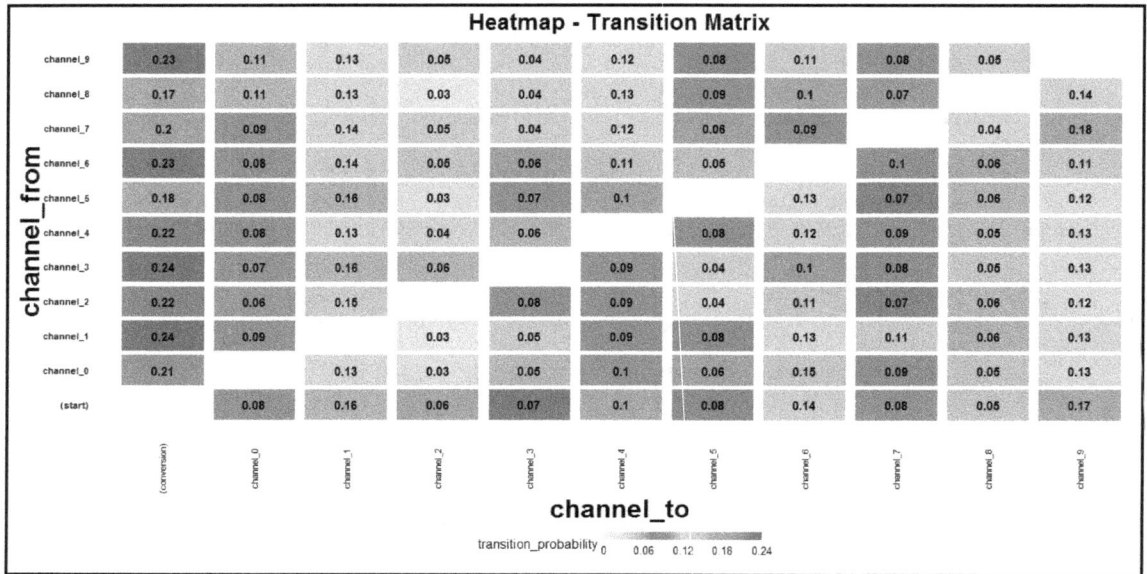

Heatmap - Transition Matrix

channel_from \ channel_to	(conversion)	channel_0	channel_1	channel_2	channel_3	channel_4	channel_5	channel_6	channel_7	channel_8	channel_9
channel_9	0.23	0.11	0.13	0.05	0.04	0.12	0.08	0.11	0.08	0.05	
channel_8	0.17	0.11	0.13	0.03	0.04	0.13	0.09	0.1	0.07		0.14
channel_7	0.2	0.09	0.14	0.05	0.04	0.12	0.06	0.09		0.04	0.18
channel_6	0.23	0.08	0.14	0.05	0.06	0.11	0.05		0.1	0.06	0.11
channel_5	0.18	0.08	0.16	0.03	0.07	0.1		0.13	0.07	0.06	0.12
channel_4	0.22	0.06	0.13	0.04	0.06		0.08	0.12	0.09	0.05	0.13
channel_3	0.24	0.07	0.16	0.06		0.09	0.04	0.1	0.08	0.05	0.13
channel_2	0.22	0.06	0.15		0.08	0.09	0.04	0.11	0.07	0.06	0.12
channel_1	0.24	0.09		0.03	0.05	0.09	0.08	0.13	0.11	0.06	0.13
channel_0	0.21		0.13	0.03	0.05	0.1	0.06	0.15	0.09	0.05	0.13
(start)		0.08	0.16	0.06	0.07	0.1	0.08	0.14	0.08	0.05	0.17

transition_probability 0   0.06   0.12   0.18   0.24

Markov chains - the car rental agency service

Suppose a car rental agency has three locations in Ottawa: A downtown location (labeled A), A East End location (labeled B), and a West End location (labeled C). The agency has a group of delivery drivers to serve all three locations. The agency's statistician has determined the following:

- Of the calls to the Downtown location, 30% are delivered in the Downtown area, 30% are delivered in the East end, and 40% are delivered in the West end
- Of the calls to the East end location, 40% are delivered in the downtown area, 40% are delivered in the East end, and 20% are delivered in the West end
- Of the calls to the West end location, 50% are delivered in the Downtown area, 30% are delivered in the East end, and 20% are delivered in the West end

After making a delivery, a driver goes to the nearest location to make the next delivery. This way, the location of a specific driver is determined only by their previous location.

How to do it...

Let's get into the details.

Step 1 - preparing the dataset

Load the following packages:

```
> install.packages("markovchain")
> library(markovchain)
```

Version info: Code for this page was tested in R version 3.2.2 (2015-08-14).

Creating the data sample. The `c()` function combines arguments to form a vector. All the arguments passed to the function are combined to form a common type that is the type of the returned value. We will be saving the data to the `RentalStates` data frame:

```
> RentalStates <- c("Downtown", "East", "West")
```

Printing the value of `RentalStates`:

```
> RentalStates
```

The result is as follows:

```
[1] "Downtown" "East"     "West"
```

Creating the matrix. The `matrix()` function creates a matrix from the given set of values. The `byrow = T` matrix is filled by rows. `nrow = 3` represents the desired number of rows. The `c()` function combines arguments to form a vector. All the arguments passed to the function are combined to form a common type that is the type of the returned value:

```
> RentalTransitionMatrix <- matrix(c(0.3, 0.3, 0.4,
                                      0.4, 0.4, 0.2,
                                      0.5, 0.3, 0.2),
         byrow = T, nrow = 3, dimnames = list(RentalStates, RentalStates))
```

Printing the value of `RentalTransitionMatrix`:

```
> RentalTransitionMatrix
```

The result is as follows:

```
         Downtown East West
Downtown     0.3  0.3  0.4
East         0.4  0.4  0.2
West         0.5  0.3  0.2
```

Step 2 - preparing the model

Creating a Markov chain object. The `new()` function creates object of the type `markovchain`. States represents the `RentalStates` as defined previously. `byrow = T` matrix is filled by rows. The result is then stored in the data frame `mcRental`:

```
> mcRental <- new("markovchain", states = RentalStates, byrow = T,
transitionMatrix = RentalTransitionMatrix, name = "Rental Cars")
```

Printing the `mcRental` data frame:

```
> mcRental
```

The result is as follows:

```
Rental Cars
 A  3 - dimensional discrete Markov chain defined by the following states:
 Downtown, East, West
 The transition matrix  (by rows)  is defined as follows:
          Downtown East West
Downtown     0.3  0.3  0.4
East         0.4  0.4  0.2
West         0.5  0.3  0.2
```

Accessing the transition matrix by calling the `mcRental` object as follows:

```
> mcRental[2]
```

The result is as follows:

```
      Downtown        East        West
           0.4         0.4         0.2
```

Ploting the `mcRental` object. `plot()` is a generic function to plot R objects:

```
> plot(mcRental)
```

The result is as follows:

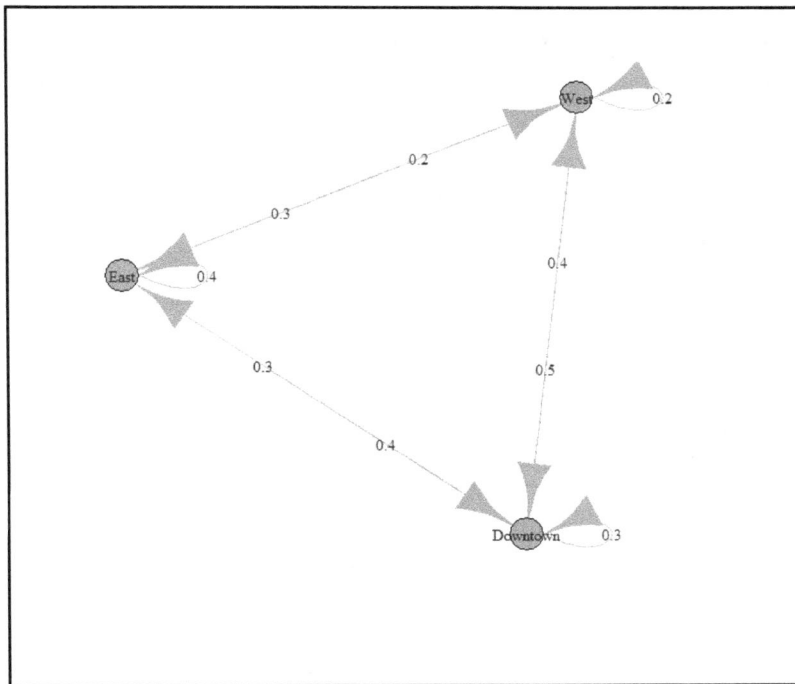

Calculating the transition probability. `transitionProbability()` provides direct access to transition probabilities.

```
> transitionProbability(mcRental, "East", "West")
```

The result is as follows:

```
[1] 0.2
```

Step 3 - improving the model

Calculating the probability of being in Downtown in two trips; Downtown to Downtown:

```
> x <- 0.3 * 0.3
```

Calculating the probability of going Downtown from the East location; East to Downtown:

```
> y <- 0.3 * 0.4
```

Calculating the probability of going Downtown from the West location; West to Downtown:

```
> z <- 0.4 * 0.5
> x + y + z
```

The result is as follows:

```
[1] 0.41
```

Squaring the `mcRental` matrix to calculate the probability, we will be downtown in two trips:

```
> mcRental ^ 2
```

The result is as follows:

```
Rental Cars^2
 A  3 - dimensional discrete Markov Chain defined by the following states:
 Downtown, East, West
 The transition matrix  (by rows)  is defined as follows:
          Downtown East West
Downtown     0.41 0.33 0.26
East         0.38 0.34 0.28
West         0.37 0.33 0.30
```

Checking the probability that we will be downtown in 20 trips using the `mcRental` matrix probability calculation as follows:

```
> mcRental ^ 20
```

The result is as follows:

```
Rental Cars^20
 A  3 - dimensional discrete Markov Chain defined by the following states:
 Downtown, East, West
 The transition matrix  (by rows)  is defined as follows:
           Downtown      East       West
Downtown 0.3888889 0.3333333 0.2777778
East     0.3888889 0.3333333 0.2777778
West     0.3888889 0.3333333 0.2777778
```

Checking the probability that we will be downtown in three trips using the `mcRental` matrix probability calculation as follows:

```
> mcRental ^ 30
```

The result is as follows:

```
Rental Cars^30
 A  3 - dimensional discrete Markov Chain defined by the following states:
 Downtown, East, West
 The transition matrix  (by rows)  is defined as follows:
           Downtown      East      West
Downtown 0.3888889 0.3333333 0.2777778
East       0.3888889 0.3333333 0.2777778
West       0.3888889 0.3333333 0.2777778
```

This method returns the stationary vector in matrix form of a markovchain object:

```
> 70 * steadyStates (mcRental)
```

The result is as follows:

```
          Downtown      East      West
    [1,]  27.22222 23.33333 19.44444
```

Printing the summary of mcRental:

```
> summary (mcRental)
```

The result is as follows:

```
Rental Cars  Markov chain that is composed by:
Closed classes:
Downtown East West
Recurrent classes:
{Downtown,East,West}
Transient classes:
NONE
The Markov chain is irreducible
The absorbing states are: NONE
```

Extracting the conditional distribution of the subsequent state, given the current state. mcRental is the markov chain object that is passed while "Downtown" is the next state:

```
> conditionalDistribution(mcRental, "Downtown")
```

The result is as follows:

```
        Downtown        East        West
             0.3         0.3         0.4
```

```
> conditionalDistribution(mcRental, "West")
```

The result is as follows:

```
        Downtown        East        West
             0.5         0.3         0.2
```

```
> conditionalDistribution(mcRental, "East")
```

The result is as follows:

```
        Downtown        East        West
             0.4         0.4         0.2
```

Continuous Markov chains - vehicle service at a gas station

A gas station has a single pump. There is no space for vehicles to wait. If a vehicle arrives at the pump and there is no place the vehicle leaves without filling at the pump. Vehicles arrive at the gas station following a Poisson process with a rate of 3/20 vehicles per minute. Of the vehicles arriving at the pump, 75% are cars and 25% are motorcycles. The refueling time can be modeled with an exponential random variable with a mean of eight minutes for cars and three minutes for motorcycles.

Getting ready

In order to perform continuous Markov chains for vehicle service at a gas station we shall be simulating data.

How to do it...

Let's get into the details.

Step 1 - preparing the dataset

Load the following packages:

```
> install.packages("simmer")
> install.packages("ggplot2")
> library(simmer)
> library(ggplot2)
```

Version info: Code for this page was tested in R version 3.2.2 (2015-08-14)

Initializing the vehicle arrival rate:

```
> ArrivalRate <- 3/20
```

Printing the `ArrivalRate` data frame:

```
> ArrivalRate
```

The result is as follows:

```
[1] 0.15
```

Initializing the service rate of the vehicles and create the data sample. The `c()` function combines arguments to form a vector. All the arguments passed to the function are combined to form a common type that is the type of the returned value. We will be saving the data to the `ServiceRate` data frame:

```
> ServiceRate <- c(1/8, 1/3)
```

Printing the `ServiceRate` data frame:

```
> ServiceRate
```

The result is as follows:

```
[1] 0.1250000 0.3333333
```

Initializing the probability of the arrival of the car:

```
> p <- 0.75
```

Creating a transition matrix. `matrix()` as a function creates a matrix from a given set of values. The result is stored in the `TransitionMatrix` data frame:

```
> TransitionMatrix <- matrix(c(1,     ServiceRate[1],      0,
1,    -ArrivalRate,       (1-p)*ArrivalRate,
1,    ServiceRate[2],     -ServiceRate[2]), byrow=T, ncol=3)
```

Printing the `TransitionMatrix` data frame:

```
> TransitionMatrix
```

The result is as follows:

```
           [,1]          [,2]          [,3]
[1,]         1    0.1250000     0.0000000
[2,]         1   -0.1500000     0.0375000
[3,]         1    0.3333333    -0.3333333
```

Initializing the vector:

```
> B <- c(1, 0, 0)
```

Step 2 - computing the theoretical resolution

Solving the linear system of equations. `solve()` is used to compute the linear equation. `t(A)` represents the transition matrix while `B` is the vector. The result is then stored in `P`:

```
> P <- solve(t(A), B)
```

Printing the `P` data frame:

```
> P
```

The result is as follows:

```
[1] 0.44720497 0.49689441 0.05590062
```

Computing the theoretical resolution. `sum()` computes the sum. The result is then stored in `Resolution`:

```
> Resolution <- sum(P * c(1, 0, 1))
```

Printing the `Resolution` data frame:

```
> Resolution
```

The result is as follows:

```
[1] 0.5031056
```

Step 3 - verifying the convergence of a theoretical solution

Simulating the system and verify that it converges to a theoretical solution:

```
> set.seed(1234)
```

Defining the option.1 function. A create_trajectory() function creates the trajectory object of car and motorcycle types. These objects comprise a chain of activities that is to be attached to a generator object. Activities for seizing the pump object by name are carried out. amount=1 means the number of objects that require to be seized. The timeout() function inserts the delays based on the user definition. The timeout() function also takes in the rexp() function that randomly generates the exponential distribution with a rate defined as ServiceRate[1] = 1/8 for the car object and ServiceRate[1] = 1/3 for the motorcycle object.

Then a simulator object is created as follows. The method initializes a simulation environment. The car and motorcycle objects are created with the exponential distribution with the rate defined as p*ArrivalRate where ArrivalRate = 0.15. Then a new generator of arrivals in a simulation environment is created:

```
> option.1 <- function(t) {
  car <- create_trajectory() %>%
      seize("pump", amount=1) %>%
      timeout(function() rexp(1, ServiceRate[1])) %>%
      release("pump", amount=1)

  motorcycle <- create_trajectory() %>%
      seize("pump", amount=1) %>%
      timeout(function() rexp(1, ServiceRate[2])) %>%
      release("pump", amount=1)

  simmer() %>%
      add_resource("pump", capacity=1, queue_size=0) %>%
```

```
        add_generator("car", car, function() rexp(1, p*ArrivalRate)) %>%
        add_generator("motorcycle", motorcycle, function() rexp(1, (1-
p)*ArrivalRate)) %>%
        run(until=t)
    }
```

Defining the `option.2` function. Define a single generator for all kinds of vehicles and a single trajectory. In order to distinguish between cars and motorcycles, define a branch after seizing the resource to select the proper service time.

A `create_trajectory()` function creates the trajectory object of the `vehicle` type. This object comprises a chain of activities that is to be attached to a generator object. Activities for seizing the pump object by name are carried out. `amount=1` means the number of objects that are required to be seized. The `create_trajectory()` function then calls the `timeout()` function that inserts the delays based on the user definition. The `timeout()` function, also takes in the `rexp()` function which randomly generates the exponential distribution with the rate defined as `ServiceRate[1] = 1/8` for a car object and `ServiceRate[1] = 1/3` for a `motorcycle` object.

Then a simulator object is created as follows. The method initializes a simulation environment. The `car` and `motorcycle` objects are created with the exponential distribution with the rate defined as `p*ArrivalRate`. `ArrivalRate = 0.15`. The `run()` function then continues to run until the user-defined time out, as mentioned in `until=t`:

```
> option.2 <- function(t) {
  vehicle <- create_trajectory() %>%
        seize("pump", amount=1) %>%
        branch(function() sample(c(1, 2), 1, prob=c(p, 1-p)), merge=c(T,
T),
                create_trajectory("car") %>%
                    timeout(function() rexp(1, ServiceRate[1])),
                create_trajectory("motorcycle") %>%
                    timeout(function() rexp(1, ServiceRate[2]))) %>%
        release("pump", amount=1)

    simmer() %>%
        add_resource("pump", capacity=1, queue_size=0) %>%
        add_generator("vehicle", vehicle, function() rexp(1,
ArrivalRate)) %>%
        run(until=t)
    }
```

Defining the `option.3` function. `option.2` adds an unnecessary overhead. An additional call is made to select the branch, and therefore performance decreases. Select the service time directly inside the `timeout()` function:

```
> option.3 <- function(t) {
    vehicle <- create_trajectory() %>%
    seize("pump", amount=1) %>%
    timeout(function() {
        if (runif(1) < p) rexp(1, ServiceRate[1])
        else rexp(1, ServiceRate[2])
    }) %>%
release("pump", amount=1)

simmer() %>%
add_resource("pump", capacity=1, queue_size=0) %>%
add_generator("vehicle", vehicle, function() rexp(1, ArrivalRate)) %>%
run(until=t)
}
```

Call the options created as follows:

```
> gas.station <- option.3(5000)
```

Step 4 - plotting the results

Plotting the results. `plot_resource_usage()` is used to plot the usage of a resource over the simulation time frame. `gas.station` represents a single simmer environment. `"pump"` represents the name of the resource. `items="system"` refers to the components of the resource to be plotted. The result is then stored in an object of `ggplot2` type graph:

```
> graph <- plot_resource_usage(gas.station, "pump", items="system")
> graph + geom_hline(yintercept = Resolution)
```

The result is as follows:

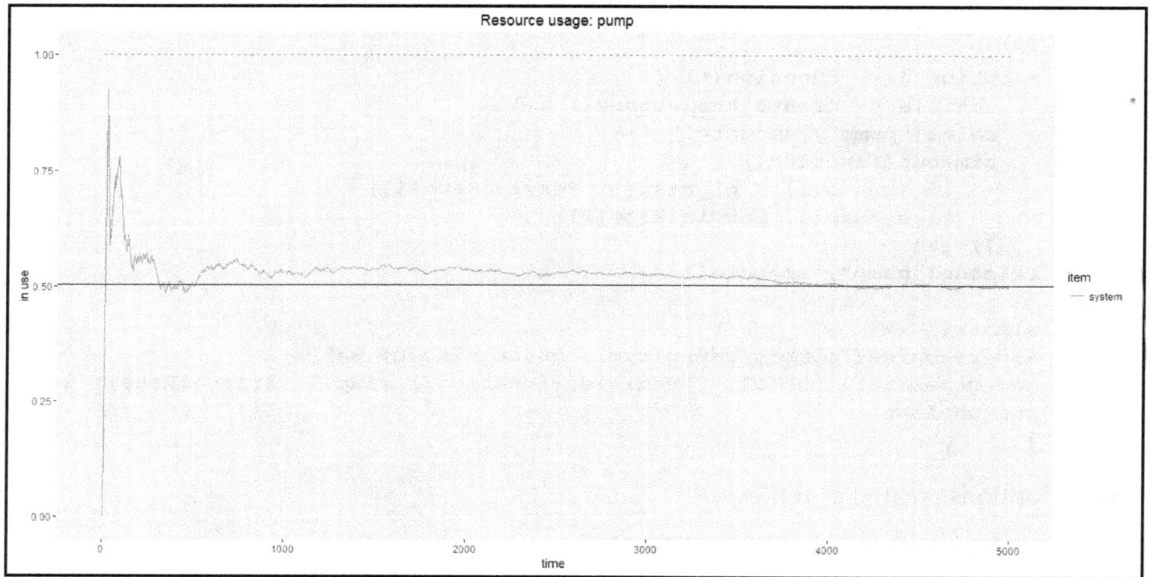

Monte Carlo simulations - calibrated Hull and White short-rates

Monte Carlo simulation is a stochastic simulation of system behavior. The simulation uses sampling experiments to be performed on the model and it then conducts numerical experiments using the computer to obtain a statistical understanding of the system behavior.

Getting ready

In order to perform Monte Carlo simulations for calibrated hull and white short-rates, data is taken from sample code that has been shipped with `QuantLib` 0.3.10, market data used to construct the term structure of interest rates and swaption volatility matrix with corresponding maturities and tenors.

Step 1 - installing the packages and libraries

Load the following packages:

```
>install.packages("RQuantLib", type="binary")
>install.packages("ESGtoolkit")
>library(RQuantLib)
>library(ESGtoolkit)
```

Version info: Code for this page was tested in R version 3.2.2 (2015-08-14)

In order to make part of the Quantlib package accessible to the R environment RQuantLib is used. The Quantlib package provides a comprehensive software framework for quantitative finance. The goal of the RQuantLib is to provide source libraries for modeling, trading, quantitative analysis, and risk management of financial assets.

type="binary" indicates the type of package to be downloaded and installed. This means that the nature of the package to be installed is not a source package.

How to do it...

Let's get into the details.

Step 2 - initializing the data and variables

Initializing the variables:

```
> freq <- "monthly"
> delta_t <- 1/12
```

Printing the value of delta_t:

```
> delta_t
```

The result is as follows:

```
[1] 0.08333333
```

Initializing the variables from the sample code integrated with `QuantLib` 0.3.10. A list specifying the `tradeDate` (month/day/year), `settleDate`, forward rate time span `dt`, and two curve construction options: `interpWhat` (with possible values discount, forward, and zero) and `interpHow` (with possible values linear, loglinear, and spline). spline here means cubic spline interpolation of the `interpWhat` value.

The result is then stored in the `params` data frame:

```
> params <- list(tradeDate=as.Date('2002-2-15'),
              settleDate=as.Date('2002-2-19'),
              payFixed=TRUE,
              dt=delta_t,
              strike=.06,
              method="HWAnalytic",
              interpWhat="zero",
              interpHow= "spline")
```

Initializing the market data. The term structure is constructed for interest rates, deposits, and swaps. The result is then stored in `TermQuotes`:

```
> TermQuotes  <- list(d1w =0.0382, # 1-week deposit rate
              d1m =0.0372,# 1-month deposit rate
              d3m = 0.0363,# 3-month deposit rate
              d6m = 0.0353,# 6-month deposit rate
              d9m = 0.0348,# 9-month deposit rate
              d1y = 0.0345,# 1-year deposit rate
              s2y = 0.037125,# 2-year swap rate
              s3y =0.0398,# 3-year swap rate
              s5y =0.0443,# 5-year swap rate
              s10y =0.05165,# 10-year swap rate
              s15y =0.055175)# 15-year swap rate
```

Initializing the `Swaptionmaturities`:

```
> SwaptionMaturities <- c(1,2,3,4,5)
```

Printing the value of `SwaptionMaturities`:

```
> SwaptionMaturities
```

The result is as follows:

```
[1] 1 2 3 4 5
```

Initializing the swap tenors:

```
> SwapTenors <- c(1,2,3,4,5)
```

Printing the value of SwapTenors:

```
> SwapTenors
```

The result is as follows:

```
[1] 1 2 3 4 5
```

Initializing the volatility matrix. The matrix() function creates a matrix from the given set of values. ncol=5 denotes the number of desired of columns. byrow=TRUE means the matrix is filled by rows. The result is then stored in VolatilityMatrix:

```
> VolatilityMatrix <- matrix(
  c(0.1490, 0.1340, 0.1228, 0.1189, 0.1148,
    0.1290, 0.1201, 0.1146, 0.1108, 0.1040,
    0.1149, 0.1112, 0.1070, 0.1010, 0.0957,
    0.1047, 0.1021, 0.0980, 0.0951, 0.1270,
    0.1000, 0.0950, 0.0900, 0.1230, 0.1160),
  ncol=5, byrow=TRUE)
```

Step 3 - pricing the Bermudan swaptions

Price the Bermudan swaption as follows. BermudanSwaption is part of the Quantlib package. This is accessible to the R environment using RQuantLib. BermudanSwaption prices a Bermudan swaption with specified strike and maturity (in years), after calibrating the selected short-rate model to an input swaption volatility matrix. Swaption maturities and swap tenors are in years. It is assumed that the Bermudan swaption is exercisable on each reset date of the underlying swaps. Passing params, TermQuotes, SwaptionMaturities, SwapTenors, and VolatilityMatrix as inputs is used to compute Bermudan swaption. The result is stored in BermudanSwaption:

```
> BermudanSwaption <- RQuantLib::BermudanSwaption(params, TermQuotes,
SwaptionMaturities, SwapTenors, VolatilityMatrix)
```

The BermudanSwaption valuation is displayed. The result is as follows:

```
Hull-White (analytic) calibration
0x0: model 0.106204, market 0.114800, diff -0.008596
0x0: model 0.106296, market 0.110800, diff -0.004504
0x0: model 0.106341, market 0.107000, diff -0.000659
0x0: model 0.106443, market 0.102100, diff 0.004343
0x0: model 0.106613, market 0.100000, diff 0.006613
```

Printing the summary of BermudanSwaption:

```
> summary(BermudanSwaption)
```

The result is as follows:

```
           Summary of pricing results for Bermudan Swaption

Price (in bp) of Bermudan swaption is   24.92137
Stike is   NULL (ATM strike is   0.05 )
Model used is: Hull-White using analytic formulas
Calibrated model parameters are:
a =   0.04641
sigma =   0.005869
```

Printing the valuations of `BermudanSwaption`:

```
> BermudanSwaption
```

The result is as follows:

```
$a
[1]  0.04641377

$sigma
[1]  0.005869286

$price
[1]  24.92137

$ATMStrike
[1]  0.05000001

attr(,"class")
[1] "HWAnalytic"          "BermudanSwaption"
```

Step 4 - constructing the spot term structure of interest rates

Initializing the vector of times at which to return the discount factors, forward rates, and zero rates. Times are specified such that the largest time plus `delta_t` does not exceed the longest maturity of the instruments used for calibration (no extrapolation):

```
> times <- seq(from = delta_t, to = 5, by = delta_t)
```

`DiscountCurve` constructs the spot term structure of interest rates based on input market data including the settlement date, deposit rates, and swap rates. It returns the corresponding discount factors, zero rates, and forward rates for a vector of times that is specified as input. params represents a list that specifies the `tradeDate` (month/day/year), `settleDate`, forward rate time span, and two curve construction options: `interpWhat` (with possible values discount, forward, and zero) and `interpHow` (with possible values `linear`, `loglinear`, and `spline`). spline here means cubic spline interpolation of the `interpWhat` value. `TermQuotes` represents market quotes to construct the spot term structure of interest rates. Use the following command:

```
> DiscountCurve <- RQuantLib::DiscountCurve(params, TermQuotes, times)
```

Exploring the internal structure of the `DiscountCurve` data frame. The `str()` function displays the internal structure of the data frame. The `DiscountCurve` is passed as an R object to the `str()` function:

```
> str(DiscountCurve)
```

The result is as follows:

```
List of 7
 $ times     : num [1:60] 0.0833 0.1667 0.25 0.3333 0.4167 ...
 $ discounts : num [1:60] 0.997 0.994 0.991 0.988 0.985 ...
 $ forwards  : num [1:60] 0.0365 0.0358 0.0349 0.0342 0.0338 ...
 $ zerorates : num [1:60] 0.0376 0.037 0.0366 0.0362 0.0358 ...
 $ flatQuotes: logi FALSE
 $ params    :List of 8
  ..$ tradeDate : Date[1:1], format: "2002-02-15"
  ..$ settleDate: Date[1:1], format: "2002-02-19"
  ..$ payFixed  : logi TRUE
  ..$ dt        : num 0.0833
  ..$ strike    : num 0.06
  ..$ method    : chr "HWAnalytic"
  ..$ interpwhat: chr "zero"
  ..$ interpHow : chr "spline"
 $ table     :'data.frame':    183 obs. of  2 variables:
  ..$ date    : Date[1:183], format: "2002-02-19" "2002-03-20" "2002-04-22" "2002-05-22" ...
  ..$ zeroRates: num [1:183] 0.0387 0.0376 0.037 0.0366 0.0362 ...
 - attr(*, "class")= chr "DiscountCurve"
```

Finding the maturity time at which to return the discount factors, forward rates, and zero rates:

```
> maturities <- DiscountCurve$times
```

Printing the value of maturities:

```
> maturities
```

The result is as follows:

```
 [1] 0.08333333 0.16666667 0.25000000 0.33333333 0.41666667 0.50000000 0.58333333 0.66666667 0.75000000 0.83333333
 0.91666667
[12] 1.00000000 1.08333333 1.16666667 1.25000000 1.33333333 1.41666667 1.50000000 1.58333333 1.66666667 1.75000000
 1.83333333
[23] 1.91666667 2.00000000 2.08333333 2.16666667 2.25000000 2.33333333 2.41666667 2.50000000 2.58333333 2.66666667
 2.75000000
[34] 2.83333333 2.91666667 3.00000000 3.08333333 3.16666667 3.25000000 3.33333333 3.41666667 3.50000000 3.58333333
 3.66666667
[45] 3.75000000 3.83333333 3.91666667 4.00000000 4.08333333 4.16666667 4.25000000 4.33333333 4.41666667 4.50000000
 4.58333333
[56] 4.66666667 4.75000000 4.83333333 4.91666667 5.00000000
```

Finding zero coupon rates:

```
> MarketZeroRates <- DiscountCurve$zerorates
```

Printing the value of zero coupon rates:

```
> MarketZeroRates
```

The result is as follows:

```
[1] 0.03760349 0.03704203 0.03662016 0.03618554 0.03578598 0.03546280 0.03521342 0.03500431 0.03482148 0.03462910
0.03445629
[12] 0.03438130 0.03440817 0.03448436 0.03460322 0.03475813 0.03494245 0.03514953 0.03537275 0.03560546 0.03584102
0.03607281
[23] 0.03629418 0.03649850 0.03669634 0.03690156 0.03711288 0.03732899 0.03754861 0.03777043 0.03799317 0.03821553
0.03843622
[34] 0.03865395 0.03886741 0.03907533 0.03928021 0.03948630 0.03969335 0.03990105 0.04010912 0.04031728 0.04052524
0.04073270
[45] 0.04093939 0.04114501 0.04134928 0.04155191 0.04175261 0.04195110 0.04214709 0.04234029 0.04253041 0.04271717
0.04290028
[56] 0.04307945 0.04325440 0.04342484 0.04359047 0.04375102
```

Finding discount factors:

```
> MarketPrices <- DiscountCurve$discounts
```

Printing the discount factors:

```
> MarketPrices
```

The result is as follows:

```
[1] 0.9968713 0.9938453 0.9908867 0.9880106 0.9851998 0.9824249 0.9796684 0.9769340 0.9742220 0.9715548 0.9689087
0.9662030
[13] 0.9634107 0.9605668 0.9576681 0.9547133 0.9517034 0.9486415 0.9455327 0.9423840 0.9392047 0.9360059 0.9328006
0.9296036
[25] 0.9263986 0.9231594 0.9198874 0.9165845 0.9132529 0.9098950 0.9065138 0.9031126 0.8996949 0.8962647 0.8928262
0.8893842
[37] 0.8859330 0.8824616 0.8789710 0.8754620 0.8719358 0.8683934 0.8648360 0.8612648 0.8576813 0.8540867 0.8504826
0.8468704
[49] 0.8432517 0.8396281 0.8360013 0.8323730 0.8287451 0.8251193 0.8214976 0.8178818 0.8142740 0.8106761 0.8070902
0.8035185
```

Step 5 - simulating Hull-White short-rates

Setting the time horizons:

```
> horizon <- 5
```

Setting the number of simulations:

```
> NoSimulations <- 10000
> a <- BermudanSwaption$a
```

Printing the value of a:

```
> a
```

```
[1] 0.04641377
```

```
> sigma <- BermudanSwaption$sigma
```

Printing the value of sigma:

```
> sigma
```

```
[1] 0.005869286
```

Simulating Gaussian shocks. simshocks() create a simulated version of correlated or dependent Gaussian shocks for risk factors. n = NoSimulations denotes number of simulations. horizon = 5 means the time horizons. frequency = monthly. The result is then stored in the GaussianShocks data frame:

```
> GaussianShocks <- ESGtoolkit::simshocks(n = NoSimulations, horizon = horizon, frequency = freq)
```

`simdiff()` makes simulations of diffusion processes. `n = NoSimulations` represents the number of independent observations. `frequency = freq` is monthly. `model = "OU"` stands for the Ornstein-Uhlenbeck method. `x0 = 0` is the starting value of the process. `eps = GaussianShocks` represents Gaussian shocks:

```
> x <- ESGtoolkit::simdiff(n = NoSimulations, horizon = horizon,
frequency = freq, model = "OU", x0 = 0, theta1 = 0, theta2 = a, theta3 =
sigma, eps = GaussianShocks)
```

Calculating the forward rates. `ts()` creates time series objects. `replicate(nb.sims, DiscountCurve$forwards)` creates a vector of time-series values. `start = start(x)` represents the time of the first observation. `deltat = deltat(x)` represents the fraction of the sampling period between successive observations. The result is then stored in the `ForwardRates` data frame:

```
> ForwardRates <- ts(replicate(nb.sims, DiscountCurve$forwards), start
= start(x), deltat = deltat(x))
```

Generating regular sequences. `from = 0, to = horizon` denotes the starting and end values of sequences. `by = delta_t` denotes the increments in sequence:

```
> t.out <- seq(from = 0, to = horizon, by = delta_t)
> param.alpha <- ts(replicate(NoSimulations, 0.5*(sigma^2)*(1 - exp(-
a*t.out))^2/(a^2)), start = start(x), deltat = deltat(x))
> alpha <- ForwardRates + param.alpha
```

Generating the short-term rates:

```
> ShortRates <- x + alpha
```

Calculating stochastic discount values. `r = ShortRates` denotes the short term rates, `X = 1` denotes the asset's price:

```
> StochasticDiscount <- ESGtoolkit::esgdiscountfactor(r = ShortRates, X
= 1)
```

Calculating the mean of stochastic discount values:

```
> MonteCarloPrices <- rowMeans(StochasticDiscount)
```

Printing the values of `MonteCarloPrices`:

```
> MonteCarloPrices
```

The result is as follows:

```
[1] 0.9969646 0.9939972 0.9911117 0.9882912 0.9855078 0.9827449 0.9800036 0.9772856 0.9746132 0.9719634 0.9692537
0.9664558
[13] 0.9636063 0.9607016 0.9577400 0.9547254 0.9516572 0.9485439 0.9453912 0.9422074 0.9390047 0.9357938 0.9325895
0.9293760
[25] 0.9261312 0.9228538 0.9195472 0.9162110 0.9128457 0.9094549 0.9060440 0.9026178 0.8991789 0.8957324 0.8922809
0.8888213
[37] 0.8853405 0.8818385 0.8783182 0.8747819 0.8712305 0.8676639 0.8640836 0.8604893 0.8568831 0.8532672 0.8496438
0.8460148
[49] 0.8423810 0.8387448 0.8351062 0.8314680 0.8278328 0.8242010 0.8205761 0.8169591 0.8133518 0.8097557 0.8061732
0.8025957
```

Calculating the zero rates of stochastic discount values:

```
> MonteCarloZeroRates <- -log(MonteCarloPrices)/maturities
```

Printing the values of `MonteCarloZeroRates`:

```
> MonteCarloZeroRates
```

The result is as follows:

```
[1] 0.03648056 0.03612541 0.03571211 0.03533363 0.03503568 0.03481134 0.03462698 0.03446451 0.03428612 0.03412455
0.03406787
[12] 0.03411972 0.03422072 0.03436407 0.03454314 0.03474862 0.03497678 0.03521811 0.03546727 0.03571789 0.03596274
0.03619645
[23] 0.03641224 0.03662097 0.03683488 0.03705436 0.03727730 0.03750368 0.03773315 0.03796394 0.03819385 0.03842104
0.03864484
[34] 0.03886362 0.03907689 0.03928637 0.03949716 0.03970938 0.03992196 0.04013419 0.04034595 0.04055738 0.04076813
0.04097840
[45] 0.04118768 0.04139545 0.04160121 0.04180462 0.04200561 0.04220371 0.04239914 0.04259133 0.04277979 0.04296464
0.04314516
[56] 0.04332135 0.04349296 0.04365987 0.04382170 0.04398085
```

Performing the student t test on the difference between stochastic discount terms and market prices. `t.test(x)` performs the t test. `conf.int` means confidence interval for the mean appropriate:

```
> ConfidenceInterval <- t(apply((StochasticDiscount - MarketPrices)[-1,
], 1, function(x) t.test(x)$conf.int))
```

The `head()` function returns the first part of the `ConfidenceInterval` frame. The `ConfidenceInterval` frame is passed as an input parameter as follows:

```
> head(ConfidenceInterval)
```

```
              [,1]         [,2]
[1,]  0.0001491098  0.0001545721
[2,]  0.0002189103  0.0002310291
[3,]  0.0002704573  0.0002907584
[4,]  0.0002932542  0.0003228398
[5,]  0.0003000920  0.0003400166
[6,]  0.0003095954  0.0003607932
```

Set the graphical parameters as follows:

```
> par(mfrow = c(2, 2))
```

`esgplotbands()` plots color bands confidence intervals as follows. `ShortRates` represents the confidence interval:

```
> ESGtoolkit::esgplotbands(ShortRates, xlab = "maturities", ylab =
  "short-rate quantiles", main = "Short Rate Quantiles")
```

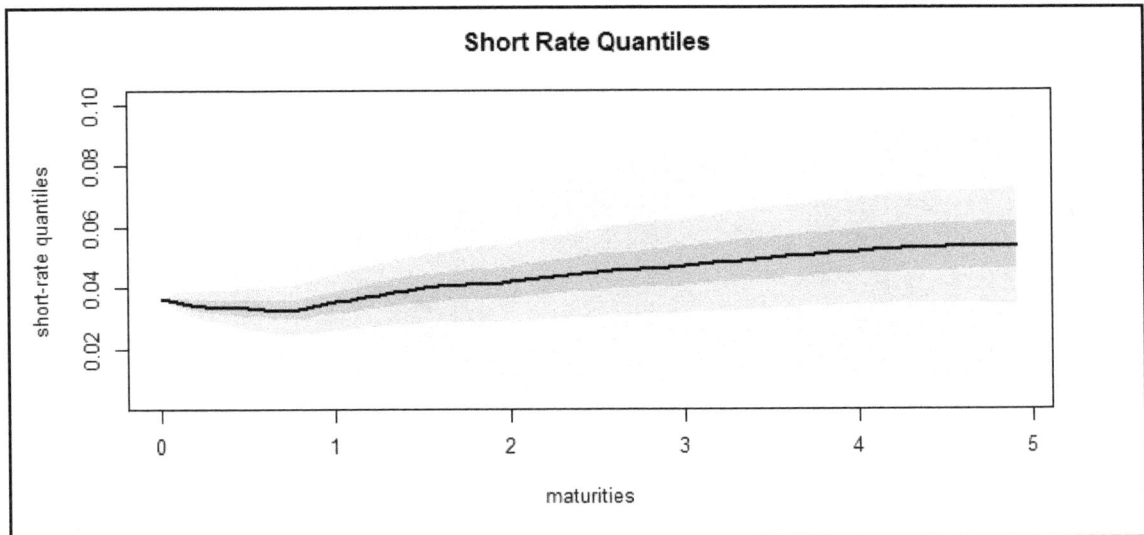

Plotting the **Monte Carlo v/s Market n Zero Rates** as follows. maturities, `MonteCarloZeroRates` represents the time series:

```
> plot(maturities, MonteCarloZeroRates, type='l', col = 'blue', lwd =
1, main = "Monte Carlo v/s Market n Zero Rates")
```

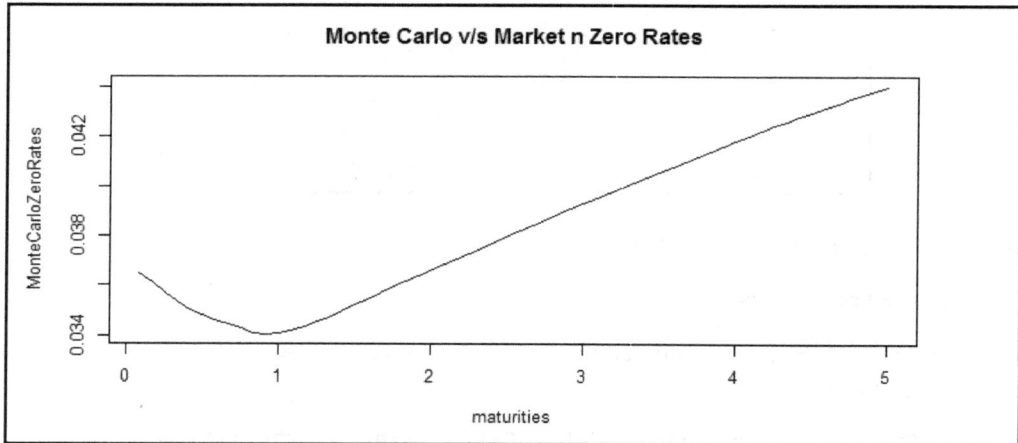

Adding a sequence of points at the specified coordinates of the plot between maturities, `MonteCarloZeroRates`:

```
> points(maturities, MonteCarloZeroRates, col = 'red')
```

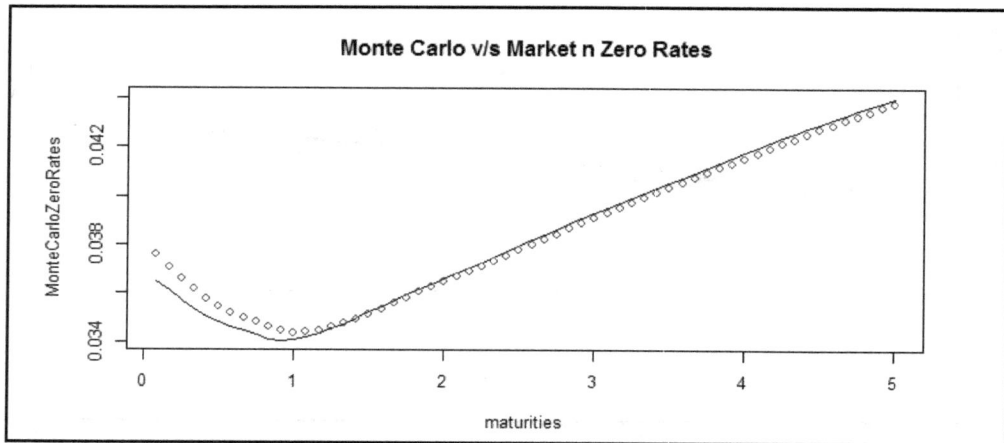

Plotting the Monte Carlo v/s Market Prices as follows. maturities, `MonteCarloPrices` represents the time series:

```
> plot(maturities, MonteCarloPrices, type='l', col = 'blue', lwd = 1,
main = "Monte Carlo v/s Market Prices")
```

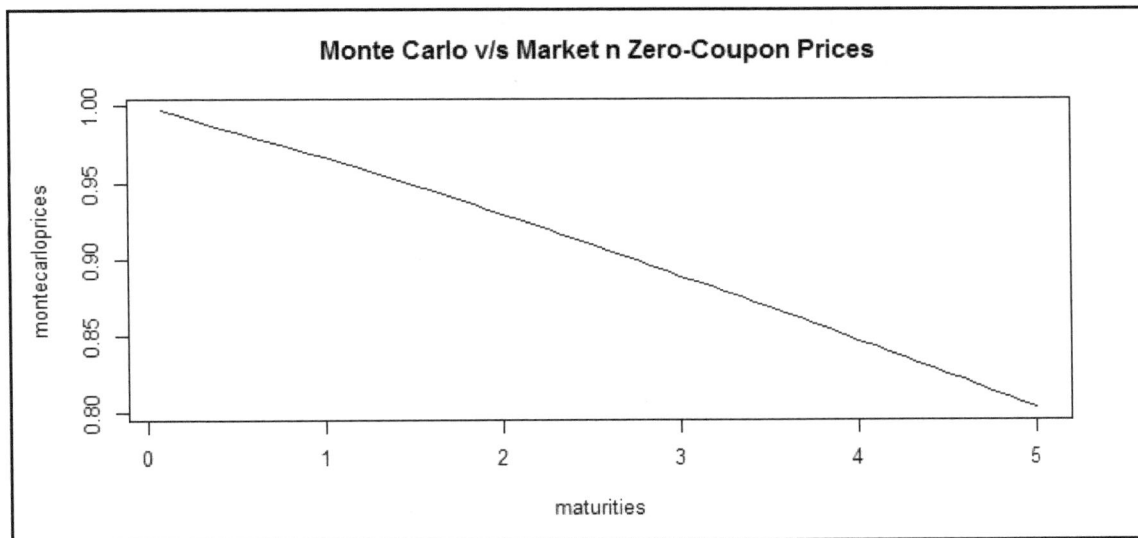

Adding a sequence of points at the specified coordinates of the plot between maturities, `MonteCarloPrices`:

```
> points(maturities, MonteCarloPrices, col = 'red')
```

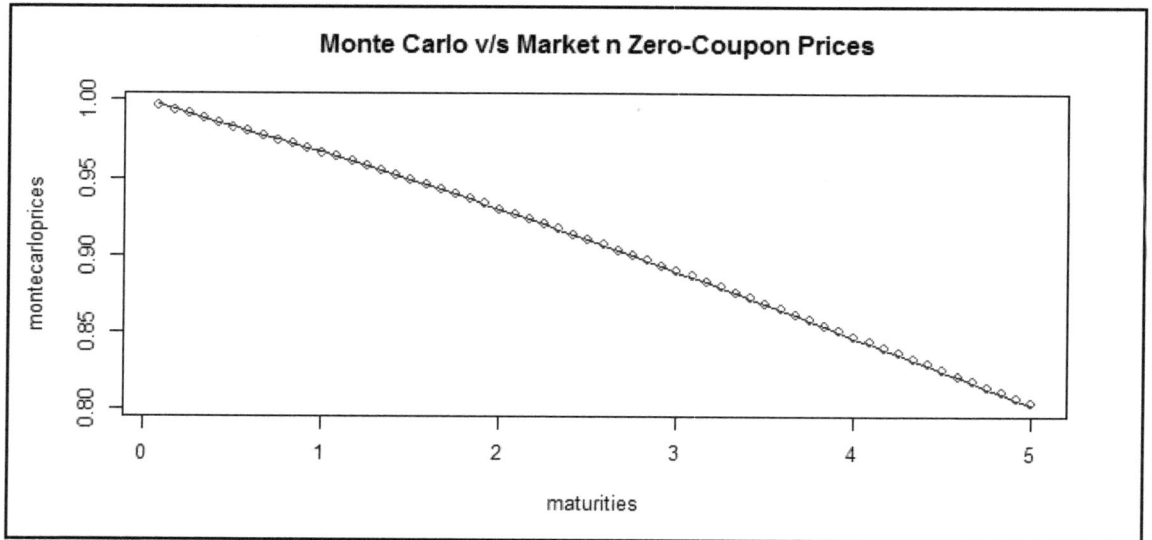

```
> matplot(maturities[-1], conf.int, type = 'l', main = "Confidence
Interval for the price difference")
```

9
Structured Prediction

In this chapter, we will cover the following recipes:

- Hidden Markov models - EUR and USD
- Hidden Markov models for regime detection

Introduction

The **hidden Markov model** (**HMM**) is a very powerful statistical method of characterizing the observed data samples of a discrete-time series. Not only can it provide an efficient way to build parsimonious parametric models, it can also incorporate the dynamic programming principle in its core for a unified pattern segmentation and pattern classification of time-varying data sequences. The data samples in the time series can be discretely or continuously distributed; they can be scalars or vectors. The underlying assumption of the HMM is the the data samples can be well characterized as a parametric random process, and the parameters of the stochastic process can be estimated in a precise and well-defined framework.

Hidden Markov models - EUR and USD

The EUR/USD is the most commonly traded pair in the Forex market. Their popularity can be attributed to the fact that each currency represents the world's two largest economic and trading blocks and many multinational corporations that conduct business across the Atlantic.

Price movements for this currency pair are generally related to factors that influence the value of either the EUR or the USD. As the world's most liquid currency pair, the EUR/USD offers tight spreads and constant liquidity for traders who are looking to instantly buy or sell. The combination of stability and volatility makes the EUR/USD an excellent pair for beginner and advanced traders. The EUR/USD pair offers traders high liquidity and has very tight and competitive spreads. The relative strength of the US economy and the European economy, which can be tracked through the daily news, generally influence this pair.

Getting ready

In order to apply the hidden Markov model to find different market regimes, and to therefore optimize a trading strategy, we will be using a dataset collected on the Euro Dollar dataset.

Step 1 - collecting and describing data

The dataset titled `EURUSD1d.csv` shall be used. This dataset is available in CSV format and called `EURUSD1d.csv`. The dataset is in a standard format. There are 1,008 rows of data and five variables. The numeric variables are as follows:

- `Open`
- `High`
- `Low`
- `Close`

The non-numeric variable is:

- `Open Timestamp`

How to do it...

Let's get into the details.

Step 2 - exploring data

The following packages need to be loaded as the first step:

```
> install.packages("depmixS4")
> install.packages("quantmod")
> install.packages("ggplot2")
> library(depmixS4)
> library(quantmod)
> library(ggplot2)
```

> Version info: Code for this page was tested in R version 3.2.2 (2015-08-14)

Let's explore the data and understand the relationships among the variables:

We'll begin by importing the CSV data file named EURUSD1d.csv. We will be saving the data to the EuroUSD data frame as follows:

```
> EuroUSD <- read.csv("d:/EURUSD1d.csv", header = TRUE)
```

Printing the EuroUSD frame: The head() function returns the first part of the EuroUSD frame. The EuroUSD frame is passed as an input parameter:

```
> head(EuroUSD)
```

The result is as follows:

```
> head(EuroUSD)
        Open.Timestamp     Open     High      Low    Close
1 2012.01.03 00:00:00   1.29357  1.30760  1.29343  1.30528
2 2012.01.04 00:00:00   1.30528  1.30718  1.28967  1.29295
3 2012.01.05 00:00:00   1.29295  1.29427  1.27688  1.27905
4 2012.01.06 00:00:00   1.27905  1.28116  1.26961  1.27136
5 2012.01.08 00:00:00   1.27136  1.27136  1.26649  1.26778
6 2012.01.09 00:00:00   1.26778  1.27843  1.26762  1.27712
```

Printing the summary of the EuroUSD data frame: The summary() function is a multipurpose function. The summary() is a generic function that provides a summary of the data related to the individual object or data frame. The EuroUSD data frame is passed as an R object to the summary() function:

```
> summary(EuroUSD)
```

The result is as follows:

```
          Open.Timestamp        Open             High             Low              Close
2012.01.03 00:00:00:   1    Min.   :1.048    Min.   :1.050    Min.   :1.046    Min.   :1.048
2012.01.04 00:00:00:   1    1st Qu.:1.272    1st Qu.:1.277    1st Qu.:1.267    1st Qu.:1.272
2012.01.05 00:00:00:   1    Median :1.311    Median :1.316    Median :1.306    Median :1.311
2012.01.06 00:00:00:   1    Mean   :1.300    Mean   :1.304    Mean   :1.296    Mean   :1.300
2012.01.08 00:00:00:   1    3rd Qu.:1.349    3rd Qu.:1.353    3rd Qu.:1.346    3rd Qu.:1.349
2012.01.09 00:00:00:   1    Max.   :1.393    Max.   :1.399    Max.   :1.391    Max.   :1.393
(Other)            :1002
```

Exploring the internal structure of the EuroUSD data frame: The str() function displays the internal structure of the data frame. The EuroUSD is passed as an R object to the str() function:

```
> str(EuroUSD)
```

The result is as follows:

```
'data.frame':   1008 obs. of  5 variables:
 $ Open.Timestamp: Factor w/ 1008 levels "2012.01.03 00:00:00",..: 1 2 3 4 5 6 7 8 9 10 ...
 $ Open          : num  1.29 1.31 1.29 1.28 1.27 ...
 $ High          : num  1.31 1.31 1.29 1.28 1.27 ...
 $ Low           : num  1.29 1.29 1.28 1.27 1.27 ...
 $ Close         : num  1.31 1.29 1.28 1.27 1.27 ...
```

Step 3 - turning data into a time series

Creating objects of the type character: The as.character() function represents real and complex numbers to 15 significant digits. The entire EuroUSD data frame is passed apart from the 1st column:

```
> Date <- as.character(EuroUSD[,1])
```

Manipulating the `Date` data frame to represent calendar dates. The result is then stored in the data frame `DateTimeSeries`:

```
> DateTimeSeries <- as.POSIXlt(Date, format = "%Y.%m.%d %H:%M:%S")
```

Creating tightly coupled data frames. `data.frame()` creates the data frame for `EuroUSD[,2:5]`. `row.names = DateTimeSeries` gives the row names for the data frame created:

```
> TimeSeriesData <- data.frame(EuroUSD[,2:5], row.names =
  DateTimeSeries)
```

Printing the `TimeSeriesData` frame. The `head()` function returns the first part of the `TimeSeriesData` frame. The `TimeSeriesData` frame is passed as an input parameter:

```
> head(TimeSeriesData)
```

The result is as follows:

```
                 Open     High      Low   Close
2012-01-03  1.29357  1.30760  1.29343  1.30528
2012-01-04  1.30528  1.30718  1.28967  1.29295
2012-01-05  1.29295  1.29427  1.27688  1.27905
2012-01-06  1.27905  1.28116  1.26961  1.27136
2012-01-08  1.27136  1.27136  1.26649  1.26778
2012-01-09  1.26778  1.27843  1.26762  1.27712
```

The `as.xts()` function converts the `TimeSeriesData` data object to the `xts` class without losing any attributes of the `TimeSeriesData` data frame as follows:

```
> TimeSeriesData <- as.xts(TimeSeriesData)
```

Measuring the volatility of a high-low-close series. The `ATR()` function measures the average volatility of the high-low-close series of `TimeSeriesData`. `TimeSeriesData[,2:4]` indicates the high-low-close of the `TimeSeriesData`. The result is then stored in the `ATRindicator` data frame:

```
> ATRindicator <- ATR(TimeSeriesData[,2:4],n=14)
```

Printing the `ATRindicator` frame. The `head()` function returns the first part of the `ATRindicator` frame. The `ATRindicator` frame is passed as an input parameter:

```
> head(ATRindicator)
```

The result is as follows:

```
                 tr atr trueHigh trueLow
2012-01-03       NA  NA       NA      NA
2012-01-04 0.01751  NA  1.30718 1.28967
2012-01-05 0.01739  NA  1.29427 1.27688
2012-01-06 0.01155  NA  1.28116 1.26961
2012-01-08 0.00487  NA  1.27136 1.26649
2012-01-09 0.01081  NA  1.27843 1.26762
```

Measuring the volatility of a high series. `ATRindicator [,2]` indicates the high of the `TimeSeriesData`. The result is then stored in the `TrueRange` data frame:

```
> TrueRange <- ATRindicator[,2]
```

Printing the `TrueRange` data frame:

```
> head(TrueRange)
```

The result is as follows:

```
           atr
2012-01-03 NA
2012-01-04 NA
2012-01-05 NA
2012-01-06 NA
2012-01-08 NA
2012-01-09 NA
```

Calculating the difference between the `LogReturns` of close and open values. The result is then stored in the `LogReturns` data frame:

```
> LogReturns <- log(EuroUSD$Close) - log(EuroUSD$Open)
```

Printing the summary of the `LogReturns` data frame. The `summary()` function is used to provide a summary of the data related to the individual object or data frame. The `LogReturns` data frame is passed as an R object to the `summary()` function:

```
> summary(LogReturns)
```

The result is as follows:

```
     Min.    1st Qu.     Median       Mean     3rd Qu.        Max.
-2.335e-02  -2.347e-03  -4.967e-05  -1.779e-04   2.155e-03   2.624e-02
```

Step 4 - building the model

Creating a data frame for the HMM model. The `data.frame()` function creates tightly coupled data frames of variables that share many of the properties of matrices:

```
> HMMModel <- data.frame(LogReturns, TrueRange)
```

Removing the data where the indicators are being calculated for the `HMMModel`:

```
> HMMModel <- HMMModel[-c(1:14),]
```

Printing the `HMMModel` frame:

```
> head(HMMModel)
```

The result is as follows:

```
              LogReturns            atr
2012-01-19  0.0075360408  0.01244214
2012-01-20 -0.0025263367  0.01226342
2012-01-22 -0.0032387061  0.01176603
2012-01-23  0.0106681264  0.01213846
2012-01-24  0.0007752087  0.01205285
2012-01-25  0.0054554841  0.01254551
```

Naming the columns. The `c()` function combines arguments to form a vector. All the arguments passed to the function are combined to form a common type that is the type of the returned value:

```
> colnames(HMMModel) <- c("LogReturns","TrueRange")
```

Printing the column's names:

```
> colnames(HMMModel)
```

The result is as follows:

```
[1] "LogReturns" "TrueRange"
```

```
> set.seed(1)
```

Building a three-state regime and set response distribution to the Gaussian state. The `depmix()` function creates the hidden Markov model. The `LogReturns~1, TrueRange~1` represents the response to be modeled. `data = HMMModel` represents the data frame to interpret the variables in response, while `nstates=3` is the number of states:

```
> HMM <- depmix(list(LogReturns~1, TrueRange~1), data = HMMModel,
  nstates=3, family=list(gaussian(), gaussian()))
```

Fitting the HMM model to the defined dataset. The `fit()` function optimizes the parameters of the HMM model, subject to linear inequality. HMM is an object of class HMM, while `verbose = FALSE` depicts that the information should not be displayed on screen. The optimized parameters are stored in object `HMMfit` of class `depmix`:

```
> HMMfit <- fit(HMM, verbose = FALSE)
```

```
converged at iteration 29 with logLik: 9503.258
```

Comparing the log likelihood and AIC and BIC values. The `print()` function prints the arguments for `HMMfit`:

```
> print(HMMfit)
```

The result is as follows:

```
Convergence info: Log likelihood converged to within tol. (relative change)
'log Lik.' 9503.258 (df=20)
AIC:  -18966.52
BIC:  -18868.48
```

```
> summary(HMMfit)
```

Printing the summary of the `LogReturns` data frame. The `summary()` function is used to provide a summary of the data related to the individual object or data frame. The `LogReturns` data frame is passed as an R object to the `summary()` function:

The result is as follows:

```
      state           S1             S2 S3
1         3   0.000000e+00 0.000000e+00  1
2         3 3.024478e-110 4.676808e-20   1
3         3   5.413285e-54 5.129597e-17  1
4         3   5.597014e-60 3.165933e-20  1
5         3   1.888606e-56 1.182525e-18  1
6         3   3.550974e-61 4.009794e-22  1
```

Finding the posterior for each of the state of datasets. The result is stored in HMMstate:

```
> HMMstate <- posterior(HMMfit)
```

Printing the HMMstate data frame. The probability for each state for every day and the class of highest probability is displayed:

```
> head(HMMstate)
```

The result is as follows:

```
      state           S1             S2 S3
1         3   0.000000e+00 0.000000e+00  1
2         3 3.024478e-110 4.676808e-20   1
3         3   5.413285e-54 5.129597e-17  1
4         3   5.597014e-60 3.165933e-20  1
5         3   1.888606e-56 1.182525e-18  1
6         3   3.550974e-61 4.009794e-22  1
```

Step 5 - displaying the results

The calculated HMMstate data frame will be displayed by following these steps:

Creating the data frame for the HMM model. The data.frame() function creates tightly coupled data frames of variables that share many of the properties of matrices. DateTimeSeries, LogReturns, and TrueRange data frames are passed to be tightly coupled. The result is then stored in DFIndicators:

```
> DFIndicators <- data.frame(DateTimeSeries, LogReturns, TrueRange)
> DFIndicatorsClean <- DFIndicators[-c(1:14), ]
```

Creating a data frame as follows:

```
> Plot1Data <- data.frame(DFIndicatorsClean, HMMstate$state)
```

Plotting the results using ggplot():

```
> LogReturnsPlot <-
ggplot(Plot1Data,aes(x=Plot1Data[,1],y=Plot1Data[,2]))+geom_line(color="dar
kred")+labs(,y="Log Return Values",x="Date")
> LogReturnsPlot
```

The result is as follows:

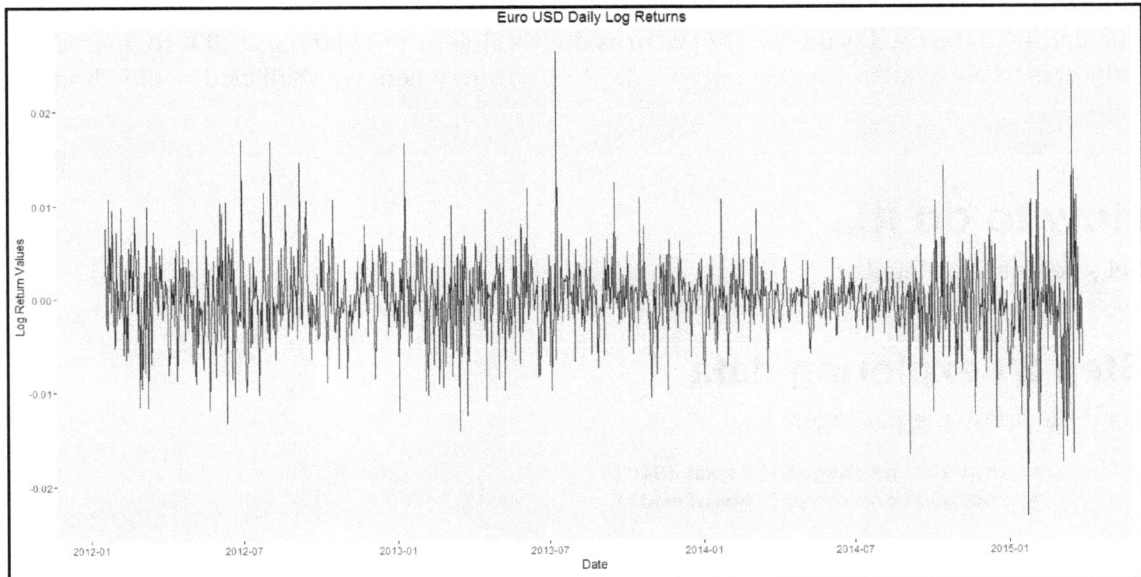

Hidden Markov models - regime detection

Standard & Poor's 500 Index (S&P 500) is an American Stock market index of 500 stocks. It is a leading indicator of US equities and reflects the performance of large-cap companies selected by economists. Experts, when determining the 500 stocks, consider factors that are included in the index, including market size, liquidity, and industry grouping. It is a market value-weighted index and one of the common benchmarks for the US stock market. Investment products based on the S&P 500 include index funds and exchange-traded funds are available to investors. Investors have a challenge replicating the S&P 500 since the portfolio would need stocks of 500 companies in ratio to the entire portfolio to replicate the index's market cap methodology. For investors it would be easier to purchase one of the S&P 500 investment products such as the Vanguard S&P 500 ETF, the SPDR S&P 500 ETF, or the Shares S&P 500 Index ETF.

Getting ready

In order to perform hidden Markov models we shall be using a dataset collected on the S&P500 returns set.

Step 1 - collecting and describing data

The dataset to be used is the S&P500 returns daily value from 1st January, 2004 to date. This dataset is freely available on https://yahoo.com/ from where we shall be downloading the data.

How to do it...

Let's get into the details.

Step 2 - exploring data

Load the following packages:

```
> install.packages("depmixS4")
> install.packages("quantmod")
```

Version info: Code for this page was tested in R version 3.3.0 (2016-05-03)

Each of the preceding libraries needs to be installed.

```
> library("depmixS4 ")
> library("quantmod")
> set.seed(1)
```

Let's download the data. We will begin by marking the start date and the end date for the time period in which the data is desired.
Loading the data using the getSymbols() function as follows. The function loads data from multiple sources, either local or remote sources. GSPC is the character vector that specifies the name of the symbol to be loaded:

```
> getSymbols( "^GSPC", from="2004-01-01" )
```

```
    As of 0.4-0, 'getSymbols' uses env=parent.frame() and
auto.assign=TRUE by default.

This behavior will be phased out in 0.5-0 when the call will
default to use auto.assign=FALSE. getOption("getSymbols.env") and
getOptions("getSymbols.auto.assign") are now checked for alternate defaults

This message is shown once per session and may be disabled by setting
options("getSymbols.warning4.0"=FALSE). See ?getSymbols for more details.
[1] "GSPC"
```

Calculating the log difference between each of the closing prices. The result is then saved in the GSPCDiff data frame:

```
> GSPCDiff = diff( log( Cl( GSPC ) ) )
```

Exploring the internal structure of the GSPCDiff frame. The str() function displays the internal structure of the data frame. The GSPCDiff is passed as an R object to the str() function:

```
> str(GSPCDiff)
```

The result is as follows:

```
An 'xts' object on 2004-01-02/2016-11-30 containing:
  Data: num [1:3252, 1] NA 0.01232 0.00129 0.00236 0.00495 ...
  - attr(*, "dimnames")=List of 2
  ..$ : NULL
  ..$ : chr "GSPC.Close"
  Indexed by objects of class: [Date] TZ: UTC
  xts Attributes:
List of 2
 $ src    : chr "yahoo"
 $ updated: POSIXct[1:1], format: "2016-12-01 23:38:20"
```

Printing the GSPCDiff data frame as follows:

```
> head(GSPCDiff)
```

The result is as follows:

```
                GSPC.Close
2004-01-02              NA
2004-01-05      0.012319151
2004-01-06      0.001291313
2004-01-07      0.002364367
2004-01-08      0.004950824
2004-01-09     -0.008927336
```

Creating the numeric value of the GSPCDiff data frame:

```
> returns = as.numeric(GSPCDiff)
```

Plotting the `GSPCDiff` data frame:

```
> plot(GSPCDiff)
```

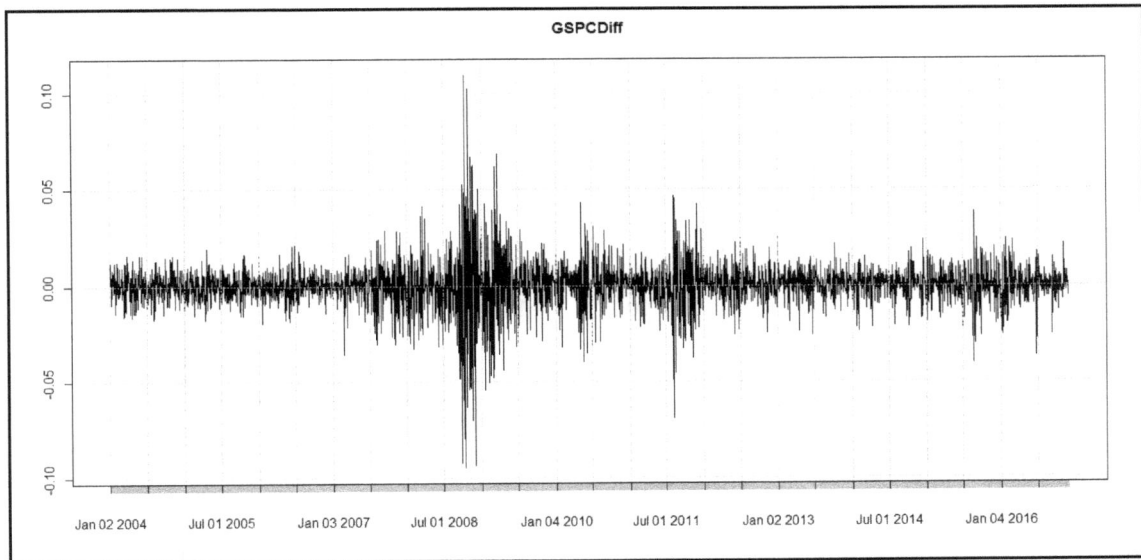

Step 3 - preparing the model

Fitting a hidden Markov model with two states to the S&P returns. Creating a hidden Markov model for two states.

The `depmix()` function creates the hidden Markov Model. The `returns ~ 1` represents the response to be modeled. `data=data.frame(returns=returns)` represents the data frame to interpret the variables in response, while `nstates = 2` is the number of states:

```
> hmm2states <- depmix(returns ~ 1, family = gaussian(), nstates = 2,
data=data.frame(returns=returns))
> hmm2states
```

The results are as follows:

```
Initial state probabilties model
pr1 pr2
0.5 0.5

Transition matrix
        toS1 toS2
fromS1  0.5   0.5
fromS2  0.5   0.5

Response parameters
Resp 1 : gaussian
     Re1.(Intercept) Re1.sd
St1                0      1
St2                0      1
```

Fitting the HMM model to the defined dataset. The `fit()` function optimizes the parameters of the HMM model, subject to linear inequality. `hmm2states` is an object of class HMM, while `verbose = FALSE` instructs that the information should not be displayed on screen. The optimized parameters are stored in object `hmmfit2states` of the `depmix` class:

```
> hmmfit2states <- fit(hmm2states, verbose = FALSE)
```

```
converged at iteration 37 with logLik: 10518.77
```

Comparing the log likelihood and AIC and BIC values:

```
> hmmfit2states
```

The results are as follows:

```
Convergence info: Log likelihood converged to within tol. (relative change)
'log Lik.' 10518.77 (df=7)
AIC:  -21023.55
BIC:  -20980.95
```

Finding the posterior for each of the state of datasets. The result is stored in
`PosteriorProbs`:

```
> PosteriorProbs <- posterior(hmmfit2states)
```

Printing the `PosteriorProbs` frame. The `head()` function returns the first part of the
`PosteriorProbs` frame. The `PosteriorProbs` frame is passed as an input parameter:

```
> head (PosteriorProbs)
```

The results are as follows:

```
    state           S1           S2
1       2 0.000000000 1.0000000
2       2 0.007586430 0.9924136
3       2 0.002517719 0.9974823
4       2 0.002560062 0.9974399
5       2 0.002888478 0.9971115
6       2 0.005725764 0.9942742
```

Plotting the two states results. `type='l'` signifies for line plot:

```
> plot(returns, type='l', main='Regime Detection', xlab='No of
Observations', ylab='Returns')
```

The results are as follows:

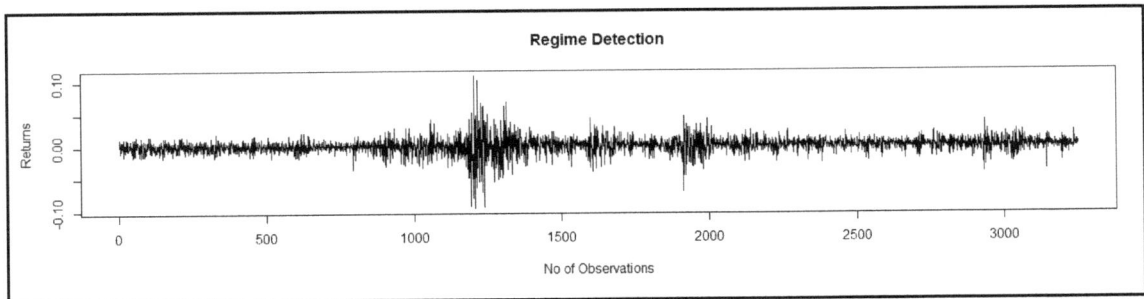

Plotting the columns of the `PosteriorProbs` data frame:

```
> matplot(PosteriorProbs[,-1], type='l', main='Regime Posterior
Probabilities', xlab='No of Observations', ylab='Probability')
```

The results are as follows:

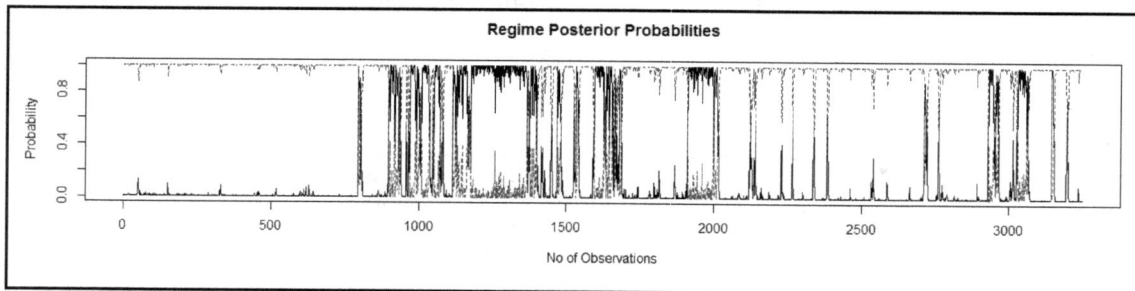

Creating a hidden Markov model for three states:

```
> hmm3states <- depmix(returns ~ 1, family = gaussian(), nstates = 3,
data=data.frame(returns=returns))
> hmm3states
```

The results are as follows:

```
Initial state probabilties model
  pr1   pr2   pr3
0.333 0.333 0.333

Transition matrix
        toS1  toS2  toS3
fromS1 0.333 0.333 0.333
fromS2 0.333 0.333 0.333
fromS3 0.333 0.333 0.333

Response parameters
Resp 1 : gaussian
    Re1.(Intercept) Re1.sd
St1               0      1
St2               0      1
St3               0      1
```

Fitting the HMM model to the defined dataset:

```
> hmmfit3states <- fit(hmm3states, verbose = FALSE)
```

```
converged at iteration 102 with logLik: 10659.7
```

Finding the posterior for each of the dataset states:

```
> PosteriorProbs <- posterior(hmmfit3states)
```

Printing the PosteriorProbs frame:

```
> head(PosteriorProbs)
```

The results are as follows:

```
     state        S1          S2           S3
1        1 1.0000000 0.00000000 0.000000000
2        1 0.9780159 0.01904906 0.002935031
3        2 0.9196440 0.07866273 0.001693291
4        2 0.8488129 0.14960389 0.001583215
5        2 0.7605025 0.23798856 0.001508972
6        2 0.8433328 0.15467220 0.001995043
```

```
> plot(returns, type='l', main='Regime Detection', xlab='No of
Observations', ylab='Returns')
```

The results are as follows:

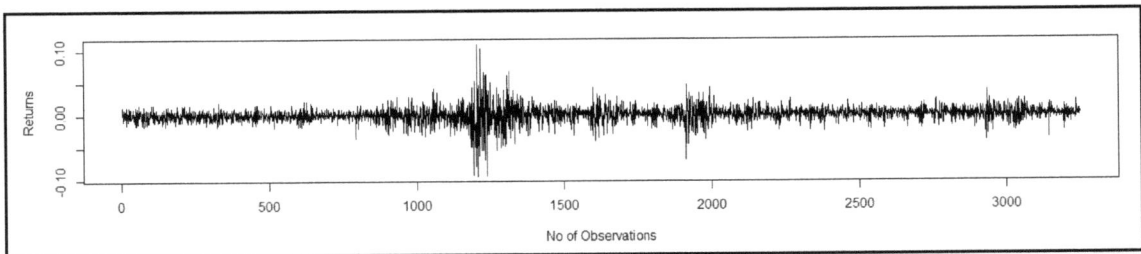

```
> matplot(PosteriorProbs[,-1], type='l', main='Regime Posterior
Probabilities', xlab='No of Observations', ylab='Probability')
```

The results are as follows:

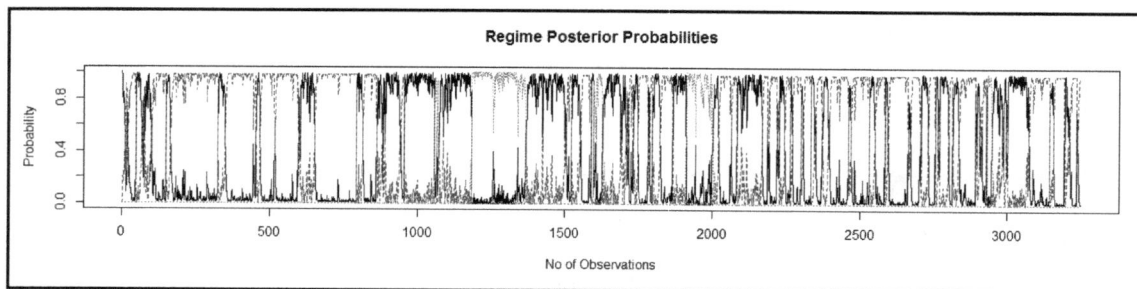

Regime Posterior Probabilities

Creating a hidden Markov model for four states:

```
> hmm4states <- depmix(returns ~ 1, family = gaussian(), nstates = 4,
data=data.frame(returns=returns))
> hmm4states
```

The results are as follows:

```
Initial state probabilties model
 pr1  pr2  pr3  pr4
0.25 0.25 0.25 0.25

Transition matrix
        toS1 toS2 toS3 toS4
fromS1 0.25 0.25 0.25 0.25
fromS2 0.25 0.25 0.25 0.25
fromS3 0.25 0.25 0.25 0.25
fromS4 0.25 0.25 0.25 0.25

Response parameters
Resp 1 : gaussian
    Re1.(Intercept) Re1.sd
St1              0      1
St2              0      1
St3              0      1
St4              0      1
```

Fitting the HMM model to the defined dataset:

```
> hmmfit4states <- fit(hmm4states, verbose = FALSE)
```

```
converged at iteration 426 with logLik: 10684.96
```

Finding the posterior for each of the datasets states:

```
> PosteriorProbs <- posterior(hmmfit4states)
> plot(returns, type='l', main='Regime Detection', xlab='No of
Observations', ylab='Returns')
```

The results are as follows:

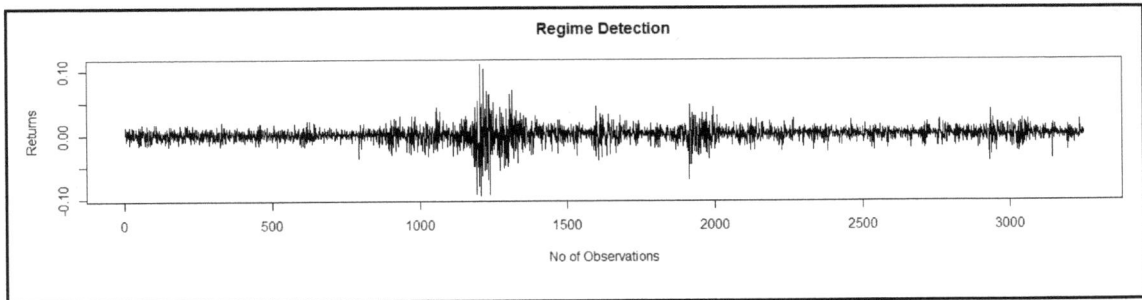

```
> matplot(PosteriorProbs[,-1], type='l', main='Regime Posterior
Probabilities', xlab='No of Observations', ylab='Probability')
```

The results are as follows:

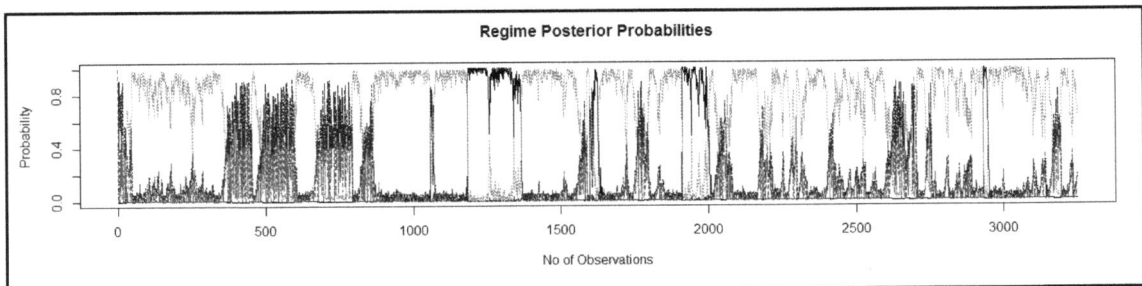

10
Neural Networks

In this chapter, we will cover the following recipes:

- Modeling S&P 500
- Measuring the unemployment rate

Introduction

Neural networks: A neural network is a sorted triple (α, β, γ) where α is the set of a neuron, and β is a set $\{(x, y) | x, y \in \mathbb{N}\}$ whose elements are called connections between neuron x and neuron y. The function $\gamma : \beta \rightarrow \mathcal{R}$ defines the weights, where $\gamma(x, y)$ is the weight of the connection between neuron x and neuron y. Data is transferred between neurons via connections, with the connecting weight being either excitatory or inhibitory.

Modelling SP 500

The value of the stocks of the 500 largest corporations by market capitalization listed on the New York Stock Exchange or Nasdaq Composite is measured by the S&P 500. Standard & Poor's provides a quick look at the movement of the stock market and economy on the basis of stock prices. The S&P 500 index is the most popular measure used by the financial media and professionals. The S&P 500 index is calculated by taking the sum of the adjusted market capitalization of all S&P 500 stocks and then dividing it with an index divisor developed by Standard & Poor's. The divisor is adjusted when there are stock splits, special dividends, or spinoffs that could affect the value of the index. The divisor ensures that these non-economic factors do not affect the index.

Getting ready

In order to model the S&P 500 index using neural networks, we shall be using a dataset collected from the GSPC dataset.

Step 1 - collecting and describing data

The dataset to be used is the GSPC daily closing stock value between January 1, 2009 and January 1, 2014. This dataset is freely available on https://www.yahoo.com/, from which we shall be downloading the data.

How to do it...

Let's get into the details.

Step 2 - exploring data

First, the following packages need to be loaded:

```
> install.packages("quantmod")
> install.packages("neuralnet")
> library(quantmod)
> library(neuralnet)
```

Let's download the data. We will begin by marking the start and the end dates for the desired time period.

The as.Date() function is used to convert the character representation and objects of the Date class, which represents calendar dates.

The start date for the dataset is stored in startDate, which represents a character vector representation of the calendar date. The format for this representation is YYYY-MM-DD:

```
> startDate = as.Date("2009-01-01")
```

The end date for the dataset is stored in endDate, which represents the character vector representation of the calendar date. The format for this representation is YYYY-MM-DD:

```
> endDate = as.Date("2014-01-01")
```

Loading the data using the `getSymbols()` function: The function loads data from multiple sources, either local or remote. `GSPC` is the character vector that specifies the name of the symbol to be loaded. `src = yahoo` specifies the sourcing method:

```
> getSymbols("^GSPC", src="yahoo", from=startDate, to=endDate)
```

```
    As of 0.4-0, 'getSymbols' uses env=parent.frame() and
auto.assign=TRUE by default.

This  behavior  will be  phased out in 0.5-0  when the call  will
default to use auto.assign=FALSE. getOption("getSymbols.env") and
getOptions("getSymbols.auto.assign") are now checked for alternate defaults

This message is shown once per session and may be disabled by setting
options("getSymbols.warning4.0"=FALSE). See ?getSymbols for more details.
[1] "GSPC"
```

Step 3 - calculating the indicators

Calculating the relative strength index: This is a ratio between the recent upward price movements and the absolute price movement. The `RSI()` function is used to calculate the **Relative Strength Index**. The `GSPC` data frame is used as a price series. `n = 3` represents the number of periods for moving averages. The result is then stored in the `relativeStrengthIndex3` data frame:

```
> relativeStrengthIndex3 <- RSI(Op(GSPC),n=3)
```

Exploring the summary of the change in prices: The `summary()` function is used for this. The function provides a range of descriptive statistics to produce result summaries of the `relativeStrengthIndex3` data frame:

```
> summary(relativeStrengthIndex3)
```

The result is as follows:

```
        Index                     EMA
Min.    :2009-01-02    Min.    : 1.244
1st Qu. :2010-04-05    1st Qu. :35.562
Median  :2011-06-30    Median  :61.666
Mean    :2011-07-02    Mean    :57.358
3rd Qu. :2012-09-27    3rd Qu. :80.360
Max.    :2013-12-31    Max.    :99.364
                       NA's    :3
```

The EMA() function uses the GSPC symbol as a price series. n = 5 represents the time period to average over. The result is then stored in the exponentialMovingAverage5 data frame:

```
> exponentialMovingAverage5 <- EMA(Op(GSPC),n=5)
```

Printing the exponentialMovingAverage5 data frame: The head() function returns the first part of the exponentialMovingAverage5 data frame. The exponentialMovingAverage5 data frame is passed as an input parameter:

```
> head(exponentialMovingAverage5)
```

The result is as follows:

```
                       EMA
2009-01-02             NA
2009-01-05             NA
2009-01-06             NA
2009-01-07             NA
2009-01-08  919.3020
2009-01-09  916.1713
```

Exploring the summary of the change in prices. For this, the summary() function is used. This function provides a range of descriptive statistics to produce result summaries of the exponentialMovingAverage5 data frame.

```
> summary(exponentialMovingAverage5)
```

The result is as follows:

```
        Index                    EMA
Min.    :2009-01-02    Min.    : 692
1st Qu.:2010-04-05    1st Qu.:1103
Median :2011-06-30    Median :1281
Mean    :2011-07-02    Mean    :1275
3rd Qu.:2012-09-27    3rd Qu.:1411
Max.    :2013-12-31    Max.    :1836
                      NA's    :4
```

Calculating the difference between the exponential opening price for GSPC and exponentialMovingAverage5:

```
> exponentialMovingAverageDiff <- Op(GSPC) - exponentialMovingAverage5
```

Now let's print the exponentialMovingAverageDiff data frame. The head() function returns the first part of the exponentialMovingAverageDiff data frame. The exponentialMovingAverageDiff data frame is passed as an input parameter:

```
> head(exponentialMovingAverageDiff)
```

The result is as follows:

```
                  GSPC.Open
2009-01-02              NA
2009-01-05              NA
2009-01-06              NA
2009-01-07              NA
2009-01-08  -13.572010
2009-01-09   -6.261344
```

Exploring the summary of the change in prices: For this, the summary() function is used. This function provides a range of descriptive statistics to produce result summaries of the exponentialMovingAverageDiff data frame.

```
> summary(exponentialMovingAverageDiff)
```

The result is as follows:

```
         Index               GSPC.Open
Min.      :2009-01-02   Min.      :-75.717
1st Qu.   :2010-04-05   1st Qu.   : -5.220
Median    :2011-06-30   Median    :  3.261
Mean      :2011-07-02   Mean      :  1.451
3rd Qu.   :2012-09-27   3rd Qu.   :  8.777
Max.      :2013-12-31   Max.      : 38.711
                        NA's      :4
```

We will now compare the fast-moving average of a GSPC series with a slow-moving average for the GSPC series. To do this, GSPC is passed as the price matrix. fast = 12 represents periods for the fast-moving average, slow = 26 represents periods for the slow-moving average, and signal = 9 represents the signal for the moving average:

```
> MACD <- MACD(Op(GSPC),fast = 12, slow = 26, signal = 9)
```

Printing the MACD data frame: The tail() function returns the last part of the MACD data frame. The MACD data frame is passed as an input parameter:

```
> tail(MACD)
```

The result is as follows:

```
                  macd      signal
2013-12-23   0.4584068   0.4360493
2013-12-24   0.5525735   0.4593541
2013-12-26   0.6503602   0.4975553
2013-12-27   0.7544246   0.5489292
2013-12-30   0.8202862   0.6032006
2013-12-31   0.8671819   0.6559969
```

Exploring the summary of the change in prices with the summary() function:

```
> summary(MACD)
```

The result is as follows:

```
      Index               macd                signal
 Min.    :2009-01-02   Min.   :-5.62181   Min.    :-4.77728
 1st Qu.:2010-04-05   1st Qu.:-0.09344   1st Qu.:-0.04305
 Median :2011-06-30   Median : 0.63804   Median : 0.61565
 Mean   :2011-07-02   Mean   : 0.39505   Mean    : 0.40129
 3rd Qu.:2012-09-27   3rd Qu.: 1.13639   3rd Qu.: 1.08340
 Max.    :2013-12-31   Max.   : 2.94747   Max.    : 2.63443
                       NA's   :25         NA's    :33
```

Next, we will grab the signal line to use as an indicator. The result is stored in the `MACDsignal` data frame:

```
> MACDsignal <- MACD[,2]
```

Calculating the **Bollinger Bands**: They are range-bound indicators that calculate the standard deviation from the moving average. Bollinger Bands operate under the logic that a currency pair's price is most likely to gravitate towards its average; thus when it strays too far, say two standard deviations away, it will fall back to its moving average. The `BBands()` function is used to calculate Bollinger Bands. `GSPC` is passed as an object and `n=20` indicates the number of periods for the moving average. `sd=2` indicates two standard deviations:

```
> BollingerBands <- BBands(Op(GSPC),n=20,sd=2)
```

Now let's print the `BollingerBands` data frame:

```
> tail(BollingerBands)
```

The result is as follows:

```
                dn       mavg       up        pctB
2013-12-23  1773.709  1798.316  1822.924  0.9999155
2013-12-24  1771.752  1799.401  1827.050  1.0175470
2013-12-26  1769.309  1801.005  1832.701  1.0356273
2013-12-27  1766.374  1802.980  1839.586  1.0462175
2013-12-30  1764.382  1804.619  1844.856  0.9579193
2013-12-31  1762.902  1806.422  1849.942  0.9157658
```

Exploring the summary of the change in prices:

```
> summary(BollingerBands)
```

The result is as follows:

```
      Index                dn               mavg              up               pctB
Min.    :2009-01-02  Min.    : 650.2  Min.    : 736.7  Min.    : 805.1  Min.    :-0.3308
1st Qu.:2010-04-05  1st Qu.:1060.2  1st Qu.:1103.0  1st Qu.:1141.1  1st Qu.: 0.3790
Median :2011-06-30  Median :1245.6  Median :1282.9  Median :1322.8  Median : 0.7077
Mean    :2011-07-02  Mean    :1232.2  Mean    :1273.7  Mean    :1315.1  Mean    : 0.6110
3rd Qu.:2012-09-27  3rd Qu.:1380.8  3rd Qu.:1408.0  3rd Qu.:1440.0  3rd Qu.: 0.8649
Max.    :2013-12-31  Max.    :1779.4  Max.    :1806.4  Max.    :1849.9  Max.    : 1.2875
                    NA's    :19      NA's    :19      NA's    :19      NA's    :19
```

Now let's grab the signal line from `BollingerBands` to use as an indicator:

```
> PercentageChngpctB <- BollingerBands[,4]
```

Printing the `PercentageChngpctB` data frame:

```
> tail(PercentageChngpctB)
```

The result is as follows:

```
                 pctB
2013-12-23  0.9999155
2013-12-24  1.0175470
2013-12-26  1.0356273
2013-12-27  1.0462175
2013-12-30  0.9579193
2013-12-31  0.9157658
```

Exploring the summary of this change in `PercentageChngpctB`:

```
> summary(PercentageChngpctB)
```

The result is as follows:

```
        Index                    pctB
Min.    :2009-01-02    Min.     :-0.3308
1st Qu. :2010-04-05    1st Qu. : 0.3790
Median  :2011-06-30    Median  : 0.7077
Mean    :2011-07-02    Mean    : 0.6110
3rd Qu. :2012-09-27    3rd Qu. : 0.8649
Max.    :2013-12-31    Max.    : 1.2875
                       NA's     :19
```

Finding the difference between the closing and opening prices:

```
> Price <- Cl(GSPC)-Op(GSPC)
```

Printing the price data frame:

```
> tail(Price)
```

The result is as follows:

```
              GSPC.Close
2013-12-23     5.069946
2013-12-24     5.299926
2013-12-26     7.060059
2013-12-27    -1.569947
2013-12-30    -0.400025
2013-12-31     5.750000
```

Combining the relativeStrengthIndex3, expMvAvg5Cross, MACDsignal, and PercentageChngpctB, Price data frames: the result is then stored in the DataSet data frame:

```
> DataSet <- data.frame(relativeStrengthIndex3, expMvAvg5Cross,
MACDsignal, PercentageChngpctB, Price)
```

Exploring the internal structure of the `DataSet` data frame: The `str()` function displays the internal structure of the data frame. The `DataSet` is passed as an R object to the `str()` function:

```
> str(DataSet)
```

The result is as follows:

```
'data.frame':    1258 obs. of  5 variables:
 $ EMA        : num   NA NA NA 88.3 43.7 ...
 $ GSPC.Open  : num   NA NA NA NA -13.6 ...
 $ signal     : num   NA NA NA NA NA NA NA NA NA NA ...
 $ pctB       : num   NA NA NA NA NA NA NA NA NA NA ...
 $ GSPC.Close : num   28.81 -1.72 3.53 -20.8 4 ...
```

Calculating the indicators, creating the dataset, and removing the points:

```
> DataSet <- DataSet[-c(1:33),]
```

Exploring the dimensions of the `DataSet` data frame: The `dim()` function returns the dimension of the `DataSet` frame. The `DataSet` data frame is passed as an input parameter. The result clearly states that there are 1,176 rows of data and 5 columns:

```
> dim(DataSet)
```

The result is as follows:

```
[1] 1176     5
```

Naming the columns: The `c()` function is used to combine the arguments into vectors:

```
> colnames(DataSet) <-
c("RSI3","EMAcross","MACDsignal","BollingerB","Price")
```

Exploring the dimensions of the `DataSet` data frame:

```
> str(DataSet)
```

The result is as follows:

```
'data.frame':    1225 obs. of  5 variables:
 $ RSI3      : num  6.99 6.32 2.47 46.69 41.4 ...
 $ EMAcross  : num  -21.45 -16.05 -29.74 -2.53 -4.94 ...
 $ MACDsignal: num  -1.78 -1.98 -2.24 -2.45 -2.64 ...
 $ BollingerB: num  -0.06817 -0.00641 -0.10584 0.138 0.1466 ...
 $ Price     : num  -5.82 -29.92 28.45 -5.74 -12.93 ...
```

Step 4 - preparing data for model building

Normalizing the dataset to be bound between 0 and 1:

```
> Normalized <- function(x) {(x-min(x))/(max(x)-min(x))}
```

Calling the function to normalize the dataset:

```
> NormalizedData <- as.data.frame(lapply(DataSet,Normalized))
```

Printing the `NormalizedData` data frame:

```
> tail(NormalizedData)
```

The result is as follows:

```
            RSI3       EMAcross    MACDsignal    BollingerB        Price
1220 0.8949682266 0.8039542230 0.7033909706 0.8223095381 0.6403435993
1221 0.9168950078 0.7862496259 0.7065352979 0.8332047211 0.6420948929
1222 0.9425533165 0.7851664068 0.7116894675 0.8443772077 0.6554982746
1223 0.9637450977 0.7906786046 0.7186209104 0.8509212683 0.5897809313
1224 0.8805725768 0.7389470017 0.7259432951 0.7963585576 0.5986898667
1225 0.8917172659 0.7198402887 0.7330666522 0.7703103038 0.6455221985
```

Building the training dataset: Data elements from `1:816` in the `NormalizedData` data frame will be used as the training dataset. The training dataset shall be stored in `TrainingSet`:

```
> TrainingSet <- NormalizedData[1:816,]
```

Exploring the dimension of the `TrainingSet` data frame:

```
> dim(TrainingSet)
```

The result is as follows:

```
[1] 816    5
```

Exploring the summary of the change in `TrainingSet`:

```
> summary(TrainingSet)
```

The result is as follows:

```
      RSI3                EMACross            MACDsignal          BollingerB          Price
 Min.   :0.004723371   Min.   :0.0000000   Min.   :0.0000000   Min.   :0.0000000   Min.   :0.0000000
 1st Qu.:0.345216893   1st Qu.:0.6129767   1st Qu.:0.6219857   1st Qu.:0.4313891   1st Qu.:0.5609580
 Median :0.621185723   Median :0.6903207   Median :0.7327540   Median :0.6440188   Median :0.6109499
 Mean   :0.571760152   Mean   :0.6733781   Mean   :0.6966899   Mean   :0.5788036   Mean   :0.6071108
 3rd Qu.:0.808167123   3rd Qu.:0.7399376   3rd Qu.:0.8091630   3rd Qu.:0.7358875   3rd Qu.:0.6604099
 Max.   :1.000000000   Max.   :1.0000000   Max.   :1.0000000   Max.   :1.0000000   Max.   :1.0000000
```

Building the testing dataset: Data elements from `817:1225` in the `NormalizedData` data frame will be used as the training dataset. This testing dataset shall be stored in `TestSet`:

```
> TestSet <- NormalizedData[817:1225 ,]
```

Exploring the dimension of the `TrainingSet` data frame:

```
> dim(TestSet)
```

The result is as follows:

```
[1] 409    5
```

Exploring the summary of the change in `TestSet`:

```
> summary(TestSet)
```

The result is as follows:

```
Relative Strength Index3 Exp Moving Avg5Cross  MACD Signal      Bollinger Bands Percentage   Price Diff
Min.    : 4.671          Min.    :-30.553       Min.    :-1.0854 Min.    :-0.2714            Min.    :-36.480
1st Qu. :39.035          1st Qu. : -3.277       1st Qu. : 0.3320 1st Qu. : 0.4582            1st Qu. : -4.952
Median  :64.992          Median  :  3.927       Median  : 0.6771 Median  : 0.7307            Median  :  1.360
Mean    :59.845          Mean    :  2.684       Mean    : 0.5522 Mean    : 0.6464            Mean    :  1.290
3rd Qu. :80.769          3rd Qu. :  8.664       3rd Qu. : 0.9498 3rd Qu. : 0.8767            3rd Qu. :  7.453
Max.    :98.988          Max.    : 28.171       Max.    : 1.3574 Max.    : 1.2709            Max.    : 36.230
NA's    :49              NA's    :49            NA's    :49      NA's    :49                 NA's    :49
```

Step 5 - building the model

Building the neural network: The `neuralnet()` function trains neural networks using a back-propagation algorithm without weight backtrackings.
`Price~RSI3+EMAcross+MACDsignal+BollingerB` is a description of the model to be fitted. `data=TrainingSet` is the data frame containing the variables specified in the formula. `hidden=c(3,3)` specifies the number of hidden neurons (vertices) in each layer. `learningrate=.001` signifies the learning rate used by the back-propagation algorithm. `algorithm="backprop"` refers to the back propagation algorithm:

```
> nn1 <-
neuralnet(Price~RSI3+EMAcross+MACDsignal+BollingerB,data=TrainingSet,
hidden=c(3,3), learningrate=.001,algorithm="backprop")
```

Plotting the neural network:

```
> plot(nn1)
```

The result is as follows:

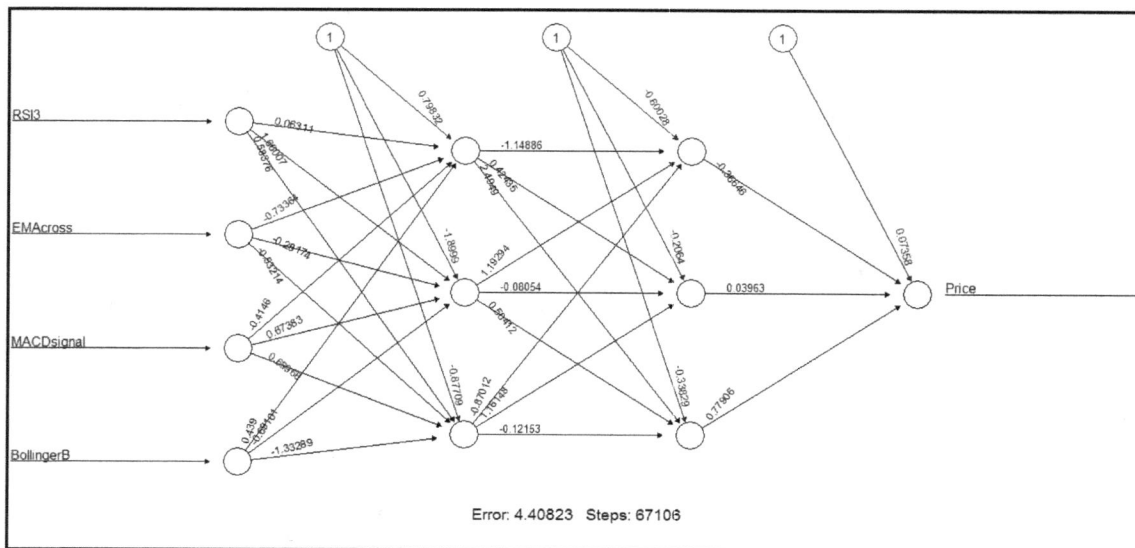

Error: 4.40823   Steps: 67106

Measuring the unemployment rate

The unemployment rate is defined as the percentage of the total labor force that is unemployed, but actively seeking employment and willing to work. As defined by the **International Labor Organization** (**ILO**), an unemployed person is someone who is actively looking for work but does not have a job. The unemployment rate is a measure of the number of people who are both jobless *and* looking for a job.

Getting ready

In order to perform a measurement of the unemployment rate using neural networks, we shall be using a dataset collected on the unemployment rate in Wisconsin.

Step 1 - collecting and describing data

For this, we will be using a CSV dataset titled `FRED-WIUR.csv`. There are 448 rows of data. There are two numeric variables as follows:

- `Date`
- `Value`

This dataset shows the unemployment rate in Wisconsin between January 1, 1976 and April 1, 2013.

How to do it...

Let's get into the details.

Step 2 - exploring data

First, the following packages need to be loaded:

```
> install.packages("forecast ")
> install.packages("lmtest")
> install.packages("caret ")
> library(forecast)
> library(lmtest)
> library(caret)
```

Version info: Code for this page was tested in R version 3.3.0

Let's explore the data and understand the relationships among the variables. We'll begin by importing the CSV data file named `FRED-WIUR.csv`. We will be saving the data to the `ud` data frame:

```
> ud <- read.csv("d:/FRED-WIUR.csv", colClasses=c('Date'='Date'))
```

Printing the `ud` data frame: The `tail()` function returns the last part of the `ud` data frame. The `ud` data frame is passed as an input parameter:

```
> tail(ud)
```

The result is as follows:

```
            DATE VALUE
443 1976-06-01   5.4
444 1976-05-01   5.5
445 1976-04-01   5.6
446 1976-03-01   5.7
447 1976-02-01   5.9
448 1976-01-01   6.0
```

Naming the columns: The `c()` function is used to combine the arguments into vectors:

```
> colnames(ud) <- c('date', 'rate')
```

The `as.Date()` function is used to convert the character representation and objects of the `Date` class, which represents calendar dates:

```
> ud$date <- as.Date(ud$date)
```

Exploring the summary of unemployment data: For this, the `summary()` function is used. The function provides a range of descriptive statistics to produce result summaries of the `ud` data frame:

```
> summary (ud)
```

The result is as follows:

```
      date                  rate
Min.    :1976-01-01   Min.    : 3.000
1st Qu. :1985-04-23   1st Qu. : 4.400
Median  :1994-08-16   Median  : 5.100
Mean    :1994-08-16   Mean    : 5.675
3rd Qu. :2003-12-08   3rd Qu. : 7.000
Max.    :2013-04-01   Max.    :11.900
```

Now let's create base data from rows 1 to 436:

```
> ud.b <- ud[1:436,]
```

Exploring the summary of the base unemployment data. For this, the summary() function is used. The function provides a range of descriptive statistics to produce result summaries of the ud.b data frame:

```
> summary(ud.b)
```

The result is as follows:

```
      date                   rate
Min.    :1977-01-01   Min.    : 3.000
1st Qu. :1986-01-24   1st Qu. : 4.400
Median  :1995-02-15   Median  : 5.000
Mean    :1995-02-15   Mean    : 5.679
3rd Qu. :2004-03-08   3rd Qu. : 7.100
Max.    :2013-04-01   Max.    :11.900
```

Now let's create the test data from rows 437 to 448:

```
> ud.p <- ud[437:448,]
```

Exploring the summary of the test unemployment data:

```
> summary(ud.p)
```

The result is as follows:

```
      date                   rate
Min.    :1976-01-01   Min.    :5.400
1st Qu. :1976-03-24   1st Qu. :5.400
Median  :1976-06-16   Median  :5.450
Mean    :1976-06-16   Mean    :5.550
3rd Qu. :1976-09-08   3rd Qu. :5.625
Max.    :1976-12-01   Max.    :6.000
```

Creating the base time series data from 1976: ts() as a function creates time series objects. ud.b$rate represents the vector of observed time series values:

```
> ud.ts <- ts(ud.b$rate, start=c(1976, 1), frequency=12)
```

Printing the value of the `ud.ts` data frame:

```
> ud.ts
```

The result is as follows:

	Jan	Feb	Mar	Apr	May	Jun	Jul	Aug	Sep	Oct	Nov	Dec
1976	6.8	6.9	6.9	6.9	6.9	6.9	6.9	7.0	7.0	7.1	7.1	7.1
1977	7.1	7.1	7.1	7.1	7.2	7.4	7.5	7.6	7.7	7.8	7.8	7.8
1978	7.9	7.9	7.9	8.0	8.1	8.2	8.3	8.3	8.4	8.4	8.5	8.7
1979	8.9	9.0	9.1	9.2	9.2	9.1	9.1	9.0	9.0	9.0	8.9	8.8
1980	8.6	8.2	7.7	7.2	6.6	6.0	5.6	5.2	5.0	4.8	4.6	4.5
1981	4.4	4.4	4.5	4.6	4.8	4.9	5.0	5.0	5.1	5.0	5.0	4.9
1982	4.9	4.9	4.9	4.9	4.9	4.9	4.8	4.8	4.8	4.7	4.7	4.7
1983	4.7	4.7	4.7	4.7	4.8	4.8	4.8	4.8	4.7	4.7	4.6	4.6
1984	4.6	4.6	4.7	4.7	4.8	4.8	4.8	4.9	4.9	5.0	5.0	5.1
1985	5.1	5.2	5.3	5.3	5.4	5.5	5.6	5.7	5.8	5.8	5.8	5.8
1986	5.8	5.8	5.7	5.6	5.5	5.4	5.4	5.3	5.3	5.3	5.3	5.4
1987	5.4	5.5	5.5	5.4	5.3	5.1	4.9	4.8	4.6	4.5	4.5	4.4
1988	4.3	4.2	4.1	3.9	3.8	3.7	3.7	3.7	3.7	3.7	3.6	3.5

Creating the test time series data: The `ts()` function creates time series objects. `ud.b$rate` represents the vector of observed time series values:

```
> ud.p.ts <- ts(ud.p$rate, start=c(2012, 5), frequency=12)
```

Printing the value of the `ud.ts` data frame:

```
> ud.ts
```

The result is as follows:

	Jan	Feb	Mar	Apr	May	Jun	Jul	Aug	Sep	Oct	Nov	Dec
2012					5.5	5.4	5.4	5.4	5.4	5.4	5.4	5.5
2013	5.6	5.7	5.9	6.0								

Plotting the base time series data:

```
> plot.ts(ud.ts)
```

The result is as follows:

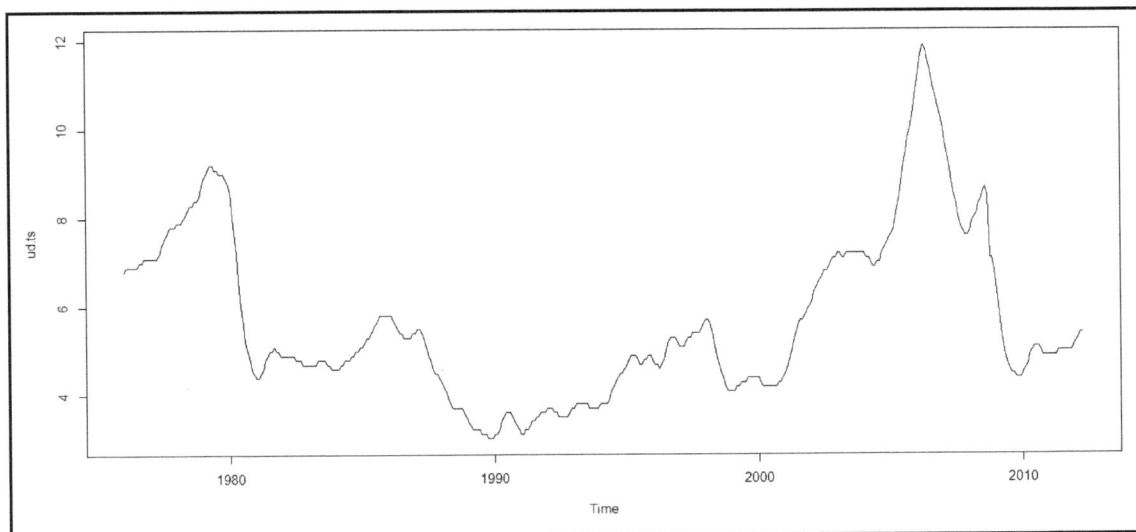

Plotting the test time series data:

```
> plot.ts(ud.p.ts)
```

The result is as follows:

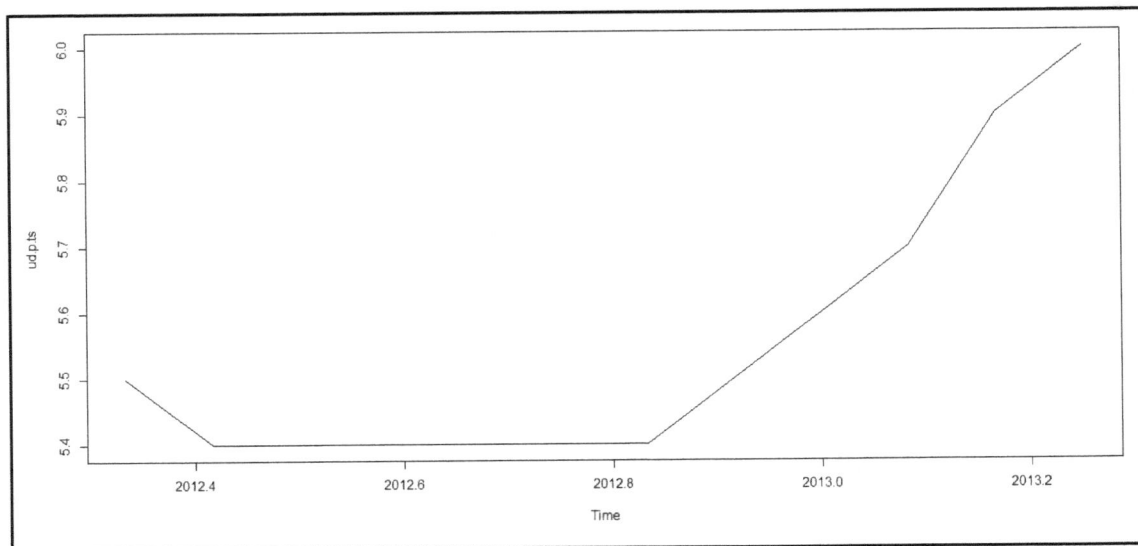

Step 3 - preparing and verifying the models

Calculating the mean of the base time series dataset. The `meanf()` function returns forecasts and prediction intervals for an **i.i.d** model applied on the `ud.ts` dataset. `12` indicates the period for forecasting:

```
> mean <- meanf(ud.ts, 12)
```

Forecasting and predicting the intervals for a random walk with a drift base time series. The `rwf()` function forecasts and returns for a random walk performed on the time series `ud.ts`. The parameter `12` indicates the period for forecasting:

```
> forecast_randomwalk <- rwf(ud.ts, 12)
```

Forecasting and predicting intervals for a random walk from an ARIMA(0,0,0)(0,1,0)m base time series: The `snaive()` function forecasts and returns results for an ARIMA(0,0,0)(0,1,0)m performed on the time series `ud.ts`. The parameter `12` indicates the period for forecasting:

```
> forecast_arima <- snaive(ud.ts, 12)
```

Forecasting and predicting the drift for the base time series. The `rwf()` function forecasts and returns for a random walk performed on the time series `ud.ts`. The parameter `12` indicates the period for forecasting. `drift=T` is a logical flag that fits a random walk with the drift model:

```
> drift <- rwf(ud.ts, 12, drift=T)
```

Next, we will prepare linear fit models for the base time series data for trend. The `tslm()` function fits linear models to the `ud.ts` time series. `ud.ts~trend` is the formula that indicates that the trend components have to be taken into consideration:

```
> m1 <- tslm(ud.ts~trend)
```

Preparing the linear fit models for the base time series data for trend and seasonality: The `tslm()` function fits linear models to `ud.ts` time series. `ud.ts~trend+season` is the formula that indicates that the trend and seasonality components have to be taken into consideration:

```
> m2 <- tslm(ud.ts~trend+season)
```

`residuals()` is a generic function that extracts model residuals from object `m1` after returned after fitting models for the base time series data for trend.

```
> residual_1 <- residuals(m1)
```

Plotting the residual model:

```
> plot(residual_1, ylab="Residuals",xlab="Year", title("Residual -
Trends"), col = "red")
```

The result is as follows:

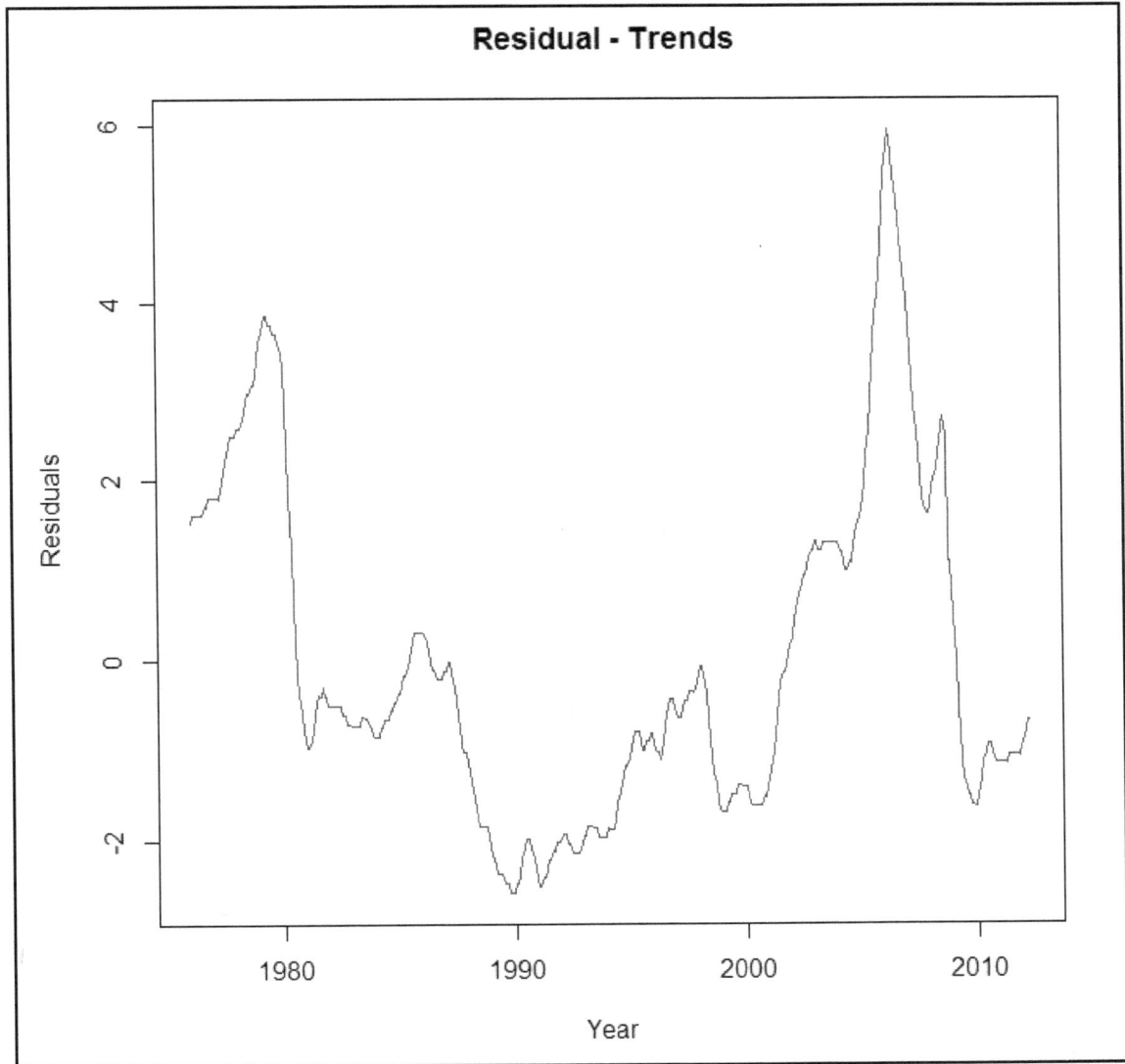

Now let's look at how to estimate the `autocovariance` function. `residual_1` is the univariate numeric time series object:

```
> acf(residual_1, main="ACF of residuals")
```

The result is as follows:

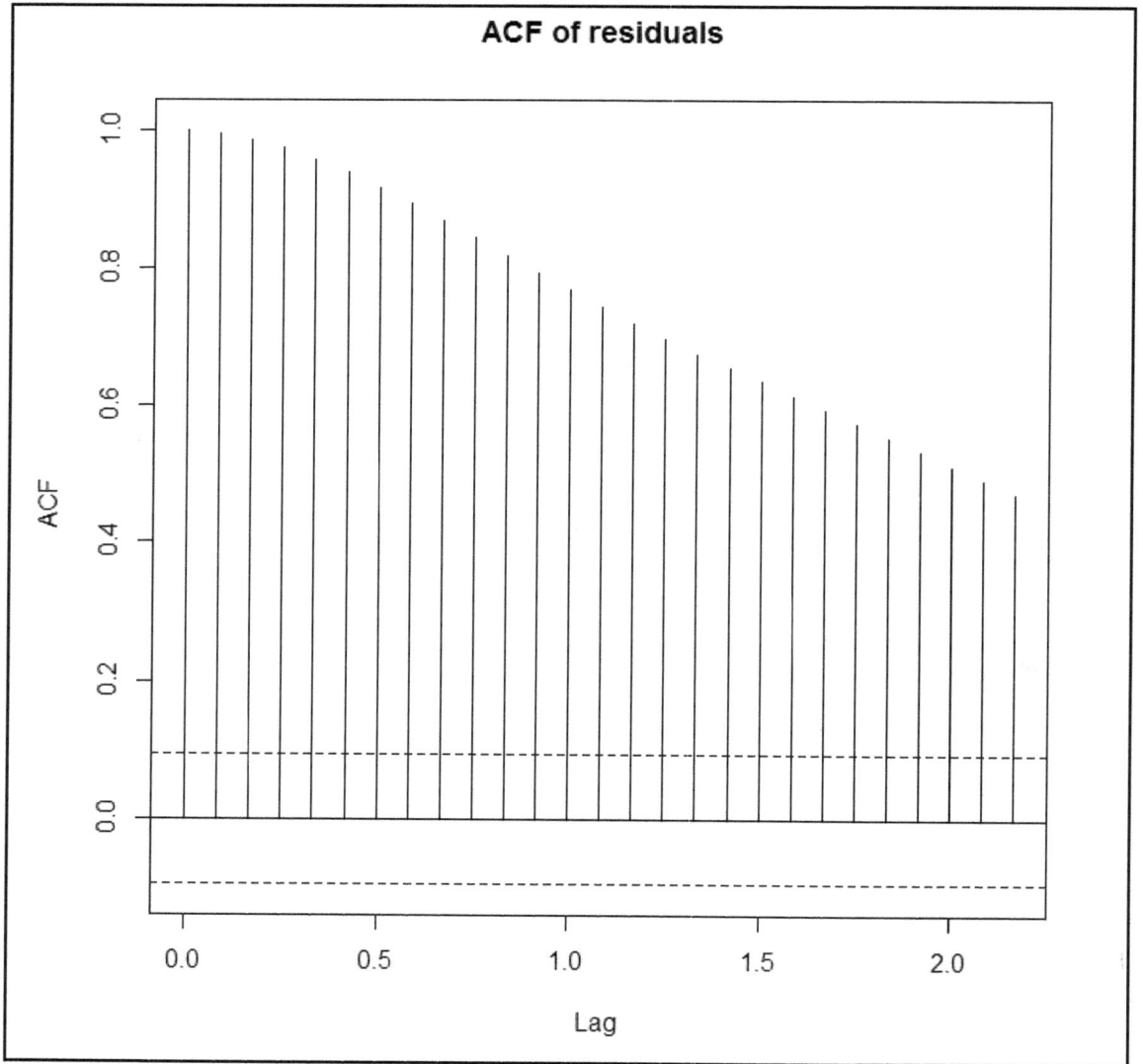

residuals() is a generic function that extracts model residuals from object m2 after returned after fitting models for base time series data for trend.

```
> residual_2 <- residuals(m2)
```

Ploting the residual model:

```
> plot(residual_2, ylab="Residuals",xlab="Year",title("Residual -
Trends + Seasonality"), col = "red")
```

The result is as follows:

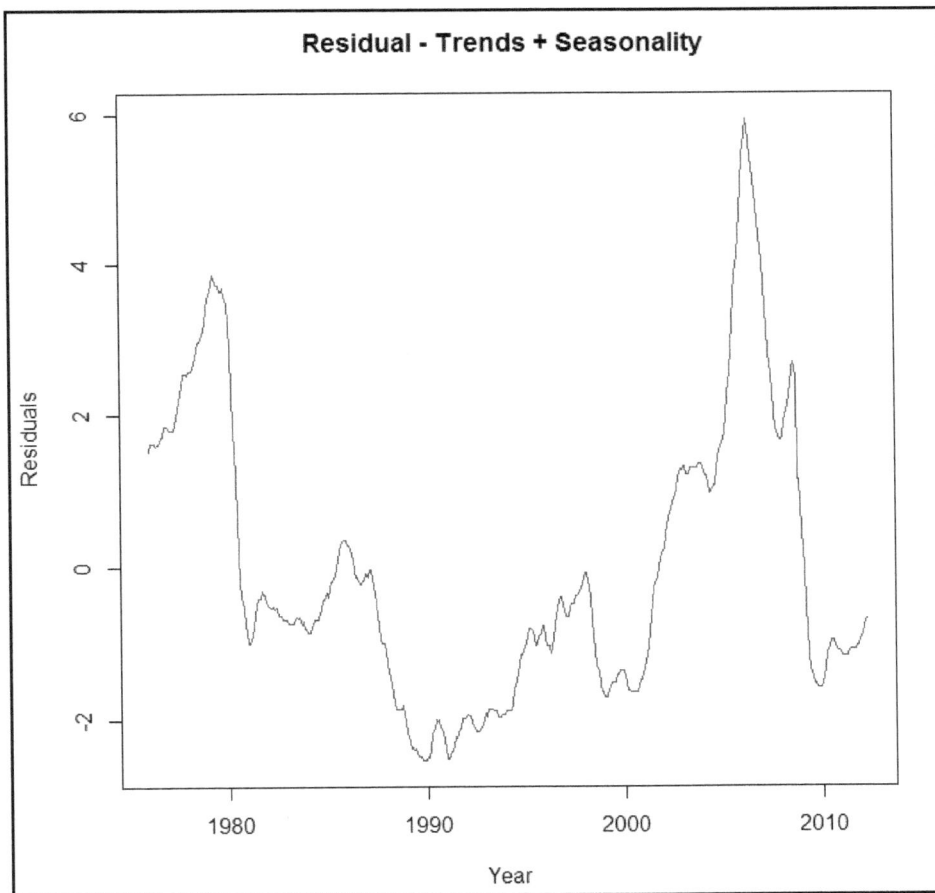

```
> acf(residual_2, main="ACF of residuals")
```

The result is as follows:

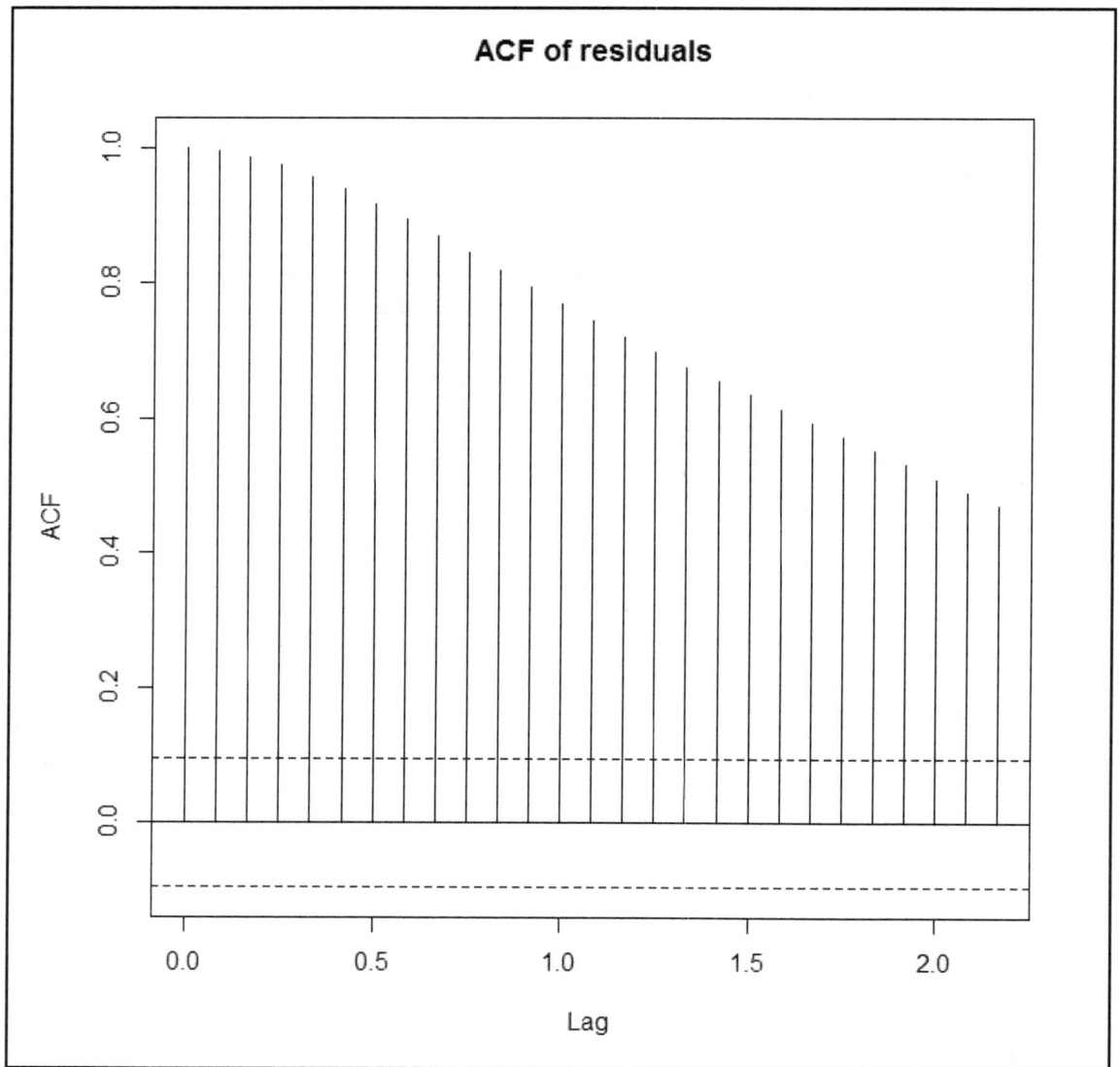

The Durbin-Watson test is performed to find out if the residuals from a linear regression or multiple regressions are independent. The hypotheses usually considered in the Durbin-Watson test are as follows:

$H_0 : \rho = 0$

$H_1 : \rho > 0$

The test statistics are given as follows:

$$d = \frac{\sum_{i=2}^{n}(e_1 - e_{i-1})^2}{\sum_{i=1}^{n}e_1{}^2}$$

In this equation, $e_1 = y_1 - \hat{y_i}$, y_1 is the observed value of for individual i, and $\hat{y_i}$ is the predicted value of for individual i.

The value of d decreases as the serial correlations increase. The upper and lower critical values, d_U and d_L, have been tabulated for different values of k--the number of explanatory variables and n:

If $d < d_L$ reject $H_0 : \rho = 0$

If $d > d_U$ do not reject $H_0 : \rho = 0$

If $d_L < d < d_U$ the test is inconclusive.

Performing the Durbin-Watson test on linear fit models for the base time series data for trend:

```
> dwtest(m1, alt="two.sided")
```

The result is as follows:

```
            Durbin-watson test

data:   m1
DW = 0.0065342, p-value < 2.2e-16
alternative hypothesis: true autocorrelation is not 0
```

Performing the Durbin-Watson test on linear fit models for the base time series data for trend and seasonality:

```
> dwtest(m2, alt="two.sided")
```

The result is as follows:

```
                    Durbin-watson test

data:   m2
DW = 0.0065138, p-value < 2.2e-16
alternative hypothesis: true autocorrelation is not 0
```

Decomposing the base data time series into period, seasonal, trend, and irregular components using LOESS:

```
> m3 <- stl(ud.ts, s.window='periodic')
```

Plotting the decomposed base data time series:

```
> plot(m3)
```

The result is as follows:

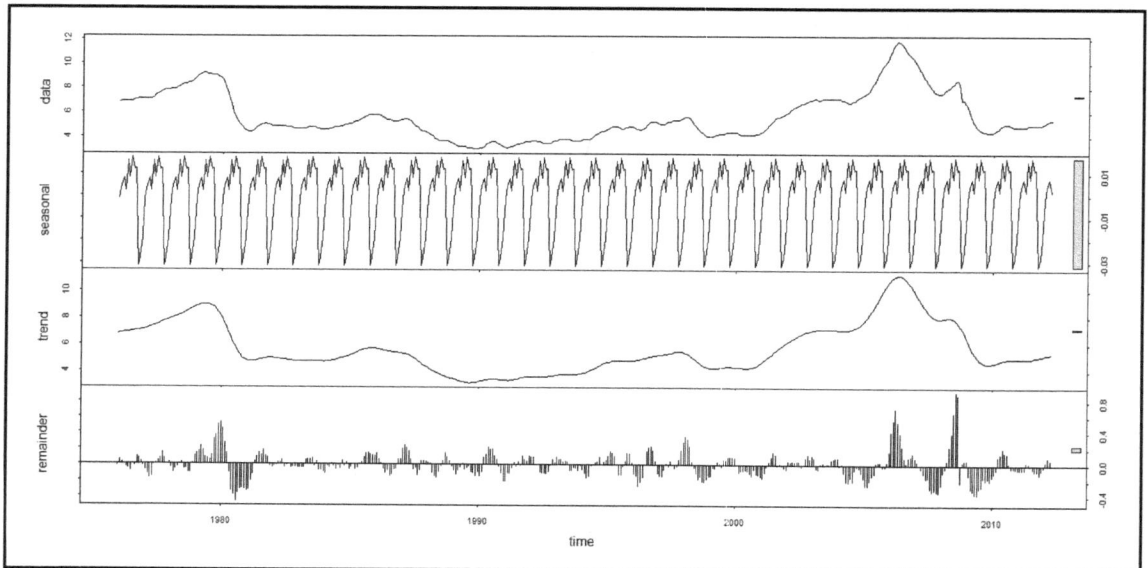

Performing the exponential smoothing state space model for the base data time series. The `ets()` function returns the `ets` model on the `ud.ts` time series. `ZZZ` – `"Z"` signifies an automatic selection. The first letter denotes the error type, the second letter denotes the trend type, and the third letter denotes the season type:

```
> m4 <- ets(ud.ts, model='ZZZ')
```

Plotting the exponential smoothing state space model for the base data time series:

```
> plot(m4)
```

The result is as follows:

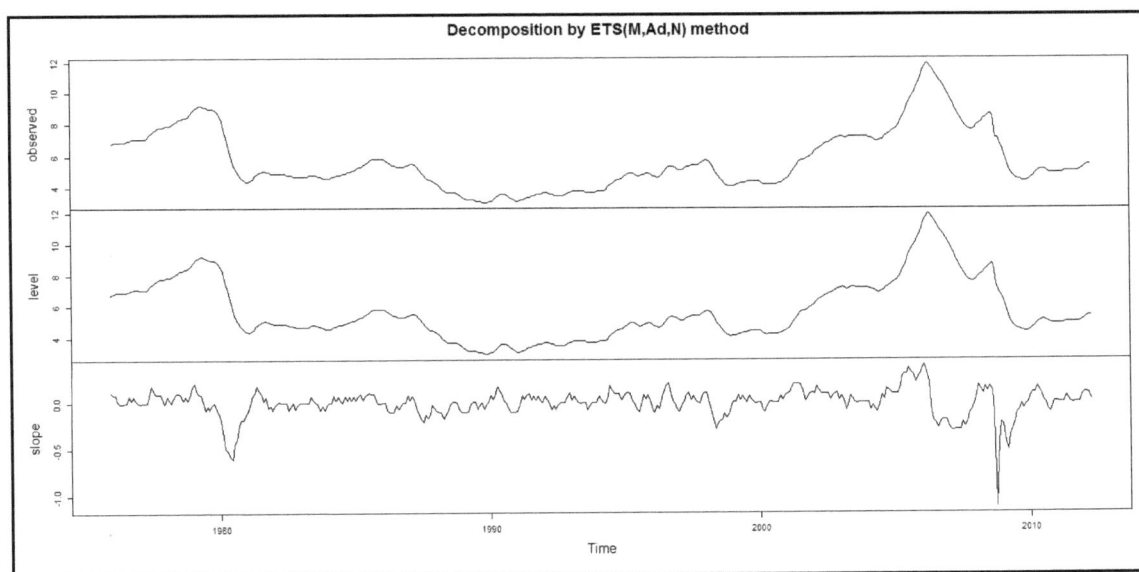

Returning the order of a univariate ARIMA for the base data time series:

```
> m5 <- auto.arima(ud.ts)
```

Ploting the univariate ARIMA for the base data time series:

```
> plot(forecast(m5, h=12))
```

The result is as follows:

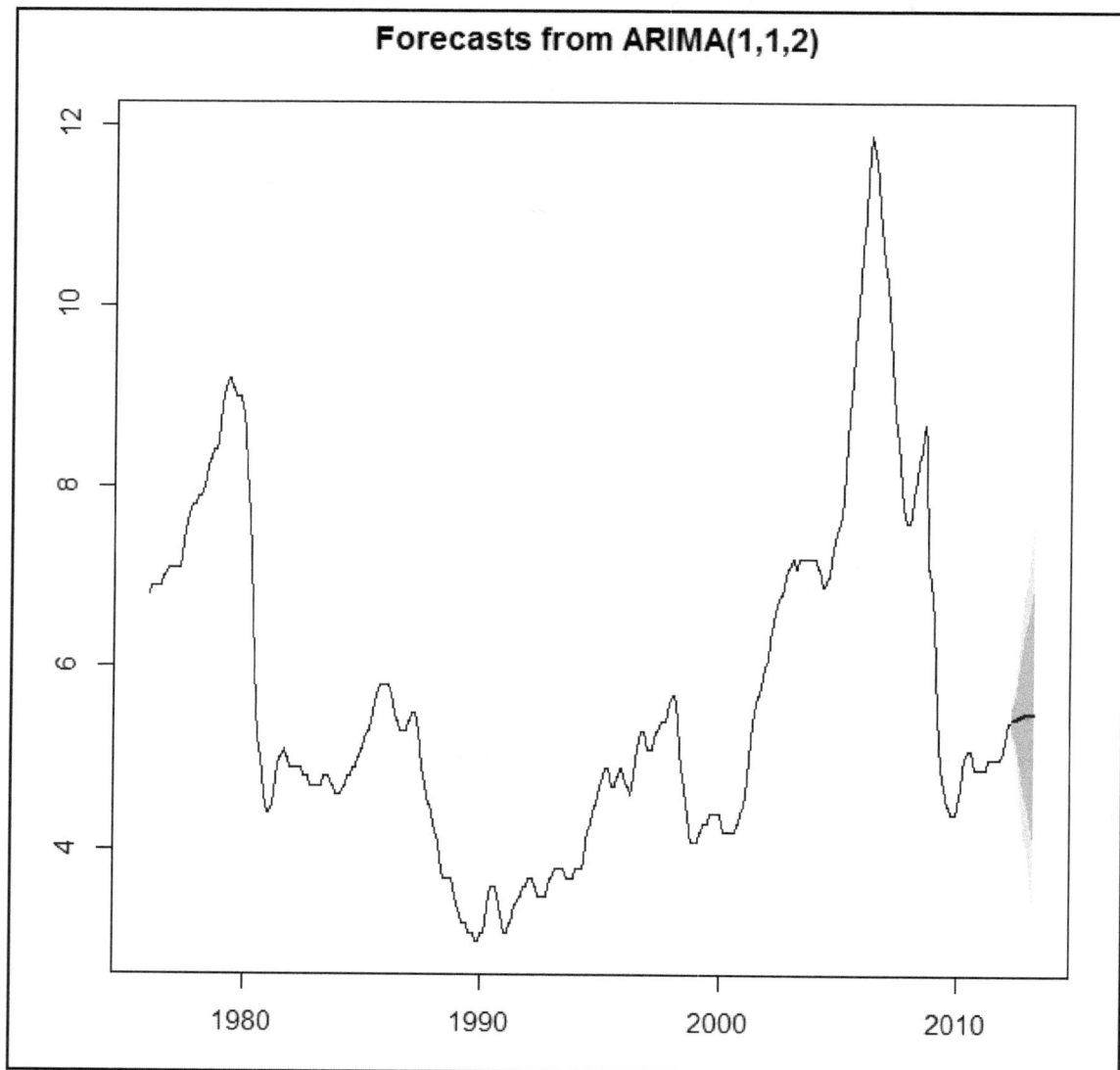

Forecasts from ARIMA(1,1,2)

Building the feed-forward neural network model: The `nnetar()` function builds the feed-forward neural network with a single hidden layer and lagged inputs for forecasting the base data univariate time series:

```
> m6 <- nnetar(ud.ts)
```

Printing the values of the feed-forward neural network model:

```
> m6
```

The result is as follows:

```
Series: ud.ts
Model:    NNAR(26,1,14)[12]
Call:     nnetar(y = ud.ts)

Average of 20 networks, each of which is
a 26-14-1 network with 393 weights
options were - linear output units

sigma^2 estimated as 0.002508
```

Plotting the feed-forward neural network model:

```
> plot(forecast(m6, h=12))
```

The result is as follows:

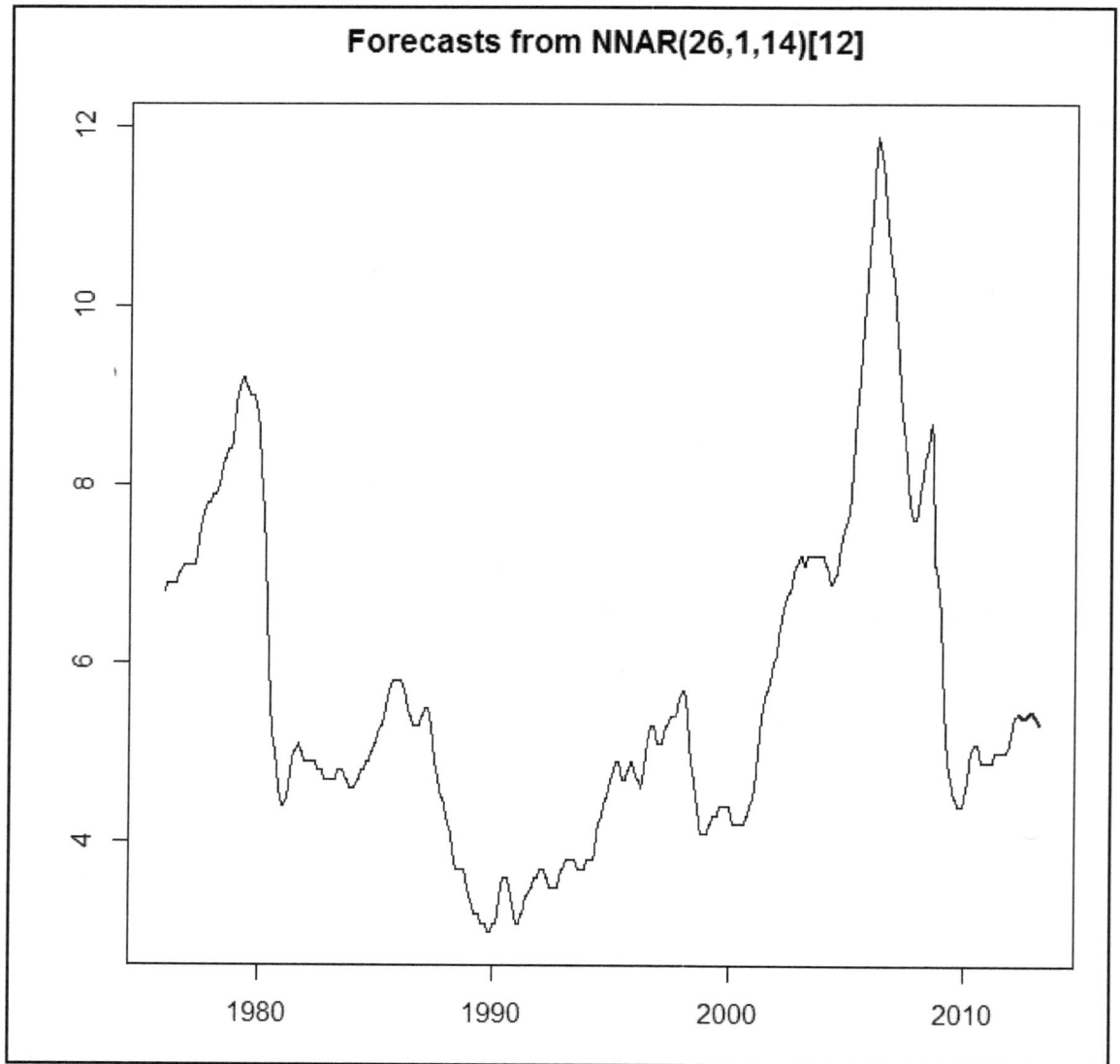

Forecasts from NNAR(26,1,14)[12]

Step 4 - forecasting and testing the accuracy of the models built

Testing the accuracy of the mean value of the base data time series with the test data time series. The accuracy() function returns the range of summary measures of the forecast accuracy. ud.p.ts is the test data time series:

```
> a1 <- accuracy(mean, ud.p.ts)
```

Testing the accuracy of the forecasted and predicted base data time series with a drift:

```
> a2 <- accuracy(forecast_randomwalk, ud.p.ts)
```

Testing the accuracy of the forecasted and predicted base data time series with an ARIMA(0,0,0)(0,1,0)m:

```
> a3 <- accuracy(forecast_arima, ud.p.ts)
```

Testing the accuracy of the drift of the base data time series:

```
> a4 <- accuracy(drift, ud.p.ts)
```

Combining the results in a table:

```
> a.table <- rbind(a1, a2, a3, a4)
```

Printing the result:

```
> a.table
```

The result is as follows:

```
                       ME       RMSE        MAE        MPE       MAPE       MASE       ACF1 Theil's U
Training set  9.159009e-17  1.9019099 1.53702129 -10.31273981 28.302156 1.8593353 0.9963622        NA
Test set     -1.288991e-01  0.2396838 0.22278287  -2.45281447  4.031039 0.2695005 0.6989796  2.763092
Training set -3.218391e-03  0.1526773 0.09287356  -0.08228355  1.582567 0.1123492 0.6931248        NA
Test set      1.500000e-01  0.2516611 0.15000000   2.57879386  2.578794 0.1814551 0.6989796  2.818489
Training set -5.212264e-02  1.2587336 0.82665094  -2.87696955 14.538198 1.0000000 0.9830841        NA
Test set      4.333333e-01  0.4377975 0.43333333   7.78692151  7.786922 0.5242035 0.3333333  4.842820
Training set  1.837714e-16  0.1526433 0.09443467  -0.01973132  1.613285 0.1142377 0.6931248        NA
Test set      1.532184e-01  0.2535926 0.15321839   2.63685674  2.636857 0.1853484 0.6989796  2.839636
```

Forecasting the linear fit models for the base time series data for trend. h=12 indicates the period of forecasting:

```
> f1 <- forecast(m1, h=12)
```

Forecasting the linear fit models for the base time series data for trend and seasonality:

```
> f2 <- forecast(m2, h=12)
```

Forecasting the decomposed base data time series into period, seasonal, trend, and irregular components using LOESS:

```
> f3 <- forecast(m3, h=12)
```

Forecasting the exponential smoothing state space model for the base data time series:

```
> f4 <- forecast(m4, h=12)
```

Forecasting the ordered univariate ARIMA for the base data time series:

```
> f5 <- forecast(m5, h=12)
```

Forecasting the feed-forward neural network model with a single hidden layer:

```
> f6 <- forecast(m6, h=12)
```

Testing the accuracy of the forecasted linear fit models for the base time series data for trend:

```
> a5 <- accuracy(f1, ud.p.ts)
```

Testing the accuracy of the forecasted linear fit models for the base time series data for trend and seasonality:

```
> a6 <- accuracy(f2, ud.p.ts)
```

Testing the accuracy of the forecasted decomposed base data time series into period, seasonal, trend, and irregular components using LOESS:

```
> a7 <- accuracy(f3, ud.p.ts)
```

Testing the accuracy of the forecasted exponential smoothing state space model for the base data time series:

```
> a8 <- accuracy(f4, ud.p.ts)
```

Testing the accuracy of the forecasted ordered univariate ARIMA for the base data time series:

```
> a9 <- accuracy(f5, ud.p.ts)
```

Testing the accuracy of the forecasted feed-forward neural network model with a single hidden layer:

```
> a10 <- accuracy(f6, ud.p.ts)
```

Combining the results in a table:

```
> a.table.1 <- rbind(a5, a6, a7, a8, a9, a10)
```

Printing the result:

```
> a.table.1
```

The result is as follows:

	ME	RMSE	MAE	MPE	MAPE	MASE	ACF1	Theil's U
Training set	4.475375e-16	1.88722530	1.53083801	-10.161145296	28.1539971	1.85185539	0.995828645	NA
Test set	-5.487103e-01	0.58297971	0.54871027	-10.023338649	10.0233386	0.66377505	0.695878741	6.671710
Training set	-6.195430e-16	1.88705289	1.53086653	-10.158672457	28.1523947	1.85188990	0.995849775	NA
Test set	-5.492242e-01	0.58206536	0.54922422	-10.029107757	10.0291078	0.66439678	0.687555685	6.623429
Training set	-9.854464e-04	0.10432066	0.06381823	0.018096634	1.1601990	0.07720094	0.111597690	NA
Test set	6.097884e-02	0.19531345	0.13899105	0.983630329	2.4283009	0.16813754	0.683262346	2.197669
Training set	-1.015557e-03	0.10565958	0.06330050	0.017500191	1.1509450	0.07657464	0.094513111	NA
Test set	7.002618e-02	0.20305522	0.14225925	1.143733343	2.4813827	0.17209107	0.686501904	2.279852
Training set	-7.528991e-04	0.10522503	0.06285967	0.022495362	1.1488709	0.07604136	0.003619751	NA
Test set	7.395984e-02	0.20312273	0.14102062	1.215641649	2.4575079	0.17059271	0.685511079	2.277821
Training set	1.892526e-04	0.05007881	0.03839996	-0.007259723	0.7362521	0.04645245	-0.192874177	NA
Test set	1.551299e-01	0.27955692	0.16401471	2.652956228	2.8174896	0.19840867	0.676462478	3.137278

11
Deep Learning

In this chapter, we will cover the following recipe:

Recurrent neural networks - predicting periodic signals

Introduction

Most of the machine learning algorithms work well due to predefined representations and input features. Machine learning algorithms optimize weights to best make a final prediction, while representation learning attempt to automatically learn good features or representations. Deep learning algorithms attempt to learn at multiple levels of representation by increasing complexity. Deep architectures are composed of multiple levels of non-linear operations, such as neural nets with many hidden layers. The main goal of deep learning techniques is to learn feature hierarchies. Deep learning techniques can be divided into three major classes; deep networks for unsupervised or generative learning, deep networks for supervised learning and hybrid deep networks

Recurrent neural networks - predicting periodic signals

Oscillators are circuits that produce specific, periodic waveforms such as square, triangular, sawtooth, and sinusoidal. In order to generate output, oscillators generally use some form of active device-lamp, which is surrounded by resistors, capacitors, and inductors. Two main classes of oscillators are relaxation and sinusoidal. Triangular, sawtooth and other non-sinusoidal waveforms are generated using relaxation oscillators, while sinusoidal oscillators consist of amplifiers with external components to generate oscillation. Normally, no harmonics are present in pure sine waves and they consist of a single frequency.

Getting ready...

The task is to predict a cosine from a noisy sine wave. 5Hz frequency waves are used for the sine wave with some normally distributed noise and a smooth cosine wave. The dataset created is a set of 10 sequences, each of which consists of 40 observations.

How to do it...

The following packages need to be loaded as the first step to be carried out:

```
> install.packages("rnn")
> library(rnn)
```

Setting the initial seed as a random number for the purpose of reproducibility:

```
> set.seed(10)
```

Initializing the required frequency:

```
> f <- 5
```

Creating the vector required:

```
> w <- 2*pi*f
```

Generating sequences: The seq() function generates regular sequences. 0.005 is the starting value while 2 is the ending value. by=0.005 determines the incremental sequence:

```
> t <- seq(0.005,2,by=0.005)
```

Generating sin and cos values:

```
> x <- sin(t*w) + rnorm(200, 0, 0.25)
> y <- cos(t*w)
```

Generating samples of time series: The matrix() function creates a matrix from x and y values. nrow = 40 indicates the number of rows required:

```
> X <- matrix(x, nrow = 40)
> Y <- matrix(y, nrow = 40)
```

Plotting the noisy wave:. The `plot()` function is a generic function for the plotting of R objects. The `as.vector(X)` data frame is passed as a function value. `type='l'` signifies lines:

```
> plot(as.vector(X), col='blue', type='l', ylab = "x-matrix, y-matrix",
main = "Noisy waves")
```

The result is as follows:

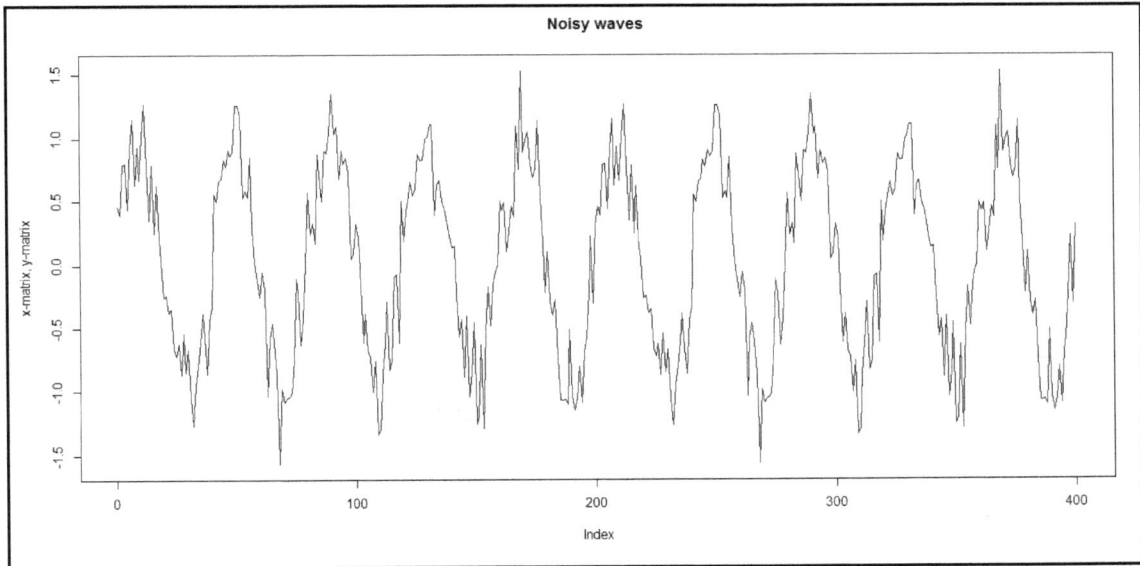

```
> lines(as.vector(Y), col = "red")
```

The result is as follows:

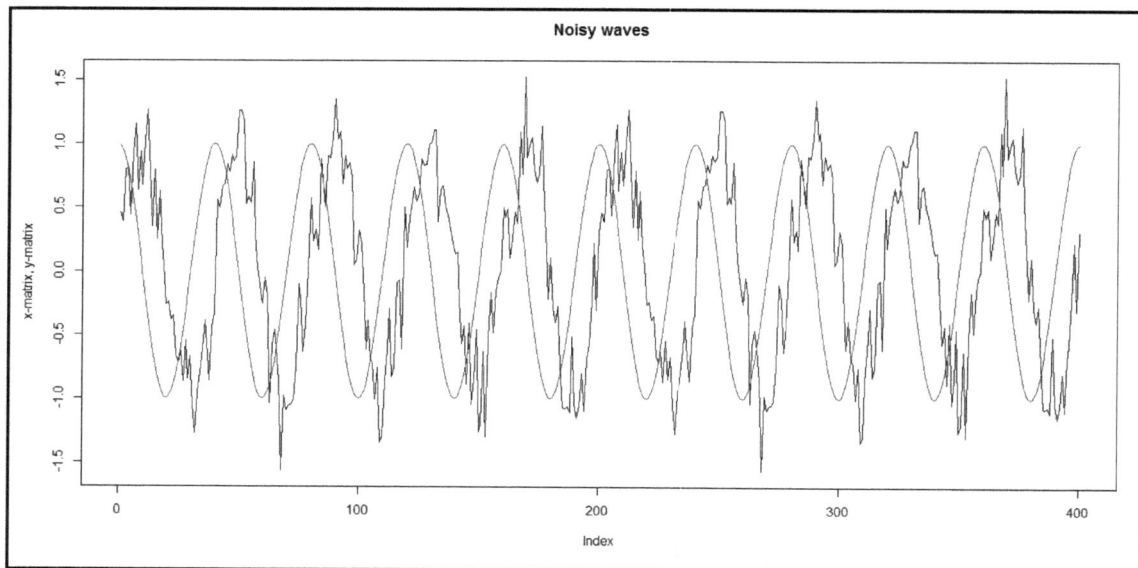

Noisy waves

Standardizing the values of x. The range of values lies between 0 and 1:

```
> X <- (X - min(X)) / (max(X) - min(X))
```

Printing the values of x:

```
> X
```

The result is as follows:

```
             [,1]      [,2]      [,3]      [,4]      [,5]      [,6]      [,7]      [,8]      [,9]     [,10]     [,11]     [,12]
 [1,] 0.5451726 0.5796069 0.5282779 0.6387957 0.7546948 0.7972073 0.6898536 0.7815417 0.6871595 0.8071538 0.9178127 0.8761765
 [2,] 0.6354409 0.5307202 0.5741530 0.7599904 0.6479934 0.7618196 0.8116367 0.7868224 0.7673894 0.8842260 0.7908040 0.7840033
 [3,] 0.5937034 0.5763600 0.7044705 0.7500259 0.7670115 0.7776825 0.8477539 1.0000000 0.7245861 0.8225836 0.7894753 0.7960983
 [4,] 0.5028951 0.6123338 0.6415219 0.5883772 0.7825188 0.6869214 0.8130090 0.7224553 0.7939027 0.7268006 0.9454927 0.8658338
 [5,] 0.5988042 0.5487380 0.6882531 0.6303222 0.6926913 0.7069975 0.8730621 0.6881716 0.8402071 0.7075135 0.7285208 0.7772329
 [6,] 0.5451726 0.5796069 0.5282779 0.6387957 0.7546948 0.7972073 0.6898536 0.7815417 0.6871595 0.8071538 0.9178127 0.8761765
 [7,] 0.6354409 0.5307202 0.5741530 0.7599904 0.6479934 0.7618196 0.8116367 0.7868224 0.7673894 0.8842260 0.7908040 0.7840033
 [8,] 0.5937034 0.5763600 0.7044705 0.7500259 0.7670115 0.7776825 0.8477539 1.0000000 0.7245861 0.8225836 0.7894753 0.7960983
 [9,] 0.5028951 0.6123338 0.6415219 0.5883772 0.7825188 0.6869214 0.8130090 0.7224553 0.7939027 0.7268006 0.9454927 0.8658338
[10,] 0.5988042 0.5487380 0.6882531 0.6303222 0.6926913 0.7069975 0.8730621 0.6881716 0.8402071 0.7075135 0.7285208 0.7772329
            [,13]     [,14]     [,15]     [,16]     [,17]     [,18]     [,19]     [,20]     [,21]     [,22]     [,23]     [,24]
 [1,] 0.7718405 0.8477304 0.7924695 0.6970002 0.5634776 0.5786857 0.6218280 0.5315196 0.3873829 0.2014617 0.2801250 0.1127961
 [2,] 0.9076216 0.9449744 0.7725552 0.7559216 0.5679354 0.6402321 0.4889864 0.5152894 0.3331712 0.3476343 0.2669833 0.3206857
 [3,] 0.7978590 0.8619244 0.7800906 0.5694356 0.5083825 0.6706676 0.5561135 0.5944188 0.3733927 0.4216502 0.2492627 0.3520874
 [4,] 0.6231765 0.7066160 0.6909037 0.6063421 0.6860786 0.6565409 0.5999989 0.5714045 0.2961664 0.2843159 0.1712096 0.4162656
 [5,] 0.8041476 0.8540351 0.6815423 0.7974153 0.6635038 0.5690770 0.6247283 0.5370858 0.4737641 0.4405969 0.2221804 0.2751527
 [6,] 0.7718405 0.8477304 0.7924695 0.6970002 0.5634776 0.5786857 0.6218280 0.5315196 0.3873829 0.2014617 0.2801250 0.1127961
 [7,] 0.9076216 0.9449744 0.7725552 0.7559216 0.5679354 0.6402321 0.4889864 0.5152894 0.3331712 0.3476343 0.2669833 0.3206857
 [8,] 0.7978590 0.8619244 0.7800906 0.5694356 0.5083825 0.6706676 0.5561135 0.5944188 0.3733927 0.4216502 0.2492627 0.3520874
 [9,] 0.6231765 0.7066160 0.6909037 0.6063421 0.6860786 0.6565409 0.5999989 0.5714045 0.2961664 0.2843159 0.1712096 0.4162656
[10,] 0.8041476 0.8540351 0.6815423 0.7974153 0.6635038 0.5690770 0.6247283 0.5370858 0.4737641 0.4405969 0.2221804 0.2751527
            [,25]     [,26]     [,27]       [,28]     [,29]      [,30]         [,31]     [,32]     [,33]     [,34]     [,35]      [,36]
 [1,] 0.1446305 0.1855372 0.1312774 0.09536614 0.1481058 0.13109154 7.508331e-17 0.1625059 0.2712798 0.2327581 0.1349303 0.17058057
 [2,] 0.3417331 0.3199320 0.2515934 0.12841562 0.2042807 0.04718597 1.889101e-01 0.0481722 0.1007691 0.1986537 0.1256320 0.39106986
 [3,] 0.1980562 0.2647339 0.2452782 0.02892975 0.2436258 0.24789822 4.848882e-02 0.2645255 0.1501646 0.1904320 0.3297219 0.29845516
 [4,] 0.2830731 0.3072307 0.2342600 0.17771651 0.2697995 0.15991971 1.236458e-01 0.1479723 0.2870491 0.1440244 0.1783199 0.09572346
 [5,] 0.3039392 0.3919639 0.1635932 0.19287067 0.2151497 0.15646443 1.662634e-01 0.2532369 0.1318188 0.1091675 0.1274274 0.26543369
 [6,] 0.1446305 0.1855372 0.1312774 0.09536614 0.1481058 0.13109154 0.000000e+00 0.1625059 0.2712798 0.2327581 0.1349303 0.17058057
 [7,] 0.3417331 0.3199320 0.2515934 0.12841562 0.2042807 0.04718597 1.889101e-01 0.0481722 0.1007691 0.1986537 0.1256320 0.39106986
 [8,] 0.1980562 0.2647339 0.2452782 0.02892975 0.2436258 0.24789822 4.848882e-02 0.2645255 0.1501646 0.1904320 0.3297219 0.29845516
 [9,] 0.2830731 0.3072307 0.2342600 0.17771651 0.2697995 0.15991971 1.236458e-01 0.1479723 0.2870491 0.1440244 0.1783199 0.09572346
[10,] 0.3039392 0.3919639 0.1635932 0.19287067 0.2151497 0.15646443 1.662634e-01 0.2532369 0.1318188 0.1091675 0.1274274 0.26543369
```

Standardizing the values of Y. The range of values lies between 0 and 1:

```
> X <- (X - min(X)) / (max(X) - min(X))
```

Printing the values of X:

```
> X
```

The result is as follows:

```
          [,1]      [,2]      [,3]      [,4]      [,5]      [,6]      [,7]      [,8]      [,9] [,10]     [,11]     [,12]     [,13]
 [1,] 0.9938442 0.9755283 0.9455033 0.9045085 0.8535534 0.7938926 0.7269952 0.6545085 0.5782172   0.5 0.4217828 0.3454915 0.2730048
 [2,] 0.9938442 0.9755283 0.9455033 0.9045085 0.8535534 0.7938926 0.7269952 0.6545085 0.5782172   0.5 0.4217828 0.3454915 0.2730048
 [3,] 0.9938442 0.9755283 0.9455033 0.9045085 0.8535534 0.7938926 0.7269952 0.6545085 0.5782172   0.5 0.4217828 0.3454915 0.2730048
 [4,] 0.9938442 0.9755283 0.9455033 0.9045085 0.8535534 0.7938926 0.7269952 0.6545085 0.5782172   0.5 0.4217828 0.3454915 0.2730048
 [5,] 0.9938442 0.9755283 0.9455033 0.9045085 0.8535534 0.7938926 0.7269952 0.6545085 0.5782172   0.5 0.4217828 0.3454915 0.2730048
 [6,] 0.9938442 0.9755283 0.9455033 0.9045085 0.8535534 0.7938926 0.7269952 0.6545085 0.5782172   0.5 0.4217828 0.3454915 0.2730048
 [7,] 0.9938442 0.9755283 0.9455033 0.9045085 0.8535534 0.7938926 0.7269952 0.6545085 0.5782172   0.5 0.4217828 0.3454915 0.2730048
 [8,] 0.9938442 0.9755283 0.9455033 0.9045085 0.8535534 0.7938926 0.7269952 0.6545085 0.5782172   0.5 0.4217828 0.3454915 0.2730048
 [9,] 0.9938442 0.9755283 0.9455033 0.9045085 0.8535534 0.7938926 0.7269952 0.6545085 0.5782172   0.5 0.4217828 0.3454915 0.2730048
[10,] 0.9938442 0.9755283 0.9455033 0.9045085 0.8535534 0.7938926 0.7269952 0.6545085 0.5782172   0.5 0.4217828 0.3454915 0.2730048
         [,14]     [,15]     [,16]      [,17]      [,18]      [,19] [,20]     [,21]      [,22]      [,23]     [,24]     [,25]     [,26]
 [1,] 0.2061074 0.1464466 0.0954915 0.05449674 0.02447174 0.00615583     0 0.00615583 0.02447174 0.05449674 0.0954915 0.1464466 0.2061074
 [2,] 0.2061074 0.1464466 0.0954915 0.05449674 0.02447174 0.00615583     0 0.00615583 0.02447174 0.05449674 0.0954915 0.1464466 0.2061074
 [3,] 0.2061074 0.1464466 0.0954915 0.05449674 0.02447174 0.00615583     0 0.00615583 0.02447174 0.05449674 0.0954915 0.1464466 0.2061074
 [4,] 0.2061074 0.1464466 0.0954915 0.05449674 0.02447174 0.00615583     0 0.00615583 0.02447174 0.05449674 0.0954915 0.1464466 0.2061074
 [5,] 0.2061074 0.1464466 0.0954915 0.05449674 0.02447174 0.00615583     0 0.00615583 0.02447174 0.05449674 0.0954915 0.1464466 0.2061074
 [6,] 0.2061074 0.1464466 0.0954915 0.05449674 0.02447174 0.00615583     0 0.00615583 0.02447174 0.05449674 0.0954915 0.1464466 0.2061074
 [7,] 0.2061074 0.1464466 0.0954915 0.05449674 0.02447174 0.00615583     0 0.00615583 0.02447174 0.05449674 0.0954915 0.1464466 0.2061074
 [8,] 0.2061074 0.1464466 0.0954915 0.05449674 0.02447174 0.00615583     0 0.00615583 0.02447174 0.05449674 0.0954915 0.1464466 0.2061074
 [9,] 0.2061074 0.1464466 0.0954915 0.05449674 0.02447174 0.00615583     0 0.00615583 0.02447174 0.05449674 0.0954915 0.1464466 0.2061074
[10,] 0.2061074 0.1464466 0.0954915 0.05449674 0.02447174 0.00615583     0 0.00615583 0.02447174 0.05449674 0.0954915 0.1464466 0.2061074
         [,27]     [,28]     [,29] [,30]     [,31]     [,32]     [,33]     [,34]     [,35]     [,36]     [,37]     [,38]     [,39] [,40]
 [1,] 0.2730048 0.3454915 0.4217828   0.5 0.5782172 0.6545085 0.7269952 0.7938926 0.8535534 0.9045085 0.9455033 0.9755283 0.9938442     1
 [2,] 0.2730048 0.3454915 0.4217828   0.5 0.5782172 0.6545085 0.7269952 0.7938926 0.8535534 0.9045085 0.9455033 0.9755283 0.9938442     1
 [3,] 0.2730048 0.3454915 0.4217828   0.5 0.5782172 0.6545085 0.7269952 0.7938926 0.8535534 0.9045085 0.9455033 0.9755283 0.9938442     1
 [4,] 0.2730048 0.3454915 0.4217828   0.5 0.5782172 0.6545085 0.7269952 0.7938926 0.8535534 0.9045085 0.9455033 0.9755283 0.9938442     1
 [5,] 0.2730048 0.3454915 0.4217828   0.5 0.5782172 0.6545085 0.7269952 0.7938926 0.8535534 0.9045085 0.9455033 0.9755283 0.9938442     1
 [6,] 0.2730048 0.3454915 0.4217828   0.5 0.5782172 0.6545085 0.7269952 0.7938926 0.8535534 0.9045085 0.9455033 0.9755283 0.9938442     1
 [7,] 0.2730048 0.3454915 0.4217828   0.5 0.5782172 0.6545085 0.7269952 0.7938926 0.8535534 0.9045085 0.9455033 0.9755283 0.9938442     1
 [8,] 0.2730048 0.3454915 0.4217828   0.5 0.5782172 0.6545085 0.7269952 0.7938926 0.8535534 0.9045085 0.9455033 0.9755283 0.9938442     1
 [9,] 0.2730048 0.3454915 0.4217828   0.5 0.5782172 0.6545085 0.7269952 0.7938926 0.8535534 0.9045085 0.9455033 0.9755283 0.9938442     1
[10,] 0.2730048 0.3454915 0.4217828   0.5 0.5782172 0.6545085 0.7269952 0.7938926 0.8535534 0.9045085 0.9455033 0.9755283 0.9938442     1
```

Transposing the values of X and Y:

```
> X <- t(X)
> Y <- t(Y)
```

Creating training and testing sets:

```
> train <- 1:8
> test <- 9:10
```

Training the recurrent neural network. `Y = Y[train,]` signifies an array of output values. `X = X[train,]` signifies an array of input values. `learningrate = 0.05` means the rate to be applied for weight iteration. `hidden_dim = 16` is the dimension of hidden layers. `numepochs = 1500` is the number of times the whole dataset undergoes training.

This phase will take time. The time taken depends on the learning rate, the number of dimensions, and the number of times the whole dataset undergoes training:

```
> model <- trainr(Y = Y[train,],X = X[train,],learningrate =
0.05,hidden_dim = 16,numepochs = 1500)
```

The result is as follows:

```
Trained epoch: 1310 - Learning rate: 0.05
Epoch error: 0.660961658599474
Trained epoch: 1311 - Learning rate: 0.05
Epoch error: 0.669677942923603
Trained epoch: 1312 - Learning rate: 0.05
Epoch error: 0.790488223916989
Trained epoch: 1313 - Learning rate: 0.05
Epoch error: 0.604705780466322
Trained epoch: 1314 - Learning rate: 0.05
Epoch error: 0.736036716583117
Trained epoch: 1315 - Learning rate: 0.05
Epoch error: 0.846403635114378
Trained epoch: 1316 - Learning rate: 0.05
Epoch error: 0.705399512762672
Trained epoch: 1317 - Learning rate: 0.05
Epoch error: 0.655253881236524
Trained epoch: 1318 - Learning rate: 0.05
Epoch error: 0.683256850600975
Trained epoch: 1319 - Learning rate: 0.05
Epoch error: 0.664219260959064
Trained epoch: 1320 - Learning rate: 0.05
Epoch error: 0.609030183713622
Trained epoch: 1321 - Learning rate: 0.05
Epoch error: 0.783214788737956
Trained epoch: 1322 - Learning rate: 0.05
Epoch error: 0.717855276763514
Trained epoch: 1323 - Learning rate: 0.05
Epoch error: 0.648403367406859
Trained epoch: 1324 - Learning rate: 0.05
Epoch error: 0.665843170375635
Trained epoch: 1325 - Learning rate: 0.05
Epoch error: 0.716409342111275
Trained epoch: 1326 - Learning rate: 0.05
Epoch error: 0.616071661248296
Trained epoch: 1327 - Learning rate: 0.05
Epoch error: 0.65502734088982
```

Predicting the output of the recurrent neural network:

```
> Y_predicted <- predictr(model, X)
```

Plotting the **Actual values vs the Predicted values**. The output constitutes the training set and the testing set:

```
> plot(as.vector(t(Y)), col = 'red', type = 'l', main = "Actual values
vs Predicted values", ylab = "Y, Y-predicted")
```

The result is as follows:

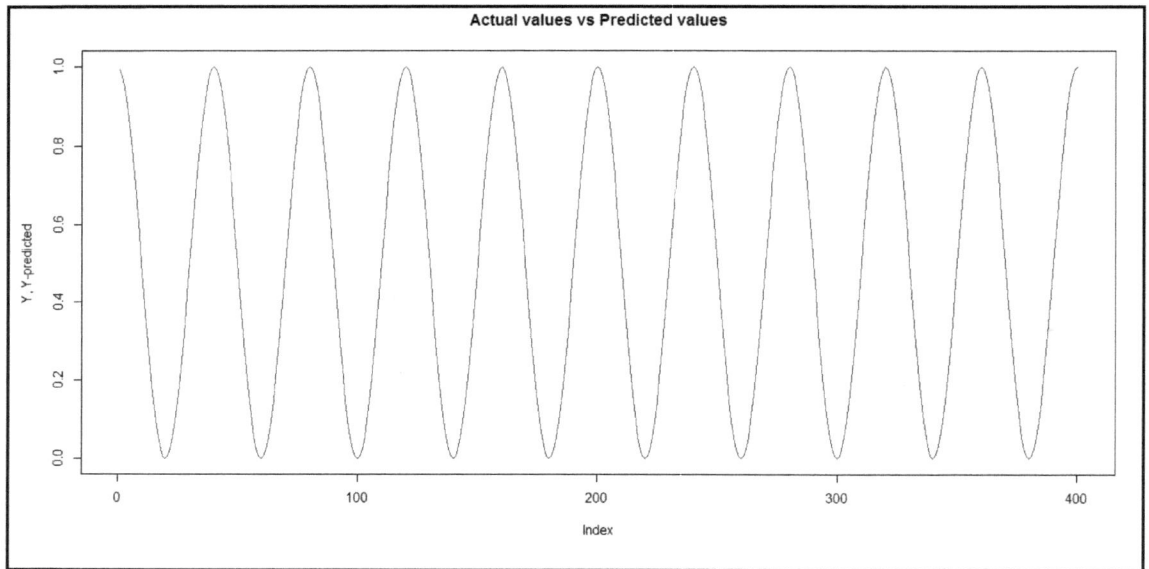

```
> lines(as.vector(t(Y_predicted)), type = 'l', col = 'blue')
```

The result is as follows:

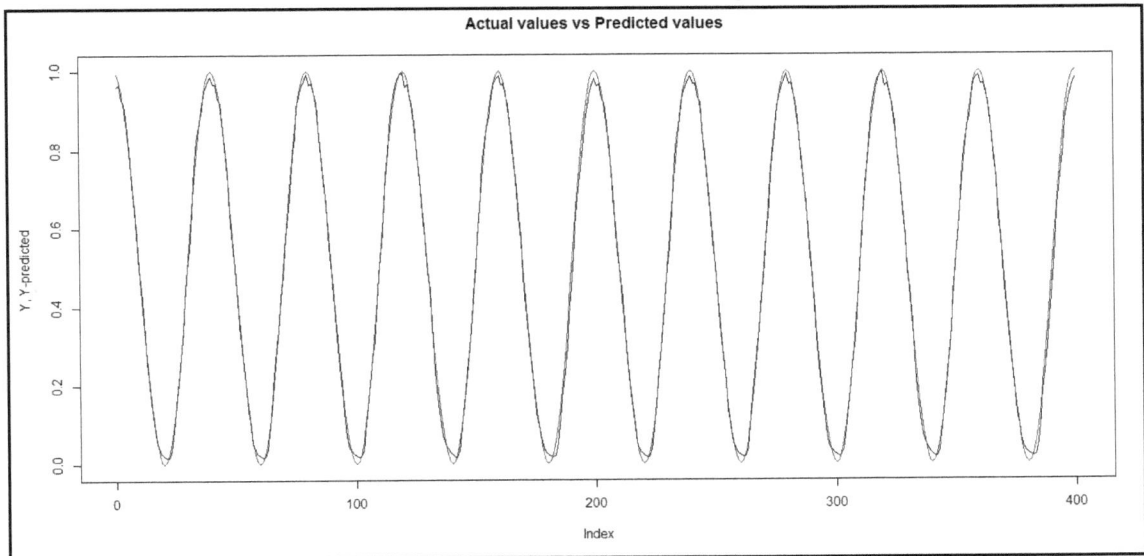

Plotting the **Actual values vs the Predicted values**. The output constitutes the testing set only:

```
> plot(as.vector(t(Y[test,])), col = 'red', type='l', main = "Actual vs
predicted: testing set", ylab = "Y,Y-predicted")
```

The result is as follows:

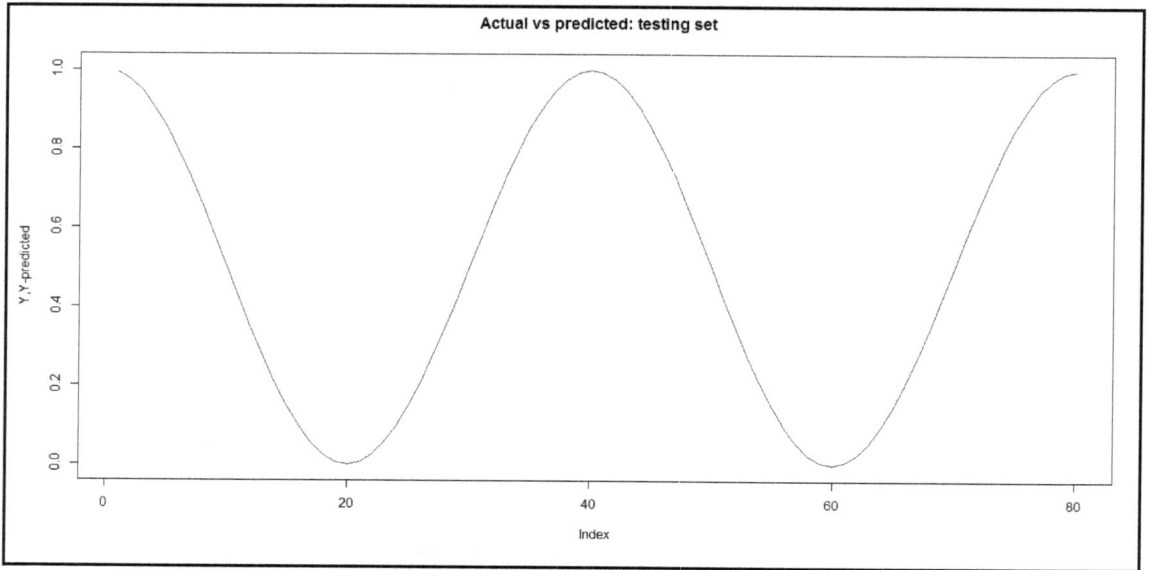

Actual vs predicted: testing set

```
> lines(as.vector(t(Y_predicted[test,])), type = 'l', col = 'blue')
```

The result is as follows:

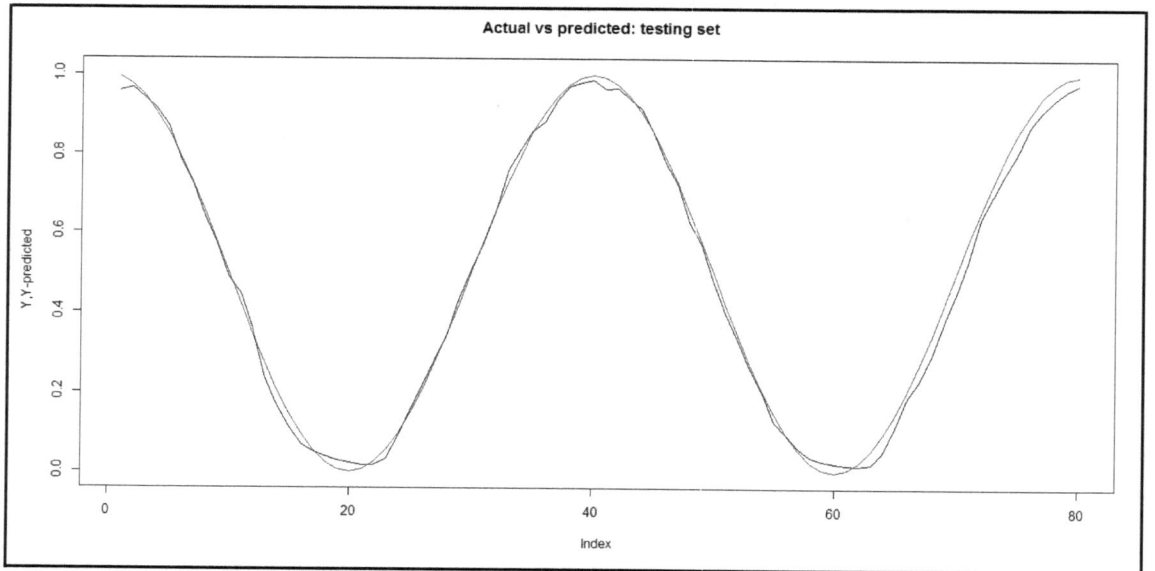

Actual vs predicted: testing set

12

Case Study - Exploring World Bank Data

Introduction

World Bank Indicators (**WDI**) is the World Bank's compilation of internationally comparable and measurable statistics about the growth of global development and its impact on the quality of people's lives measuring the state of development in countries, regions and income groups by looking into data collected from over 200 economies and more than 50 partner organizations to present more than 1400 indicators. On September 25, 2015, the United Nations General Assembly formally adopted the 2030 agenda for sustainable development, to guide global action over the next 15 years. The five main focus themes of SDG's are people, planet, prosperity, peace, and partnership. Countries have resolved to end poverty and hunger and ensure that all people can fulfill their potential in dignity and equality and in a healthy environment; to protect the planet from degradation and take urgent action on climate change; to ensure that all people can enjoy prosperous and fulfilling lives and that progress takes place in harmony with nature; to foster peaceful, just, and inclusive societies free from fear and violence; and to mobilize the means to implement agenda 2030, focused on the poorest and most vulnerable, through strong global partnership. A World Bank group perspective, for each of the 17 goals, experts from the World Bank's Development Data Group, global practices and cross-cutting solution areas have selected indicators to identify and analyze important trends and challenges, and to elicit discussion on measurement issues. World Development Indicators is the result of a collaboration of numerous international agencies, over 200 national statistical offices and many others.

Exploring World Bank data

In 2012, 13 percent of the world's population lived below the international poverty line of $1.90 a day, down from 37 percent in 1990. Declines in all regions contributed to the early success of meeting the Millennium Development Goal target of halving extreme poverty globally. The aim is to eliminate poverty in all forms by 2030 and to achieve social protection for poor, increase access to basic services, and to support people harmed by conflict and climate-related disaster.

More than half the deaths recorded in low income countries is due to communicable diseases or maternal, prenatal, or nutrition conditions. While, in the middle and high-income countries more than two-thirds of the recorded deaths are due to non communicable diseases. Energy use increased about 54 percent between 1990 and 2013 worldwide. Access to energy is fundamental to development, but as economies evolve, rising incomes and growing populations demand more energy. Energy, especially electricity, is crucial to improving the standard of living for people in low and middle income countries.

Getting ready...

In order to carry out the pricing of reinsurance contracts we shall be using a dataset collected from the Hurricane dataset.

In order to carry out the data pattern analysis of the World Bank we shall be using a dataset collected from the following:

- Total world population (1960-2015)
- Life expectancy at birth for all the countries and regions (1960-2014)
- Fertility rate (births per woman) for all the countries and regions (1960-2014)
- GDP as measured in US$ for all the countries and regions (1960-2015)
- Poverty head count ratio for all the countries and regions (1960-2016)
- Access to sanitation for all the countries and regions (1960-2016)
- Percentage of population with access to electricity for all countries and regions (1960-2016)
- CO_2 emissions for all countries and regions (1960-2016)

Step 1 - collecting and describing data

The World Bank's dataset for the analysis is available from the World Bank data bank and can be downloaded freely.

How to do it...

Let's get into the details.

Step 2 - downloading the data

Load the following packages:

```
> install.packages("wbstats")
> install.packages("data.table")
> install.packages("googleVis")
```

Version info: Code for this page was tested in R version 3.3.0 (2016-05-03)

Each of the following libraries needs to be installed:

```
> library(wbstats)
> library(data.table)
> library(googleVis)
```

Let's download the data and understand the relationships among the variables. We will begin by downloading data from the World Bank website. `data.table()` as a function allows fast aggregation of large datasets, ordering joins, adding/modifying/deleting of columns by group using no copies, listing of columns, a friendly file reader, and a parallel file writer. The `wb()` function uses the World Bank API to download the requested information. indicator represents the character vector of indicator codes.

The indicator codes are as follows:

- `SP.POP.TOTL`: Total world population (1960-2015)
- `SP.DYN.LE00.IN`: Life expectancy at birth for all the countries and regions (1960-2014)
- `SP.DYN.TFRT.IN`: Fertility rate (births per woman) for all the countries and regions (1960-2014)

The result is stored in the `Pop_LifeExp_FertRt` data frame. Use the following command:

```
> Pop_LifeExp_FertRt <- data.table(wb(indicator = c("SP.POP.TOTL",
"SP.DYN.LE00.IN", "SP.DYN.TFRT.IN"), startdate = 1960, enddate = 2016))
```

The indicator codes are as follows:

- `SP.POP.TOTL`: Total world population (1960-2015)
- `NY.GDP.MKTP.CD-GDP`: GDP as measured in US$ for all the countries and regions (1960-2015)
- `SI.POV.2DAY`: Poverty head count ratio for all the countries and regions (1960-2016)

The result is stored in the `Pop_GDPUSD_HeadCnt` data frame. Use the following command:

```
> Pop_GDPUSD_HeadCnt <- data.table(wb(indicator = c("SP.POP.TOTL",
"NY.GDP.MKTP.CD", "SI.POV.2DAY"), startdate = 1960, enddate = 2016))
```

The indicator codes are as follows:

- `SP.POP.TOTL`: Total world population (1960-2015)
- `NY.GDP.MKTP.CD`: GDP as measured in US$ for all the countries and regions (1960-2015)
- `SH.STA.ACSN`: Access to sanitation for all the countries and regions (1960-2016)

The result is stored in the `Pop_GDPUSD_Sanitation` data frame. Use the following command:

```
> Pop_GDPUSD_Sanitation <- data.table(wb(indicator = c("SP.POP.TOTL",
"NY.GDP.MKTP.CD", "SH.STA.ACSN"), startdate = 1960, enddate = 2016))
```

The indicator codes are as follows:

- `NY.GDP.MKTP.CD`: GDP as measured in US$ for all the countries and regions (1960-2015)
- `EG.ELC.ACCS.ZS`: Percentage of population with access to electricity for all countries and regions (1960-2016)
- `EN.ATM.CO2E.KT`: Electricity consumption KWh per capita for all countries and regions (1960-2016)

The result is stored in the GDPUSD_Electricity_CO2 data frame. Use the following command:

```
> GDPUSD_Electricity_CO2 <- data.table(wb(indicator =
c("NY.GDP.MKTP.CD", "EG.ELC.ACCS.ZS", "EN.ATM.CO2E.KT"), startdate = 1960,
enddate = 2016))
```

Step 3 - exploring data

Exploring the dimension of the Pop_LifeExp_FertRt data frame: The dim() function returns the dimension of the Pop_LifeExp_FertRt data frame. The Pop_LifeExp_FertRt data frame is passed as an input parameter. The result clearly states that there are 41150 rows of data and six columns:

```
> dim(Pop_LifeExp_FertRt)
```

The result is as follows:

```
[1] 41150      6
```

Exploring the dimension of the Pop_LifeExp_FertRt data frame: The result clearly states that there are 27023 rows of data and six columns:

```
> dim(Pop_GDPUSD_HeadCnt)
```

The result is as follows:

```
[1] 27023      6
```

Exploring the dimension of the `Pop_GDPUSD_Sanitation` data frame: The result clearly states that there are 31884 rows of data and six columns:

```
> dim(Pop_GDPUSD_Sanitation)
```

The result is as follows:

```
[1] 31884      6
```

Exploring the dimension of the `GDPUSD_Electricity_CO2` data frame: The result clearly states that there are 23994 rows of data and six columns:

```
> dim(GDPUSD_Electricity_CO2)
```

The result is as follows:

```
[1] 23994      6
```

Exploring the internal structure of the `Pop_LifeExp_FertRt` data frame: The `str()` function displays the internal structure of the data frame. The `Pop_LifeExp_FertRt` is passed as an R object to the `str()` function:

```
> str(Pop_LifeExp_FertRt)
```

The result is as follows:

```
Classes 'data.table' and 'data.frame':  41150 obs. of  6 variables:
 $ value       : num  3.92e+08 3.84e+08 3.77e+08 3.69e+08 3.61e+08 ...
 $ date        : chr  "2015" "2014" "2013" "2012" ...
 $ indicatorID : chr  "SP.POP.TOTL" "SP.POP.TOTL" "SP.POP.TOTL" "SP.POP.TOTL" ...
 $ indicator   : chr  "Population, total" "Population, total" "Population, total" "Population, total" ...
 $ iso2c       : chr  "1A" "1A" "1A" "1A" ...
 $ country     : chr  "Arab World" "Arab World" "Arab World" "Arab World" ...
 - attr(*, ".internal.selfref")=<externalptr>
```

Exploring the internal structure of the `Pop_GDPUSD_HeadCnt` data frame:

> **str(Pop_GDPUSD_HeadCnt)**

The result is as follows:

```
Classes 'data.table' and 'data.frame':  27023 obs. of  6 variables:
 $ value     : num  3.92e+08 3.84e+08 3.77e+08 3.69e+08 3.61e+08 ...
 $ date      : chr  "2015" "2014" "2013" "2012" ...
 $ indicatorID: chr  "SP.POP.TOTL" "SP.POP.TOTL" "SP.POP.TOTL" "SP.POP.TOTL" ...
 $ indicator : chr  "Population, total" "Population, total" "Population, total" "Population, total" ...
 $ iso2c     : chr  "1A" "1A" "1A" "1A" ...
 $ country   : chr  "Arab world" "Arab world" "Arab world" "Arab world" ...
 - attr(*, ".internal.selfref")=<externalptr>
```

Explore the internal structure of the `Pop_GDPUSD_Sanitation` data frame:

> **str(Pop_GDPUSD_Sanitation)**

The result is as follows:

```
Classes 'data.table' and 'data.frame':  31884 obs. of  6 variables:
 $ value     : num  3.92e+08 3.84e+08 3.77e+08 3.69e+08 3.61e+08 ...
 $ date      : chr  "2015" "2014" "2013" "2012" ...
 $ indicatorID: chr  "SP.POP.TOTL" "SP.POP.TOTL" "SP.POP.TOTL" "SP.POP.TOTL" ...
 $ indicator : chr  "Population, total" "Population, total" "Population, total" "Population, total" ...
 $ iso2c     : chr  "1A" "1A" "1A" "1A" ...
 $ country   : chr  "Arab world" "Arab world" "Arab world" "Arab world" ...
 - attr(*, ".internal.selfref")=<externalptr>
```

Exploring the internal structure of the `GDPUSD_Electricity_CO2` data frame:

> **str(GDPUSD_Electricity_CO2)**

The result is as follows:

```
Classes 'data.table' and 'data.frame':  23994 obs. of  6 variables:
 $ value     : num  2.57e+12 2.89e+12 2.83e+12 2.73e+12 2.50e+12 ...
 $ date      : chr  "2015" "2014" "2013" "2012" ...
 $ indicatorID: chr  "NY.GDP.MKTP.CD" "NY.GDP.MKTP.CD" "NY.GDP.MKTP.CD" "NY.GDP.MKTP.CD" ...
 $ indicator : chr  "GDP (current US$)" "GDP (current US$)" "GDP (current US$)" "GDP (current US$)" ...
 $ iso2c     : chr  "1A" "1A" "1A" "1A" ...
 $ country   : chr  "Arab world" "Arab world" "Arab world" "Arab world" ...
 - attr(*, ".internal.selfref")=<externalptr>
```

Exploring the internal structure of the `GDPUSD_Electricity_CO2` data frame:

> **str(GDPUSD_Electricity_CO2)**

The result is as follows:

```
Classes 'data.table' and 'data.frame':  23994 obs. of  6 variables:
$ value     : num  2.57e+12 2.89e+12 2.83e+12 2.73e+12 2.50e+12 ...
$ date      : chr  "2015" "2014" "2013" "2012" ...
$ indicatorID: chr  "NY.GDP.MKTP.CD" "NY.GDP.MKTP.CD" "NY.GDP.MKTP.CD" "NY.GDP.MKTP.CD" ...
$ indicator : chr  "GDP (current US$)" "GDP (current US$)" "GDP (current US$)" "GDP (current US$)" ...
$ iso2c     : chr  "1A" "1A" "1A" "1A" ...
$ country   : chr  "Arab World" "Arab World" "Arab World" "Arab World" ...
- attr(*, ".internal.selfref")=<externalptr>
```

Printing the `Pop_LifeExp_FertRt` data frame: The `head()` function returns the first part of the `Pop_LifeExp_FertRt` data frame. The `Pop_LifeExp_FertRt` data frame is passed as an input parameter:

> **head(Pop_LifeExp_FertRt)**

The result is as follows:

```
     value date indicatorID          indicator iso2c    country
1: 392022276 2015 SP.POP.TOTL Population, total    1A Arab World
2: 384222592 2014 SP.POP.TOTL Population, total    1A Arab World
3: 376504253 2013 SP.POP.TOTL Population, total    1A Arab World
4: 368802611 2012 SP.POP.TOTL Population, total    1A Arab World
5: 361031820 2011 SP.POP.TOTL Population, total    1A Arab World
6: 353112237 2010 SP.POP.TOTL Population, total    1A Arab World
```

Printing the `Pop_GDPUSD_HeadCnt` data frame:

> **head(Pop_GDPUSD_HeadCnt)**

The result is as follows:

```
     value date indicatorID          indicator iso2c    country
1: 392022276 2015 SP.POP.TOTL Population, total    1A Arab World
2: 384222592 2014 SP.POP.TOTL Population, total    1A Arab World
3: 376504253 2013 SP.POP.TOTL Population, total    1A Arab World
4: 368802611 2012 SP.POP.TOTL Population, total    1A Arab World
5: 361031820 2011 SP.POP.TOTL Population, total    1A Arab World
6: 353112237 2010 SP.POP.TOTL Population, total    1A Arab World
```

Printing the `Pop_GDPUSD_Sanitation` data frame:

> **head(Pop_GDPUSD_Sanitation)**

The result is as follows:

```
      value date indicatorID            indicator iso2c      country
1: 392022276 2015 SP.POP.TOTL Population, total      1A Arab world
2: 384222592 2014 SP.POP.TOTL Population, total      1A Arab world
3: 376504253 2013 SP.POP.TOTL Population, total      1A Arab world
4: 368802611 2012 SP.POP.TOTL Population, total      1A Arab world
5: 361031820 2011 SP.POP.TOTL Population, total      1A Arab world
6: 353112237 2010 SP.POP.TOTL Population, total      1A Arab world
```

Printing the `GDPUSD_Electricity_CO2` data frame:

> **head(GDPUSD_Electricity_CO2)**

The result is as follows:

```
       value date    indicatorID           indicator iso2c      country
1: 2.565871e+12 2015 NY.GDP.MKTP.CD GDP (current US$)    1A Arab world
2: 2.889755e+12 2014 NY.GDP.MKTP.CD GDP (current US$)    1A Arab world
3: 2.830820e+12 2013 NY.GDP.MKTP.CD GDP (current US$)    1A Arab world
4: 2.733908e+12 2012 NY.GDP.MKTP.CD GDP (current US$)    1A Arab world
5: 2.497297e+12 2011 NY.GDP.MKTP.CD GDP (current US$)    1A Arab world
6: 2.103839e+12 2010 NY.GDP.MKTP.CD GDP (current US$)    1A Arab world
```

Exploring the dimension of the `SP.POP.TOTL` data frame: The `dim()` function returns the dimension of the `SP.POP.TOTL` data frame. The `SP.POP.TOTL` data frame is passed as an input parameter. The result clearly states that there are 14623 rows of data and six columns:

> **dim(wb(indicator = "SP.POP.TOTL"))**

The result is as follows:

```
[1] 14623     6
```

Exploring the dimension of the SP.DYN.LE00.IN data frame:

```
> dim(wb(indicator = "SP.DYN.LE00.IN"))
```

The result is as follows:

```
[1] 13253      6
```

Exploring the dimension of the SP.DYN.TFRT.IN data frame:

```
> dim(wb(indicator = " SP.DYN.TFRT.IN "))
```

The result is as follows:

```
[1] 13274      6
```

Exploring the dimension of the NY.GDP.MKTP.CD data frame:

```
> dim(wb(indicator = " NY.GDP.MKTP.CD"))
```

The result is as follows:

```
[1] 11050      6
```

Exploring the dimension of the SI.POV.2DAY data frame:

```
> dim(wb(indicator = " SI.POV.2DAY "))
```

The result is as follows:

```
[1] 1350      6
```

Exploring the dimension of the SH.STA.ACSN data frame:

```
> dim(wb(indicator = " SH.STA.ACSN "))
```

The result is as follows:

```
[1] 6211      6
```

Exploring the dimension of the EG.ELC.ACCS.ZS data frame:

```
> dim(wb(indicator = "EG.ELC.ACCS.ZS"))
```

The result is as follows:

```
[1] 1032      6
```

Exploring the dimension of the EN.ATM.CO2E.KT data frame:

```
> dim(wb(indicator = "EN.ATM.CO2E.KT"))
```

The result is as follows:

```
[1] 11912      6
```

Downloading the updated country and region information from the World Bank API using `wbcountries()` as a function:

```
> Countries <- data.table(wbcountries())
```

Printing the `Countries` data frame: The `head()` function returns the first part of the `Countries` data frame:

```
> head(Countries)
```

The result is as follows:

```
    iso3c iso2c      country        capital    long     lat regionID                    region adminID
1:   ABW    AW        Aruba     Oranjestad -70.0167  12.5167      LCN Latin America & Caribbean      NA
2:   AFG    AF  Afghanistan          Kabul  69.1761  34.5228      SAS                South Asia     SAS
3:   AFR    A9       Africa             NA       NA      NA       NA                Aggregates      NA
4:   AGO    AO       Angola         Luanda  13.242  -8.81155      SSF        Sub-Saharan Africa     SSA
5:   ALB    AL      Albania         Tirane  19.8172  41.3317      ECS     Europe & Central Asia     ECA
6:   AND    AD      Andorra Andorra la Vella  1.5218  42.5075      ECS     Europe & Central Asia      NA
                                           admin incomeID               income lendingID          lending
1:                                            NA      HIC          High income       LNX Not classified
2:                                    South Asia      LIC           Low income       IDX              IDA
3:                                            NA       NA           Aggregates        NA       Aggregates
4:      Sub-Saharan Africa (excluding high income)     UMC Upper middle income       IBD             IBRD
5: Europe & Central Asia (excluding high income)     UMC Upper middle income       IBD             IBRD
6:                                            NA      HIC          High income       LNX Not classified
```

Step 4 - building the models

Sorting the `Pop_LifeExp_FertRt` data table: The `setkey()` function sorts a `Pop_LifeExp_FertRt` data table and marks it as sorted. The sorted columns are the key. The key is in column `iso2c`; the column `iso2c` is always sorted in ascending order. The table is changed by reference and is therefore very memory efficient:

```
> setkey(Pop_LifeExp_FertRt, iso2c)
```

Sorting the `Pop_GDPUSD_HeadCnt` data table:

```
> setkey(Pop_GDPUSD_HeadCnt, iso2c)
```

Sorting the `Pop_GDPUSD_Sanitation` data table:

```
> setkey(Pop_GDPUSD_Sanitation, iso2c)
```

Sorting the `GDPUSD_Electricity_CO2` data table:

```
> setkey(GDPUSD_Electricity_CO2, iso2c)
```

Sorting the `Countries` data table:

> **setkey(Countries, iso2c)**

Printing the `Countries` data table:

> **head(setkey(Countries, iso2c))**

The result is as follows:

```
   iso3c iso2c                                                        country capital long lat
1:   ARB    1A                                                      Arab world      NA   NA  NA
2:   WLD    1W                                                           world      NA   NA  NA
3:   EAP    4E                      East Asia & Pacific (excluding high income)      NA   NA  NA
4:   DXS    6D                         IDA total, excluding Sub-Saharan Africa      NA   NA  NA
5:   FXS    6F IDA countries classified as fragile situations, excluding Sub-Saharan Africa      NA   NA  NA
6:   NLS    6L      Non-resource rich Sub-Saharan Africa countries, of which landlocked      NA   NA  NA
   regionID     region adminID admin incomeID     income lendingID     lending
1:       NA Aggregates      NA    NA       NA Aggregates        NA Aggregates
2:       NA Aggregates      NA    NA       NA Aggregates        NA Aggregates
3:       NA Aggregates      NA    NA       NA Aggregates        NA Aggregates
4:       NA Aggregates      NA    NA       NA Aggregates        NA Aggregates
5:       NA Aggregates      NA    NA       NA Aggregates        NA Aggregates
6:       NA Aggregates      NA    NA       NA Aggregates        NA Aggregates
```

Removing aggregates from the `Pop_LifeExp_FertRt` dataset while adding regions to the dataset:

> **Pop_LifeExp_FertRt <- Countries[Pop_LifeExp_FertRt][! region %in% "Aggregates"]**

Printing the `Pop_LifeExp_FertRt` data table:

> **head(Pop_LifeExp_FertRt)**

The result is as follows:

```
   iso3c iso2c country     capital        long     lat regionID               region adminID admin incomeID
1:   AND    AD Andorra Andorra la Vella 1.5218 42.5075      ECS Europe & Central Asia      NA    NA      HIC
2:   AND    AD Andorra Andorra la Vella 1.5218 42.5075      ECS Europe & Central Asia      NA    NA      HIC
3:   AND    AD Andorra Andorra la Vella 1.5218 42.5075      ECS Europe & Central Asia      NA    NA      HIC
4:   AND    AD Andorra Andorra la Vella 1.5218 42.5075      ECS Europe & Central Asia      NA    NA      HIC
5:   AND    AD Andorra Andorra la Vella 1.5218 42.5075      ECS Europe & Central Asia      NA    NA      HIC
6:   AND    AD Andorra Andorra la Vella 1.5218 42.5075      ECS Europe & Central Asia      NA    NA      HIC
        income lendingID       lending value date indicatorID          indicator i.country
1: High income       LNX Not classified 70473 2015 SP.POP.TOTL Population, total   Andorra
2: High income       LNX Not classified 72786 2014 SP.POP.TOTL Population, total   Andorra
3: High income       LNX Not classified 75902 2013 SP.POP.TOTL Population, total   Andorra
4: High income       LNX Not classified 79316 2012 SP.POP.TOTL Population, total   Andorra
5: High income       LNX Not classified 82326 2011 SP.POP.TOTL Population, total   Andorra
6: High income       LNX Not classified 84419 2010 SP.POP.TOTL Population, total   Andorra
```

Removing aggregates from the `Pop_GDPUSD_HeadCnt` dataset while adding regions to the dataset:

```
> Pop_GDPUSD_HeadCnt <- Countries[Pop_GDPUSD_HeadCnt][ ! region %in%
"Aggregates"]
```

Removing aggregates from the `Pop_GDPUSD_Sanitation` dataset while adding regions to the dataset:

```
> Pop_GDPUSD_Sanitation <- Countries[Pop_GDPUSD_Sanitation][ ! region
%in% "Aggregates"]
```

Removing aggregates from the `GDPUSD_Electricity_CO2` dataset while adding regions to the dataset:

```
> GDPUSD_Electricity_CO2 <- Countries[GDPUSD_Electricity_CO2][ ! region
%in% "Aggregates"]

> wPop_LifeExp_FertRt <- reshape(Pop_LifeExp_FertRt[, list(country,
region, date, value, indicator)], v.names = "value", idvar=c("date",
"country", "region"), timevar="indicator", direction = "wide")

> wPop_GDPUSD_HeadCnt <- reshape(Pop_GDPUSD_HeadCnt[, list(country,
region, date, value, indicator)], v.names = "value", idvar=c("date",
"country", "region"), timevar="indicator", direction = "wide")

> wPop_GDPUSD_Sanitation <- reshape(Pop_GDPUSD_Sanitation[,
list(country, region, date, value, indicator)], v.names = "value",
idvar=c("date", "country", "region"), timevar="indicator", direction =
"wide")

> wGDPUSD_Electricity_CO2 <- reshape(GDPUSD_Electricity_CO2[,
list(country, region, date, value, indicator)], v.names = "value",
idvar=c("date", "country", "region"), timevar="indicator", direction =
"wide")
```

Printing the contents of the data frame `wPop_LifeExp_FertRt`:

```
> wPop_LifeExp_FertRt
```

The result is as follows:

	country	region	date	value.Population, total	value.Fertility rate, total (births per woman)
1:	Andorra	Europe & Central Asia	2015	70473	NA
2:	Andorra	Europe & Central Asia	2014	72786	NA
3:	Andorra	Europe & Central Asia	2013	75902	NA
4:	Andorra	Europe & Central Asia	2012	79316	NA
5:	Andorra	Europe & Central Asia	2011	82326	NA

12053:	Zimbabwe	Sub-Saharan Africa	1964	4279561	7.347
12054:	Zimbabwe	Sub-Saharan Africa	1963	4140804	7.311
12055:	Zimbabwe	Sub-Saharan Africa	1962	4006262	7.267
12056:	Zimbabwe	Sub-Saharan Africa	1961	3876638	7.215
12057:	Zimbabwe	Sub-Saharan Africa	1960	3752390	7.158

	value.Life expectancy at birth, total (years)
1:	NA
2:	NA
3:	NA
4:	NA
5:	NA

12053:	52.97166
12054:	52.62932
12055:	52.27790
12056:	51.91495
12057:	51.54246

Printing the contents of the data frame wGDPUSD_Electricity_CO2:

```
> wGDPUSD_Electricity_CO2
```

The result is as follows:

	country	region	date	value.GDP (current US$)	value.Access to electricity (% of population)	value.CO2 emissions (kt)
1:	Andorra	Europe & Central Asia	2013	3248924588	NA	491.378
2:	Andorra	Europe & Central Asia	2012	3146151869	100	491.378
3:	Andorra	Europe & Central Asia	2011	3427022519	NA	491.378
4:	Andorra	Europe & Central Asia	2010	3346516556	100	517.047
5:	Andorra	Europe & Central Asia	2009	3650083356	NA	517.047

10483:	Zimbabwe	Sub-Saharan Africa	1964	1217138000	NA	4473.740
10484:	Zimbabwe	Sub-Saharan Africa	1963	1159511700	NA	NA
10485:	Zimbabwe	Sub-Saharan Africa	1962	1117601600	NA	NA
10486:	Zimbabwe	Sub-Saharan Africa	1961	1096646600	NA	NA
10487:	Zimbabwe	Sub-Saharan Africa	1960	1052990400	NA	NA

Converting the wPop_LifeExp_FertRt, wPop_GDPUSD_HeadCnt, wPop_GDPUSD_Sanitation, and wGDPUSD_Electricity_CO2 datasets from character format to integer format:

```
> wPop_LifeExp_FertRt[, date := as.integer(date)]
> wPop_GDPUSD_HeadCnt[, date := as.integer(date)]
> wPop_GDPUSD_Sanitation[, date := as.integer(date)]
> wGDPUSD_Electricity_CO2[, date := as.integer(date)]
```

Setting names: The `setnames()` function sets the names of the `wPop_LifeExp_FertRt`, `wPop_GDPUSD_HeadCnt`, `wPop_GDPUSD_Sanitation`, and `wGDPUSD_Electricity_CO2` objects:

```
> setnames(wPop_LifeExp_FertRt, names(wPop_LifeExp_FertRt),
c("Country", "Region", "Year", "Population", "Fertility",
"LifeExpectancy"))
> setnames(wPop_GDPUSD_HeadCnt, names(wPop_GDPUSD_HeadCnt),
c("Country", "Region", "Year", "Population", "GDPUSD", "PovertyHead"))
> setnames(wPop_GDPUSD_Sanitation, names(wPop_GDPUSD_Sanitation),
c("Country", "Region", "Year", "Population", "GDPUSD", "SanitationAccess"))
> setnames(wGDPUSD_Electricity_CO2, names(wGDPUSD_Electricity_CO2),
c("Country", "Region", "Year", "GDPUSD", "ElectricityConsumption",
"CO2Emissions"))
```

Step 5 - plotting the models

Plotting the `wPop_LifeExp_FertRt` data frame models with the following steps. The `gvisMotionChart()` function reads the `wPop_LifeExp_FertRt` data frame. It uses the Google Visualization API to create text output which is included in a web page. The chart is rendered by the web browser in Flash. A motion chart which is dynamic in nature explores indicators. `wPop_LifeExp_FertRt` is the data frame. `idvar = "Country"` represents the column name of data which is to be analyzed. `timevar = "Year"` is the column name of data which represents the time dimension. `xvar = "LifeExpectancy"` is the numerical vector of the data to be plotted on the x axis. `yvar = "Fertility"` is the numerical vector of the data to be plotted on the y axis. `sizevar = "Population"` represents the values of the column which are to be mapped to actual pixel values. `colorvar = "Region"` identifies the bubbles. Use the following commands:

```
> pltPop_LifeExp_FertRt <- gvisMotionChart(wPop_LifeExp_FertRt, idvar =
"Country", timevar = "Year", xvar = "LifeExpectancy", yvar = "Fertility",
sizevar = "Population", colorvar = "Region")
> plot(pltPop_LifeExp_FertRt)
```

Plotting the `wPop_GDPUSD_HeadCnt` data frame models:

```
> pltPop_GDPUSD_HeadCnt <- gvisMotionChart(wPop_GDPUSD_HeadCnt, idvar =
"Country", timevar = "Year", xvar = "GDPUSD", yvar = "PovertyHead", sizevar
= "Population", colorvar = "Region")
> plot(pltPop_GDPUSD_HeadCnt)
```

Plotting the `wPop_GDPUSD_Sanitation` data frame models:

```
> pltPop_GDPUSD_Sanitation <- gvisMotionChart(wPop_GDPUSD_Sanitation,
idvar = "Country", timevar = "Year", xvar = "GDPUSD", yvar =
"SanitationAccess", sizevar = "Population", colorvar = "Region")
> plot(pltPop_GDPUSD_Sanitation)
```

Plotting the `pltGDPUSD_Electricity_CO2` data frame models:

```
> pltGDPUSD_Electricity_CO2 <- gvisMotionChart(wGDPUSD_Electricity_CO2,
idvar = "Country", timevar = "Year", xvar = "GDPUSD", yvar =
"ElectricityAccess", sizevar = "CO2Emissions", colorvar = "Region")
> plot(pltGDPUSD_Electricity_CO2)
```

The results are as follows, Fertility vs life expectancy:

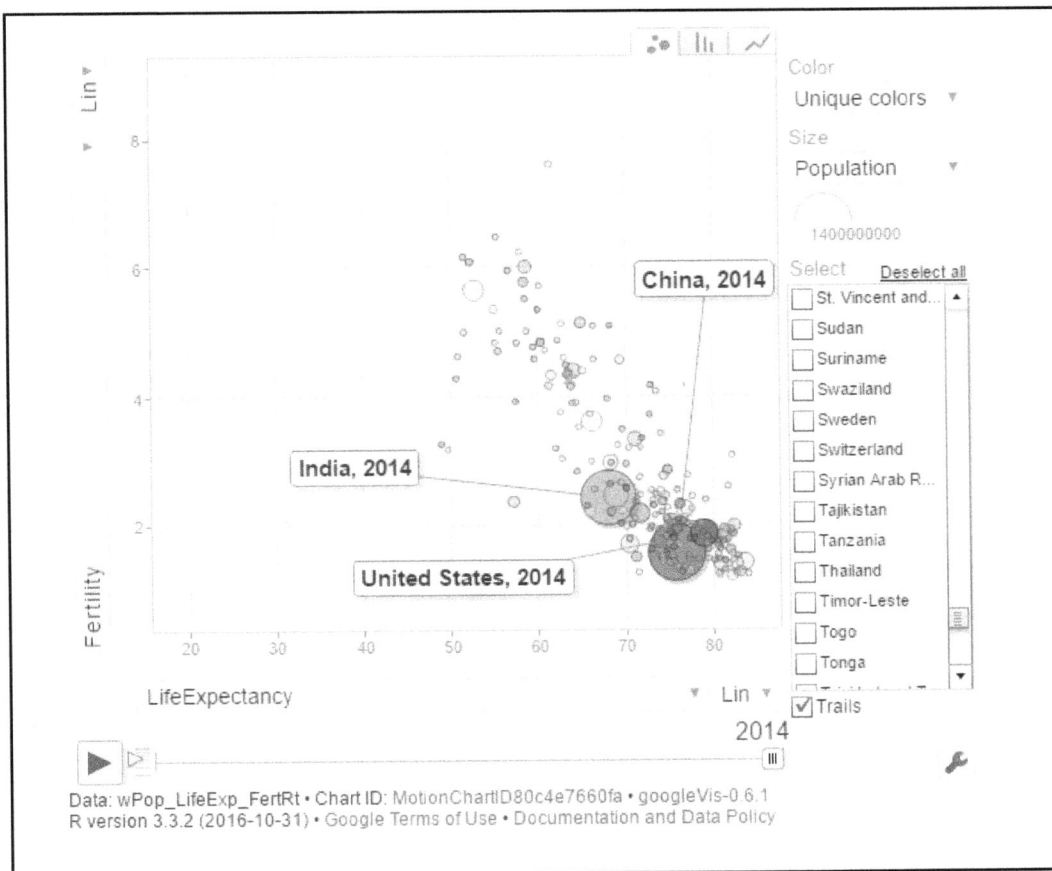

Population growth:

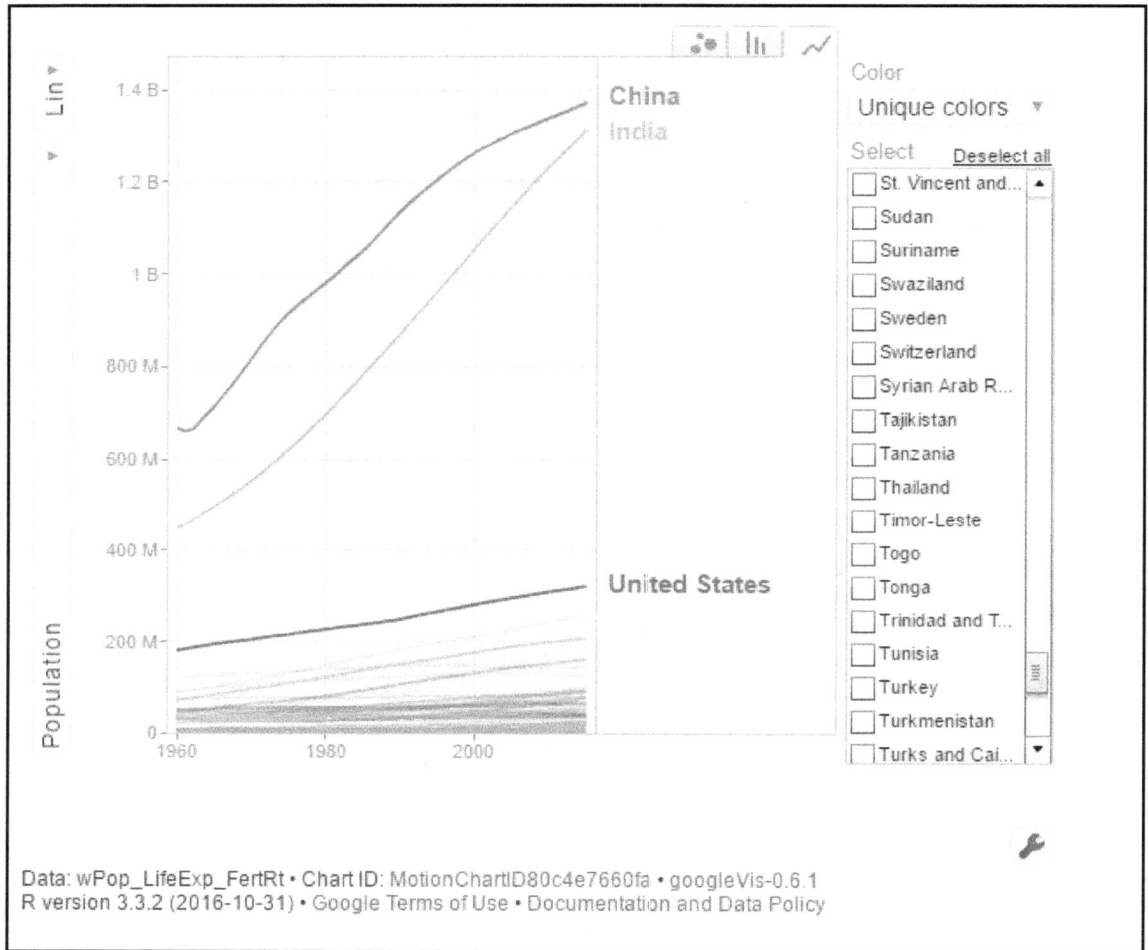

Growth of GDP as measured in US$:

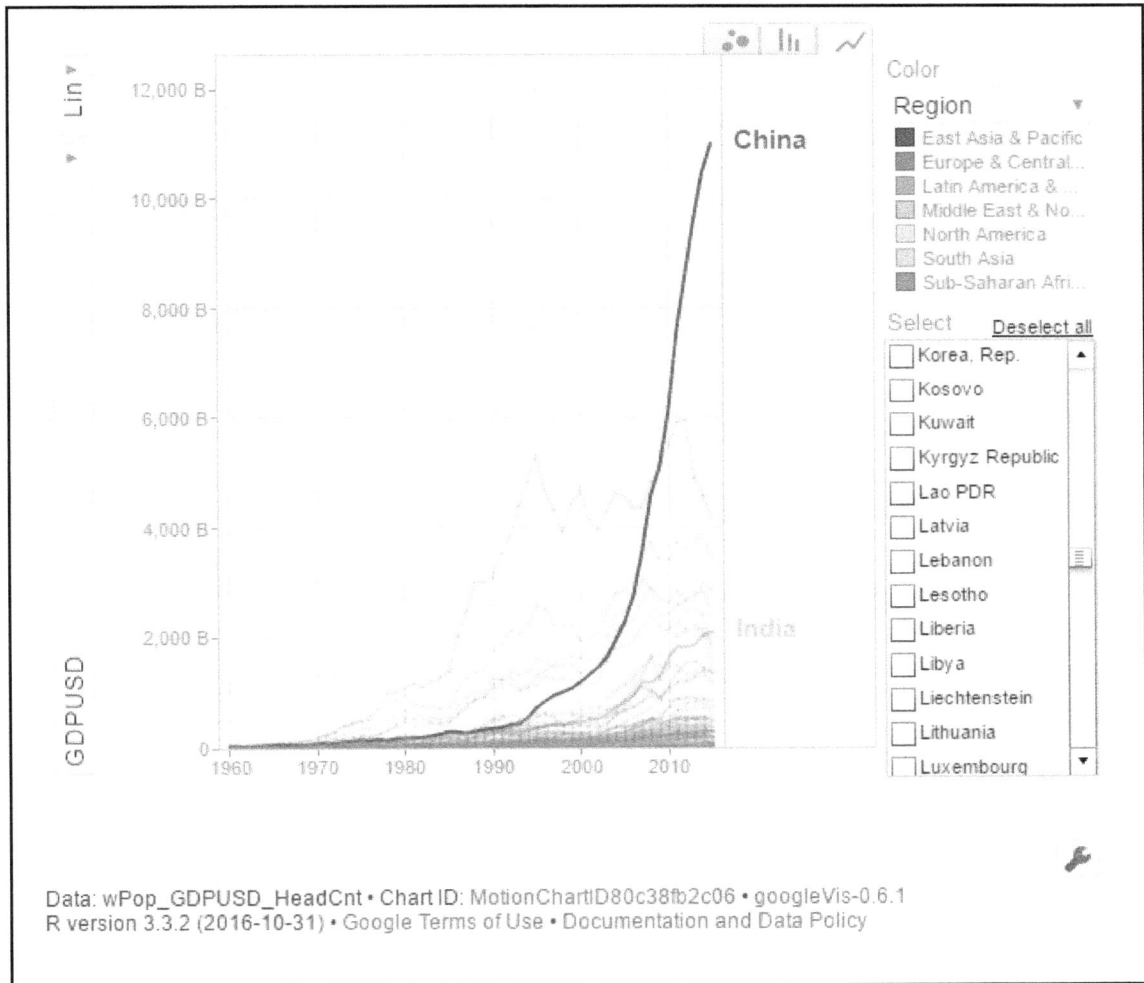

Data: wPop_GDPUSD_HeadCnt • Chart ID: MotionChartID80c38fb2c06 • googleVis-0.6.1
R version 3.3.2 (2016-10-31) • Google Terms of Use • Documentation and Data Policy

Poverty head count ratio vs population growth:

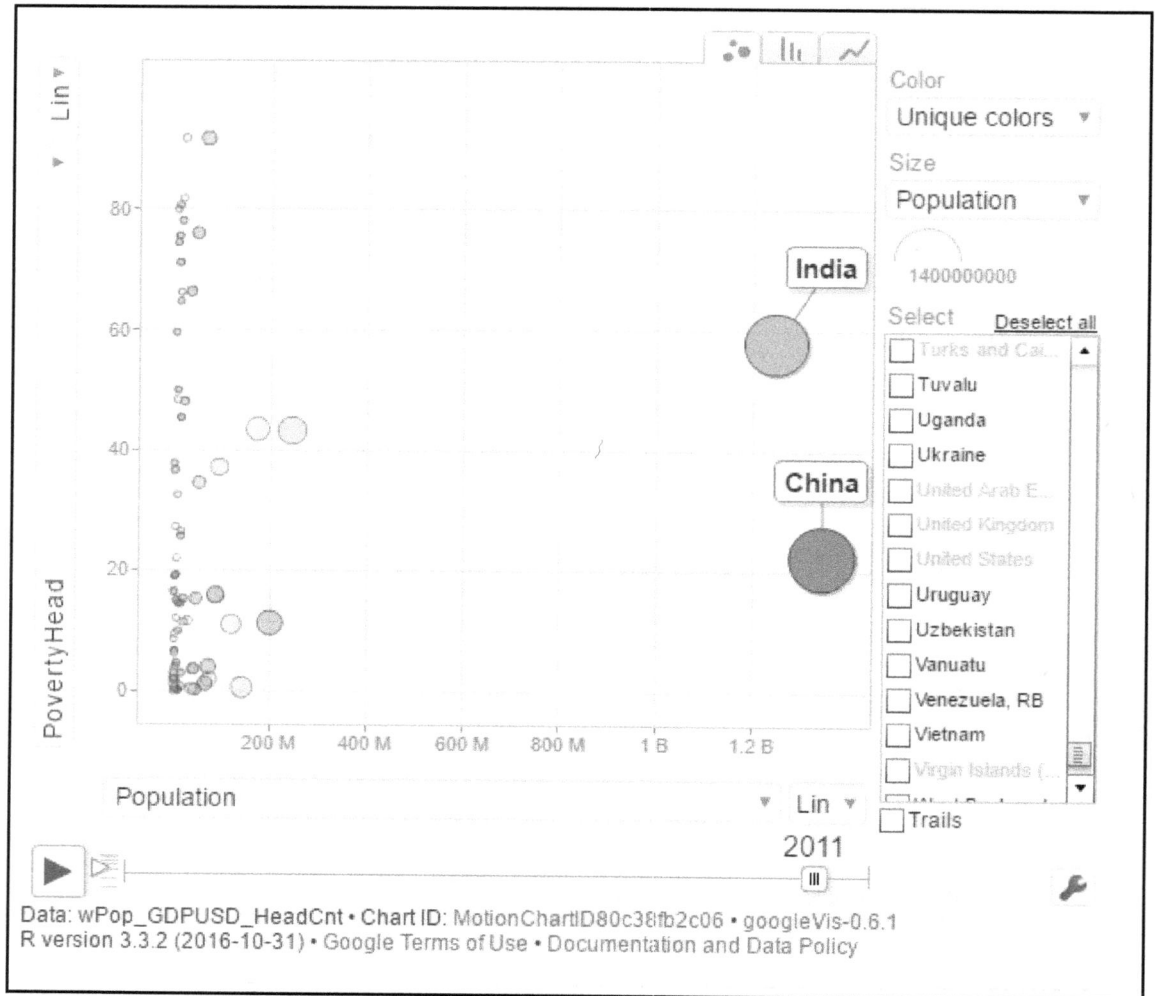

Growth in access of population to sanitation:

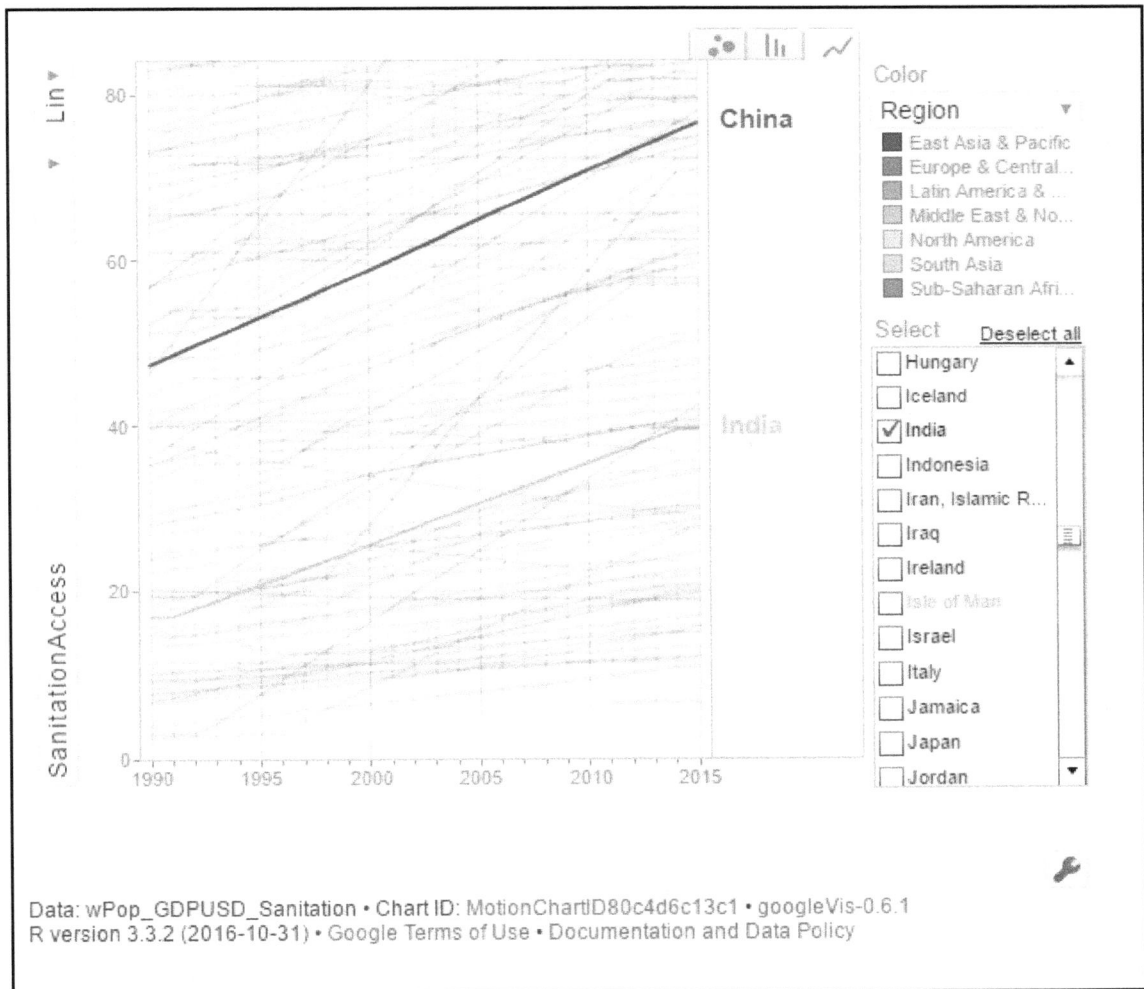

Data: wPop_GDPUSD_Sanitation • Chart ID: MotionChartID80c4d6c13c1 • googleVis-0.6.1
R version 3.3.2 (2016-10-31) • Google Terms of Use • Documentation and Data Policy

Sanitation access:

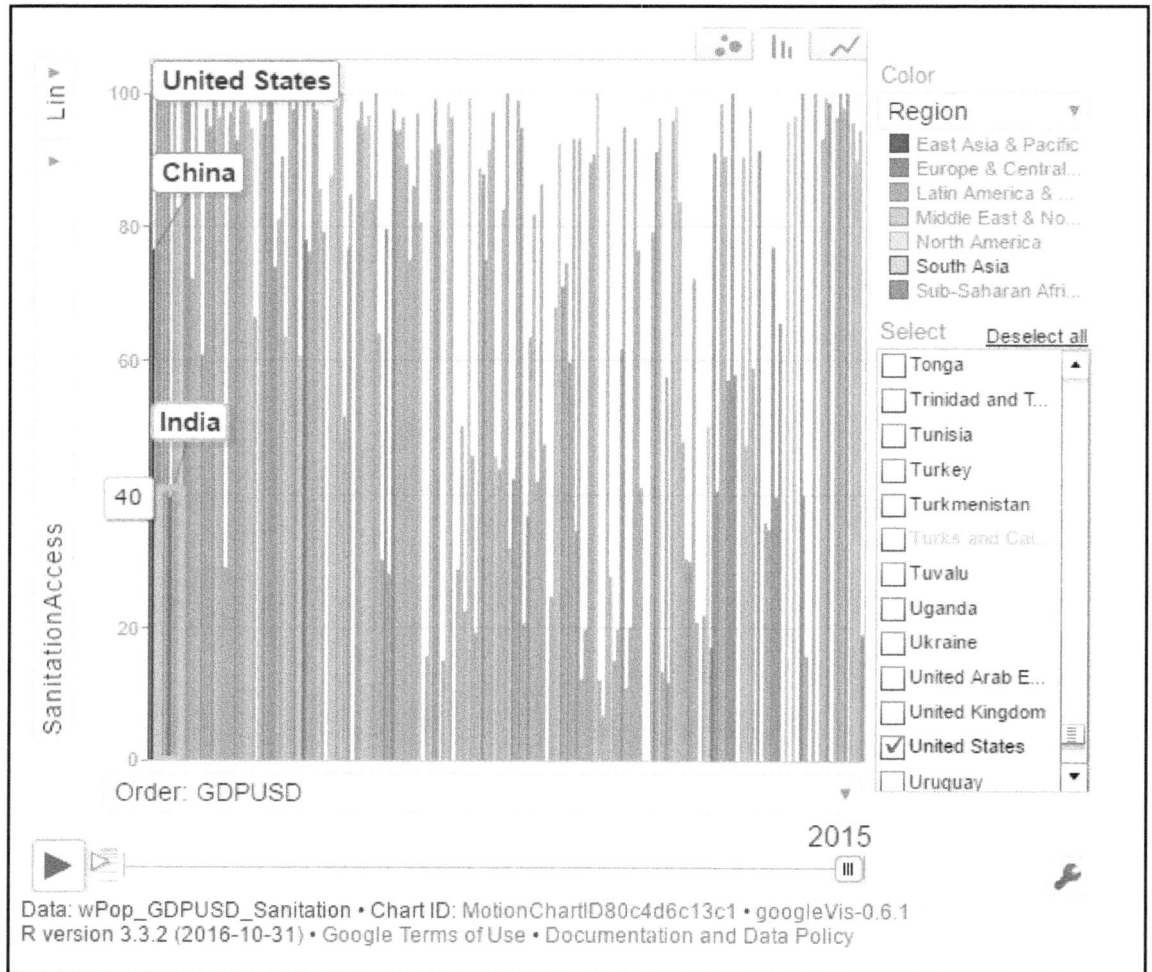

Improvement in sanitation access vs population growth:

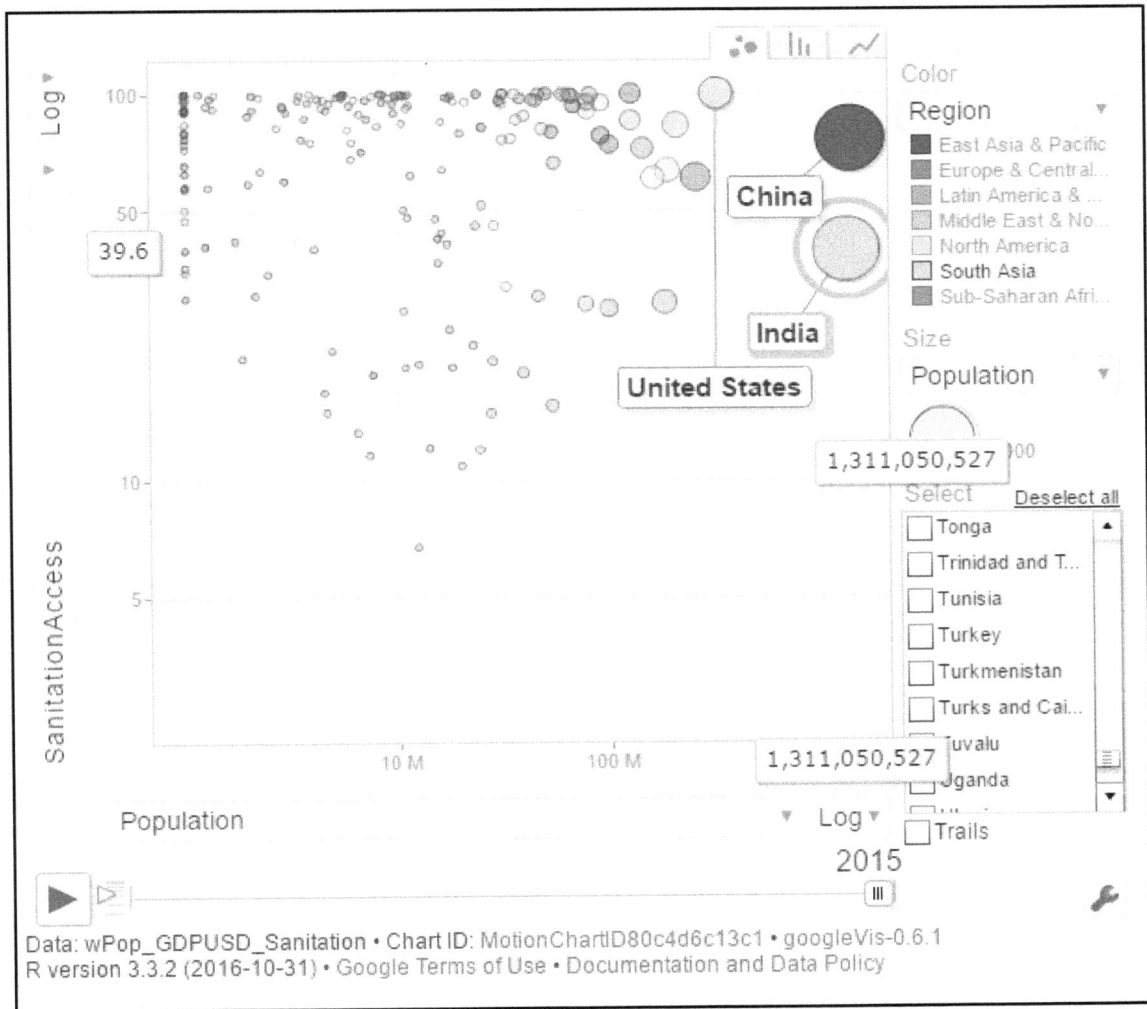

Population with access to electricity for all countries and regions:

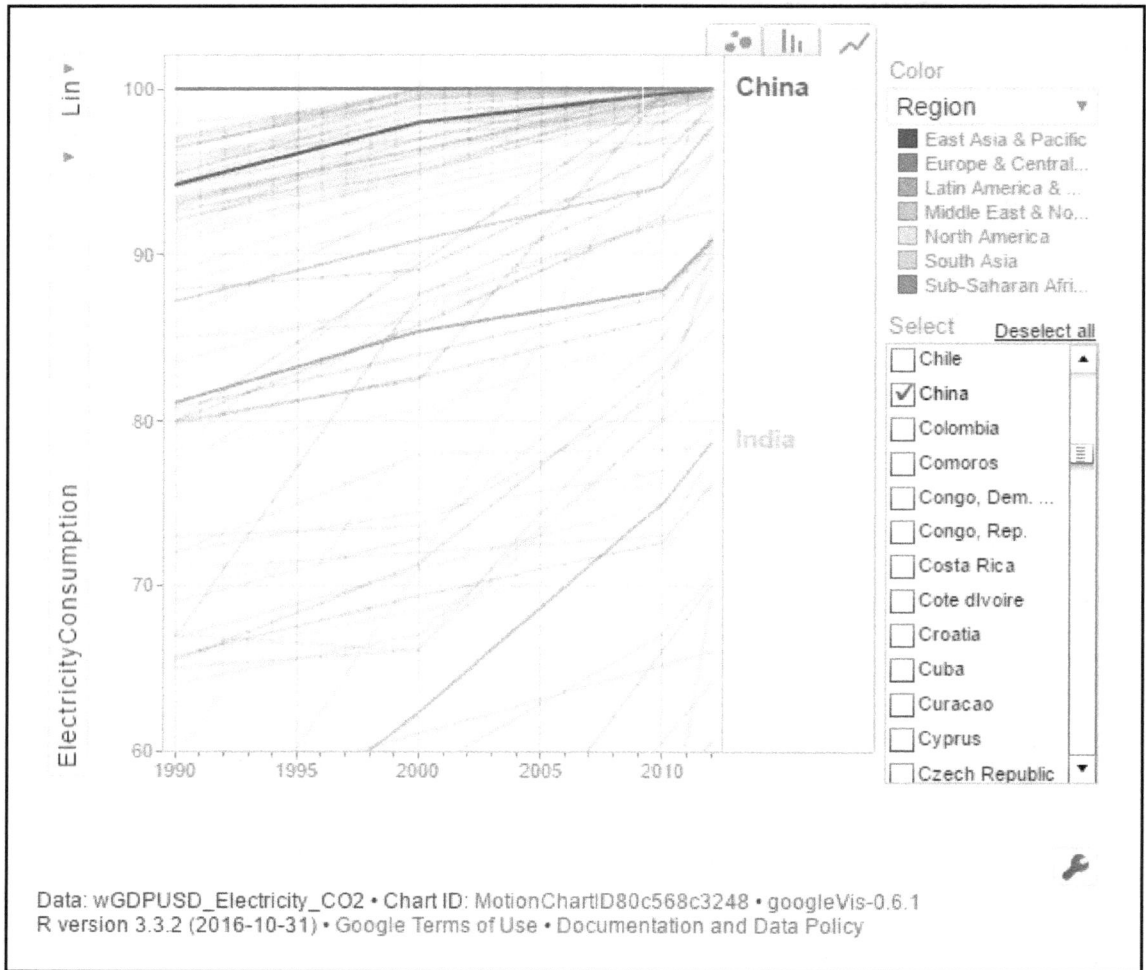

Data: wGDPUSD_Electricity_CO2 • Chart ID: MotionChartID80c568c3248 • googleVis-0.6.1
R version 3.3.2 (2016-10-31) • Google Terms of Use • Documentation and Data Policy

CO$_2$ emissions (log scale):

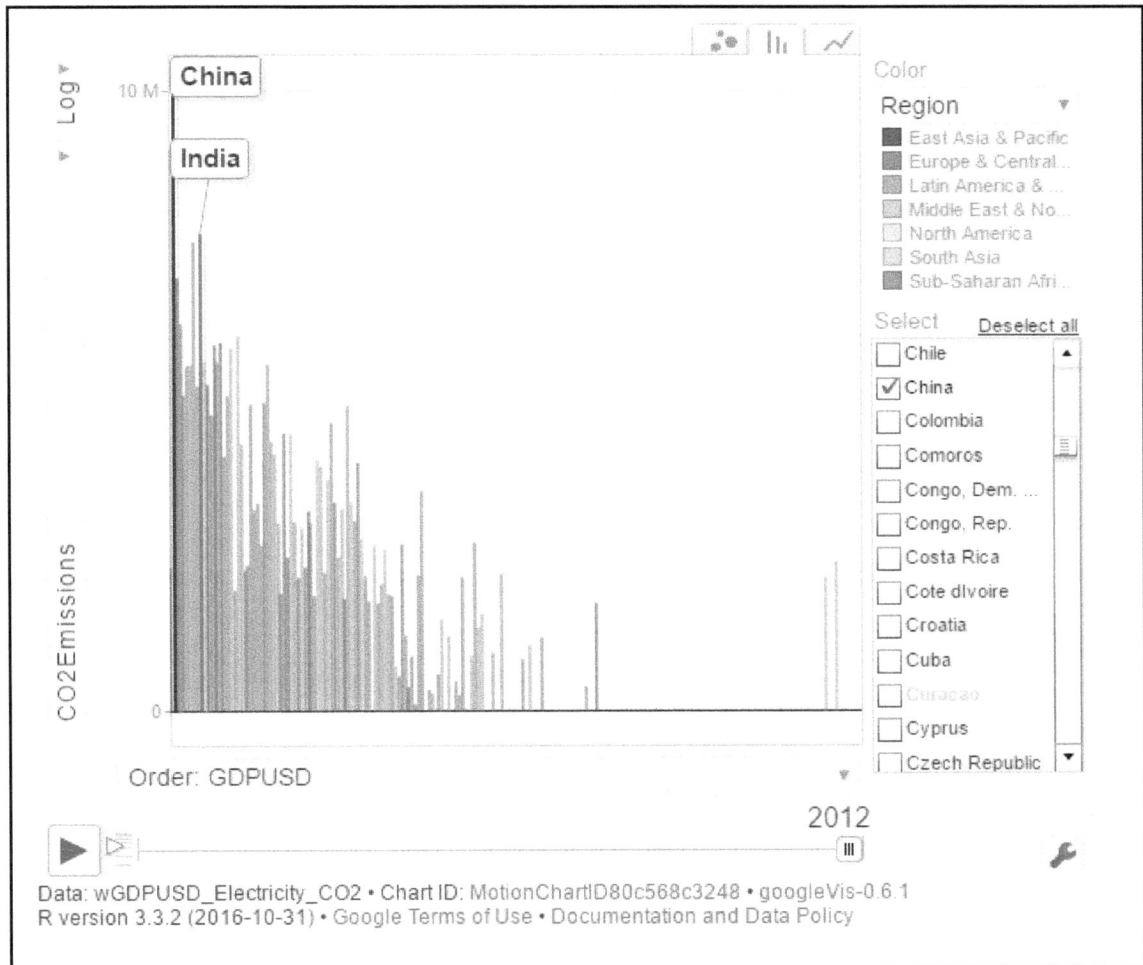

CO_2 emission vs electricity consumption:

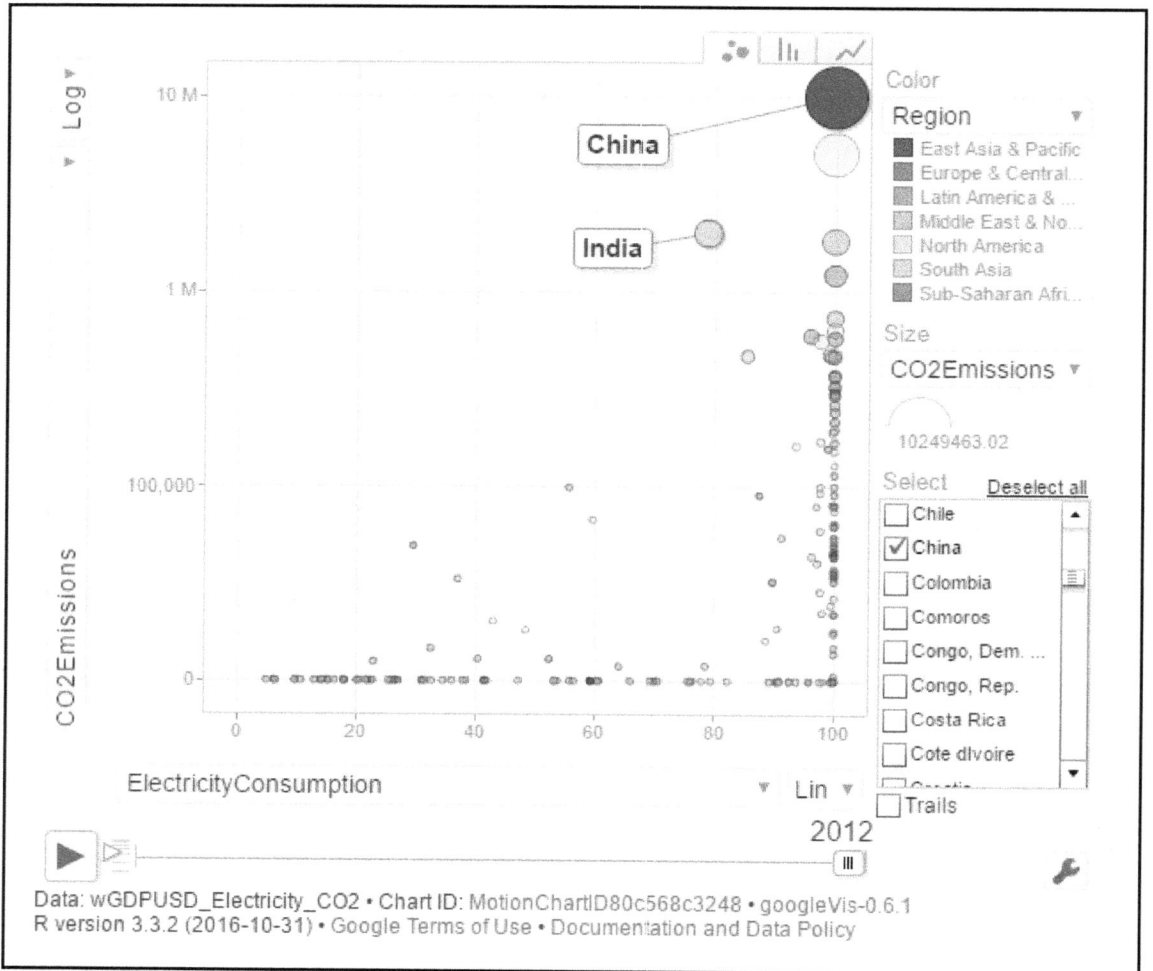

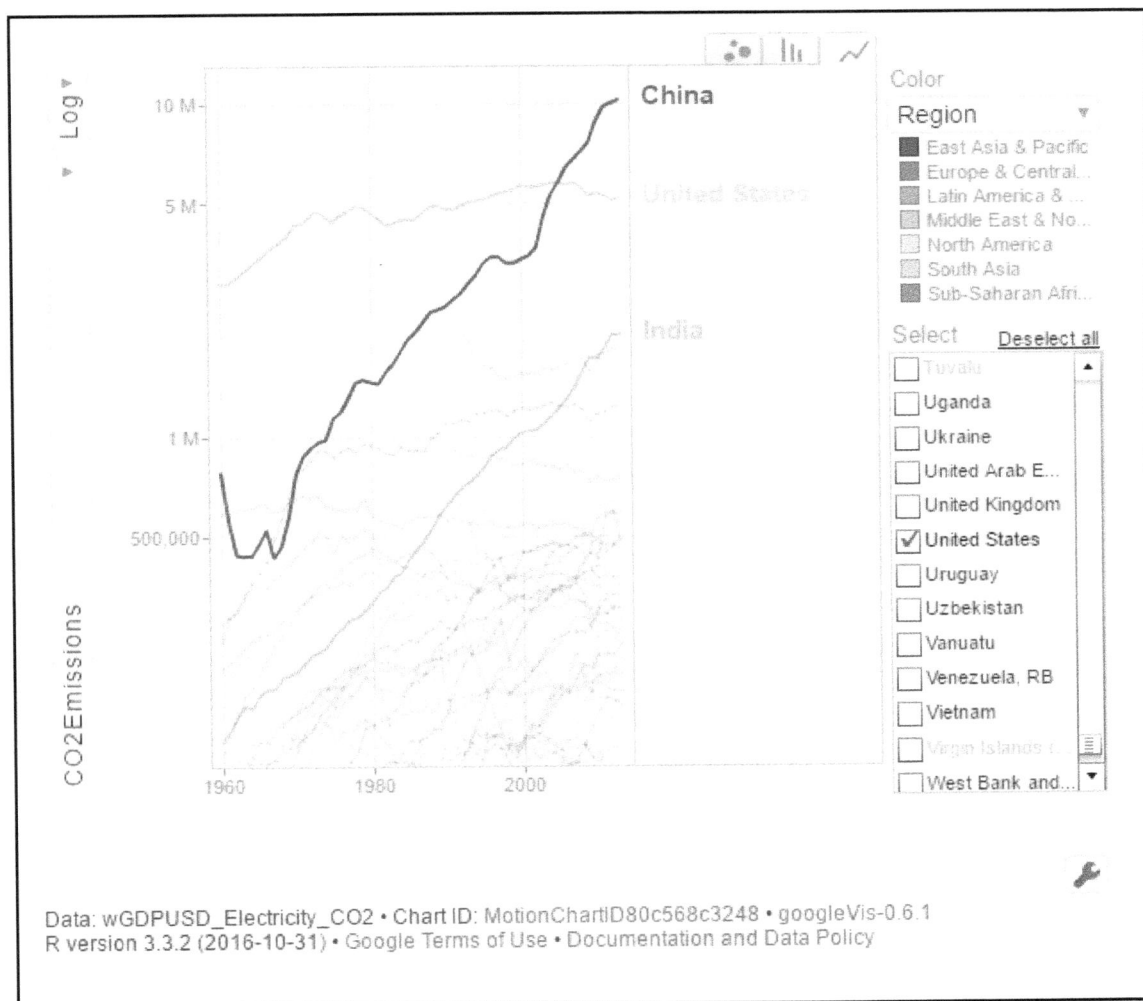

13

Case Study - Pricing Reinsurance Contracts

Introduction

Reinsurance, as the name implies, has developed from insurance business and the extent of its use will depend not only upon the amount but also upon the characteristics of the risks to be underwritten by the direct insurer. The volume of reinsurance business which can be transacted depends primarily upon the volume of direct business available at any given time. The idea of reinsurance is rooted in the same human instinct that brought insurance into being, that is, the desire that the loss of one shall be shared by many.

Pricing reinsurance contracts

The key objectives of an insurer in arranging reinsurance are inter alia; increasing capacity to handle larger risks by passing to the re insurer that part of the exposure which would not normally bear, because of financial constraints; enhancing ability to accept larger lines than capital allows; stabilizing operating results from year to year with the re insurer absorbing larger claims or catastrophe losses; increasing the chances making a profit by reinforcing the underwriter's attempts to establish an account which is homogeneous in both size and quality of risk; ability to write and new risk exposures. The functions of reinsurance can be considered as providing services to protect increased capacity, financial stability, stabilization of claims ratio, accumulation of claims under different classes, spread of risks, protection of solvency margins and stabilize profits. The reinsurance helps to absorb newer risk exposure arising from economic changes, social changes, changes in insurance methods and changes caused by scientific development.

There are only two ways a reinsurance contract can be arranged either by Facultative reinsurance one-off for a single policy or Treaty reinsurance automatic for a defined group of policies.

Getting ready...

In order to carry out the pricing of reinsurance contracts, we shall be using a dataset collected on the Hurricane dataset.

Step 1 - collecting and describing the data

The dataset, available in XLS format, called `publicdatamay2007.xls`, will be used. The dataset is in a standard format. There are 207 rows of data. There are seven variables. The numeric variables are as follows:

- `Year`
- `Base economic damage`
- `Normalized PL05`
- `Normalized CL05`

The non-numeric variables are as follows:

- `Hurricane description`
- `State`
- `Category`

How to do it...

Let's get into the details.

Step 2 - exploring the data

Load up the following packages:

```
> install.packages("gdata")
> install.packages("evir")
> library(gdata)
> library(evir)
```

> Version info: Code for this page was tested in R version 3.2.2

Let's explore the data and understand the relationships among the variables as follows. We'll begin by importing the XLS data file called `publicdatamay2007.xls`. We will be saving the data to the `StormDamageData` data frame:

```
> StormDamageData <- read.xls("d:/publicdatamay2007.xls", sheet = 1)
```

Printing the `StormDamageData` frame: The `head()` function returns the first part of `StormDamageData` frame. The `StormDamageData` data frame is passed as an input parameter:

```
> head(StormDamageData)
```

The result is as follows:

```
   Year Hurricane.Description State Category Base.Economic.Damage Normalized.PL05 Normalized.CL05  X X.1
1  1900        Galveston (1)    TX        4           30,000,000   77,961,217,075  71,883,312,422 NA  NA
2  1901                   4  LA,MS        1            1,000,000      160,419,111     194,228,565 NA  NA
3  1903                   3     FL        1              700,000    5,233,590,783   4,205,750,228 NA  NA
4  1904                   2     SC        1            2,000,000      884,746,945   1,521,808,490 NA  NA
5  1906                   5  AL,MS        2            4,000,000    1,781,764,478   2,013,732,631 NA  NA
6  1906                   8     FL        3              200,000    1,449,580,271   1,180,430,774 NA  NA
```

The `tail()` function returns the last part of `StormDamageData` frame as follows. The `StormDamageData` frame is passed as an input parameter.

```
> tail(StormDamageData)
```

The result is as follows:

	Year	Hurricane.Description	State	Category	Base.Economic.Damage	Normalized.PL05	Normalized.CL05	X	X.1
202	2005	Cindy	LA	1	320,000,000	320,000,000	320,000,000	NA	NA
203	2005	Dennis	FL	3	2,230,000,000	2,230,000,000	2,230,000,000	NA	NA
204	2005	Katrina	LA,MS	3	81,000,000,000	81,000,000,000	81,000,000,000	NA	NA
205	2005	Ophelia	NC	1	1,600,000,000	1,600,000,000	1,600,000,000	NA	NA
206	2005	Rita	TX	3	10,000,000,000	10,000,000,000	10,000,000,000	NA	NA
207	2005	Wilma	FL	3	20,600,000,000	20,600,000,000	20,600,000,000	NA	NA

Exploring the dimension of the StormDamageData data frame: The dim() function returns the dimension of the StormDamageData frame. The StormDamageData data frame is passed as an input parameter. The result clearly states that there are 207 rows of data and nine columns:

```
> dim(StormDamageData)
```

The result is as follows:

```
[1] 207    9
```

Step 3 - calculating the individual loss claims

Formatting the data: The wrapper function, ChangeFormat, eliminates the comma (,) from the values passed and returns the result as a numeric value:

```
> ChangeFormat <- function(x){
  x = as.character(x)
  for(i in 1:10){x=sub(",","",as.character(x))}
    return(as.numeric(x)) }
```

Storing the StormDamageData data frame in base:

```
> base <- StormDamageData[,1:4]
```

Calling the wrapper function, ChangeFormat: The Base.Economic.Damage of the StormDamageData data frame is passed as an input. The Vectorize() function creates the wrapper to the function ChangeFormat(). The result is then stored in the base$Base.Economic.Damage data frame:

```
> base$Base.Economic.Damage <-
  Vectorize(ChangeFormat)(StormDamageData$Base.Economic.Damage)
```

Call the wrapper function, ChangeFormat: The Normalized.PL05 of the
StormDamageData data frame is passed as an input. The result is then stored in the base$
Normalized.PL05 data frame:

```
> base$Normalized.PL05 <-
Vectorize(ChangeFormat)(StormDamageData$Normalized.PL05)
```

Call the wrapper function, ChangeFormat: The Normalized.CL05 of the
StormDamageData data frame is passed as an input. The result is then stored in the base$
Normalized.CL05 data frame:

```
> base$Normalized.CL05 <-
Vectorize(ChangeFormat)(StormDamageData$Normalized.CL05)
```

Printing the base data frame: The head() function returns the first part of the base data
frame. The base data frame is passed as an input parameter:

```
> head(base)
```

The result is as follows:

```
     Year Hurricane.Description State Category Base.Economic.Damage Normalized.PL05 Normalized.CL05
1 1900         Galveston (1)     TX       4                  3e+07       77961217075     71883312422
2 1901                     4  LA,MS       1                  1e+06         160419111       194228565
3 1903                     3     FL       1                  7e+05        5233590783      4205750228
4 1904                     2     SC       1                  2e+06         884746945      1521808490
5 1906                     5  AL,MS       2                  4e+06        1781764478      2013732631
6 1906                     8     FL       3                  2e+05        1449580271      1180430774
  .
```

Plotting the normalized cost of 207 hurricanes: plot() is a generic function.
base$Normalized.PL05/1e9 represents the *x* coordinates of the plot. type="h"
represents the histogram representational style. ylim=c(0,155) sets the upper limit of the
y axis representation as 0 as the lower limit and 155 as the upper limit. The x axis represents
the index of loss:

```
> plot(base$Normalized.PL05/1e9, type="h", ylim=c(0,155), main = "207
Hurricanes, Normalized Costs: 1900 - 2005", xlab = "Index of Loss", ylab =
"Normalized Costs", col = "red")
```

The result is as follows:

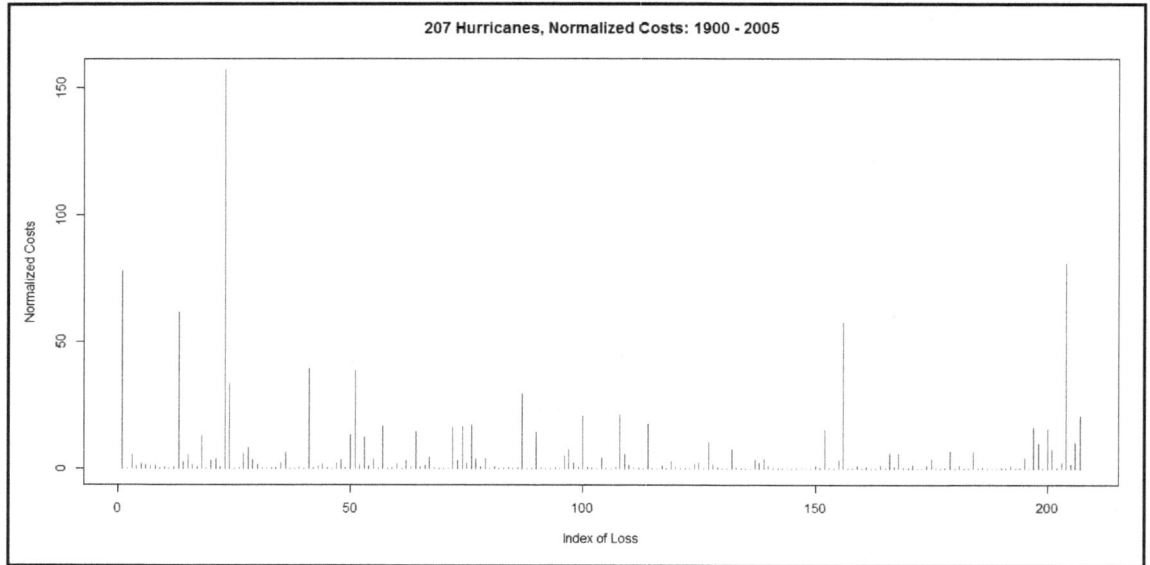

207 Hurricanes, Normalized Costs: 1900 - 2005

Step 4 - calculating the number of hurricanes

Extracting the year and the frequency of the hurricanes count for each year: The base data frame contains the details as shown in the preceding text. `table()` uses `base$Year` to build a contingency table of the hurricanes count for each year. The result is stored in the `TestBase` data frame:

```
> TestBase <- table(base$Year)
```

Printing the contents of the `TestBase` data frame:

```
> TestBase
```

The result is as follows:

1900	1901	1903	1904	1906	1909	1910	1911	1913	1915	1916	1918	1919	1920	1921	1926	1928	1929	1932	1933	1934	1935	1936	1938	1940	1941	1942
1	1	1	1	2	3	1	1	1	2	2	1	1	1	1	3	1	2	1	4	3	2	3	2	2	2	2

1943	1944	1945	1946	1947	1948	1949	1950	1951	1952	1953	1954	1955	1956	1957	1958	1959	1960	1961	1962	1963	1964	1965	1966	1967	1968	1969
1	3	2	2	5	3	2	2	1	1	2	3	3	1	2	1	4	4	2	2	1	5	2	2	1	3	1

1970	1971	1972	1973	1974	1975	1976	1977	1978	1979	1980	1981	1982	1983	1984	1985	1986	1987	1988	1989	1990	1991	1992	1993	1994	1995	1996
1	4	2	1	2	1	1	1	1	5	1	1	2	1	2	6	2	2	5	4	1	1	1	2	3	5	3

1997	1998	1999	2000	2001	2002	2003	2004	2005
1	6	5	2	3	6	3	6	6

Extracting the year from the `TestBase` data frame: The `names()` function extracts the name of each year. `as.numeric()` converts each of the extracted names of the years into a numeric value. The result is stored in the years data frame:

```
> years <- as.numeric(names(TestBase))
```

Printing the contents of the `years` data frame:

```
> years
```

The result is as follows:

```
 [1] 1900 1901 1903 1904 1906 1909 1910 1911 1913 1915 1916 1918 1919 1920 1921 1926 1928 1929 1932 1933 1934 1935 1936 1938 1940 1941
[27] 1942 1943 1944 1945 1946 1947 1948 1949 1950 1951 1952 1953 1954 1955 1956 1957 1958 1959 1960 1961 1962 1963 1964 1965 1966 1967
[53] 1968 1969 1970 1971 1972 1973 1974 1975 1976 1977 1978 1979 1980 1981 1982 1983 1984 1985 1986 1987 1988 1989 1990 1991 1992 1993
[79] 1994 1995 1996 1997 1998 1999 2000 2001 2002 2003 2004 2005
```

Extracting the frequency of hurricanes count for each year from the `TestBase` data frame: `names()` extracts the frequency of hurricanes count for each year. `as.numeric()` converts each of the extracted frequency of hurricanes count into a numeric value. The result is stored in the frequency data frame:

```
> frequency <- as.numeric(TestBase)
```

Printing the contents of the `frequency` data frame:

```
> frequency
```

The result is as follows:

```
 [1] 1900 1901 1903 1904 1906 1909 1910 1911 1913 1915 1916 1918 1919 1920 1921 1926 1928 1929 1932 1933 1934 1935 1936 1938 1940 1941
[27] 1942 1943 1944 1945 1946 1947 1948 1949 1950 1951 1952 1953 1954 1955 1956 1957 1958 1959 1960 1961 1962 1963 1964 1965 1966 1967
[53] 1968 1969 1970 1971 1972 1973 1974 1975 1976 1977 1978 1979 1980 1981 1982 1983 1984 1985 1986 1987 1988 1989 1990 1991 1992 1993
[79] 1994 1995 1996 1997 1998 1999 2000 2001 2002 2003 2004 2005
```

Extracting the frequency of the hurricanes count for each year where there were no hurricane occurrences from the `TestBase` data frame: The result is stored in the `years0frequency` data frame:

```
> years0frequency <- (1900:2005)[which(!(1900:2005)%in%years)]
```

Printing the contents of the `years0frequency` data frame:

```
> years0frequency
```

The result is as follows:

```
[1] 1902 1905 1907 1908 1912 1914 1917 1922 1923 1924 1925 1927 1930 1931 1937 1939
```

Extracting all the counts of hurricanes for each year. The result is stored in the `StormDamageData` data frame:

```
> StormDamageData <- data.frame(years=c(years, years0frequency),
  frequency=c(frequency, rep(0,length(years0frequency))))
```

Printing the `StormDamageData` data frame. The `head()` function returns the first part of the `StormDamageData` data frame. The `StormDamageData` data frame is passed as an input parameter:

```
> head(StormDamageData)
```

The result is as follows:

```
  years frequency
1  1900         1
2  1901         1
3  1903         1
4  1904         1
5  1906         2
6  1909         3
```

Ploting the years and frequency count for hurricanes for each year between 1900 and 2005: `plot()` is a generic function. years represents the *x* coordinates of the plot, while frequency represents the y coordinates of the plot. `type="h"` represents the histogram representational style:

```
> plot(years, frequency, type="h", main = "Frequency of Hurricanes:
1900 - 2005", xlab = "Time (Years)", ylab = "Annual Frequency", col =
"red")
```

The result is as follows:

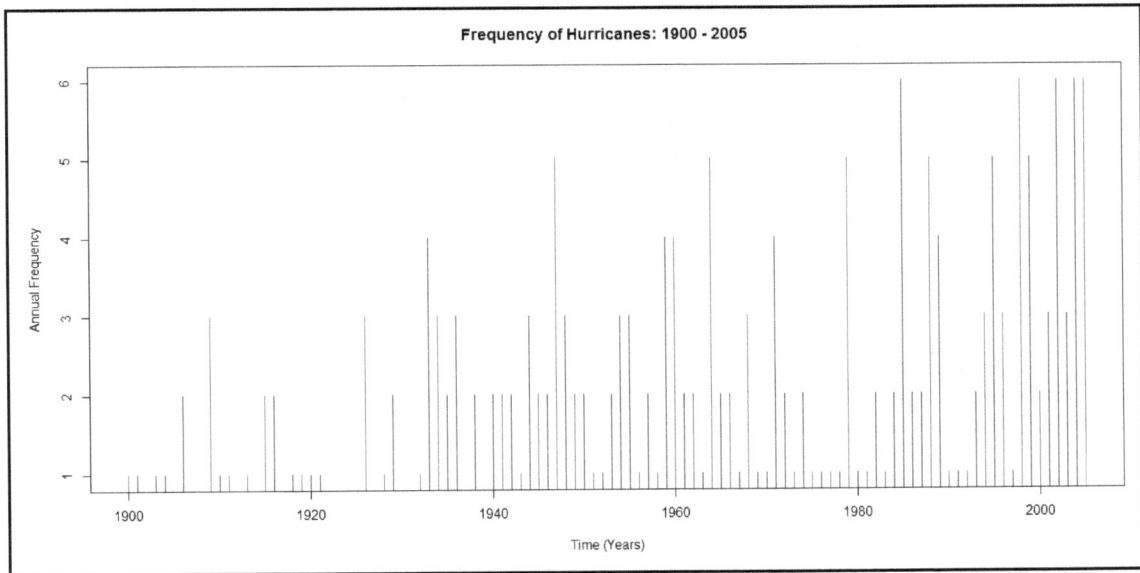

Calculating the mean of the hurricane counts for all the years between 1900 to 2005:

```
> mean(StormDamageData$frequency)
```

The result is as follows:

```
[1] 1.95283
```

On average there have been two hurricanes per year.

Step 5 - building predictive models

Let's find out the possible linear trend in the hurricane occurrence frequency. The `glm()` function is used to fit generalized linear models. `frequency~years` defines the formula. `data = StormDamageData` defines the dataset for the formula. The `family=poisson(link="identity")` function signifies the Poisson distribution.

The `lm()` function is used to fit linear models. `frequency~years` defines the formula. `data = StormDamageData` defines the dataset for the formula. Use the following commands:

```
> LinearTrend <- glm(frequency~years, data = StormDamageData,
family=poisson(link="identity"), start=lm(frequency~years, data =
StormDamageData)$coefficients)
```

Printing the details of the `LinearTrend`:

```
> LinearTrend
```

The result is as follows:

```
call:  glm(formula = frequency ~ years, family = poisson(link = "identity"),
    data = StormDamageData, start = lm(frequency ~ years, data = StormDamageData)$coefficients)

coefficients:
(Intercept)        years
  -48.69248      0.02594

Degrees of Freedom: 105 Total (i.e. Null);   104 Residual
Null Deviance:        143
Residual Deviance: 105.1          AIC: 342
```

Finding out the possible exponential trend in the hurricane occurrence frequency:

The glm() function is used to fit generalized linear models. frequency~years defines the formula. data = StormDamageData defines the dataset for the formula. The family=poisson(link="identity") function signifies the Poisson distribution. We do this by using the following command:

> **ExpTrend <- glm(frequency~years, data=StormDamageData, family = poisson(link="log"))**

Printing the details of ExpTrend:

> **ExpTrend**

The result is as follows:

```
call:  glm(formula = frequency ~ years, family = poisson(link = "log"),
    data = StormDamageData)

coefficients:
(Intercept)        years
  -27.66036      0.01446

Degrees of Freedom: 105 Total (i.e. Null);   104 Residual
Null Deviance:        143
Residual Deviance: 104.7          AIC: 341.7
```

Plotting the years and frequency count for hurricanes for each year between 1900 and 2005: plot() is a generic function. years represents the *x* coordinates of the plot, while frequency represents the y coordinates of the plot. type="h" represents the histogram representational style. The ylim=c(0,6) function sets the upper limit of the *y* axis representation as 0 as the lower limit and 6 as the upper limit:

```
> plot(years, frequency, type='h', ylim=c(0,6), main = "No. of Major
Hurricanes Predicted for 2014", xlim=c(1900,2020))
```

The result is as follows:

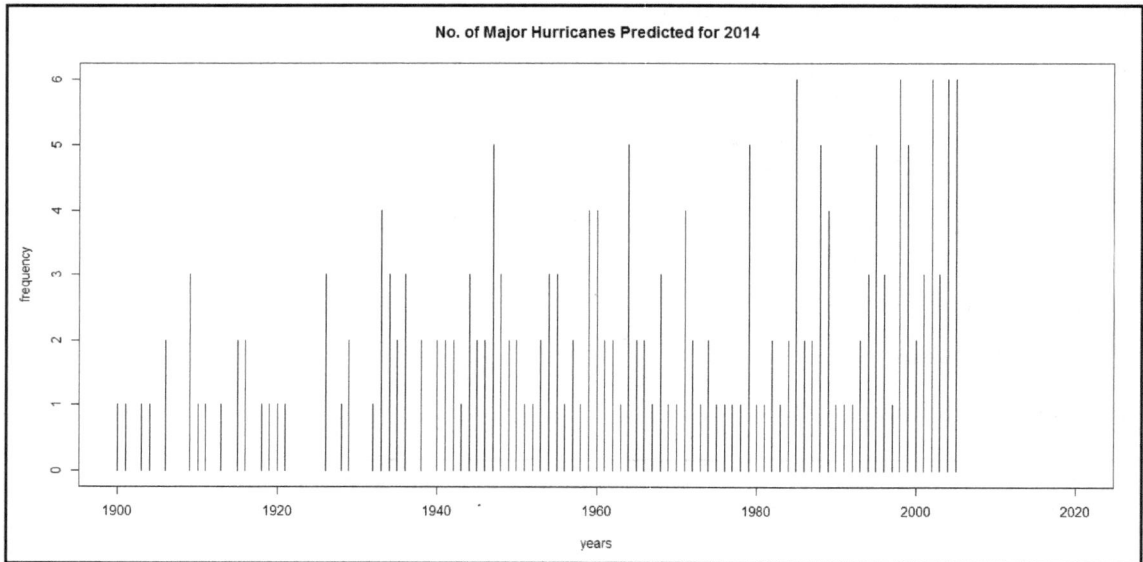

Predicting the trend for 2014 based on the exponential trend: The predict() function is used to predict values based on the linear model object. ExpTrend represents the object of the class inheriting from lm. The newdata = data.frame(years=1890:2030) function represents the data frame in which to look for variables with which to predict:

```
> cpred1 <- predict(ExpTrend, newdata = data.frame(years=1890:2030),
type="response")
```

Printing the details of cpred1:

```
> cpred1
```

The result is as follows:

1	2	3	4	5	6	7	8	9	10	11
0.7185495	0.7290154	0.7396337	0.7504067	0.7613365	0.7724256	0.7836762	0.7950907	0.8066714	0.8184208	0.8303413
12	13	14	15	16	17	18	19	20	21	22
0.8424355	0.8547058	0.8671549	0.8797852	0.8925995	0.9056005	0.9187908	0.9321733	0.9457507	0.9595258	0.9735015
23	24	25	26	27	28	29	30	31	32	33
0.9876809	1.0020667	1.0166621	1.0314701	1.0464937	1.0617362	1.0772007	1.0928905	1.1088087	1.1249588	1.1413442
34	35	36	37	38	39	40	41	42	43	44
1.1579682	1.1748343	1.1919461	1.2093072	1.2269211	1.2447915	1.2629223	1.2813171	1.2999798	1.3189144	1.3381248
45	46	47	48	49	50	51	52	53	54	55
1.3576149	1.3773890	1.3974511	1.4178053	1.4384561	1.4594076	1.4806643	1.5022306	1.5241110	1.5463101	1.5688326
56	57	58	59	60	61	62	63	64	65	66
1.5916830	1.6148664	1.6383874	1.6622509	1.6864621	1.7110259	1.7359475	1.7612320	1.7868849	1.8129114	1.8393170
67	68	69	70	71	72	73	74	75	76	77
1.8661071	1.8932875	1.9208638	1.9488417	1.9772272	2.0060260	2.0352444	2.0648883	2.0949640	2.1254777	2.1564359
78	79	80	81	82	83	84	85	86	87	88
2.1878450	2.2197116	2.2520423	2.2848440	2.3181234	2.3518875	2.3861434	2.4208983	2.4561594	2.4919340	2.5282298
89	90	91	92	93	94	95	96	97	98	99
2.5650541	2.6024149	2.6403198	2.6787768	2.7177940	2.7573794	2.7975414	2.8382884	2.8796289	2.9215715	2.9641250
100	101	102	103	104	105	106	107	108	109	110
3.0072984	3.0511005	3.0955407	3.1406281	3.1863723	3.2327827	3.2798691	3.3276413	3.3761094	3.4252833	3.4751736
111	112	113	114	115	116	117	118	119	120	121
3.5257905	3.5771446	3.6292468	3.6821078	3.7357387	3.7901508	3.8453554	3.9013641	3.9581886	4.0158408	4.0743326
122	123	124	125	126	127	128	129	130	131	132
4.1336765	4.1938846	4.2549698	4.3169446	4.3798221	4.4436155	4.5083380	4.5740033	4.6406249	4.7082170	4.7767935
133	134	135	136	137	138	139	140	141		
4.8463688	4.9169576	4.9885745	5.0612345	5.1349528	5.2097449	5.2856263	5.3626129	5.4407209		

Joining the points of `cpred1` with line segments: `lines()` is a generic function that takes the value of the `cpred1` data frame as the coordinates of the *y* axis and joins the corresponding points with line segments. $1890:2030$ represents the *x* axis:

```
> lines(1890:2030,cpred1,col="blue")
```

The result is as follows:

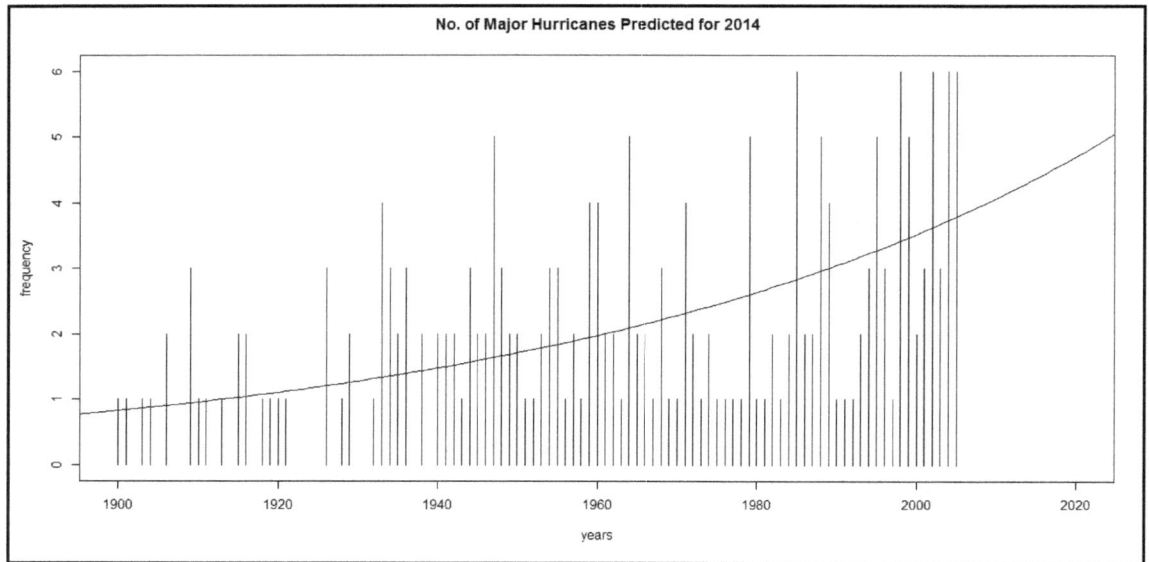

No. of Major Hurricanes Predicted for 2014

Predicting the trend for 2014 based on the linear trend: The `predict()` function is used to predict values based on the linear model object. `LinearTrend` represents the object of the class inheriting from `lm`. The `newdata = data.frame(years=1890:2030)` function represents the data frame in which to look for variables with which to predict:

```
> cpred0 <- predict(LinearTrend, newdata=data.frame(years=1890:2030),
type="response")
```

Printing the details of `cpred0`:

```
> cpred0
```

The result is as follows:

1	2	3	4	5	6	7	8	9	10	11
0.3316616	0.3576003	0.3835390	0.4094777	0.4354164	0.4613551	0.4872938	0.5132325	0.5391711	0.5651098	0.5910485
12	13	14	15	16	17	18	19	20	21	22
0.6169872	0.6429259	0.6688646	0.6948033	0.7207420	0.7466807	0.7726194	0.7985581	0.8244968	0.8504355	0.8763742
23	24	25	26	27	28	29	30	31	32	33
0.9023129	0.9282516	0.9541903	0.9801290	1.0060677	1.0320064	1.0579451	1.0838838	1.1098225	1.1357612	1.1616999
34	35	36	37	38	39	40	41	42	43	44
1.1876386	1.2135773	1.2395160	1.2654547	1.2913934	1.3173321	1.3432708	1.3692095	1.3951482	1.4210869	1.4470256
45	46	47	48	49	50	51	52	53	54	55
1.4729643	1.4989030	1.5248417	1.5507804	1.5767191	1.6026578	1.6285965	1.6545352	1.6804739	1.7064126	1.7323513
56	57	58	59	60	61	62	63	64	65	66
1.7582900	1.7842287	1.8101673	1.8361060	1.8620447	1.8879834	1.9139221	1.9398608	1.9657995	1.9917382	2.0176769
67	68	69	70	71	72	73	74	75	76	77
2.0436156	2.0695543	2.0954930	2.1214317	2.1473704	2.1733091	2.1992478	2.2251865	2.2511252	2.2770639	2.3030026
78	79	80	81	82	83	84	85	86	87	88
2.3289413	2.3548800	2.3808187	2.4067574	2.4326961	2.4586348	2.4845735	2.5105122	2.5364509	2.5623896	2.5883283
89	90	91	92	93	94	95	96	97	98	99
2.6142670	2.6402057	2.6661444	2.6920831	2.7180218	2.7439605	2.7698992	2.7958379	2.8217766	2.8477153	2.8736540
100	101	102	103	104	105	106	107	108	109	110
2.8995927	2.9255314	2.9514701	2.9774088	3.0033475	3.0292862	3.0552249	3.0811636	3.1071022	3.1330409	3.1589796
111	112	113	114	115	116	117	118	119	120	121
3.1849183	3.2108570	3.2367957	3.2627344	3.2886731	3.3146118	3.3405505	3.3664892	3.3924279	3.4183666	3.4443053
122	123	124	125	126	127	128	129	130	131	132
3.4702440	3.4961827	3.5221214	3.5480601	3.5739988	3.5999375	3.6258762	3.6518149	3.6777536	3.7036923	3.7296310
133	134	135	136	137	138	139	140	141		
3.7555697	3.7815084	3.8074471	3.8333858	3.8593245	3.8852632	3.9112019	3.9371406	3.9630793		

Joining the points of `cpred0` with line segments: `lines()` is a generic function which takes the value of the `cpred0` data frame as coordinates of the *y*-axis and joins the corresponding points with line segments. `1890:2030` represents the *x*-axis:

```
> lines(1890:2030, cpred0, col="red"))
```

The result is as follows:

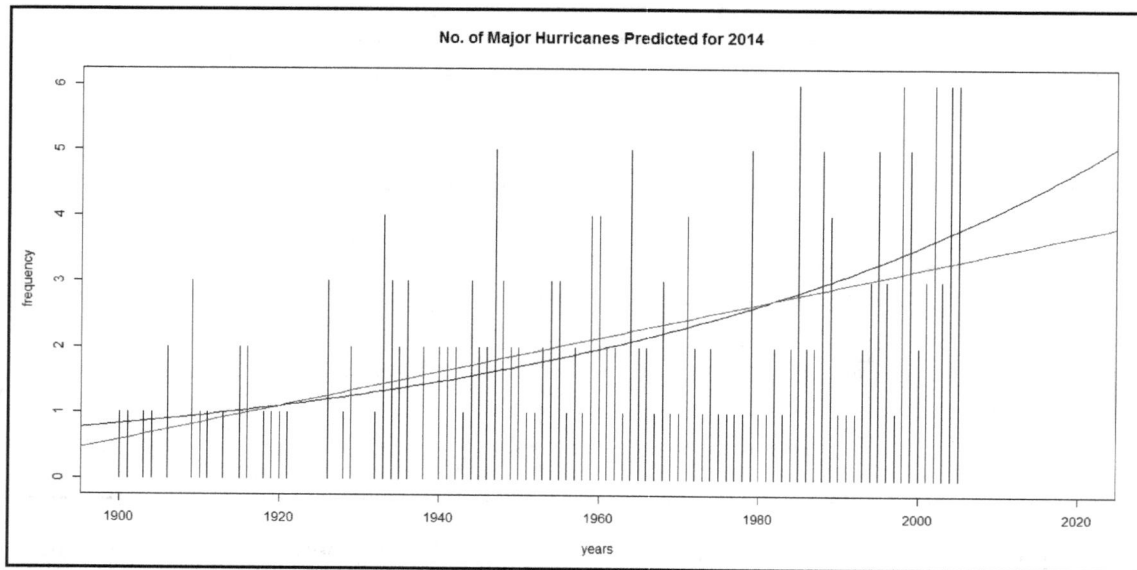

No. of Major Hurricanes Predicted for 2014

Plotting the mean value: `abline()` as a function plots the straight line using the mean value of the `StormDamageData$frequency` which is `1.95283`. `h = mean(StormDamageData$frequency)` is the *y*-value for horizontal line:

```
> abline(h = mean(StormDamageData$frequency), col="black")
```

The result is as follows:

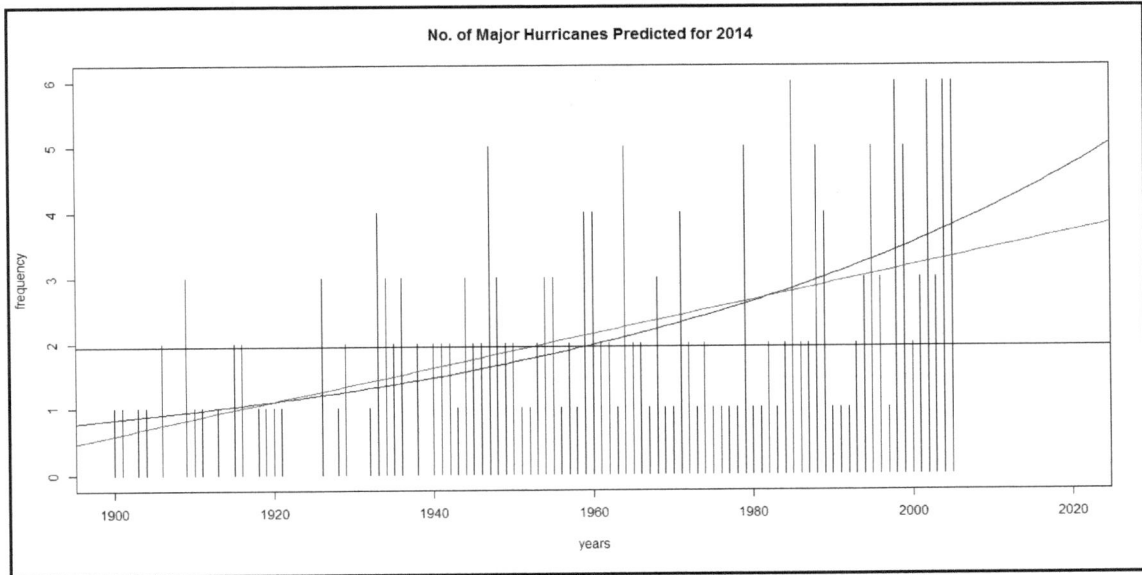

Combine the data frame values for the mean of the `StormDamageData$frequency`, `cpred0` and `cpred1`:

```
> predictions <- cbind(constant = mean(StormDamageData$frequency),
linear = cpred0[126], exponential=cpred1[126])
```

Printing the details of the predictions:

```
> predictions
```

The result is as follows:

```
        constant   linear  exponential
126   1.95283  3.573999     4.379822
```

Plotting the points of the predictions on the graph for the year 2014:

```
> points(rep((1890:2030)[126],3), predictions,
col=c("black","red","blue"), pch=19)
```

The result is as follows:

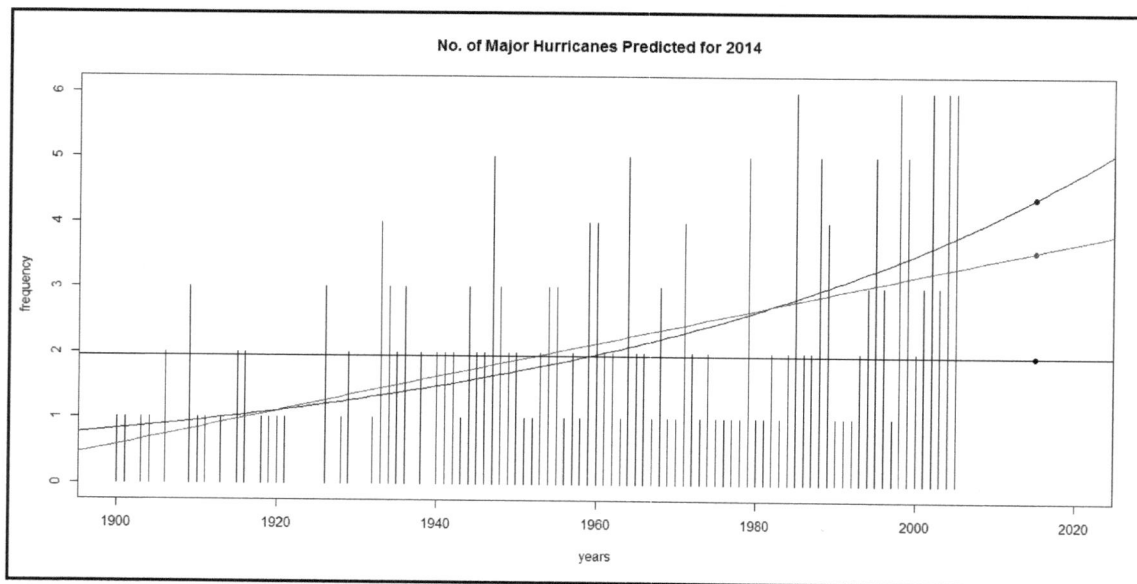

It is important to observe that by changing the predictive model there will be a change in the premium. With a flat prediction, there are less than two (major) hurricanes, but with the exponential trend, there are more than four (major) hurricanes.

Step 6 - calculating the pure premium of the reinsurance contract

Now we find a suitable model to compute the premium of a reinsurance treaty, with a deductible and limited cover. Estimate the tail index using Hill's tail-index estimator as follows. `hill()` is the function for estimating the tail of the index of the heavy-tailed data, `base$Normalized.PL05`:

```
> hill(base$Normalized.PL05)
```

The result is as follows:

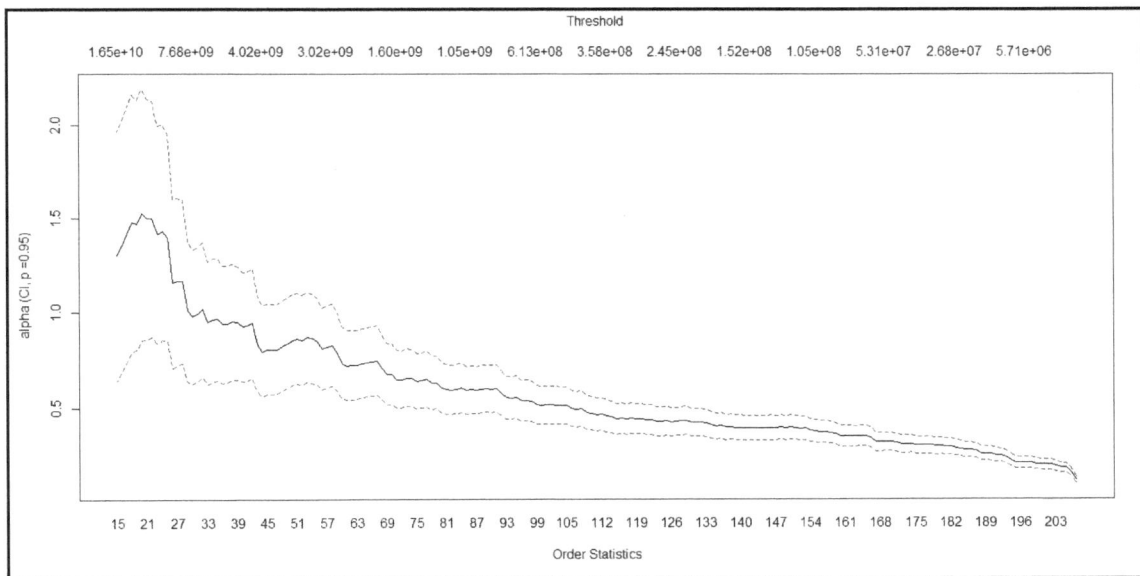

The preceding figure shows that the costs of major hurricanes are heavy tailed.

Set the threshold of losses above 500 million for the Pareto model as follows:

```
> threshold <- .5
```

We return an object of the class, gpd, representing the fit of a generalized Pareto model to excesses over a threshold (0.5) with the following command. The dataset is represented by base$Normalized.PL05/1e9/20:

```
> gpd.PL <- gpd(base$Normalized.PL05/1e9/20, threshold)$par.ests
```

The result is as follows:

```
      xi        beta
0.4424669 0.6705315
```

Calculating the mean of the base$Normalized.CL05/1e9/20 data frame above the threshold value of 0.5:

```
> mean(base$Normalized.CL05/1e9/20> .5)
```

The result is as follows:

```
[1] 0.1256039
```

Given that the loss exceeds 500 million, we can now compute the expected value of the reinsurance contract:

$$\int_{d}^{d+c} (x - d) \, dF_{(\varepsilon,\mu,\sigma)}(x)$$

```
> ExpectedValue <- function(yinf,ysup,xi,beta){
+ as.numeric(integrate(function(x) (x-yinf) *
dgpd(x,xi,mu=threshold,beta),
+ lower=yinf,upper=ysup)$value +
+ (1-pgpd(ysup,xi,mu=threshold,beta))*(ysup-yinf))
+ }
```

Find the mean value of the predictions data frame as follows:

```
> predictions[1]
```

The result is as follows:

```
[1] 1.95283
```

Calculating the mean of the `base$Normalized.PL05/1e9/20` data frame above the threshold value of 0.5:

```
> mean(base$Normalized.PL05/1e9/20>.5)
```

The result is as follows:

```
[1] 0.1256039
```

This indicates that each hurricane has a 12.5% chance of costing more than 500 million for the insurance company.

Calculating the expected value of the reinsurance contract:

```
> ExpectedValue(2,6,gpd.PL[1],gpd.PL[2])*1e3
```

The result is as follows:

```
[1] 330.9865
```

This indicates that the expected repayment by the reinsurance company is about 330.9865 million.

Calculating the premium of the reinsurance contract:

```
> predictions[1] * mean(base$Normalized.PL05/1e9/20> .5) *
ExpectedValue(2, 6, gpd.PL[1], gpd.PL[2]) * 1e3
```

The result is as follows:

```
[1] 81.18538
```

14

Case Study - Forecast of Electricity Consumption

Introduction

Electricity is the only commodity that is produced and consumed simultaneously; therefore, a perfect balance between supply and consumption in the electricity power market must always be maintained. Forecasting electricity consumption is of national interest to any country since electricity is a key source of energy. A reliable forecast of energy consumption, production, and distribution meets the stable and long-term policy. The presence of economies of scale, focus on environmental concerns, regulatory requirements, and a favorable public image, coupled with inflation, rapidly rising energy prices, the emergence of alternative fuels and technologies, changes in life styles, and so on, has generated the need to use modeling techniques which capture the effect of factors such as prices, income, population, technology, and other economic, demographic, policy, and technological variables.

Underestimation could lead to under-capacity utilization, which would result in poor quality of service including localized brownouts, or even blackouts. While on the other hand, an overestimation could lead to the authorization of a plant that may not be needed for several years. The requirement is to ensure optimal phasing of investments, a long-term consideration, and rationalizing pricing structures and designing demand-side management programs, to meet the nature of short- or medium-term needs. The forecast further drives various plans and decisions on investment, construction, and conservation.

Getting ready

In order to carry out forecasting of electricity consumption, we shall be using a dataset collected on smart meter data with time series aggregated by four located industries.

Step 1 - collecting and describing data

The dataset titled `DT_4_ind` shall be used. The numeric variable is as follows:

- `value`

The non-numeric variables are as follows:

- `date_time`
- `week`
- `date`
- `type`

How to do it...

Let's get into the details.

Step 2 - exploring data

The following packages need to be loaded as a first step to be carried out:

```
> install.packages("feather")
> install.packages("data.table")
> install.packages("ggplot2")
> install.packages("plotly")
> install.packages("animation")
> library(feather)
> library(data.table)
> library(ggplot2)
> library(plotly)
> library(animation)
```

Version info: Code for this page was tested in R version 3.2.2

Let's explore the data and understand the relationships between the variables.

Checking whether an object is `as.data.table()`: Binary columnar serialization for data frames is carried out using `feather`. In order to share, read, and write data across data analysis languages easily, `feather` is used. The `read_feather()` function is used to read feather files.

We'll begin by importing the `DT_4_ind` dataset. We will be saving the data to the `AggData` data frame:

```
> AggData <- as.data.table(read_feather("d:/DT_4_ind"))
```

Exploring the internal structure of the `AggData` data frame: The `str()` function displays the internal structure of the data frame. `AggData` is passed as an R object to the `str()` function:

```
> str(AggData)
```

The result is as follows:

```
classes 'data.table' and 'data.frame':    70080 obs. of   5 variables:
 $ date_time: POSIXct, format: "2012-01-02 00:00:00" "2012-01-02 00:30:00" "2012-01-02 01:00:00" "2012-01-02 01:30:00"
 ...
 $ value    : num  1590 1564 1560 1585 1604 ...
 $ week     : chr  "Monday" "Monday" "Monday" "Monday" ...
 $ date     : Date, format: "2012-01-02" "2012-01-02" "2012-01-02" "2012-01-02" ...
 $ type     : chr  "Commercial Property" "Commercial Property" "Commercial Property" "Commercial Property" ...
 - attr(*, ".internal.selfref")=<externalptr>
```

Printing the `AggData` frame. The `head()` function returns the first part of the base data frame. The `AggData` data frame is passed as an input parameter:

```
> head(AggData)
```

The result is as follows:

```
             date_time    value   week       date                   type
1: 2012-01-02 00:00:00 1590.210 Monday 2012-01-02 Commercial Property
2: 2012-01-02 00:30:00 1563.772 Monday 2012-01-02 Commercial Property
3: 2012-01-02 01:00:00 1559.914 Monday 2012-01-02 Commercial Property
4: 2012-01-02 01:30:00 1584.671 Monday 2012-01-02 Commercial Property
5: 2012-01-02 02:00:00 1604.281 Monday 2012-01-02 Commercial Property
6: 2012-01-02 02:30:00 1566.582 Monday 2012-01-02 Commercial Property
```

Plotting the aggregated time series data of electricity consumption by industry.

The ggplot() function declares the input data frame for a graphic and specifies the set of plot aesthetics intended to be common throughout. data = AggData is the dataset to be used for plotting while aes() describes how variables in the data are mapped to visual properties. geom_line() produces the single line that tries to connect all the observations:

```
> ggplot(data = AggData, aes(x = date, y = value)) +
+ geom_line() +
+ facet_grid(type ~ ., scales = "free_y") +
+ theme(panel.border = element_blank(),
+ panel.background = element_blank(),
+ panel.grid.minor = element_line(colour = "grey90"),
+ panel.grid.major = element_line(colour = "green"),
+ panel.grid.major.x = element_line(colour = "red"),
+ axis.text = element_text(size = 10),
+ axis.title = element_text(size = 12, face = "bold"),
+ strip.text = element_text(size = 9, face = "bold")) +
+ labs(title = "Electricity Consumption - Industry", x = "Date", y =
"Load (kW)")
```

The result is as follows:

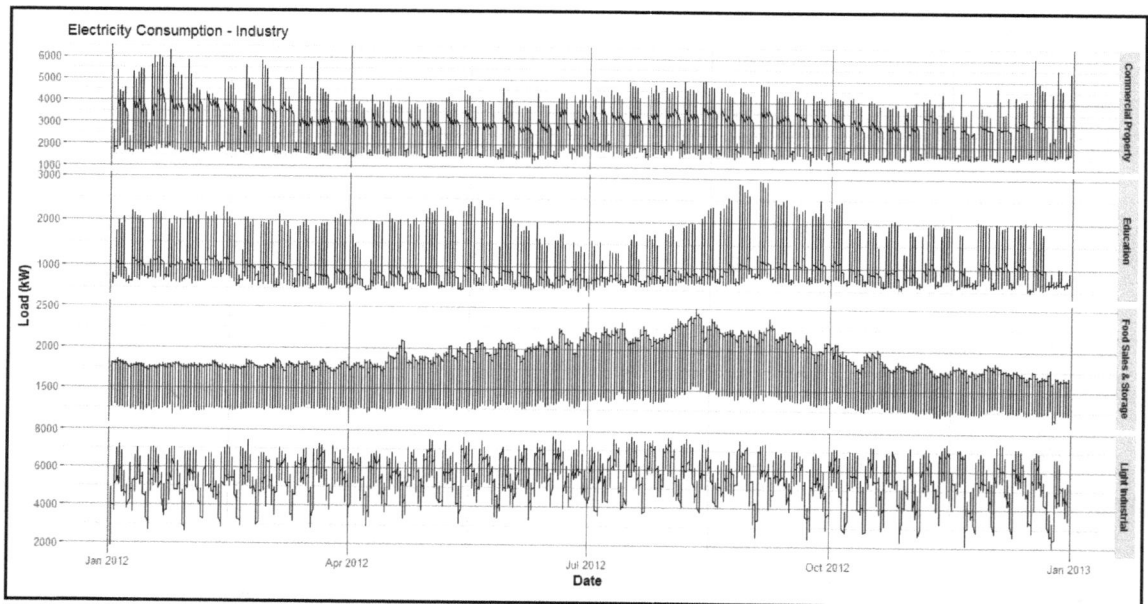

It is important to note that the consumption of the industry Food Sales & Storage does not change much during holidays compared to others.

Step 3 - time series - regression analysis

The regression model is formulated as follows:

$$y_i = \beta_1 d_{i1} + \beta_2 d_{i2} + \ldots + \beta_{48} d_{i48} + \beta_{49} w_{i1} + \ldots + \beta_{54} w_{i6} + \varepsilon_i$$

Variables (inputs) are of two types of seasonal dummy variables--daily $(d_1, \ldots, d_{48})$ and weekly $(w_1, \ldots, w_6)$. y_i is the electricity consumption at the time i, where $i = 1, \ldots, N$. $\beta_1 \cdots \beta_{54}$ are the regression coefficients to be estimated.

Printing the contents of the `AggData` data frame:

```
> AggData
```

The result is as follows:

```
                date_time    value   week       date              type
    1: 2012-01-02 00:00:00 1590.210 Monday 2012-01-02 Commercial Property
    2: 2012-01-02 00:30:00 1563.772 Monday 2012-01-02 Commercial Property
    3: 2012-01-02 01:00:00 1559.914 Monday 2012-01-02 Commercial Property
    4: 2012-01-02 01:30:00 1584.671 Monday 2012-01-02 Commercial Property
    5: 2012-01-02 02:00:00 1604.281 Monday 2012-01-02 Commercial Property
   ---
70076: 2012-12-31 21:30:00 3548.279 Monday 2012-12-31   Light Industrial
70077: 2012-12-31 22:00:00 3488.161 Monday 2012-12-31   Light Industrial
70078: 2012-12-31 22:30:00 3510.200 Monday 2012-12-31   Light Industrial
70079: 2012-12-31 23:00:00 3533.678 Monday 2012-12-31   Light Industrial
70080: 2012-12-31 23:30:00 3414.966 Monday 2012-12-31   Light Industrial
```

Transforming the characters of weekdays to integers: The `as.factor()` function is used to encode a vector as a factor. The `as.integer()` function creates the `AggData[, week]` object of the integer type:

```
> AggData[, week_num := as.integer(as.factor(AggData[, week]))]
```

Printing the contents of the `AggData` data frame after the change:

```
> AggData
```

The result is as follows:

```
                date_time    value    week       date                  type week_num
    1: 2012-01-02 00:00:00 1590.210 Monday 2012-01-02 Commercial Property        2
    2: 2012-01-02 00:30:00 1563.772 Monday 2012-01-02 Commercial Property        2
    3: 2012-01-02 01:00:00 1559.914 Monday 2012-01-02 Commercial Property        2
    4: 2012-01-02 01:30:00 1584.671 Monday 2012-01-02 Commercial Property        2
    5: 2012-01-02 02:00:00 1604.281 Monday 2012-01-02 Commercial Property        2
   ---
70076: 2012-12-31 21:30:00 3548.279 Monday 2012-12-31     Light Industrial      2
70077: 2012-12-31 22:00:00 3488.161 Monday 2012-12-31     Light Industrial      2
70078: 2012-12-31 22:30:00 3510.200 Monday 2012-12-31     Light Industrial      2
70079: 2012-12-31 23:00:00 3533.678 Monday 2012-12-31     Light Industrial      2
70080: 2012-12-31 23:30:00 3414.966 Monday 2012-12-31     Light Industrial      2
```

Extracting unique industry types from the `AggData` data frame using the following:

```
> n_type <- unique(AggData[, type])
```

Printing the contents of the data frame n_type after the change:

```
> n_type
```

The result is as follows:

```
[1] "Commercial Property"  "Education"            "Food Sales & Storage" "Light Industrial"
```

Extracting unique dates from the `AggData` data frame using the following:

```
> n_date <- unique(AggData[, date])
```

Extracting unique weekdays from the `AggData` data frame using the following:

```
> n_weekdays <- unique(AggData[, week])
```

Setting the `period` value using the following:

```
> period <- 48
```

Performing regression analysis on a sample dataset.

We extract education (schools) buildings over a period of 2 weeks. The result is stored in the `data_reg` data frame. `n_type[2]` represents education buildings and `n_date[57:70]` denotes a 2-week period:

```
> data_reg <- AggData[(type == n_type[2] & date %in% n_date[57:70])]
```

Printing the contents of the `data_reg` data frame after the change:

```
> data_reg
```

The result is as follows:

```
              date_time    value   week        date        type week_num
  1: 2012-02-27 00:00:00 652.0693 Monday 2012-02-27 Education        2
  2: 2012-02-27 00:30:00 646.6226 Monday 2012-02-27 Education        2
  3: 2012-02-27 01:00:00 658.3790 Monday 2012-02-27 Education        2
  4: 2012-02-27 01:30:00 669.0898 Monday 2012-02-27 Education        2
  5: 2012-02-27 02:00:00 675.9707 Monday 2012-02-27 Education        2
---
668: 2012-03-11 21:30:00 514.5865 Sunday 2012-03-11 Education        4
669: 2012-03-11 22:00:00 505.0426 Sunday 2012-03-11 Education        4
670: 2012-03-11 22:30:00 508.6684 Sunday 2012-03-11 Education        4
671: 2012-03-11 23:00:00 511.6602 Sunday 2012-03-11 Education        4
672: 2012-03-11 23:30:00 522.0277 Sunday 2012-03-11 Education        4
```

Plotting the sample dataset of education (school buildings) over a period of 2 weeks (February 27 to March 12)

The `ggplot()` function declares the input data frame for a graphic and specifies the set of plot aesthetics intended to be common throughout. `data_reg` is the dataset to be used for plotting while `aes()` describes how variables in the data are mapped to visual properties. `geom_line()` produces the single line that tries to connect all the observations:

```
> ggplot(data_reg, aes(date_time, value)) +
+ geom_line() +
+ theme(panel.border = element_blank(),
+ panel.background = element_blank(),
+ panel.grid.minor = element_line(colour = "grey90"),
+ panel.grid.major = element_line(colour = "green"),
+ panel.grid.major.x = element_line(colour = "red"),
+ axis.text = element_text(size = 10),
+ axis.title = element_text(size = 12, face = "bold")) +
+ labs(title = "Regression Analysis - Education Buildings", x = "Date",
y = "Load (kW)")
```

The result is as follows:

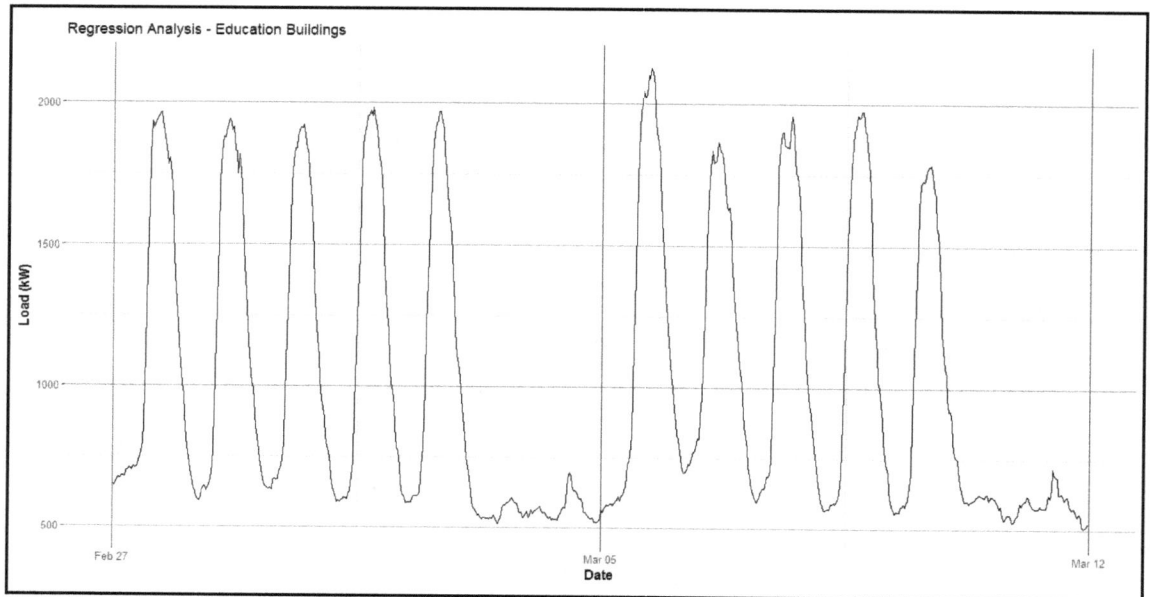

Regression Analysis - Education Buildings

Extracting the number of rows from the data_reg data frame:

```
> N <- nrow(data_reg)
```

Calculating the number of days in the training set:

```
> trainset_window <- N / period
```

Creating independent seasonal dummy variables--daily $(d_1, \dots, d_{48})$ and weekly $(w_1, \dots, w_6)$. The daily seasonal value is extracted from *1,.....period, 1,.......period* for 48 vectors of daily variables. The weekly value is extracted from week_num. The result is then stored in one vector, matrix_train:

```
> matrix_train <- data.table(Load = data_reg[, value], Daily =
as.factor(rep(1:period, trainset_window)), Weekly = as.factor(data_reg[,
week_num]))
```

Printing the contents of the `matrix_train` data frame after the change:

```
> matrix_train
```

The result is as follows:

```
        Load Daily Weekly
  1: 652.0693     1      2
  2: 646.6226     2      2
  3: 658.3790     3      2
  4: 669.0898     4      2
  5: 675.9707     5      2
---
668: 514.5865    44      4
669: 505.0426    45      4
670: 508.6684    46      4
671: 511.6602    47      4
672: 522.0277    48      4
```

Creating a linear model. The `lm()` function fits the linear models: `Load ~ 0 + .` is the formula. Since `lm()` automatically adds to the linear model intercept, we define it now as `0`. `data = matrix_train` defines the data frame which contains the data:

```
> linear_model_1 <- lm(Load ~ 0 + ., data = matrix_train)
```

Printing the contents of the `linear_model_1` data frame after the change:

```
> linear_model_1
```

The result is as follows:

```
Call:
lm(formula = Load ~ 0 + ., data = matrix_train)

coefficients:
  Daily1    Daily2    Daily3    Daily4    Daily5    Daily6    Daily7    Daily8    Daily9   Daily10   Daily11   Daily12
  964.46    925.54    874.87    842.27    821.33    799.04    767.56    737.28    722.42    715.04    708.85    709.57
 Daily13   Daily14   Daily15   Daily16   Daily17   Daily18   Daily19   Daily20   Daily21   Daily22   Daily23   Daily24
  712.85    712.02    724.55    729.16    729.94    732.19    750.64    760.74    798.12    839.97   1006.45   1171.81
 Daily25   Daily26   Daily27   Daily28   Daily29   Daily30   Daily31   Daily32   Daily33   Daily34   Daily35   Daily36
 1319.01   1458.93   1555.40   1603.95   1623.88   1628.66   1637.48   1658.36   1657.23   1653.48   1654.59   1623.13
 Daily37   Daily38   Daily39   Daily40   Daily41   Daily42   Daily43   Daily44   Daily45   Daily46   Daily47   Daily48
 1573.42   1540.26   1514.78   1487.84   1427.99   1334.33   1239.45   1172.62   1108.44   1073.54   1013.76    973.76
 weekly2   weekly3   weekly4   weekly5   weekly6   weekly7
  100.99   -516.80   -539.96     54.58     86.11     61.52
```

Producing result summaries of the model `linear_model_1`:

```
> summary_1 <- summary(linear_model_1)
```

Printing the contents of the `summary_1` data frame after the change:

```
> summary_1
```

The result is as follows:

```
Call:
lm(formula = Load ~ 0 + ., data = matrix_train)

Residuals:
    Min      1Q  Median      3Q     Max
-561.87 -149.34  -15.13  181.13  477.75

Coefficients:
         Estimate Std. Error t value Pr(>|t|)
Daily1     964.46      71.40  13.508  < 2e-16 ***
Daily2     925.54      71.40  12.963  < 2e-16 ***
Daily3     874.87      71.40  12.253  < 2e-16 ***
Daily4     842.27      71.40  11.797  < 2e-16 ***
Daily5     821.33      71.40  11.503  < 2e-16 ***
Daily6     799.04      71.40  11.191  < 2e-16 ***
Daily7     767.56      71.40  10.750  < 2e-16 ***
Daily8     737.28      71.40  10.326  < 2e-16 ***
Daily9     722.42      71.40  10.118  < 2e-16 ***
Daily10    715.04      71.40  10.015  < 2e-16 ***
Daily11    708.85      71.40   9.928  < 2e-16 ***
Daily12    709.57      71.40   9.938  < 2e-16 ***
Daily13    712.85      71.40   9.984  < 2e-16 ***
Daily14    712.02      71.40   9.972  < 2e-16 ***
Daily15    724.55      71.40  10.148  < 2e-16 ***
Daily16    729.16      71.40  10.212  < 2e-16 ***
Daily17    729.94      71.40  10.223  < 2e-16 ***
Daily18    732.19      71.40  10.255  < 2e-16 ***
Daily19    750.64      71.40  10.513  < 2e-16 ***
Daily20    760.74      71.40  10.655  < 2e-16 ***
Daily21    798.12      71.40  11.178  < 2e-16 ***
Daily22    839.97      71.40  11.764  < 2e-16 ***
Daily23   1006.45      71.40  14.096  < 2e-16 ***
Daily24   1171.81      71.40  16.412  < 2e-16 ***
```

```
Signif. codes:  0 '***' 0.001 '**' 0.01 '*' 0.05 '.' 0.1 ' ' 1

Residual standard error: 251.9 on 618 degrees of freedom
Multiple R-squared:  0.9547,    Adjusted R-squared:  0.9508
F-statistic: 241.3 on 54 and 618 DF,  p-value: < 2.2e-16
```

Extracting the coefficient of determination using the r.squared attribute from the summary_1 data frame:

```
> paste("R-squared: ", round(summary_1$r.squared, 3), ", p-value of F
test: ", 1-pf(summary_1$fstatistic[1], summary_1$fstatistic[2],
summary_1$fstatistic[3]))
```

```
[1] "R-squared:  0.955 , p-value of F test:  0"
```

Creating one data.table from a list of data_reg and linear_model_1:

```
> datas <- rbindlist(list(data_reg[, .(value, date_time)],
data.table(value = linear_model_1$fitted.values, date_time = data_reg[,
date_time])))
```

Printing the contents of the datas data frame after the change:

```
> datas
```

The result is as follows:

```
            value          date_time
   1: 652.0693 2012-02-27 00:00:00
   2: 646.6226 2012-02-27 00:30:00
   3: 658.3790 2012-02-27 01:00:00
   4: 669.0898 2012-02-27 01:30:00
   5: 675.9707 2012-02-27 02:00:00
   ---
1340: 632.6548 2012-03-11 21:30:00
1341: 568.4755 2012-03-11 22:00:00
1342: 533.5817 2012-03-11 22:30:00
1343: 473.8017 2012-03-11 23:00:00
1344: 433.7951 2012-03-11 23:30:00
```

Plotting fitted values for `linear_model_1`.

`data = datas` is the dataset to be used for plotting while `aes()` describes how variables in the data are mapped to visual properties. `geom_line()` produces the single line that tries to connect all the observations:

```
> ggplot(data = datas, aes(date_time, value, group = type, colour =
type)) + geom_line(size = 0.8) + theme_bw() +
+ labs(x = "Time", y = "Load (kW)", title = "Fit from Multiple Linear
Regression")
```

The result is as follows:

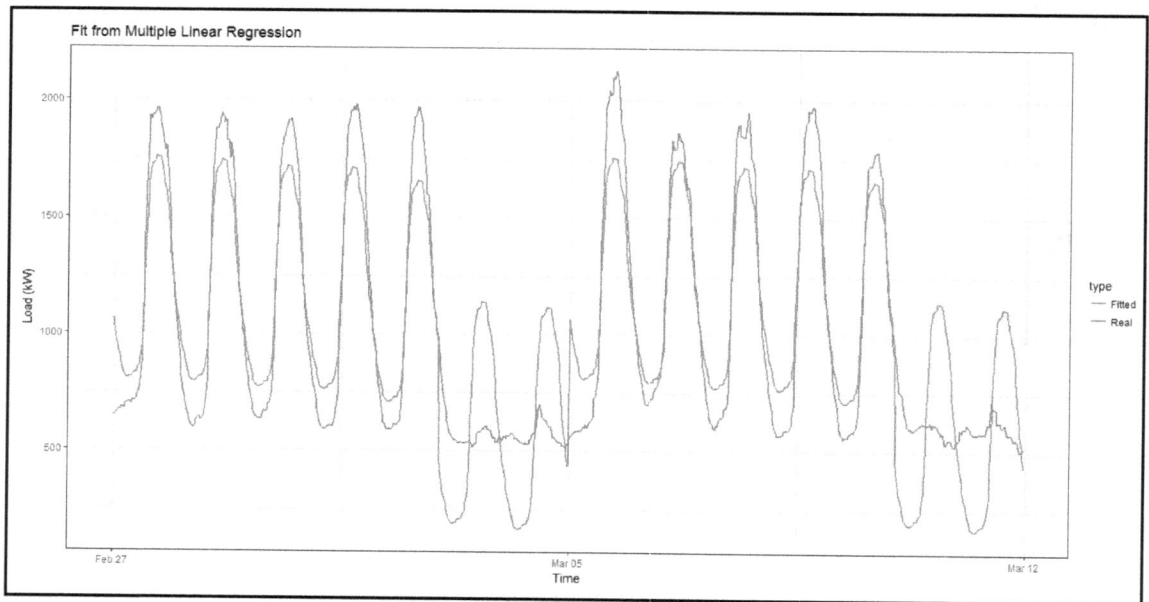

Plotting fitted values versus residual values.

`data` is the dataset to be used for plotting while `aes()` describes how variables in the data are mapped to visual properties:

```
> ggplot(data = data.table(Fitted_values =
linear_model_1$fitted.values,Residuals =
linear_model_1$residuals),aes(Fitted_values, Residuals))
    + geom_point(size = 1.7) +
    + geom_smooth() +
    + geom_hline(yintercept = 0, color = "red", size = 1) +
    + labs(title = "Fitted values vs Residuals")
```

The result is as follows:

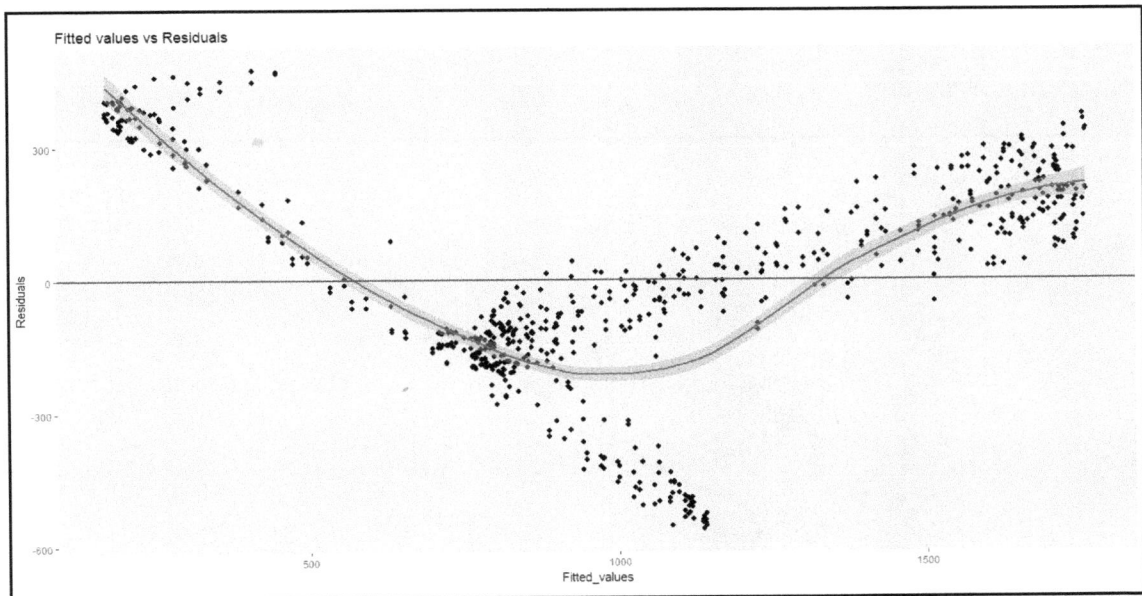

The function first gives the standardized residual from the linear model. It then calculates the 1Q and 4Q lines. Then, the quantile distribution is generated from the normal distribution. The slope and intercept is then calculated which is then plotted:

```
> ggQQ <- function(lm) {
# extracting residuals from the fit
+ d <- data.frame(std.resid = rstandard(lm))
# calculate 1Q, 4Q line
+ y <- quantile(d$std.resid[!is.na(d$std.resid)], c(0.25, 0.75))
# calculate 1Q, 4Q line
+ x <- qnorm(c(0.25, 0.75))
+ slope <- diff(y)/diff(x)
```

```
+ int <- y[1L] - slope * x[1L]
+
+ p <- ggplot(data = d, aes(sample = std.resid)) +
+ stat_qq(shape = 1, size = 3) +
+ labs(title = "Normal Q-Q",
+ x = "Theoretical Quantiles",
+ y = "Standardized Residuals") +
+ geom_abline(slope = slope, intercept = int, linetype = "dashed",
+ size = 1, col = "firebrick1")
+ return(p)
+ }
```

We can plot Q-Q with the following command:

```
> ggQQ(linear_model_1)
```

The result is as follows:

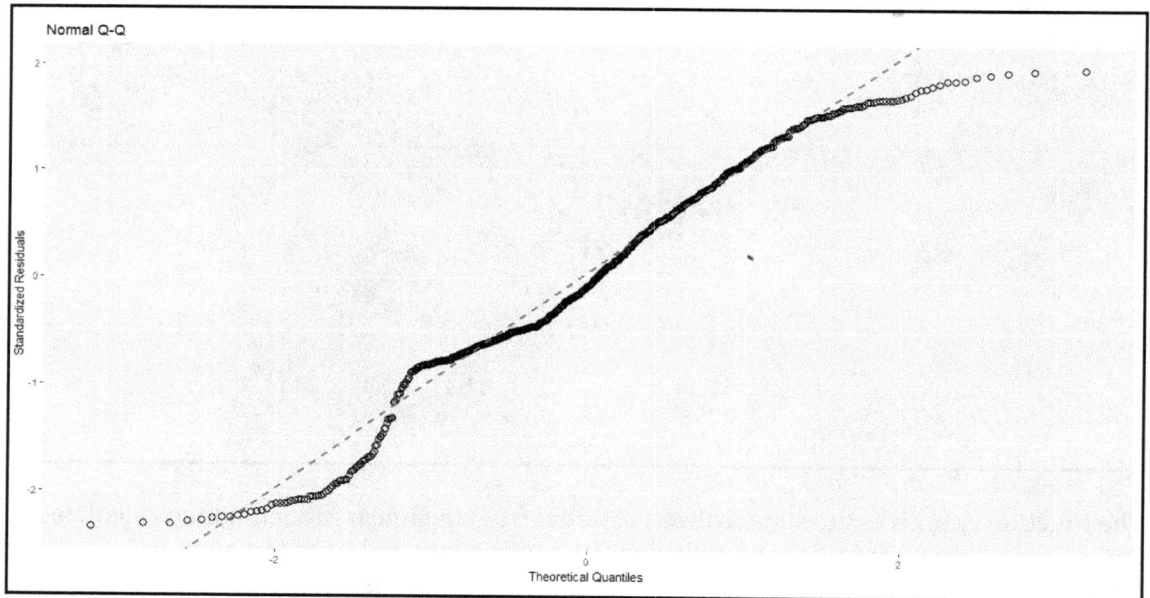

As is clearly visible, the points are not normal as they are away from the red line. The measurements during the day were moved constantly by the estimated coefficient of the week variable, but the behavior during the day wasn't captured. We need to capture this behavior because weekends, especially, behave absolutely differently.

Step 4 - time series - improving regression analysis

Creating a linear model: The `lm()` function fits the linear models. `Load ~ 0 + Daily + Weekly + Daily:Weekly` is the new formula. Since `lm()` automatically adds to the linear model intercept, we define it now as `0`. `data = matrix_train` defines the data frame which contains the data:

```
> linear_model_2 <- lm(Load ~ 0 + Daily + Weekly + Daily:Weekly, data = matrix_train)
```

Printing the contents of the `linear_model_2` data frame after the change:

```
> linear_model_2
```

The result is as follows:

```
Call:
lm(formula = Load ~ 0 + Daily + weekly + Daily:weekly, data = matrix_train)

Coefficients:
      Daily1          Daily2          Daily3          Daily4          Daily5          Daily6          Daily7
     963.6868        910.1281        832.4827        767.9888        746.0964        709.4052        646.7310
      Daily8          Daily9         Daily10         Daily11         Daily12         Daily13         Daily14
     607.0952        593.1229        579.3818        571.4749        577.7818        575.1910        576.0727
     Daily15         Daily16         Daily17         Daily18         Daily19         Daily20         Daily21
     590.8817        596.6877        599.9783        596.8332        605.5058        617.2628        685.2319
     Daily22         Daily23         Daily24         Daily25         Daily26         Daily27         Daily28
     742.3322        951.7756       1158.7365       1339.7397       1530.8187       1680.5525       1772.6732
     Daily29         Daily30         Daily31         Daily32         Daily33         Daily34         Daily35
    1812.0905       1827.8779       1834.1506       1869.0104       1875.9046       1860.0126       1846.6024
     Daily36         Daily37         Daily38         Daily39         Daily40         Daily41         Daily42
    1789.6251       1731.6673       1682.2293       1586.0122       1571.6402       1496.8899       1358.2929
     Daily43         Daily44         Daily45         Daily46         Daily47         Daily48         weekly2
    1245.7848       1166.1215       1091.9825       1066.7010        997.4765        955.2032       -355.3522
     weekly3         weekly4         weekly5         weekly6         weekly7     Daily2:weekly2  Daily3:weekly2
     -42.9479       -383.8207        -47.4477         43.1739         38.2679         46.9318        138.6611
  Daily4:weekly2  Daily5:weekly2  Daily6:weekly2  Daily7:weekly2  Daily8:weekly2  Daily9:weekly2 Daily10:weekly2
     211.0272        238.7233        273.2973        342.3193        382.9568        393.0218        420.0024
 Daily11:weekly2 Daily12:weekly2 Daily13:weekly2 Daily14:weekly2 Daily15:weekly2 Daily16:weekly2 Daily17:weekly2
     433.0777        432.5059        439.6293        428.7760        429.8100        424.0835        429.2114
 Daily18:weekly2 Daily19:weekly2 Daily20:weekly2 Daily21:weekly2 Daily22:weekly2 Daily23:weekly2 Daily24:weekly2
     441.2555        483.8489        489.4588        450.5552        461.8552        547.1952        614.2202
 Daily25:weekly2 Daily26:weekly2 Daily27:weekly2 Daily28:weekly2 Daily29:weekly2 Daily30:weekly2 Daily31:weekly2
     635.9273        645.8638        629.4519        538.6554        531.7929        506.9881        510.5959
 Daily32:weekly2 Daily33:weekly2 Daily34:weekly2 Daily35:weekly2 Daily36:weekly2 Daily37:weekly2 Daily38:weekly2
     516.8237        507.8630        524.8920        514.2205        531.7239        513.5249        515.8282
 Daily39:weekly2 Daily40:weekly2 Daily41:weekly2 Daily42:weekly2 Daily43:weekly2 Daily44:weekly2 Daily45:weekly2
     603.7991        572.5889        557.3761        561.1792        551.5947        539.1175        529.6320
 Daily46:weekly2 Daily47:weekly2 Daily48:weekly2  Daily2:weekly3  Daily3:weekly3  Daily4:weekly3  Daily5:weekly3
     491.0887        477.7638        443.8735          5.5692         10.2973         32.1318         32.9816
```

Comparing R-squared values from the summaries of the `linear_model_1` and `linear_model_2` models:

```
> c(Previous = summary(linear_model_1)$r.squared, New =
summary(linear_model_2)$r.squared)
```

The result is as follows:

```
 Previous       New
0.9547247 0.9989725
```

There is a significant improvement in the R-squared value of the second model.

Comparing the residuals of the `linear_model_1` and `linear_model_2` models graphically:

```
> ggplot(data.table(Residuals = c(linear_model_1$residuals,
linear_model_2$residuals), Type = c(rep("Multiple Linear Reg - simple",
nrow(data_reg)), rep("Multiple Linear Reg with interactions",
nrow(data_reg)))), aes(Type, Residuals, fill = Type)) + geom_boxplot()
    > ggplotly()
```

The result is as follows:

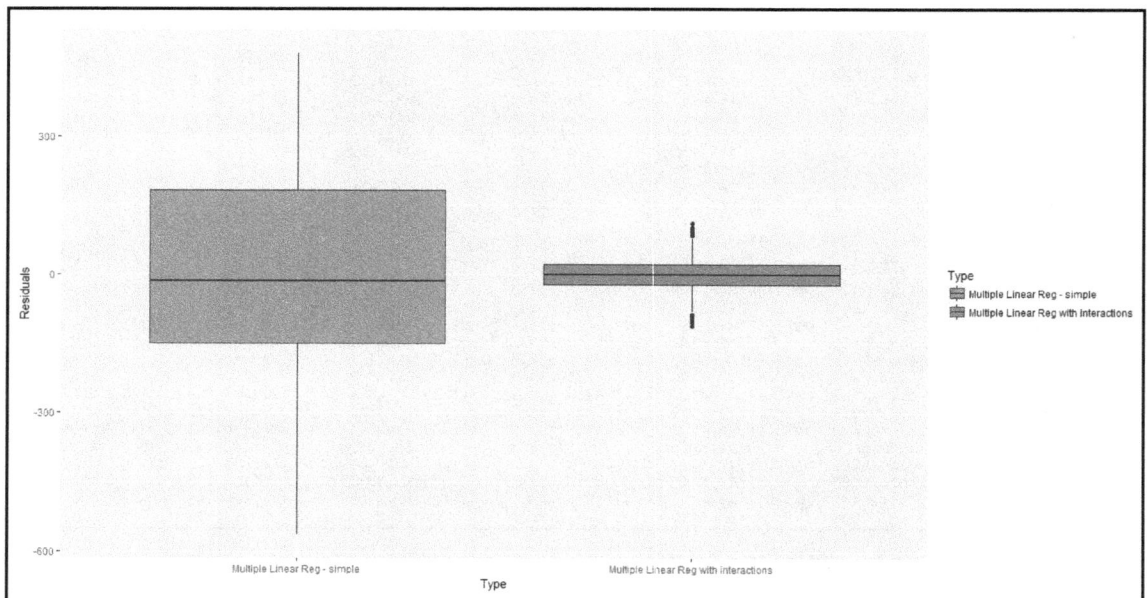

Details of residuals of `linear_model_1`.

The result is as follows:

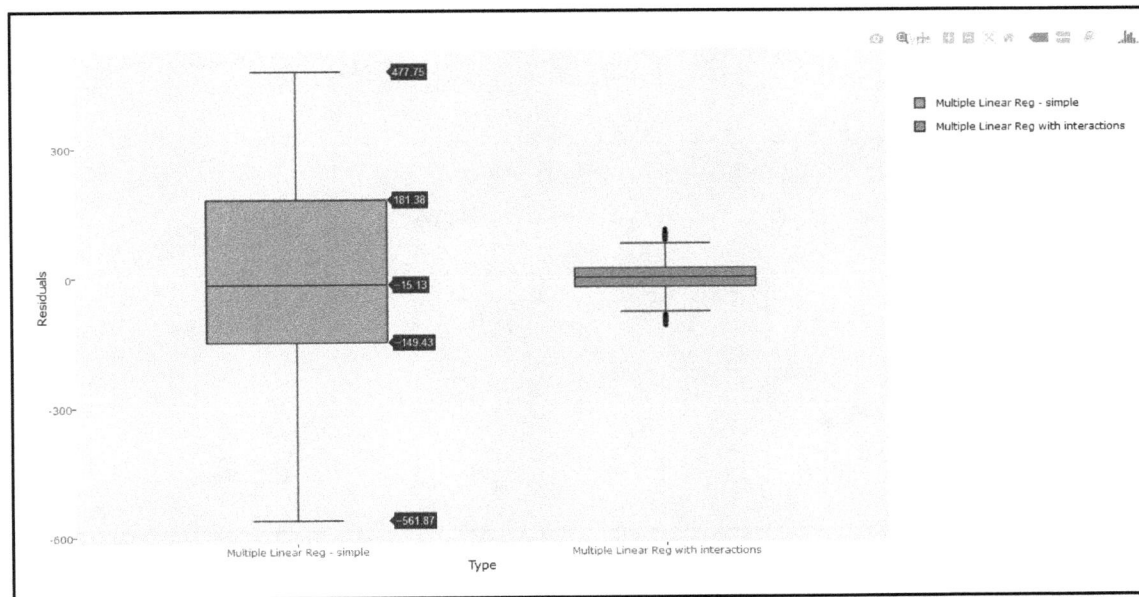

Details of residuals of `linear_model_2`.

The result is as follows:

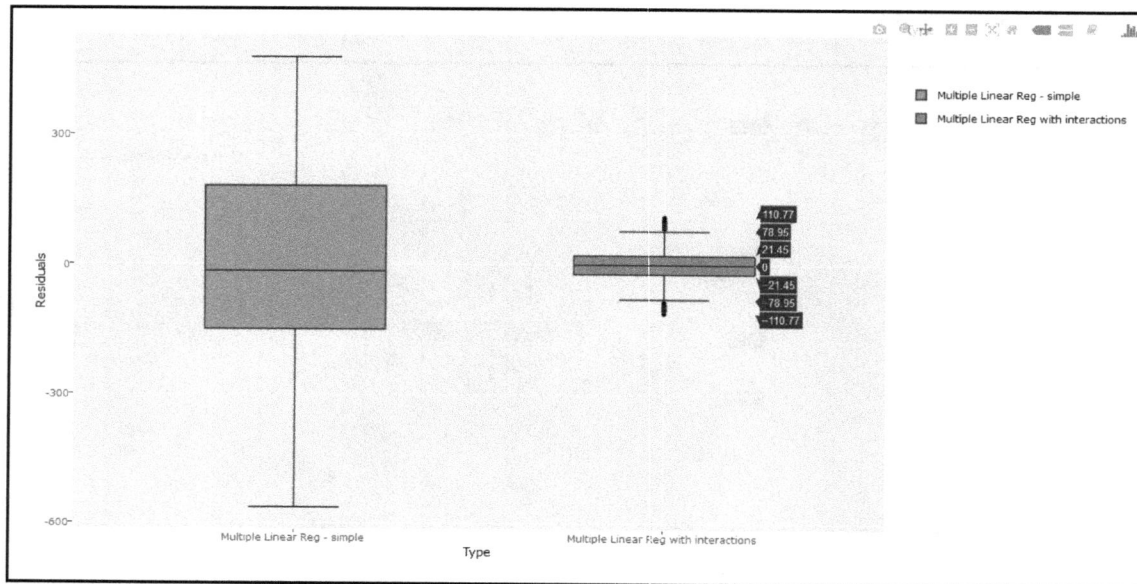

Creating one `data.table` from a list of `data_reg` and `linear_model_2`:

```
> datas <- rbindlist(list(data_reg[, .(value, date_time)],
data.table(value = linear_model_2$fitted.values, data_time = data_reg[,
date_time])))
```

Printing the contents of the `datas` data frame after the change:

```
> datas
```

The result is as follows:

```
              value              date_time
   1:  652.0693  2012-02-27  00:00:00
   2:  646.6226  2012-02-27  00:30:00
   3:  658.3790  2012-02-27  01:00:00
   4:  669.0898  2012-02-27  01:30:00
   5:  675.9707  2012-02-27  02:00:00
  ---
1340:  517.3413  2012-03-11  21:30:00
1341:  512.7296  2012-03-11  22:00:00
1342:  513.3986  2012-03-11  22:30:00
1343:  517.8433  2012-03-11  23:00:00
1344:  527.1080  2012-03-11  23:30:00
```

Adding `Real` and `Fitted` columns to `datas`:

```
> datas[, type := rep(c("Real", "Fitted"), each = nrow(data_reg))]
```

Printing the contents of the `datas` data frame after the change:

```
> datas
```

The result is as follows:

```
              value              date_time    type
   1:  652.0693  2012-02-27  00:00:00    Real
   2:  646.6226  2012-02-27  00:30:00    Real
   3:  658.3790  2012-02-27  01:00:00    Real
   4:  669.0898  2012-02-27  01:30:00    Real
   5:  675.9707  2012-02-27  02:00:00    Real
  ---
1340:  517.3413  2012-03-11  21:30:00  Fitted
1341:  512.7296  2012-03-11  22:00:00  Fitted
1342:  513.3986  2012-03-11  22:30:00  Fitted
1343:  517.8433  2012-03-11  23:00:00  Fitted
1344:  527.1080  2012-03-11  23:30:00  Fitted
```

Plotting fitted values for `linear_model_2`.

`data = datas` is the dataset to be used for plotting while `aes()` describes how variables in the data are mapped to visual properties. `geom_line()` produces the single line that tries to connect all the observations:

```
> ggplot(data = datas, aes(date_time, value, group = type, colour =
type)) + geom_line(size = 0.8) + theme_bw() +
+ labs(x = "Time", y = "Load (kW)", title = "Fit from Multiple Linear
Regression")
```

The result is as follows:

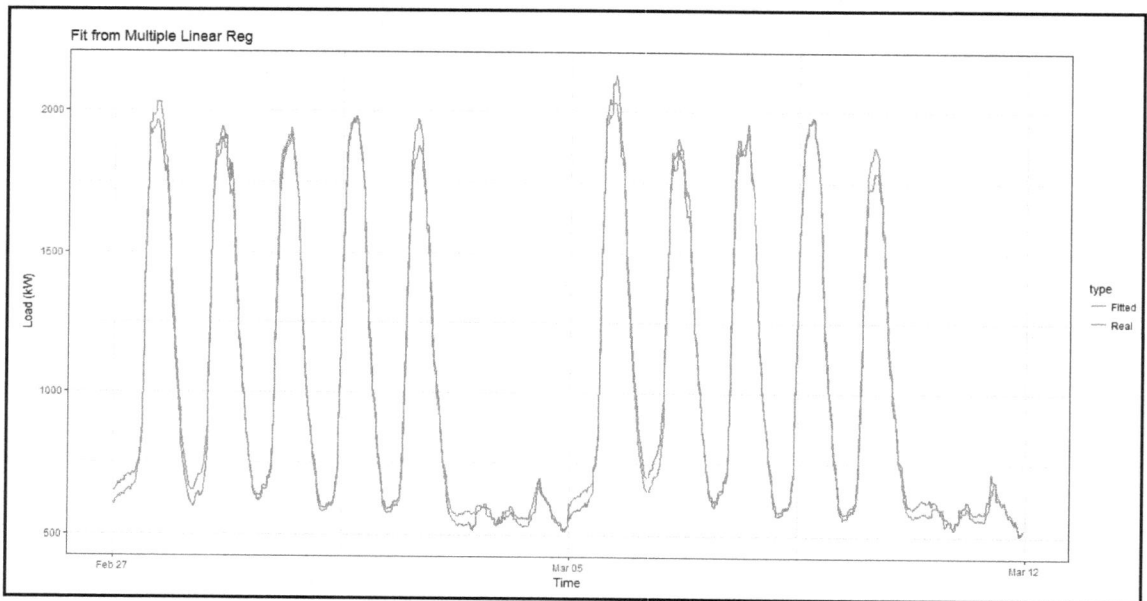

The fitted and real values closely match compared to the earlier plot of `linear_model_1`.

Plotting fitted values versus residual values. `Data` is the dataset to be used for plotting while `aes()` describes how variables in the data are mapped to visual properties:

```
> ggplot(data = data.table(Fitted_values =
linear_model_2$fitted.values, Residuals = linear_model_2$residuals),
aes(Fitted_values, Residuals)) + geom_point(size = 1.7)
+ geom_hline(yintercept = 0, color = "red", size = 1) +
+ labs(title = "Fitted values vs Residuals")
```

The result is as follows:

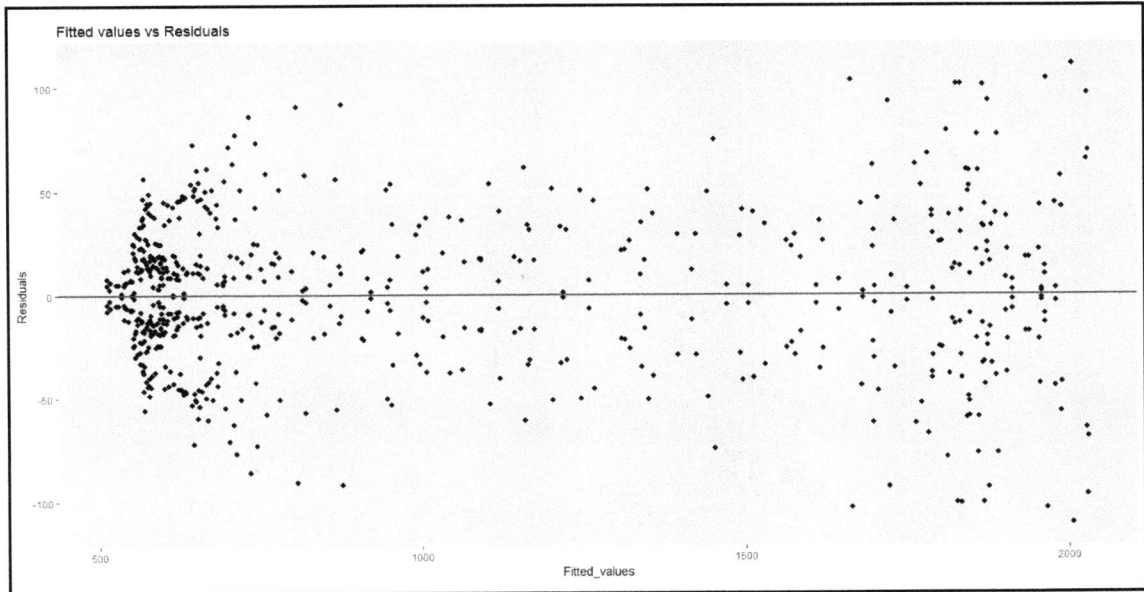

The plots appear to be closer to the residual line compared to the earlier plot of `linear_model_1`.

We can plot Plotting Q-Q using the following:

```
> ggQQ(linear_model_2)
```

The result is as follows:

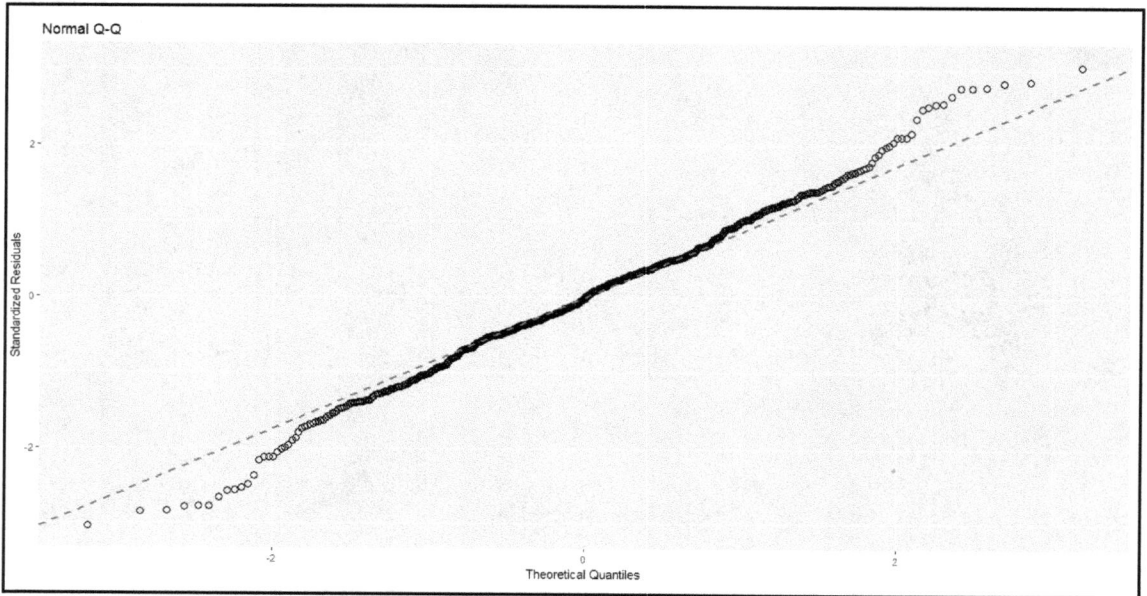

Step 5 - building a forecasting model

We can define a function to return the forecast for a 1 week ahead prediction. The input parameters are data and set_of_date:

```
> predWeekReg <- function(data, set_of_date){
+ #creating the dataset by dates
+ data_train <- data[date %in% set_of_date]
+ N <- nrow(data_train)
+
+ # number of days in the train set
+ window <- N / period # number of days in the train set
+
+ #1, ..., period, 1, ..., period - daily season periods
+ #feature "week_num"- weekly season
+ matrix_train <- data.table(Load = data_train[, value],
+ Daily = as.factor(rep(1:period, window)),
+ Weekly = as.factor(data_train[, week_num]))
+
+ #creating linear model.
+ # formula - Load ~ 0 + Daily + Weekly + Daily:Weekly
+ # dataset - data = matrix_train
```

```
+ lm_m <- lm(Load ~ 0 + Daily + Weekly + Daily:Weekly, data =
matrix_train)
    +
    + #forecast of one week ahead
    + pred_week <- predict(lm_m, matrix_train[1:(7*period), -1, with =
FALSE])
    + return(as.vector(pred_week))
    + }
```

Defining the mean absolute percentage error for evaluating the forecast:

```
> mape <- function(real, pred){
+ return(100 * mean(abs((real - pred)/real)))
+ }
```

Setting the training set of the length for 2 weeks, therefore deducting 2. A forecast for 50 weeks will be produced. Using a sliding window approach for training forecasting is done for every type of industry:

```
> n_weeks <- floor(length(n_date)/7) - 2
```

Printing the number of weeks:

```
> n_weeks
```

The result is as follows:

```
[1] 50
```

Calculating the forecast for each type of industry for 1 week ahead.

Calling the function to return the forecast for a 1 week ahead prediction for the AggData commercial property and dataset:

```
> lm_pred_weeks_1 <- sapply(0:(n_weeks-1), function(i)
+ predWeekReg(AggData[type == n_type[1]],
  n_date[((i*7)+1):((i*7)+7*2)]))
```

Calling the function to return the forecast for a 1 week ahead prediction for the AggData - education and date set:

```
> lm_pred_weeks_2 <- sapply(0:(n_weeks-1), function(i)
+ predWeekReg(AggData[type == n_type[2]],
  n_date[((i*7)+1):((i*7)+7*2)]))
```

Calling the function to return the forecast for a 1 week ahead prediction for the `AggData` food and sales and date set:

```
> lm_pred_weeks_3 <- sapply(0:(n_weeks-1), function(i)
+ predWeekReg(AggData[type == n_type[3]],
n_date[((i*7)+1):((i*7)+7*2)]))
```

Calling the function to return the forecast for a 1 week ahead prediction for the `AggData` lighting industry and date set:

```
> lm_pred_weeks_4 <- sapply(0:(n_weeks-1), function(i)
+ predWeekReg(AggData[type == n_type[4]],
n_date[((i*7)+1):((i*7)+7*2)]))
```

Calculate the mean absolute percentage error for each type of industry for evaluating the forecasts. Call the function to return the mean absolute percentage. Calculate the error for evaluating the forecast for the `AggData` lighting industry and date set:

```
> lm_err_mape_1 <- sapply(0:(n_weeks-1), function(i)
+ mape(AggData[(type == n_type[1] & date %in%
n_date[(15+(i*7)):(21+(i*7))]), value],
+ lm_pred_weeks_1[, i+1]))
```

Printing the `lm_err_mape_1` data frame:

```
> lm_err_mape_1
```

The result is as follows:

```
[1] 15.651678 11.885790 13.711592  7.216850  5.261544  8.074024  6.046631  5.175894 10.175659  6.573435  7.249069  5.189729
[13]  3.966611  3.537241  4.517766  4.259040  3.865752  4.564565  4.540562 14.533468  7.091113  6.321064 10.747477  8.175696
[25] 12.011780 10.181759  9.469939  5.571468  6.054342  5.065741  5.013238  7.510948  4.157744 15.843159  8.724484  7.609050
[37]  3.712756  3.912121  5.448236  3.866538  3.244851  6.641563  8.244843  8.190629 18.194939  6.481096  6.339300  8.457155
[49] 11.176872 15.880014
```

Calling the function to return the mean absolute percentage error for evaluating the forecast for the `AggData` education and date set:

```
> lm_err_mape_2 <- sapply(0:(n_weeks-1), function(i)
+ mape(AggData[(type == n_type[2] & date %in%
n_date[(15+(i*7)):(21+(i*7))]), value],
+ lm_pred_weeks_2[, i+1]))
```

Printing `lm_err_mape_2` data frame:

```
> lm_err_mape_2
```

The result is as follows:

```
 [1] 10.084345  8.452523  8.100982 10.779631 12.290251 13.748548 13.185274  8.708880 13.608198  7.976265  7.786389 22.951015
[13] 12.754905 11.052129  5.624771  6.243265  4.557871  7.842977  5.464003  9.951756 13.658921 11.571770  7.876418 10.951769
[25] 10.921287  8.672482  7.639304 10.006915  9.030679  6.077076  9.848483  6.445102 14.021887 14.064280 13.624932  9.057978
[37]  4.276840  5.329250 11.452156 13.313456  9.835459 11.187358 12.744013  9.460053 34.312551 13.113285 12.155385  8.036420
[49] 10.614472 51.541775
```

Calling the function to return the mean absolute percentage error for evaluating the forecast for the `AggData` food and sales and date set:

```
> lm_err_mape_3 <- sapply(0:(n_weeks-1), function(i)
+ mape(AggData[(type == n_type[3] & date %in%
n_date[(15+(i*7)):(21+(i*7))]), value],
+ lm_pred_weeks_3[, i+1]))
```

Printing the `lm_err_mape_3` data frame:

```
> lm_err_mape_3
```

The result is as follows:

```
 [1] 1.3494435 1.6115792 1.1212235 1.2100342 1.0249229 0.9645256 0.9538736 1.6206521 3.3962925 2.3641598 1.3481740 1.5083682
[13] 1.8310301 5.8381717 1.8980476 1.3625701 2.3412257 2.3754512 2.8773237 3.1063138 2.9674816 2.5777905 4.1572684 3.8093668
[25] 3.5908706 4.2735190 2.3578053 4.5968416 4.0791122 7.9821166 3.2058152 5.3319568 3.2213241 2.9283188 2.6655705 4.7280836
[37] 5.4562748 2.8417542 6.4128534 2.9900441 3.5614321 4.6741020 3.9244749 3.3571312 1.9261284 2.6419782 2.4853783 2.7261717
[49] 2.3941716 6.1437349
```

Calling the function to return the mean absolute percentage error for evaluating the forecast for the `AggData` lighting industry and date set:

```
> lm_err_mape_4 <- sapply(0:(n_weeks-1), function(i)
+ mape(AggData[(type == n_type[4] & date %in%
n_date[(15+(i*7)):(21+(i*7))]), value],
+ lm_pred_weeks_4[, i+1]))
```

Printing the `lm_err_mape_4`data frame:

```
> lm_err_mape_4
```

The result is as follows:

```
 [1]  8.647721  7.375660  5.463200  7.180215  6.029445  5.736619  8.209645 10.220787  8.049561  7.831923  5.942506  7.537182
[13]  5.957011  5.871259  5.924100  7.175428  7.107502  6.602283  5.144848 13.114200  7.087625  9.881252  5.949965  5.529862
[25] 12.620649 11.001515  8.630602  5.249746  5.037242  4.541921  6.132860 11.573741 10.771706 21.248055  9.164510 15.612347
[37]  9.994092  7.129103  8.642347  5.765497  7.846388 13.715063  9.045185 10.814154 29.182009 12.573626 12.319590  5.138492
[49]  6.550366 35.256450
```

Step 6 - plotting the forecast for a year

Plotting the results:

You need to have ImageMagick-7.0.4-Q16 installed for `saveGIF` to work.

```
> datas <- data.table(value = c(as.vector(lm_pred_weeks_1),
  AggData[(type == n_type[1]) & (date %in% n_date[-c(1:14,365)]),
value]),
  date_time = c(rep(AggData[-c(1:(14*48), (17473:nrow(AggData))),
date_time], 2)),
  type = c(rep("MLR", nrow(lm_pred_weeks_1)*ncol(lm_pred_weeks_1)),
  rep("Real", nrow(lm_pred_weeks_1)*ncol(lm_pred_weeks_1))),
  week = c(rep(1:50, each = 336), rep(1:50, each = 336)))

> saveGIF({
oopt = ani.options(interval = 0.9, nmax = 50)
for(i in 1:ani.options("nmax")){
  print(ggplot(data = datas[week == i], aes(date_time, value, group =
type, colour = type)) +
  geom_line(size = 0.8) +
  scale_y_continuous(limits = c(min(datas[, value]), max(datas[,
value]))) +
  theme(panel.border = element_blank(), panel.background =
element_blank(),
  panel.grid.minor = element_line(colour = "grey90"),
  panel.grid.major = element_line(colour = "grey90"),
  panel.grid.major.x = element_line(colour = "grey90"),
  title = element_text(size = 15),
  axis.text = element_text(size = 10),
  axis.title = element_text(size = 12, face = "bold")) +
  labs(x = "Time", y = "Load (kW)",
  title = paste("Forecast of MLR (", n_type[1], "); ", "week: ", i, ";
MAPE: ",
  round(lm_err_mape_1[i], 2), "%", sep = "")))
ani.pause()
}
}, movie.name = "industry_1.gif", ani.height = 450, ani.width = 750)
```

The result is as follows:

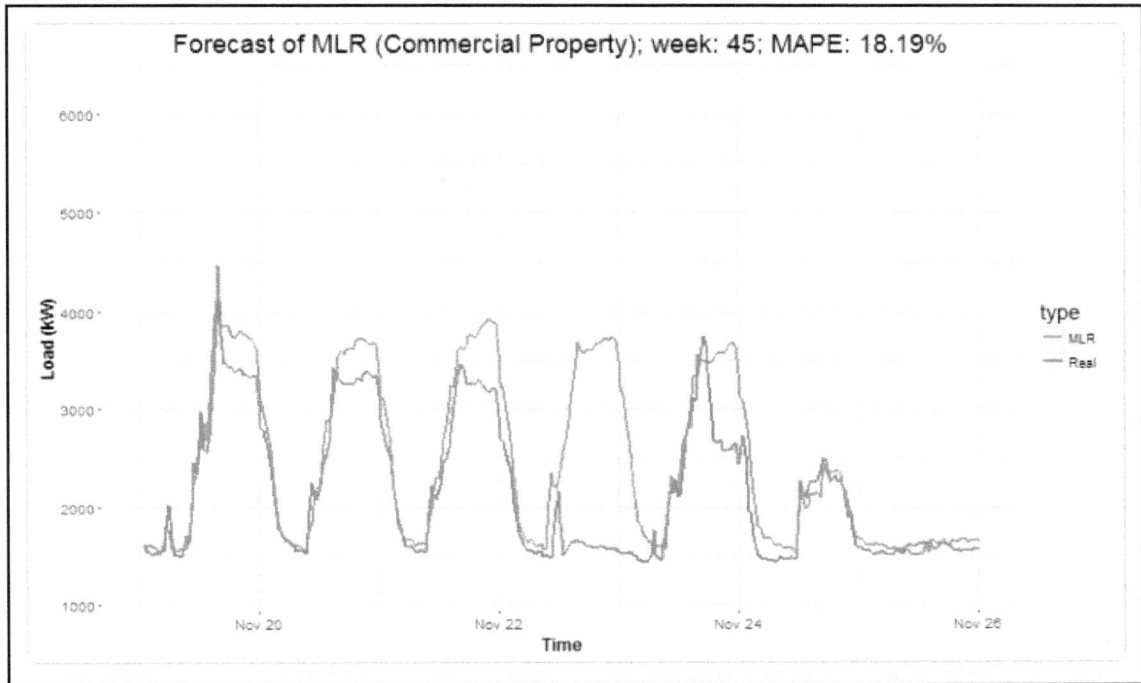

Forecast of MLR (Commercial Property); week: 45; MAPE: 18.19%

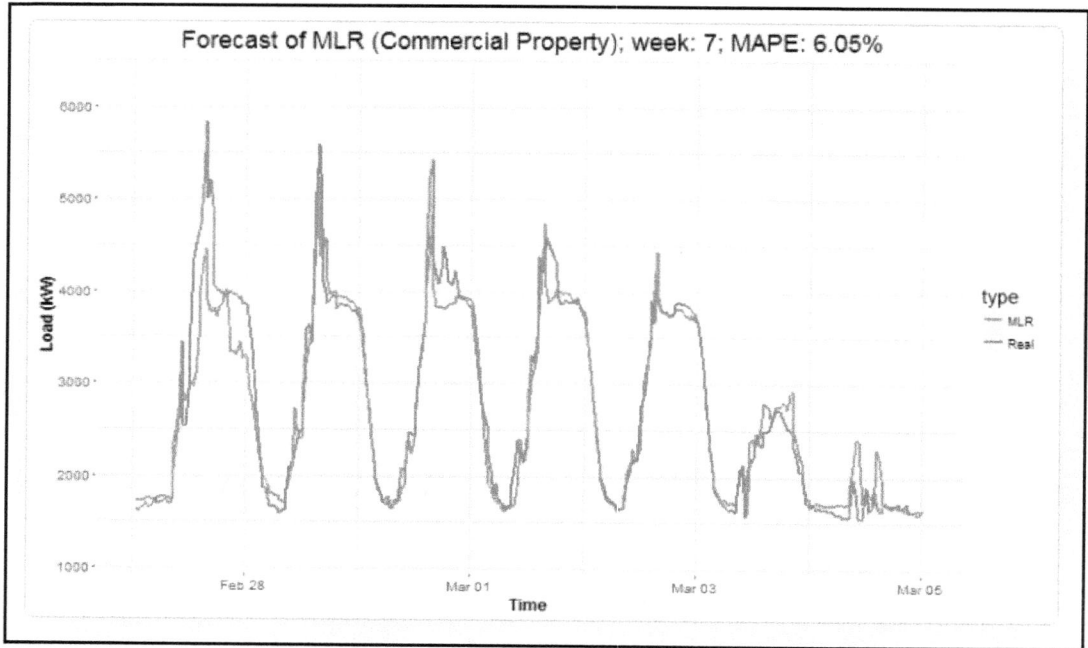

Forecast of MLR (Commercial Property); week: 7; MAPE: 6.05%

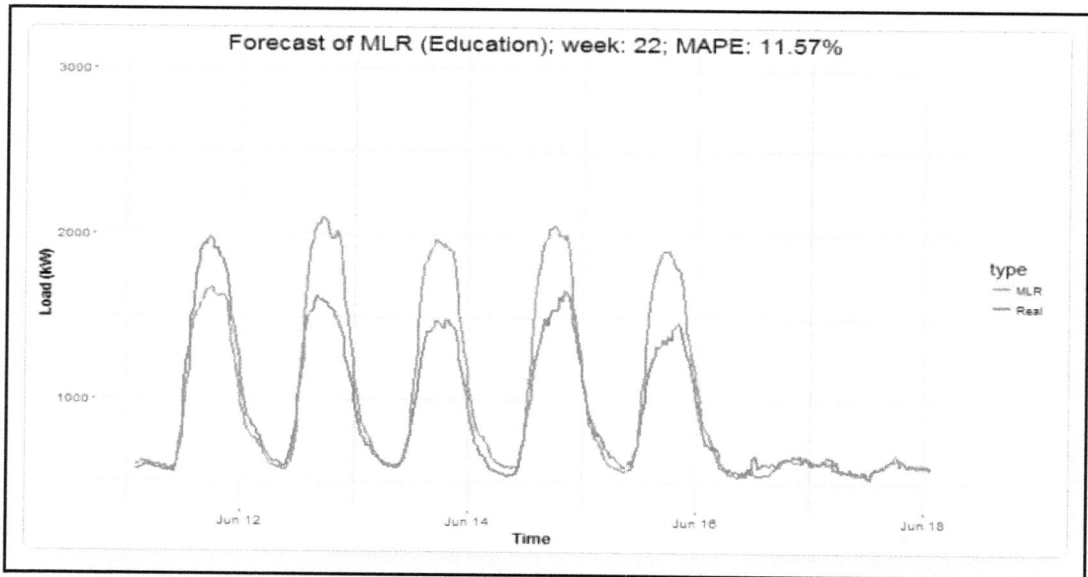

Forecast of MLR (Education); week: 22; MAPE: 11.57%

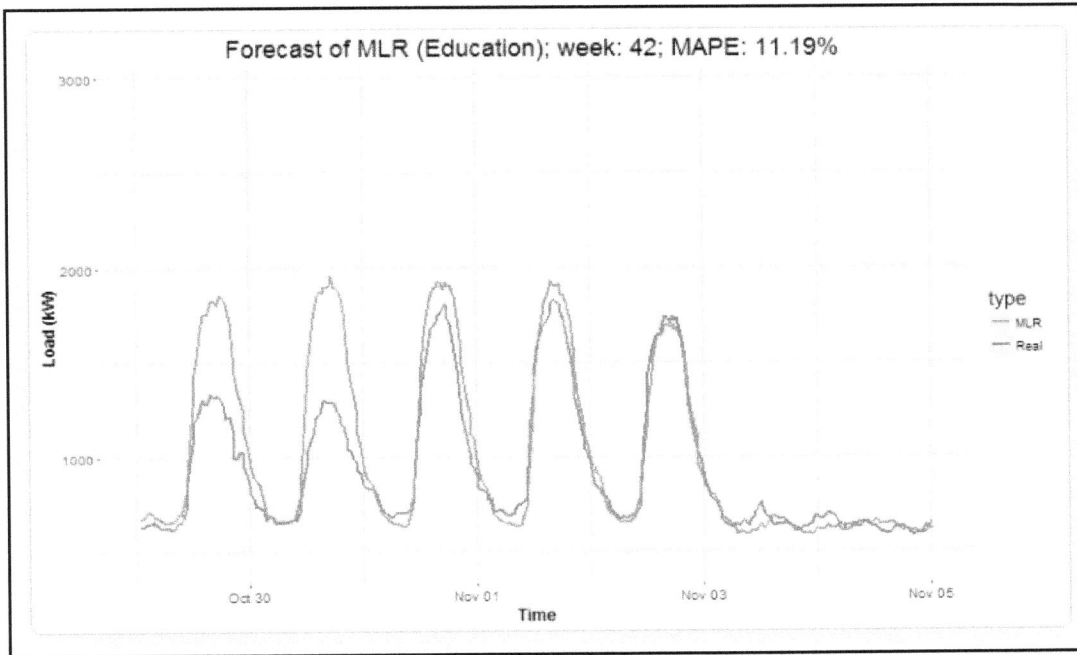

Forecast of MLR (Education); week: 42; MAPE: 11.19%

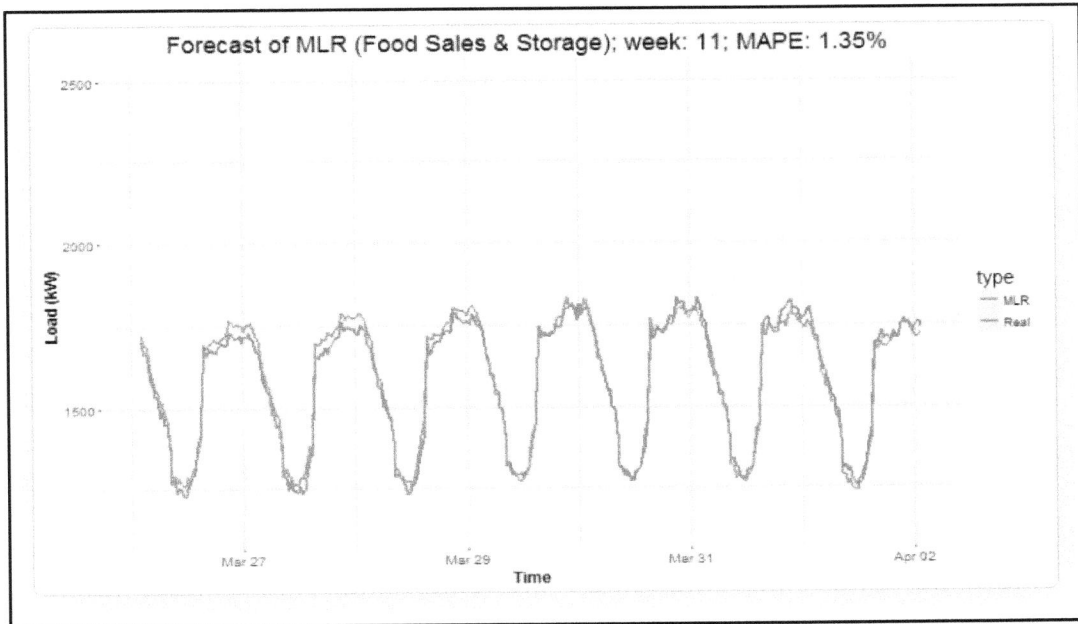

Forecast of MLR (Food Sales & Storage); week: 11; MAPE: 1.35%

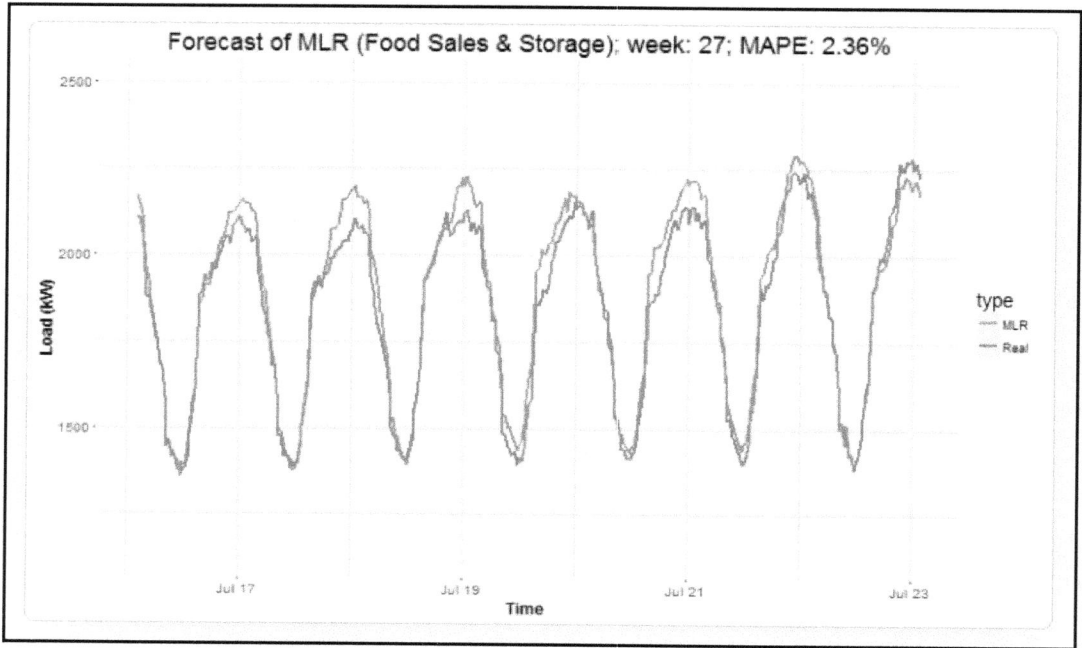
Forecast of MLR (Food Sales & Storage); week: 27; MAPE: 2.36%

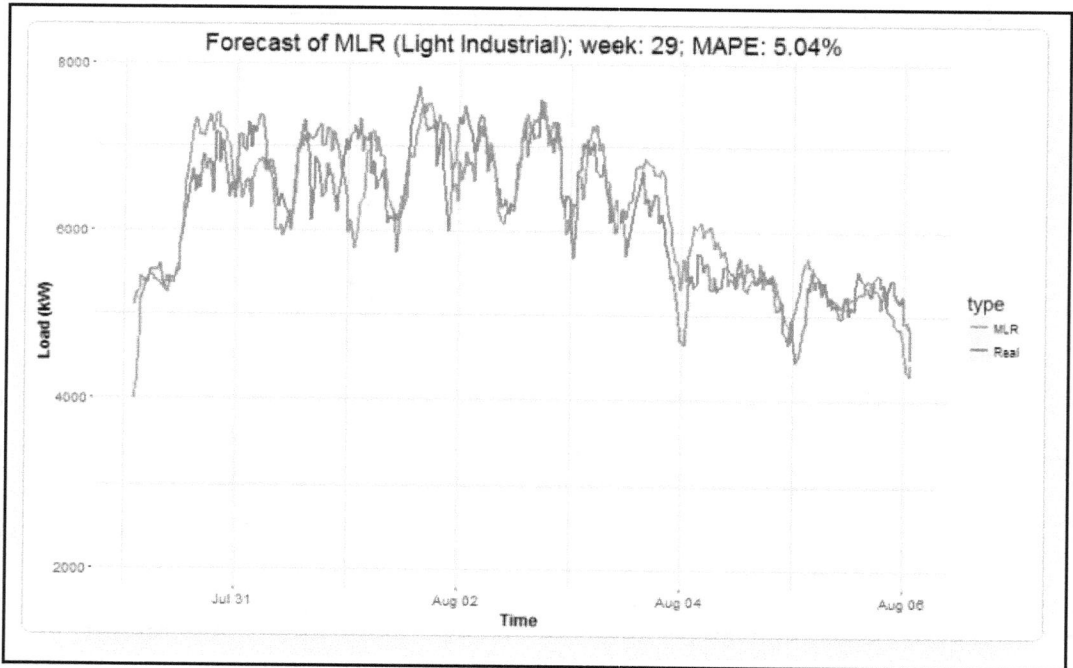
Forecast of MLR (Light Industrial); week: 29; MAPE: 5.04%

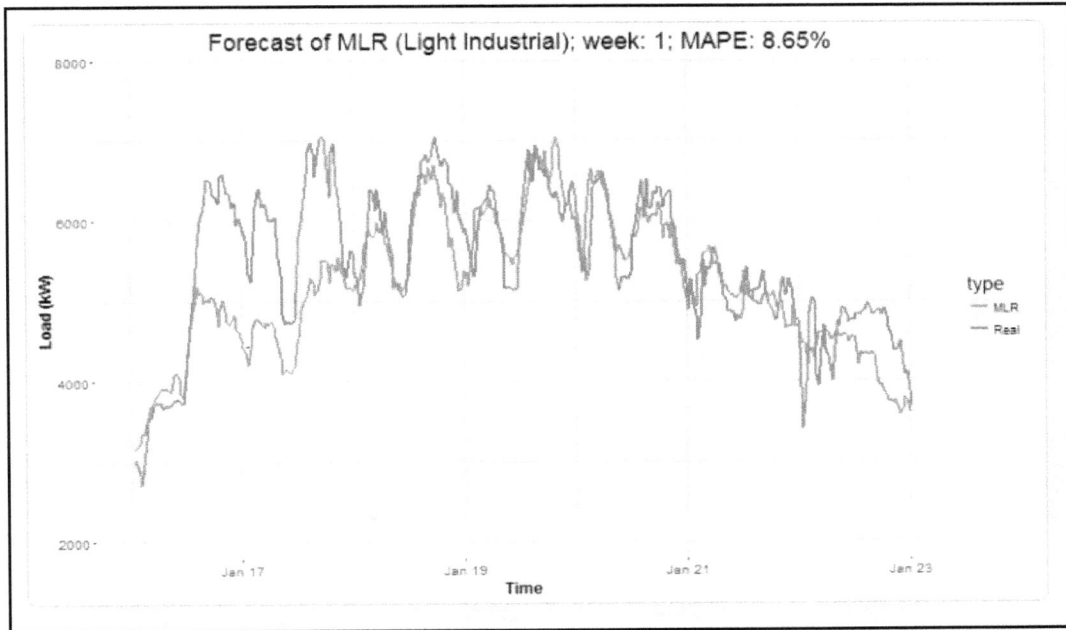

Forecast of MLR (Light Industrial); week: 1; MAPE: 8.65%

The preceding results prove that the consumption of the electricity pattern is based on external factors such as holidays, weather, nature of property, and so on. The consumption pattern is very stochastic in nature.

> The aim is to introduce to the reader the application of multiple linear regressions for forecasting double seasonal time series. It is very effective to include interactions of independent variables to ensure the effectiveness of the model.

Index